THE
JESUS
CRISIS

THE
JESUS
CRISIS

THE INROADS OF HISTORICAL CRITICISM INTO EVANGELICAL SCHOLARSHIP

Robert L. Thomas
F. David Farnell

kregel
PUBLICATIONS

Grand Rapids, MI 49501

The Jesus Crisis: The Inroads of Historical Criticism into Evangelical Scholarship

Copyright © 1998 by Robert L. Thomas and F. David Farnell

Published by Kregel Publications, a division of Kregel, Inc., P.O. Box 2607, Grand Rapids, MI 49501. Kregel Publications provides trusted, biblical publications for Christian growth and service. Your comments and suggestions are valued.

Cover design: Sarah Slattery
Book design: Nicholas G. Richardson

Library of Congress Cataloging-in-Publication Data
Thomas, Robert L.
    The Jesus crisis: the inroads of historical criticism into evangelical scholarship / coedited by Robert L. Thomas and F. David Farnell.
        p.   cm.
    Includes bibliographical references and indexes.
        1. Bible—Criticism, interpretation, etc.—History.
2. Bible—Evidences, authority, etc.—History of doctrines.
3. Evangelicalism—History of doctrines. I. Thomas, Robert L. II. Farnell, F. David.
BS520.J47   1998   226'.06'01—dc21   98-5608
                                                            CIP

ISBN 0-8254-3811-x

Printed in the United States of America

1 2 3 / 04 03 02 01 00 99 98

To those who taught us the traditional view
of Synoptic Gospel relationships.

*"The things that you have heard from
me through many witnesses, these commit to faithful men,
the kind who will be competent to teach others also"*
(2 Timothy 2:2).

Contents

Foreword

MORE THAN A HUNDRED years ago religious liberals began mixing rationalism and Christianity on an unprecedented scale. The elixir that resulted from that blend turned out to be a deadly poison.

One of the more highly touted products of this turn-of-the-century religious modernism was a new approach to the Scriptures known as *higher criticism*, a principal aspect of which was Historical Criticism. The historical critics subjected the Bible to a cynical brand of scholarship. They devised speculative literary theories—all rooted in skepticism—about the authorship and origin of various biblical books. They routinely denied both the authenticity and the historicity of Scripture. Before long the critics' theories themselves were canonized, and the word *scholarship* became synonymous with higher criticism in many people's minds.

By the early part of this century, most of the mainline Protestant denominations had embraced one form or another of Historical Criticism. And as they did so, one denomination after the other began the inevitable process of decay and decline. Today many of those denominations are mere shells of what they once were. Their churches, once bustling, are now lifeless and empty—monuments to skepticism, liberalism, and humanistic rationalism. The damning and destructive fruits of Historical Criticism were thus made manifest for all to see.

But the movement itself is far from dead. In recent years the higher critics have undertaken a public-relations campaign to breathe life and interest into their dying movement. For example, the secular media has trumpeted the work of "The Jesus Seminar." This is a group of liberal intellectuals who claim they are engaged in a "quest for the historical Jesus." This is a modern catchphrase signifying an approach to "scholarship" that starts with the presupposition that the Scriptures are *not* a reliable historical record.

This movement is hostile to the Christian faith. It is also antagonistic to historic Christianity's high esteem for the Word of God. This movement furthermore is the very spirit of antichrist (1 John 2:22) and a doctrine of demons (1 Tim. 4:1).

In light of Historical Criticism's anti-God origin and incontestable

9

deadening effect on churches, it is staggering to see how easily some of the notions of higher criticism have made deep inroads in recent years into evangelical seminaries, colleges/universities, and churches. I have interacted with a variety of institutions and ecclesiastical situations, and I am amazed that Higher Criticism, with its secular orientation and subtle ways, has infiltrated classrooms and pulpits that were previously theologically conservative. These are places where such compromise with liberalism would never have been expected.

Some of evangelicalism's best-known theologians and seminary and college professors are now debating among themselves ideas that would have been deemed entirely nonnegotiable before the last quarter of the twentieth century. Destructive applications of redaction theories, source criticism, literary speculations, and so on have always been the theological liberals' stock in trade. However, to see evangelicals applying this sort of Historical Criticism in order to cast doubt on the authenticity or historicity of the biblical text is wholly unprecedented. Tragically, the prevailing attitude among evangelical scholars today closely mirrors the extreme tolerance that left the door wide open for Historical Criticism in the leading mainline schools and denominations of a hundred years ago.

Dr. Robert Thomas is eminently qualified to confront this trend. And toward that end, he along with Dr. David Farnell, has summoned several other gifted scholars and able defenders of the faith. In this book they examine in scholarly fashion several of the dangerous trends that are luring many from the evangelical camp down the well-worn path toward skeptical rationalism and theological liberalism.

The Jesus Crisis aims to sort out the confusion that modern historical-critical approaches to Scripture so often leave in their wake. The book answers with clarity and precision the arguments set forth by the so-called "evangelical" critics. It shows that despite all the bluster and noise heard from these critics, the rock-solid foundation of biblical truth remains unshaken. And just as the Word of God did in the past, it will continue to stand long after all its critics have been laid to rest.

Evangelicals *must* recover their steadfast confidence in the truth of the Scriptures. Because I know that *The Jesus Crisis* can be instrumental in helping to reestablish that proper focus, I commend it eagerly to the reading public, and especially to all leaders within the evangelical movement.

JOHN MACARTHUR

Preface

DURING THE LAST DECADES of the twentieth century, Historical Criticism has penetrated deeply into the ranks of evangelical New Testament scholarship, affecting radically how many people view the historical accuracy of the Synoptic Gospels. *The Jesus Crisis* endeavors to expose those inroads, explain where they originated, and note their effects on evangelical exegesis and theology. The editors pray that this volume will serve to enhance the reader's appreciation for the accuracy and truthfulness of the Synoptic Gospels. The Introduction to follow will amplify the goals of the volume.

We want to thank those who have contributed to *The Jesus Crisis*. They include the following:

Thomas R. Edgar, Th.D., Professor of New Testament, Capital Bible Seminary
Paul W. Felix, Th.M., Pastor of Berean Bible Church, Denver, Colorado
Dennis A. Hutchison, Th.D., Pastor of Frenchtown Community Church, Frenchtown, Montana
Kelly Osborne, Ph.D., Associate Professor of Classics, Hope College
Robert W. Yarbrough, Ph.D., Associate Professor of New Testament Studies, Trinity Evangelical Divinity School

Contributors do not necessarily endorse every opinion expressed in the following pages, but on the following point all are in full agreement: Each gospel writer worked independently, namely, without relying on another canonical gospel as a source of information.

We express our gratitude to Mr. Dennis M. Swanson, Seminary Librarian at The Master's Seminary, who has graciously served in compiling the indexes of *The Jesus Crisis*.

Robert L. Thomas, Professor of New Testament,
The Master's Seminary

F. David Farnell, Associate Professor of New Testament,
The Master's Seminary

The "Jesus Crisis": What Is It?

Robert L. Thomas

THE CRISIS DEFINED AND EXPLAINED: AN OVERVIEW

DOES A CRISIS CONNECTED with Jesus exist? To answer that question, there are two considerations worth noting.

(1) Since about the middle of the twentieth century, a movement known as evangelicalism[1] has had a considerable impact in thwarting the advance of liberalism in Christian circles. Evangelicals have been a major force in the creation of new organizations, seminaries, denominations, and local churches that honor the Bible as the inerrant Word of God. Historically, the evangelical role is vital. Alister McGrath, a well-known contemporary theologian, writes the following:

> Evangelicalism is historic Christianity. Its beliefs correspond to the central doctrines of the Christian churches down the ages. . . . In its vigorous defense of the biblical foundations, theological legitimacy, and spiritual relevance of these doctrines, evangelicalism has shown itself to have every right to claim to be a modern standard bearer of historic, orthodox Christianity.[2]

McGrath adds, "[T]he future of Christianity may come increasingly to depend on evangelicalism."[3] In other words, what happens among evangelicals is of critical significance for the future of the church.

(2) Evangelical New Testament scholars have conceded much ground to critical methodologies that question the accuracy of the Synoptic Gospels—Matthew, Mark, and Luke. By adopting the methodology of those who are less friendly to a high view of Scripture, most evangelical specialists have surrendered traditional, orthodox understandings of historicity in various parts of the first three gospels.

13

In light of these two factors, a crisis in studies about Jesus most definitely has arisen. If those whose special trust it has been to guard the veracity of Scripture are affirming that those gospels are not as trustworthy as the church for centuries has deemed them to be, who remains to assert the inerrancy of the Bible? The Gospels are a particularly crucial part of Scripture, since they are the only reliable sources for the church's detailed knowledge about the historical Jesus.

The Jesus Seminar, as an opponent of biblical inerrancy, has attracted much media attention during the last decade of the twentieth century. That seminar, which is composed of liberal scholars under the leadership of Robert Funk, began its twice-a-year meetings in 1985. Its highly publicized findings have denied the authenticity of 82 percent of what the four gospels indicate that Jesus said. Their conclusions about Jesus' sayings appeared in 1993 in *The Five Gospels: The Search for the Authentic Words of Jesus*.[4]

The Seminar has continued its meetings to vote on the authenticity of the deeds of Jesus as recorded in the Gospels. The already published work prints Jesus' alleged sayings in four colors—red, pink, gray, and black—to match the colors of the symbolic beads members used to cast votes in their meetings. Red means that Jesus definitely said it; pink means that Jesus probably said it; gray means that Jesus probably did not say it; and black means that Jesus definitely did not say it. Only one red statement appears in the gospel of Mark and none in the gospel of John. In comparison, the appearance in red of three sayings in the gospel of Thomas illustrates the skepticism of this group toward the canonical gospels.

The evangelical community has reacted strongly against the pronouncements of the Jesus Seminar because of that group's rejection of many historical aspects of the Gospels.[5] The number of specific evangelical responses to this Seminar is growing.[6]

Yet most of these evangelical responses come from those who utilize the same methodology in gospel study as do the Jesus Seminar personnel. Further, a closer look at studies done by some of the evangelical critics shows that achieving their goal of refuting the seminar is practically impossible if not impossible. To a degree, they must attack the same presuppositional framework that they themselves utilize. In their acceptance of the same historical-critical assumptions as the Jesus Seminar, they have rejected the wisdom of B. B. Warfield, who many years ago wrote, "And in general, no form of criticism is more uncertain than that, now so diligently prosecuted, which seeks to explain the several forms of narratives in the Synoptics as modifications of one another."[7] The following discussion will reflect the similarity in methodology and results of evangelical scholars to the Jesus Seminar. This in turn will exemplify the serious crisis that now faces evangelicalism and the Christian church.

Evangelical Similarities to the Jesus Seminar

Outspoken evangelical critics have engaged in the same type of dehistoricizing activity as the Jesus-Seminar people with whom they differ. If they were to organize among themselves their own evangelical "Jesus

Seminar,"[8] the following is a sampling of the issues they would vote on, most of which they would probably pass:[9]

1. The author of Matthew, not Jesus, created the Sermon on the Mount.
2. The commissioning of the Twelve in Matthew 10 is a group of instructions compiled and organized by the author of the first gospel, not spoken by Jesus on a single occasion.
3. The parable accounts of Matthew 13 and Mark 4 are anthologies of parables that Jesus uttered on separate occasions.
4. Jesus did not preach the Olivet Discourse in its entirety, as found in three of the gospel accounts.
5. Jesus gave His teaching on divorce and remarriage without the exception clauses found in Matthew 5:32 and 19:9.
6. In Matthew 19:16–17, the writer changed the words of Jesus and the rich man either to obtain a different emphasis or to avoid a theological problem involved in the wording of Mark's and Luke's accounts of the same event.
7. The scribes and Pharisees were in reality decent people whom Matthew painted in an entirely negative light because of his personal bias against them.
8. The genealogies of Jesus in Matthew 1 and Luke 3 are figures of speech and not accurate records of Jesus' physical and/or legal lineage.
9. The magi who, according to Matthew 2, visited the child Jesus after His birth are fictional, not real, characters.
10. Jesus uttered only three or four of the eight or nine beatitudes in Matthew 5:3–12.

Recognizably, the listed conclusions impinge upon the historical accuracy of the gospel records. Various evangelicals have opted for the stated unhistorical choice in each of the suggested instances. Granted, their reduction of historical precision in the Gospels is not the wholesale repudiation of historical data as is that of the original Jesus Seminar, but that it is a repudiation is undeniable. An acceptance of imprecision is even more noticeable in light of the fact that the above questions are only the tip of the iceberg. An exhaustive list would reach staggering proportions.[10]

In the spring of 1991, the *Los Angeles Times* religion staff planned to run two articles, one a pro-Jesus Seminar piece and the other an anti-Jesus Seminar one. The cochairman of the Jesus Seminar—Robert Funk—wrote the former, and a professor at a prominent evangelical seminary—Robert Guelich—wrote the other.[11] The plan to represent the two sides failed, however. Some staff person for this newspaper recognized that the antiseminar article was not "anti" at all, but took the same essential viewpoint as the Jesus Seminar. This came to light when a *Times* editor called me and asked if I would do an "anti" article the following week, for the evangelical contributor approached the Gospels in the same way as those he was supposed to oppose.[12] This observation by someone on the editorial staff—to this day I do not know who—was shrewd, for it recognized that the evangelical in what was to have been the "con" article supported the same general methodological and presuppositional mold as those whom he purposed to refute.

A Standard Methodology

Methodological Framework

What do evangelical scholars who surrender this or that historical aspect of the first three gospels have in common? They all build on the same presuppositional construct, which also happens to be the one followed by the more radical Jesus Seminar.[13] They thereby render themselves all but powerless to respond to the radical conclusions of that seminar.

A title appropriate to the methodology common to Jesus-Seminar personnel and many evangelicals is Historical Criticism. Various subdisciplines that have come into vogue under this broad heading include Source Criticism, Tradition Criticism, Form Criticism, and Redaction Criticism. Source Criticism was the earliest of these to arise, having its origin in the nineteenth century. The others sprang up at various points in the twentieth century. The stated purpose of all the subdisciplines is to *test* the historical accuracy of New Testament historical narrative,[14] but in one way or another, they actually *reduce* the historical accuracy of the Synoptic Gospels.

The claim of these evangelical scholars is that the widely practiced Historical Criticism is not necessarily antithetic to finding the Gospels historically reliable. Yet the results of their research belie their claim. They profess that their methodology is neutral and does not necessitate negative presuppositions regarding the integrity of the gospel accounts,[15] but the same people question Matthew's and Mark's representation that Jesus taught the parables of Matthew 13 and Mark 4 on a single occasion[16] and Matthew's and Luke's indications that Jesus preached the whole Sermon on the Mount and Sermon on the Plain to one audience.[17] The evangelical stance of those who thus question historicity dictates that in all probability the theories do not arise from conscious antisupernaturalistic predispositions. Their questionings must issue from a flawed methodology, one that inevitably leads to diminishing historical accuracy in the Gospels.

A basic tenet of Historical Criticism is the assumption that the authors of the three Synoptic Gospels depended on one another's writings. Various schemes regarding who depended on whose writings have surfaced, the most widely held current theory being that Mark wrote first and Matthew and Luke depended on Mark.[18] The other element of the theory maintains the existence of another document called "Q" on which Matthew and Luke depended also. No one in recent centuries has ever seen Q, if indeed it ever existed.[19]

Attempted Proof of Literary Dependence

Rarely does one find a defense of the general theory of literary dependence. It is most often just an assumption with no serious attempt at proof.[20] One exception to the unsupported assumption is the argumentation by

Stein favoring a common literary source for the Synoptic Gospels. He cites agreements (1) in wording, (2) in order, (3) in parenthetical material, and (4) the Lukan prologue (Luke 1:1–4) as proof of literary dependence.[21]

(1) Stein lists a number of places to illustrate agreements in wording, but makes no allowance in his argument for places of disagreement. He fails to note that these disagreements include three categories: Matthew and Mark against Luke, Matthew and Luke against Mark, and Mark and Luke against Matthew.[22] This factor argues strongly against any type of literary dependence and favors a random type of composition through which no writer ever saw another's work before writing his own gospel.[23]

(2) Stein also notices agreements in sequence in the Gospels,[24] but fails to give more than passing notice to disagreements in order, which are adverse to the case he builds for literary dependence. He does not endorse the possibility that agreements in order could result from the sequence of historical occurrences they describe. Yet such a possibility offers a natural explanation for the agreements in essentially all cases.

(3) Stein's first illustration of agreements in parenthetical material lies in the words "let the reader understand," found in Matthew 24:15 and Mark 13:14. Yet he cites this acknowledging only in a footnote the widely held opinion that these words were not parentheses added by Matthew and Mark, but were the words of Jesus Himself, referring to the reader of Daniel, not the reader of Matthew and Mark.[25] Stein's other three instances of agreement in parenthetical material are not verbatim agreements with each other and could easily be coincidental words of explanation from writers working independently, without seeing each other's work.

(4) Stein's final reason in proof of literary dependence is the prologue of Luke's gospel. In defending his use of the prologue for this purpose, he reflects no awareness of the possibility that Luke's sources mentioned therein do not include another canonical book.[26] This is the traditional understanding of the prologue, an understanding quite defensible exegetically, modern Source Criticism notwithstanding. The best understanding of Luke's prologue excludes Mark from, not includes Mark among, the sources used by the author of the third gospel.[27]

So a tabulation of tangible evidence shows the case for literary dependence is essentially nonexistent. It is merely an assumption, incidentally an assumption possibly shared by only one early church figure—Augustine— and that he took that position is highly doubtful (see chapter 1 of this volume for further discussion of the Synoptic Gospels in the early church). Essentially, the church for her first eighteen hundred years held the first three gospels to be independent of each other in regards to literary matters.[28] Substantial opinion in support of independence has emerged recently,[29] but most in the historical-critical school apparently do not take the possibility seriously.

Consequences of Literary Dependence

Where has the theory of literary dependence among the synoptists led? Does it impact one's view of the inerrancy of Scripture? To many, this foundational plank of Historical Criticism appears inconsequential. Yet when pursued to its logical end, the theory has quite serious repercussions.

The type of dependence advocated by most is the one described above, namely, Mark and Q are the earliest documents and Matthew and Luke are copies of and elaborations on these two. The usual name assigned to this theory is the Two-Source (or Two-Document) Theory.[30] To many, this assumption does no harm. After all, literary collaboration between the writers of Kings and Chronicles in the Old Testament is obvious,[31] and did not Jude depend on 2 Peter in writing his epistle (or vice versa, as some would have it)?[32]

Yet the consequences are more serious when dealing with Matthew, Mark, and Luke and their similar records of the life of Christ. McKnight elaborates on the nature of the consequences in his observations about comparing the Gospels and identifying authorial reasons for editorial changes:

> For example, a redaction critic, usually assuming Markan priority, inquires into the nature of and rationale for Matthew's addition of Peter's unsuccessful attempt to walk on the water (cf. Mark 6:45–52 with Matt. 14:22–33). The critic seeks to discover whether the confession at the end of the story (Matt. 14:33) is materially different from Mark's rather negative comment (Mark 6:52). . . . Alteration . . . involves direct alterations of the tradition to avoid misunderstandings, as when Matthew alters Mark's comment which could suggest inability on the part of Jesus (Mark 6:5; Matt. 13:53) or when he changes Mark's form of address by the rich young ruler (Mark 10:17–18; Matt. 19:16–17).[33]

In those words, McKnight—himself a proponent of Historical Criticism—acknowledges the necessity of assuming editorial changes if Matthew depended on Mark's texts in writing his gospel. If literary dependence of any type explains the origin of the Synoptic Gospels, someone did some changing that affected the historicity of the three accounts.

To illustrate how authorial changes impact historical accuracy, a closer look at the ten sample issues listed above in this Introduction is in order. For clarity's sake, the illustrations will lie in three categories that redaction critics find useful to describe the types of editorial changes allegedly made by the Synoptic Gospel writers: arrangement, modification, and creativity.[34] The first category is that of arrangement of material, by which they mean the writer rearranged material from a chronological to a nonchronological sequence. Four samples are of this type.[35]

Arrangement of Material

(1) *The Sermon on the Mount.* According to many evangelical practitioners of Historical Criticism, the traditional credit given to Jesus for preaching the Sermon on the Mount is a mistake. Guelich has written the following:

When one hears the phrase "the Sermon on the Mount," one generally identifies it with Matthew's Gospel and correctly so, not only because of the presence of the Sermon in the first Gospel but because the Sermon on the Mount, as we know it, is ultimately the literary product of the first evangelist.[36]

Mounce's opinion clarifies Guelich's position somewhat: "We are not to think of the Sermon on the Mount as a single discourse given by Jesus at one particular time. Undoubtedly there was a primitive and historic sermon, but it has been enlarged significantly by Matthew."[37] Stein goes even further regarding the creativity of the gospel writers:

> The Sermon on the Mount (Matt. 5:1–7:29) and the Sermon on the Plain (Luke 6:20–49) are literary creations of Matthew and Luke in the sense that they are collections of Jesus' sayings that were uttered at various times and places and have been brought together primarily due to topical considerations, i.e., in order to have an orderly account (1:3). There is no need, however, to deny that a historical event lies behind the scene. Jesus' teaching on a mountain/plain has been used as an opportunity by the Evangelists (or the tradition) to bring other related teachings of Jesus in at this point.[38]

Hagner concurs: "The 'sermon' is clearly a compilation of the sayings of Jesus by the evangelist, rather than something spoken by Jesus on a single occasion."[39] Others share the view that teachings in the Sermon on the Mount did not all come at the same time in Jesus' ministry, but were the result of the "clustering" of similar themes by the gospel writers.[40]

Going the route of these evangelical scholars entails explaining away Matthew's introduction to the Sermon (5:1–2)—which indicates Jesus began at a certain point to give the Sermon's contents—and His conclusion to the Sermon (7:28)—which indicates Jesus' ending of that same portion. Dispensing with the factuality of the introduction is what Wilkins does in his remarks:

> Instead Matthew's editorial activity in the introduction to the Sermon serves to make an explicit distinction between them [namely, the *mathētai* and the *ochloi*]. . . . Since the underlying Sermon tradition clearly had the disciples as the audience (cf. Lk. 6:20), this writer suggests that Matthew has maintained that tradition and has added that the crowds were also there, but as a secondary object of teaching because of their interest in his mission (4:23–25).[41]

In other words, the introductory and concluding formulas are no more than literary devices adopted by Matthew to give the impression (for whatever reason) that Jesus preached just such a sermon to the crowds and the disciples on one given occasion. The historical reality of the situation was that Jesus did not preach it all at that time. Rather, Matthew grouped various teachings of Jesus given at different times to create the sermon.

It is difficult to locate an explanation for why Matthew bracketed the sermon with "And seeing the crowds, He ascended into the mountain; and having sat down, His disciples came to Him; and having opened His mouth, He began teaching them, saying" (5:1–2) and "and it came about that when Jesus finished these words, the crowds were amazed at His teaching" (7:28). If Jesus did not preach such a sermon on a single occasion, why would the gospel writer mislead his readers to think that Christ did? This question has no plain answer.[42]

Yet the proponents of Historical Criticism, because of their proclivity to compare parts of the sermon with words of Christ uttered at other times and to assume Matthew's dependence on other writings (such as Mark and Q), find themselves compelled to visualize the sermon as made up of many small pieces that the writer of Matthew assembled in a masterful manner. This theory devastates the historical accuracy of the Gospels.

(2) Commissioning of the Twelve. A number of evangelical leaders have proposed that Jesus did not on a single occasion commission the twelve disciples as described in Matthew 10:5–42, but that Matthew has drawn together sayings of Jesus from several different occasions and combined them into a single flowing discourse. Carson, for example, is of the opinion that if the sermon came from Q, conceived as a variety of sources, oral and written and not necessarily recorded in the historical setting in which the teaching was first uttered, the effect on historical conclusions would be "not much."[43] He finds it plausible that Matthew, without violating the introductory and concluding formulas in 10:5a and 11:1, collapsed the discourse to the seventy-two in Luke 10:1–16 with the commissioning of the Twelve in Matthew 10 to form a single discourse.[44] Carson thus concludes that the Matthew 10 instructions are a mingling of what Jesus gave the seventy-two with what He told the Twelve when He sent them out.[45]

However, Carson's explanation of how such liberties are possible without violating the sermon's introduction and conclusion is unconvincing. Certainly Matthew left no clues for his first readers to alert them to the fact that this sermon was a compilation of Jesus' teachings from more than one occasion.[46]

Wilkins agrees that Matthew 10:5–42 is a composite of Jesus' utterances on several occasions. Wilkins evidences his agreement in allowing that Matthew used a statement from a separate occasion when he borrowed from Mark 9:41–42 in recording Jesus' words in the last verse of Matthew 10.[47] The episode in Mark came later in Jesus' life when Jesus warned His disciples against causing believers to stumble, and the passage is parallel to Matthew 18:6.

Wilkins shows his view further in stating that the interpretation and context of Matthew 10:24–25 differs from that of the similar statement in Q (Luke 6:40).[48] The context of the latter is that of Luke's Sermon on the Plain, which came chronologically earlier than the commissioning of the

Twelve in Matthew 10. Wilkins' conclusion is that Matthew used the statement from Q in two different places, once in its correct historical context and once in the context of Matthew 10. Thus Wilkins groups himself with those who view Matthew 10:5–42 as a combination of Jesus' words from different periods of His ministry, in disregard for the historical markers found in the discourse's introduction and conclusion.

Blomberg also notes how the latter part of the discourse in Matthew 10 (Matt. 10:17–42) parallels Jesus' eschatological discourse (especially, Mark 13:9–13; Luke 21:12–17) and scattered excerpts in Luke elsewhere (for example, 12:2–9, 51–53; 14:26–27). On this basis and because of what Blomberg calls the vague wording of Matthew 11:1, he concludes that a theory of composite origins is more plausible here than it is in Matthew's other four discourses.[49]

Gundry joins in the opinion that in Matthew 10:16–42 "Matthew brings together various materials scattered in Mark and Luke and relates them to the persecution of the twelve disciples, who stand for all disciples of Jesus."[50]

The theory of literary dependence again has caused its advocates to sacrifice historical particularity in the gospel accounts. It has also caused a disregard for the discourse's introduction (Matt. 10:5a)—"Jesus sent these twelve, charging them, saying"—and conclusion (Matt. 11:1a)—"and it came about when Jesus finished giving orders to His twelve disciples"—which to Matthew's earliest readers and to readers for almost twenty centuries have meant that Matthew 10:5–42 constituted a commissioning of Jesus delivered on one occasion, not several.

(3) The Parables of Mark 4 and Matthew 13. Bock proposes that the parable accounts of Mark 4 and Matthew 13 are probably anthologies.[51] He notes the difficulty in placing the parable of the soils chronologically in light of the possibility that either Matthew or Mark, or both, may have done some rearranging of material. Bock sees the parables as having been uttered by Jesus on separate occasions and grouped in these chapters for topical reasons. He gives little or no historical weight to Matthew 13:1–3 and 13:53, another introduction and conclusion that bracket the parabolic teachings in 13:4–52.[52]

In dealing with the Mark sequence of parables, Brooks isolates 4:10–12 and 4:21–25 as words not spoken by Jesus on this particular occasion.[53] Regarding the former, he favors those as words applying to Jesus' whole ministry and not just to Jesus' teachings in parables, as Mark indicates. Regarding the latter, Brooks sees those as five or six sayings of Jesus spoken at various times, with Mark bringing them together and attributing them to Jesus at this point in His ministry. It is clear that Mark's introduction and conclusion to the parabolic discourse (Mark 4:1–2, 33) are of no historical consequence to Brooks.

Stein suggests the possibility that the three synoptic writers, Luke in particular (Luke 8:11–15), interpreted the parable of the soils in light of their own theological interests.[54] Without concluding that the interpretation was a pure creation of the early church, he still sees that interpretation as being strongly influenced by early church circumstances in which existed a real danger of falling away from allegiance to Christ. Again, this questions the historical integrity of such indicators as Luke's clear statement that Jesus Himself gave the interpretation of Luke 8:9–10.

Stein's statement about the parabolic series in Mark 4:3–32 confirms his reluctance to attribute historical worth to introductory and concluding formulas: "It is clear that Mark sees the parables of Mark 4:3–32 as a summary collection and not a chronology of consecutive parables that Jesus taught in a single day."[55] With this perspective Stein can allow Matthew to add parables to Mark's collection and Luke to put some of the parables in other locations.[56] This is all without regard to how it erodes the historicity of the biblical text.

(4) The Olivet Discourse. Brooks expresses the following opinion regarding Jesus' Olivet discourse:

> This claim that the substance of the discourse goes back to Jesus himself should not be extended to claim that it is a verbatim report or free from any adaptation and application on Mark's part or spoken on one occasion. That portions of it are found in other contexts in Matthew and Luke suggests Mark included some comments Jesus spoke on other occasions.[57]

Blomberg concurs with this position:

> Sayings of Jesus may appear in different contexts. The Sermon on the Mount (Mt. 5–7) and the Olivet Discourse (Mt. 24–25) gather together teachings which are scattered all around the Gospel of Luke. Some of these may simply reflect Jesus' repeated utterances; others no doubt reflect the common practice of creating composite speeches. Again, no one questioned the integrity of ancient historians when they utilized a device that modern readers often find artificial.[58]

Yet one must ask Brooks and Blomberg what to make of the introductory and concluding formulas of this discourse, which in Matthew read, "Jesus answered and said to them" (Matt. 24:4) and "and it came about when Jesus finished all these words" (Matt. 26:1). Despite what the practice of ancient historians may have been, Matthew's intention to cite a continuous discourse from a single occasion is conspicuous. Was he mistaken? Hopefully, an evangelical would not propose that he was.

Regarding the discourse, Stein writes the following:

> Although Luke added additional material to the discourse (cf. 21:12, 15, 18, 20–22, 23b–26a, 28), his main source appears to have been Mark. Whether his additional material came from

another source or sources (L, proto-Luke, some apocalyptic source) is debated.[59]

Like others of the historical-critical school, Stein sees in this discourse (as recorded in all three Synoptic Gospels) sayings that Jesus uttered on other occasions.[60] Stein even attributes to Luke a widening of the audience of the discourse from that to whom it was addressed in Mark, his source.[61] Later in his comments, Stein suggests, "Luke changed Mark 13:19; Matt 24:21 . . . in order to avoid confusing Jerusalem's destruction, which he was describing, with the final tribulation that precedes the return of the Son of Man, which Mark and Matthew were describing."[62] All this raises the question as to what were the circumstances and words of Jesus on the occasion of the sermon. Were they as Mark and Matthew described them, as Luke described them, or neither?

Modifying of material

The second type of alteration is that of modifying material. This editorial activity accounts for places where a writer changed material when incorporating it into his gospel. Illustrations (5), (6), and (7) are of this type.

(5) The Exception Clause. Hagner is one of those who cannot endorse the exception clauses in Matthew 5:32 and 19:9 as having come from Jesus. One of the reasons he gives for this is the absolute prohibition of divorce in Mark 10:11, which Matthew allegedly used as his source.[63] With this to work from, either Matthew or someone else in the traditional handling of Jesus' teaching must have added it.[64]

Gundry's reasoning is similar as he draws the conclusion, "It [the exception clause in Matthew 5:32] comes from Matthew, not from Jesus, as an editorial insertion to conform Jesus' words to God's Word in the Old Testament."[65] Stein likewise reasons that "the 'exception clause' is an interpretative comment added by Matthew" because of its nonappearance in Mark, Q, and Paul.[66] Bruner says the exception clause came from the creative thought of Jesus' spokesman, not from Jesus Himself.[67] In other words, Jesus never uttered the clause.

Here is another instance where the assumption of literary dependence forces scholars to diminish the historical precision of a gospel account. This is no different in kind from decisions of the Jesus Seminar. Granted, these evangelicals do not carry their dehistoricizing to the same degree as those who radically reduce the biographical data in the Gospels, but it is nevertheless the same type of dehistoricizing.

(6) Dialogue with the Rich Man. The writer of Matthew supposedly found the words of Jesus and the rich man in Mark 10:17–18 theologically unacceptable and changed them in his account to solve a Christological problem:

Mark 10:17–18	Matthew 19:16–17
. . . Having run up and knelt before Him, one was asking Him, "Good Teacher, what should I do to inherit eternal life?" And Jesus said to him, "Why do you call me good? No one is good but God alone."	. . . Having come up to Him, one said, "Teacher, what good thing should I do to have eternal life?" And He said to him, "Why do you ask me about what is good? One there is who is good."

The impression given by Stein and others is that Mark's wording implies that Jesus was less than deity. Thus Matthew felt compelled to change the young man's question and Jesus' answer to convey a high view of Christology.[68] Even Stonehouse sacrificed the historical accuracy of Matthew's account in theorizing that Matthew changed Mark's wording and thereby attributed to Jesus words that He never spoke.[69]

All these recent writers part company with Warfield on this issue. It was in connection with this passage that Warfield reached the sensible conclusion already noted: "And in general, no form of criticism is more uncertain than that, now so diligently prosecuted, which seeks to explain the several forms of narratives in the Synoptics as modifications of one another."[70] It is not difficult to harmonize Matthew's account of the rich man with the one in Mark and Luke if one drops the assumption that Matthew embellished Mark's account and assumes that all three writers worked independently of each other.[71]

(7) The Pharisees. It is a recent tendency among evangelicals to dwell on the positive qualities of the Pharisees of Jesus' time, even though Jesus emphatically denounced the group on many occasions, such as in Matthew 23:13–36 when He pronounced woes against them and the scribes. Hagner laments as follows:

> It is a tragedy that from this ch. in Matthew [chapter 23] that the word "Pharisee" has come to mean popularly a self-righteous, hypocritical prig. Unfortunately not even Christian scholarship was able over the centuries to rid itself of an unfair bias against the Pharisees.[72]

Wyatt proposes that an accurate description of the Pharisees is possible only by a comparison of three major sources: Josephus, the New Testament, and the rabbinic literature.[73] The resultant picture differs from how the New Testament pictures them, namely, almost always in a negative light.

Hagner notes, "Pharisaism was at heart, though tragically miscarried, a movement for righteousness. . . . This basic drive for righteousness accounts for what may be regarded as attractive and Biblical both about Pharisaic and rabbinic Judaism."[74] One can only marvel at how radically this appraisal differs from that of Jesus: "For I say to you, unless your righteousness exceeds that of the scribes and Pharisees, you shall in no way enter the kingdom of heaven" (Matt. 5:20).

How has Historical Criticism managed to formulate a picture of this group so diverse from the one painted by Jesus? Largely through assuming that the gospel writers, particularly Matthew, took great editorial liberties in describing the life of Christ. Matthew allegedly was writing about the church of his day late in the first century more than about the actual experiences and words of Jesus. By comparing Matthew with his source, Mark, one can reputedly see how Matthew's embellishments were intended to make the Pharisees look so bad. The cause of these embellishments is traceable to the presumed tension that existed between Matthew's community and "a noticeable Jewish presence" in which Matthew wrote his gospel.[75] It supposedly was this hostility between the late first-century church and the synagogue that left its impact on the material found in Matthew 23.[76]

This type of reasoning once again highlights the implications of theorizing a form of literary dependence among the Synoptic-Gospel writers. In trying to explain why Matthew changed his source material to convey new emphases, the historical critic must postulate that the writers took editorial liberties that exceeded the limits of historical precision. In the case of the Pharisees, that liberty included reading into the life of Jesus circumstances that prevailed in the surroundings of Matthew when he wrote his gospel.[77]

Creation of Material

The third kind of editorial change is that of creativity. In this case, according to historical critics, the writer inserted new material that was not a part of the source(s) from which he worked. Examples (8), (9), and (10) come under this classification.

(8) The Genealogies. In regard to the two genealogies in Luke and Matthew, Marshall and Gundry assume that the two writers worked from a common source, presumably "Q." By comparing Luke's genealogy with the one in Matthew, Marshall detects that Luke's genealogy is not historically accurate.[78] On the other hand, when Gundry compares Matthew's genealogy with the one in Luke, he finds that Matthew has made more revisions in the traditional material than Luke.[79] This leads Gundry to the conclusion that Matthew's "genealogy has become a large figure of speech for Jesus' messianic kingship,"[80] thereby removing it from the realm of historical data. Marshall concludes that it is impossible "to be sure that the genealogy in Lk. is accurate in detail," and may have resulted from Luke's use of midrashic techniques.[81]

Here are two evangelical treatments that dehistoricize the genealogies. The starting point for both is apparently the assumption that the two gospel writers used a common source. In other words, the two commentators feel compelled to explain discrepancies in the genealogies as traceable to editorial liberties taken by the gospel writers, liberties that injected nonhistorical elements into the apparent ancestral lists. They choose the assumption that the writers worked from a common source rather than the possibility that they worked from different sources and that the genealogies lend themselves to rational harmonization.[82]

(9) Visit of the Magi. Because of his assumption that Matthew follows the same tradition as represented in Luke 2:8–20 (presumably the tradition found in Q), Gundry concludes that Matthew 2:1–12 transforms the visit of local Jewish shepherds into adoration by Gentile magi from foreign parts.[83] Gundry sees the necessity of a transformation because of his foregone conclusion that literary collaboration must explain the origin of the Synoptic Gospels.

Such compulsion forces the conclusion that the author of Matthew takes editorial liberty with his sources, a liberty justified by allowing that Matthew incorporated lessons for the church of his day into his gospel. Gundry alleges that for Matthew the coming of the magi previews the bringing of Gentiles into the church at a later time.[84] To further his emphasis on Jesus as the star of David, Matthew supposedly also replaces the tradition about the angel and the heavenly host (Luke 2:8–15a) with that about a star.[85] Here is another example of the extremes to which an assumption of literary dependence among the synoptists will drive a scholar.

(10) The Beatitudes. Opinion is also widespread among evangelical advocates of Historical Criticism that Jesus is not the source of all the beatitudes in Matthew 5:3–12. Hagner allows that eight of them (5:3–10) may have originated with Jesus Himself—though Jesus spoke them in the second person rather than the third as Matthew has them—but that the ninth (5:11–12) is probably an addition by Matthew himself.[86] Guelich is of the opinion that the core beatitudes (5:3, 4, 6; also 5:11–12) go back to Jesus Himself, but that four more (5:5, 7, 8, 9) developed in church tradition after Jesus and before Matthew wrote. The gospel writer himself created one beatitude (5:10).[87] Gundry's approach has four beatitudes coming from the lips of Jesus (5:3, 4, 9, 10) and four resulting from Matthew's redaction (5:5, 6, 7, 8).[88]

Gundry assumes Matthew's source (Q?)[89] had only four beatitudes because Luke's Sermon on the Plain has only four. So, Gundry concludes, Matthew must have added the other four.[90] Guelich understands several stages in the growth of three to eight beatitudes. Jesus originated the first three for the sake of the "desperate ones of his day."[91] Tension between what Jesus was accomplishing and the future consummation was the cause for adding the fourth (5:11–12) to the list. The Christian community later added four more (5:5, 7–9) through the use of the Psalms and Jesus' sayings. Finally, Matthew added the last (5:10) as he adapted the rest to Isaiah 61.[92] Hagner sees the first eight beatitudes as a unity in themselves, with the ninth probably being added by Matthew himself.[93]

In one way or another the positions of all three men arise through the assumption that Matthew worked from the same source (presumably Q) as Luke did in creating the Sermon on the Plain. So they must explain Matthew's differences from Luke under the assumption that they arose through Matthew's editorial activity. This assumption forces them to grant Matthew unusual liberties in attributing to Jesus either one, four, or five of the beatitudes that He never spoke, which amounts to a dehistoricizing of the gospel accounts. Even the Jesus Seminar has allowed that Jesus probably spoke three of the beatitudes, the same number granted by Guelich.[94]

AN ANALYSIS OF THE CRISIS: ITS ROOTS AND ITS FRUITS

The above ten "tip-of-the-iceberg" illustrations are revealing. The hazards of Historical Criticism have entered the evangelical camp, raising questions about how much of the Gospels is accurate history and how much is editorial embellishment. McKnight's rejoinder that redaction is not a matter that impinges on history, but that it is a matter of style[95] makes an "either-or" issue out of one that is rightly a matter of "both-and." If authorial style introduces historical inaccuracy, it is not "contorted historiography and logic"—as McKnight contends—to conclude that it is *both* authorial style *and* historical distortion.[96] A factual misrepresentation is an inaccuracy, regardless of its cause.

Yes, a "Jesus crisis" does exist because evangelicals, the expected defenders of "Gospel truth," have yielded important ground to enemies of the truth. Who will defend the integrity of the Synoptic Gospels if those expected to do so have gone over to the side of the enemy?

How has all this transpired? How did the enemy get his foot in the door to cause those of an otherwise conservative theological orientation to surrender the historical accuracy of the Gospels? How does this defection affect specific areas of biblical study and application? The following pages propose to answer these and other questions according to the following plan.

Part 1

The first portion of this volume will explore the roots of Historical Criticism. The six chapters in it will show how evangelicalism has absorbed more and more of what was in the beginning a liberal theological ideology.

Chapter 1	This chapter presents an investigation of the views of the ancient church regarding the Synoptic Gospels. The following question will be addressed: Did early church fathers show any signs of embracing historical-critical views?
Chapter 2	This chapter conducts an examination of philosophical and theological influences that gave rise to Historical Criticism. The following question will be addressed: In what sort of theological environment did the system come into existence?
Chapter 3	This chapter probes Source Criticism in general and the Two-Source Theory in particular. The following question

will be addressed: What influences produced this way of explaining the origin of the Synoptic Gospels?

Chapter 4   This chapter takes a look at Eta Linnemann. She is a renowned scholar who at one time was an internationally known historical critic but who has since broken ranks with Historical Criticism. The following question will be addressed: How have evangelicals and others responded to her embracing of a traditional view of the Synoptic Gospels?

Chapter 5   This chapter delves into Form Criticism and Tradition Criticism. The following question will be addressed: How were these two fields the natural outgrowth of widely accepted theories of Source Criticism?

Chapter 6   This chapter presents an analysis of Redaction Criticism. The following question will be addressed: How did it grow from a subdiscipline of Form Criticism into a discipline of its own?

Part 2

The second portion of *The Jesus Crisis* will look at some of the fruits of Historical Criticism. The five chapters in it will show how the results of Historical Criticism reflect the unhealthy theological origin of the ideology.

Chapter 7   This chapter presents an exegetical study of the Lukan prologue (Luke 1:1–4) from the standpoint of whether it supports literary dependence among the synoptists, as historical critics have alleged. The following question will be addressed: Did Luke acknowledge his use of another canonical gospel as a source in writing his own gospel account?

Chapter 8   This chapter presents an exegetical study in which the traditional understanding of the rich ruler passage in Luke (Luke 18:18–30) is compared with a contemporary understanding of the same passage by Historical Criticism. The following question will be addressed: How great of an effect does Historical Criticism have on exegetical study of the Gospels?

Chapter 9   This chapter notes the effect of Historical Criticism on hermeneutics. The following question will be addressed: Can Historical Criticism legitimately claim to follow principles of traditional grammatical-historical exegesis?

Chapter 10   This chapter discusses the impact of Historical Criticism on preaching. The following question will be addressed: Does Historical Criticism allow for an expository treatment of a synoptic text?

Chapter 11   This chapter contemplates some of the results of Historical Criticism in the fields of theology and apologetics. The

following questions will be addressed: Can a historical
critic defend the Christian faith against its enemies? Is it
possible for Historical Criticism to delineate a precise theology of Jesus Himself?

The Epilogue

The epilogue summarizes the major points and suggests measures to
alleviate and/or eliminate the existing Jesus crisis.

ENDNOTES

1. The ensuing discussion will not attempt a close definition of the term "evangelical" or "evangelicalism." The loose sense envisioned allows the word to
   apply to individuals who probably think of themselves as being in the evangelical camp.
2. Alister McGrath, "Why Evangelicalism is the Future of Protestantism," *Christianity Today* 39, no. 7 (June 19, 1995): 20.
3. Ibid.
4. Robert W. Funk, Roy W. Hoover, and the Jesus Seminar, *The Five Gospels:
   The Search for the Authentic Words of Jesus* (New York: Macmillan, 1993).
5. For example, D. A. Carson, "Five Gospels, No Christ," *Christianity Today*
   38, no. 5 (April 25, 1994): 30–33; Ben Witherington III, *The Jesus Quest:
   The Third Search for the Jew of Nazareth* (Downers Grove: InterVarsity,
   1995), 42–43; James R. Edwards, "Who Do Scholars Say That I Am?" *Christianity Today* 40, no. 3 (March 4, 1996): 14–20.
6. For example, Michael J. Wilkins and J. P. Moreland, gen. eds., *Jesus Under
   Fire* (Grand Rapids: Zondervan, 1995); Gregory A. Boyd, *Cynic, Sage, or
   Son of God?* (Wheaton: Victor, 1995); Witherington, *Jesus Quest*, 42–57.
   Jesus Under Fire includes chapters by Craig L. Blomberg, Scot McKnight,
   and Darrell L. Bock, among others.
7. Benjamin Breckinridge Warfield, *Christology and Criticism* (New York:
   Oxford, 1929), 115.
8. Carson alludes to such a possibility ("Five Gospels," 30).
9. A detailed discussion about and the documentation for the same ten issues
   enumerated here appears later in this introductory chapter under the heading "Consequences of Literary Dependence."
10. Marshall comments as follows regarding Ernst Käsemann: "Many people who
    read his works may well be highly shocked by the amount of material in the
    Gospels which even he regards as unhistorical" (I. Howard Marshall, *I Be-
    lieve in the Historical Jesus* [Grand Rapids: Eerdmans, 1977], 12). The same
    observation would hold true regarding many evangelical scholars, if Chris-
    tians in evangelical churches were to have access to an exhaustive compila-
    tion of their conclusions about unhistorical facets in the Gospels.
11. See "How Should the Jesus Seminar's Conclusions Be Viewed?" *Los Ange-
    les Times* (April 6, 1991): F18–F19.
12. See "Did the Jesus Seminar Draw from Faulty Assumptions?" *Los Angeles
    Times* (April 13, 1991): F18–F19.
13. Craig L. Blomberg argues for an "evidentialist" approach in responding to
    radical excesses in dehistoricizing the Gospels (*The Historical Reliability of
    the Gospels* [Downers Grove, Ill.: InterVarsity, 1987], 9–10). He contrasts
    this with a "presuppositionalist" approach, which assumes the inspiration of
    the Scriptures. What he means by "evidentialist"—namely, defending the

accuracy of Scripture on purely historical grounds—includes an embracing of the same methodology as those of radical persuasions (cf. ibid., 12–18). That is the methodology outlined below in this section.

14. I. Howard Marshall, "Historical Criticism," in *New Testament Interpretation*, ed. I. Howard Marshall (Grand Rapids: Eerdmans, 1977), 126–27.
15. For example, William W. Klein, Craig L. Blomberg, and Robert L. Hubbard, Jr., *Introduction to Biblical Interpretation* (Dallas: Word, 1993), 95; Robert H. Stein, *The Synoptic Problem, An Introduction* (Grand Rapids: Baker, 1987), 217–18; Blomberg, *Historical Reliability*, 20; Edwards, "Who Do Scholars," 20.
16. For example, Klein et al., *Biblical Interpretation*, 164.
17. For example, Stein, *Synoptic Problem*, 96, 149–50, 219–20.
18. The proposal of Markan priority originated relatively recently. France recalls that Matthean priority was the unanimous opinion of the church for seventeen hundred years, until the theory of Markan priority emerged (R. T. France, *Matthew, Evangelist and Teacher* [Grand Rapids: Zondervan, 1989], 25–27).
19. See Eta Linnemann, "Is There a Gospel of Q?" *Bible Review* (August 1995): 19–23, 42, for strong evidence that Q never existed.
20. For example, Darrell L. Bock, *Luke 1:1–9:50*, in Baker Exegetical Commentary on the New Testament, Moisés Silva, ed. (Grand Rapids: Baker, 1994), 7; D. A. Carson, "Matthew," in *EBC*, Frank E. Gaebelein, gen. ed. (Grand Rapids: Zondervan, 1984), 8:13; John Nolland, *Luke, Volume 1: 1:1–9:50*, vol. 35A of *Word Biblical Commentary*, David A. Hubbard and Glenn W. Barker, gen. eds. (Dallas: Word, 1989), xxix.
21. Robert H. Stein, *Synoptic Problem*, 29–44. Scot McKnight builds a case for literary dependence that is similar to Stein's (*Interpreting the Synoptic Gospels* [Grand Rapids: Baker, 1988], 37–40).
22. See Robert L. Thomas, "The Agreements Between Matthew and Luke Against Mark," *JETS* 19 (1976): 110–11; idem, "The Rich Young Man in Matthew," *Grace Theological Journal* 3, no. 2 (fall 1982): 244–48.
23. Thomas, "Agreements," 112; see also idem, "Rich Young Man," 249–51, 259.
24. Stein, *Synoptic Problem*, 34–37.
25. For example, Robert H. Gundry, *Matthew, A Commentary on His Handbook for a Mixed Church under Persecution*, 2d ed. (Grand Rapids: Eerdmans, 1994), 481.
26. Cf. Stein, *Synoptic Problem*, 42, 194; idem, *Luke*, vol. 24 of *The New American Commentary* (Nashville: Broadman, 1992), 28–29, 63.
27. See Chapter 7 of this volume for a full discussion of the Lukan Prologue.
28. For example, see Wayne A. Meeks, "Hypomnemata from an Untamed Skeptic: A Response to George Kennedy," *The Relationships Among the Gospels*, William O. Walker, Jr., ed. (San Antonio: Trinity University, 1978), 171.
29. For example, Albert B. Lord, "The Gospels as Oral Tradition Literature," in *The Relationships Among the Gospels*, William O. Walker, Jr., ed. (San Antonio: Trinity University, 1978), 82; Leander F. Keck, "Oral Tradition Literature and the Gospels," in *The Relationships Among the Gospels*, 116; Eta Linnemann, *Is There a Synoptic Problem?* (Grand Rapids: Baker, 1992), 155–91; cf. R. T. France, *Matthew, Evangelist and Teacher* (Grand Rapids: Zondervan, 1989), 25.
30. A closely related theory goes by the name Four-Source, the two additional documents being "M" (on which Matthew relied) and "L" (on which Luke relied). Like "Q," these two documents are also phantoms. No one in modern times—if indeed at any time during the Christian era—has ever seen them.

31. Everett F. Harrison, *Introduction to the New Testament* (Grand Rapids: Eerdmans, 1964), 145.

32. Jude gives credit to Peter indirectly as his source in Jude 17. The theory that ancient writers never gave credit for their sources—a precedent that the synoptists allegedly followed in copying and editing one another's works—runs counter to available evidence. Eusebius, the early church historian, regularly gives the sources of information found in his writings. If a gospel writer's source had been anything other than what he represents it to be—namely, the activities and spoken words of Jesus—he would surely have stated it.

33. Scot McKnight, *Interpreting the Synoptic Gospels* (Grand Rapids: Baker, 1988), 84, 87.

34. Cf. Donald A. Hagner, "Interpreting the Gospels: The Landscape and the Quest," *JETS* 24, no. 1 (March 1981): 30–31.

35. In which category each example belongs is a subjective judgment. Recategorizing from one category to another does not affect the thrust of this discussion. As they stand, perhaps the order of the categories reflects an increasing degree of departure from historical accuracy, with arrangement having the smallest impact. Nevertheless, even with arrangement, a degree of dehistoricization is present.

36. Robert A. Guelich, *The Sermon on the Mount, A Foundation for Understanding* (Dallas: Word, 1982), 33.

37. Robert H. Mounce, *Matthew,* A Good News Commentary, W. Ward Gasque, ed. (San Francisco: Harper & Row, 1985), 34.

38. Stein, *Luke,* 198; cf. also idem, *Synoptic Problem,* 96, 219–20.

39. Donald A. Hagner, *Matthew 1–13,* vol. 33A of *Word Biblical Commentary,* David A. Hubbard and Glenn W. Barker, gen. eds. (Dallas: Word, 1993), 83. Regarding the conclusion of the Sermon on the Mount (Matt 7:28–29), Hagner writes, "Matthew will not miss the opportunity here at the end of a *masterful distillation* of the teaching of Jesus to call his readers' attention to the supreme authority of this Teacher" (194, emphasis added). Hagner apparently means the Sermon is "masterful" because of Matthew's knack for distillation, not because of Jesus' preaching.

40. For example, William W. Klein, Craig L. Blomberg, and Robert L. Hubbard, Jr., *Introduction to Biblical Interpretation* (Dallas: Word, 1993), 164 n. 10; C. R. Blomberg, "Gospels (Historical Reliability)," in *Dictionary of Jesus and the Gospels,* Joel B. Green, Scot McKnight, and I. Howard Marshall, eds. (Downers Grove, Ill.: InterVarsity, 1992), 295; G. R. Osborne, "Round Four: The Redaction Debate Continues," *JETS* 28, no. 4 (December 1985): 406; France, *Matthew,* 162–64. McKnight writes, "I would suggest that Matthew (or a previous Christian teacher) has thematically combined two teachings on prayer for reasons other than strict chronology, augmenting 6:5–6 with 6:7–13 (14–15)" (*Synoptic Gospels,* 53 n. 2). In other words, Jesus did not utter 6:7–13 on the same occasion as He gave the words of 6:5–6.

41. Michael J. Wilkins, *The Concept of Disciple in Matthew's Gospel, As Reflected in the Use of the Term* Mathētēs (Leiden: E. J. Brill, 1988), 149–50. Gundry is similar in treating the introduction and conclusion to the Sermon, observing that "and seeing the crowds" (Matt 5:1) is a Matthean addition that makes Jesus' teaching applicable to the universal church, that Matthew derives "He went up a mountain" (Matt 5:1) from Mark 3:13a, that "and it came about when He completed these words" (7:28) is a rewording of Luke 7:1a, and that "the crowds were amazed at His teaching" is the writer's reworking of Mark 1:22 (*Matthew,* 65–66, 136).

42. D. A. Carson comments on those who see the introductory and concluding notes that frame each of Matthew's five discourse as "artistic, compositional devices" ("Matthew," in *Expositor's Bible Commentary*, Frank E. Gaebelein, gen. ed. [Grand Rapids: Zondervan, 1984], 124). He objects to this premise because such introductory and concluding brackets do not appear in any other first-century literature. This means they were not merely artistic devices to show the reader that they meant anything other than to furnish the historical setting they profess to describe (124–25).
43. Carson, "Matthew," 243. When Carson sees the effect of this theory on historical accuracy as "not much," he in essence concedes that it does make *some* difference. Yet he endorses the theory anyway. The effect on the meaning of the words is significant rather than "not much," when he casts them in a different historical context.
44. Ibid., 241–42; cf. Blomberg, *Historical Reliability*, 145–46.
45. Carson, "Matthew," 241.
46. See R. Morosco, "Redaction Criticism and the Evangelical: Matthew 10 a Test Case," *JETS* 22 [1979]: 323–31, for an attempt to prove that "seams" in the discourse are a sign of such a compilation. Except for the last two centuries, however, Morosco's proposed clues have escaped readers since the time of Christ. The reason is they are nonexistent in the discourse. See also idem, "Matthew's Formation of a Commissioning Type-Scene out of the Story of Jesus' Commissioning of the Twelve," *JBL* 103 (1984): 539–56.
47. Wilkins, *Matthew*, 131.
48. Ibid., 145.
49. Craig L. Blomberg, *Matthew*, vol. 22 of *The New American Commentary*, David S. Dockery, gen. ed. (Nashville, Tenn.: Broadman, 1992), 166.
50. Gundry, *Matthew*, 190–91.
51. Bock, *Luke 1:1–9:50*, 718, 742–43. R. T. France also views the parables of Matthew 13 as a compilation, not uttered by Jesus on the same occasion: "This is hardly a 'single sermon', and it seems that the larger part of it is not addressed to the audience stated in verse 2 at all" (*Matthew*, 157).
52. Blomberg follows a slightly different path in concluding that the parables of Matthew 13:1–52 came on a single occasion, but that Mark and Luke redistributed them elsewhere in their gospels. He gives Mark and Q as Matthew's source for the parables, but then says that Mark along with Luke have scattered these parables elsewhere. He evidences a lack of concern for Mark's introduction and conclusion that bracket his section of parables, two of which parallel those in Matthew 13 (cf. Mark 4:1–2, 33) (*Matthew*, 211).
53. James A. Brooks, *Mark*, vol. 23 of *The New American Commentary*, David S. Dockery, gen. ed. (Nashville: Broadman, 1991), 82–83.
54. Stein, *Luke*, 243–44.
55. Stein, *Synoptic Problem*, 36.
56. Ibid. Cf. also Gundry, *Matthew*, 250; Klein, Blomberg, and Hubbard, *Biblical Interpretation*, 164.
57. Brooks, *Mark*, 205.
58. Blomberg, "Gospels (Historical Reliability)," 295. Blomberg attributes a higher degree of accuracy to modern historians than to Spirit-inspired writers of the Gospels in ancient times.
59. Stein, *Luke*, 510 n. 57.
60. Ibid., 510.
61. Ibid.
62. Ibid., 522.

63. Hagner, *Matthew 1–13,* 123, cf. xlvii–xlviii.
64. Ibid., 123.
65. Gundry, *Matthew,* 90.
66. Stein, *Synoptic Problem,* 152.
67. Frederick Dale Bruner, *The Christbook, A Historical/Theological Commentary: Matthew 1–12* (Dallas: Word, 1987), 191.
68. Stein, *Synoptic Problem,* 67, 75–76; cf. also Gundry, *Matthew,* 385; Blomberg, *Matthew,* 297; Carson, "Matthew," 421–23.
69. Ned B. Stonehouse, *Origins of the Synoptic Gospels* (Grand Rapids: Eerdmans, 1963), 108–9. For further discussion of Stonehouse's theory, see chapter 11 of this volume, "Impact of Historical Criticism on Theology and Apologetics." However, Stonehouse saw Matthew's motive for change as a desire to bring a different emphasis to the words, not to convey a higher view of Christology.
70. Warfield, *Christology and Criticism,* 115 n.
71. Cf. Thomas, "Rich Young Man," 251–56; cf. also Carson, "Matthew," 423.
72. D. A. Hagner, "Pharisees," *The Zondervan Pictorial Encyclopedia of the Bible,* Merrill C. Tenney, gen. ed. (Grand Rapids: Zondervan, 1975), 4:750.
73. R. J. Wyatt, "Pharisees," *The International Standard Bible Encyclopedia,* Geoffrey W. Bromiley, gen. ed. (Grand Rapids: Eerdmans, 1986), 3:823.
74. Hagner, "Pharisees," 752.
75. S. Westerholm, "Pharisees," *Dictionary of Jesus and the Gospels,* Joel B. Green and Scot McKnight, eds. (Downers Grove, Ill.: InterVarsity, 1992), 613.
76. Donald A. Hagner, *Matthew 14–28,* vol. 33B of *Word Biblical Commentary* (Dallas: Word, 1995), 654–55.
77. Westerholm expresses the position of Historical Criticism thus: "The Gospels' depictions of Pharisees reflect both memories from the career of Jesus *and subsequent developments in the Christian communities*" (Westerholm, "Pharisees," 613, emphasis added).
78. I. Howard Marshall, *The Gospel of Luke, Commentary on the Greek Text,* in The New International Greek Testament Commentary (Grand Rapids: Eerdmans, 1978), 157–60.
79. Gundry, *Matthew,* 13–14.
80. Gundry, *Matthew,* 15.
81. Marshall, *Luke,* 160. Nolland sees difficulty in reading biblical genealogies with a strict historical and biographical interest. He concludes that this difficulty precludes ancestry as the exclusive factor in interpreting the Lukan genealogy (*Luke 1–9:20,* 169).
82. For possible ways to harmonize the genealogies, see Robert L. Thomas, ed., and Stanley N. Gundry, assoc. ed., *A Harmony of the Gospels with Explanations and Essays, Using the Text of the New American Standard Bible* (San Francisco: Harper & Row, 1978), 313–19; idem, *The NIV Harmony of the Gospels* (San Francisco: Harper & Row, 1988), 304–10.
83. Gundry, *Matthew,* 26–27, 651 n. 25.
84. Ibid., 27.
85. Ibid.
86. Hagner, *Matthew 1–13,* 90.
87. Guelich, *Sermon on the Mount,* 117–18. Bock calls Guelich's analysis "helpful," but is less confident than Guelich as to whether Matthew and his sources are responsible for additional beatitudes beyond what Jesus actually spoke (Bock, *Luke . . . 1:1–9:50,* 552).
88. Gundry, *Matthew,* 67–70. Hagner, Guelich, and Gundry differ conspicuously

among themselves regarding which beatitudes came from Jesus, which from church tradition, and which from Matthew.

89. See Robert H. Gundry, *Mark: A Commentary on His Apology for the Cross* (Grand Rapids: Eerdmans, 1993), 17, for an indication that Gundry understands Q to have been a written source.
90. Gundry, *Matthew*, 67–70.
91. Guelich, *Sermon on the Mount*, 17.
92. Ibid.
93. Hagner, *Matthew 1–13*, 90.
94. Funk, Hoover et al., *Five Gospels*, 138.
95. McKnight, *Synoptic Gospels*, 89–90.
96. Marshall crystallizes the issue in the following: "It is certainly impossible to practise the historical method without concluding that on occasion the correct solution to a difficulty lies in the unhistorical character of a particular narrative. Several cases of this kind have been cited above, but in many of them we have claimed that to establish that a particular statement is unhistorical is not to establish the presence of an error which would call into question the reliability of the New Testament writer. Very often the reader may be demanding a kind of historical truth from the narrative which it was never intended to provide" ("Historical Criticism," 136). Marshall proceeds to admit that the ordinary reader would view matters differently from the way scholars would. When Marshall and Blomberg speak about "reliable," they obviously distinguish the word from "accurate" or "errorless." When a writer says something happened that did not happen, he can still be reliable even though he has reported the event inaccurately or erroneously (Blomberg, *Historical Reliability*, 151–52; cf. also Marshall, "I Believe," 19). These writers distinguish sharply between what is *generally reliable* and what is *historically factual* as does Graham Stanton, who writes, "Gospel truth cannot be confirmed by historical evidence, but it does depend on *general reliability* of the evangelists' portraits of Jesus. . . . I have chosen the term 'general reliability' deliberately. We do not have precise historical *records* in the Gospels . . ." (*Gospel Truth? New Light on Jesus and the Gospels* [Valley Forge, Pa.: Trinity Press International, 1995], 193, emphasis in the original).

PART I

The Roots of
Historical Criticism

CHAPTER ONE

The Synoptic Gospels in the Ancient Church

Robert L. Thomas and
F. David Farnell

IN A COMPARISON OF HISTORICAL-CRITICAL theories regarding the Synoptic Gospels with writings originating in the early church, two focal points emerge. One relates to the sequence in which the three writers composed their books, and the other with whether they collaborated with one another in a literary manner. Those two topics will constitute the major substance of this chapter. Though this study is dealing only with the first three gospels, the fourth gospel—the gospel of John—will come up for mention now and then, for the early fathers often dealt with it along with Matthew, Mark, and Luke.

The writings of the early fathers were not inerrant, making it impossible to put them on a plane with inspired Scripture. They are, however, reliable to the point of presenting a generally consistent picture regarding the sequence of the Synoptic Gospels, literary dependence/independence, or any other issue with which they may deal. They may seem to contradict one another occasionally; indeed, a given father may seem to contradict himself at times, but a closer look will usually correct any misimpression of contradiction. Taken as a whole, they agree in reflecting what the early church thought about the order of the Gospels and the possibility/impossibility of literary collaboration among the synoptic writers.

Their view of the sequence of composition is the first item to investigate.

PART 1: THE ORDER OF COMPOSITION

Introduction

The gospel of Matthew was the church's most popular gospel in the decades up to the time of Irenaeus (c. A.D. 180). After an extensive analysis of Matthew's influence on early Christianity, Massaux relates the following:

> Of all the New Testament Writings, the Gospel of Mt. was the one whose literary influence was the most widespread and the most profound in Christian literature that extended into the last decades

of the second century. . . . Until the end of the second century,
the first gospel remained the gospel par excellence. . . . The Gospel was, therefore, the normative fact of Christian life. It created
the background for ordinary Christianity.[1]

Moreover, the unanimous and unquestioned consensus of the church
fathers was that Matthew was the first gospel written, and almost without
exception, the early church placed the gospel of Matthew first in the canon
of the New Testament. Petrie observes, "Until the latter half of the eighteenth century, the apostolic authorship of 'the Gospel according to Matthew' seems to have been generally accepted."[2]

However, the Enlightenment and its spawning of historical-critical methodologies—particularly that aspect of the system called "Source Criticism"—
marked the beginning of the end of that viewpoint.[3] Most New Testament
scholars at the turn of the twenty-first century resoundingly reject the unanimous testimony of the early church regarding Matthean priority in favor
of the Two- or Four-Source Theory[4] of how the Synoptic Gospels came
into existence.[5] That rejection characterizes not only those of a liberal-
theological perspective. It extends also to include many who probably would
classify themselves as conservative evangelicals, people such as Hill, Carson
(along with Moo and Morris), Martin, and France. Each of them explains
away the evidence from Papias and church tradition regarding Matthean
priority in deference to a theory of modern vintage that requires the priority of Mark.[6] Few conservative evangelicals today dare to challenge the
"findings" of Source Criticism.

The theory of Mark's being written first flies in the face of what is quite
clear from the writings in the early church, as Massaux has pointedly
demonstrated:

The literary influence of the Gospel of Mk. is practically nil of
these writings [namely, the church writings of the first two centuries up to Irenaeus]. This characteristic of the early tradition constitutes a strange phenomenon. How can we explain this silence
of tradition, if, as is generally believed, Mk. was the first of the
canonical gospels? How can we explain the first Christians hardly
resorted to it, so that it appeared almost nonexistent? Did it not
respond, perhaps to the exigencies and concrete needs of the
community of the time? Or have we been wrong to elevate it to
the detriment of the Gospel of Mt.?[7]

Someone besides Massaux needs to set the record straight. The church
fathers must have their hearing, apart from a dogmatism that bases itself
on a late-blooming theory regarding gospel sequence. They lived much
closer to the composition of the Gospels than anyone associated with the
Enlightenment. Also, they were scholars in their own right. Thus it is a
grave mistake to dismiss their testimony so casually as moderns have tended
to do. The church fathers bear a unified testimony against critical

assumptions of the last two centuries that have supported the priority of Mark and the associated Two- (or Four-) Source Theory. The discussion of their writings will also evidence the shortcomings of the avenue of Source Criticism that results in the Two-Gospel Theory.[8]

Papias

Early in the first half of the second century A.D., Papias was bishop of Hierapolis in the Phrygian region of the province of Asia—a city about twenty miles west of Colosse and six miles east of Laodicea.[9] Nothing much is known about Papias's life beyond the comment of Irenaeus that he was "one of the ancients."[10] His writing activity dates between approximately A.D. 95 and 110.[11] That early dating makes his works crucial, for he is one of only a few witnesses to a very early period of church history.

Papias (along with his friend and contemporary Polycarp) was a disciple and personal acquaintance of the apostle John, for Irenaeus wrote that Papias was "the hearer of John."[12] Unfortunately, Papias's writings are no longer extant. Only fragments of his works remain and are largely known through quotations by later fathers, especially Eusebius. Papias wrote a series of five treatises entitled *Interpretation of the Oracles of the Lord* (*Logiōn kyriakōn exēgēseōs*) in which he draws information from the remaining, living-eyewitness sources, namely, the apostle John himself and another original disciple of Jesus named Ariston, concerning what the apostles had said or done.[13] In essence, Papias's assertions had their foundation in direct "eyewitness" (namely, firsthand) reports.[14] If Papias wrote approximately A.D. 95–110, then the information that he imparts reaches well back into the first century and is an invaluable source of information regarding the Gospels.

Papias included a brief account in his *Expositions* regarding the composition of Matthew: "Matthew collected (*synetaxato*) the oracles (*ta logia*) in the Hebrew language (*Hebraïdi dialektō*), and each interpreted (*hermēneusen*) them as best he could."[15] A great deal of conflict, however, has raged around this short statement, especially regarding the meaning and significance of the words "the oracles" (*ta logia*) and the phrase "in the Hebrew language" (*Hebraïdi dialektō*). An understanding of the latter expression has some impact on how one interprets the former.

Ta logia as an independent collection of Jesus' sayings. Regarding the meaning of "the oracles" (*ta logia*), scholars exhibit several major interpretations. Some think that it refers to an independent collection of Jesus' sayings, perhaps Q.[16] T. W. Manson popularized the view:

> In Eusebius we find a quotation from Papias stating that "Matthew composed the oracles (*ta logia*) in the Hebrew language, and each one interpreted them as he was able." This obviously cannot refer to the first Gospel, which is essentially a Greek work based on Greek sources, of which Mark is one. It is, however, possible that what is meant is the document which we now call Q.[17]

Adding support to this conclusion was the fact that *ta logia* is not the usual way of referring to a "gospel" and would be rather unique, for the normal descriptive term already seen by the time of Papias and evidenced in early manuscripts of the Gospels would be *to euangelion*.[18]

That explanation of *ta logia*, however, is dubious for several reasons. First, Papias does not use *ta logia* to refer only to sayings but also to the deeds of Jesus. The title of Papias' work, *Interpretation of the Oracles of the Lord (Logiōn kyriakōn exēgēseōs)* implies that more than Jesus' words are encompassed in its meaning, for enough is known regarding this work that it is safe to say that Papias did not restrict it in scope to an exposition merely of Jesus's words.[19]

Second, in Eusebius's *Ecclesiastical History* 3.39.15–16, Papias commented that in composing his gospel, Mark, being Peter's interpreter, "wrote accurately all that he remembered . . . of the things said *or done* by the Lord" [emphasis added] and immediately after this spoke of Peter as "not making, as it were, an arrangement of the Lord's oracles *[syntaxin tōn kyriakōn poioumenos logiōn]*, so that Mark did nothing wrong in thus writing down single points as he remembered them." Since Mark's gospel included deeds as well as words, *tōn . . . logiōn* must include both too.

Third, the parallelism between these two phrases "things said *or done*" and "the oracles of the Lord" in immediate juxtaposition demonstrates that the expression *tōn kyriakōn . . . logiōn* ("the oracles of the Lord") can encompass both the deeds as well as the words of Jesus. Fourth, immediately after these statements regarding Mark's gospel, Papias applies the term *ta logia* ("the oracles") to Matthew's work, thus making it hard to avoid the conclusion that he refers to Matthew's gospel rather than some hypothetical sayings source like Q.[20] Therefore, the *ta logia* ("the oracles") is most naturally understood as a synonym for the gospel.[21]

No evidence exists that such a document as "Q" ever existed at Papias' time or any other time. The increasing skepticism of a wide spectrum of New Testament scholars regarding the nature (for example, makeup and extent) of Q and whether such a document ever really existed in church history make this suggestion highly dubious.[22]

Ta logia as a collection of Old Testament proof texts. A second view similar to the first is that *ta logia* refers to an Old Testament *testimonia* collection (namely, a book of Old Testament proof texts). This allegedly was compiled by Matthew from the Hebrew canon for use in Christian apologetics, and the collection eventually was incorporated into canonical Matthew. Hunt forcefully argues as follows:

> [L]ogia has nothing to do with the title of any book, but is a technical term meaning O.T. oracles. That is to say that *logia* was not the *name* of a book composed by St. Matthew, or by anyone else, but was a description of the contents of the book; it was composed of *logia*, which had been arranged by St. Matthew.[23]

For Hunt, those who would see the term *logia* as meaning "gospel" most likely "have been hypnotized by tradition" and "for whatever *ta logia* may have been taken as meaning at a later period, it could not have meant *The Gospel according to St. Matthew* when originally written; since nobody will maintain that a gospel was ever called *ta logia*."[24] Similarly, Grant asserts that *tōn kyriakōn . . . logiōn* ("the oracles of the Lord") predominately refer to "divine utterances" such as those contained in the Old Testament.[25] Therefore, Papias seems to refer to Matthew's collection of Old Testament prophecies of the Messiah, "a collection of the kind embedded in the gospel of Matthew."[26]

Yet, this view seems unlikely for significant reasons. First, a similar criticism applies to this view as to the first view above, namely, in the context of Papias' writings, *ta logia* ("the oracles") most likely refers to both deeds and sayings of Jesus and not to a hypothesized collection of Old Testament proof-texts. This view, therefore, supplies an aberrant meaning to Papias' words. It also makes Grant's assumption regarding *tōn kyriakōn... logiōn* ("the oracles of the Lord") as referring to Old Testament oracles tenuous, for Papias, in the context of Eusebius' discussion, refers to Jesus' sayings and deeds rather than Old Testament sayings. In fact, the latter is not in view at all in that context.[27]

Second, the view cannot account for the diversity of text forms in Old Testament quotations in Matthew and for the way he often parallels the LXX rather than the Hebrew Old Testament (for instance, Matt. 1:23; 5:21, 27, 38, 43; 13:14–15; 21:16).[28] Third, the most likely understanding of the term *hermēneusen* ("interpret") refers to "translation" of a language, especially in light of the phrase "in the Hebrew language" *(Hebraïdi dialektǭ)*, rather than "interpretation" of Old Testament sayings, the latter being the sense required under this view.[29] Furthermore, this Hebrew (namely, Aramaic) *testimonia* collection may not need to be "translated," especially since the LXX would have been well-established.

Ta logia as an error by Papias. Yet, if some scholars find neither of these two views satisfactory regarding *ta logia*, then they often envision two alternatives in their discussion about its meaning: either Papias was inaccurate and his testimony should be discounted, or Papias was referring to some other composition of Matthew which is not now extant.

Carson, Moo, and Morris prefer the idea that Papias' statement was partially in error when he asserted a Semitic (namely, Aramaic) original of Matthew, labeling it as "an intelligent, albeit erroneous, guess."[30] From their point of view Papias spoke from ignorance, especially if he "had no real knowledge of just how much Greek was spoken in first-century Palestine, especially in Galilee."[31] At times, they are ambivalent as to who wrote the gospel bearing Matthew's name, for after discussing the evidence, both pros and cons, for apostolic authorship of the gospel, they conclude "at one level very little hangs on the question of the authorship of this [Matthew's] gospel. By and large, neither its meaning nor its authority are greatly changed if one decides that its author was not an apostle."[32] For them, apostolic, eyewitness origin ultimately carries little weight for the validity of this gospel. Martin holds the same perspective.[33]

Harrison deprecates Papias in a fashion similar to Carson, Moo, and Morris, arguing that "Papias, like Jerome, confused the *Gospel according to the Hebrews* or something like it with an Aramaic Matthew."[34] Similarly, Hill comments, "[T]he tradition of Matthean priority rests . . . on a misinterpretation of Papias' statements, or on Papias' misunderstanding of the actual matter to which he was referring."[35]

Significantly, most of these evangelicals who dismiss the testimony of Papias apparently do so because of their acceptance of the historical-critical conclusion that Mark was the first gospel, as expressed in the Two- or Four-Source Hypothesis.[36] For them, current (and dogmatic) source-critical conclusions are sufficient to override strong and ancient historical testimony.[37] Yet, in reply, apostolic origin of the Gospels is vital for a document that purports to be a record of Jesus' historical ministry on earth. The anonymity of the Matthean gospel argues strongly for the validity of tradition that attached Matthew's name to it, for such anonymity is inexplicable apart from its direct association with the apostle Matthew. Matthew was a relatively obscure figure among the Twelve, so no adequate reason exists to explain why the early church would have chosen his name rather than a better-known apostle if he had not indeed written it.

Furthermore, the more reasonable explanation is that Papias, possessing information from highly placed apostolic and eyewitness testimony regarding Matthew, was correct and that attempts at deprecating Papias border on intellectual presumptuousness. Petrie describes such a casual dismissal of the evidence: "This is the kind of unintentional belittling guess that easily hardens from 'may be' to a firm statement and then becomes a dogmatic basis for further adventures in criticism."[38]

Since Papias is not relating his own opinion but citing information derived from firsthand reports of the apostle John and the disciple Ariston, a supposition of Papias' confusion is unlikely. For as Gundry observes, "Possibilities of confusion decrease the closer we approach the time of writing. It is especially hard to think that one of the twelve apostles, John himself, fell into such an error."[39] Interestingly, Papias uses the imperfect tense (*elegen*, "he was saying") to depict how John repeatedly transmitted information to him about Mark's arrangement of topics.[40] Theirs was not just a onetime conversation. Petrie best summarizes Historical Criticism's attack on Papias' credibility:

> This testimony is on much firmer ground than the best speculative guesses of the twentieth century, and it must be fairly and fully reckoned with in the quest for Gospel backgrounds. Failing substantial evidence to contradict it or to turn its meaning, it is not to be dismissed because of its inconvenience for current hypotheses. If it does not accord with these hypotheses, it is the hypotheses that must be considered anew. For the one is tangible evidence from a competent, informed, and credible witness; the rest, however attractive or even dazzling they appear, lack its substantiality.[41]

Ta logia *as a canonical Greek Matthew.* A fourth view of Papias' meaning takes *ta logia* to refer to the canonical Greek version of Matthew's gospel and exonerates Papias as an accurate reporter, but says his readers misunderstood him. Reflecting a concept similar to Kürzinger,[42] Gundry asserts that rather than a linguistic sense, Papias' expression "in the Hebrew dialect" *[Hebraïdi dialektō]* has a literary sense, referring to a Semitic style: "In describing Matthew, then, 'a Hebrew dialect' means a Hebrew way of presenting Jesus' messiahship."[43] With this approach, the verb *hermēneusen* ("interpreted") had the sense of "explain" rather than "translate."

Moreover, Kürzinger points out that immediately before Papias' statement regarding Matthew, he describes Mark's composition of his gospel as reflecting Peter's testimony. There Papias calls Mark the "interpreter" (*hermēneutes* [Eusebius *Ecclesiastical History* 3.39.15]) of Peter. Kürzinger insists that this cannot mean that Mark was Peter's "translator," but must have been the "interpreter" of that preached or spoken by Peter.[44] Thus, Papias' statement regarding Matthew must mean that everyone "passed on" or "interpreted" Matthew's Greek gospel to the world as he was able.

A first response to that analysis notes that although the sense of argumentational style is a possible meaning of *dialektō*,[45] it is a more remote and secondary sense. The most natural understanding of *dialektos* is "language," not "interpretation."[46] Also, the term in combination with the noun *Hebraïdi* (literally "Hebrew" but most likely a reference the Aramaic language) and the verb *hermēneuein* points to the latter's natural meaning of "translate (a language)" rather than to an alleged Semitic style. Second, the church fathers understood Papias' statement as referring to language. Without exception they held that the apostle Matthew wrote the canonical Matthew and that he wrote it first in a Semitic language.[47] Third, all six occurrences of the word *dialektos* in the New Testament refer to human languages rather than to a particular style of argument (Acts 1:19; 2:6, 8; 21:40; 22:2; 26:14).[48] These arguments render the view of Kürzinger and Gundry as very improbable.

A significant observation notes that the common thread of all four viewpoints of Papias' words discussed so far is an *a priori* assumption of validity of the Two-Document Hypothesis. As a result, they all attempt to find a way either to diminish the force of Papias' words, dismiss his information as inaccurate or wrong, or superimpose a totally foreign understanding. Survival of the cherished synoptic hypothesis drives them to pursue such tactics as Gundry illustrates in his discussion of Papias' words: "[I]t is the currently prevalent and well-substantiated opinion that our Greek Matthew shows many signs of drawing in large part on the Gospel of Mark, also written in Greek."[49]

Gundry goes one step further in his analysis of Papias' words. He takes them to indicate that Matthew deliberately corrected Mark. Immediately before Papias' comments about Matthew (Eusebius, *Ecclesiastical History* 3.39.16), Eusebius quotes Papias' description of the composition of Mark:

"And the Presbyter [John] used to say this, 'Mark became Peter's interpreter and wrote accurately all that he remembered, not, indeed, in order, of the things said or done by the Lord. For he had not heard the Lord, nor had he followed him, but later on, as I said, followed Peter, who used to give teaching as necessity demanded but not making, as it were, an arrangement of the Lord's oracles, so that Mark did nothing wrong in thus writing down single points as he remembered them. For to one thing he gave attention, to leave out nothing of what he had heard and to make no false statements in them.'" This is related by Papias about Mark.[50]

Since the statements come before Papias' comments about Matthew's gospel, Gundry contends that they prove that Mark wrote before Matthew. In a nutshell, Gundry argues that the sequence and nature of discussion in this section indicate that Matthew should be understood as a deliberate corrective to Mark. Gundry notes that Papias' statements that Mark's gospel was written "not, indeed, in order" and "not making . . . an arrangement of the Lord's oracles" comes immediately before Papias' discussion of Matthew and how he "collected" (synetaxato) his oracles. Gundry contends, Matthew did it "for the precise purpose of bringing order out of the chaos in Mark."[51]

However, a few observations show Gundry's contentions to be tenuous. First, Eusebius is quoting detached statements of Papias regarding Mark and Matthew so that the sequence of the Gospels means nothing, and there does not arise any alleged dependence among the Gospels in the order of discussion in the text. Second, such a theory underscores the absolute paucity of evidence in ancient tradition for the Two-Document Hypothesis. Its proponents must endeavor to make something out of nothing in a vain attempt at proving their a priori and dogmatic assumption that colors everything they analyze.

Papias' words (and Eusebius' citation and discussion) do not constitute any type of proof for Markan priority or literary dependence between Matthew and Mark. They add absolutely nothing to an understanding of any relationship between Matthew or Mark (or the other gospels for that matter). Eusebius' disjointed citation of Papias' words about Mark coming before that same historian's citation of Papias' words about Matthew's gospel have no relevance to that issue. Such alleged evidence goes far beyond what the statements indicate and is blatantly non sequitur. As a matter of fact, Papias' statements here actually constitute evidence against an assumed literary dependence, for he remarked that Mark depended on Peter for the contents of his gospel!

Ta logia as an early edition of Matthew's gospel. A final view, distinct from the others (and also from their synoptic hypotheses) is that Papias referred to an earlier edition of Matthew. This was written entirely in Hebrew (namely, Aramaic) and preceded the Greek version of the gospel. That was perhaps a proto-Matthew, namely, a shorter version that eventually came to be incorporated into (not necessarily translated from but contained within) an expanded Greek version, namely, the canonical gospel of Matthew.[52] Thus, Papias indicated that Matthew wrote first (prior to the other gospels) and that in so doing, he produced an initial Aramaic edition. The Aramaic edition served as a model and/or source for some of the contents of his Greek edition that he most likely produced as a fresh work soon after he wrote the Aramaic one.[53]

Several arguments support this proposal. First, it permits Papias to speak for himself and allows for an understanding of his words in their natural sense. Since he was closest to the events and relied on excellent sources, his information must have priority over speculative modern hypotheses.

Second, an expanded Greek version would have been quickly helpful among Matthew's targeted Jewish audience, especially those hellenized Jews who no longer spoke Hebrew (the *Diaspora* [Acts 6:1]). Although Matthew concentrated his efforts at first among Hebraistic Jews who spoke Aramaic, such a gospel would have limited appeal outside of the land of the Jews. Tradition has it that Matthew eventually left the environs of Jerusalem to minister among non-Aramaic-speaking peoples.[54] The dominance of Greek in the Hellenistic world would have impelled him to produce another edition. Because he was a former tax collector for the Romans, he would most likely have been conversant in Greek as well as Aramaic,[55] thus facilitating the writing of both versions. Once the Greek Matthew became current in the church, the limited appeal of Aramaic caused that edition to fall into disuse. Papias' statement that "each interpreted" Matthew's gospel (Aramaic version) "as best he could" probably hints at the reason why Matthew would have quickly produced a Greek version: to facilitate the understanding of his gospel in the universal language of Greek.

Third, this view accords with the very early and consistent manuscript ascription of the gospel to Matthew *(KATA MATHTHAION)*.[56] The title is not a part of the original text, but no positive evidence exists that the book ever circulated without this title. Moreover, the ascription has a very early date, approximately A.D. 125.[57] As Guthrie notes, "the title cannot be dismissed too lightly, for it has the support of ancient tradition and this must be the starting point of the discussion regarding authorship."[58]

Fourth, though patristic witnesses like Papias uniformly spoke about an Aramaic original for the gospel, they accepted the Greek Matthew as unquestionably authoritative and coming from the apostle Matthew himself.[59] They offered no explanation concerning the change in language.[60] Most likely, that indicates their regard for the Greek Matthew as authoritative and substantially representative of the Hebrew *ta logia*.[61] Besides, all references to the gospel of Matthew in the early church fathers reflect the Greek Matthew rather than the Hebrew. They never viewed the Greek gospel of Matthew as inferior but as equal or better than the other Greek canonical gospels in terms of its authority and influence.

Fifth, the universal ascription of the Greek Matthew to the apostle Matthew and the failure of tradition to mention any other possible author except Matthew renders unconvincing any suggestion that the early church forgot the true author of the work. Only a brief span of fifty to sixty years passed between its composition and the statements of Papias. A less-prominent apostle such as Matthew would not have been a likely candidate to receive credit for such an important and influential document as the Greek Matthew unless he did indeed write it.

As indicated earlier in this chapter, "of all the New Testament Writings, the Gospel of Mt. was the one whose literary influence was the most wide-spread and the most profound in Christian literature that extended into the last decades of the second century. . . . [T]he first gospel remained the gospel par excellence. . . . The gospel was, therefore, the normative fact of Christian life. It created the background for ordinary Christianity."[62] The only explanation for the gospel's influence and overwhelming popularity in the early church is its apostolic authorship. That one of the Twelve wrote it soon after writing his Aramaic *ta logia* and before Mark and Luke wrote their gospels is far and away the most satisfactory explanation for the facts that remain from early church history.

In light of the evidence, unless someone feels compelled to embrace historical-critical scholarship's *a priori* assumption of Markan priority, the testimony of Papias is credible and supportive of Matthean priority and Matthean authorship of the gospel that bears Matthew's name.

Irenaeus

Irenaeus (born c. A.D. 115–120 and martyred c. A.D. 200) was an immigrant from Asia Minor and a presbyter of the church at Lyons in Gaul. He was one of the early church's most able apologists and theologians, writing against Marcion and the Gnostics with his work *Refutation and Overthrow of Knowledge Falsely So-called*, which tradition has more conveniently labeled *Against Heresies* (completed c. A.D. 185).[63]

In his youth Irenaeus claims to have been a disciple of Polycarp (born c. A.D. 70 and died c. A.D. 155–160). Irenaeus writes, "Polycarp . . . was not only instructed by apostles and conversed with many who had seen the Lord, but was also appointed bishop by apostles in Asia in the church in Smyrna."[64] Irenaeus continues, "We also saw him [namely, Polycarp] in our childhood. . . . He [namely, Polycarp] constantly taught those things which he had learnt from the apostles, which also are the tradition of the church, which alone are true."[65] As reported by Eusebius, Polycarp, in turn, was a disciple of the apostle John:

> I [namely, Irenaeus] remember the events of those days more clearly than those which happened recently, for what we learn as children grows up with the soul and is united to it, so that I can speak even of the place in which the blessed Polycarp sat and disputed, how he came in and went out, the character of his life, the discourses which he made to the people, how he [Polycarp] reported his intercourse with John and with the others who had seen the Lord, how he remembered their words, and what were the things concerning the Lord which he had heard from them . . . and how Polycarp had received them from the eyewitnesses of the word of life.[66]

Besides Polycarp, Irenaeus also had met and conversed with many apostolic and sub-apostolic fathers of Asia Minor and obtained information from them about the life and teachings of the Lord and the activities of the early church.[67] He thus reflected information from many sources and not only from his own childhood memories. Irenaeus also had traveled extensively (for instance, from Asia Minor to Gaul and also the church in Rome), so that his information is not from an isolated region but widespread.

Irenaeus wrote the following regarding the Gospels:

> Now Matthew published among the Hebrews a written gospel also in their own tongue, while Peter and Paul were preaching in Rome and founding the church. But after their death, Mark also, the disciple and interpreter of Peter, himself handed down to us in writing the things which were preached by Peter, and Luke also, who was a follower of Paul, put down in a book the gospel which was preached by him. Then John, the disciple of the Lord, who had even rested on his breast, himself also gave forth the gospel, while he was living in Ephesus in Asia.[68]

Proponents of the Two-Document Hypothesis dismiss Irenaeus' assertion as useless, for they assert he was merely repeating Papias. Filson argues, "But note this: Papias is the key witness. Irenaeus, for example, obviously knows and uses Papias as an authority. No tradition demonstrably independent of Papias exists."[69] Nineham asserts the same: "The testimony of early Christian writers subsequent to Papias, such as Irenaeus, Clement of Alexandria, Origen, and Jerome, need not be discussed at length, for it is not clear that these writers had any trustworthy source of information other than the Papias tradition."[70] Streeter, the great advocate of the Four-Document Hypothesis, deprecates Irenaeus' ability to testify regarding Polycarp's connection to John. Streeter dismisses the evidence because of Irenaeus' youth. He says Irenaeus was too young to tell to which "John" Polycarp referred.[71]

Petrie drives to the heart of their problem, noting, "There is in the document [namely, the writings of Irenaeus] no hint of dependence [namely, on Papias]. Indeed, Irenaeus was sufficiently close to the authorities of Papias to have gathered this information on his own."[72] In addition, Irenaeus was more than likely at least fifteen years old, old enough "to understand the meaning of Polycarp's words and also to distinguish between the Apostle John and any other John."[73] As Lightfoot reasoned, "A pupil of Polycarp, at all events, was not likely to be misinformed here."[74] Besides nullifying the Two- or Four-Source Theory's view of Markan priority, Irenaeus' testimony also negates literary dependence of Mark on Matthew as proposed by the Two-Gospel Hypothesis, for it states that Mark depended on Peter's preaching, not on the other written gospels of Matthew or Luke, for his information.

In sum, proponents of Two-Document Hypothesis must either reject, ignore, or explain away much of the evidence by any means possible, for acceptance of its credibility would reinforce the fact of Matthew's gospel being written prior to the other gospels. That constitutes a strong testimony either against their assumption of the priority of Mark or, for that matter, against the idea that Mark depended on Matthew instead of Peter's preaching, as held by the Two-Gospel Hypothesis. The belittling of Irenaeus by advocates of the Two-Document Hypothesis notwithstanding, Irenaeus' testimony is credible and important in its own right, constituting an independent and reliable witness for information regarding Matthew as the first gospel.

Worthy of observation also in this section is Irenaeus' failure to make a substantial distinction between the Aramaic and Greek versions as coming from Matthew.[75] For example, in *Against Heresies* 3.1.1 Irenaeus discusses all four gospels. In this discussion he mentions only the Hebrew Matthew. Yet, in the work he shows a close familiarity with the Greek Matthew by referring to it frequently.[76] That indicates that he equated the Aramaic Matthew with the Greek Matthew and intimately connected them with each other.

Although the statement cited follows the order Matthew, Mark, Luke, and John, the sequence in this passage is unique to Irenaeus.[77] He generally follows the order of Matthew, Luke, Mark, and John at other places, which, as Campenhausen notes, "would seem therefore to be the order most familiar to Irenaeus himself."[78] Yet, in another place he follows the sequence John-Luke-Matthew-Mark (*Against Heresies* 3.2.8) perhaps because of theological rather than historical, reasons.[79] Since Irenaeus follows a variety of sequences when mentioning the Gospels, he is not of much help in establishing a sequence of composition, but he does offer support for the priority of Matthew as first to be composed and apparent support for the composition of Luke before Mark.

Clement of Alexandria

The origins of Christianity in Alexandria are obscure. The movement must have appeared there at a relatively early date, for it seems firmly established at least as early as around the late second century.[80] According to Eusebius, Pantaenus was the earliest leader of the catechetical school in Alexandria around A.D. 185. He was a converted Stoic philosopher whom Eusebius describes as "especially eminent."[81] Eventually, Pantaenus was "appointed as a herald for the gospel of Christ to the heathen in the East, and was sent as far as India."[82] Upon arrival, Pantaenus allegedly discovered that the Hebrew version of Matthew's gospel had preceded him there, being left by the apostle Bartholomew.[83] That tradition corroborates information from both Papias and Irenaeus about Matthew writing originally in Hebrew (or Aramaic).

Clement of Alexandria (c. A.D. 150–215) lived in Alexandria and became a pupil of Pantaenus.[84] In time, Clement distinguished himself as a scholar and became a teacher for over twenty years in Alexandria, succeeding Pantaenus as the leader of the school. At the outbreak of persecution under

Severus in A.D. 202, Clement left Alexandria, never to return. In spite of periods of intense persecution, the school gained great prominence and importance.

Beyond that, few facts regarding Clement are available. Nothing certain is known concerning his parentage or early training.[85] Most likely, he was not a Christian during his early years. According to Eusebius, however, he was "the namesake of the pupil of the apostles who had once ruled the church of Rome."[86] Clement's name, of course, reflects his connection with the Egyptian city of Alexandria, where he wrote all his important works. His extant works are *Exhortation to the Greeks, Pedagogue, Stromateis or Miscellanies, Who is the rich man that shall be saved?* and some fragments from *Selections from the Prophets,* which is a brief commentary on portions of the Scripture.

Information from Clement is of basic importance in determining the order of composition of the Gospels, for not only was he a preeminent early church scholar as head of the Alexandrian school, but was also in personal contact with a number of church elders from different parts of the Mediterranean world and their information regarding that order. The following quotation of Clement by Eusebius reveals Clement's widespread network of information:

> This work [namely, *Stromateis*] is not a writing composed for show, but notes stored up for my old age, a remedy against forgetfulness, an image without art, and a sketch of those clear and vital words which I was privileged to hear, and of blessed and truly notable men. Of these one, the Ionian, was in Greece, another in South Italy, a third in Coele-Syria, another in Egypt, and there were others in the East, one of them an Assyrian, another in Palestine of Hebrew origin. But when I had met the last, and in power he was indeed the first, I hunted him out from his concealment in Egypt and found rest.[87]

The last elder in Egypt referred to is most likely Pantaenus. Since Clement probably met Pantaenus in the latter part of the second century, the testimony that the various elders passed on would reflect well back into the first half of that century.[88]

What is important for the present study is that Clement's widespread information furnishes important additional information about the order of the synoptics. Eusebius quotes him as follows regarding this order:

> And again in the same books Clement has inserted a tradition of the primitive elders with regard to the order of the Gospels, as follows. He said that those Gospels were first written which include the genealogies, but that the Gospel according to Mark came into being in this manner: When Peter had publicly preached the word at Rome, and by the Spirit had proclaimed the Gospel, that those present, who were many, exhorted Mark,

as one who had followed him for a long time and remembered what had been spoken, to make a record of what was said; and that he did this, and distributed the Gospel among those that asked him. And that when the matter came to Peter's knowledge he neither strongly forbade it nor urged it forward. But that John, last of all, conscious that the outward facts had been set forth in the Gospels, was urged on by his disciples, and, divinely moved by the Spirit, composed a spiritual Gospel. This is Clement's account.[89]

Several important features emerge from those words. First, Clement supplies *unique* information when revealing that the gospels with genealogies (Matthew and Luke) originated before Mark. A scholar of his stature was not likely merely to repeat information without careful investigation. Though Clement does not reveal whether Matthew was first and Luke second or Matthew second and Luke first, he does clearly indicate Mark's third position after Matthew and Luke and not before them. This view is contrary to what modern historical-critical theories such as Two- and Four-Document Hypotheses maintain.

Moreover, the information from Clement does not contradict Matthew's being first but is an important supplement to information gleaned from other church fathers (for example, Papias, Irenaeus, and Tertullian). The others make plain that Matthew was first, thereby placing Luke second in sequence when combined with Clement's information. Like Irenaeus, Clement places the apostle John's gospel last, saying that John wrote it with full awareness of the other three and designed it to supplement the "synoptic" accounts as a "spiritual Gospel." The order of composition, then, was Matthew first, Luke second, Mark third, and John last.

Third, very important in evaluating Clement's information in regard to any proposed solution to the Synoptic Problem is that the tradition he passed on did not come just from a single elder in a single locality but from "a tradition of the primitive elders" scattered widely throughout the Christian community. That indicates that it was a tradition known and received in different places some time in the early to mid-second century. Clement's wide travels made this information all the more significant, for it represents a strong tradition in the early church, not merely a fanciful whim of Clement and a few others. As a result, one cannot easily dismiss such information.

Fourth, according to Eusebius in *Ecclesiastical History* 2.16.1, Mark helped found the church at Alexandria and was its first overseer. For Clement to place Mark's gospel third in order of composition is, therefore, all the more important. Gamba notes, "He [Clement] would have no reason at all to place Mark's gospel after the other two that contain a genealogy of Jesus, unless it was for a definite and grounded persuasion of historical nature."[90] That reinforces the strength and reliability of Clement's testimony.

Tertullian

Tertullian (c. A.D. 160–c. 225) was a contemporary of Clement of Alexandria. Tertullian constitutes a prime witness to the faith of the African church regarding the authenticity of the Gospels. Despite his eventual Montanist proclivities, he was the outstanding apologist of the Western church of his time.[91]

Little is known about Tertullian's life except that he was a native of Carthage and that his father had been a Roman centurion on duty in that city. Tertullian knew and used both Latin and Greek and loved the classics. He became a proficient lawyer, and taught public speaking and law in Rome, where he became a convert to Christianity. His goal was the development of a sound Western theology and the defeat of all false philosophical and pagan forces opposed to Christianity.[92]

Tertullian's importance for gospel study lies especially in the fact that he verified the tradition of all Western Christianity, especially the tradition of Rome. His treatise, *Against Marcion* (around A.D. 207–212), is especially relevant to the composition of the Gospels, for he affirms that apostles wrote Matthew and John, that Mark's gospel reflects Peter's preaching, and that Paul was the sponsor of Luke.

Regarding the four gospels, Tertullian reported that "the evangelical Testament has Apostles as its authors."[93] Here Tertullian makes no distinction between an Aramaic and Hebrew Matthew, but considers that the Greek Matthew has come from the apostle Matthew himself. Since Tertullian was a lawyer and orator by profession and an outstanding apologist against the heretic Marcion in his *Treatise Against Marcion*, where he mentions the Gospels' composition, he most probably had his information correct concerning the traditions behind the four gospels. Tertullian saw no grounds at all for setting aside this tradition as he attacked Marcion's stance. Any possibility of the facts being wrong would have weakened Tertullian's attack against Marcion. That Tertullian's comments corroborate as well as supplement the traditions of Papias, Irenaeus, and Clement strengthens his case even more.

Origen

Origen (c. A.D. 185–253) was born into a Christian family at Alexandria. In A.D. 202, the persecution under Septimius Severus forced Clement to leave the city. Origen was eighteen years old at the time. Because of his renowned scholarship, he became Clement of Alexandria's successor.[94] Although an eclectic Middle Platonism that was prevalent in Alexandria and in the East adversely affected Origen's thought and gave him a strong propensity toward an allegorical hermeneutic, he was the most remarkable scholar of his time in depth and breadth of learning.

Origen's extant works evidence his profound scholarship. Tragically, most of his writings have perished, but he may have written over six thousand works. Several salient examples of his scholarship are representative of the rest. His *Hexapla*, in which several Hebrew and Greek versions of the Old Testament are arranged in parallel columns, constitutes the beginnings of textual criticism. One of his greatest contributions was his work *De Principiis* (around A.D. 230), which exists only in a Latin version by Rufinus. It is the first Christian treatise of systematic theology. In the fourth book of that work, he set forth his allegorical method of interpretation. In *Against Celsus,* Origen devised an apologetic defense against the anti-Christian Platonist Celsus. Yet, the majority of Origen's writings took the form of an exegetical commentary on Scripture.

Origen was also widely traveled, having visited Rome (c. A.D. 211–212), where he met Hippolytus, and Arabia (c. A.D. 213–214). Around A.D. 215 when the emperor Caracalla drove all teachers of philosophy from Alexandria, Origen traveled to Caesarea in Palestine. He resumed his teaching in Alexandria around A.D. 216 and continued there until around A.D. 230–231. Therefore, the information that he imparts regarding the Synoptic Gospels is from a man not only of great learning and research but also one who was widely traveled.

Eusebius records the following from Origen's *Commentary on the Gospel of Matthew*:

> But in the first of his *[Commentaries]* on the Gospel According to *Matthew*, defending the canon of the Church, he gives his testimony that he knows only four Gospels, writing somewhat as follows: ". . . as having learnt by tradition concerning the four Gospels, which alone are unquestionable in the Church of God under heaven, that first was written that according to Matthew, who was once a tax-collector but afterwards an apostle of Jesus Christ, who published it for those who from Judaism came to believe, composed as it was in the Hebrew language. Secondly, that according to Mark, who wrote it in accordance with Peter's instructions, whom also Peter acknowledged as his son in the catholic epistle. . . . And thirdly, that according to Luke, who wrote, for those who from the Gentiles [came to believe], the Gospel that was the praise of Paul. After them all, that according to John.[95]

Here Origen's statement reflects an order of Matthew, Mark, Luke, and John, but nothing in the context requires this to be an assumed chronological order for Mark and Luke. Origen's explicit statement is that Matthew wrote first and John last, but otherwise Eusebius' discussion centers in Origen's view of the exact number of the Gospels rather than in the order of their composition.[96] Most likely, Eusebius included Origen's statement because of its bearing on the *number* (not the *order*) of gospels in the canon of the church. He probably accepted Origen's order as reflecting the *canonical* order of appearance in New Testament manuscripts. On the other hand, Eusebius included Clement's statement cited earlier in this chapter, for it related directly to the *chronological* sequence of composition of the Gospels (namely, Matthew, Luke, Mark, and John).[97]

In another place, Origen stressed the apostolic origin of the four gospels and rejected numerous apocryphal gospels as spurious. Origen accepted only four gospels: "For Matthew did not 'take in hand' but wrote by the Holy Spirit, and so did Mark and John and also equally Luke."[98] In this quotation, Origen does not distinguish between Greek and Aramaic versions of Matthew, but includes the Greek Matthew as written by the apostle himself along with the other three gospels (namely, John, Mark, and Luke). Though Origen was aware that Matthew originally wrote in Hebrew (see earlier quotation from his *Commentary on the Gospel of Matthew*), this latter statement implies that he made no distinction between the Aramaic and Greek versions, but included the Greek as equally authoritative with the other three gospels and also stressed its origin from the Holy Spirit.

Just as with Tertullian and Clement, to doubt Origen's assertions that Matthew and John were written by apostles and that men associated with the apostles wrote the gospels that bear their names (in other words, Luke and Mark) would be to repudiate Origen's intelligence as a preeminent, careful scholar and also to question his integrity.

Eusebius

Eusebius of Caesarea (c. A.D. 260–c. 340) was bishop of Caesarea in Palestine and a pupil of the presbyter Pamphilus, who was himself a student of Origen. Many look on Eusebius as the Father of Church History, especially in light of his most famous work *Ecclesiastical History,* which surveyed the history of the church from apostolic times until A.D. 324.[99] His purpose was to compose a record of past trials of the church at the end of its long struggle and the beginning of its era of prosperity. The work is particularly valuable since Eusebius had access to the excellent library housed at Caesarea and also the imperial archives. He also records that he exerted great effort to be honest and objective in using the best and most reliable of the primary sources available to him.[100] Therefore, in many respects Eusebius is an invaluable source of knowledge concerning the history of the church during her first three centuries of existence. Eusebius was also a participant in the Council of Nicaea (A.D. 325).

Much of the earlier information in this chapter has come from Eusebius' *Ecclesiastical History.* Much of *Ecclesiastical History* is a record of what others said and did, but at times Eusebius appears to give his own personal views. He mentions that only two apostles, Matthew and John, left their recollections and that they wrote under the pressure of necessity: "[T]hey took to writing perforce."[101] Though Eusebius mentions that Matthew first wrote in the Hebrew language, he also considers Greek Matthew to have come from the apostle's hand.[102] He notes that John was aware of Matthew, Mark, and Luke, and confirmed their accuracy when he composed his gospel.[103] Eusebius refers to sections of the Greek Matthew and ascribes them to the apostle as their author.[104]

Also, according to Eusebius, Mark composed his gospel on the basis of Peter's preaching,[105] while Luke's gospel came about through his association "with Paul and his [Luke's] conversation with other apostles."[106]

Augustine

Augustine (around A.D. 354–430) was a younger contemporary of Jerome. In Augustine's youth, he studied grammar, Latin classics, and rhetoric with parental hopes for his becoming a lawyer or a high civil servant in the imperial government. After his conversion, he became a priest in A.D. 391 and in A.D. 396 the bishop of Hippo in North Africa. Some have acclaimed Augustine as the greatest of the church fathers.[107] He left over one hundred books, five hundred sermons, and two hundred letters. His influence became pervasive not only in the African church but in the Western Church, even surpassing that of Jerome. His most widely known work is his *Confessions*, one of the great autobiographical works of all time. His *City of God* may be his greatest apologetic work. He also wrote many other significant works, including *The Harmony of the Gospels* and *Christian Doctrine*.

Augustine's position on the order of the composition of the Gospels appears in his *Harmony of the Gospels*: "Now, these four evangelists . . . are believed to have written in the order which follows: first Matthew, then Mark, thirdly Luke, lastly John."[108] Augustine here passes on a tradition of the order of composition as in the present New Testament canon. His assignment of Matthew as first and John as last is in overall harmony with earlier tradition as reviewed above in this chapter.

Yet, the Augustinian order conflicts with Clement's sequence in reversing the order of Mark and Luke. Militating against assigning too much weight to the aspect of Augustine's order of Mark being prior to Luke is that he, in contrast to Clement, does not clearly identify the origin of his information or show how widespread or general was the acceptance of his sequence. Augustine merely states that they "are believed to have written in the order which follows." Significant questions remain unanswered as to who held the views he espouses, how widespread was the belief, and what evidence was available for the information he imparts.

In contrast, Clement's information has better documentation, for it is much earlier, reaching back into the early part of the second century and reflecting a widespread consensus. Augustine's is much later and unspecified as to source. Overall, such factors make Clement's information decidedly more weighty in molding a decision regarding the order of composition of the synoptics.

Within the same context, Augustine remarks as follows:

> [A]s respects the task of composing that record of the gospel which is to be accepted as ordained by divine authority, there were (only) two, belonging to the number of those whom the Lord chose before the passover, that obtained places,—namely, the first place and the last. For the first place in order was held by Matthew, and the last by John. And thus the remaining two, who did not belong to the number referred to, but who at the same time had become followers of the Christ who spoke in those others, were supported on either side by the same, like sons who were to be embraced, and who in this way were set in the midst between these twain.[109]

Here Augustine implicitly accepts that the Greek Matthew came from the apostle Matthew as its author and that John was written by the apostle John. This latter quotation, however, appears most likely to deal with the order of the Gospels within the canon and is not necessarily helpful for giving the order of composition. Neither does it specify whether Luke was prior to Mark or Mark prior to Luke.[110]

Augustine goes on to note that prior to the Greek version of Matthew, the apostle wrote first in the Hebrew language, once again confirming the tradition set forth in the other church fathers: "Of these four, it is true, only Matthew is reckoned to have written in the Hebrew language; the others in Greek." Yet as with other church fathers, Augustine does not explain the transition from Aramaic to Greek, but accepts without question that the Greek version was from the apostle.[111] He confirmed that latter point by following up his comments on the order of the Gospels and on Matthew's composition of his gospel in Greek before the others with his analysis of the Greek Matthew (as well as the other Greek gospels) as to their themes and character, thereby leaving the strong impression that he saw no significant difference between the Aramaic and Greek versions of Matthew's gospel.[112]

At another place, Augustine commented that "Mark follows him [namely, Matthew] closely and looks like his attendant and epitomizer."[113] That statement, however, appears not to be based on tradition but on Augustine's personal analysis of Matthew in comparison with Mark. Hence, no real significance attaches to it beyond the fact of reflecting Augustine's personal reflections and observations in explaining agreements between Matthew and Mark. Moreover, as the next section of this chapter will reveal, the church fathers viewed the Gospels as being composed independently of one another. Augustine's *Harmony of the Gospels* evidences no indications to the contrary. As a matter of fact, it indicates just the opposite.

At another place, Augustine discusses the canonical order as follows:

> Now the whole canon of Scripture on which we say this judgment is to be exercised, is contained in the following books. . . . That of the New Testament, again, is contained within the following:—Four books of the Gospel, according to Matthew, according to Mark, according to Luke, according to John.[114]

Here again Augustine apparently reflects the compositional order of Matthew, Mark, Luke, and John.

One other place deserves mention as possibly significant, for Augustine relates the following distinguishing characteristics of the contents of the Gospels:

> [I]t is a clearly admitted position that the first three—namely, Matthew, Mark and Luke—have occupied themselves chiefly with the humanity of our Lord Jesus Christ. . . . And in this way, Mark . . . either appears to be preferentially the companion of Matthew

. . . or else, in accordance with the more probable account of the matter, he holds a course in conjunction with both [the other synoptists]. For although he is at one with Matthew in a large number of passages, he is nevertheless at one rather with Luke in some others.[115]

Peabody, who favors the Two-Gospel Hypothesis, argues from this statement that Augustine has changed his mind regarding his relegation of Luke to third position in order of composition, reasoning that after Augustine's extensive analysis of the Gospels, "Augustine's new, more probable view of Mark is that Mark is literarily dependent upon both Matthew and Luke" and "Augustine had not one but two views of the relationships among the Gospels."[116] That conclusion is not warranted, however. Peabody has a strong desire to explain away the apparent Augustinian order of composition of Matthew, Mark, Luke, and John in hopes of establishing him as supportive of the Two-Gospel Hypothesis and its order of Matthew, Luke, Mark, and John. As a result, Peabody reads too much into Augustine's statement. Augustine, in context, is merely describing the similarities and differences between the gospel of John and the three Synoptic Gospels. Furthermore, in the immediate context, Augustine refers to the Gospels in the order Matthew, Mark, and Luke, thus giving strong indication that he has not changed his mind regarding his assumed order of composition. Another explanation for Augustine's assertions is that he may have identified any established canonical order (Matthew, Mark, Luke, and John) with the order of composition, but demonstrating that beyond a reasonable doubt is impossible.

Above all, one point is important. Regardless of the difference of opinion between Clement and Augustine on the order of composition of the Gospels, neither Augustine nor Clement place Mark first in order of composition as the Two-Document Theory supposes. Virtually *all* church fathers place Matthew earliest. Although they may mention a Hebrew or Aramaic original of Matthew, the fathers accepted without any serious question that the Greek Matthew came from the apostle Matthew, the gospel of Luke from Luke's association with Paul, Mark from his association with Peter's preaching, and the apostle John's gospel came last in order of composition.

Conclusion Regarding Order of Composition

An analysis of data from the church fathers results in one conspicuous conclusion: they do not support either the Two-Document Hypothesis or the Two-Gospel Hypothesis. The assumed dependence of Matthew and Luke on Mark is totally without historical foundation as is the assumed dependence of Mark on Matthew and Luke instead of on Peter's preaching. Strained and desperate interpretations by proponents of the Two-Document Hypothesis as well as by those of the Two-Gospel Hypothesis stand as a monumental testimony to their dismal failure in mustering any support among the fathers.

Papias' testimony answers the question as to whether Mark was in any sense dependent on Matthew as the Two-Gospel Theory would require, for Mark wrote on the basis of Peter's preaching, not on the basis of literary dependence on Matthew. Besides, the church fathers were not merely unthinkingly reflecting Papias, because they (for example, Irenaeus, Clement, Tertullian, and Origen) were renowned scholars in their own right who had information from widespread and independent sources. They did not need to rely solely on Papias for their information.

Far from contradicting each other, the information that these fathers supply is largely complementary, consistent, and congruent. The apostle Matthew wrote first, the apostle John last, and Luke and Mark wrote between these two. Some difference of opinion exists as to whether Luke or Mark wrote second, but probability is on the side of Luke's being second. Mark derived his material from the preaching of Peter, not from Matthew and Luke.

Sadly, the overarching reason why modern scholarship rejects or explains away the testimony of the Gospels is an adherence to an assumed hypotheses of literary dependence, which is the basic assumption of Historical Criticism (hereafter HC). The church fathers stand solidly against the stultifying dogma of modern Source Criticism, which blindly upholds the Two- (or Four-) Document Hypothesis and the Two-Gospel Hypothesis. These are theories that suppress, dismiss, or ridicule any evidence contrary their assumed tenets. Instead of being blindly rejected, explained away, or enervated by a preconceived agenda or predilection toward a particular synoptic hypothesis, the statements of the fathers should have their full weight in any discussion of the synoptic issue. Their voices, when objectively analyzed, constitute a united witness against the concept of the priority of Mark based on literary dependence, and in turn, provide a cogent testimony for the chronological priority of the writing of Matthew.

PART 2: THE INDEPENDENCE OF THE GOSPELS

Whether the "Synoptic Problem" exists is open to question. The practice of HC presupposes the existence of a Synoptic Problem, for it assumes that writers of the Synoptic Gospels exercised some type of mutual literary dependence, whatever the nature of that dependence may have been. Proposed solutions to that problem have sought unsuccessfully to explain who depended on whom and in what sequence the writers wrote.

A comparison of how leaders in the early church stood on the issue of literary independence or dependence (namely, interdependence) among the three synoptic writers is helpful in evaluating historical-critical theories. Upon a review of several of the early fathers, Meeks has written the following:

> Most surprisingly, in view of the use to which they [namely, the fathers and their reports] have often been put, they are completely uninterested in the "Synoptic Problem." Both Papias and Clement write as if there were *no literary connection* between any of

the gospels. The insistence that Mark was the *hermēneutes* of Peter precludes, in Papias' picture of things, Mark's having depended on Matthew. Papias mentions Matthew after he mentions Mark, and he contrasts the two, but he does not suggest that Matthew depended on Mark. Clement and Origen, on the other hand, mention the gospels in the orders, respectively, Matthew, Luke, Mark, John and Matthew, Mark Luke, John, but neither has a word to say about dependence.[117]

With an issue such as the dependence/independence one, the burden of proof rests on advocates of dependence, in light of the many differences between parallel accounts in the Synoptic Gospels. With Meeks' summary in mind—namely, the clear stand of the fathers in favor of independence—the burden of proof for those favoring dependence becomes that much heavier. But the case cannot rest there. Several observations based on detailed statements in early church writings demonstrate conclusively that, as far as the fathers were concerned, no gospel writer depended on the gospel written by another.

The Absence of References to Literary Dependence

Writers from early church history never mention interdependence, even though they had every opportunity to do so, many more opportunities than those to which Meeks alludes. A number of examples will furnish insights into the nature of those opportunities. In each of the excerpts, the early writer cites more than one Synoptic Gospel in the same immediate context, but gives no indication that a gospel writer depended on another for his material. It is true that they were discussing other subjects in their writings. But one would think that in the midst of the large number of such treatments, they would have mentioned in passing dependence of one on the writings of another, if they thought such dependence had occurred. Yet no such mention ever appears in their writings.

Second-century writers. Early in the second century, Papias wrote the following: "Mark having been the interpreter of Peter, wrote accurately . . . all that he recalled. . . . Matthew compiled the oracles in the Hebrew language, and everyone interpreted them as he was able."[118]

Irenaeus wrote during the last half of the second century and mentioned the Gospels often. He makes the following summary of his earlier comments: "The opinion of the apostles, therefore, and of those (Mark and Luke) who learned from their words, concerning God has been made manifest."[119] Earlier in his *Against Heresies*, Irenaeus had written the following:

> Matthew also issued a written Gospel among the Hebrews in their own dialect, while Peter and Paul were preaching at Rome, and laying the foundations of the Church. After their departure, Mark, the disciple and interpreter of Peter, did also hand down to us in

writing what had been preached by Peter. Luke also, the companion of Paul, recorded in a book the Gospel preached by him.[120]

In another place, Irenaeus writes, "Thus hath Matthew set it down, and Luke in like manner, and Mark the very same."[121] Irenaeus indicates a similarity of accounts, but obviously not an identity of wording that would result from copying.

After a strong defense of the gospel of Luke, Tertullian writes the following:

> The same authority of the apostolic churches will afford evidence to the other Gospels also, which we possess equally through their means, and according to their usage—I mean the Gospels of John and Matthew—whilst that which Mark published may be affirmed to be Peter's whose interpreter Mark was.[122]

Tertullian also makes the following contribution:

> We lay it down as our first position, that the evangelical Testament has apostles for its authors, to whom was assigned by the Lord Himself this office of publishing the gospel. . . . Of the apostles, therefore, John and Matthew first instill faith into us; whilst of apostolic men, Luke and Mark renew it afterwards.[123]

Still in the second century, Clement of Alexandria, in commenting on 1 Peter, wrote the following:

> Mark, the follower of Peter, while Peter publicly preached the Gospel at Rome before some of Caesar's equities, and adduced many testimonies to Christ, in order that thereby they might be able to commit to memory what was spoken, of what was spoken by Peter wrote entirely what is called the Gospel according to Mark. As Luke also may be recognized by the style, . . . to have composed the Acts of the Apostles.[124]

In his comments on the epistle of Jude, Clement wrote the following:

> Now, in the Gospel according to Mark, the Lord being interrogated by the chief of the priests if He was the Christ, the Son of the blessed God, answering, said, "I am. . . ." In the other Gospels, however, He is said not to have replied to the high priest, on his asking if He was the Son of God.[125]

Eusebius cites Clement's words after Clement had noted that the gospels with the genealogies were written first:

> Peter having preached the word publicly at Rome, and by the Spirit proclaimed the Gospel, those who were present, who were

numerous, entreated Mark, inasmuch as he had attended him from an early period, and remembered what had been said, to write down what had been spoken.[126]

Third-century writers. Origen, writing in the third century, said the following:

> The Gospels then being four, I deem the first fruits of the Gospels to be that which you have enjoined me to search into according to my powers, the Gospel of John, that which speaks of him whose genealogy had already been set forth, but which begins to speak of him at a point before he had any genealogy. For Matthew, writing for the Hebrews who looked for Him who was to come of the line of Abraham and of David, says: "The book of the generation of Jesus Christ, the son of David, the son of Abraham." And Mark, knowing what he writes, narrates the beginning of the Gospel; we may perhaps find what he aims at in John; in the beginning the Word, God the Word. But Luke, though he says at the beginning of Acts, "The former treatise did I make about all that Jesus began to do and to teach," yet leaves to him who lay on Jesus breast the greatest completest discourses about Jesus.[127]

In commenting on a conversation between John the Baptist and Jesus, Origen reports the following:

> John the disciple does not tell us where the Savior comes from to John the Baptist, but we learn this from Matthew, who writes: "Then cometh Jesus from Galilee to Jordan to John, to be baptized of him." And Mark adds the place in Galilee; he says, "And it came to pass in those days that Jesus came from Nazareth in Galilee and was baptized by John in Jordan." Luke does not mention the place Jesus came from, but on the other hand he tells us what we do not learn from the others.[128]

Writing about Jesus' departure into Galilee, the same father notes, "Matthew and Luke represent that he was first at Nazara, and then left them and came and dwelt in Capernaum. Matthew and Mark also state a certain reason why He departed thither, namely, that He had heard that John was cast into Prison."[129]

Regarding preparations for the triumphal entry, Origen makes the following statement:

> From Beth-phage Matthew says the disciples are sent out who are to fetch the ass and the colt. . . . Mark and Luke say that the two disciples, acting on their Master's instructions, found a foal tied,

on which no one had ever sat, and that they loosed it and brought it to the Lord.[130]

Regarding the Gospels, Origen also writes the following:

> Concerning the four Gospels which alone are uncontroverted in the Church of God under heaven, I have learned by tradition that the Gospel according to Matthew, who was at one time a publican and afterwards an Apostle of Jesus Christ, was written first; and that he composed it in the Hebrew tongue and published it for the converts from Judaism. The second written was that according to Mark, who wrote it according to the instruction of Peter, who, in his General Epistle, acknowledged him as a son, saying, "The church that is in Babylon, elect together with you, saluteth you; and so doth Mark my son." And third, was that according to Luke, the Gospel commended by Paul, which he composed for the converts from the Gentiles. Last of all, that according to John.[131]

Regarding the tomb in which Joseph laid Jesus' body, Origen made the following observation:

> [H]e who examines the words of the narrative may see something worthy of consideration, both in them and in the newness of the tomb,—a point mentioned by Matthew and John—and in the statement of Luke and John, that no one had ever been interred therein before.[132]

Regarding the angels at the tomb of Jesus, the same writer indicates, "Matthew and Mark speak of one, and Luke and John of two, which statements are not contradictory."[133]

Dionysius, another second-century father, writes the following about the time of Christ's resurrection: "It was 'in the end of the Sabbath,' as Matthew has said; it was 'early, when it was yet day,' as John writes; it was 'very early in the morning,' as Luke puts it; and it was 'very early in the morning, at the rising of the sun,' as Mark tells us."[134]

Regarding Jesus' prayer in the Garden of Gethsemane, Dionysius records the following:

> Besides, Matthew has indicated most clearly that He did indeed pray that the cup might pass from Him, but yet that His request was that this should take place not as He willed, but as the Father willed it. The words given by Mark and Luke, again, ought to be introduced in their proper connection. For Mark says, "Nevertheless, not what I will, but what Thou wilt"; and Luke says, "Nevertheless not my will, but Thine be done."[135]

Fourth-century writers. John Chrysostom was an important fourth-century preacher and writer who, concerning the Gospels, wrote the following:

> And why can it have been, that when there were so many disciples, two write only from among the apostles, and two from among their followers? (For one that was a disciple of Paul, and another of Peter, together with Matthew and John, wrote the Gospels.) It was because they did nothing for vainglory, but all things for use.[136]

Augustine wrote during the late fourth and early fifth centuries. Regarding the sequence of the Gospels, he says the following:

> Now, those four evangelists whose names have gained the most remarkable circulation over the whole world, and whose number has been fixed as four . . . are believed to have written in the order which follows: first Matthew, then Mark, thirdly Luke, lastly John.[137]

Among the early fathers, Augustine is alone in indicating that writers of later gospels had any knowledge of an earlier one or earlier ones:

> And however they may appear to have kept each of them in a certain order of narration proper to himself, this certainly is not to be taken as if each individual writer chose to write in ignorance of what his predecessor had done, or left out as matters about which there was no information things which another nevertheless is discovered to have recorded. But the fact is, that just as they received each of them the gift of inspiration, they abstained from adding to their several labors any superfluous conjoint compositions.[138]

That opinion of Augustine differs from the one ventured by Clement during the second century, namely, that only John was aware of the contents of other canonical gospels before he wrote his gospel. Writing at a much later time, he chose to write an account much different from them. Rather than copying from Matthew, Mark, or Luke, John verified their truthfulness and supplemented their contents with material that is largely missing from the synoptics.[139]

The opinion of some has been that Augustine advocated some manner of literary dependence among the synoptic writers.[140] A careful review of Augustine's words cited above, however, reveals that he said that the three wrote by virtue of "the gift of inspiration" and "abstained from adding to their several labors any superfluous conjoint compositions." In other words, they did not copy the works of an earlier writer, which action would have made someone's work superfluous. They rather worked independently under the inspiration of the Holy Spirit. How that is consistent with Augustine's later statement that "Mark follows him [namely, Matthew] closely, and looks like his attendant and epitomizer"[141] is a bit puzzling. This chapter's later discussion of gospel harmonization by the early fathers will show the probability that Augustine must have meant that Mark followed Matthew in his choice of subject matter and/or was a personal acquaintance of Matthew, but was not literarily dependent on him.

Regardless of whether Augustine is right in supposing that the synoptic writers were aware of one another's works, the important fact is this: *like all of the other ancient fathers, Augustine did not understand the writers of the Synoptic Gospels to have depended on each other in a literary way.* That fact will become obvious under the section below dealing with how the fathers harmonized the Gospels.

Contrasts with historical-critical writings by evangelicals. Regarding literary dependence among the synoptists, recent evangelicals who have represented the historical-critical perspective express an exactly opposite viewpoint. They constantly refer to the dependence of one writer upon another, a characteristic that is *never* observable among the early fathers in the quotations cited or in any other that a historical critic has cited.

Many examples of this literary interdependence viewpoint appear in recent evangelical volumes. Stein advances four arguments that he says prove "the use of a common written source by Matthew, Mark, and Luke—or the use of one of these Gospels by the other two."[142] Marshall concludes, "The view that Luke used Mk. substantially as we have it seems to me to be beyond reasonable doubt."[143]

Illustrative of this are statements appearing throughout Marshall's commentary on Luke. From these one can clearly detect Marshall's theory of literary interdependence:

"The wording follows Mk. fairly closely."

"The wording [of Luke] is based on Mk."

"Luke . . . has abbreviated his Markan material at this point."

"Still following Mk. Luke goes on to give the specific meaning of the parable of the sower."

"The sentence structure in Mk. is extremely involved, and both Luke and Matthew attempt to simplify it."[144]

A seemingly endless stream of such comments flows from Marshall's work as well as from other recent Synoptic Gospel commentaries by other evangelicals. Such statements differ radically from anything found in writings of the early church fathers. The reason for that difference lies in the perspective of the fathers that no literary collaboration existed among the writers.

The Separate Apostolic Origin of Each Gospel

Early Christian writers unite in their verification that the sources of the three Synoptic Gospels were apostolic, with each being traceable to a different apostle.

Matthew. Early Christian writers regularly declare that Matthew's source of information was his own experiences with the Lord as one of His apostles. Justin Martyr writes, "For the apostles, in the memoirs composed by them which are called Gospels, have thus delivered unto us what was enjoined upon them."[145] Irenaeus, in speaking about the Lord's disciples and the need to follow their testimonies, refers to what "Matthew the apostle" has written in his gospel. After a lengthy discussion about Matthew's account of Jesus' birth and baptism, Irenaeus concludes the section with the words, "Such, then, [is the witness] of Matthew."[146]

Tertullian states, "[T]he evangelical Testament has apostles for its authors. . . . Since there are apostolic men also, they are not alone, but appear with the apostles and after apostles."[147] Tertullian then names as apostles John and Matthew, and as apostolic men Luke and Mark, who possessed "the authority of the masters [namely, of the apostles]."[148] Tertullian called "Matthew, that most faithful chronicler of the Gospel, because the companion of the Lord."[149] Hippolytus, a disciple of Irenaeus, added his testimony that the apostle "Matthew wrote the Gospel in the Hebrew tongue."[150] Augustine, in speaking about a statement of Jesus that Matthew allegedly was not present to hear, writes, "In this way, the Gospels of Luke and Mark, who were companions of the disciples, as well as the Gospel of Matthew, have the same authority as that of [the Gospel of] John."[151]

Clearly, the fathers viewed Matthew's source of material not as written, but as firsthand, apostolic information. The apostle recorded matters that he had witnessed and heard himself or received directly from another apostle.

Mark. Papias makes clear that Mark's source of information was Peter:

> Mark having become the interpreter of Peter, wrote down accurately whatsoever he remembered. . . . Wherefore Mark made no mistake in thus writing some things as he remembered them. For of one thing he took especial care, not to omit anything he had heard, and not to put anything fictitious into the statements.[152]

Clement of Alexandria agrees:

> Mark, the follower of Peter, while Peter publicly preached the Gospel at Rome before some of Caesar's equities, and adduced many testimonies to Christ, in order that thereby they might be able to commit to memory what was spoken, of what was spoken by Peter wrote entirely what is called the Gospel according to Mark.[153]

In another place, Clement writes as follows:

> And such a ray of godliness shone forth on the minds of Peter's
> hearers, that they were not satisfied with the once hearing or with
> the unwritten teaching of the divine proclamation, but with all
> manner of entreaties importuned Mark, to whom the Gospel is
> ascribed, he being the companion of Peter, that he would leave in
> writing a record of the teaching which had been delivered to them
> verbally; and did not let the man alone till they prevailed upon
> him; and so to them we owe the Scripture called the "Gospel by
> Mark."[154]

In another place, Eusebius reported Clement's words:

> Peter having preached the word publicly at Rome, and by the Spirit
> proclaimed the Gospel, those who were present, who were numer-
> ous, entreated Mark, inasmuch as he had attended him from an
> early period, and remembered what had been said, to write down
> what had been spoken.[155]

The same would appear to be the gist of Irenaeus' words: "The opinion
of the apostles, therefore, and of those (Mark and Luke) who learned from
their words, concerning God, has been made manifest."[156]

The discussion above has already cited the testimony of Origen to the
same effect, namely, that Mark wrote according to the instruction of Peter.

Luke. Irenaeus reports the following:

> Thus did the apostles simply, and without respect of persons, de-
> liver to all what they had themselves learned from the Lord. Thus
> also does Luke, without respect of persons, deliver to us what he
> had learned from them, as he has himself testified, saying, "Even
> as they delivered them to us, who from the beginning were eye-
> witnesses and ministers of the Word."[157]

As noted already under the discussion of Mark's gospel, Irenaeus indicated that both Mark and Luke had learned from the apostles.

Tertullian sees Luke as an "apostolic man":

> Luke, however, was not an apostle, but only an apostolic man; not
> a master, but a disciple, and so inferior to a master—at least as far
> subsequent to him as the apostle whom he followed (and that, no
> doubt, was Paul) was subsequent to the others. . . . Inasmuch,
> therefore, as the enlightener of St. Luke himself desired the au-
> thority of his predecessors for both his own faith and preaching,
> how much more may not I require for Luke's Gospel that which
> was necessary for the Gospel of his master.[158]

Luke himself describes his sources in the prologue to his gospel (Luke 1:1–4), a description that precludes his use of another canonical gospel (see chapter 7 of this volume for further discussion of Luke's prologue).

Differentiated from HC. The above citations demonstrate that the fathers consistently viewed the sources of the Synoptic Gospels to be three different apostles and not the written product of another gospel writer. They held Matthew's source to be himself, Mark's source to be Peter, and Luke's source to be Paul and the other apostles. That is a drastic difference from contemporary HC's view that Matthew and Luke depended on Mark for their material or that Luke depended on Matthew and Mark depended on Matthew and Luke for their material.

The Insistence on Harmonizing the Gospels

Incompatibility of harmonization with literary dependence. A factor that demonstrates quite conclusively that the ancient church did not view the Gospels as dependent on each other is the consistent effort of early writers to harmonize the gospel accounts with each other. Their method was exactly the method that historical-critical writers of the present strongly disparage.

Historical Criticism with its assumption of literary interdependence has little room for harmonizing apparent discrepancies in parallel accounts of the Synoptic Gospels. That is the inevitable result of assuming literary dependence. In fact, evangelicals who practice HC have shown strong rejection for traditional methods of harmonization practiced by evangelicalism, methods such as those exhibited by the early fathers. They accept the existence of "outright discrepancies" in the Gospels caused by such things as redactional activity of the gospel writers.[159] (See chapters 9 and 11 of this volume for more discussion of HC's differing attitude toward traditional harmonization, an attitude that a presumption of literary dependence creates.)

Without question, early Christian writers held to traditional methods of harmonization, thus adding further confirmation to their view of literary independence. If two of the gospel writers depended on another for their material, recent methods of accounting for differences between them is to assume substantial changes by early Christian communities or by dependent gospel writers. But early Christians knew nothing about such changes and "redactions." They harmonized the parallel passages, explaining the differences in other ways. The following quotations will demonstrate this.

Irenaeus. Regarding Matthew's statement, "No man knows the Son, but the Father," Irenaeus writes, "Thus hath Matthew set it down, and Luke in like manner, and Mark the very same."[160] Irenaeus insisted on agreement in essence—obviously not verbal agreement—among the synoptists who wrote about the same statements. In other words, he harmonized parallel accounts.

Tatian, Ammonius, and Eusebius. Also in the second century, Tatian composed what is thought to be the first harmony of the Gospels, in which he wove together the four gospels into one continuous narrative. Construction of such a harmony presupposes the full agreement of the Gospels with one another in every matter of detail. In the third century Ammonius of Alexandria, the teacher of Origen, did the same. Then early in the fourth century, Eusebius devised a system of divisions like that of Ammonius to indicate parallel sections of the Gospels.[161]

Clement of Alexandria. In connection with mutual agreement of the gospels, Clement of Alexandria writes, "These things are written in the Gospel according to Mark; and in all the rest correspondingly; although perchance the expressions vary slightly in each, yet all show identical agreement in meaning."[162] In regard to the day of the Lord's crucifixion, he adds, "With this precise determination of the days both the whole Scriptures agree, and the Gospels harmonize."[163]

Origen. With third-century heretics claiming that the Gospels were inconsistent with each other, writers of that period had more to say about harmonization. In responding to Celsus, Origen says, "Now, with respect to our Lord's silence when false witness was born against Him, it is sufficient at present to quote the words of Matthew, for the testimony of Mark is to the same effect."[164] Origen also speaks about "the harmony of the three evangelists" in regard to the place of Jesus' burial.[165] Responding to a claim of inconsistency regarding the number of angels at the tomb after Jesus' resurrection, Origen makes the following report:

> I think, that Matthew and Mark speak of one, and Luke and John of two, which statements are not contradictory. For they who mention "one," say that it was he who rolled away the stone from the sepulcher; while they who mention "two," refer to those who appeared in shining raiment to the women that repaired to the sepulcher, or who were seen within sitting in white garments.[166]

At another point Origen compares John the Baptist's words, "Offspring of vipers," in Matthew and Luke, noting in Matthew's case that John spoke the words to the Pharisees and Sadducees and in Luke's case to the multitudes. Origen harmonizes the two thus: "But Matthew, as the careful observer will see, does not speak of the multitudes in the way of praise, and he probably means the Baptist's address, Offspring of vipers, etc., to be understood as addressed to them also."[167] Origen at one point spoke about "stitch[ing] together into one statement what is written in the various Gospels" when harmonizing the statements about John the Baptist in John 1 and Matthew 3.[168]

Origen was not consistent in his harmonizing efforts, however, because of his well-known proclivity toward allegorizing the text of Scripture. In fact, at some points he disparaged literal interpretation and spoke about discrepancies in the gospel accounts when limiting analyses to that method.[169] Because of his attempt to integrate Greek philosophy with Scripture, Origen understood three senses in Scripture. There were the obvious matter-of-fact sense, the moral sense, and the spiritual sense. Origen made the historical facts conveyed in the Gospels subservient to the spiritual sense, which to him was mystical and supremely important.[170] Origen wrote regarding the four accounts of Jesus cleansing of the temple, "I conceive it to be impossible for those who admit nothing more than the history in their interpretation to show that these discrepant statements are in harmony with each other."[171]

In such deviations from historical interest, only Origen among the early fathers shows a similarity to modern HC, though he was not exactly the same as modern historical critics. The Enlightenment had not impacted him the way it has historical critics in modern times (see chapter 2 of this volume for more discussion about the influence of the Enlightenment on gospel studies). Origen's great weakness, one that removes him from the ranks of mainstream orthodox Christianity, was his hermeneutical approach to Scripture. In a real sense, he is the father of Christian allegorism.

John Chrysostom. John Chrysostom's consistent literal interpretation of the Gospels offers a clear-cut example of how he and other orthodox fathers of the early church harmonized the Gospels. To criticisms that the Gospels presented differing pictures of the same miraculous healing by Jesus, Chrysostom responds as follows:

> And it is possible to collect many other instances of this kind from the Gospels, which seem to have a suspicion of contradiction, where there is no real contradiction, the truth being that some incidents have been related by this writer, others by that; or if not occurring at the same hour one author has related the earlier event another the later; but in the present case there is nothing of this kind, but the multitude of the evidences which I have mentioned proves to those who pay any attention whatever to the matter, that the paralytic was not the same man in both instances. And this would be no slight proof to demonstrate that *the evangelists were in harmony with each other* and not at variance. For if it were the same man the discord is great between the two accounts: but if it be a different one all material for dispute has been destroyed.[172]

Regarding the four gospels, Chrysostom proposed, "But the harmony between them we will establish, both by the whole world, which hath received their statements, and by the very enemies of the truth."[173]

In comparing the accounts of Mark and Matthew in connection with the feeding of the four thousand, Chrysostom observes, "So completely do the evangelists harmonize one with another."[174] He also reports on the accounts of Peter's denials in Matthew and Mark by discussing whether the cock crowed once (Matthew) or twice (Mark).

> How then is what is said true, when Matthew affirms that Christ said, "Verily I say unto thee, that before the cock crow thou shalt deny me thrice"; and Mark declares after the third denial, that

"The cock crew the second time?" Nay, most certainly is it both
true and in harmony. . . . So that both things are true.[175]

Chrysostom's explanation of *how* two or more passages harmonize need
not prevail over another explanation. The point made in the present discussion is that he and other fathers harmonized parallel passages in the
Synoptic Gospels without recourse to positing historical or editorial changes
made by early Christian communities or the synoptic writers.

Augustine. The writings of Augustine climax the movement among early
writers toward harmonization. He wrote his harmony in response to accu-
sations by both heathen and heretics of his day that the four gospels contradicted each other. In his own words,

> [W]e have undertaken in this work to demonstrate the errors or
> the rashness of those who deem themselves able to prefer charges,
> the subtlety of which is at least sufficiently observable, against
> those four different books of the gospel which have been written
> by these four several evangelists. And in order to carry out this
> design to a successful conclusion, we must prove that the writers
> in question do not stand in any antagonism to each other.[176]

Augustine's principles of harmonization were simple and governed by
common sense. He circumvented apparently divergent accounts of the same
events by proposing different instances of the same circumstances or repeated utterances of the same words. Never does he explain differences as
changes in tradition by early Christian communities or redactional changes
of another gospel by a writer.

Examples of Augustine's methodology abound, as several instances will
illustrate. In response to an opponent's claim of inconsistency in the two
genealogies of Christ, Augustine responds in part,

> Since, therefore, the practice of adoption is common among our
> fathers, and in Scripture, is there not irrational profanity in the
> hasty condemnation of the evangelists as false because the gene-
> alogies are different, as if both could not be true, instead of con-
> sidering calmly the simple fact that frequently in human life one
> man may have two fathers, one of whose flesh he is born, and
> another of whose will he is afterwards made a son by adoption?[177]

Though one may choose to disagree with Augustine's solution to harmonizing the genealogies, the important fact for this discussion is that he
did not resort to assumptions of historical or redactional changes as do
recent evangelical historical critics. That is because Augustine does not
display any indication that Matthew and Luke could have been working
from a common literary source in composing the genealogies.

Faustus—one of Augustine's opponents—objects to a number of discrepancies between Matthew and Luke in the account of Jesus' healing of the

centurion's servant. As to whether the centurion came himself or sent others to Jesus, Augustine answers, "The explanation is, that Matthew's narrative is correct, but brief, mentioning the centurion's coming to Jesus, without saying whether he came himself or by others, or whether the words about his servant were spoken by himself or through others."[178] Augustine follows that up with the following words:

> In Matthew we have a not infrequent form of expression, and at the same time a symbolical import; while in Luke there is a simple narrative of the whole event, such as to draw our attention to the manner in which Matthew has recorded it. I wish one of those people who found their silly objections to the Gospels on such trifling difficulties would himself tell a story twice over, honestly giving a true account of what happened, and that his words were written down and read over to him.[179]

Note again that Augustine had no use for any of the tools of HC, for he had no room for any species of literary dependence.

In harmonizing the events immediately after Christ's birth, Augustine states the principle that Matthew includes material omitted by Luke and vice versa:

> On this principle, therefore, we understand that where he tells us how the wise men were warned in a dream not to return to Herod, and how they went back to their own country by another way, Matthew has simply omitted all that Luke has related respecting all that happened to the Lord in the temple, and all that was said by Simeon and Anna; while, on the other hand, Luke has omitted in the same place all notice of the journey into Egypt, which is given by Matthew, and has introduced the return to the city of Nazareth as if it were immediately consecutive.[180]

Did Jesus command the Twelve to take a staff on their mission or not? Matthew and Luke answer no, but Mark answers yes. How did Augustine harmonize these?

> For the sentence might also have been briefly expressed in this way: "Take with you none of the necessaries of life, neither a staff, save a staff only." So that the phrase "neither a staff" may be taken to be equivalent to "not even the smallest things"; while the addition, "save a staff only," may be understood to mean that, in virtue of that power which they received from the Lord, and which was signified by the name "staff" [or, "rod"], even those things which were not carried with them would not be wanting to them. Our Lord used both phrases. But inasmuch as one and the same evangelist has not recorded them both, the writer who has told us that the rod, as introduced in the one sense, was to be taken, is

supposed to be in antagonism to him who has told us that the rod, as occurring again in the other sense, was not to be taken. After this explanation of the matter, no such supposition ought to be entertained.[181]

That explanation differs radically from the usual evangelical redaction critic of today, who resorts to Source Criticism or some other tool of HC in explaining the difference as a conflation by Matthew of accounts in Mark and Q.[182] Augustine knew nothing about the theory of literary dependence that lies behind such an explanation. If he had, such would have been in evidence here.

This is an appropriate time to return to Augustine's statement to the effect that later gospel writers knew what an earlier one had written (see above under "The Absence of References to Literary Dependence," "Fourth-century writers"). Specifically, it is important to discuss what he meant in stating that "just as they [namely, the writers] received each of them the gift of inspiration, they abstained from adding to their several labors any superfluous conjoint compositions."[183] Orchard renders that part of Augustine's statement more clearly: "[E]ach has added without any superfluity the cooperation of his own work, according to the manner in which he was inspired."[184] Attention of historical critics has focused most often on other statements of Augustine shortly thereafter:

> For in his [namely, Mark's] narrative he gives nothing in concert with John apart from the others: by himself separately, he has little to record; in conjunction with Luke, as distinguished from the rest, he has still less; but in concord with Matthew, he has a very large number of passages. Much, too, he narrates in words almost numerically and identically the same as those used by Matthew, where the agreement is either with that evangelist alone, or with him in connection with the rest.[185]

Understandably, a post-Enlightenment environment that assumes some sort of literary dependence interprets Augustine's citation of the close verbal agreement of Mark with Matthew as indicating his belief that one writer copied from another. Yet several indicators oppose such a conclusion. (1) One is the statement immediately before about the three synoptists adding "without any superfluity the cooperation of his own work."[186] The expression indicates that the writers did not incorporate any extra material into their accounts, which presumably means that they did not precisely duplicate one another so as to provide two or more identical accounts of the same thing. The most natural meaning of the words excludes literary collaboration among the gospel writers, for copying from one another would have been an overkill. Most probably in the broader context, Augustine was referring to how the two gospels cover the same historical phases of Jesus' life and even evidence a personal relationship between Matthew and Mark—rather than a literary one between their gospels—when Augustine spoke about Mark's following Matthew closely and looking like "his attendant and epitomizer."[187] But Augustine carefully indicates that no duplication appears in the accounts as would have been the case with literary collaboration.

(2) For Augustine to have intended to convey that Mark copied from Matthew would directly contradict testimony from all the fathers before him, thereby placing himself outside the mainstream of Christian tradition. Earlier reports agree that Mark's source of information was Peter, as previous discussion in this chapter has shown. It is doubtful that someone so well-informed as Augustine would have contradicted earlier testimony about an oft-emphasized point without some kind of elaboration to explain why he did so. Without elaboration he differed with Clement of Alexandria regarding the sequence of Luke and Mark, but that issue did not receive nearly as much attention in early church writings as did Mark's dependence on Peter.

(3) Augustine's method of harmonization excludes the possibility of one writer's copying from another, so he must have meant that though later writers knew about an earlier writing or earlier writings, they made no literary use of it or them. Had he known of any such interdependence, he would have proceeded as contemporary historical critics do and explained how a later community or writer changed what an earlier one had handed down. Augustine never did that. He views each of the four as having written independently and warns against a conclusion "that any one of all the four evangelists has stated what is false, or has fallen into error in a position of authority at once so elevated and holy."[188]

The remote possibility that Augustine did advocate some sort of literary dependence—a very dubious possibility—would make him a lone dissenter among all the writers before him and contemporary with him. If that were the case, the verdict would have to be that he was an exception to the early consensus that advocated literary independence. Yet the case stated above indicates the strong probability that he was not alone, but stood with the others in favoring literary independence.

Direct Statement of Literary Independence

Like Augustine, Chrysostom makes a somewhat vague statement that someone might interpret as advocating literary interdependence. In reasoning why Mark has no genealogy, Chrysostom wrote the following:

It seems to me that Matthew was before the rest in entering on the subject (wherefore he both sets down the genealogy with exactness, and stops at those things which require it): but that Mark came after him, which is why he took a short course, as putting his hand to what had been already spoken and made manifest.[189]

What did Chrysostom mean by Mark's "putting his hand to what had been already spoken and made manifest"? One could interpret the words in two ways. Did he mean that the gospel of Mark is an abridgement of the gospel of Matthew? Or did Chrysostom mean that Mark composed his gospel by independently putting his hand to the same historical material that Matthew had covered? Chrysostom answers that question decisively in favor of the latter alternative in an extended statement where he indicates explicitly that the gospel writers worked independently of one another:

> And why can it have been, that when there were so many disciples, two write only from among the apostles, and two from among their followers? (For one that was a disciple of Paul, and another of Peter, together with Matthew and John, wrote the Gospels.) It was because they did nothing for vainglory, but all things for use.
>
> What then? Was not one evangelist sufficient to tell all? One indeed was sufficient; but if there be four that write, not at the same times, nor in the same places, neither after having met together, and conversed one with another, and then they speak all things as it were out of one mouth, this becomes a very great demonstration of the truth.
>
> But the contrary, it may be said, hath come to pass, for in many places they are convicted of discordance. Nay, this very thing is a very great evidence of their truth. For if they had agreed in all things exactly even to time, and place, and to the very words, none of our enemies would have believed but that they had met together, and had written what they wrote by some human compact; because such entire agreement as this cometh not of simplicity. But now even that discordance which seems to exist in little matters delivers them from all suspicion, and speaks clearly in behalf of the character of the writers.
>
> But if there be anything touching times or places, which they have related differently, this nothing injures the truth of what they have said. And these things too, so far as God shall enable us, we will endeavor, as we proceed, to point out; requiring you, together with what we have mentioned, to observe, that in the chief heads, those which constitute our life and furnish out our doctrine, nowhere is any of them found to have disagreed, no not ever so little.[190]

Quite clearly from his extended statement, Chrysostom's view was that the four gospel writers worked independently of one another, without either immediate personal consultation or literary collaboration. That direct statement confirms the consensus opinion of the fathers seen in the earlier discussion of their views endorsing literary independence. The extent of their disagreements with one another relieves them of any suspicion of having contrived a false story. But it also shows that they worked separately from each other in recording events and speeches based on their separate apostolic witnesses to historical occurrences.

Agreements in the Synoptic Gospels

If the early Christian writers held to the literary independence of the Synoptic Gospels, as they so clearly did, how did they explain the large degree of agreement among the gospel writers? After all, those agreements are the chief argument used by HC to support its theory of literary interdependence. The fathers explained them through inspiration of the Spirit and historical accuracy.

The Muratorian Canon records, "[A]lthough different points are taught us in the several books of the Gospels, there is no difference as regards the faith of Believers, inasmuch as in all of them all things are related under one imperial Spirit."[191] Augustine agrees: "But the fact is, that just as they [namely, the gospel writers] received each of them *the gift of inspiration,* they abstained from adding to their several labors any superfluous conjoint compositions."[192] Dionysius adds, "The Holy Spirit therefore, apportioned among the evangelists, makes up the full account of our Savior's whole disposition by the expressions of these several narrators [namely, the gospel writers] together."[193] So speak all the early church leaders.

The early Christian writers also refer frequently to the historical accuracy of what is recorded. Julius Africanus, an early third-century father, defends the historical accuracy of the genealogies of Christ and speaks about the folly of those who claimed the Gospels were contrived:

> The evangelists, therefore, would thus have spoken falsely, affirming what was not truth, but a fictitious commendation. . . . Therefore, that we may expose the ignorance also of him who speaks thus, and prevent any one from stumbling at this folly, I shall set forth the true history of these matters.[194]

Origen spoke strongly against heretics who dared "to trifle with the Gospels" and "corrupt the Gospel histories."[195] Regarding people that Jesus raised from the dead, Origen asserted that the accounts are "no fiction of those who composed the Gospels."[196] So speak all the rest of the early Christian writers.

Thus the earliest church leaders proposed that the high degree of agreements in the Synoptic Gospels resulted from the writers' Spirit-inspired accuracy in recording historical happenings.

SUMMARY

Five factors have proven that the earliest Christian leaders believed that writers of the Synoptic Gospels worked independently of each other:

1. The church fathers do not refer to one writer's use of the work of another, even though they had every opportunity to do so when discussing the Synoptic Gospels in the same context.
2. The church fathers give specific indication of a distinctive apostolic origin of each one of the Synoptic Gospels.
3. The constant effort of the church fathers to harmonize apparently

contradictory parallel passages indicates a belief in the independent origin of each.

4. The direct statement of John Chrysostom is representative of the rest of the fathers. It makes explicit that he viewed the writers as working strictly on their own and without any sort of literary collaboration.

5. The church fathers held the agreements between the Synoptic Gospels to be traceable to the Spirit's work in guiding the writers to record history accurately.

By viewing the Gospels in that manner, the fathers stand directly opposed to the viewpoint expressed by contemporary evangelical historical critics. The theory that some sort of literary dependence existed among the Synoptic Gospels did not originate in the early church. It came into existence in modern times, as subsequent chapters in this work will detail.

As indicated at the outset of this chapter, the writings of the early church fathers were not inerrant as are the Scriptures. But their stand on the priority of Matthew, Mark's dependence on Peter, and the literary independence of each gospel deserves full weight in light of their unanimity on each of these issues. Together with other considerations, their setting the tone for all of church history is an important factor in evaluating viewpoints about the Synoptic Gospels. The Two- (or Four-) Source Hypothesis and the Two-Gospel Hypothesis have directly reversed the perspective of the fathers regarding the Gospels and need to be viewed in that light. If the fathers were so consistently wrong, the burden of proof rests squarely on the shoulders of HC to prove them wrong. If the fathers were right, the foundational plank of HC—literary dependence—completely disappears.

ENDNOTES

1. Édouard Massaux, *The Influence of the Gospel of Saint Matthew on Christian Literature Before Saint Irenaeus*, trans. Norman J. Belval and Suzanne Hecht, Arthur J. Bellinzoni, ed., 3 vols. (Macon, Ga.: Mercer University, 1993), 3:186–87.

2. C. Steward Petrie, "The Authorship of 'The Gospel According to Matthew': A Reconsideration of the External Evidence," *New Testament Studies* 14 (1967–1968):15. Stonehouse, a leading advocate of Markan priority, admitted, "[T]he tradition concerning the apostolic authorship of Matthew is as strong, clear, and consistent and . . . the arguments advanced against its reliability are by no means decisive . . . the apostolic authorship of Matthew is as strongly attested as any fact of ancient church history" (Ned B. Stonehouse, *The Origins of the Synoptic Gospels* [Grand Rapids: Eerdmans, 1963], 46–47, cf. 76–77).

3. Bernard Orchard and Harold Riley, *The Order of the Synoptics, Why Three Synoptic Gospels?* (Macon, Ga.: Mercer, 1987), 111; see also chapter 2 of this volume.

4. The Two-Source Theory contends that Mark was written first, then Matthew and Luke wrote in dependence on Mark and a document called "Q," which contained material common to Matthew and Luke but not found in Mark.

The Four-Source Theory adds documents called "M" (used by Matthew in addition to the others) and "L" (used by Luke in addition to the others).

5. See Bernard Orchard and Thomas R. W. Longstaff, *J. J. Griesbach: Synoptic and text-critical studies 1776–1976* (Cambridge: Cambridge University, 1978), 134; William R. Farmer, *The Synoptic Problem* (Macon, Ga.: Mercer University, 1976), 48–49; Burnett Hillman Streeter, *The Four Gospels, A Study of Origins* (New York: Macmillan and Co., 1924), 151–98. Orchard and Longstaff cite Griesbach as an example of one who criticized the early fathers. Farmer cites the lack of evidence supporting the Two- (or Four-Source) Theory.

6. David Hill, *The Gospel of Matthew*, in The New Century Bible Commentary (Grand Rapids: Eerdmans, 1972), 28; D. A. Carson, Douglas J. Moo, and Leon Morris, *An Introduction to the New Testament* (Grand Rapids: Zondervan, 1992), 70–71; R. T. France, *Matthew*, Tyndale New Testament Commentary (Grand Rapids: Eerdmans, 1985), 34–38; Ralph P. Martin, *New Testament Foundations*, vol. 1 of *The Four Gospels* (Grand Rapids: Eerdmans, 1975), 139–60, 225.

7. Massaux, *Gospel of Saint Matthew*, 3:188.

8. The Two-Gospel Theory holds that Matthew was written first, then Luke wrote depending on Matthew, and finally Mark wrote in dependence on Matthew and Luke.

9. See Eusebius, *Ecclesiastical History* 3.36.1–2.

10. Irenaeus, *Against Heresies* 5.33.3–4; cf. Eusebius *Ecclesiastical History* 3.39.1–2.

11. For the strong evidence linking Papias to the date of approximately 95–110, see Robert W. Yarbrough, "The Date of Papias: A Reassessment," *Journal of the Evangelical Theological Society* 26 (June 1983): 181–91; Robert H. Gundry, *Matthew, A Commentary on His Handbook for a Mixed Church under Persecution*, 2d ed. (Grand Rapids: Eerdmans, 1994), 611–13.

12. See Irenaeus, *Against Heresies* 5.33.4; also quoted by Eusebius *Ecclesiastical History* 3.39.1. Regarding Eusebius' skeptical attitude about whether Papias ever heard the apostle John (*Ecclesiastical History* 3.39.1–2) see William R. Schoedel, *Polycarp, Martyrdom of Polycarp, Fragments of Papias*, vol. 5 of *The Apostolic Fathers*, Robert M. Grant, ed. (Camden, N.J.: Thomas Nelson, 1967), 89–92; Rudolf Helm, *Eusebius Werke*, vol. VII of *Die Chronik des Hieronymus*, in Die Griechischen Christlichen Schriftsteller der Ersten Jahrhunderte (Akademie-Verlag: Berlin, 1956): 193–94; 412–13. For persuasive evidence that Papias *did* have direct contact with the apostle, see Robert H. Gundry, Matthew, *A Commentary on His Handbook for a Mixed Church under Persecution*, 2d ed. (Grand Rapids: Eerdmans, 1994), 611–13. Eusebius' skepticism may have stemmed from his anti-chiliastic view as opposed to that of Papias (and Irenaeus), who strongly affirmed a physical reality of the millennium (see Eusebius, *Ecclesiastical History* 3.39.12–13). Or, it may have resulted from Papias' alleged preference for oral tradition rather than authorized books as his sources (see Eusebius, *Ecclesiastical History* 3.39.4; cf. also Robert M. Grant, ed., "An Introduction," in vol. 1 of *The Apostolic Fathers, A New Translation and Commentary* [New York: Thomas Nelson and Sons, 1964], 86).

13. Eusebius denied that Papias was a direct hearer of the apostle John by inferring that another John, John the Elder who was different from John the apostle, lived in Ephesus at the time (*Ecclesiastical History* 3.39.5–6). A close reading of Papias's words, however, indicates that he neither affirmed nor denied that he was hearer or eyewitness of the apostles. He does not

mention it in the passage. Petrie argues, "[T]here is nothing to justify the careless confidence with which Eusebius contradicts Irenaeus" (C. Stewart Petrie, "Authorship of 'The Gospel According to Matthew'," 15–32 [esp. 17–18]). Furthermore, even if Papias was not a personal disciple of John, as Lightfoot contended, "still his age and country place him in more or less close connection with the traditions of the Apostles; and it is this fact which gives importance to his position and teaching" (J. B. Lightfoot, *Essays on the Work Entitled Supernatural Religion* [London: Macmillan and Co., 1889], 142).

14. Eusebius, *Ecclesiastical History* 3.39.15–16. Papias's statement regarding John the disciple and the Elder John probably referred to one and the same person, namely, John the apostle (Petrie, "Authorship," 18–24; Gundry, *Matthew*, 611–13).

15. Eusebius, *Ecclesiastical History* 3.39.16. All quotes of Papias and Eusebius in part 1 of this chapter are taken from the Loeb Classical Library Series. See Eusebius, *The Ecclesiastical History*, with an English translation by Kirsopp Lake, 2 vols. (London: William Heinemann, 1926).

16. According to most, the designation "Q" stands for the first letter of the German word for "source," *Quelle*. That position, however, is debated. See the discussion in John J. Schmitt, "In Search of the Origin of the Siglum Q," *Journal of Biblical Literature* 100 (1981): 609–11.

17. T. W. Manson, *The Teaching of Jesus* (London: SCM Press, 1957), 18–20; cf. also idem, *The Sayings of Jesus* (London: SCM Press, 1949), 18–19; idem, "The Gospel of Matthew," in *Studies in the Gospels and Epistles*, Matthew Black, ed. (Manchester: Manchester University, 1962), 82–83.

18. Lampe cites only two examples of this phrase referring to "the gospels" contained in the *Chronicon Paschale* (seventh century A.D.) (see "*logion, to*" in G. W. H. Lampe, *A Patristic Greek Lexicon* (Oxford: At the Clarendon, 1961), 806.

19. Eusebius, *Ecclesiastical History* 3.39.1.

20. Kittel argues that Papias' use of the term *logia* cannot be confined to mere sayings or collections of sayings, but more likely has reference to the whole gospel, namely, words and deeds of Jesus: "[I]t is just as clear and indisputable that in the light of the usage of the LXX, New Testament and early Church the more comprehensive meaning is also possible" Gerhard Kittel, "*logion*," *TDNT*, 4:141.

21. See Lightfoot, *Essays on Supernatural Religion*, 172–76.

22. See Stewart Petrie, "Q is Only What You Make It," *Novum Testamentum* 3 (1959): 28–33. Petrie points out that the wide variety and conflicting hypotheses concerning the nature and extent of Q have cast great suspicion on the validity of the hypothesis for its existence. Farrar, though holding to the idea that Matthew and Luke utilized Mark, nonetheless, argues that against the existence of Q (A. M. Farrar, "On Dispensing with Q," in *Studies in the Gospels*, Essays in Memory of R. H. Lightfoot, D. E. Nineham, ed. [Oxford: Blackwell, 1955]: 55–88). After an extensive analysis, Linnemann, a former post-Bultmannian who at one time was a staunch advocate of the Two-Source Hypothesis, concludes that any idea of Q is a "fantasy," is "based in error," and "proves untenable" (Eta Linnemann, "Gospel of Q," *Bible Review* XI [August 1995]: 19–23, 42–43).

23. B. P. W. Stather Hunt, *Primitive Gospel Sources* (London: James Clarke & Co., 1951), 184; cf. also Rendel Harris, *Testimonies*, 2 vols. (Cambridge: University Press, 1920), 1:118–123, 130–131, 2:1–11, and F. C. Grant, *The*

Gospels: Their Origin and Their Growth (New York: Harper, 1957): 65, 144.
24. Hunt, Primitive Gospel Sources, 184.
25. Grant, Gospels, Their Origin and Growth, 65, 144; cf. Eusebius Ecclesiastical History 3.39.1, 14.
26. Grant, Gospels, Their Origin and Growth, 65.
27. Eusebius, Ecclesiastical History 3.39.1, 14.
28. Gundry notes, "Of the twenty formal quotations peculiar to Mt., seven are Septuagintal. Seven are non-Septuagintal. In six there is a mixture of Septuagintal and non-Septuagintal" (Robert H. Gundry, The Use of the Old Testament in St. Matthew's Gospel [Leiden: E. J. Brill, 1967], 149).
29. Martin, New Testament Foundations, 1:239.
30. Carson et al., Introduction to the New Testament, 70.
31. Ibid., 71.
32. Ibid., 74; cf. D. A. Carson, "Matthew," vol. 8 of Expositor's Bible Commentary, Frank E. Gaebelein, gen. ed. (Grand Rapids: Zondervan, 1984), 19.
33. Martin, New Testament Foundations, 1:240.
34. Everett F. Harrison, Introduction to the New Testament (Grand Rapids: Eerdmans, 1971), 169.
35. Hill, Gospel of Matthew, 29.
36. For example, Carson, Moo, and Morris, Introduction to the New Testament, 61–85 (esp. 68–69); Martin, New Testament Foundations, 1:139–60; 224–43; Hill, Matthew, 29–34.
37. For example, Carson, "Matthew," 13.
38. Petrie, "Authorship of 'The Gospel According to Matthew,'" 29.
39. Gundry, Matthew, A Commentary, 618.
40. Eusebius, Ecclesiastical History 3.39.15.
41. Petrie, "The Authorship of Matthew," 32. Strangely, Hagner, a Markan prioritist, agrees: "[I]t seems better to take this early piece of evidence seriously rather than to dismiss it as being dead wrong. Papias had reason for saying what he did. . . . [W]e do well to attempt to make sense of his testimony" (Donald A. Hanger, Matthew 1–13, vol. 33A of Word Biblical Commentary, David A. Hubbard and Glenn W. Barker, eds. (Waco, Tex.: Word, 1993), xlvi.
42. Josef Kürzinger, "Das Papiaszeugnis und die Erstgestalt des Matthäusevangeliums," Biblische Zeitschrift 4 (1960): 19–38; cf. idem, "Irenäus und sein Zeugnis zur Sprache des Matthäusevangeliums," New Testament Studies 10 (1963), 108–15.
43. Gundry, Matthew: A Commentary, 619–20.
44. Cf. Kürzinger, "Das Papiaszeugnis," 22–23, 27–30.
45. For example, cf. Liddell and Scott, A Greek English Lexicon, rev. and augmented by Henry Stuart Jones, with a 1968 Supplement (Oxford: At the Clarendon, 1940), 401.
46. For example, BAGD, 185; James P. Louw and Eugene A. Nida, Greek-English Lexicon of the New Testament Based on Semantic Domains (New York: United Bible Societies, 1988), 1:389 (33.1).
47. For example, Irenaeus, Against Heresies 3.1.1 (quoted in Eusebius Ecclesiastical History 5.8.2); Tertullian (Against Marcion 4.2); Pantaenus, cited by Eusebius (Ecclesiastical History 5.10.3); Origen (quoted by Eusebius in Ecclesiastical History 6.25.3–6); Eusebius himself (Ecclesiastical History 3.24.5–6); and Jerome, Preface to the Commentary on Saint Matthew; Lives of Illustrious Men 2.3.

48. Gundry argues that these New Testament occurrences of *dialektos* are articular (and thus definite) so that human language is clearly in mind in these passages. In contrast, Papias's reference does not have the article (*Hebraïdi dialektǭ*—"Hebrew dialect"). He concludes that Papias's reference should be considered indefinite ("a Hebrew way of presenting Jesus' messiahship" or Semitic style of argument) rather than definite ("the Semitic language"). See Gundry, *Matthew*, 619–20. Yet, in reply, the article is not necessary for Papias to mean "language." The force of *Hebraïdi* ("Hebrew") with *dialektǭ* ("dialect") is sufficient to make the term definite without the article. For instances where the article is not necessary to make a noun definite, consult Daniel B. Wallace, *Greek Grammar Beyond the Basics* (Grand Rapids: Zondervan, 1996), 245–54.

49. Gundry, *Matthew: A Commentary,* 618.

50. Eusebius, *Ecclesiastical History* 3.39.15.

51. Gundry, *Matthew: A Commentary,* 614.

52. The canonical Greek version shows no signs of being translated from Aramaic. For example, in certain places it transliterates Aramaic into Greek before giving a Greek translation—for instance, Matt. 1:23, *Emmanouēl, ho estin methermēneuomenon Meth' hēmōn ho theos* ("Immanuel, which is interpreted 'God with us'"); Matt. 27:33, *Golgotha, ho estin Kraniou Topos legomenos* ("Golgotha, which is called 'the Place of the Skull'"); cf. also Matt. 27:46. Also, the Greek Matthew provides explanations of local customs among the Jews that would have been unnecessary for an Aramaic-speaking audience (for instance, Matt. 27:15). Though the Greek Matthew is not a translation, Matthew may have produced an expanded version of the life of Christ that incorporated much of the original Aramaic without being a direct translation of it. Such an entirely reworked version would have suited the needs of the Diaspora Jews and others.

53. Louis Berkhof, *New Testament Introduction* (Grand Rapids: Eerdman-Sevensma, 1915), 64–71; Henry Clarence Thiessen, *Introduction to the New Testament* (Grand Rapids: Eerdmans, 1943), 137.

54. Eusebius, *Ecclesiastical History* 3.24.5–6; Hippolytus *On the Twelve Apostles* 7; cf. D. A. Hagner, "Matthew," in vol. 3 of *ISBE*, Geoffrey W. Bromiley, gen. ed. (Grand Rapids: Eerdmans, 1986), 280.

55. Matt. 9:9–14; Mark 2:13–17; Luke 5:27–32; cf. Gundry, *Use of the Old Testament,* 183; Edgar J. Goodspeed, *Matthew, Apostle and Evangelist* (Philadelphia: John C. Winston, 1959), 42–47.

56. Davies and Allison try to explain away the title in light of their assumption that Mark wrote first and the Matthean gospel could not have been written by an apostle. However, their case lacks persuasiveness in light of consistent manuscript evidence (cf. W. D. Davies and Dale C. Allison, *The Gospel According to Matthew,* International Critical Commentary [Edinburgh: T & T Clark, 1988], 1:58).

57. Ropes reasons, "Probably as early in the second century as the year 125, someone, in some place, or some group of persons, assembled for the use and convenience of the churches the only four Greek books describing the life and teachings of Jesus Christ which were then believed to be of great antiquity and worthy of a place in such a collection" (J. H. Ropes, *The Synoptic Gospels,* 2d Impression with New Preface [Cambridge, Mass.: Harvard University, 1960], 103).

58. Donald Guthrie, *New Testament Introduction,* 2d ed. (Downers Grove, Ill.: InterVarsity, 1990), 156–57.

59. See note 47 for a list of fathers who supported this.
60. Jerome, who wrote, "who afterwards translated it into Greek is not certainly known," is a possible exception (Jerome, *Lives of Illustrious Men* 2.3).
61. Hiebert, *Introduction to the New Testament,* 1:53.
62. Massaux, *Influence of the Gospel of Saint Matthew,* 3:186–87.
63. Eusebius, *Ecclesiastical History* 5.7.1. Two major writings of Irenaeus have survived. In addition to *Against Heresies,* he also wrote *Demonstration of the Apostolic Preaching,* the latter being an instructional book demonstrating that the Christian faith fulfills the Old Testament, first published in the twentieth century.
64. Eusebius, *Ecclesiastical History* 4.14.3.
65. Ibid., 4.14.3–4; 5.20.5–6; cf. Irenaeus *Against Heresies* 3.3.4.
66. Eusebius, *Ecclesiastical History* 5.20.5–6.
67. Irenaeus, *Against Heresies* 2.22.5; 4.27.1; 4.32.1; 5.36.2.
68. Ibid., 3.1.1–4; cited also in Eusebius's *Ecclesiastical History* 5.8.1–4.
69. Floyd Filson, *A Commentary on the Gospel According to Matthew,* 2d ed. (London: Adam & Charles Black, 1971), 16.
70. D. E. Nineham, *St. Mark* (Philadelphia: Westminster, 1963), 39 n.
71. Streeter apparently held that the apostle John and the Elder John to whom Papias referred were two different individuals (Streeter, *Four Gospels,* 444).
72. Petrie, "Authorship of 'The Gospel According to Matthew,'" 29.
73. A. C. Perumalil, "Are not Papias and Irenaeus competent to report on the Gospels?" *Expository Times* 91 (August 1980): 336.
74. J. B. Lightfoot, *Supernatural Religion,* 142.
75. Irenaeus, *Against Heresies* 3.1.1; also cited by Eusebius, *Ecclesiastical History* 5.8.2.
76. To cite only a few random examples, compare Irenaeus, *Against Heresies* "Preface" 2 with Matt. 10:26; compare 1.1.3 with Matt. 20:1–16; compare 1.3.5 with Matt. 10:21, 34; compare 1.6.1 with Matt. 5:13–14; compare 1.8. with Matt. 26:38–39; 27:46; compare 3.8.1 with Matt. 6:24.
77. Irenaeus in this context appears to be setting forth an apologetic regarding the content of each gospel as being inspired by the Holy Spirit and united in testimony about the true contents of the gospel in contrast to the teaching of heretics. He is not necessarily setting forth a strict compositional order (cf. *Against Heresies* 3.2.1).
78. Hans von Campenhausen, *The Formation of the Christian Bible* (Philadelphia: Fortress, 1972), 195 n. 243; cf. for example, Irenaeus *Against Heresies* 3.9.1–11.8; 4.6.1.
79. Campenhausen explains this order of John-Luke-Matthew-Mark as corresponding "to the various epochs of salvation history" from Irenaeus's perspective (Campenhausen, *Formation of the Christian Bible,* 195 n. 243).
80. Williston Walker, Richard A. Norris, David W. Lotz, and Robert T. Handy, *A History of the Christian Church,* 4th ed. (New York: Charles Scribner's Sons, 1985), 87.
81. Eusebius, *Ecclesiastical History* 5.10.1–2.
82. Ibid., 5.10.2.
83. Ibid., 5.10.2–3.
84. Ibid., 5.11.1–2.
85. Butterworth says he may have been an Athenian by birth (G. W. Butterworth, "Introduction," *Clement of Alexandria,* trans. G. W. Butterworth, The Loeb Classical Library [London: William Heinemann, 1919], xi).
86. Eusebius, *Ecclesiastical History* 5.11.1.

87. Ibid., 5.11.3–4; Clement, *Stromateis* 1.1.1.11; cf. also J. Stevenson, *The New Eusebius*, rev. by W. H. C. Frend (London: SPCK, 1987), 180 [*Stromateis* 1.1.11.1–3; *Ecclesiastical History* 5.11.3–5].

88. William R. Farmer, "The Patristic Evidence Reexamined: A Response to George Kennedy," in *New Synoptic Studies*, William R. Farmer, ed. (Macon, Ga.: Mercer University, 1983), 7.

89. Eusebius, *Ecclesiastical History* 6.14.5–7; Clement, *Hypotyposeis* 6. The quotation comes from Eusebius, *The Ecclesiastical History, Volume II*, trans. J. E. L. Oulton, The Loeb Classical Library (Cambridge, Mass.: Harvard University Press, 1932), 46–59.

90. Giuseppe Fiov. Gamba, "A Further Reexamination of Evidence from Early Tradition," in *New Synoptic Studies*, William R. Farmer, ed. (Macon, Ga.: Mercer University, 1983), 21 n. 10. For further discussion of other ancient documents that support Clement's tradition, see ibid., 21–29.

91. Tertullian became a Montanist in the very early part of the third century A.D. (cf. Earle E. Cairns, *Christianity Though the Centuries* [Grand Rapids: Zondervan, 1996], 106–7).

92. Cairns, *Christianity Through the Centuries*, p. 106.

93. Tertullian, *Against Marcion* 4.5.3; cf. ibid., 4.2.1–5.

94. Cf. Eusebius, *Ecclesiastical History* 6.1–8, 16, 29, 23–27, 32.

95. Ibid., 6.25.3–6.

96. The larger context deals with Origen's view of the number of sacred writings in the Old Testament and New Testament (ibid., 6.25.1–14).

97. Farmer, "Patristic Evidence Reexamined," 14.

98. Origen, *Homily in Luke* I; cf. also Orchard and Riley, *Order of the Synoptics*, 137.

99. *Ecclesiastical History* consists of ten books, the first seven of which recount the history of the church from the beginning to A.D. 303 and the last three some events in Eusebius's own lifetime until the Council of Nicaea in A.D. 325. He wrote in a strict chronological order.

100. Eusebius, *Ecclesiastical History* 1.1.1–8.

101. Ibid., 3.24.6.

102. Ibid., 3.24.5–7.

103. Ibid., 3.24.7–8.

104. Ibid., 3.24.9–10.

105. Ibid., 2.15.1–2.

106. Ibid., 3.24.15.

107. Augustine's *Confessions* 1–10 give the story of his life until shortly after his conversion. He gives an account of his conversion in 8.12.

108. Augustine, *The Harmony of the Gospels* 1.2.3. Quotations from Augustine's *Harmony* come from Philip Schaff, ed., vol. 6 of *The Nicene and Post-Nicene Fathers*, here after designated *NPNF*.

109. Ibid.

110. Cf. David Peabody, "Augustine and the Augustinian Hypothesis: A Reexamination of Augustine's Thought in De Consensu Evangelistarum," in *New Synoptic Studies*, William R. Farmer, ed. (Macon, Ga.: Mercer, 1983), 38.

111. Augustine, *The Harmony of the Gospels* 1.2.4. Augustine refers to the Hebrew Matthew at least two other times in his Harmony (2.66.128 and 2.80.157), in both of which places he refers to or quotes the Greek Matthew while talking about a Hebrew original. He never denies that the Greek version came from Matthew himself.

112. Ibid., 1.2.5–6.

113. Ibid., 1.2.4.
114. Ibid., 2.8.13.
115. Ibid., 4.10.11.
116. Peabody, "Augustine and the Augustinian Hypothesis," 61–62.
117. Wayne A. Meeks, "Hypomnemata from an Untamed Sceptic: A Response to George Kennedy," *The Relationships Among the Gospels: An Interdisciplinary Dialogue,* William O. Walker, Jr., ed. (San Antonio, Tex.: Trinity University, 1978), 170–71 [emphasis in the original].
118. Cited by Eusebius, *Ecclesiastical History* 3.39.15–16.
119. Irenaeus, *Against Heresies* 3.15.3 (*ANF*, 1:440). All quotations in part 2 of this chapter come from A. Roberts and J. Donaldson, eds., *The Ante-Nicene Fathers* (hereafter *ANF*, 1:440) or from *NPNF*, unless otherwise noted. For example, the quotation cited from Irenaeus appears in vol. 1 on p. 440 of *ANF*.
120. Ibid., 3.1.1 (*ANF*, 1:414).
121. Ibid., 4.6.1 (*ANF*, 1:467–68).
122. Tertullian, *The Five Books Against Marcion* 4.5 (*ANF*, 3:350).
123. Ibid., 4.2 (*ANF*, 3:347).
124. Clement Alexandrinus, *Fragments* 1 ("Comments on the First Epistle of Peter") (*ANF*, 2:573).
125. Clement Alexandrinus, *Fragments* 2 ("Comments on the Epistle of Jude") (*ANF*, 2:574).
126. Eusebius, *Ecclesiastical History* 6.14.
127. Origen, *Commentary on the Gospel of John* 1.6 (*ANF*, 10:299–300).
128. Ibid., 6.31 (*ANF*, 10:367).
129. Ibid., 10.1 (*ANF*, 10:381).
130. Ibid, 10.18 (*ANF*, 10:398).
131. Origen, *Commentary on Matthew* Book 1 (*ANF*, 10:412).
132. Origen, *Against Celsus* 2.69 (*ANF*, 4:459).
133. Ibid., 5.56 (*ANF*, 4:568).
134. Dionysius, *The Works of Dionysius* 5.1 (*ANF*, 6:94).
135. Ibid., 3 (*ANF*, 6:118).
136. John Chrysostom, *Homilies of St. John Chrysostom on the Gospel According to St. Matthew* 1.5 (*NPNF*, 10:2).
137. Augustine, *The Harmony of the Gospels* 1.2.3 (*NPNF*, 6:78).
138. Ibid., 1.2.4 (*NPNF*, 6:78).
139. Cited by Eusebius *Ecclesiastical History* 3.24.7; 6.14.7; cf. Friedrich Bleek, *An Introduction to the New Testament,* William Urwick, ed. (Edinburgh: T & T Clark, 1873), 1:192.
140. For example, Robert H. Stein has written, "Augustine was probably the first to seek to explain how they [namely, the Synoptic Gospels] were related literarily" (*The Synoptic Problem: An Introduction* [Grand Rapids: Baker, 1987], 130).
141. Augustine, *The Harmony of the Gospels* 1.2.4 (*NPNF*, 6:78).
142. Stein, *Synoptic Gospels,* 29–44, esp. 44.
143. I. Howard Marshall, *The Gospel of Luke: A Commentary on the Greek Text,* I. Howard Marshall and W. Ward Gasque, eds. (Grand Rapids: Eerdmans, 1978), 30.
144. Ibid., 228, 241, 317, 323, 325.
145. Justin Martyr, *The First Apology of Justin* 66 (*ANF*, 1:185).
146. Irenaeus, *Against Heresies* 3.9.3 (*ANF*, 1:423).
147. Tertullian, *The Five Books Against Marcion* 4.2 (*ANF*, 3:347).

148. Ibid.
149. Tertullian, *On the Flesh of Christ* 22 (*ANF*, 3:540).
150. Hippolytus, *On the Twelve Apostles* 7 (*ANF*, 5:255).
151. Augustine, *Reply to Faustus the Manichaean* 17.3 (*NPNF*, 4:235).
152. Papias, *Fragments of Papias* 6 (*ANF*, 1:154–55).
153. Clement Alexandrinus, *Fragments* 1, cited by Cassiodorus (*ANF*, 2:573).
154. Ibid., 3 (*ANF*, 2:579), cited by Eusebius, *Ecclesiastical History* 2.15.1.
155. Ibid., cited by Eusebius, *Ecclesiastical History* 6.14.
156. Irenaeus, *Against Heresies* 3.15.3 (*ANF*, 1:440).
157. Ibid., 3.14.2 (*ANF*, 1:438).
158. Tertullian, *The Five Books against Marcion* 4.2 (*ANF*, 3:347–48).
159. For example, Gundry, *Matthew: A Commentary*, 624; cf. Blomberg, "The Legitimacy and Limits of Harmonization," in *Hermeneutics, Authority and Canon*, D. A. Carson and John D. Woodbridge, eds. (Grand Rapids: Baker, 1995), 145.
160. Irenaeus, *Against Heresies* 4.6.1 (*ANF*, 1:467–68).
161. M. B. Riddle, "Introductory Essay to Augustine's 'The Harmony of the Gospels,'" *The Nicene and Post-Nicene Fathers*, Philip Schaff, ed. (1980 reprint, Grand Rapids: Eerdmans, n.d.), 6:68–69.
162. Clement Alexandrinus, *Salvation of the Rich Man* 5 (*ANF*, 2:592).
163. Clement Alexandrinus, *Fragments* 11 (*ANF*, 2:581).
164. Origen, *Against Celsus* Preface to Book 1 (*ANF*, 4:395).
165. Ibid., 2.69 (*ANF*, 4:459).
166. Ibid., 5.56 (*ANF*, 4:568).
167. Origen, *Commentary on the Gospel of John* 6.14 (*ANF*, 10:364).
168. Ibid., 6.13 (*ANF*, 10:362).
169. Ibid., 10.15 (*ANF*, 10:693).
170. Allan Menzies, "Introduction to Commentaries of Origen," *The Ante-Nicene Fathers*, 5th ed., Alan Menzies, A. Roberts and J. Donaldson, eds. (1974 reprint, Grand Rapids: Eerdmans, n.d.), 10:292.
171. Origen, *Commentary on the Gospel of John* 10.15 (*ANF* Supplement, 10:393).
172. John Chrysostom, *Homily on the Paralytic Let Down Through the Roof* 4 (*NPNF*, 9:214–15) [emphasis added].
173. John Chrysostom, *Homilies of St. John Chrysostom on the Gospel according to St. Matthew* Homily 1.8 (*NPNF*, 10:4).
174. Ibid., Homily 53.1 (*NPNF*, 10:327).
175. Ibid., Homily 85.2 (*NPNF*, 10:507).
176. Augustine, *The Harmony of the Gospels* 1.7.10 (*NPNF*, 6:81).
177. Augustine, *Reply to Faustus the Manichaean* 3.3 (*NPNF*, 4:160).
178. Ibid., 33.7 (*NPNF*, 4:344).
179. Ibid., 33.8 (*NPNF*, 4:344).
180. Augustine, *The Harmony of the Gospels* 2.5.16 (*NPNF*, 6:109).
181. Ibid., 2.30.74 (*NPNF*, 6:138).
182. For example, Blomberg, "Legitimacy and Limits," 154–55.
183. Augustine, *Harmony of the Gospels* 1.2.4 (*NPNF*, 6:78).
184. Bernard Orchard and Harold Riley, *The Order of the Synoptics: Why Three Synoptic Gospels* (Macon, Ga.: Mercer University, 1987), 213.
185. Ibid.
186. The Latin behind this translation is *superfluam cooperationem* (Sancti Aurelii Augustini, *De Consensu Evangelistarum* 1.2.4, in *Opera Omnia* [Parisiis: Venit Apud Editorem in Vico Dicto Montrouge, Juxta *Portam*

Inferni, 1841], 1044), the former term denoting a "surplus" or an "over-flowing" and the latter word a "working together" or "cooperation" (cf. C. T. Lewis and C. Short, *A Latin Dictionary* [Oxford: Clarendon, 1879]; P. G. W. Glare, ed., *Oxford Latin Dictionary* [Oxford: Clarendon, 1982]). In other words, nothing "extra" appears in the accounts.

187. Cf. Peabody, "Augustine and the Augustinian Hypothesis," 40–41.
188. Augustine, *The Harmony of the Gospels* 3.13.43 (*NPNF*, 6:199).
189. John Chrysostom, *Homilies of St. John Chrysostom on the Gospel according to St. Matthew*, Homily 4.1 (*NPNF*, 10:20).
190. Ibid., Homily 1.5–6 (*NPNF*, 10:2–3).
191. *Canon Muratorianus* 1 (*ANF*, 5:603).
192. Augustine, *The Harmony of the Gospels* 1.2.4 (*NPNF*, 6:78) [emphasis added].
193. Dionysius, *The Works of Dionysius, Exegetical Fragments* 3 (*ANF*, 6:117).
194. Julius Africanus, "The Epistle to Aristides," *The Extant Writings of Julius Africanus* 1 (*ANF*, 6:125).
195. Origen, *Against Celsus* 2.27 (*ANF*, 4:43).
196. Ibid., 2.48 (*ANF*, 4:449).

CHAPTER TWO

Philosophical and Theological Bent of Historical Criticism

F. David Farnell

AN EVALUATION OF HISTORICAL Criticism must include an analysis of its presuppositions. Its roots are not scientific, but are philosophically presuppositional. These philosophical roots are hostile to biblical inerrancy. The method cannot impartially investigate the Bible. The question is not whether the method impugns the Bible, but when and in what way it does so.

Ingrained in the discipline is a prevailing antisupernaturalism that intuitively suspects any document describing the miraculous. Historical Criticism is in reality an ideology whose very nature negates the Scriptures.

Philosophical opposition to the supernatural is not new. Paul encountered such in Athens (Acts 17:16–34), for his biblical world-view included the resurrection of a material body, but that of his philosophical listeners had no room for the supernatural. Philosophy's clash with Christianity in the New Testament appears also in Colossians, 1 John, 2 Peter, Jude, and Revelation 2–3. It emerged early in the post-Apostolic church and continued throughout the Middle Ages. It was not until the Reformation corrected the hermeneutical abuses of philosophy that a resolution of the problem surfaced. But just over a hundred years after the Reformers, philosophy reasserted itself to haunt the church. Scholars began finding errors in the Bible "because theologians had capitulated to alien philosophical presuppositions. . . . Philosophical premises . . . undermined the historic belief in an infallible and inerrant Bible."[1] The collection of articles in *Biblical Errancy* traces the underpinnings of Historical Criticism to baneful philosophical methodologies.[2] They accepted "certain philosophical or scientific assumptions that are inimical to evangelical theology."[3]

Linnemann, a former student of form-critic Rudolf Bultmann and new-hermeneutic proponent Ernst Fuchs, has noticed that evangelicals—faithful heirs of the Reformation—have acquiesced to Historical Criticism and its devastating hermeneutical results. She notes how inappropriate this is because the discipline has "its foundation in philosophies which made bold to define truth so that God's Word was excluded as the source of truth. . . . These philosophies simply presupposed that man could have no valid knowledge of the God of the Bible."[4] She stresses that the Enlightenment laid an atheistic starting point for the sciences and for biblical criticism as a whole.[5] One of her comments is especially insightful:

> What is concealed from the student is the fact that science itself, including and especially theological science, is by no means unbiased and presuppositionless. The presuppositions which determine the way work is carried on in each of its disciplines are at work behind the scenes and are not openly set forth.[6]

Consequently the associated disciplines of Historical Criticism (such as Source, Form, Redaction, and Tradition Criticisms) cannot be studied in isolation from the philosophical "isms" that buttressed and underpinned their developments. They all share the same foundation with biblical fallibility.

Yet the philosophically oriented, theological community brands all attempts to such resist that methodology as "unscientific," though it is the practitioners of such methods who are in reality "unscientific." They are presuppositionally controlled in their investigations. Conservative evangelicals need to consider this intrinsic bias and heed the following scriptural warning: "See to it that no one takes you captive through hollow and deceptive philosophy" (Col. 2:8).

Specific antibiblical philosophical systems foundational to Historical Criticism include inductivism, materialism, rationalism, deism, skepticism, agnosticism, idealism, romanticism, evolution, and existentialism. Though not exhaustive, the list provides typical examples of philosophical thought that are at odds with an orthodox view of the Bible. A survey of each of the ten systems and its leading representative(s) will clarify the nature of the system and its impact on historical-critical methodologies.

1. INDUCTIVISM: FRANCIS BACON

Sir Francis Bacon (1561–1626) was a writer, orator, lawyer, and philosopher-scientist. In 1618, he rose to the position of Lord Chancellor in England. In 1620, just over a century after the Reformation, Bacon published his *Novum Organum*. This work was foundational for not only modern biblical criticism but also the resultant historical-critical methodologies. British empiricism grew out of the thought of Francis Bacon.[7]

In this work, Bacon made the inductive method—namely, what is learned by experience and experiment—the basis of discovering all truth.[8] Furthermore, science and not religion becomes the true model of the world.[9] For Bacon, truth becomes known pragmatically, for whatever works is truth. Truth and whatever works are synonymous.[10]

Bacon also separated science from the Bible.[11] One must keep science and reason entirely distinct from religion and faith. For Bacon, science deals with the physical universe, but religion deals with faith. One not dare build science on the Bible but on inductive methods through an examination of the physical universe.[12]

Linnemann characterizes Bacon's inductivism as excluding Holy Scripture from being the source of truth and replacing it with whatever people can discover through their own reason and experimentation.[13] The ascendancy of Bacon's thinking pictured Scripture as infallible in matters of only faith and practice, but not science and history. However, the separation of faith and practice from science and history is unbiblical. The grammatical-historical hermeneutic of the Reformation linked the historical and scientific implications of Scripture inseparably to the theological implications of Scripture (for example, compare Genesis 3 with Romans 5). So Bacon cleared the way for the historical-critical view that the Bible is infallible only in "spiritual matters" but does not speak inerrantly on "historical and/or scientific matters." Instead of Scripture serving as a guide to science, scientific interpretations became the exclusive avenue to all truth and stand in judgment on Scripture.[14]

So Bacon began the gradual process of separating faith from science, a road that would lead eventually to the mythological interpretations of Strauss and Bultmann and fully developed Historical Criticism.

2. MATERIALISM: THOMAS HOBBES

Thomas Hobbes (1588–1679) was secretary to Francis Bacon for a brief period. Hobbes was also the most prominent proponent of materialistic philosophy. His *magnum opus* was *Leviathan* (1651). Although Hobbes professed to be Christian, the extreme views in this work cost him the support of many Anglican and Catholic authorities in England and France and raised questions about the genuineness of his profession.[15] After noting that religion was not central in Hobbes' thinking, Brown comments as follows:

> The kind of philosophy that Hobbes advocated was an attempt to work out a world view and a prescription for human conduct and public life in secular terms. Hobbes himself saw it as a version of rationalism in which geometry was seen as a model for reasoning. . . . He excluded from philosophy all appeals to experience (for experience had no part in "original knowledge") and to supernatural revelation (for knowledge alleged to be attained by such means was not acquired reasoning).[16]

As a forerunner of skeptical empiricism and rationalism in religion, Hobbes advocated materialistic sensationalism, namely, the origin of all ideas in the mind are reducible to sensations.[17] Reality consists of materiality and nothing else, no provision being made for spiritual reality.[18] So one should not speak about the soul as a separate entity from the body, for human beings are merely living bodies with death being the cessation of bodily functions.[19] To Hobbes, although one cannot say that no God exists, the idea of God is not a philosophical subject.[20]

Hobbes also doubted the miraculous. To him, the supernatural reflects "fear" and "ignorance of causes."[21] For Hobbes, such things were the "natural seed of religion."[22] If any alleged miraculous event happened, a rational, rather than supernatural, explanation must exist.[23] If people only realized the natural cause of an event, they would not in ignorance call it supernatural.

Hobbes therefore removed everything supernatural from the biblical record and became one of the first modern writers to engage in Historical Criticism of Scripture. He rejected all appeals to divine inspiration and supernatural revelation, for reason was not the means of obtaining knowledge purportedly gained by such means.[24] He explained away Jesus' exorcism of demon-possessed people, calling the cases mental illness, not demon possession.[25] Supernatural elements in the Gospels are merely parabolic or symbolic, not historical or factual.

Furthermore, Hobbes claimed that "many things in God's word [are] above reason; that is to say, which cannot by natural reason be either demonstrated or confuted," so that "we then captivate our understanding and reason when we forbear contradiction."[26] Hobbes meant that reason and contradiction (namely, ecclesiastical dogma) may coexist, but natural reason is "the undoubted Word of God."[27] However, contradictions are acceptable whether or not they make sense logically. He called the deity of Christ and the Trinity "absurdities."[28] Geisler captures the heart of the matter:

> If these [Hobbes'] words are taken seriously, it is one of the most blatant forms of blind fideism ever proposed. What is significant . . . is the radical separation of faith and reason and the apparent relegation of matters of faith to the unverifiable and paradoxical realm of the absurd and contradictory.[29]

Hobbes saw faith (namely, blind faith) and obedience as critical elements in religion and ecclesiastical tradition, even if their objects are "absurdities" and contrary to "reason."[30]

Hobbes' long-range effect on Historical Criticism and theological development is visible in his anticipation of existentialism and its "blind leap of faith" advocated by Kierkegaard. Yet, Hobbes system even went further.[31] His deprecation of miracles laid the groundwork for later deist and naturalist denials of everything miraculous. His system also previewed modern liberal theory that the Bible is not itself the revelation of God but a record of that revelation.[32]

Hobbes's interest was not in Scripture as a revelation of God's actions in history or as a source of Christian theology. He was a political philosopher who regarded Scripture as a book containing rules and regulations for religion or ecclesiastical institutions.[33] Yet he held none of the propositions of the Bible to be meaningful descriptions of God. In other words, the Bible contains no propositional truth.[34]

Linnemann's opinion is that through the work of Hobbes "a radical separation between faith and thought" occurred. Consequently, through Bacon's and Hobbes's works

> not only were the foundations of biblical criticism laid . . . but the atheistic starting point of the sciences as a whole was likewise fixed.

Spinoza, Descartes, Kant—just to name some of many—only stated more precisely what was already laid down in the beginning stages of the Enlightenment.[35]

The cumulative effect of Hobbes' work was to diminish increasingly the Scriptures as relevant and authoritative for people. Reason now ascends the throne.

3. RATIONALISM: SPINOZA

Baruch de (or Benedictus) Spinoza (1632–1677) was born in Amsterdam of Jewish lineage. Although he was a Jew, in 1656 Spinoza's free thinking resulted in his expulsion from the synagogue for "abominable heresies which he practices and teaches."[36] Spinoza's ideas were not only repugnant to Jewish authorities but also to Christians.[37] Sometimes described as a hideous atheist and other times as God-intoxicated, Spinoza was a rationalistic pantheist.[38]

"Rationalism" is a system that assigns reason, not sensory experience, as the primary means of gaining knowledge. In other words, all truth is discoverable by human reason.[39] Rationalism extols the power of deductive reasoning in one's ability to grasp substantial truths about self, others, and the world, and correspondingly tends to regard natural science as a basically *a priori* enterprise.[40] For seventeenth-century rationalists, mathematical axioms and postulates were the ideal of all knowledge.[41]

Rationalism, however, as a specific movement refers especially to a philosophy that developed in the seventeenth and early eighteenth centuries.[42] Rationalistic philosophy arose partly as a response to Pyrrhonianism (doctrines of ancient extreme skepticism that were unable to decide anything about reality), which raised questions about scientific as well as religious beliefs.[43] Rationalism challenged this skepticism and provided a basis for reality.[44] Spinoza, Descartes (1596–1650),[45] and Leibniz (1646–1716) were the three most prominent rationalistic philosophers.[46]

Arguing from a strongly deductive perspective, Spinoza pushed the "reason only" view to an extreme by arguing that all truth, even religious truth, is knowable only through self-evident mathematical axioms.[47] Anything contrary to these axioms or not reducible to them is irrational and to be rejected—whether it is in the Bible or not. Spinoza supported the existence of only one substance: "Whatsoever is, is in God, and nothing can be or be conceived without God."[48] Spinoza therefore identified God with the universe, a species of rationalistic pantheism. In his system, God is not personal, and He could not have failed to create the universe for it reflects God's essence. God is not transcendent or apart from creation for God and nature are the same. Spinoza argued, "God is the immanent, not the transitive, cause of all things."[49] Also, he argued for determinism, a theory holding all types of phenomena to be determined by preceding events of natural causes.[50] In Spinoza's system, a loving personal God was impossible.[51] In pantheistic fashion, he defined religion as "the Mind's intellectual love of God."[52]

Spinoza's philosophy has been characterized as both skeptical and antiskeptical.[53] It was antiskeptical in that it gave a place to the concept of God, but it was profoundly skeptical about biblical religion as reflected in Judaism and Christianity.[54] Though he allowed that biblical religion had a place in history, he felt it was of no foundational importance.[55]

In *Tractatus*, Spinoza detailed his views of Scripture. Like Bacon and Hobbes, he limited the authority of Scripture to religious matters, asserting, "We now have shown that Scripture can only be called the Word of God in so far as it affects religion."[56] As long as Scripture is for religious purposes, it is sacred, because rationalistic pantheism views faith and reason as completely separate realms.[57] Spinoza's essential argument was that science is the domain of the intellect or reason (thinking rationalistically and pantheistically), but religion's domain is that of obedience.[58]

Spinoza supported what came to be the classic liberal formula of Scripture: the Bible is not the Word of God; rather, it merely contains the Word of God. Spinoza affirmed, "In so far as it [the Bible] contains the Word of God, it has come down to us uncorrupted."[59] He also wrote the following:

> Those who look upon the Bible as a message sent down by God from Heaven to men, will doubtless cry out that I have committed the sin against the Holy Ghost because I have asserted that the Word of God is faulty, mutilated, tampered with, and inconsistent.[60]

Because Spinoza's rationalistic pantheism equated God with nature, he was one of the most antisupernatural philosophers in history. To him, a belief in miracles stems from ignorance. Promotion of miracles was a propaganda tool of religious authorities to protect their own authority.[61] Miracles were merely misapprehensions of natural law. Since they are contrary to nature, they are also contrary to reason. Whatever is contrary to reason is absurd and worthy of rejection.[62]

Following such a rationale, Spinoza engaged in a historical-critical analysis of Scripture and became "the father of much modern biblical criticism."[63] For example, he denied the Mosaic authorship of the Pentateuch,[64] the traditional authorship of other Old Testament books (for example, Joshua),[65] and the Danielic authorship of the first seven chapters of Daniel.[66] Spinoza questioned the divine inspiration of the New Testament epistles.[67] He impugned the gospel accounts by asserting that "it is scarcely credible that God can have designated to narrate the life of Christ four times over, and to communicate it thus to mankind."[68]

Spinoza also advocated allegorical interpretation: "Many things are narrated in Scripture as real, and were believed to be real, which were in fact only symbolical and imaginary."[69] Geisler's summarizes Spinoza's influence accurately:

> It is clear . . . that over a century before Johann Semler (1725–1791), and two centuries before Julius Wellhausen (1844–1918),

Spinoza engaged in systematic antisupernatural criticism of the Bible. Indeed, virtually all of the central emphases in modern liberalism—"the Bible contains the Word of God . . ." issue, the accommodation theory, rationalism, naturalism, the religious-only view, the moral criterion for canonicity, and even the allegorical interpretation of Scripture—are found in Spinoza.[70]

Though Spinoza's view attracted little attention in his day, in the Age of Enlightenment he had many followers. Hasel notes that the rationalists had great impact, calling their influences "powerful catalysts toward the formation of the full-fledged historical-critical method."[71]

Gotthold Ephraim Lessing (1729–1781), one of the principal thinkers of the Enlightenment, professed to be a Spinozist in his later years.[72] His two German articles "Theses from the History of the Church" (1776) and "New Hypothesis Concerning the Evangelists Regarded as Merely Human Historians" (1778) proposed that the three Synoptic Gospels are independent of each other but depended on a common source, namely, a heretical Aramaic gospel of the Nazarenes. This view is called the *Urevangelium* hypothesis or theory of a lost original gospel.[73] Thus, Lessing paved the way for other theories of literary dependence to explain the similarities in the first three gospels.

Without denying the possibility of miracles or prophecy, Lessing in another German work (English, *Concerning the Proof from the Spirit and Power*) denied their relevance for religious truth and for proving Christianity's reality. He also rejected Christianity as a historical religion, for *"accidental truths of history can never become the proof of necessary truths of reason."*[74] Like Descartes and Spinoza, Lessing maintained that only clear and distinct ideas such as geometric and self-evident axioms—not miracles and prophecy—are a basis for any system of thought. He also rejected "orthodox ideas of the deity." His own creed was a pantheistic approach, *Hen kai Pan* ("One and All"), like Spinoza.[75]

Spinoza profoundly influenced Schleiermacher,[76] often described as "the greatest exponent of liberal Protestantism."[77] Like Spinoza, Schleiermacher believed God was at work in the world, but the notion of an absolute miracle was inconceivable to him, for it contradicted nature.[78] For both men, faith was not dependent on but was separate from miracles.[79] Schleiermacher knew that his thinking had much in common with Spinoza and urged his readers to offer tribute to "the holy, rejected Spinoza" who exhibited "the high World-Spirit."[80] D. F. Strauss referred to some of Schleiermacher's work as Spinozian formulations.[81] Spinoza was also heavily influential in the formulation of the absolute idealism of Hegel (1770–1831), who himself was important in the Tübingen school of F. C. Baur. Hegel gave Spinoza a prominent place in his *Lectures on the Philosophy of History*.[82]

Brown accurately summarizes Spinoza's influence: "What is beyond dispute is the fact that from this time [the period of Lessing's writings] onwards an increasing number of writers professed admiration for Spinoza."[83]

The Enlightenment's emphasis on reason as the sole guide and its re-sultant extreme historical skepticism has pervaded the historical-critical method. Krentz makes that point:

> The rationalist Enlightenment radicalized the claim of reason and history; as a result it placed the claims of religion outside the realm of reason. In this division Orthodox theology lost its foundations in history. . . . Few orthodox scholars learned the historical method without taking over rationalist antisupernaturalism.[84]

The roots of Historical Criticism show it is not an objective science for it is replete with prejudices that make objectivity impossible.

4. DEISM: TOLAND, COLLINS, TINDAL, AND OTHERS

As a general system, deism teaches the separation of God from the world as Theism does, but, unlike theism, it denies that God also interacts and is involved with the world.[85] Deism applies to a small number of heterogeneous thinkers of the seventeenth and early eighteenth centuries who rejected supernatural revelation and revealed mysteries.[86] French and German deism made some contributions, but English deism had an "extraordinary effect . . . on the whole intellectual life of the eighteenth century."[87]

Halyburton viewed Herbert of Cherbury (1583–1648) as the "father" of English deism.[88] Herbert delineated five "Common Notions" about reli-gion: the existence of a supreme God, the worship of God, the need for a moral life, repentance from sin, and eternal life with reward or punish-ment. Common reason was the primary authority for the "notions" that he took to be the foundation of world religions and the essence of true religion.[89]

Like some deists, Herbert saw reason as supporting orthodox Chris-tianity—though he himself was not orthodox[90]—but other deist systems refuted Christianity.[91] After Herbert's death, Charles Blount (1654–1693) became the most zealous early promoter of his ideas. Using Apollonius, a reputed miracle worker who died around A.D. 98, he denigrated the unique-ness of Jesus Christ.[92] Echoing a common maneuver in the deistic polemic against Christian miracles, Blount alleged that miracle stories like those tied to Jesus were commonplace among religious figures of that time.[93] Blount reflected the influence of Hobbes and Spinoza in his thinking about miracles.

With the expiration of the Licensing Act in Great Britain, John Toland (1670–1722) was among those taking advantage of this new era in free speech regarding religion when he published his landmark work *Chris-tianity Not Mysterious* (1696).[94] In part, the volume drew upon the Com-mon Notions of Lord Herbert and the empirical approach of Locke, but in substance, it drew heavily on continental rationalism, attempting to elimi-nate everything beyond the scope of reason. Toland asserted that the mysteries of Christianity resulted from pagan ideas and priestcraft. Jesus allegedly preached a simple, moral religion. The book caused such an uproar in England that even John Locke repudiated Toland's approval of his own thinking.

In 1718, Toland published another significant work entitled *Nazarenus*.[95] In this work, Toland argued that Jews and Gentiles mistook the purpose of Jesus, who did not come to abolish the law but to recognize its moral validity. Toland also furnished a preview of Lessing's views of institutional religion and the Synoptic Gospels' being based on the gospel of the Nazarenes. Toland's position was that the Nazarenes, or Ebionites, were the first Christians, so their view about Jesus was more authentic than that in the canonical gospels and the rest of the New Testament. To Toland, the Gospels present an unhistorical and falsely supernatural portrait of the real Jesus.

Another significant English deist was Anthony Collins (1676–1729). Although Collins was a friend of John Locke, he attacked Locke's assertions that miracles and fulfilled prophecy demonstrate the divine origin of revelation.[96] In 1713, Collins published anonymously *A Discourse on Free Thinking*, advocating that only through free inquiry is truth about religious questions available. In 1724, Collins turned to biblical criticism in his work *A Discourse on the Grounds and Reasons of the Christian Religion* and in a sequel entitled *The Scheme of Literal Prophecy Consider'd* (1727). Both works were refutations of the Christian apologetic of fulfilled prophecy. They denied that Christ fulfilled any Old Testament predictions and said fulfillments came in the time of the prophets themselves (for example, Matt. 1:22–23 with Isa. 7:14; Matt. 2:15 with Hos. 11:1; Matt. 11:14 with Mal. 4:5; Matt. 13:34–35 with Isa. 6:9). Collins rejected literal hermeneutics in the fulfillment of prophecy, calling New Testament claims of fulfillment a kind of allegorical interpretation based on rabbinical methods.[97]

Deism reached its zenith with Oxford scholar Matthew Tindal (1655–1733), perhaps the most historically significant of the English deists.[98] In 1730, he wrote *Christianity as Old as the Creation: Or, the Gospel, a Republication of the Religion of Nature*, a work eventually regarded as a kind of deistic Bible.[99] Tindal asserted that one cannot rely on the Gospels to teach anything beyond the bounds of reason and nature. Orthodox Christianity and rational religion are not the same, for certain doctrines such as the Fall, original sin, and the Atonement are unacceptable. For Tindal, true religion consisted of moderation and living according to one's nature.

In such movements as deism, the seventeenth-century doctrine of the necessity of reason was slowly giving way to a belief in the complete sufficiency of reason in the discovery of truth.[100] Although deism was not completely unified, it generally affirmed the absolute unity of God's nature and person. Deism also rejected the Christian concept of the Trinity as being meaningless (or at best polytheistic). Deism furthermore conceived God as being beyond the universe but not in it and as not being supernaturally active in the finite world He created. Rather, everything operated by natural law flowing from God's nature. In fact, natural law was humankind's sole revelation of God.

Deists rejected any Christian claims to supernatural revelation, for God does not reveal Himself in any other way but through His creation. They rejected the possibility of miracles, for miracles would violate natural law. Belief in miracles, therefore, represents superstition and an ignorance of natural law. God has given people through reason and science the rational ability to discover in nature all that they need to know to live a full and happy life. Happiness is said to be the innate principle in people and is achievable through reason. Even human morality finds its foundation in nature. Individual works (good and bad) determine reward and punishment in a person's afterlife.[101]

The profound influence of deism "was all out of proportion" to the number of scholars supporting it.[102] Peter Gay writes the following regarding the profound impact of the deists:

> While their intellectual limitations are evident and their defeats at the hands of Bishop Butler and David Hume were devastating, their historical significance was considerable: they redrew the religious map of Europe. . . . The deists came at the right historic moment with the right arguments.[103]

Along with Spinoza, "the English deists may be regarded as the forerunners of biblical criticism and the initiators of the quest for the historical Jesus."[104] Though English deists disappeared by 1750, their position that reason precludes the supernatural took root everywhere, particularly regarding their rejection of the historicity of miracles and the fulfillment of prophecy. This presupposition eventually led to a search for the real Jesus of history, since the historical Jesus could not have been the supernatural person performing the miracles depicted in the New Testament.[105]

Gotthold Ephraim Lessing, a Spinozist (see discussion of rationalism above), published a German work whose title in English meant "Fragments by an Unknown Person" (1774–1778).[106] It was written anonymously by rationalist and deist Hermann Samuel Reimarus (1694–1768), a personal friend of Lessing. In this work, Reimarus's purpose was to discredit the origins of Christianity.[107] He saw Jesus as an unsuccessful messianic pretender and the disciples as disappointed charlatans who stole Jesus' body. They allegedly invented the resurrection story to start a new religious movement in order to avoid working for a living.

David Friedrich Strauss (1808–1874)[108] held views close to those of Reimarus. In fact, Strauss characterized Reimarus as one of the "most courageous and worthy representatives" of biblical criticism in the eighteenth century.[109] In 1835–36, Strauss wrote "The Life of Jesus Critically Examined" (English title of German work). In it he identified mythical elements in the gospel accounts and denied the historicity of all supernatural parts. He saw a closed-continuum of cause and effect that allowed no divine intervention. To Strauss, whenever the biblical data presents the supernatural—or abnormal, as he called it—the mythopoeic faculty has been at work. Allowing only a minimal historical framework for the life of Jesus, Strauss considered the vast majority of the Gospels to be myth.[110] If his interpretation had won the day, Christianity as known through the centuries would have ended.[111]

Albert Schweitzer (1875–1965) viewed Reimarus as the deist who inaugurated the search for the historical Jesus,[112] but Reimarus was far from the originator. He built his views on a foundation of the Enlightenment, deism, and rationalism that pervaded the intellectual climate of his time. Welch corrects Schweitzer's wrong evaluation: "Reimarus was much influenced by radical English deism, in which the opposition of natural religion and Christianity had long been proclaimed by men like Anthony Collins."[113] Reimarus was a deist (and a rationalist) whose attempts to discredit Christianity arose in great part through his presupposition of deism.[114]

Ernst Troeltsch's essay entitled "On Historical and Dogmatic Method in Theology" (1898) delineated the principles of Historical Criticism. He believed that the unifying thought of the Enlightenment was the rejection of the supernatural and that deism was its religious philosophy.[115] His three principles of Historical Criticism evidence the antisupernatural bias of both deism and the Enlightenment: (1) The principle of criticism or methodological doubt: in the realm of history, probability, not certainty, is the basis of judgment, necessitating a rigorous scrutiny of religious tradition (namely, miraculous events); (2) the principle of analogy: present experience is the criterion for determining probability; an absence of the supernatural today means that such events did not occur in the past; (3) the principle of correlation or mutual interdependence: a closed continuum of cause and effect exists, thus excluding the possibility of miracles.[116] Troeltsch contended, "It was not until the Enlightenment that an essentially historical [namely, historical-critical] outlook emerged."[117] Krentz concurs: "Historical method is the child of the Enlightenment."[118]

In his adoption of the principle of a closed continuum, Rudolf Bultmann illustrates Troeltsch's influence on Form Criticism:

> The historical method includes the presupposition that history is a unity in the sense of a closed continuum of effect in which individual events are connected by the succession of cause and effect. . . . This closedness means that the continuum of historical happenings is not rent by the interference of supernatural, transcendent powers and that therefore there is no "miracle" in the sense of the word. Such a miracle would be an event whose cause did not lie within history. . . . It is in accordance with such a method as this that the science of history goes to work on all historical documents. And there cannot be any exceptions in the case of biblical texts if the latter are at all to be understood historically.[119]

Deism and rationalism had a formative influence on Redaction Criticism too. Schweitzer identified Reimarus as showing the necessity of "a creative element in the tradition" to which must be ascribed "the miracles, the stories which turn on the fulfillment of messianic prophecy, the universalistic traits and the predictions of the passion and resurrection."[120] Taking up this thought, Norman Perrin concludes, "So far as redaction criticism is concerned, it is this 'creative element in the tradition,' as Albert Schweitzer calls it, which concerns us, and in calling attention to it Reimarus is the father of our discipline [namely, Redaction Criticism], as he is of the Life of Jesus research altogether."[121]

Remairus rejected the historicity of the Gospels. He also saw a creative element in the gospel tradition. The disciples allegedly fabricated their claims (for example, about miracles, the fulfillment of messianic prophecy, and Jesus' passion and resurrection) to win as many converts as possible to their new religion.[122] Perrin correctly identifies the deist Reimarus as a leading figure in the development of historical-critical methodologies and as a primary impetus to the modern search for the historical Jesus.

Wilhelm Wrede's *Messianic Secret* (German original, 1901) rejected the historicity of Mark and asserted that Mark's gospel represents creative, dogmatic ideas that the evangelist and the post-resurrection church imposed on the tradition. In other words, during Jesus' lifetime, He never claimed to be the Messiah.[123] Perrin remarks, "Wilhelm Wrede (1859–1906) . . . sounded the death knell" for the historicity of Mark "by demonstrating that a major aspect of the Marcan narratives was precisely the 'mythic' and, in so doing, opened the door for the entry of redaction criticism upon the scene."[124]

The presuppositions of deism are ample evidence that Historical Criticism *a priori* denigrates the Scriptures, especially—though not exclusively—in the area of the supernatural. The question is not whether Historical Criticism challenges the Bible's historical accuracy, but when and in what manner or degree it does so.

5. SKEPTICISM: HUME

Skepticism was a predominant element in the Enlightenment. White describes this period as follows:

> The Enlightenment attitude of mind was complex and internally varied, but it can be characterized roughly as a dedication of human reason, science, and education as the best means of building a stable society for free men on earth. This meant that the Enlightenment was inherently suspicious of religion, hostile to tradition, and resentful of any authority based on custom or faith alone.[125]

Gay describes the main characters of the Enlightenment: "Theirs was a paganism directed against their Christian inheritance and dependent upon the paganism of classical antiquity, but it was also a *modern* paganism, emancipated from classical thought as much as from Christian dogma."[126]

Several strains of thinking dominated Enlightenment philosophy to produce negativity toward religion in general and Christianity in particular.

The discussion above has already dealt with two of them: the rationalism of Descartes, Spinoza, and Leibniz and the deism of Herbert of Cherbury, Matthew Tindal, and John Toland. A third significant element was that of British empiricism.[127] This last philosophy came from Francis Bacon, who in many respects pioneered this approach. Within the empirical tradition were John Locke (1632–1704), George Berkeley (c. 1685–1753), and David Hume (1711–1776).

These three philosophical traditions—rationalism, deism, and empiricism—relate closely to one another. And besides dominating the Enlightenment as a whole, they provide the background for Hume's skepticism.[128] Moreover, Historical Criticism emerged from this philosophical milieu.[129]

Between Spinoza and Kant, the philosopher who probably had the most lasting harmful effect on biblical authority was the skeptic David Hume.[130] Gay calls Hume "the complete modern pagan."[131] The three major Enlightenment philosophies—rationalism, deism, and empiricism—provided the foundation for Hume's skepticism, though in many ways he went beyond these systems.[132] Although Hume lies within the tradition of British empiricism, his thinking was more radical and often critical of all three major movements of the Enlightenment.[133] Because of his philosophical reasoning, one has aptly called him "a vigorous and often scornful critic of evangelical doctrine."[134]

Hume believed that all ideas of the mind are traceable to one or more perceptions deriving from the five senses. Nothing exists in the mind that the senses did not perceive first. In his *Treatise of Human Nature* (1739),[135] Hume wrote, "The idea of substance as well as that of a mode, is nothing but a collection of simple ideas, that are united by the imagination, and have a particular name assigned them, by which we are able to recall, either to ourselves or others, that collection."[136] We perceive the data of our senses, but cannot know that there is anything beyond. In Hume's thought, one could not even prove the existence of the human self. Hume related the following:

> For my part, when I enter most intimately into what I call *myself,* I always stumble on some particular perception or, of heat or cold, light or shade, love or hatred, pain or pleasure. I never can catch *myself* at any time without a perception, and never can observe anything but the perception.[137]

Thus, Hume's theory was that knowledge has definite limits so that people can know nothing for sure, not even their own existence or that of the external world.

Hume's skepticism went further, questioning the principle of cause and effect. We observe successive events, but no one can discover the exact link between them.[138] People can only accept cause and effect by instinct or faith. All that someone perceives as cause and effect is a matter of sequence; it is not something that happens between objects; it is really a product of the imagination.[139] Nothing is certain or known for sure: "I much

doubt whether it is possible for a cause to be known only by its effect . . .
or to be of so singular and particular a nature as to have no parallel and
no similarity with any other cause or object, that has ever fallen under our
observation."[140] Yet Hume did not deny the whole idea of cause and effect,
only that it was impossible to know such to be true in the sense of proof.[141]

Hume's approach to Scripture and miracles was no less radical. He saw
only two kinds of meaningful statements: definitional and factual.[142] Hume
came to the following conclusion:

> When we run over libraries, persuaded of these principles, what
> havoc must we make? If we take in our hand any volume; of di-
> vinity or school metaphysics, for instance; let us ask, *Does it con-
> tain any abstract reasoning concerning quantity or number?* No.
> *Does it contain any experimental reasoning concerning matter
> of fact and existence?* No. Commit it then to the flames: for it
> can contain nothing but sophistry and illusion.[143]

Carried to its logical conclusion, this statement takes all metaphysical
and theological statements to be neither true nor false, for they are not
subject to any empirical verification through the senses. Thus they have
no meaning. They are not statements of reality but expressions of "soph-
istry and illusion." Only assertions that involve abstract reasoning and correspond to empirical data are knowable (for example, mathematics and
logic). Geisler's comment captures the problem with Hume's logic:

> The result of Hume's empiricism is semantical atheism. The im-
> plications for propositional revelation are severe. No proposition
> in the Bible could be cognitively true. Likewise, no biblical decla-
> ration about God could really be informative. At best, biblical lan-
> guage is in this view, evocative of religious commitment; at worse,
> it is purely emotive expressions of the religious feelings of the hu-
> man writers.[144]

Hume also argued against miracles. He defined a miracle as *"a
transgression of a law of nature by a particular volition of the Deity, or
by the interposition of some invisible agent."*[145] Hume added further, "A
miracle is a violation of the laws of nature; and as a firm and unalterable
experience has established these laws, the proof against a miracle, from
the very nature of the fact, is as entire as any argument from experience
can possibly be imagined."[146] However, Hume did not claim to demonstrate
the impossibility of miracles, for his system did not preclude the intuitive
acceptance of them "brought home to everyone's breast, by the immediate
operation of the Holy Spirit."[147] His argument was essentially defensive.
He argued that one could never know for certain that a miracle had ever
occurred. Flew notes, "Most especially he is asking—and urging that we
must answer in the negative—a more particular question: 'whether a miracle
can [ever] be proved, so as to be the foundation of a system of religion.'"[148]

Hume could not prove conclusively that a miracle could not happen, but he reasoned also that no one could prove that a miracle had actually happened. Thus, Christian apologetics could not use miracles to support its claims, since for Hume Christianity was founded on faith, not reason.[149] Hume's influence in Historical Criticism is pervasive. Peirce remarks, "The whole of modern 'higher criticism' of ancient history in general, and of Biblical history in particular, is based upon the same logic that is used by Hume."[150] Randall states the following:

> Since Hume's critique of miracles in the eighteenth century, religious liberals have refused to believe in any such interferences with the order of natural law. The records they explain as the product of the natural causes of human credulity, imagination, and legend. . . . In the eighteenth century, miracles were the chief support of the faith; in the next, they became the chief problem to be explained.[151]

Hume's work affected many who practiced historical-critical methods. Habermas makes the following observation:

> In rejecting miracles, nineteenth-century liberal theologians not only followed Hume's insistence that the laws of nature cannot be violated, but they also accepted Hume's suggestion that naturalistic alternatives to miraculous events are more probable than the actual miracles.[152]

Among the many nineteenth-century thinkers who followed Hume's lead in rejecting miracles were Strauss (1808–1874), Schleiermacher (see the section on "rationalism" above), Ernst Renan (1823–1892), and Adolf Harnack (1851–1930).[153]

Yet the nineteenth century did not have a monopoly on the rejection of miracles. Hume's thinking also pervades twentieth-century theology.[154] Among affected theologians of this century have been Rudolf Bultmann (1884–1976) and Paul Tillich (1886–1965).[155]

Brown summarizes Hume's impact on Historical Criticism:

> Hume's approach anticipated the doctrine of analogy developed by Ernst Troeltsch in the nineteenth century. . . . Troeltsch argued that in order to recognize anything we need to compare it with our experience of life and our understanding of the way in which things work.[156]

That is, if one cannot observe miracles in present experience, miracles could not occur in past experience.

A pattern emerges from the above. Hume's philosophical thinking pervaded not only the philosophical world of his day, but has generated devastating consequences down to the present in terms of Historical

Criticism. His thinking has so permeated the historical-critical method as to remove the very foundations of the Christian faith.

6. AGNOSTICISM: KANT

Immanuel Kant (1724–1804) stands as the pivotal thinker and creative genius of modern philosophy.[157] His influence in theology as well as philosophy has been profound. Although Kant began as a rationalist influenced by Hume's writings, his lasting philosophical achievement was the persuasive synthesizing of empiricism and rationalism.[158] That resulted in an agnosticism about reality.

In 1781, Kant wrote *Critique of Pure Reason* (2d ed., 1787). It is difficult to formulate a brief overview of this book's concepts, but a summarization is feasible. The work examined the scope and limitations of human thought through a prior investigation of human reason, in which Kant sought to determine how knowledge is possible.

Accepting the view of the empiricists "that all our knowledge begins with experience there can be no doubt," Kant differed from them when he reasoned, "It by no means follows, that all arises out of experience."[159] He accepted the empiricists' view that the senses are passive receptors of sensations as the only means through which the mind can process data.[160] The raw material for knowledge comes from outside us, yet the mind has a part in processing that material through its own built-in concepts. Since the senses perceive this raw material, the mind processes it. In this perception, the mind employs the Forms of Intuition (for example, space and time) and Categories or the Pure Concepts of the Understanding (for example, quantity and quality).[161]

These categories of understanding enable the mind to classify and interpret the objects of experience, thereby making understanding possible. However, the mind does not perceive these things as they actually are in themselves, for the mind reshapes what it perceives: "For this reason, in respect to the form of appearances, much may be said *a priori*, whilst of the thing itself, which may lie at the foundation of these appearances, it is impossible to say anything."[162] In other words, the mind conditions (perhaps better, "colors") everything that it encounters.[163] Kant intended to counteract Hume's skepticism, but Kant's logic resulted in further skepticism.[164] One can know only what appears *(phenomenal)*, not what really is *(noumenal)*.[165] The thing-in-itself is unknowable.[166] The very nature of the knowing processes places an inseparable barrier between the phenomenal and noumenal realms.

The implications of Kant's thought for Christianity were profound. Though he was skeptical about knowing material things as they actually are, he was even more skeptical about knowing nonmaterial religious or metaphysical realities. For Kant, the forms of intuition were "valid only for objects of possible experience."[167] The mind cannot know rationally anything beyond its immediate experience of the world. When the human mind goes beyond the material order, *Antinomies* (namely, irreconcilable self-contradictions) arise.[168]

In light of this, Kant's agnosticism regarding religion, especially Christianity, is acute. The existence and nature of God, the condition and destiny of humanity, the status and source of values, and so on, are all unknowable. Reducing the arguments for the existence of God to three (ontological, cosmological, and teleological [or, Kant's term, physico-theological]), he rejected them all, arguing that they do not afford rationally compelling proof.[169] Yet, his system contended that the objective reality of God "can neither be proved or disproved by pure reason."[170] For Kant, even if it was impossible for reason to prove the existence of God, one must live as though God exists. Kant believed God existed, but no rational proofs existed to demonstrate that existence, only a moral assumption to that effect. That is, one must presume about both God and morality.[171] Kant's scheme was paradoxical in advocating that morality is autonomous and needs no idea of God and, at the same time, points to religion and God.[172]

Agreeing with deists, Kant saw "the Christian Religion as a Natural Religion."[173] Reason must replace the traditional Christian view of revelation (namely, God revealing Himself in history and through propositional revelation): "universal human reason" is "the supremely commanding principle."[174] Christian concepts of God's grace for a helpless humanity become "an unbending religion of self-help."[175] Consistently avoiding use of the name "Jesus," Kant held Jesus to be just another naturally begotten man. Kant viewed Him as "the ideal of a humanity pleasing to God."[176] Indeed, Kant argued that he was divesting theological ideas of their "mystical veil" and replacing them with "rational meaning."[177]

Kant's discussion of miracles followed a similar tactic:

> If a moral religion (which must consist not in dogmas and rites but in the heart's disposition to fulfil all human duties as divine commands) is to be established, all miracles which history connects with its inauguration must themselves in the end render superfluous the belief in *miracles* in general; for it bespeaks a culpable degree of moral unbelief not to acknowledge as completely authoritative the commands of duty—commands primordially engraved upon the heart of man through reason—unless they are in addition accredited through miracles.[178]

Kant's identification of Christianity's true nature as a religion of reason made miracles unnecessary and irrelevant to natural religion in general, so he did not try to disprove them. He merely attributed them to unknown causes.[179] True to his agnosticism, he asserted, "We cannot know anything about supernatural aid."[180]

In spite of Kant's agnosticism, however, he viewed the physical world as a closed system of cause and effect. No one can determine what might lie within it and beyond, for the mind thinks only in terms of causation and other categories through which it perceives reality. So in essence, Kant declared that reason required that miracles never happen.[181]

The impact of Kant's thinking on Historical Criticism is significant. Before Strauss and Bultmann, Kant reinterpreted biblical ideas in a rationalistic mode. Brown summarizes Kant's purpose to divest theological ideas of their "mystical veil": "It was a secularization and rationalization of biblical ideas. In the twentieth century the process might have been called one of demythologization."[182]

Though some have described Kant as the philosopher of Protestantism, his agnosticism was essentially a form of deism.[183] The strong consensus of recent observers is that his system in one way or another has affected all later philosophical thought and a large portion of theology.[184]

From Kant, the line of influence has progressed to Schleiermacher to nineteenth century liberalism to contemporary neoliberalism. Geisler states, "In making the moral imperative the criterion for true religion, Kant is the forerunner of . . . Schleiermacher."[185] Wilhelm Martin Leberechte de Wette (1780–1849) adopted Kantian philosophy in his work *Biblische Dogmatik des Alten und Neuen Testaments* (English, "Biblical Dogmatics of the Old and New Testaments") (1813). This book shattered the material unity of the Old and New Testaments and resulted in a subsequent history-of-religions approach to biblical theology.[186] Kantian thought also influenced Hegel who, in turn, influenced Bruno Bauer, Ludwig Feuerbach, D. F. Strauss, and F. C. Baur.[187] Albrecht Ritschl (1822–1889) developed a theology with strong Kantian distinctions between scientific and religious knowledge.[188] More recently, Rudolf Otto (1869–1937) reflected Kant's thinking in his formulation of higher critical methodology.[189]

Kant's influence on Bultmann was significant. Morgan writes, "His theology was shaped above all by the pious neo-Kantianism of his teacher Wilhelm Herrmann (1846–1922), a devout follower of Ritschl."[190] The post-Bultmannian Schubert Ogden expressed some of his theology in Kantian form.[191]

Yet, Brown's remark is insightful regarding Kant's philosophical successors:

> Even though they may have taken Kant as their starting point, in one way or another they found illumination in Spinoza. But in the end, what they accepted from him was not his philosophical system but his anti-supernaturalistic attitude toward philosophy and religion.[192]

The death of Kant marked the end of the Age of Enlightenment.[193]

7. ROMANTICISM: SCHLEIERMACHER

Romanticism began in Europe in about the last decade of the eighteenth century. It reacted against the dominance of philosophical systems emphasizing reason and order—the systems of classicism and the Enlightenment.[194] By the eighteenth century the term "romanticism" referred to what was sentimental, full of expression, and melancholy.[195] Technically, Romanticism was not so much a philosophy as a mood affecting literature, music, painting, philosophy, and theology. Its impact on theology was as an artistic-literary movement whose underlying philosophy affected religious thinking.[196]

In opposition to the cold, unemotional, intellectual questioning that the Enlightenment engendered, Romanticism stressed the need for feelings, emotionalism, sensualism, fantasy, mystery, imagination, and heroic men and movements of the past over against order and control. It protested against the formalism and structure evident in neoclassicism, rationalism, and moral asceticism. In contrast with rationalism, which stressed the universal, Romanticism emphasized the individual. It sought a new freedom and spontaneity, instead of the mechanical perfection of an ordered universe that reason had conceptualized.[197]

An early advocate of Romanticism was the Frenchman Jean Jacques Rousseau (1712–1778). However, the movement was most predominant in Germany where Johann Wolfgang Goethe (1749–1832), Friedrich Schiller (1759–1805), and Friedrich Hölderlin (1770–1843) were its proponents.[198] However, the person most identified with the theology of the period was the philosopher-theologian, Friedrich Ernst Daniel Schleiermacher (1768–1834).[199]

Schleiermacher profoundly affected nineteenth-century theology. Sometimes hailed as the father of Protestant liberalism and the most influential theologian of the nineteenth century,[200] he received education in Moravian schools where mystical pietism impressed him. In 1787, he entered the University of Halle and studied the writings of Kant and Spinoza. Karl Barth described Schleiermacher with the same words that Schleiermacher applied to Frederick the Great: "He did not found a school, but an era."[201]

Schleiermacher developed what is known as *positive theology*.[202] As he relied heavily on personal experience, the influences of Romanticism and of the philosophies of Spinoza, Leibniz, and Kant were great. Schleiermacher was conscious of these influences and praised especially the rationalist and pantheist Spinoza.[203] Schleiermacher sought to combine the pietistic stress on religious experience with the new liberal attitude toward Christianity advocated by the intellectuals of his day.[204] He joined with the romantic writers and poets in rebelling against the rationalistic views of the Enlightenment, emphasizing instead imagination, feeling, and mystery.

In line with the rationalists, Schleiermacher no longer accepted the Bible as an actual history of divine interventions and collections of divine utterances.[205] Instead, he stressed the Bible as a record of religious experience. Brown recounts, "It meant that he no longer needed to take the Bible seriously in every detail. . . . What Schleiermacher endeavored to do was to analyze religious experience and extract from it the essence of religion."[206] His goal was to reinterpret the Christian faith in terms that would find acceptance to modern people both inside and outside the church.

In Schleiermacher's view, the essence of religion was neither activity nor knowledge, but something common to both: "The piety which forms the basis of all ecclesiastical communions is . . . neither a Knowing, nor a Doing, but a modification of Feeling, or of immediate self-consciousness."[207]

Thus, one should base religion on an intuition and awareness, independent of all dogma.[208] At one point, Schleiermacher defined religion almost exclusively in aesthetic and metaphysical terms: "True religion is sense and taste for the Infinite."[209] He described its essence or "common element" as "the consciousness of being absolutely dependent, or . . . of being in relation with God."[210] Some have said he emphasized subjective religious "feelings," but it is better to see his emphasis as being on an "awareness" or "consciousness" of absolute dependence.[211]

From this concept, Schleiermacher proceeded to measure all religious experience, including Christian teaching. He reinterpreted the whole range of Christian doctrine. Accordingly, inspiration for Schleiermacher was exclusively a human activity, for the medium of revelation originated from this sense of absolute dependence.[212] Because he rejected traditional proofs for the existence of God, this sense of absolute dependence also constituted for him the proof for the existence of God.[213] God's attributes *are to be taken as denoting not something special in God, but only something special in the manner in which the feeling of absolute dependence is related to him.*[214]

Schleiermacher defined sin as an interference with this sense of absolute dependence, not as a transgression of divine commandments. He referred to it as anything "that has arrested the free development of the God-consciousness."[215] He also rejected orthodox concepts of original sin through Adam[216] and identified redemption with a restoration of this absolute sense of dependence. Christ's unique part in redemption is His restoration of this sense of dependence.[217] The early Christian creeds of orthodoxy—namely, that deity took on humanity in the incarnation—were wrong about Jesus' uniqueness. That uniqueness consisted in fact that Jesus had an exemplary sense of God consciousness, which serves as an example to all others.[218] The redemptive work of Christ enables believers to come *"into the power of His God-consciousness."*[219]

Schleiermacher agreed with Hume that it is people ignorant of natural law who most often report miracles. One must reject supernatural occurrences, for they destroy the concept of nature and no known examples of them exist.[220] He also seems to explain Jesus' resurrection as a resuscitation after apparent death.[221]

Schleiermacher has had a profound effect on theology in helping lay a foundation for neo-orthodoxy by retaining orthodox vocabulary, but imbuing it with radically different meaning.[222] Brown aptly comments, "Schleiermacher retains some of the vocabulary of the older Christian theology and even something of its contents. But the meaning he gives it is considerably stretched or all but completely changed."[223]

Schleiermacher's highly subjective and abstract thought also anticipated existentialism. Robinson[224] and Tillich[225] have recast much of Schleiermacher's thought, using his motivation to make God relevant for their generation and describing God as the object of "ultimate concern" or as the "depth" or "ground of being."

Schleiermacher's revision of Christian theology "had its most radical impact on the issue of authority, because he argued that no external authority, whether it be Scripture, church, or historic creedal statement, takes precedence over the immediate experience of believers."[226] He rejected doctrine not commensurate with his subjective interpretation of religious experience (for example, the Trinity, the virgin birth, and the return of Christ). Influenced by Kant's insistence that nothing is knowable beyond the scope of direct human experience, Schleiermacher formulated his whole theology on the basis of subjective feeling-states.[227] After he rejected orthodox Christian beliefs and understanding, the only kernel he had left was ambiguous concepts of religious experience. For Schleiermacher, the Bible could not be true, propositional revelation.

In relation to Historical Criticism, Schleiermacher's hermeneutics influenced such twentieth-century theologians as Rudolf Bultmann. Duke offers this analysis: "Schleiermacher's *Hermeneutics* has been characterized as a watershed in the history of the field. Although he drew freely from his Enlightenment predecessors . . . Schleiermacher attempted a full-scale reconception of hermeneutical theory."[228] He marked a shift from language-oriented hermeneutics to one that emphasized the subjective understanding and intentions of the author.[229] For Schleiermacher, hermeneutics was more an art than a science. He perceived it as communication between persons, analogous to conversation. He asserted that the message of Scripture must be historical, yet he also held that since history has to do with persons, psychological and subjective meaning must be the concern of hermeneutics.[230] Therefore, the New Testament requires a special hermeneutic that is sensitive to the perceived message of the Bible. Interpretation must also deal with the life of the author and the forces that moved the author to communicate.[231] Dockery has said, "Schleiermacher contended for a pre-understanding that must take place before interpretation can happen."[232]

With these psychological and subjective factors evident from Schleiermacher's hermeneutical system, he delineated the "inner kernel" of the Christian faith.[233] His hermeneutical concern was "what does their [namely, the biblical writers'] message mean to readers and hearers in the different context of today?"[234] In other words, Schleiermacher approached hermeneutics rationalistically and thereby negated much historicity in the New Testament text—particularly the supernatural elements—by interpreting it subjectively.[235] Schleiermacher read back into the text perceived psychological elements, thus contributing to the confusion between interpretation and application in the exegesis.[236] Along with his title "Father of Theological Liberalism," he also earned the title "'founder' of modern hermeneutics."[237]

Schleiermacher's rationalism caused him to differentiate between the Jesus of history in the synoptics and the Christ of faith in the fourth gospel.[238] In Schleiermacher's *Life of Jesus* (1864) and *Einleitung ins Neue Testament* (1845; English: "Introduction to the New Testament"), he also set forth portions of his synoptic theory.[239] He rejected the proposal that Papias's *logia* is the gospel of Matthew,[240] claiming instead that it was a collection of sayings. Schleiermacher favored an oral tradition that crystallized in a number of disconnected written fragments. He rejected the independence of the three Synoptic Gospels, stating that "strictly speaking we have to say *that so far as our four canonical Gospels are concerned, we have actually only two different sources.* The Gospel of John is one, and the other three taken together are the other."[241] He also rejected traditional views of authorship of the Synoptics Gospels, viewing them instead as late collections of assorted material whose historicity varied from section to section: "when we are thinking in terms of a historical view—our sources cause us much embarrassment."[242] Yet he did allow that an eyewitness wrote the gospel of John.[243]

Anticipating Form Criticism, Schleiermacher assumed an early period during which no written traditions existed and contended that the gospel material had earlier circulated in the form of brief memorabilia on which the gospel writers later worked. He contended, "The first three Gospels are compilations of many accounts that earlier stood by themselves."[244]

Schleiermacher had enormous influence on later Protestant theologians such as Albrecht Ritschl[245] and Bultmann.[246] Duke records, "Via Wilhelm Dilthey [1833–1911], especially, his [Schleiermacher's] influence has extended far into the twentieth century, to Rudolf Bultmann and beyond."[247] Dilthey continued Schleiermacher's assertion that a subjective imposition of the interpreter's experience is the only way to obtain the biblical author's meaning.[248] Furthermore, through Dilthey Schleiermacher's psychological and historical conception of religion "gave considerable impetus to the comparative study of religions and to the scientific analysis and classification of religious phenomena . . . in the work of the twentieth century historians of religion Ernst Troeltsch [1855–1923] and Rudolf Otto [1869–1937]."[249] Other theologians affected by Schleiermacher's emphasis on religious experience were Adolf von Harnack (1851–1931), John Oman (1860–1939), H. H. Farmer (1892–1981), and John Baille (1886–1960).[250]

In summary, for Schleiermacher the Bible may not be propositional authoritative revelation or historically accurate, but it still conveyed religious "experience" relevant for people. He did not speak about the Jesus of history but about the Christ of faith and about the search for the "historical Jesus." In terms of historical-critical interpretation, "what it means to me in my present situation" (namely, eisegesis and application) was more important for Schleiermacher than the original meaning of Scripture (exegesis and interpretation).

8. ABSOLUTE IDEALISM: HEGEL

Broadly speaking, "idealism" is the view that the mind and spiritual values are more fundamental than material ones.[251] It is the opposite of realism—the view that things exist independently of being perceived—and of naturalism that explains the mind and spiritual values via materialism. Idealism came to be a technical philosophical term in the eighteenth century and was applied to the philosophy of Berkeley. Berkeley himself, however, preferred the term "immaterialism" for his system because he advocated the nonexistence of material substance.[252]

Other philosophical systems, such as those of Plato and Descartes, eventually acquired the label of idealism.[253] Kant adopted the term, calling his philosophy "Transcendental Idealism" in order to distinguish it from Descartes and Berkeley.[254] From Kant's background, the German idealist movement emerged, as Brown describes: "It was partly in reaction to Kant and partly owing to inspiration from him that the next generation of German philosophers developed what came to be known as Absolute Idealism."[255] Their view that reality was ultimately spiritual or mental in character explains the addition of "absolute" to "idealism."

Three figures were significant in German Idealism: Johann Gottlieb Fichte (1762–1814), Friedrich Wilhelm Joseph von Schelling (1775–1854), and Georg Wilhelm Friedrich Hegel (1770–1831),[256] among whom Hegel was the most influential.[257] One source has called Hegel "possibly the most stupendous of all nineteenth century thinkers."[258]

Hegel's absolute idealism was an all-encompassing system, for he "more than most other philosophers in history, is known for building a system in which each constituent part is intricately related to the whole."[259] He carried idealism to its absolute limits.[260]

Kant's philosophy strongly influenced Hegel, as did the works of Plato and Aristotle.[261] Kroner writes that Hegel

> became a Kantian the moment he understood the revelation brought about by Kant's Critical Philosophy; and he remained a Kantian throughout his life, no matter how much he disputed many of Kant's doctrines and even his fundamental position. Hegel would never have found his dialectical method without the "Transcendental Dialectic" in Kant's *Critique of Pure Reason.*[262]

The deist Lessing was also one of Hegel's heroes.[263]

Hegel's basic conceptual idea in his writings was that of the German word *Geist*.[264] One may translate the word *Geist* as "Mind"—emphasizing the rational aspect—or "Spirit"—emphasizing the immaterial and religious aspect of reality. Hegel wrote the following:

> Spirit is alone Reality. It is the inner being of the world, that which essentially is, and is *per se;* it assumes objective, determinative form, and enters into relations with itself—it is externality (otherness), and exists for itself; yet, in this determination, and in its otherness, it is still one with itself—it is self-contained and self-complete, in itself and for itself at once.[265]

Thus, Hegel's philosophy simply put is that all reality is the outworking of the Spirit.[266] The sum total of human knowledge is the Absolute Spirit thinking its thoughts through human minds. In other words, history, nature, and thought are aspects of the Absolute Spirit coming to self-consciousness.

In his work *Leben Jesu* (English, "The Life of Jesus"), Hegel eliminated the supernatural and miraculous elements of the Gospels. Kantian thinking saturated the work. Even the vocabulary used to interpret the Sermon on the Mount was directly from Kant.[267] For Hegel, the goal of all religion was obtaining Virtue.[268] Spinoza was also prominent in Hegel's writings, since he viewed Spinozism as an important development toward his formulation of absolute idealism.[269]

Hegel's system in terms of the Spirit's outworking is sometimes known as Dialectic, namely, the process of thesis, antithesis, and synthesis. However, this is inaccurate.[270] Although Hegel occasionally uses these terms, they more aptly characterize the philosophical system of Fichte.[271] However, as Brown concludes, "The basic idea is there, and the notion of Dialectic is paramount."[272] For Hegel, the Dialectic of Spirit permeated everything. He even detected it in the broad sweeps of history.[273]

One group influenced by Hegel interpreted his philosophy as destroying the need for religion. Such theologians as Bruno Bauer (1809–1882), Ludwig Feuerbach (1804–1872), D. F. Strauss (1808–1874), and F. C. Baur (1792–1860) represent this movement that heavily influenced succeeding generations of thought.

Bruno Bauer went from Hegelianism to radical skepticism. One of his pupils was Karl Marx. In Bauer's work on the gospel of John, *Kritik der evangelischen Geschichte des Johannes* (1840, English, "Criticism of the Gospel History of John"), he contended that John was not a work of history but of art written under the influence of Philo. In *Kritik der evangelischen Geschichte der Synoptiker* (2 vols., 1841–42, English, "Criticism of the Gospel History of the Synoptics"), he declared Mark to be a literary, not a historical, work. Building on the foundation of Weisse and Wilke, Bauer contended that Matthew and Luke were dependent on Mark in the composition of their gospels.

Bauer labeled the birth narratives in the Gospels as literary inventions, the product of Christian self-consciousness. In his *Kritik der Evangelien und Geschichte ihres Ursprungs* (3 vols., 1850–51, English, "Criticism of the Gospels and History of Their Origins"), he denied the historical existence of Jesus. And in *Kritik der Paulinischen Briefe* (3 vols., 1850–52, English, "Criticism of the Pauline Epistles"), reflecting an even more radicalized concept than F. C. Baur, Bauer attributed Pauline letters to a late second-century author. At the end of his life, he wrote *Christus und die Caesaren* (1877, English, "Christ and Caesar"). In this work Bauer alleged that Seneca and Philo, rather than Jesus and Paul, were the ideological progenitors of Christianity. This latter work, although having little theological influence, appealed to Marx and Engels and was authoritative for socialist, Marxist groups. Bauer anticipated both Form and Redaction Criticism in their assertion of a radical creativity on the part of the Christian community and the gospel writers.[274]

Feuerbach viewed the concept of God as a product of humankind's mind and hence denied the existence of God.[275] He saw the Bible as full of errors and discrepancies that make it unacceptable to human reason. Feuerbach said the resurrection of Christ never occurred.[276]

Discussions of rationalism, deism, skepticism, and agnosticism above have disclosed much about David Friedrich Strauss and his famous work, *The Life of Jesus Critically Examined*. Strauss applied Hegelian philosophy to the critical analysis of the Gospels. In his application Strauss constructed the concept of myth.[277] Strimple notes the following:

> Here is where Strauss's Hegelian roots are exposed. A myth, as Strauss presented the concept, may be defined as an idea clothed in a form of history. Hegel had stressed the need to distinguish between the Idea *(Begriff)* and the Form *(Vorstellung)*, which is the historical representation of the Idea at a particular stage in history. Since the Idea is the important thing, we may, at no loss, dispense with the particular Form in which the Idea is presented at a particular time in history.[278]

Thus, Strauss's starting point in analyzing the life of Jesus was philosophical. The basic premise of his work is that spiritual reality is of a different order than historical reality. Thereby he advanced a basic dichotomy between factual and spiritual revelation.[279] Nothing about the historical Jesus is certain, but even though the Bible is myth, it still may convey spiritual and philosophical truth.[280]

Bultmann also followed Strauss in his mythical interpretation. Harris notes, "Both Strauss and Bultmann . . . have the same view of myth, in that everything supernatural or other-worldy is regarded as unhistorical and therefore mythical."[281]

Another Hegelian was Ferdinand Christian Baur, founder and uncontested leader of the "Tübingen School" of German radical biblical criticism and a tutor of Strauss.[282] He represents a more moderate approach to Hegel's philosophy, as Corduan notes: "Baur's appropriation of Hegel is far more subtle than those of other Hegelians."[283] In 1831, Baur published a German essay (English title, "The Christ-party in the Corinthian Community") in which he asserted that apostolic Christianity was marked by deep cleavage between the Jerusalem church and the Pauline mission. On the one side was Jewish Christianity represented by Peter and maintaining a Judaizing form of Christianity, and on the other side was Paul who insisted on the abolition of Jewish legalism. After the publication of this essay, Baur came under increasing influence from Hegel in the formulation of this theology.

Vorlesungen über Neutestamentliche Theologie (English, "Lectures on New Testament Theology"), published posthumously in 1864, represented Baur's conclusions. In a somewhat dialectical manner, he viewed the history of Christianity as a struggle between the thesis of Jewish Christianity (Petrine materials, Matthew, and Revelation) and the antithesis of Gentile Christianity (Galatians, 1–2 Corinthians, Romans, and Luke). Baur posited that this tension resolved itself early in the second century into an incipient Catholicism (Mark, John, and Acts). Based on this theory, he dated all the books of the New Testament, placing the Gospels in the mid-second century, long after the deaths of eyewitnesses of Jesus' life and resurrection. Baur also asserted that only four genuine epistles of Paul exist: Galatians, 1–2 Corinthians, and Romans.[284] He considered the teaching of Jesus as a prehistory of the New Testament and not a part of the theology of the New Testament itself. This emphasis lay behind Bultmann's statement that *"the message of Jesus* is a presupposition for the theology of the New Testament rather than a part of that theology itself."[285]

From the widespread influence of Hegel on other influential thinkers, it is evident how he earned the title "the Father of Historical Criticism."[286] He forms an important link in the chain of philosophers and theologians that constitute the roots of Historical Criticism.

9. EVOLUTION: DARWIN

Examinations of Historical Criticism have often neglected the impact of evolutionary hypotheses on the discipline. Evolution is not just a "scientific" hypothesis. It is also an all-encompassing philosophy that pervades not only the scientific community but every aspect of life, including theology.[287] Morris has demonstrated correctly that as a "science" and philosophy "evolution permeates and dominates modern thought in every field."[288] To a large extent, the hypothesis of evolution resulted from a presuppositional exclusion of God and religion from science and stemmed from the philosophies prevalent immediately before and during the Enlightenment (for example, deism, agnosticism, uniformitarianism—"the present is the key to the past"—and atheism).[289]

Although popularized by Charles Darwin (1809–1882) in his *Origin of Species* (1859) and *The Descent of Man* (1871), evolutionary concepts originated long before his time.[290] Yet Darwin brought them to the forefront in a renewed way.[291] In the late nineteenth and early twentieth centuries, evolutionary ideas had a strong, quick, and saturating impact in Britain (Darwin's homeland) and in Germany, where many new theories regarding the origin and development of the New Testament were arising. However, the current status of evolution is subject to question. Even philosophical naturalism has raised doubts about evolution, not as a science but as a faith postulate.[292]

Evolution's weak interpretation of the Genesis account of creation[293] is not directly relevant in this discussion, but a few examples will show how evolutionary thinking affects historical-critical theory.

The Documentary (namely, Graf-Wellhausen) Hypothesis originated during the height of evolution's popularity in philosophical circles.[294] Rejecting Mosaic authorship of the Pentateuch, it posited a gradual development (long after Moses) of the Old Testament from simple documents (JEDP) into the complexity of the first five books.[295] The hypothesis developed with a backdrop of philosophical speculations by the rationalist and pantheist Spinoza (who suggested Ezra composed the Torah), the deists, Hegelianism, and the increasing popularity of evolutionary philosophy. Twentieth-century scholarship has tended to discount the Graf-Wellhausen hypothesis.[296]

Later in life, Wellhausen (1844–1918) applied his theory to the New Testament,[297] with the help of Hermann Gunkel and others.[298] Gunkel was the father of Form Criticism in the Old Testament and a strong proponent of the evolutionary-based history-of-religions school. This eventually led to the form-critical analysis of the New Testament popularized by Karl L. Schmidt (1891–1956)—*Der Rahmen der Geschichte Jesu* (1919; English, "The Framework of the Story of Jesus"), Martin Dibelius (1883–1947)—*Die Formgeschichte des Evangeliums* (1919, English, "From Tradition to Gospel"), and Rudolf Bultmann—*Die Geschichte der synoptischen Tradition* (1921; English, "The History of the Synoptic Tradition"). These three works proposed the Christian community's gradual development of the gospel stories from simple, brief, oral accounts to complex written documents.[299]

Bultmann sought to "demythologize" the Gospels, asserting, "The cosmology of the New Testament is essentially mythical in character" and "*Man's knowledge and mastery of the world* have advanced to such an extent through science and technology that it is no longer possible for anyone seriously to hold the New Testament view of the world—in fact, there is no one who does."[300] He contended, "Modern science has destroyed the old creation stories, even that of the Old Testament."[301] Furthermore, "To speak . . . of God as creator, no longer involves speaking of His creatorship in the sense of the old myth" [namely, the Genesis account of creation].[302] Bultmann felt compelled to demythologize such concepts.

Source criticism offers another example of the strong influence of evolution, especially in the Two- and Four-Source Theories of gospel origins that assume that Mark was the first gospel written. The Two-Source Theory was synthesized and popularized by Heinrich J. Holtzmann (1832–1910) in *Die Synoptischen Evangelien* (1863) in Germany, and the Four-Source by Burnett Hillman Streeter (1874–1937) in *The Four Gospels* (1924) in Britain. Here again the idea of simple to complex appears: the combining of Mark, the alleged "Q" source *(Quelle)*, material peculiar to Matthew (M), and material peculiar to Luke (L) into the complex documents of Matthew and Luke.[303] The Two- and Four-Source Hypotheses unfolded at the same time evolutionary philosophy was rocketing to prominence in Britain and on the continent of Europe.

Farmer identifies the evolutionary "intellectual climate" of the late nineteenth century as propelling the Four-Source Hypothesis to prominence.[304] Thomas Huxley (1825–1895), one of the greatest of evolutionary propagandists, championed the Markan-priority hypothesis when he wrote the following:

> Our canonical second Gospel (the so-called "Mark's" Gospel) is that which most closely represents the primitive groundwork of the three. That I take to be one of the most valuable results of New Testament criticism, of immeasurably greater importance than the discussion about dates and authorship.[305]

In *Oxford Studies,* Streeter wrote an essay entitled "The Literary Evolution of the Gospels."[306] *Oxford Studies'* editor, William Sanday (1843–1920), an outstanding propagandist for the British Four-Source Theory, praised Streeter's essay with the following:

> I do not remember to have seen, within anything like the same compass, a picture at once so complete, so sound, and (to my mind) so thoroughly scientific, of the whole course of development in the Apostolic and sub-Apostolic age in its bearing upon literary composition in general and the composition of the Gospels in particular. It is a real evolution, and an evolution conceived as growth, in which each stage springs naturally, spontaneously, and inevitably out of the last.[307]

Farmer remarks as follows:

> Darwin's epoch-making *Origin of Species* had been published during Sanday's student days at Oxford and there is no doubt that in the years following, like many of the best minds of his generation, he [Sanday] drank deeply from the cup of salvation offered by the cult of "scientism," that is, faith in science.[308]

In addition, Edwin Abbott (1838–1926) provided another important evidence for the acceptance of Mark as the first and most "primitive" gospel: antisupernaturalism. Abbott based his acceptance of the "antiquity" of Mark on its failure to mention some "supernatural events" found in Matthew and Luke—namely, the virgin birth, the visit of angels, and the star in Bethlehem—and its inclusion of "only the barest prediction of [Jesus'] resurrection."[309] Because Mark was relatively "simple," without any reference to the miraculous birth narratives and post-Resurrection appearances, the antisupernatural climate of the time naturally gravitated to the Marcan hypothesis.[310]

Another example of the influence of evolution upon historical-critical methodologies is that of the history-of-religions school. This was a group of influential German biblical scholars between 1880 and 1920 who advocated an evolutionary framework in explaining Christianity as a natural development from religions in the Near East. They explained Christianity in terms of a near-Eastern religious syncretism. An example was Wilhelm Bousset (1865–1920), who alleged that in Hellenistic Christianity the "Kyrios Christos" (English, "Lord Christ") concept replaced the eschatological Son of Man of earlier Christianity, and that it along with other biblical concepts was based on ancient myths of non-Jewish origin (for example, Babylonians and Egyptians).[311] Bousset claimed that in many cases Christians followed mystery religions before being converted, and transferred such concepts of the mystery-gods to Christianity.

Ernst Troeltsch, who formulated the three basic principles of Historical Criticism (criticism, analogy, and correlation), was also a member of the history-of-religions School.[312] He labeled himself "the systematic theologian of this approach."[313]

Another strong advocate was Bultmann, who urged that the evolutionary *religionsgeschichtliche* (English, "religion history") method be applied not only to Jesus but also to the entire history of New Testament theology, especially its Christology. He stipulated that one must carry out the practice of Form Criticism in terms of the presuppositions of *Religionsgeschichte*.[314] For Bultmann, the concept of evolutionary development and change in religious environments must be the interpretive grid that sifts all New Testament ideas about Jesus.

Without question, evolutionary thinking was another significant contribution to the historical-critical method's origin.

10. EXISTENTIALISM: KIERKEGAARD

Existentialism is not easy to define. Making it even more difficult to define is the fact that writers who claim to be existentialists might not agree on any one cardinal point. MacIntyre remarks "to define existentialism by means of a set of philosophical formulas could be very misleading."[315] Existentialism is not so much a movement with a common program as it is a tendency or attitude.[316] Kaufmann argues that "Existentialism is not a philosophy but a label for several widely different revolts against traditional philosophy."[317] He holds that the label "existentialism" ought to be abandoned.[318] One describes existentialism as an attempt to philosophize from the standpoint of the actor rather than from that of a detached spectator like traditional philosophy.[319] Existentialist philosophy arises in response to personal problems in the life of the existentialist. Copleston has expressed it thus:

> Philosophy and biography go together in the sense that the former arises in response to . . . personal problems in which . . . [the existentialist] is involved and which are solved on the existential level, by choice, rather than simply on the abstract or theoretical level.[320]

Existentialism's name reflects its primary concern regarding human existence.[321] It asserts that existence is always particular and individual; existence is primarily the problem of existence's mode of being, and thus it investigates the meaning of Being; this investigation is continually faced with diverse possibilities to which those who exist (namely, people) must make a selection and commit themselves; existence is always a being-in-the-world—namely, in a concrete and historically determinate situation that limits or conditions choice. Thus, people are called *Dasein* ("there being"), for they are defined by the fact that they exist or are in the world and inhabit it.[322]

In terms of its approach to religion and to Christianity in particular, two general branches of existentialism exist. Søren Kierkegaard (1813–1855, considered by many the father of existentialism), Karl Jaspers (1883–1969), and Gabriel Marcel (1889–1973) represent the theistic branch. Jean-Paul

Sartre (1905–1980), Martin Heidigger (1889–1976), and Albert Camus (1913–1960) represent the atheistic branch.[323]

In Germany existentialism became prominent as a distinct movement after World War I. In France, it arose after World War II. Theistic existentialism's roots went back into the nineteenth century to the dead orthodoxy of Danish Lutheranism, but atheistic existentialism's primary impetus was a reaction to the philosophy of nihilism that dominated the intellectual world around the time of the first World War. By the 1950s, existentialism became a significant worldview.[324]

Many consider Søren Abby Kierkegaard as the great-grandfather of existentialism. Before 1918, his writings were not widely known outside Denmark. For some, Kierkegaard's existentialism replaces idealism as the philosophical basis of Christianity. But for others, Kierkegaard represents the bankruptcy of Western philosophy. His anxiety-ridden pietistic upbringing produced a melancholy that affected much of his philosophical thinking.[325]

The Greek philosopher Socrates also greatly influenced Kierkegaard's thinking. He accepted Socrates's view of Recollection, which asserts that the human soul participates in eternal truth. In other words, truth lies latent within the Soul. However, he also allowed for the view that people may be strangers to the truth and need to learn from a teacher. Kierkegaard called his concept "Repetition" instead of "Recollection."[326] He also used Socrates indirect means of communication called "dialogue."

Kierkegaard expressed high regard for Gotthold Ephraim Lessing (1729–1781):

> [Lessing's] merit consists precisely in having prevented this: he closed himself off in the isolation of subjectivity, did not allow himself to be tricked into becoming world-historical or systematic with regard to the religious, but he understood, and knew how to maintain, that the religious pertains to Lessing and Lessing alone, just as it pertains to every human in the same way, understood that he had infinitely to do with God, but nothing, nothing to do directly with any human being. . . . This is the objection of my expression, the object of my gratitude.[327]

Kierkegaard reacted against the predominant Hegelian philosophy of his era. He viewed Hegel's philosophical system as no good and not true, for it was indemonstrable, irrelevant, and based on a confusion of categories.[328] Kierkegaard wrote, "Hegelian philosophy confuses existence by not defining its relation to an existing person, by disregarding the ethical."[329] It "makes men into heathens, *into a race of animals gifted with reason.*"[330] Hegel's reality has no relationship to the reality of human existence.[331]

In attacking Hegel, Kierkegaard was reacting ultimately against the "modern gratuitous assumption that truth is impersonal, that it can be attained simply by thinking dispassionately."[332] Although Kierkegaard did not necessarily assert that truth is subjective or that objective truth does not exist, he dismissed objectivity as a way of knowing ultimate or religious truth.[333] Kierkegaard asserted, "Truth is subjectivity" and "An objective uncertainty, held fast through appropriation with the most passionate inwardness, is the truth, the highest truth there is for an existing person."[334] For Kierkegaard, subjectivity was the key. He wrote, "It is perfectly true, isolated subjectivity is, in the opinion of the age, evil; but 'objectivity' as a cure is not one whit better. The only salvation is subjectivity, i.e. God, as infinite compelling subjectivity."[335]

For Kierkegaard, truth was paradoxical: "When subjectivity, inwardness, is truth, then truth, objectively defined, is a paradox; and that truth is objectively a paradox shows precisely that subjectivity is truth."[336] He goes on to reason, "The paradox is the objective uncertainty that is the expression for the passion of inwardness that is truth."[337] Yet, for Kierkegaard, this paradox rests not in religious truth itself but in the finitude of man.[338] Geisler evaluates Kierkegaard thus: "Truth is a subjective encounter with God for which one has no good reason but which one must appropriate by a passionate 'leap' of faith."[339] Kierkegaard commented, "And so I say to myself: I choose; that historical fact means so much to me that I decide to stake my whole life upon that if. . . . That is called risking; and without risk faith is an impossibility."[340]

Kierkegaard never denied that Christianity was objectively or historically true,[341] but he felt that the results of historical research are uncertain. Though asserting his personal belief in the historicity of the Bible and Christ,[342] he maintained that objective truth is not essential to Christianity.[343] Brown notes, "For Kierkegaard the paradox of faith means that belief must be proportioned in inverse proportion to the evidence. The less evidence, the better. Faith and reason are mutually exclusive opposites."[344] Kierkegaard made the following argument:

> Even if the contemporary generation had not left anything behind except these words, "We have believed that in such and such a year the god appeared in the humble form of a servant, lived and taught among us, and then died"—this is more than enough. The contemporary generation would have done what is needful, for this little announcement, this world-historical *nota bene*, is enough to become an occasion for someone who comes later, and the most prolix report can never in all eternity become more for the person who comes later.[345]

The importance, for Kierkegaard, is not what you know but how you react: "What makes the difference in life is not what is said, but how it is said."[346] The goal in faith is not more factual knowledge but a greater understanding of oneself and human existence.[347]

Kierkegaard did not engage in higher criticism of the biblical text, for he maintained that even the most destructive forms of criticism would not harm Christianity, even if such criticism negated the genuineness or authenticity of Scripture.[348] Geisler's comment is correct: "Kierkegaard left a gaping hole in the wall of the historic church, through which modern higher criticism has made its destructive march."[349]

Kierkegaard did not personally deny the inspiration and authority of Scripture. He accepted the Bible as the word of God. However, he argued that the inspiration of Scripture is a subjective matter of faith and denied that belief in its inspiration has any objective basis. Instead, he deprecated the great apologetic efforts that were made to defend Scripture and termed the concept of inspiration "a dogmatic guarantee."[350] Geisler comments, "We witness in Kierkegaard the continuation of the Kantian fact/value dichotomy. No fact can ever disconfirm the realm of religious value, which is forever reserved for faith alone."[351]

Kierkegaard also asserted that God is suprarational.[352] Human reason cannot prove or know Him, for He is beyond the reach of reason. In seeking to describe/define what God is, Kierkegaard asks, "What is this unknown against which the understanding in its paradoxical passion collides and which disturbs man and his self-knowledge?" He concludes, "It [God] is the unknown."[353] For Kierkegaard, the existence of God "is impossible to demonstrate" and "if he does exist, then it is foolishness to want to demonstrate it . . . since I, in the very moment the demonstration commences, would presuppose it not as doubtful."[354] He goes on to ask, "How could it [reason] understand the absolutely different? . . . . for if the god is absolutely different from a human being, then a human being is absolutely different from the god—but how is the understanding to grasp this? At this point, we seem to stand at a paradox."[355] For Kierkegaard, this paradox continues in the incarnation.[356]

Kierkegaard's thought has had profound impact on twentieth-century neo-orthodoxy and neo-evangelicalism. Nygren remarks, "He [Kierkegaard] can claim a vast posterity who, like him, have a great distrust of reason as a means of approaching God and of history as a means of discovering Jesus Christ."[357] Karl Barth echoed Kierkegaardian thought when he asserted that the Gospel requires faith, for it "can . . . neither directly be communicated nor directly apprehended."[358] Like Kierkegaard he maintained that the Gospel can only be "received and understood" as "contradiction."[359] Echoing Kierkegaard, Barth argued that Christ also must be "unknown," since He is God. For Barth, "We do not demand belief in our faith. . . . It is unbelievable."[360]

The historical-critical method of the New Hermeneutic is a descendent of Kierkegaard and a product of existentialist thinking.[361] Two of the leading proponents of the method are Ernst Fuchs (b. 1903) and Gerhard Ebeling (b. 1912).[362] The New Hermeneutic ignores the text's original context and interprets existentially/experientially in the contemporary context. It asks, "What does the text mean to me today?"

According to Wolf, Bultmann also reflected existential thinking.[363] Kierkegaard's hypothesis maintained the alleged paradoxical nature of God and the idea that Christianity must be accepted by a "leap of faith." His thinking has had a profound effect on the search for the historical Jesus, which was conducted by such historical-critical theologians as Bultmann.[364]

Influenced by Kierkegaard's reliance on a leap of faith rather than fact, Bultmann argued, "It is only when there is no such objective guarantee that faith acquires meaning and strength, for only then is it authentic decision."[365] Bultmann joins Kierkegaard in holding that God is "the hidden and mysterious . . . . unknown God."[366] While at Marburg University, Bultmann came under the influence of Martin Heidegger (1889–1976), the existentialist philosopher,[367] and wrote, "The work of existential philosophy, which I came to know through my discussion with Martin Heidegger, has become of decisive significance for me."[368]

Paul Tillich also rejected reliance upon the historicity of the biblical accounts. Acceptance must be solely upon the basis of faith. Tillich wrote, "There is no way of meeting the 'historical Jesus' (i.e., the product of Historical Criticism) because the Jesus of whom we have reports was from the very beginning the 'Christ of faith.'"[369]

In the last decade of the twentieth century, the existential "road" has led to "deconstructionism." This point of view negates the existence of theological truth altogether as a coherent process of inquiry. Indeed, not only is God "dead," but the term "God" ("the Transcendental Signified") has no meaning. The long, winding road of Historical Criticism has come to a lonely, dead end with deconstructionism.[370]

CONCLUSION

Francis Schaeffer drove to the heart of the problem that evangelicals are facing today: a disregard of presuppositions.[371] Christian leaders have been inattentive to the need for correct presuppositions and, as a result, are reaping the fruit of confusion and negative thinking. Schaeffer's opinion was that *"Presuppositional Apologetics Would Have Stopped the Decay"* rampant in evangelical thinking. He related the following:

It was indeed unfortunate that our Christian "thinkers" . . . did not teach and preach with a clear grasp of presuppositions. . . . The really foolish thing is . . . many Christians still do not know what is happening. And this is because they are still not being taught the importance of thinking in terms of presuppositions, especially concerning truth.[372]

Unfortunately, the world of biblical scholarship and the practitioners of New Testament criticism and interpretation continue to be careless in this regard, especially in their utilization of Historical Criticism. Failure to consider presuppositions and their subsequent impact upon the interpretation of Scripture *is* the true scandal of the evangelical mind.[373]

ENDNOTES

1. Norman L. Geisler, "Inductivism, Materialism, and Rationalism: Bacon, Hobbes, and Spinoza," in *Biblical Errancy: An Analysis of Its Philosophical Roots*, ed. Norman L. Geisler (Grand Rapids: Zondervan, 1981), 11.
2. Ibid.

3. Stephen Davis, *The Debate about the Bible* (Philadelphia: Westminster, 1977), 139.
4. Eta Linnemann, *The Historical Criticism of the Bible,* trans. Robert W. Yarbrough (Grand Rapids: Baker, 1990), 17–18.
5. Ibid., 29.
6. Ibid., 107.
7. John Locke (1632–1704), George Berkeley (1685–1753), and David Hume (1711–1776) are among those included in the empirical tradition.
8. Bacon wrote, "And as common logic, which regulates matters by syllogisms, is applied not only to natural, but also to every other science, so our inductive method likewise comprehends them all" (Francis Bacon, *Novum Organum,* vol. 30 in *Great Books of the Western World,* ed. Robert M. Hutchins et al. [Chicago: William Benton, 1952], 1.127 [p. 134]).
9. Bacon, *Novum Organum* 1.124 (p. 133).
10. Ibid. Bacon argued, "Truth . . . and utility are . . . perfectly identical."
11. Ibid., 1.65 (p. 114).
12. Ibid., 1.65 (p. 114).
13. Linnemann, *Historical Criticism,* 28–29.
14. Geisler, "Inductivism," 13.
15. "Biographical Note," in Thomas Hobbes, *Leviathan,* vol. 23 of *Great Books of the Western World,* ed. Robert Maynard Hutchins et al. (Chicago: William Benton, 1952), 41; Geisler, "Inductivism," 14.
16. Colin Brown, *Christianity and Western Thought* (Downers Grove: InterVarsity, 1990), 200.
17. Hobbes, *Leviathan* 1.1 (p. 49).
18. Hobbes, *Leviathan* 4.46 (p. 269); cf. Frederick Copleston, *A History of Philosophy,* part 2, vol. 5: *Hobbes to Hume* (New York: Doubleday, 1960), 5.
19. Hobbes, *Leviathan* 4.46 (p. 270).
20. Ibid., 1.3 (p. 54); cf. Copleston, *History of Philosophy, Hobbes to Hume,* 5.
21. Ibid., 1.12 (p. 79).
22. Ibid., 1.12 (p. 80).
23. Ibid., 1.12 (p. 80); see also 3.37 (pp. 188–91).
24. Ibid., 1.8 (p. 70); see also Brown, *Christianity and Western Thought,* 200.
25. *Leviathan* 1.8 (pp. 70–71).
26. Ibid., 3.32 (p. 165).
27. Ibid., 3.32 (p. 165).
28. Ibid., 1.10 (p. 71).
29. Geisler, "Inductivism, Materialism, and Rationalism," 15.
30. Cf. Norman L. Geisler, *Miracles and the Modern Mind* (Grand Rapids: Baker, 1992), 85.
31. Geisler, "Inductivism, Materialism, and Rationalism," 15. See discussion of "Existentialism" below.
32. Cf. *Leviathan* 3.32 (p. 165); cf. also Robert M. Grant, *A Short History of the Interpretation of the Bible* (New York: Macmillan, 1963), 145.
33. Grant, *Short History,* 146.
34. Geisler, "Inductivism, Materialism, and Rationalism," 14.
35. Linnemann, *Historical Criticism,* 29.
36. "Biographical Note, Benedict de Spinoza," in *Great Books of the Western World,* ed. Robert M. Hutchins et al. (Chicago: William Benton, 1952), 31:354.
37. See Letter LIV, March 30, 1673, in R. H. M. Elwes, *The Chief Works of Spinoza* (London: George Bell, 1883), 2:374–75.

38. Brown, *Christianity and Western Thought*, 185–86.
39. Of the various shades of rationalism, this description characterizes the three seventeenth-century rationalists, Descartes, Leibnitz, and Spinoza (cf. Norman L. Geisler and Paul D. Feinberg, *Introduction to Philosophy, A Christian Perspective* [Grand Rapids: Baker, 1980], 110–11).
40. See Bernard Williams, "Rationalism," in *The Encyclopaedia of Philosophy*, ed. P. Edwards (New York: Macmillan, 1967), 7:69.
41. Diogenes Allen, *Philosophy for Understanding and Theology* (Atlanta: John Knox, 1973), 172; cf. Geisler and Feinberg, *Introduction to Philosophy*, 110.
42. Ibid.
43. See the section on skepticism below and Richard H. Popkin, *The History of Skepticism from Erasmus to Descartes*, rev. ed. (New York: Harper, 1968).
44. See Colin Brown, *Miracles and the Critical Mind* (Grand Rapids: Eerdmans, 1984), 23–30, for further information on the rise of rationalism.
45. René Descartes was the catalyst in the development of modern philosophy (Allen, *Philosophy for Understanding and Theology*, 170).
46. Allen, *Philosophy for Understanding and Theology*, 171–202.
47. Benedict De Spinoza, *The Collected Works of Spinoza*, ed. and trans. Edwin Curley (Princeton, N.J.: Princeton University, 1985), 1:439–46, citing Spinoza's work entitled *Ethics, Demonstrated in Geometrical Order* (1677).
48. Ibid., 1:420.
49. Ibid., 1:428.
50. Ibid., 1:599.
51. Ibid., 1:604.
52. Ibid., 1:612; cf. Brown, *Christianity and Western Thought*, 187–88.
53. Cf. Popkin, *History of Skepticism*, 229–48.
54. Brown, *Christianity and Western Thought*, 187.
55. Benedict De Spinoza, *The Chief Works of Benedict de Spinoza*, trans. R. H. M. Elwes (New York: Dover, 1951), 1:194, citing Spinoza's work *Tractatus Theologico–Politicus* (1670).
56. Ibid., 1:171–72.
57. Ibid., 1:190.
58. Geisler, "Inductivism, Materialism, and Rationalism," 17.
59. Spinoza, *Chief Works*, 1:165.
60. Ibid., 1:165.
61. Ibid., 1:443–44.
62. Ibid., 1:92.
63. Geisler, "Inductivism, Materialism, and Rationalism," 19.
64. Spinoza, *Chief Works*, 1:130–31.
65. Ibid., 1:127.
66. Ibid., 1:150.
67. Ibid., 1:159.
68. Ibid., 1:171.
69. *Tractatus VI* (*Chief Works* 1:93).
70. Geisler, "Inductivism, Materialism, and Rationalism," 19.
71. Gerhard Hasel, *New Testament Theology: Basic Issues in the Current Debate* (Grand Rapids: Eerdmans, 1978), 26; cf. also William Baird, *History of New Testament Research* Philadelphia: Fortress, 1992), 1:6; Leo Strauss, *Spinoza's Critique of Religion*, trans. E. M. Sinclair (New York: Schocken, 1965).
72. Colin Brown, *Jesus in European Protestant Thought, 1778–1860* (Durham, North Carolina: Labyrinth, 1985), 22.

73. Cf. Werner Georg Kümmel, *The New Testament: The History of the Investigation of Its Problems* (Nashville: Abingdon, 1972), 76–77.
74. Henry Chadwick, *Lessing's Theological Writings: Selections in Translation with an Introductory Essay* (Stanford, Calif.: Stanford University, 1956), 53.
75. Cf. Brown, *Jesus in European Protestant Thought*, 22.
76. Baird, *History of New Testament Research*, 211.
77. Brown, *Miracles and the Critical Mind*, 103.
78. Friedrich Schleiermacher, *The Christian Faith*, trans. H. R. Mackintosh and J. S. Steward (Philadelphia: Fortress, 1976), 1:179.
79. Schleiermacher, *Christian Faith*, 1:71.
80. F. Schleiermacher, *On Religion: Speeches to its Cultured Despisers* (reprint, New York: Harper & Brothers, 1958), 40.
81. D. F. Strauss, *Die christliche Glaubenslehre* (Tübingen: C. F. Osiander, 1841), 2:175–76.
82. Georg Hegel, *Lectures on the History of Philosophy,* trans. E. S. Haldane and Frances H. Simson (New York: Humanities Press, 1968), 3:252–90; cf. Horton Harris, *The Tübingen School: A Historical and Theological Investigation of F. C. Baur* (Grand Rapids: Baker, 1990), 25–26.
83. Brown, *Christianity and Western Thought*, 309.
84. Edgar Krentz, *The Historical-Critical Method* (Philadelphia: Fortress, 1975), 21–22.
85. Cf. Brown, *Miracles and the Critical Mind*, 333 n. 1; cf. also E. C. Mossner, "Deism," in *The Encyclopedia of Philosophy*, 2:326–36.
86. Copleston, *History of Philosophy*, 5:162–63; James W. Sire, *The Universe Next Door,* updated and expanded ed. (Downers Grove, Ill.: InterVarsity, 1988), 50; R. M. Burns, *The Great Debate on Miracles: From Joseph Glanvill to David Hume* (Lewisburg: Buckness University, 1981), 13.
87. Ernst Cassirer, *The Philosophy of the Enlightenment,* trans. Fritz C. A. Koelln and James P. Pettegrove (Princeton, N.J.: Princeton University, 1979), 174.
88. Thomas Halyburton's *Natural Religion Insufficient, and Revealed Necessary to Man's Happiness in his Present State* (1714).
89. Herbert of Cherbury, *De Veritate,* trans. Meyrick H. Carré (Bristole: Arrowsmith, 1937), 289–307 (a 1624 work whose title in English is *On Truth*).
90. Cf. Brown, *Miracles and the Skeptical Mind*, 48–49.
91. Cf. Gary Habermas, "Skepticism: Hume," in *Biblical Errancy: An Analysis of Its Philosophical Roots,* ed. Norman L. Geisler (Grand Rapids: Zondervan, 1981), 27.
92. Charles Blount, *The First Two Books of Philostratus Concerning the Life of Apollonius Tyaneus* (1680); cf. Philostratus, *The Life of Apolloneus of Tyana,* Greek text and English translation by F. C. Conybeare, Loeb Classical Library, 2 vols., rev. ed. (Cambridge, Mass.: Harvard University, 1950).
93. Some think that the work was originally anti-Christian propaganda based on historical romances of the time and that no parallel exists (John Ferguson, *The Religion of the Roman Empire* [London: Thames and Hudson, 1970], 182).
94. The full title of the work was *Christianity Not Mysterious: Or, a Treatise Showing that there is Nothing in the Gospel Contrary to Reason, nor above it; And that No Christian Doctrine can properly be Called a Mystery.* Robert E. Sullivan, *John Toland and the Deist Controversy: A Study in Adaptations* (Cambridge, Mass.: Harvard University Press, 1982), and Stephen H. Daniel, *John Toland: His Methods, Manners, and Mind* (Kingston and Montreal: McGill–Queen's University Press, 1984) are two recent studies about Toland.

95. The full title was *Nazarenus: Or, Jewish, Gentile, and Mahometan Christianity. Containing The History of the ancient Gospel of Barnabus. . . . The Original Plan of Christianity occasionally explained in the history of the Nazarenes, whereby diverse Controversies about this divine (but highly perverted) Institution may be happily terminated.*
96. John Locke, *The Reasonableness of Christianity,* ed. I. T. Ramsey (Stanford, Calif.: Stanford University Press, 1958), describes Locke's view on miracles.
97. For evidence of Collins' influence on Reimarus, see Brown, *Jesus in European Protestant Thought,* 39 n. 61.
98. Brown, *Miracles and the Critical Mind,* 49.
99. Copleston, *A History of Philosophy,* 4:163.
100. Pete Medawar, "On 'The Effecting of All Things Possible,'" *The Listener* (October 2, 1969): 438.
101. Cf. Norman L. Geisler and William D. Watkins, *Worlds Apart, A Handbook on World Views,* 2d ed. (Grand Rapids: Baker, 147–85).
102. Brown, *Christianity and Western Thought,* 203.
103. Peter Gay, *The Enlightenment, An Interpretation: The Rise of Modern Paganism* (New York: W. W. Norton, 1966), 374–75.
104. Brown, *Miracles and the Critical Mind,* 47; Brown, *Jesus in European Protestant Thought,* 29.
105. Brown, *Christianity and Western Thought,* 212.
106. See Colin Brown, *Jesus in European Thought,* 1.
107. See particularly the sixth and seventh fragments, "Concerning the Resurrection Story" and "On the Purpose of Jesus and that of his Disciples."
108. Strauss himself espoused Hegel's philosophy. See Cornelio Fabro, *God in Exile,* trans. and ed. Arthur Gibson (Westminster, Md.: Newman, 1968); Bruno Bauer, *The Trumpet of the Last Judgement Against Hegel, the Atheist and Antichrist,* trans. Lawrence Stepelevich (Lewiston, New York: Edwin Mellen, 1989).
109. David Friedrich Strauss, "Hermann Samuel Reimarus and His Apology," in Hermann Samuel Remairus, *Reimarus: Fragments,* ed. Charles H. Talbert, trans. Ralph S. Fraser (Philadelphia: Fortress, 1970), 44.
110. Cf. David Friedrich Strauss, *The Life of Jesus Critically Examined,* ed. Peter C. Hodgson (Philadelphia: Fortress, 1972), 52–91.
111. Stephen Neill and Tom Wright, *The Interpretation of the New Testament, 1861–1986,* 2d ed. (Oxford: Oxford University, 1988), 14.
112. Albert Schweitzer, *The Quest for the Historical Jesus,* trans. W. Montgomery (New York: Macmillan, 1968), 22, 26.
113. Claude Welch, *Protestant Thought in the Nineteenth Century* (New Haven, Connecticut: Yale University Press, 1972), 1:38.
114. Cf. Brown, *Jesus in Protestant European Thought,* 50–55.
115. Ernst Troeltsch, *Gesammelte Schriften* (Leipzig and Berlin: Teubner, 1927), 3:131.
116. Ernst Troeltsch, "Historical and Dogmatic Method in Theology (1898)," in Ernst Troeltsch, *Religion in History,* essays trans. James Luther Adams and Walter F. Bense with an Introduction by James Luther Adams (Minneapolis: Fortress, 1991), 13–15.
117. Troeltsch, "Historical and Dogmatic Method," 24.
118. Krentz, *Historical-Critical Method,* 55.
119. Rudolf Bultmann, "Is Exegesis Without Presuppositions Possible?" *Existence and Faith,* ed. Schubert M. Ogden (New York: Meridian Books, 1960), 291–92.
120. Schweitzer, *Quest,* 24.

121. Norman Perrin, *What Is Redaction Criticism?* (Philadelphia: Fortress, 1969), 4.

122. Cf. Remairus, *Reimarus: Fragments,* 135–269.

123. This work was not translated into English until 1971: William Wrede, *The Messianic Secret,* trans. J. C. G. Greig (Cambridge: James Clarke, 1971), 11; James D. G. Dunn refutes Wrede's assertions in "The Messianic Secret in Mark," in *The Messianic Secret,* ed. Christopher Tuckett (Philadelphia: Fortress, 1983), 116–31.

124. Perrin, *Redaction Criticism?* 7.

125. Hayden White, "Editor's Introduction," in Robert Anchor, *The Enlightenment Tradition,* reprinted and updated (Berkeley, Calif.: University of California, 1979), ix. Cf. Geisler and Feinberg, *Introduction to Philosophy,* 139, 665.

126. Gay, *Enlightenment,* xi.

127. British empiricists advocated an epistemology based on verification of sense experience through the inductive method, namely, testing by experience or experiment. They confined themselves to observations and remedies that worked and were skeptical of general, theoretical explanations. Cf. Colin Brown, *Philosophy and the Christian Faith* (Downers Grove: InterVarsity, 1968), 60–61; idem, *Christianity and Western Thought,* 215.

128. Cf. Gary Habermas, "Skepticism: Hume," *Biblical Errancy,* 25.

129. Krentz relates that features of the Enlightenment that produced the historical critical method were predominantly philosophical. For a succinct overview of the influence of rationalism and deism, cf. Krentz, *Historical Critical Method,* 16–22.

130. Ernest C. Mossner, *The Life of David Hume,* 2d ed. (Oxford: Clarendon, 1980), and John Vladimir Price, *David Hume,* updated ed. (Boston: Twayne Publishers, 1991), give an overview of Hume's life.

131. Gay, *Enlightenment,* 401.

132. Habermas, "Skepticism: Hume," in *Biblical Errancy,* 28.

133. Baird, *History of New Testament Research,* 57.

134. Welch, *Protestant Thought in the Nineteenth Century,* 1:42.

135. The treatise became a classic work of philosophy, but it was disappointing to Hume (cf. Mossner, *The Life of David Hume,* 612).

136. David Hume, *A Treatise of Human Nature,* ed. and Introduction by Ernest C. Mossner (New York: Penguin, 1969), 1.1.6 (p. 63).

137. Hume, *Treatise of Human Nature,* 1.4.6. (p. 300).

138. Ibid., 1.3.14 (p. 217).

139. David Hume, *Enquiries Concerning Human Understanding and Concerning the Principles of Morals,* ed. L. A. Selby-Bigge, 3d ed. with text and revised notes by P. H. Nidditch (Oxford: Clarendon, 1975), #59 (pp. 74–76).

140. Hume, *Enquiry Concerning Human Understanding,* #115 (p. 148).

141. Habermas, "Skepticism," 30; cf. Brown, *Christianity and Western Thought,* 240.

142. Geisler, "Philosophical Presuppositions of Biblical Errancy," in *Biblical Errancy,* 320.

143. Hume, *Enquiry Concerning Human Understanding,* #132 (p. 165).

144. Geisler, "Philosophical Presuppositions of Biblical Errancy," 321.

145. Hume, *Enquiry Concerning Human Understanding,* #90 (p. 115 n. 1).

146. Ibid., (p. 114); cf. #92–95 (pp. 116–122). In *David Hume's Argument Against Miracles, A Critical Analysis* (Lanham, Md.: University Press of America, 1989), Francis J. Beckwith analyzes and refutes Hume's arguments against miracles.

147. Hume, *Enquiry Concerning Human Understanding*, #86 (p. 109).
148. Anthony Flew, "Introduction," in David Hume, *Of Miracles* (La Salle, Ill.: Open Court, 1985), 4.
149. Hume, *Enquiry Concerning Human Understanding*, #101 (p. 131).
150. C. S. Peirce, *Values in the Universe of Chance*, ed. with an introduction and notes by Philip P. Wiener (New York: Doubleday Anchor, 1958), 292–93; cf. also Flew, "Introduction," 12–13.
151. John Herman Randall, Jr., *The Making of the Modern Mind. A Survey of the Intellectual Background of the Present Age*, 15th Anniv. ed. (New York: Columbia University, 1940, 1976), 293, 553–554; cf. Wilbur M. Smith, *The Supernaturalness of Christ* (Grand Rapids: Baker, 1974), 142.
152. Habermas, "Skepticism: Hume," 34; cf. David Friedrich Strauss, *A New Life of Jesus*, authorized translation, 2d ed. (Williams and Norgate, 1879), 199.
153. Schleiermacher, *The Christian Faith*, 1:178–84; Ernest Renan, *The Life of Jesus*, introduction by John Haynes Holmes (New York: Random House, 1955), 249, 257; Adolf Harnack, *What Is Christianity?* trans. Thomas Bailey Saunders; introduction by Rudolf Bultmann (Philadelphia: Fortress, 1986), 25, 28.
154. Cox and Burkholder ("A Dialog on Christ's Resurrection," *Christianity Today* [April 12, 1968]: 5–12) candidly admit that Hume's thinking is the philosophical foundation for the final rejection of miracles by many modern theologians.
155. Rudolf Bultmann, "New Testament and Mythology," in *Kerygma and Myth*, ed. Hans Werner Bartsch, rev. ed. by Reginald H. Fuller (New York: Harper & Row, 1961), 4–5; Paul Tillich, *Systematic Theology* (Chicago: University of Chicago Press, 1951), 1:115–16.
156. Brown, *Miracles and the Critical Mind*, 99; cf. Ernst Troeltsch, "Historical and Dogmatic Method in Theology," 13–14.
157. The following have information on Kant's life and thought: Ernst Cassirer, *Kant's Life and Thought*, trans. James Haden, introduction by Stephan Körner (New Haven and London: Yale University Press, 1981); J. H. W. Stuckenberg, *The Life of Immanuel Kant*, with a new Preface by Rolf George (Lanham, Md.: University Press of America, 1986); Paul Guyer, ed., *The Cambridge Companion to Kant* (Cambridge: Cambridge University, 1992).
158. Vasilis Politis, "Introduction," in Immanuel Kant, *Critique of Pure Reason*, ed. Vasilis Politis (New York: Everyman, 1993), xxvii.
159. Kant, *Critique of Pure Reason*, 30.
160. Ibid., 48–68.
161. Ibid., 85.
162. Ibid., 64–65.
163. Kant defined *a priori* knowledge as knowledge that is absolutely independent of all experience, while he defined *a posteriori* knowledge as that which denotes empirical knowledge of the world gained through the senses or experience. In his system, these types overlap to some extent (cf. Ibid., 30–32).
164. Brown, *Philosophy and the Christian Faith*, 96.
165. Ibid., 211.
166. Ibid., 65.
167. Kant, *Critique of Pure Reason*, 68.
168. Ibid., 317–40.
169. Ibid., 407–27.
170. Ibid., 433.
171. Immanuel Kant, "Preface to the First Edition," *Religion Within the Limits*

of Reason Alone, trans. Theodore M. Greene and Hoyt H. Hudson (New York: Harper, 1960), 3–5.

172. Brown, *Jesus in European Protestant Thought*, 61; cf. Kant, "Preface to the First Edition," 3.
173. Kant, *Religion Within the Limits of Reason Alone*, 145.
174. Ibid., 152.
175. Brown, *Christianity and Western Thought*, 328.
176. Kant, *Religion Within the Limits of Reason Alone*, 54, cf. 56–57; cf. Brown, *Christianity and Western Thought*, 238.
177. Ibid., 78.
178. Ibid., 79.
179. Ibid., 81.
180. Ibid., 179.
181. Ibid., 84.
182. Brown, *Jesus in European Protestant Thought*, 66; cf. Brown, *Miracles and the Critical Mind*, 106.
183. Brown, *Christianity and Western Thought*, 329; Brown, *Miracles and the Critical Mind*, 76.
184. For example, W. David Beck, "Agnosticism: Kant," in *Biblical Errancy*, 74; Neill and Wright, *Interpretation of the New Testament 1861–1986*, 2; Schubert Ogden, "The Challenge to Protestant Thought," *Continuum* 6 (summer 1968): 237; Frederic W. Farrar, *History of Interpretation* (reprint of 1886 E. P. Dutton ed., Grand Rapids: Baker, 1961), 407.
185. Norman L. Geisler and William E. Nix, *A General Introduction to the Bible* (Chicago: Moody, 1986), 141.
186. Hasel, *New Testament Theology*, 29.
187. Winfried Corduan, "Trascendentalism: Hegel," in *Biblical Errancy*, 83, 89–94.
188. Robert B. Strimple, *The Modern Search for the Real Jesus* (Phillipsburg, N.J.: Presbyterian and Reformed, 1995), 50–51.:
189. Both Kant and Otto stressed the inner subjective witness of the Spirit in determining acceptable parts of the Bible. Cf. Kant, *Religion Within the Limits of Reason Alone*, 103; Rudolf Otto, *The Idea of the Holy*, trans. John Harvey (Oxford: Oxford University, 1967), 162.
190. Robert Morgan, "Rudolf Bultmann," in *The Modern Theologians*, vol. 1 in *An Introduction to Christian Theology in the Twentieth Century*, ed. David F. Ford (New York: Basil Blackwell, 1989), 109.
191. Ogden stated moral obligation in Kantian form: "The rule here, of course, is the one stated by Kant: *Du kannst, denn du sollst* ["You can, because you should"] and unless this rule can be shown to be false—and, as we have indicated, it appears to be self-evident—the conclusion just drawn cannot be evaded" (Schubert Ogden, *Christ Without Myth, A Study Based on the Theology of Rudolf Bultmann* (New York: Harper & Brothers, 1961), 118; Ogden also based the reality of God on the idea of Kantian morality (idem, "The Reality of God," in *The Reality of God and Other Essays* (New York: Harper and Row, 1966), 10–11.
192. Brown, *Jesus in European Protestant Thought*, 67.
193. Brown, *Christianity and Western Thought*, 330.
194. Harold O. J. Brown, "Romanticism and the Bible," in *Challenges to Inerrancy*, ed. Gordon Lewis and Bruce Demarest (Chicago: Moody, 1984), 49–50.
195. Contemporary scholars differ regarding exact definitions of Romanticism, but agree on general details describing it (R. V. Pierard, "Romanticism," in

Evangelical Dictionary of Theology, ed. Walter A. Elwell [Grand Rapids: Baker, 1984], 960).

196. Brown, "Romanticism and the Bible," 51.

197. Cf. Claude Welch, *Protestant Thought in the Nineteenth Century*, 1:52–55.

198. Brown, "Romanticism and the Bible," 51.

199. Schleiermacher influenced not only theology but also philosophy. He lectured in both fields while carrying on active preaching ministry (W. A. Hoffecker, "Schleiermacher, Friedrich Daniel Ernst," in *Evangelical Dictionary of Theology*, 981–983). Brown adds, "It was in the realm of philosophical theology that Schleiermacher was to make his chief contributions" (Brown, *Protestant Religious Thought*, 106).

200. Hoffecker, "Schleiermacher," 981.

201. Karl Barth, *From Rousseau to Ritschl* (London: SCM Press, 1959), 306.

202. Brown, *Philosophy and the Christian Faith*, 110.

203. Friedrich Schleiermacher, *On Religion: Speeches to Its Cultured Despisers*, trans. John Oman (New York: Harper and Row, 1958), 40.

204. Brown, *Philosophy and the Christian Faith*, 109.

205. Schweitzer, *Quest*, 63.

206. Brown, *Philosophy and the Christian Faith*, 111.

207. Ernst Schleiermacher, *The Christian Faith*, English trans. of 2d German ed., ed. H. R. Mackintosh and J. S. Steward (New York & Evanston: Harper & Row, 1963), 1:5.

208. Schleiermacher, *On Religion*, 94.

209. Ibid., 39.

210. Schleiermacher, *Christian Faith*, 1:12.

211. Brown, *Jesus in European Protestant Thought*, 116; see Friedrich D. E. Scheiermacher, *On the Glaubenslehre, Two Letters to Dr. Locke*, trans. James Duke and Francis Fiorenza (Chico, Calif.: Scholars, 1981), 38–46.

212. *"The finding of one's self in immediate self-consciousness as absolutely dependent is always presupposed and also accordingly contained in every Christian religious self-consciousness, and this is the only way that, in general, our own being and the infinite being of God can be one in self-consciousness"* (ibid., 1:131, emphasis original); cf. Fred H. Klooster, "Revelation and Scripture in Existentialist Theology," in *Challenges to Inerrancy*, 205.

213. Schleiermacher, *Christian Faith*, 1:133–34.

214. Ibid., 1:194 [emphasis original].

215. Ibid., 1:271.

216. Ibid., 1:299–304.

217. Ibid., 2:388.

218. Ibid., 2:385.

219. Ibid., 2:425 [emphasis original].

220. Ibid., 1:178–84.

221. Friedrich Schleiermacher, *The Life of Jesus*, ed. and with an introduction by Jack C. Verheyden, trans. S. Maclean Gilmour (Philadelphia: Fortress, 1975), 415–17, 464.

222. For example, Schleiermacher speaks about the "Trinity," terming it the "coping–stone of Christian doctrine," but arguing against "the unity of Essence and trinity of Persons" (Schleiermacher, *Christian Faith*, 2:738–39).

223. Brown, *Philosophy and the Christian Faith*, 113.

224. John A. T. Robinson, *Honest to God* (Philadelphia: Westminster, 1963), 21–22, 29–83.

225. Paul Tillich, *Systematic Theology* (Chicago: University of Chicago, 1951–1963), 1:3–66, 211–89.
226. Geisler and Nix, *General Introduction*, 143.
227. Brown, *Jesus in European Protestant Thought*, 117; cf. James C. Livingston, *Modern Christian Thought From The Enlightenment to Vatican II* (New York: Macmillan, 1972), 110.
228. James Duke, "Translators' Introduction," in Friedrich Schleiermacher, *Hermeneutics: The Handwritten Manuscripts*, ed. Heinz Kimmerle, trans. James Duke and Jack Forstman (Atlanta: Scholars Press, 1977), 1.
229. Schleiermacher, *Hermeneutics*, 9.
230. Ibid., 104.
231. Ibid., 147; cf. Baird, *New Testament Research*, 212.
232. David S. Dockery, "New Testament Interpretation: A Historical Survey," in *New Testament Criticism and Interpretation*, ed. David Alan Black and David S. Dockery (Grand Rapids: Zondervan, 1991), 59; cf. Schleiermacher, *Hermeneutics*, 141.
233. Brown, *Jesus in European and Protestant Thought*, 125.
234. F. F. Bruce, "The History of New Testament Study," in *New Testament Interpretation*, ed. I. Howard Marshall (Grand Rapids: Eerdmans, 1977), 39.
235. Bruce, "History of New Testament Study," 40; cf. Schleiermacher, *Christian Faith*, 448–49; *Life of Jesus*, 392–481.
236. Brown, "Romanticism and the Bible," 61.
237. James Duke, "Translators' Introduction," in Schleiermacher, *Hermeneutics: The Handwritten Manuscripts*, 15.
238. Schleiermacher, *The Life of Jesus*, 36–44; cf. Dockery, "New Testament Interpretation: A Historical Survey," 53.
239. Cf. William R. Farmer, *The Synoptic Problem* (Macon, Ga.: Mercer, 1976), 15.
240. Cf. Eusebius, *Ecclesiastical History* 3.39.
241. Schleiermacher, *Life of Jesus*, 37 [emphasis original].
242. Ibid., 43, 433.
243. Ibid., 433.
244. Ibid.
245. Ritschl agreed with Schleiermacher in trying to extract the essence of Christianity from Christian experience (Brown, *Philosophy and the Modern Mind*, 154–155), but was not in complete agreement with Schleiermacher's system, however, as Strimple observes: "Although he had been influenced earlier by . . . Schleiermacher . . . Ritschl rejected . . . Schleiermacher's appeal to the subjective and mystical. . . . Against Schleiermacher, Ritschl emphasized the historical basis of Christian faith in the person and work of Jesus of Nazareth" (Strimple, *Modern Search*, 50). Ritschl defined Jesus' role as "the Bearer of God's ethical lordship over men" (Albrecht Ritschl, *The Doctrine of Justification and Reconciliation*, trans. H. R. Mackintosh and A. B. Macaulay [Clifton, N.J.: Reference Books, 1966], 451).
246. Rudolf Bultmann, "The Problem of Hermeneutics," in *Essays Philosophical and Theological*, trans. J. C. G. Greig (London: SCM, 1955), 234–62.
247. Dilthey's essay, "The Origin of Hermeneutics" [1900] has been decisive in understanding Schleiermacher (cf. Duke, "Translator's Introduction," and Kimmerle, "Forward to the German Edition," in *Hermeneutics, The Handwritten Manuscripts*, 1, 19, 27–28).
248. Cf. Keith W. Clements, ed. *Friedrich Schleiermacher, Pioneer of Modern Theology* (Minneapolis: Fortress, 1991), 49.

249. Livingston, *Modern Christian Thought*, 111; cf. Clements, *Friedrich Schleiermacher, Pioneer of Modern Theology*, 49.
250. Cf. Clements, *Friedrich Schleiermacher, Pioneer of Modern Theology*, 36–40.
251. Another term used to label Hegel's system of thought is "transcendentalism" (cf. Winfried Corduan, "Transcendentalism: Hegel," in *Biblical Errancy*, 81; cf. also H. B. Acton, "Idealism," in the *Encyclopedia of Philosophy*, 4:115).
252. Ibid., 4:110–11.
253. Ibid., 4:111–12.
254. Emmanuel Kant, "Transcendental Dialectic," in *The Critique of Pure Reason*, 356 including n. 1.
255. Brown, *Philosophy and the Christian Faith*, 118.
256. Cf. Copleston, *History of Philosophy*, 7:1–31.
257. Ibid., 7:30.
258. R. R. Palmer and Joel Colton, *A History of the Modern World*, 5th ed. (New York: Alfred A. Knopf, 1978), 434; cf. Acton, "Idealism," 4:114.
259. Corduan, "Transcendentalism: Hegel," 81.
260. Brown, *Jesus in European Protestant Thought*, 83.
261. G. R. G. Mure, *An Introduction to Hegel* (Oxford: Clarendon, 1940), 52; cf. Georg Hegel, *The History of Philosophy*, trans. E. S. Haldane and Frances H. Simson (New York: Humanities, 1963), 2:1–210.
262. Richard Kroner, "Introduction," in Georg Hegel, *On Christianity: Early Theological Writings*, trans. T. M. Knox with Introduction and Fragments, trans. Richard Kroner (reprint, New York: Harper Torchbook, 1961), 4–5; cf. Georg W. F. Hegel, *Three Essays: The Tübingen Essay, Berne Fragments, The Life of Jesus*, ed. and trans. Peter Fuss and John Dobbins (Notre Dame: University of Notre Dame, 1984), 104.
263. Laurence Dickey, *Hegel Religion, Economics and the Politics of Spirit, 1770–1807* (Cambridge: Cambridge University, 1987), 159, 190; Peter Singer, *Hegel* (Oxford: Oxford University, 1983), 1–8.
264. Brown, *Philosophy and the Christian Faith*, 120.
265. Georg W. F. Hegel, *The Phenomenology of Mind*, trans. and ed. J. B. Baillie (New York: Harper & Row, 1967), 86.
266. Perhaps an oversimplification, this statement summarizes the essence of Hegel's philosophy (cf. Brown, *Philosophy and the Christian Faith*, 121).
267. Hegel used Kant's vocabulary in expressing the underlying principle of the Sermon on the Mount (cf. Matt. 7:12): "'To act only on principles that you can will to become universal laws among men, laws no less binding on you than on them'—this is the fundamental law of morality, the sum and substance of all moral legislation and the sacred books of all people" (Hegel, "The Life of Jesus," in *Three Essays*, 115–116 (cf. especially editor's note).
268. Cf. Brown, *Jesus in European Protestant Thought*, 85.
269. Hegel, *History of Philosophy*, 3:252–90.
270. Corduan, "Transcendentalism: Hegel," 82.
271. John. N. Findlay, *Hegel: A Reexamination* (London: George Allen & Unwin, 1958), 69–70.
272. Brown, *Philosophy and The Christian Faith*, 121.
273. Georg W. F. Hegel, *The Philosophy of History*, ed. Charles Hegel and trans. J. Sibree (New York: Dover, 1956), 104.
274. Van A. Harvey, "Bauer, Bruno," in *The Encyclopedia of Religion*, ed. Mircea Eliade (New York: Macmillan, 1987), 2:84.

275. Ludwig Feuerbach, *The Essence of Christianity*, ed. E. Graham Waring and F. W. Strothmann (New York: Continuum, 1989), 53–65.
276. Feuerbach, *Essence of Christianity*, 57–59.
277. Strimple, *Modern Search for the Real Jesus*, 30.
278. Ibid., 30; cf. Kümmel, *New Testament*, 120; Ben F. Meyer, *The Aims of Jesus* (London: SCM, 1979), 34.
279. Cf. Strauss, *Life of Jesus Critically Examined*, 57–59, 86–87.
280. Strauss, *Life of Jesus Critically Examined*, 75–86.
281. Horton Harris, *David Friedrich Strauss and His Theology* (Cambridge: University Press, 1973), 272.
282. Harris, *Tübingen School*, 1–262; Peter C. Hodgson, "General Introduction," in Ferdinand Christian Baur, *On the Writing of Church History*, ed. Peter C. Hodgson (New York: Oxford University, 1968), 1–40; Neill and Wright, *Interpretation of the New Testament 1861–1986*, 20–30.
283. Corduan, "Transcendentalism: Hegel," 94.
284. Cf. Hasel, *New Testament Theology*, 31–32.
285. Rudolf Bultmann, *The Theology of the New Testament*, trans. Kendrick Grobel (New York: Charles Scribner's Sons, 1952), 1:3.
286. W. Ward Gasque, "Nineteenth-Century Roots of Contemporary New Testament Criticism," in *Scripture, Tradition, and Interpretation*, ed. W. Ward Gasque and William Sanford LaSor (Grand Rapids: Eerdmans, 1978), 147.
287. Thomas Gilby and William J. Duggan, "Evolution," in *Encylopedic Dictionary of Religion*, ed. Paul Kevin Meagher et al. (Washington, D.C.: Corpus, 1979), 1:1276–78; cf. Theodore Roszak, "Evolution," in *The Encyclopedia of Religion*, 5:208–14.
288. Henry M. Morris, *The Long War Against God* (Grand Rapids: Baker, 1989), 52, cf. 207–18.
289. John C. Hutchison, "Darwin's Evolutionary Theory and 19th-Century Natural Theology," *BibSac* (July–September 1995): 334–354.
290. Morris, *Long War*, 218; cf. also Henry M. Morris, *The Troubled Waters of Evolution* (San Diego, Calif.: Creation Life, 1982), 51–76.
291. Hutchison, "Darwin's Evolutionary Theory," 334.
292. For an excellent critique of evolution, consult Phillip E. Johnson, *Darwin on Trial*, 2d ed. (Downers Grove, Ill.: InterVarsity, 1993).
293. Fred Willson, "Compromise and Consequences in the Genesis Account," *Impact* 247 (1994).
294. Gleason L. Archer, *A Survey of Old Testament Introduction*, rev. and expanded (Chicago: Moody, 1994), 149–50.
295. Proponents of the Wellhausen Hypothesis largely ignored William Henry Green's effective refutations of the theory in *Unity of the Book of Genesis* (New York: Scribner, 1895) and *Higher Criticism of the Pentateuch* (New York: Scribner, 1896).
296. Archer, *A Survey of Old Testament Introduction*, 89–171.
297. Kümmel, *Introduction to the New Testament*, 281–84.
298. Ibid., 325–41; cf. also Frederick C. Grant, "Preface," in Rudolf Bultmann and Karl Kundsin, *Form Criticism, Two Essays on New Testament Research*, trans. Frederick C. Grant (New York: Harper & Brothers, 1934), vii–viii.
299. Edgar V. McKnight, *What Is Form Criticism?* (Philadelphia: Fortress, 1969), esp. 16.
300. Rudolf Bultmann, "The New Testament and Mythology" in *Kerygma and Myth*, 1–44; cf. also Roger A. Johnson, ed., *Rudolf Bultmann, Interpreting Faith for the Modern Era* (Philadelphia: Fortress, 1991), 40–43.

301. Rudolf Bultmann, "The Meaning of the Christian Faith in Creation," in *Existence and Faith* (New York: Meridian Books, 1960), 209.
302. Rudolf Bultmann, *Jesus Christ and Mythology* (New York: Charles Scribner's Sons, 1958), 67.
303. For further information on the details of the Four-Source Hypothesis, consult Burnett H. Streeter, *The Four Gospels, A Study of Origins* (London: Macmillan, 1953), 223–272.
304. Farmer, *Synoptic Problem*, 178–90.
305. Thomas H. Huxley, *Science and Christian Tradition* (New York: D. Appleton, 1899), 273.
306. Burnett H. Streeter, "The Literary Evolution of the Gospels," in *Oxford Studies in the Synoptic Problem*, ed. W. Sanday (Oxford: At the Clarendon, 1911), 209–27; cf. Streeter, *Four Gospels*, 609; cf. 526, 499 n. 1.
307. Sanday, *Oxford Studies*, xvi.
308. Farmer, *Synoptic Problem*, 181.
309. Edwin A. Abbott, "Gospels" in *Encyclopaedia Brittannica* (reprint of 1879 article, Chicago: R. S. Peale, 1892), 10:801–2.
310. Farmer, *Synoptic Problem*, 25–26, 178–79.
311. Wilhelm Bousset, *Kyrios Christos,* trans. John E. Steely (Nashville: Abingdon, 1970).
312. Ernst Troeltsch, "Christianity and the History of Religion" and "The Dogmatics of the History-of-Religions School," in *Religion in History,* 77–108.
313. Troeltsch, "The Dogmatics of the History-of-Religions School," in *Religion in History,* 87.
314. Bultmann, *Existence and Faith*, 52–53.
315. Alasdair MacIntyre, "Existentialism," in *The Encyclopedia of Philosophy,* 3:147.
316. Brown, *Philosophy and the Christian Faith*, 181.
317. Walter Kaufmann, *Existentialism From Dostoevsky to Sartre* (Cleveland: World Publishing, 1956), 11.
318. Ibid., 11.
319. Frederick Copleston, *Contemporary Philosophy, Studies of Logical Positivism and Existentialism* (New York: Barnes and Noble, 1972), 127–28.
320. Ibid., 128.
321. MacQuarrie, "Existentialism by John MacQuarrie," in *The Encyclopedia of Religion,* 5:223–24.
322. Nocola Abbagnano, "Existentialism-Western Philosophical Schools and Doctrines," in *The New Enclyclopaedia Britannica*, ed. Philip W. Goetz et al. (Chicago: University of Chicago, 1989), 25:620–26.
323. Copleston (*Contemporary Philosophy,* 148–200) describes the views of each of these existentialists.
324. Sire, *Universe Next Door,* 109–10.
325. For overviews of Kierkegaard's life, consult H. V. Martin, *Kierkegaard, The Melancholy Dane* (New York: Philosophical Library, 1950); Walter Lowrie, *A Short Life of Kierkegaard* (Princeton, N.J.: Princeton University, 1970); Bruce H. Kirmmse, *Kierkegaard in Golden Age Denmark* (Bloomington and Indianapolis, Ind.: Indiana University, 1990).
326. Søren Kierkegaard, *Repetition* (Princeton, N.J.: Princeton University, 1941), 3–4.
327. Søren Kierkegaard, *Concluding Unscientific Postscript to Philosophical Fragments,* ed. and trans. Howard V. Hong and Edna H. Hong (Princeton, N.J.: Princeton University, 1992), 1:65.

328. Ibid., 1:310–11.
329. Ibid., 1:310.
330. Søren Kierkegaard, *The Journals of Søren Kierkegaard,* ed. and trans. Alexander Dru (New York: Harper & Brothers, 1959), 187 [emphasis original].
331. For more on Kierkegaard's view of Hegel, consult Niels Thulstrup, *Kierkegaard's Relation to Hegel,* trans. George L. Stengren (Princeton, N.J.: Princeton University, 1980).
332. Brown, *Philosophy and the Christian Faith,* 128.
333. Geisler, "Philosophical Presuppositions of Biblical Inerrancy," in *Inerrancy,* 327.
334. Kierkegaard, *Concluding Unscientific Postscript,* 1:203.
335. Kierkegaard, *Journals,* 184.
336. Kierkegaard, *Concluding Unscientific Postscript,* 1:204.
337. Ibid., 1:205.
338. Ibid.
339. Geisler, "Philosophical Presuppositions of Biblical Errancy," in *Inerrancy,* 327.
340. Kierkegaard, *Journals,* 185.
341. Kierkegaard, *Concluding Unscientific Postscript,* 23.
342. Kierkegaard, *Journals,* 109.
343. Paul R. Sponheim, *Kierkegaard on Christ and Christian Coherence* (New York: Harper & Row, 1968), 173–264.
344. Brown, *Philosophy and the Christian Faith,* 130.
345. Søren A. Kierkegaard, *Philosophical Fragments, Johannes Climacus,* ed. and trans. Howard V. Hong and Edna H. Hong (Princeton, N.J.: Princeton University, 1985), 104.
346. Kierkegaard, *Journals,* 190.
347. Brown, *Philosophy and the Christian Faith,* 131; cf. Kierkegaard, *Journals,* 97.
348. Kierkegaard, *Concluding Unscientific Postscript,* 1:30.
349. Geisler, "The Philosophical Presuppositions of Errancy," in *Inerrancy,* 328.
350. Kierkegaard, *Concluding Unscientific Postscript,* 24–25.
351. Geisler, "Philosophical Presuppositions of Biblical Inerrancy," in *Inerrancy,* 330.
352. The influence of Kierkegaard and existentialism on Bultmann (and also Otto) would be seen here in the description of God as "wholly other." For further information, see Rudolf Bultmann, "The Hidden and Revealed God," in *Existence and Faith,* 23–34.
353. Kierkegaard, *Philosophical Fragments,* 39.
354. Ibid.
355. Ibid., 46.
356. Ibid., 46–47, 55–71; cf. Sponheim, *Kierkegaard on Christ and Christian Coherence,* 180–264.
357. E. Herbert Nygren, "Existentialism: Kierkegaard," in *Biblical Errancy,* 124.
358. Karl Barth, *The Epistle to the Romans* (London: Oxford University, 1933), 38.
359. Ibid., 38.
360. Ibid., 99.
361. See D. A. Carson's article, "Hermeneutics: A Brief Assessment of Some Recent Trends," *Themelios* 5 (January 1980): 12; Anthony C. Thiselton, "The New Hermeneutic," in *New Testament Interpretation,* ed. I. H. Marshall (Grand Rapids: Eerdmans, 1977), 308–33.

362. For the presuppositional thinking and methodology of the New Hermeneutic, see Ernst Fuchs, *Studies of the Historical Jesus*, trans. Andrew Scobie (Naperville, Ill.: Alec R. Allenson, 1964), 32–47, 84–103, 191–206, 207–28. For the role of various New Testament scholars advocating this method, see James M. Robinson, "Hermeneutic Since Barth," in *New Frontiers in Theology*, vol. 2 of *The New Hermeneutic*, ed. James M. Robinson and John B. Cobb, Jr. (New York: Harper & Row, 1964), 1–77.

363. Herbert C. Wolf, *Kierkegaard and Bultmann: The Quest of the Historical Jesus* (Minneapolis, Minn.: Augsburg, 1965), 62.

364. Ibid., 61–84.

365. Rudolf Bultmann, "The Case for Demythologizing: A Reply," in *Kerygma and Myth*, II, trans. R. H. Fuller, ed. H. W. Bartsch (London: SPCK, 1962), 192.

366. Rudolf Bultmann, "Concerning the Hidden and the Revealed God," in *Existence and Faith*, 28.

367. Rudolf Bultmann, "Autobiographical Reflections," in *Existence and Faith*, 288.

368. Ibid.

369. Paul Tillich, *The Protestant Era* (Chicago: University of Chicago Press, 1948), 82.

370. Carl Raschke, in *A New Handbook of Christian Theology*, ed. Donald W. Musser and Joseph L. Price (Nashville, Tenn.: Abingdon, 1992).

371. Francis Schaeffer, *The God Who Is There*, vol. 1 of *The Francis Schaeffer Trilogy* (Wheaton, Ill.: Crossway, 1990), 7.

372. Ibid.

373. Contra Mark Noll; see his view of what the scandal is in "Scandal, a Forum on the Evangelical Mind," *Christianity Today* (August 14, 1995): 21–27.

CHAPTER THREE

Source Criticism: The Two-Source Theory

Thomas R. Edgar

BACKGROUND

To MOST EVANGELICAL Christians a theory of gospel origins seems unnecessary for the Gospels were written by eyewitnesses or by someone in direct contact with eyewitnesses. Although the books have a theological purpose, they are also historically accurate accounts of Jesus' ministry. However, many scholars, including some evangelicals, do not believe this. They consider the Synoptic Gospels to be literary creations of "editors" who copied and arranged material from written "sources," and they propose assorted theories about these "sources" or "origins" of the gospels. This field of study is called "Source Criticism."

The Synoptic Gospels—Matthew, Mark, and Luke—agree with one another to a great extent, and yet they also disagree. The "Synoptic Problem" is the name given to the dilemma of defining the literary relationship between them. Of the many theories attempting to explain that relationship, the "Two-Document Theory" has held the prominent position for years.[1] One scholar describes it as "an unquestioned part of an unquestioned tradition."[2]

Another theory holds that two gospels, Matthew and Luke, are the sources for Mark. To differentiate it from this "Two-Gospel Hypothesis," which likewise considers two documents as the sources of Mark, the Two-Document Theory now goes by the name of the "Two-Source Theory." It postulates that the gospel of Mark is one source for the other two Synoptic Gospels. The other "source," known as "Q," supplies all that is not in Mark but is common to Matthew and Luke. Most proponents would also stipulate that Matthew and Luke were independently copied from these sources.[3]

The Two-Source Theory has never gone unchallenged. For example, Meijboom argued in 1866 that the Two-Source Theory arose as a reaction to the events of the day rather than because of the validity of its supporting arguments.[4] Though the Two-Source Theory still predominates among

132

New Testament scholars, research into the Synoptic Problem seems to be in flux.[5]

RELEVANCE

The public often receives deductions based on the Two-Source Theory as though they were facts. Evangelical Christians in particular accept such conclusions without realizing their implications. After all, scholars present the Two-Source Theory as a hypothesis founded on a "scientific" approach to the Synoptic Problem. Many evangelical scholars promote the theory and thus influence Christians who have neither the time nor the technical knowledge to study the issue thoroughly. Is this merely an academic question, or does it impact the beliefs of the average Christian?

Ominous potential

The issue is not merely academic. Many evangelical scholars have accepted the Two-Source Theory, but this should not produce a complacent acceptance of it. A good number of these scholars have studied under nonevangelical teachers and have trustingly accepted their "scholarly opinion." The Two-Source Theory has very serious ramifications. Farmer has written an entire book discussing the pastoral relevance of this theory.[6] Others have also pointed out serious liabilities of the theory.

In 1958, Ludlum analyzed the Synoptic Problem very astutely.[7] His analysis in the two 1958 articles he wrote on the matter is well nigh irrefutable in demonstrating the literary independence of the three synoptics, though he allows for a modified theory of literary dependence in two 1959 articles that followed. His conclusions in the earlier articles call into question many of the "results" of gospel criticism in the last 100 years. He, as others, points out that the Two-Source Theory essentially reduces three gospels to only one gospel, Mark, and an imaginary document, "Q," which is whatever its proponents make it. The one gospel, Mark, does not have an infancy narrative and thus no virgin birth. Many exclude its last twelve verses, in which case neither does it have a resurrection account.

To make the situation even more precarious, many scholars regard the gospel of Mark as unreliable. Some vocal and publicly prominent scholars do not regard John Mark as the author of the book. They describe it as late without any connection to an apostolic figure.[8] For example, Stephen J. Patterson of Eden Theological Seminary asserts that Mark was a theologian, not a historian; therefore, the gospel of Mark "can be of little value in reconstructing the life of Jesus."[9] Then assuming the Two-Source Theory, he concludes that since Matthew and Luke used Mark as a source, modern Christians really "have no historical record of Jesus' life."[10] They only know that He came from Galilee and died in Jerusalem.

Patterson and Crossan, a Catholic scholar, feel that the three documents, "Q," the apocryphal Gospel of Thomas, and Mark, are the earliest verifiable Christian tradition. But Mark is later and merely the "product of the author's creativity and imaginative theological mind."[11] Accordingly, this leaves only the hypothetical, theologically questionable document "Q," which does not connect salvation with Jesus' death,[12] and an apocryphal gospel of Thomas, as the main Christian documents.[13] In any case, the Two-Source Theory undermines Matthew and Luke as independent accounts of the Lord's life and reduces them to mere copies of Mark and an imaginary document "Q" which, as it is proposed, is not necessarily orthodox.

Evangelicals in general seem unaware of the unsound assumptions underlying much of gospel criticism. The source critic's attempt to identify the oldest extant "source" is not merely an intellectual pursuit but is also an effort to define the most reliable gospel.[14] Thus, this is not an issue of mere chronology, but one that for most scholars establishes that the later documents, Matthew and Luke, are less reliable. Relying on this theory, an evangelical scholar named D. A. Carson remarks that Matthew used sources "and perhaps his own memory as well."[15] In effect, Carson reduces the gospel of an eyewitness to a mere copy from "sources."

The Two-Source Theory has ominous potential for undermining the trustworthiness of the Gospels. It has been and is being used for just that purpose.[16] This theory should not be naively accepted, but needs to be examined for its merits and demerits. One of its demerits is the way it undermines the gospel accounts.

Scholarly Impact

The Two-Source Theory also has immense significance for gospel studies, first, because it concerns the Synoptic Gospels. Although textual criticism (the study of manuscripts to determine the best text) may seem to be a purely objective study, to a great extent much of its work has built on the Two-Source Theory.[17] The theory is inherently interrelated with Form Criticism and with one of the most prevalent areas in current gospel research, Redaction Criticism. Few scholars study, teach, or write about the Gospels apart from the assumptions of the Two-Source Theory. Redaction critical studies have supported and enhanced this theory, which in turn has done the same for Redaction Criticism.[18] The discarding of this theory would reveal that most modern scholarly work on the Gospels as belonging to the category of unsupported speculations. Consequently, proponents of the theory will not relinquish it without a battle.

ARGUMENTS FOR THE TWO-SOURCE THEORY

Underlying assumptions

Literary dependence. The presupposition of literary dependence among the Synoptic Gospels is foundational to the Two-Source Theory, as it is to most gospel criticism. Although "literary dependence" could refer to any use of literary sources by some New Testament authors,[19] it has a very specific meaning in gospel studies. It indicates that one gospel author used one of the other gospels as a source; that is, he copied extensive material from a fellow gospel-writer. The basic argument for this, other than the usual presuppositions involved in source criticism, is the allegedly close similarities between the Gospels. This includes content, order of material, and specific wording. Luke 1:1–4 is sometimes used as the centerpiece of biblical evidence that Luke used written sources, specifically Mark's gospel. Most scholars assume literary dependence as an accepted, self-evident fact.[20] Only a few question the validity of that presupposition.[21]

Accepted facts? General agreement prevails regarding the arguments for the Two-Source Theory and the relationships between the Synoptic Gospels.[22] Most agree with Streeter's description of the relationships, which in summary form states the following: (1) Matthew reproduces 90 percent of the subject matter of Mark in language very identical to that of Mark; Luke does the same for rather more than half of Mark; (2) the majority of the words used by Mark are reproduced by Matthew and Luke, alternately or together; (3) the relative order of incidents and sections in Mark finds general support in Matthew and Luke; where either deserts Mark, the other usually supports him; in addition, "Matthew and Luke have in common material, which is not found in Mark, amounting to about 200 verses, mostly discourse."[23]

These alleged facts give rise to the Synoptic Problem, and at the same time are foundational to the Two-Source Theory. If these observations are not true, the very basis for the theory disintegrates. Most of the other theories—including the Two-Gospel Hypothesis—depend on the same observations. In departing from the majority, however, some gospel critics have questioned the accuracy of this description.[24] Based on Streeter's or similar statistics, the Two-Source Theory rests on the following arguments.

Customary arguments

The argument from order. For many, the argument from order is foundational. It is the main argument. It alleges that the common order of events in the Synoptic Gospels is Mark's order.[25] This argument basically conforms to Streeter's third point, which says that the order of incidents in Mark is clearly the more original, for wherever Matthew departs from Mark's order Luke supports Mark, and whenever Luke departs from Mark, Matthew agrees with Mark.[26] This argument implicitly includes Lachmann's observation that the diversity in order is minimal, if Mark is compared with each of the other synoptics separately.[27]

The argument from brevity. Many advocates for the Two-Source Theory consider the argument from brevity one of the theory's most important arguments. They declare the shortest gospel to be the earliest, for they cannot conceive that a writer copying from Matthew or Luke would leave anything out.[28]

The primitive or original nature of Mark. Two-source theorists consider Mark's style of writing—and some of them, his theology also—to be more primitive or original than that of Matthew and Luke, thus marking it as the earliest.[29] They see Mark's style as vivid and living in contrast to the way the other two synoptists write.

The argument from psychological reflection. Stoldt accurately observes, "This is the proof which the founders of the Markan hypothesis use the most and talk about the least,"[30] when referring to the argument he calls "psychological reflection." This argument particularly interrelates with the practice of Redaction Criticism with its focus on an accumulation of details such as the following. The critic studies a parallel between Mark and either Matthew or Luke. From differences in literary details, he deduces which author copied from the other and determines why and how the copier changed the earlier gospel. The criteria used stem from what seems most reasonable to the critic, that is, from "psychological reflection."

For example, McKnight studies Mark 14:3, where Mark uses two genitive absolutes and Matthew in the parallel passage uses only one. He then asserts, "It is more likely that Matthew 'corrected' Mark than that Mark took a perfectly normal expression and made it irregular."[31] They often state their opinions in terms such as Matthew or Luke "improves" Mark, or Matthew makes clumsy "alterations" of Mark, correcting or "corrupting the sense."[32] According to this argument, the literary details in the Synoptic Gospels are more easily explainable if Matthew (and Luke) copied Mark than the other way around.[33] This procedure may have different titles, such as linguistic, theological, or redactional phenomena,[34] but it is essentially the same argument. For many, this is the main argument for the Two-Source Theory.[35]

Arguments for "Q." All the arguments for Markan priority also serve to support the "Q" hypothesis. However, two main arguments are used in proving the existence and use of Q by Matthew and Luke. These are the occurrence of "doublets" and the existence of non-Markan "agreements" of Matthew and Luke.[36]

The places where Matthew and Luke have non-Markan material in common supposedly require a common source from which the two authors copied independently. Two-Source advocates call this hypothetical source Q.[37] A doublet is an occurrence in either Matthew or Luke of what appear to be duplicate incidents, only one of which appears in Mark.[38] Presumably the author of the gospel in question would not duplicate on his own but copied the event once from Mark and then from another written source, presumably Q.

All these arguments assume that whoever wrote Matthew and Luke were merely copyists of earlier written materials or "sources."

ANALYSIS OF THE TWO-SOURCE THEORY

Suspect presuppositions

What constitutes evidence? Evidence for the priority of writing and for possible sources of the Synoptic Gospels conceivably could come from several areas. Although there is some patristic testimony on this issue, two-source theorists have largely ignored or used that testimony only selectively. Biblical evidence could be helpful; however, only Luke 1:1–4 may touch on this issue (see chapter 7 of this volume for a full discussion of Luke 1:1–4). The Synoptic Problem concerns the relationships between the Synoptic Gospels. Not only does the "problem" arise from comparing the synoptics themselves, but the comparisons have provided statistics and "evidence" for proposed solutions. Therefore, the most significant question in this discussion is precisely what is to be compared and how that comparison is to be implemented.

This perhaps would seem to be obvious, but there are a number of ways to manipulate comparisons and statistics. Whether past comparisons and "statistics" are valid has received only cursory consideration from most scholars. They seldom mention methodology, and then only in reference to very general categories. For instance, when a scholar says that Matthew contains "the substance of more than 600 verses of Mark. . . . Only 40 verses of Mark's material is missing from him,"[39] what do these vague generalities mean in precise terms?

Acceptance of various synopses should not be automatic, for they are not necessarily unbiased. Streeter feels that Augustine would have held the Two-Source Theory if he had possessed the same synopsis as Streeter, namely, Rushbrooke's *Synopticon*. Streeter recommended this work to a student as providing evidence of Markan priority.[40] Hawkins' highly lauded *Horae Synopticae* used Rushbrooke's *Synopticon* and Tischendorf's *Synopsis Evangelica*.[41] Butler, who argued against the Two-Source Theory, used Huck's synopsis.[42] Ludlum, after making a careful comparison of the synoptics, referred to the usual assertions of 90 percent agreement between Matthew and Mark as "fantastic."[43] My own study agrees with Ludlum's contention about these agreements.[44]

Several common synopses are full of inconsistencies because they follow no standards. For example, Aland parallels Matthew 1:18–25 with Luke 2:1–7 and Matthew 2:1–12 with Luke 2:8–20, but Burton and Goodspeed, Huck, and Robertson do not see these passages as parallel.[45] Synopses commonly sandwich verses from a different passage into the middle of another passage on a different subject in order to achieve similarities in wording. They regard similar sayings of Jesus given in different contexts as the same, despite the different context. They ignore the probability that Jesus must have said the same things repeatedly, for they presuppose that the accounts are not historically accurate. They assume instead that the saying was merely a "scrap" of tradition that each gospel author acquired and placed wherever he desired. In most synopses it is usually not clear what are exact parallels versus general parallels. Few evangelicals would agree with many of the alleged parallels, yet most of them accept the conclusions drawn from them without questioning.

Farmer demonstrates that presuppositions influenced the arrangement of Rushbrooke's *Synopticon,* the work which influenced Streeter so much.[46] Although Aland, Burton, and Goodspeed, as well as Lietzmann—in describing Huck's synopsis—claim that their synopses have no bias toward any theory,[47] some do not accept the possibility of an impartial synopsis. Dungan believes that all synopses of necessity must be biased.[48] An obvious fact is that all synopses do not agree. Dungan compares Huck's synopsis and its 259 pericopes with Aland's, which has 304, and concludes that around 110 (roughly 33 percent) are different. Solages' synopsis, allegedly scientific and unbiased, claims to establish systematically the Two-Source Theory.[49] However, it divides the texts into two general categories: "double or triple Marcan tradition," which includes Mark, and "double Xan tradition," which excludes Mark. The index verifies that the entire synopsis is structured around the presence or absence of Mark, and this indicates that it is hardly an unbiased approach.[50] Ludlum's synopsis regarding the relationship of the synoptics led him to statistics radically different from those usually furnished.[51]

Different methods of comparing the gospels produce different statistics. A difference of opinion has arisen even over whether to compare all three synoptics together or only one at a time with Mark.[52] No statistics describing the relationship between the synoptics can be reliable until someone establishes an accurate standard of comparison. It is disconcerting that so many evangelical scholars have accepted descriptions of these relationships, provided by liberal scholars and detrimental to orthodox theology, without questioning the basis on which they derived the statistics.

Is it possible to construct a synopsis apart from bias? Certainly! The fact that many are biased does not prove that an unbiased synopsis is impossible or even improbable. Hypothetically, before theories of synoptic origins emerged, unbiased comparisons had to exist to facilitate development of a theory. It is possible to compare any three items, including literary works, without prejudice, especially writings purporting to discuss the same events. The problem does not arise from the difficulty in comparing the three Synoptic Gospels. Rather, it stems from the underlying presuppositions regarding how the Gospels came into existence.

The three gospels purport to be actual historical accounts of Jesus Christ. That is the only scientific and objective way to compare them. Whether or not an analyst believes them to be actual historical accounts, an objective scholar must compare them in accordance with what they purport to be. To analyze and compare them on the basis of a critic's presuppositions of what is true and false is not objective or "scientific." That is not an analysis of the documents themselves but of a reconstruction of them based on the critic's opinions. Any objective analysis takes into account the literary integrity of the passages, the context, and the probability of many similar events and sayings in Jesus' ministry, and excludes all theories of sources or literary dependence. Logically, no theories about the relationship of the synoptics, including literary dependence among them, can legitimately arise until a valid comparison furnishes the necessary evidence.

Linnemann used Aland's *Synopsis* but derived statistical relationships entirely different from many source critics who used the same or a similar synopsis.[53] The precision of her comparisons in contrast to the generalities followed by others is partially responsible for the differences, but her work highlights another problem, namely, the absence of any standard by which to classify something as an agreement. The uninitiated assume that, as in most professions, the term "agreement" refers to some exact or very close agreement, but in the field of gospel comparisons, scholars have used it to describe similarities of a most general nature as well as precise agreements. In some cases, the agreement is very obscure. To correct this inaccuracy, the term "agreement" should refer only to exact agreement since, for the purposes of comparison, anything else is actually a "difference," and should be considered as such in compiling statistics.

Only when the "comparison" comes from an unbiased and accurate synopsis and refers to precise agreements as distinguished from disagreements, can one resolve any aspect of the Synoptic Problem, including whether they did indeed depend on one another in a literary way.

Literary dependence dubious. Like other theories, the Two-Source Theory depends on literary dependence among the synoptics as its starting point. Yet the probability of literary dependence is impossible to establish without a precise comparison of the three books. One scholar says that virtually every word in Mark is in Matthew and Luke.[54] What does this mean? Does he mean merely the vocabulary form, regardless of differences such as tense and case? If so, many of the words are actually different. If he means precisely the same forms—which is the only way to support literary dependence—his statement does not agree with precise comparisons of the gospels.

Goulder asserts that on a conservative count 606 out of Mark's 661 verses have parallels in Matthew.[55] But that has little significance, for Goulder's discussion following his statistics shows that he regards only about 38 percent of Mark as agreeing with Matthew in form and sequence.[56] Wenham's calculations of agreements fall far below the customary figures.[57] So do the calculations of others.

Ludlum, who allows for a degree of literary interdependence, determined that Matthew and Mark have exact agreement of one or more words in 1,887 places, for a 2.43-word average length of exact agreement. Only a little over 2 percent (38) of these places agree for ten or more words in succession.[58] He also shows that Old Testament scholars insisted that the two oldest Greek texts of the book of Judges were not literarily dependent, despite the fact that they agree twice as many times in Greek as the synoptics.

A synopsis derived by taking the Gospels as they are, apart from any presuppositions, reveals that Matthew and Mark have 68 percent of their total subject matter in common, and Luke and Mark have 41 percent.[59] However, by analyzing exact agreements rather than vague generalities, one learns that words which agree in Matthew and Mark are only 17 percent of the total, in Mark and Luke only 8 percent, and in Matthew and Luke only 6 percent. The average number of words agreeing in form and order is less than five words for any of the gospels. Of the parallel passages in Matthew and Mark, 46 percent are so diverse that they preclude either literary dependence between the two or reliance upon a common written source. Only 20 percent of the parallels have enough similarity to be considered as possible evidence for dependence. Similar results apply to comparisons of all three synoptics with one another.[60]

As Ludlum, this writer obtained the above results by first creating a synopsis based on the Synoptic Gospels as they stand, apart from any synoptic theories, and then making precise comparisons. Linnemann made her precise study of the synoptics using a standard critical synopsis and arrived at similar conclusions, in other words, that not enough agreement exists to warrant the presupposition of literary dependence. She "diligently performed the necessary drudgery."[61] As a result, she concluded that 44.54 percent of the words in Matthew do not appear in Mark and that, setting aside narratives that would be expected to follow a similar sequence—such as the Crucifixion and Resurrection—not even one-half of the sections in Mark follow the sequence of the others. She also found that a word count shows 53.51 percent of Mark is not parallel to Matthew and 63.83 percent is not parallel to Luke.[62]

Consequently, whether using a critical synopsis or one compiled more objectively, an analyst will discover that a *precise* comparison reflects statistics quite different from those based on impressions or generalities. Linnemann used a standard critical synopsis, Ludlum used a synopsis constructed by comparing the gospels in accordance with what they claim to be, and both of these scholars derived statistics radically different from those asserted by scholars who advocate literary dependence. This writer's precise study verifies the findings of Linnemann and Ludlum.[63] Thus, one of the major weaknesses of the Two-Source Theory, as well as most critical theories, is the inaccurate and misleading information that is its basis. Precise comparisons do not support literary dependence.

The gospel writers quote the Old Testament, but this is comparable to the modern practice of quoting another's work and is different from copying a large part of material, utilizing the entire framework of someone else's work, and presenting it as one's own. Though advocates of literary dependence sometimes cite Luke 1:1–4 as evidence of literary sources behind the gospels,[64] it is neither evident that Luke used the "accounts" he mentions nor were they necessarily written.[65]

Hence, the two foundations of the Two–Source Theory crumble—the alleged agreements among the synoptics, which created the Synoptic Problem in the first place, and the assumption of literary dependence. Evidence of widespread agreements on which the theory depends is inaccurate. Accordingly, no matter how credible the arguments to support the theory may seem, they are invalid because of the questionable assumptions on which the theory rests. It now remains to examine the theory's specific arguments.

Invalid Arguments

The argument from order. The argument from order holds that the relative sequence of incidents and sections in Mark finds general support in Matthew and Luke, thus making Mark the earliest gospel. How reliable is the argument from order in proving Markan priority? Proponents consider this argument fundamental, "the one solid contribution" of nineteenth century scholarship, "the foundation," the "central fact" of "decisive importance" for the theory of Markan priority.[66]

Upon first hearing the "argument from order," this writer's reaction was, "The argument does not at all prove Markan priority. In fact, it can just as easily prove the exact opposite." Butler concurs, describing it as "obviously false" and due to "a schoolboyish error of elementary reasoning at the very base of the Two-Document hypothesis as commonly proposed for our acceptance."[67] If the argument could prove anything—and obviously it cannot if one maintains literary independence—it would more naturally prove that Mark copied from the other two synoptics where they agree, thereby arguing for Mark's posteriority rather than priority and eliminating any need to postulate a hypothetical document such as Q.

A study of the Synoptic Problem reveals that "1) An argument based on the order of events in the three Synoptic Gospels can prove nothing regarding the priority of the individual gospels, and 2) The statement of relationships as usually given does not appear to be accurate."[68] More and more gospel critics are recognizing that the argument from order can just as easily prove the exact opposite of Markan priority.[69] The "Lachmann fallacy" is the name given to the error of presupposing it can prove a specific order of writing. Yet, apparently because of a statement by Butler, those advocates for the Two-Source Theory who admit that the argument from order cannot prove the priority of either Matthew or Mark, still insist that it does prove Mark to be the connecting link between the other two.[70] In addition, both Butler and Farmer hold the opinion that the usual inferences drawn from the "argument from order" would be valid if one were to recognize an "Ur-gospel."[71] A response to the argument from order is as follows.

No logical correlation exists between the order of events in a writing and the time of its writing or copying relative to other documents. Anyone can write or copy and alter the order of events in any way he chooses, whether he writes first or last. For example, three writers separated by ten-year intervals could make independent use of an account of events leading up to and during the battle of Gettysburg. They all follow the same general order of events, but one or two add additional material. Nothing precludes the first writer from adding more material from other sources and modifying the order of events nor the last or the middle writer from making the least modification of the common source. No logical relationship exists between the priority of writing and the amount of modification or order of events. Ludlum has given a thorough demonstration of this argument's lack of relevance to the sequence of the Synoptic Gospels, and concluded, "It is logically impossible to mount any argument for the priority of *Matthew* or *Mark* (or, for that matter, of *Luke*) on any kind or combination of kinds of agreement or disagreement in matters of arrangement of materials."[72]

Neither does the existence of an "Ur-gospel" make the argument from order valid. The original account from which three writers drew in the

Gettysburg illustration is in effect an Ur-gospel. As explained, the argument from order offers no logical means for discerning priority of writing, either with or without sources. For the same reason, it offers no logical basis to conclude that Mark is a connecting link between the other two gospels.

Wenham, who does not feel that the argument from order can establish the priority of any of the synoptics, thinks that the amount of agreement in order does argue for some kind of literary interdependence.[73] However, this is logical only if one assumes, as Wenham apparently does, that the Synoptic Gospels are merely the work of later editors who collected fragments of tradition and placed and arranged them in a literary rather than a historical framework. Only then can their agreement in order furnish any evidence of dependence, since historical sequence in that case cannot explain their agreement. On the other hand, since they are describing historical events, the fact that the events actually occurred in that order explains the agreement in order between these gospels.

Disbelief in the historicity of the Gospels is foundational to using the argument from order to establish literary dependence. For example, Conzelmann and Lindemann state, "One might try to explain the agreements in the order of presentation of the events by arguing for the rendering of historical incidents, but that would make the divergences inexplicable."[74] This is typical of those who discount the historical order of the events as an explanation for agreement in order, and it is also fallacious reasoning. Any three people describing a series of events may agree completely regarding sequence or for some reason may diverge from one another in their descriptions. The Synoptic Gospels are in general chronological order as a comparison of their contents demonstrates. Yet, as most recognize, they also have divergences in order. The divergences argue against literary dependence or reliance on a common written source, but agreement is explicable, for the three followed a general outline of gospel tradition based on the actual chronology of events.

Any three accounts of the same short period will normally exhibit the same patterns of order as the three Synoptic Gospels. All will agree on certain events considered essential to the narrative. Unless there is collusion, two will be longer than the other. All three will convey the essential material, but the shortest will have material basic to all three. The other two will usually have additional material, some of which is common to both and some unique to each. Mark's gospel fits the normal pattern for the shortest account.[75] This represents nothing unusual or significant, nor does it demonstrate anything regarding priority or relative importance. Some might think that the selection by all three authors of these events out of the many that Jesus performed must show dependence;[76] however, that is not necessarily so. Certainly a core of tradition existed and included certain impressive events, selected and passed on by eyewitnesses and considered basic by the three synoptic writers. Such would be true whether the gospel authors were eyewitnesses, in contact with eyewitnesses, or, as some believe, merely editors of the oral and written tradition they received.

Not only are statistics supporting the argument from order inaccurate, but usually proponents do not compare all three synoptics. They compare Matthew and Luke with Mark, but not with each other. If all three are not compared, why not compare Mark with Matthew and Luke with Matthew? A comparison of the three gospels reveals that the same general description applies to Luke as to Mark; the other two gospels follow the order of Luke, and when one departs from the Lucan order, the other supports Luke. Mark and Luke are virtually agreed in their order. They disagree in only two places where they record the order of almost simultaneous events differently. Thus, the reason Matthew and Luke do not agree together in order against Mark is because they have almost no opportunity to do so. Only Matthew differs significantly from the other two.[77]

An accurate comparison between the synoptics by merely comparing the other two with Mark, a practice that is "unscientific" and biased at the start, is impossible. Thus, the argument from order is both logically invalid as an argument to prove priority or literary dependence and is based on inaccurate statistics. It can prove nothing regarding the validity of the Two-Source Theory. If the Gospels are historically accurate, all the agreements in order are easily traceable to the historical order of events. That rules out the necessity for any kind of literary dependence, but even assuming literary dependence, the argument from order can prove nothing regarding priority of writing.

The argument from brevity. Mark is the earliest gospel, for it is the shortest. Mark, as the shortest of the synoptics, could not have copied Matthew or Luke, for Mark would surely not omit any material from those gospels. Therefore, the other two must have copied Mark. This was a major argument in the last century and still exists today.[78] However, it does not stand up under scrutiny. It assumes not only literary dependence, but also that only two possibilities of dependence exist—either Mark copied the other two or they copied Mark. The argument from brevity can arise from more than one perspective. Meijboom, writing in 1866, stated that it assumes "the premise that the purpose of the evangelists was to preserve as many reports as possible about Jesus' life and work."[79] Peabody describes modern critics thus:

> It is difficult for some critics approaching these texts to understand why this or that passage in Gospel A, being perceived as very valuable by the critic examining the text of the gospels, could possibly have been omitted by evangelist B, if that passage had appeared in his source.[80]

Farmer states that the argument based on brevity "is intellectually satisfying for many scholars."[81] The concept that the gospel authors were trying to preserve as much material as possible is not only logically improbable, but expressly denied by John, who states that he selected only some of many possibilities in order to convince the readers that Jesus was the Christ (John 20:31). Luke also states that he was selective and gathered his material to give assurance to Theophilus of what Theophilus already knew (Luke 1:1–4). It is commonly recognized that each author had a purpose for writing and was not merely collecting material or writing a biography. Thus, as Meijboom shows, Mark's purpose could easily be served by selecting fewer incidents than the other gospel authors and at the same time giving a more detailed account of many of those same incidents.[82]

The argument from brevity runs into another obstacle: where Mark records an incident, he is often longer and gives more detail than the other two gospels. Thus the argument from brevity does not apply to individual incidents and can only apply to the overall length and the number of incidents in Mark.[83]

In any three descriptions of the same events, one will usually be shorter. This does not mean it was written earlier.[84] It is no more improbable for Mark to leave out some material than for Matthew and Luke to add more material to what they allegedly found in Mark. Is every textbook on theology of the same length? If not, are the shorter ones always earlier? Is it highly unlikely that an author would leave out important information that he found in earlier textbooks, and thus the longer must have come later? Obviously not! The fact that Mark does not explicitly state a purpose for his gospel does not mean that he had none. Thus, he could well have served his purpose by writing a shorter gospel.

The argument from brevity cannot exist apart from the assumption of literary dependence. However, literary dependence is itself highly improbable. No matter how one views the Gospels, the length of a document has no logical correlation with the priority of writing or with whether the writers depended on one another.

The primitive nature of Mark. The argument that a comparison of someone's writing style with other writings can demonstrate priority is obviously unscientific. Why should an earlier writer be more "primitive" than a later one? As Stoldt says, "There is simply no law in literary or intellectual history that vividness of presentation is a measure of the sequence in which literary accounts originated."[85] After showing how authors who were not present for a historical event produced some of the most vivid descriptions of that event, Stoldt states again, "Vividness of narrative presentation is not a question of temporal proximity to the experienced object but is exclusively a matter of literary skill."[86] Style results from the personality and ability of the writer or the purpose of his writing.

The stylistic differences in question are not comparable to that between classical and modern writers. The gospel writers belonged to the same cultural, geographical, and temporal period. Nothing precludes a more polished and less vivid writer from writing an account or making a copy before a less polished and more vivid writer. The differences do not correlate with times of writing. Those using this argument refer to Mark as a "living rhapsodist," as breathing "the smell of Palestine's earth," and to Matthew and Luke as "scanty, mangled and distorted."[87] But are such comments realistic? Differences in the styles of the synoptics are not that noticeable and certainly not significant enough to justify such elaborate distinctions.

Is Mark's theology more primitive? No! The level of theology varies with the individual writer, not with the order of writing. A contemporary conservative Christian may write a "primitive" theology that is closer to that of the Bible than a liberal nineteenth-century scholar. That does not make his writing earlier than that of the scholar from the last century. The nature of a writing's theology does not correlate with the date of that writing.

Also, how does one differentiate between "primitive" theology and later theology? How does one recognize what is primitive? The argument assumes that the theology in the Synoptic Gospels is not consistent. It presupposes a long period between the events and the writing of the Gospels, allowing for "improvements" in theology. This allowed the church (namely, the later gospels) to correct the primitive theology of the earlier Christians (namely, Mark) to make it fit their ideas. The entire rationale rejects the Gospels as historically and theologically accurate.[88]

Psychological reflection. The argument from psychological reflection is decisive for many. It goes by many titles and often entails Redaction Criticism. The critic or commentator looks at a statement of Matthew, Luke, or Mark, written nineteen hundred years ago in a language that is not the critic's first language. He has never lived in that culture and knows the specific situation only through the documents in front of him. He is only indirectly familiar with the linguistic idioms and has never met the authors of the Synoptic Gospels. He knows little or nothing about their personalities or tendencies other than what these three books reveal. He compares two gospel statements and solely on the basis of what he thinks reasonable not only decides who copied from whom, but also how and why that author changed what he saw in the document from which he allegedly copied. Stoldt's description of this as "psychological reflection"[89] is quite *apropos,* for in the majority of instances the critic has no possible way to obtain such information except through psychological reflection, no matter how much he may argue for an objective basis.

For example, the modern critic in his present frame of reference decides he cannot understand why Mark would change Matthew's wording. On the other hand, he is under the impression that he can see why Matthew would change what Mark wrote. The critic concludes that it is obvious that Matthew did what he (the critic) would have done. The procedure not only lacks humility, but also is hardly objective scholarship. In most instances, it derives from circular reasoning.

Notice the reason one critic gives to explain why Matthew and Luke, in contrast to Mark, do not call Jesus a carpenter. Matthew and Luke changed this term that was used by Mark, for carpentry was not respectable enough for Jesus, and being the son of a carpenter was "more appropriate to the messianic calling of Jesus."[90] This remarkable "insight" assumes Markan priority. Neirynck states, referring to Matthew 4:24b–25, "By omitting its temporal connection . . . and its local setting . . . , this little story of Mk. 1:32, 34 can be used by Matthew in the summary before the Sermon on the Mount, in keeping with the Marcan order."[91]

Using this method, McKnight describes Mark 7:31 as giving a strange route for Jesus, and Matthew 15:29 as easier to understand. McKnight then concludes, "It is more likely that Mark gave rise to Matthew's clarification than for Mark to take this perfectly sensible statement of Matthew and make it obscure."[92] Thus, McKnight concludes that Mark is probably prior. However, Mark's statement is perfectly clear and easy to understand. A lack of clarity is not really the problem that McKnight has with this passage. He does not think that the route as Mark states it is "sensible." McKnight's problem with Mark is not lack of clarity; rather, he does not think Mark's description makes sense. Is Mark true or not? If Mark is accurate, then Jesus took the route Mark described.

The fact that Mark's description does not make sense to McKnight or some other modern scholars is irrelevant. How does a twentieth-century person know that it did not make sense at the time or what reasons may have prompted Jesus to take this route? Were they present and, therefore, cognizant of the issues affecting the choice of a route so that they could determine that it did not make sense? Assuming that Mark is accurate, then Matthew, if he were copying Mark, would agree and hardly feel a necessity to clarify a clear statement. Neither would Mark, if he were copying Matthew, be making Matthew's statement "obscure" if he accurately and clearly filled in details. The issue here, as in most of these instances, is whether we believe the Gospels are accurate. If we do, McKnight's argument does not hold up. Since this type of argument often views one of the Gospels as corrected or improved by the other, it assumes a low view of inspiration of the source-gospel solely on the basis of the critic's imagination.

However, there is an overlooked but very basic issue involved in McKnight's comparison. When comparing the supposedly parallel passages, one finds that they are quite different. Synopses often treat the passages involved, Matthew 15:29–31 and Mark 7:31–37, as parallel, but hardly one word in Matthew's account is the same as in Mark's. Matthew gives a general summary of an entire phase of Jesus' ministry, but Mark refers to a specific healing. The context easily explains the difference that McKnight notes. Further, McKnight does not mention a textual variant that could alleviate the "strangeness" of Mark's account. Of greater significance, however, is the total lack of detailed agreement, which shows that Matthew or Mark could hardly be dependent on the other.

The psychological-reflection argument normally seeks to explain *differences* between the synoptics, differences that make a literary-dependence theory difficult. Thus, most of the places where it is used actually argue against literary dependence rather than for Markan priority or literary dependence.

The entire process is circular reasoning. It uses the differences that actually show nondependence to argue for Markan priority by assuming literary dependence regardless of the differences. Then after "reflection," the critic asserts that Matthew's alleged change of Mark is evidence that Matthew did, in fact, change Mark. The critic uses the assumption of literary dependence to explain a difference that actually refutes literary dependence.

Many call this argument the main one for Markan priority.[93] However, its logic is muddled. The argument assumes literary dependence and usually also assumes that Matthew and Luke changed Mark. The argument is supposed to prove both literary dependence and Markan priority, but it assumes its conclusion. What seems reasonable to the critic is, at best, an opinion and can hardly be evidence that it actually happened that way. That type of argument can only be confirmatory. Once one establishes the Markan-priority hypothesis on objective grounds, then this type of argument could be used to show how the details of the Synoptic Gospels are explicable in light of that hypothesis. However, a hypothesis should be derived from the best explanation of available *facts* (evidence). These "redaction-critical, psychological-reflection" arguments can, at most, only confirm that the details of the Synoptics can be explained by the hypothesis. They are not *proof* of the hypothesis. They can have no logical force in deriving a hypothesis, for they *assume* the basic elements of what they set out to prove.

Lack of evidence for Q

Evidence of "agreements" insufficient. The real reason for postulating a Q document is that the Two-Source Theory needs it.[94] The material Matthew and Luke have in common that is not in Mark is assumed to require a source from which they could get that material. So the existence of Q rests on the assumptions of literary dependence and Markan priority. If either assumption is invalid, the Q theory falls. It rests on the further assumption that Matthew and Luke copied independently from Mark, for their copying from one another would explain the material common to the two.

The existence of Q also assumes that Matthew and Luke could not have obtained their information from eyewitnesses, nor could they have been eyewitnesses since frequent agreement of eyewitness testimony is not unusual. Furthermore, it must assume that these gospels are not accurate descriptions of historical events, since whether eyewitness testimony or tradition, accurate histories would agree regarding many incidents and sayings of Jesus, thus requiring no document to explain agreements.

Q has never been seen nor is there any evidence that such a document ever existed. Without all the above assumptions, there is neither need nor place for it. Finding the non-Markan passages where Matthew and Luke agree should be simple, but two-source advocates have come to little agreement regarding Q. Petrie refers to Q as follows: "Indeed the variety of conclusion that is reached concerning the hypothetical 'Q' is bewildering in its exasperating contradictoriness."[95] He lists a long series of contradictory statements by Q proponents as to the nature and contents of Q. After observing, "It were surely not unreasonable to expect some indications of a measure of unanimity in the passages claimed for 'Q.' But the expectation is overwhelmingly discouraged," Petrie then describes how in a study of seventeen different reconstructions of Q, he found that not one verse from Matthew is common to all seventeen.[96]

No uniformity of opinion has prevailed, for the existence and content of Q is entirely hypothetical. Rosche refers to 217 verses that one scholar assigns to Q. After discounting verses that may have a parallel in Mark, he found only seventy-eight verses with a verbal correspondence of 54 percent or more, and that the nature of this correspondence does not require a written document to explain it.[97]

McKnight calls Hawkins' work the "classic defense" of the Q hypothesis.[98] However, Hawkins' work does not stand up to close scrutiny, in spite of all the glowing comments by scholars willing to use it but not careful enough to verify his arguments. Hawkins stated that he intended to give "every exclusively Matthaeo-Lucan parallel, however unlikely some of them may be to have had a common written origin."[99] Hawkins regarded eighty-four passages as evidence for Q, of which fifty-four were very probable, twenty-two had a considerable amount of probability, and eight were slightly probable.[100] None of the eight alleged agreements are valid. Of the twenty-two supposedly probable agreements, twenty-one are not parallel passages, and the remaining parallel is the beatitudes with only a very slight literary similarity between the two accounts. Of the fifty-four "most probable," thirty-three are definitely not parallel. Of the remaining twenty-one, most are either questionable as to their non-Markan character or too dissimilar to furnish evidence for a common source. Only six passages out of Hawkins' eighty-four are actually non-Markan agreements, with enough similarity to provide possible evidence for a common written source. Of these, four are common, short axiomatic sayings easily explainable by other theories of transmission.[101]

Hence most of Hawkins' evidence in reality favors no common written source. If one maintains the literary integrity of the passages, a very limited amount of material consists of non-Markan parallels between Matthew and Luke. Of a total of seven parallels, three are not sayings, but are the genealogies, the healing of the centurion's son, and the cleansing of the temple. The remainder are the Sermon on the Mount, John the Baptist's question, principles of discipleship, and the thanksgiving for the Father's revelation to babes.

If Q were a full gospel account, why would Matthew and Luke not use it instead of Mark? If it had more material than Matthew and Luke had in common, why did they omit the rest? By definition, it cannot be less than the material in Matthew and Luke, so it must be a document roughly equivalent to the "non-Marcan agreements." A source made up of such material would be strange indeed. The Matthean and Lucan material in these "non-Marcan agreement" passages is so dissimilar that it is difficult to explain how both could have copied it from the same source. The few lines that are similar cannot offset the overall diversity.

Doublets? A standard definition of a "doublet" does not exist. Hawkins defines a doublet as "repetitions of the same or closely similar sentences in the same gospel."[102] Other definitions are "when two passages of the same work . . . are alike to the point of seeming to be a repetition," "texts which one evangelist has written twice," and more recently with the added specification that one must come from Mark and the other from some other source.[103] But, even with the assumption of Markan priority, how can one know that one of the two passages came from another source? And assuming that the author deliberately included the same incident twice, how would one know that he did not just repeat what he found in Mark? Another source is unnecessary.

Or could the author have unwittingly repeated the same incident? This is hardly plausible. Matthew, according to critics, is so skilled an editor that he has taken two documents and combined them so well that most cannot tell he did so. According to historical critics, Matthew can "correct" Mark, and bring Mark's theology into agreement with the church. Since Matthew feels free to make these changes and improvements, he can hardly be a slavish copier or editor of Mark. Has this same person suddenly and momentarily turned into a bumbling idiot and slavish copier who cannot tell that he is copying the same event twice? Rather, so-called "doublets" are merely descriptions of similar incidents or statements.

Is it unrealistic to deny that Jesus could have uttered the same or similar statements more than once? Jesus' ministry was highly repetitive in nature and geared for a restricted cultural entity. Is it unreasonable to believe that similar events occurred? Repetition would be both normal and expected in such a situation. Yet, regardless of these realities, most gospel critics would agree with Meyer's statement that to regard doublets as similar incidents would be true only of a "naive biblicist."[104]

However, an example of two such similar incidents occurs in Scripture. Jesus fed the five thousand in Matthew 14:15–21, and in Matthew 15:32–38, He fed the four thousand. Later, in Matthew 16:9–10, Jesus specifically referred to both feedings as separate historical events. So no objective reason forces one to assume that the so-called doublets are repetitions of the same event. Consequently, doublets do not prove the existence of another document, an alleged Q. Hawkins lists twenty-two passages as doublets, none of which appears to be caused by a repetition of the same event.[105] Stoldt also calls attention to doublet-type constructions within Mark itself, a fact that invalidates the entire argument for the existence of Q.[106] A final observation that further weakens the doublet theory is its assumption of the Two-Source Theory in order to construct the doublets, a theory that in turn depends on the doublet theory. It is circular reasoning to have two unproven theories depend on each other for their validity.

EVIDENCE AGAINST THE TWO-SOURCE THEORY

Biblical evidence

The extensive differences between the Synoptic Gospels provide evidence against literary dependence and thus against the Two-Source Theory. In these three writings describing the period of Jesus' ministry, an amazing amount of material differs, though proponents of the theory commonly stress the similarities. There are differences in content, including overall subject matter, as well as in details. Matthew and Luke agree in many details against Mark.[107] They also have a great deal of material not found in Mark. Further, Luke omits the lengthy section, Mark 6:45–8:26.[108] If Luke copied Mark, why did he omit this lengthy section, which includes Jesus' walking on the water, the healing at Gennesaret, a major conflict over the tradition of the elders, the Syrophoenician woman's faith, the healing of a deaf and dumb man, the feeding of the four thousand, the Pharisees' demand for a sign, the instruction regarding the leaven of the Pharisees and that of Herod, and the healing of a blind man at Bethsaida? The case for literary dependence falters in its inability to answer this question. Surely something in that section would have contributed to Luke's purpose.

Luke 1:1–4 gives a specific purpose for the third Synoptic Gospel. Both Matthew and Mark must have also had a purpose. Their descriptions of the same period account for the similarities between the three synoptics. Their differences in purpose account sufficiently for differences in subject matter and length. So the Synoptic Problem is nonexistent for the characteristics of the Synoptic Gospels fit normal expectations of three independent treatments, covering the same period of someone's life but with differing purposes.

Luke 1:1–4, rather than supplying evidence for Luke's use of written sources, may imply the opposite. Though Luke states that many had produced "accounts" of Jesus' ministry, whatever those accounts were, Luke tells Theophilus that their insufficiency is his reason (*epeidēper*, "inasmuch as," Luke 1:1) for writing. Luke in particular writes because he has researched everything accurately from the beginning. Based on that research, he writes to assure Theophilus about the certainty of these facts. Luke apparently regarded an accurate account as necessary to provide this *certainty,* and felt that the previous accounts could not do so. Luke states that he did his own research in contradiction to the idea that he relied on a single source or two such as Mark and Q, especially to the extent imagined by the Two-Source Theory. Research entails the use of *many* sources.

In addition, Luke seems to view the earlier accounts negatively, making it quite unlikely that he depended on them or that any of them were canonical gospels. In fact, his statement rules out his extensive use or copying of any one or two sources, for he stresses his own research.

Patristic evidence

Papias comments that Mark wrote his gospel based on Peter's information. Carson assumes that he meant Mark did not use another gospel and uses Papias' statement as evidence against the Griesbach hypothesis (namely, Matthean priority) and thus indirect support for the Two-Source Theory.[109] If this meant Mark did not depend on Matthew or Luke, it must also rule out dependence on any sources other than Peter. If Papias' statement that Mark based his writing on Peter's information rules out Mark's use of other sources, including other gospels, then Luke's statement that he writes based on his own research, equally rules out his dependence on other sources, including other gospels.

It is implausible that Matthew, an eyewitness of events he writes about, would rely to any extent on the gospel of Mark, since Mark was not an eyewitness of most of Jesus' ministry. If Mark's recording of information received from Peter precludes his use of another gospel, then Matthew's recording of information he obtained as an eyewitness also precludes reliance on another gospel.

Specific patristic testimony places Matthew as the earliest of the synoptics. Some of that testimony locates both Matthew and Luke as prior to the other gospels.[110] How objective is it to ignore this early testimony and the overall testimony of church tradition and select one possibly misconstrued statement by Papias to prop up the Two-Source Theory? The comment of Papias, at best, shows only that Mark did not depend on sources other than Peter. It says nothing about priority of writing and nothing contradictory to other patristic testimony regarding priority.

Matthew was an eyewitness of most of the events recorded in the Gospels. He was present with Jesus for three years and associated with the other apostles and disciples after Jesus' ascension. The group would have repeated descriptions of these events to the point that descriptions, including details, became fixed in their minds. They could hardly have forgotten the basic order of events. They must have developed a core of testimony, oral or written, that they passed on. It is implausible that Matthew depended on, much less copied, the gospel of a non-eyewitness for specifics or for the overall framework of events, rather than writing his own record.[111]

Cumulative biblical evidence argues against the Two-Source Theory and literary dependence among the synoptic writers. Available testimony from the church fathers agrees in that it does not fit with the Two-Source Theory.

CONCLUSION

The common arguments that the Two-Source Theory has appeal, is simple, and is useful in gospel criticism beg the question. They are circular reasoning in assuming the point to be proven. They cannot provide proof of the theory. The same type of reasoning could be used to argue for the priority of Matthew or Luke, if they are assumed as first. A group of travelers could agree in choosing the wrong road. Their decision might have appeal, be simple, and be useful in the sense that they appear to be progressing. Yet, that road leads to the wrong destination. The alleged "merits" turn out to be demerits, for they produce a false sense of progress at the same time they foster error. The issue in gospel criticism is not appeal, simplicity, or usefulness, but whether a theory is valid.

The many differences between the synoptics argue against the possibility of literary dependence. Admittedly, with even a minimal amount of similarity, one cannot prove independence. However, literary dependence is at best only speculation that is inconsistent with the heavy weight of evidence.

Even with the assumption of literary dependence, a fundamental flaw in the Two-Source Theory remains. The theory's basis is inaccurate, even misleading, comparisons of the Synoptic Gospels. Those comparisons do not come from the Gospels as they are, which is the only objective way to compare. Instead they come from reconstructed gospels derived from the assumptions of Source Criticism, especially the Two-Source Theory. Thus, the foundation of the entire approach is circular reasoning.

Even with the assumption of both literary dependence and the usual statistics of comparison, the main arguments for the theory are logically invalid. Neither the order of events, the length, nor the style can prove anything regarding priority of writing. All of the "psychological-reflection," redactional types of argument are circular in nature, personal opinion, or both; they prove nothing. Multiplying guesses and circular arguments does not increase their validity. No matter how large the number of opinions, they are still opinion, not proof, and a large number of circular arguments remain circular.

The theory grew step by step so that invalid arguments appeared to gain validity through an accumulation of presuppositions. The scholarly credentials of proponents have overwhelmed many who have been exposed to that thinking. The Christian needs to be aware that although some evangelical scholars defend the view as valid scholarship, the theory at its foundation rejects the Synoptic Gospels as factual history. Most proponents also reject any connection of those gospels with eyewitnesses.

The theory may appear "scientific" in its arguments, but upon examination the alleged scientific aspect extends only to discarding the three synoptics as accurate historical accounts by eyewitnesses or those in direct contact with eyewitnesses. Though it is not true of every two-source advocate, those who laid the foundations of this theory and those who emphasize it now, reject the idea that these gospels are what they purport to be, particularly their inspiration and accuracy. After they have used "scientific" methodology to discard inspiration, they discard scientific methodology itself, leaving only unscientific, logically incohesive arguments, circular reasoning, and speculations as a basis for the theory. The theory is neither correct nor "scientific."

Unless the documents have some direct indication of priority, such as a date or explicit statement, it is impossible by comparing the contents to ascertain whether they copied from one another and, if so, in what order. It is an illusion to think it is possible to make any scientifically certain determination. The only conceivable proof is either external testimony—such as patristic evidence—or some statement within a document—such as Luke 1:1–4. The available evidence contradicts rather than supports the Two-Source Theory.

Finally, if the Gospels report factual history, it is doubtful that a Synoptic Problem exists. All the characteristics allegedly creating the problem are quite natural for three accounts of the same historical events.

ENDNOTES

1. Bo Reicke, "The History of the Synoptic Discussion," *The Interrelations of the Gospels*, David L. Dungan, ed. (Macon, Ga.: Mercer University, 1990), 297; William R. Farmer, *The Gospel of Jesus* (Louisville: Westminster/John Knox, 1994), 146, 148; Hans-Herbert Stoldt, *History and Criticism of the Marcan Hypothesis*, trans. and ed. Donald L. Niewyk (Macon, Ga.: Mercer University, 1980), 260–61.
2. William R. Farmer, *The Synoptic Problem* (New York: Macmillan, 1964), viii.
3. Gordon D. Fee, *New Testament Exegesis* (Philadelphia: Westminster, 1983), 35–37; Robert Morgan with John Barton, *Biblical Interpretation*, The Oxford Bible Series (Oxford: Oxford University Press, 1988), 67; F. Neirynck, "The Two–Source Hypothesis," *Interrelations of the Gospels*, 3; Robert H. Stein, *The Synoptic Problem* (Grand Rapids: Baker, 1987), 46.
4. Hajo Uden Meijboom, *A History and Critique of the Origin of the Marcan Hypothesis 1835–1866*, trans. and ed. John J. Kiwiet, New Gospel Studies, vol. 8 (Macon, Ga.: Mercer, 1993), xxviii; Stoldt agrees (*History and Criticism*, 257–58).
5. Stephen Neill and Tom Wright, *The Interpretation of the New Testament 1861–1986*, 2d ed. (Oxford: Oxford University, 1988), 362.
6. Farmer, *Gospel of Jesus*.
7. John H. Ludlum, Jr., "New Light on the Synoptic Problem," *Christianity Today, Part 1* (November 10, 1958): 6–9, and *Part 2* (November 24, 1958): 10–14; cf. "Are We Sure of Mark's Priority?" *Christianity Today, Part 1* (September 14, 1959) 11–14, and *Part 2* (September 28, 1959) 9–10.
8. Cf. Gregory A. Boyd, *Cynic, Sage, or Son of God?* (Wheaton: Victor, 1995), 228.
9. Stephen J. Patterson, "Sources for a Life of Jesus," *The Search for Jesus: Modern Scholarship Looks at the Gospels*, ed. Herschel Shanks (Washington, D.C.: Biblical Archaeology Society, 1994), 18.
10. Ibid.
11. Ibid., 20.
12. Boyd, *Cynic Sage*, 136–42.
13. Ibid., 132–36.
14. H. Conzelmann and A. Lindemann, *Interpreting the New Testament*, trans. Siegfried S. Schatzmann (Peabody, Mass.: Hendrickson, 1985), 46.
15. D. A. Carson, "Matthew," in *The Expositor's Bible Commentary*, gen. ed. Frank E. Gaebelein (Grand Rapids: Zondervan, 1984), 8:16.
16. Farmer, *Gospel of Jesus*, ix, x, 3, 5, 164–201.
17. D. L. Dungan, "Synopses of the Future," *The Interrelations of the Gospels*, 318–22.
18. Neirynck, *Interrelations*, 4.
19. D. A. Carson, "Redaction Criticism," in *Scripture and Truth*, eds. D. A. Carson and John D. Woodbridge (Grand Rapids: Zondervan, 1983), 120.
20. Carson, "Matthew," 13; Conzelmann and Lindemann, *Interpreting the New Testament*, 47–48.
21. For example, Thomas R. Edgar, "An Analysis of the Synoptic Problem" (Th.D.

Dissertation, Dallas Theological Seminary, 1969); Eta Linnemann, *Is There a Synoptic Problem?* trans. Robert W. Yarbrough (Grand Rapids: Baker, 1992).

22. For example, B. C. Butler, *The Originality of Matthew* (Cambridge: University Press, 1951), 1–36; Carson, "Matthew," 13; Farmer, *Synoptic Problem*, 1–198; A. M. Farrer, "On Dispensing with Q," *Studies in the Gospels*, ed. D. E. Nineham (Oxford: Blackwell, 1955), 55–86; Everett F. Harrison, *Introduction to the New Testament* (Grand Rapids: Eerdmans, 1964), 136–45; John C. Hawkins, *Horae Synopticae* (Oxford: Clarendon, 1909), 3–13; G. E. Ladd, "More Light on the Synoptics," *Christianity Today* (March 2, 1959): 12–16. Some scholars advocate two additional sources, "M" and "L," making four sources instead of two.

23. Burnett Hillman Streeter, *The Four Gospels* (London: Macmillan, 1930), 151–53; Streeter developed the arguments for Marcan priority some sixty years after Holzmann first synthesized the Two-Source Theory. Streeter supported a Four-Source Theory, but others have used his arguments regarding Mark and Q to support the Two-Source Theory.

24. Edgar, "Analysis of the Synoptic Problem"; Linnemann, *Is There a Synoptic Problem?* Ludlum, "New Light, Part 1," 6–9; idem, "New Light, Part 2," 10–14; Robert L. Thomas, "An Investigation of the Agreements between Matthew and Luke against Mark," *JETS* 19 (spring 1976): 103–12; idem, "The Rich Young Man in Matthew," *Grace Theological Journal* 3 (fall 1982): 235–51.

25. F. C. Burkitt, *The Gospel History and its Transmission* (Edinburgh: T & T Clark, 1907), 37–38.

26. Streeter, *Four Gospels*, 151; Neirynck, "Two-Source Hypothesis," 7–8.

27. Owen E. Evans, "Synoptic Criticism since Streeter," *The Expository Times* 72 (October 1960–September 1961): 296; Neirynck, 19–22; D. L. Dungan, "Response to the Two-Source Hypothesis," *Interrelations of the Gospels*, 202–3.

28. Carson, "Matthew," 14; Conzelmann and Lindemann, *Interpreting the New Testament*, 48; Farmer, *Gospel*, 127; Meijboom, *History and Critique*, 97; Neill and Wright, *Interpretation of the New Testament*, 125; D. B. Peabody, "Response to Multi-Stage Hypothesis," *The Interrelations of the Gospels*, 221–22; Charles B. Puskas, *An Introduction to the New Testament* (Peabody, Mass.: Hendrickson, 1989), 94.

29. Joseph A. Fitzmeyer, "The Priority of Mark and the 'Q' Source in Luke," *Jesus and Man's Hope* (Pittsburgh: Pittsburgh Theological Seminary, 1970), 1:135, 39; Meijboom, *History and Critique*, 97, 104–15; Neirynck, "Two-Source," 5; Stein, *Synoptic Problem*, 76; Stoldt, *History and Criticism*, 159–68.

30. Stoldt, *History and Criticism*, 201.

31. Scot McKnight, "Source Criticism," *New Testament Criticism and Interpretation*, eds. D. A. Black and D. D. Dockery (Grand Rapids: Zondervan, 1991), 149.

32. Puskas, *Introduction to the New Testament*, 93; Lamar Cope, "The Argument Revolves: The Pivotal Evidence for Marcan Priority Is Reversing Itself," *New Synoptic Studies*, ed. W. R. Farmer (Macon, Ga.: Mercer University, 1983), 143.

33. Cope, "Argument Revolves, 144, 152f.; Fitzmeyer, *Jesus and Man's Hope*, 1:134f., 167; F. Neirynck, "Matthew 4:23–5:2 and the Matthaean Composition of 4:23–11:1," *Interrelations of the Gospels*, 26–36; Puskas, *Introduction to the New Testament*, 93; Stein, *Synoptic Problem*, 76.

34. McKnight, "Source Criticism," 149–50.

35. Ibid., 151; Stein, *Synoptic Problem*, 76.
36. Stein, *Synoptic Problem*, 89–112.
37. Stephen L. Harris, *The New Testament*, 2d. ed. (Mountain View, Calif.: Mayfield Pub., 1995), 72.
38. Fitzmeyer, *Jesus and Man's Hope*, 1:152.
39. Alfred Wikenhauser, *New Testament Introduction*, trans. Joseph Cunningham (New York: Herder & Herder, 1958), 223–27.
40. Streeter, *Four Gospels*, 157–61.
41. Neill and Wright, *Interpretation of the New Testament*, 126–27; Hawkins, *Horae Synopticae*, 65, 81.
42. Butler, *Originality of Matthew*, vi.
43. Ludlum, "New Light: Part I," 8.
44. Edgar, "Analysis of the Synoptic Problem," 212–15.
45. Kurt Aland, *Synopsis Quattuor Evangeliorum*, 2d ed. (Stuttgart: Wurtembergischese Bibelanstalt, 1964), 10–13; Ernest DeWitt Burton and Edgar J. Goodspeed, *A Harmony of the Synoptic Gospels in Greek* (Chicago: University of Chicago, 1920), ix; Albert Huck, *Synopsis of the First Three Gospels* (Oxford: Blackwell, 1951), xiii; A. T. Robertson, *A Harmony of the Gospels for Students of the Life of Christ* (London: Hodder and Stoughton, 1922), 9–12.
46. Farmer, *Synoptic Problem*, 190–96.
47. Aland, *Synopsis Quattuor Evangeliorum*, xi; Burton and Goodspeed, *Harmony of the Synoptic Gospels in Greek*, vi; Huck, *Synopsis of the First Three Gospels*, iv.
48. D. L. Dungan, "Synopses of the Future," *Interrelations of the Gospel*, 317–42; W. R. Farmer, "Introduction," *New Synoptic Studies*, x, xviii.
49. Fitzmeyer, *Jesus and Man's Hope*, 1:163–64.
50. B. de Solages, *A Greek Synopsis of the Gospels*, trans. J. Baissus (Leyden: Brill, 1959), 27, 1126.
51. Ludlum, "New Light, Part 1," 8.
52. Dungan, "Response," 202–3; Neirynck, "Two-Source," 21.
53. Linnemann, *Is There a Synoptic Problem?* 71–108.
54. Carson, "Matthew," 14.
55. M. D. Goulder, review of *On the Independence of Matthew and Mark*, JTS 30 (1979): 266; cf. John Wenham, *Redating Matthew, Mark & Luke* (Downers Grove, Ill.: InterVarsity, 1992), 6.
56. Ibid., 266.
57. Wenham, *Redating Matthew, Mark & Luke*, 251–52.
58. Ludlum, "New Light: Part I," 8.
59. Edgar, "Analysis of the Synoptic Problem," 199–222.
60. Ibid.
61. Linnemann, *Is There a Synoptic Problem?* 73.
62. Ibid., 77, 91, 103–7.
63. Edgar, "Analysis of the Synoptic Problem," 199–215.
64. Conzelmann and Lindemann, *Interpreting the New Testament*, 48; Harris, *New Testament*, 139; Puskas, *Introduction to the New Testament*, 90; Stein, *Synoptic Problem*, 42, 43, 129.
65. See chapter 8, "The Impact of Luke's Prologue on Literary Dependence."
66. Burkitt, *Gospel History*, 37–38; Dungan, "Response," 202–3; Evans, "Synoptic Criticism," 296; Farmer, *Synoptic Problem*, 50; Fitzmeyer, *Jesus and Man's Hope*, 1:165.
67. Butler, *Originality of Matthew*, 62–63.

68. Edgar, "Analysis of the Synoptic Problem," 110.
69. McKnight, "Source Criticism," 167; Neill and Wright, *Interpretation of the New Testament*, 125; Neirynck, "Two-Source," 7; C. M. Tuckett, *The Revival of the Greisbach Hypothesis* (Cambridge: Cambridge University, 1983), 145; Malcolm Lowe, "The Demise of Arguments from Order for Markan Priority," *Novum Testamentum* 24 (1982): 27–36.
70. Butler, *Originality of Matthew*, 65; cf. Farmer, *Synoptic Problem*, 50; Neill and Wright, *Interpretation of the New Testament*, 125; Wenham, *Redating Matthew, Mark & Luke*, 90.
71. Butler, *Originality of Matthew*, 65; Farmer, *Synoptic Problem*, 48–117.
72. Ludlum, "Are We Sure, Part I," 11–14.
73. Wenham, *Redating Matthew, Mark & Luke*, 6–7.
74. Conzelmann and Lindemann, *Interpreting the New Testament*, 50.
75. In some of his individual pericopes, Mark is somewhat longer; see below under the section entitled "Argument from brevity."
76. For example, George Eldon Ladd, "More Light on the Synoptics," *Christianity Today* (March 2, 1959): 12–13.
77. Edgar, "Analysis of the Synoptic Problem," 216–17.
78. Farmer, *Gospel of Jesus*, 127; Meijboom, *History and Critique*, 97f.
79. Meijboom, *History and Critique*, 98.
80. Peabody, "Responses to Multi-Stage Hypothesis," 222.
81. Farmer, *Gospel of Jesus*, 127; for possible reasons behind the intellectual satisfaction, cf. chapter 2 of this volume, "Philosophical and Theological Bent of Historical Criticism."
82. Meijboom, *History and Critique*, 97–104.
83. Farmer, *Gospel of Jesus*, 127–28.
84. Roland Mushat Frye, while Professor of English Literature at the University of Pennsylvania, observed, "The equation between greater length and later date applies primarily to the development of a single work by a single author and not to the recension of an earlier text by a later writer, where the result may at least equally well be a shortening of the text" ("The Synoptic Problems and Analogies in Other Literatures," in *The Relationships Among the Gospels*, ed. William O. Walker, Jr. [San Antonio, Tex.: Trinity, 1978], 263, cf. 271–79). D. A. Carson's rejoinder to Frye ("Matthew," 14) inadvertently ignores the last part of Frye's comparison to other literature. Frye observes that the historical examples of literary conflation he has been able to find lend support to a theory that Mark shortened Matthew and Luke and at the same time lengthened individual pericopes (Frye, "Synoptic Problems," 265–66). Thus Carson's rejoinder is valueless.
85. Stoldt, *History and Criticism*, 165.
86. Ibid., 166.
87. Cited by Stoldt, *History and Criticism*, 160–67.
88. For an explanation of the antisupernatural bias of Historical Criticism, cf. chapter 2 of this volume, "Philosophical and Theological Bent of Historical Criticism."
89. Stoldt, *History and Criticism*, 201–2.
90. Donald A. Hagner, *Matthew 1–13*, vol. 33A of *Word Biblical Commentary* (Dallas, Tex.: Word, 1993), 404.
91. Neirynck, "Matthew 4:23," 30.
92. McKnight, "Source Criticism," 148.
93. For example, McKnight, "Source Criticism," 149–51, 169; Stein, *Synoptic Problem*, 76.

94. A few Marcan prioritists reject the need for Q (for instance, Michael D. Goulder, 'Is Q a Juggernaught?" *JBL* 115, no. 4 [1996]: 667–81; cf. Arthus J. Bellinzoni, Jr., *The Two-Source Hypothesis* [Macon, Ga.: Mercer University, 1985], 5, 321–56), but that is exceptional.

95. Stewart Petrie, "'Q' is Only What You Make It," *Novum Testamentum* 3 (1959): 29–30.

96. Ibid., 31.

97. Theodore R. Rosche, "The Words of Jesus and the Future of the 'Q' Hypothesis," *JBL* 79 (1960): 217–19.

98. McKnight, "Source Criticism," 170.

99. Hawkins, *Horae Synopticae*, 108.

100. John C. Hawkins, "Probabilities as to the So-Called Double Tradition of St. Matthew and St. Luke," *Studies in the Synoptic Problem*, ed. W. Sanday (Oxford: Clarendon, 1911), 112–18.

101. Edgar, "Analysis of the Synoptic Problem," 169.

102. Hawkins, *Horae Synopticae*, 80.

103. Solages, *Greek Synopsis*, 1069; Paul Feine, Johannes Behm, and Werner Georg Kummel, *Introduction to the New Testament*, trans. A. J. Matill, Jr. (Nashville: Abingdon, 1966), 51; Fitzmeyer, *Jesus and Man's Hope*, 1:152.

104. B. F. Meyer, "Objectivity and Subjectivity in Historical Criticism of the Gospels," *Interrelations of the Gospels*, 548.

105. Hawkins, *Horae Synopticae*, 80; cf. Edgar, "Analysis of the Synoptic Problem," 33–36.

106. Stoldt, *History and Criticism*, 175–78.

107. Linnemann, *Is There a Synoptic Problem?* 99–130, 150; Thomas, "Agreements between Matthew and Luke against Mark," 104–8.

108. Robert L. Thomas, ed., *The NIV Harmony of the Gospels* (San Francisco: Harper and Row, 1988), 263.

109. Carson, "Matthew," 14.

110. S. O. Abogunrin, "The Synoptic Gospel Debate," *Interrelations of the Gospels*, 388–95; W. R. Farmer, "The Patristic Evidence Reexamined," and Guiseppe Giov. Gamba, "A Further Reexamination of Evidence from the Early Tradition," and David Peabody, "Augustine and the Augustinian Hypothesis," *New Synoptic Studies*, 3–64; cf. also chapter 1 of this volume, "The Synoptic Gospels in the Ancient Church."

111. Contra Ladd, "More Light on the Synoptics," 12–16, and Lumby, "Are We Sure of Mark's Priority? Part I," 11–14, and idem, "Are We Sure of Mark's Priority? Part II," 9–10.

CHAPTER FOUR

Eta Linnemann: Friend or Foe of Scholarship?

Robert W. Yarbrough

HISTORICAL CRITICISM IN ITS classic Troeltschian formulation has come under increasing fire in recent decades. This is so much the case that Gerald Bray argues plausibly for recognizing a new hermeneutical paradigm as characteristic of current academic study of the Christian Scriptures. No longer should one speak about "critical" study, meaning academically rigorous and in some sense "scientific" research, as over against "uncritical" or "conservative" study, meaning academically flabby, methodologically outdated, and hermeneutically naive. Rather, in existence today are, broadly speaking, three approaches to formal scholarly study of Scripture, each having its own distinct heritage, characteristics, legitimacy, and leading lights.

The first of these is what Bray calls "academic scholarship, which carries on the historical-critical tradition inherited from the last century, and seeks to integrate new approaches into its established norms."[1] From its own point of view, this approach often regards itself as the only game in town, but in point of fact it no longer possesses the monopoly status it once did, and a rival outlook has arisen. This rival, a second position, Bray characterizes by the rubric "social trends." In this world of academic discourse, current social and political issues set the agenda. Here scholars typically accept fully the critical conclusions of the first group—but view them as irrelevant. Along the lines made famous by liberation theology, they press toward a responsible and transformative orthopraxy rather than an academic critical orthodoxy that is removed from the world and its pressing social needs.

Bray's third group is that of "conservative evangelicalism." To quote Bray at some length:

> This is a movement within the Protestant churches whose adherents have rejected the critical assumptions of Enlightenment thought to a greater or lesser degree. They seek to maintain the theology of the Reformation, though in practice this has frequently

been modified. . . . Conservative evangelicals tend to regard the first world of discourse ["academic scholarship" above] as their mission field, and are ambivalent toward the second one ["social trends" above]. They frequently sympathize with the cause of fighting injustice, but doubt whether the way it is defined, or the methods adopted to combat it, are really consonant with scholarly standards or traditional theological positions.[2]

Bray's taxonomy is useful for purposes of the present discussion, for it helps contextualize the subject of this essay, namely, Professor Dr. Eta Linnemann. Bray himself alludes to her, albeit in just one sentence. Under the subheading "Alternatives to historical criticism: The conservative attack," he states the following:

> Mention might also be made of the remarkable case of Eta Linnemann, who after being trained in the standard liberalism of the German universities was converted to a conservative evangelical faith, and has subsequently devoted her life to a root-and-branch critique of her earlier views.[3]

For some reason Bray does not list any of her post-conversion writings in his otherwise full bibliographies. Is this possibly not an oversight but an understandable move to avoid seeming too familiar with, and possibly sympathetic to, Linnemann's controversial outlook and sometimes flamboyant turns of phrase?[4] Bray's recognition that her views are important enough to cite, but sufficiently problematic to pass over lightly, alerts readers to a problem, or set of problems, crying out for clarification. To provide that clarification is the aim in what follows.

To that end, subsequent discussion will first flesh out biographical information, only sketchily furnished in Dr. Linnemann's published works to date. Sources for this will be personal autobiographical statements she has made available and oral interviews granted to this writer in late 1994 and early 1995. Next, the chapter will analyze reaction to her by surveying (1) the flurry of German-language discussion that arose after her formal published renunciation of "the historical critical method" in 1985, and (2) published reviews of her two major books written since that renunciation. Finally, this investigation will seek to answer the question posed by the essay's title. For reasons to be expressed below, the conclusion will cautiously contend that overall Linnemann is a friend of the scholarly enterprise in its highest sense rather than an adversary.

BIOGRAPHY

Linnemann was born October 19, 1926, in Osnabrück, Germany, in the northwestern corner of present unified Germany, well inland from the coast and as far south in Lower Saxony as one can travel without entering the North Rhine-Westphalia area. Primary and secondary schooling stretched from April 1933 until March 1948, being prolonged by World

War II. From October 1948 until July 1953, she studied Protestant theology, which included a full range of biblical, philosophical, theological, and church-historical subjects, in Marburg, Tübingen, and Göttingen. Notable professors at Marburg were Bultmann and Dinkler in New Testament, Balla and Fohrer in Old Testament, and Benz, Maurer, and Zscharnack in church history and dogmatics. At Tübingen, her professors included Fuchs and Michel in New Testament, Würthwein and Elliger in Old Testament, Rückert and Ebeling in church history and dogmatics, and Weischedel and Krüger in philosophy. At Göttingen she heard, among others, Gogarten, Wolf, Käsemann, and Trillhaus.

Ironically, Linnemann had entered university in the hopes of becoming a schoolteacher, but all university openings for this major were full when she sought enrollment. She was advised to declare theology as her subject and then later move laterally into education. She never made the switch, becoming a theologian instead, yet continuing in her direct involvement with public school religious curriculum, as remarks below will show. By her third semester at Marburg, she says, her thought turned "in the historical-critical direction." Important books in this early period were Rudolf Bultmann's on Jesus and on the history of the synoptic tradition[5] as well as Walter Bauer's on early Christian belief and heresy.[6] Linnemann regards Ernst Fuchs as her theological father in those days and Bultmann as her grandfather. Linnemann acquired from Bultmann her exegetical method, and she acquired from Fuchs her theology and hermeneutic.

Linnemann took and passed her first state examinations on August 12–15, 1953. Then came a practicum during which she produced a scholarly, as yet unpublished treatise on the theology of Johann Adam Möhlers. Her second set of required exams took place August 17–18, 1957. She passed them as well. At this point the *Landeskirche* (state church) in Hannover assigned her to write interpretations of biblical texts for religion teachers in the German public school system. Out of this labor arose her critically acclaimed book on Jesus' parables, which was accepted as a doctoral dissertation by the *Kirchliche Hochschule* (Ecclesiastical College) of Berlin. Overseeing this work were Karl Kupisch, Ernst Fuchs, and Martin Fischer. She received her doctoral degree *summa cum laude* on July 13, 1961.

From April 16, 1961 until March 31, 1966, Linnemann taught in a seminary in Berlin,[7] lecturing in New Testament, church history, and religious education. On April 1, 1966, Linnemann received appointment to occupy the chair of Protestant theology and religious pedagogical methodology at the Teachers' College of Braunschweig. There she became associate professor on February 14, 1967. In the midst of these labors she requested permission to *habilitieren* (submit a second doctoral dissertation, required in the German theological system for the *venia legendi*, the right to full privileges as university professor), a request she made to the Protestant faculty at the Phillipps University in Marburg. Linnemann's dissertation there was entitled *Studien zur Passionsgeschichte (Studies of the Passion Story)*. She received the *venia legendi* for New Testament on February 11, 1970, and was named honorary professor at Marburg on August 10, 1971. She become full professor at Braunschweig in 1972.

Linnemann's move into evangelical Christian confession has an early stage and then a later, better known one. In 1946 she had been given a copy of the Pietist *Losungen*. This document contained Bible verses for each day of the year that were meant for personal devotions and life direction. In subsequent years, Linnemann bought them for herself, expressing her spiritual interest. Then on a holiday retreat in April 1948, following graduation from secondary school, she underwent a memorable religious experience when she responded to an evangelistic message and invitation. But apparently this rebirth barely took root, if at all; at any rate, it did not issue immediately in sweeping life change. That took place on November 5, 1977, when at the age of fifty-one, Linnemann says she gave her life to Christ. It was a month later that she "repented of my perverse theological teaching" and declared her earlier work and writing rubbish. She has elaborated on this part of her life in her first post-conversion book, *Historical Criticism of the Bible*.[8]

At Linnemann's own request, she took early retirement from the university, sensing a need to rebuild her biblical and theological outlook from the ground up. She received aid here by American missionaries in Wolfenbüttel, who were holding Bible classes that she attended. In 1983, Linnemann sensed a call to teach in a missionary capacity in Batu, Indonesia, where she has returned to teach a number of times over the years since.[9] Her other Christian service, besides local church involvement in an independent congregation near her north German residence of Leer-Loga, has been research and writing. Linnemann's initial book on Historical Criticism appeared in German in 1986, and has since been published in Dutch (1987), English (1990), Indonesian (1991), and Norwegian (1994) editions.[10] Sales of the English edition alone have far exceeded 10,000 copies. A second monograph dealing with the Synoptic Problem appeared in both German and English editions in 1992,[11] and has likewise sold several thousand copies. A third book is well along and will cover various topics, centering on questions of New Testament introduction. Just one of its chapters alone runs to forty single-spaced pages (approximately, 17,500 words), in which Linnemann subjects to close scrutiny Udo Schnelle's negative decisions regarding the authorship of most New Testament documents.[12]

Since 1991, Linnemann has conducted two extended lecture tours in the United States, speaking at several dozen colleges and seminaries and before numerous church groups. She has also produced a number of essays, among them one called "Pauline Authorship and Vocabulary Statistics,"[13] a second entitled "Historical Critical and Evangelical Theology,"[14] a third entitled "The Lost Gospel of Q—Fact or Fantasy?", which recently appeared in *Trinity Journal*,[15] and fourth "Is There a Gospel of Q?", which appeared in *Bible Review*.[16] Still unpublished, to this writer's knowledge, is a close analysis of a portion of Robert H. Stein's *The Synoptic Problem*. An example of Linnemann's German language article production is

"Echtheitsfragen und Vokabelstatistik" ("Questions of Authenticity and Vocabulary Statistics"),[17] in which she investigates the use made of statistics to call in question the traditional authorship of most New Testament books.

If being a friend of scholarship were simply a matter of authoring academically serious publications, the overarching question of this essay would virtually answer itself: of course, Linnemann is a friend of scholarship for she is producing it! But a look at reviews of her works shows that such an unqualified answer would meet with considerable disagreement.

REACTION TO LINNEMANN'S PUBLICATIONS

This section will canvass the response, first in Germany and then in North America and Britain, to Linnemann's book *Historical Criticism of the Bible,* her initial post-conversion blast against Historical Criticism and call to faith in Christ and the Bible. This section will then do likewise in North America and Britain with her second book, *Is There a Synoptic Problem?* It will deal with some minor criticisms along the way, leaving major criticisms for the next section where attention will focus on the weaknesses and merits of Linnemann's second book.

Germany: Responses to Linnemann's Conversion and Charges Against *Historical Criticism of the Bible*

In December 1985, Linnemann went public with news of her conversion and renunciation of Historical Criticism as she had previously practiced it. A newspaper article in the *Kasseler Sonntagsblatt* entitled "Radikale Wendung einer Theologin" ("A Theologian's Radical Turn") contained the same news about her disillusionment with university biblical criticism as later appeared in the foreword of her book *Historical Criticism.*[18] This report caused no small stir, and it was all negative as far as Protestant theological officialdom was concerned.

Bultmann supporter and retired bishop Erich Vellmer drew first blood in the counterattack by chiding Linnemann condescendingly in the same paper for harboring the personal misconception that faith requires the support of theology and of historical-critical work. Vellmer, sounding notes familiar to anyone conversant with Bultmann's writings, insisted that a "faith" intermixed with "facts" was not Christian faith at all. The outward form of the Bible's statements ("Aussageweise") must be separated from the meaning, the content, of the Bible's statements ("Aussageinhalt"). Biblical writers wrote with particular intentions and used time-bound conceptions whose meaning must be liberated from their antiquated forms.

This is the service that Historical Criticism provides, says Vellmer. He implied that Linnemann is an imbalanced extremist ("Schwärmer") for raising a red flag regarding the negative relation between "history" and "faith" that prevails among historical critics in Germany. For Vellmer, what "faith" asserts is completely independent of what "history" turns out to be when analyzing Scripture with the historical-critical method. To relate faith directly to facts would be to make salvation dependent on works—the work of human cognition. Linnemann is thus unfaithful to the genius of the Reformation, Vellmer concludes, as well as of the New Testament itself. Supportive media departments of the state church in several central locales picked up and publicized Vellmer's letter in coming weeks. It received additional support from a second Protestant clergyman, Walther Roth. He linked Linnemann's conversion with psychological fickleness or character weakness, thus disqualifying her testimony as a witness to anything of consequence whatsoever. The editorial staff of the paper airing the whole dispute likewise opposed Linnemann, siding with the Protestant clergy who were critical of her new outlook.

Initial mainline response to Linnemann, then, was negative if not scathing. It is worth noting that the primary means of official attack was to twist Linnemann's position. She confessed that she had quit assuming that the Bible was historically untrue, for she realized that her grounds for that critical assumption were unfounded. She also went on to speak about her new-found personal faith in Christ. However, her opponents ignored the personalistic side of her statement and represented her as saying that faith is a mere affirmation of facts. The German statement, "Glauben ist nicht bloßes Fürwahrhalten" ("Believing is not merely affirming facts to be true"), blared the title of a state church press release. Besides, at the dogmatic level Linnemann could expect little sympathy for her reported conversion in a church that teaches salvation is inherent in baptism and thus requires no conviction and decision of the sort Linnemann reported.

In the midst of all this, laity rose immediately to mount a spirited if populist defense. The newspaper in which Linnemann's initial profession of faith appeared received over a dozen formal letters of protest against Vellmer and support for Linnemann. The paper printed few of these but did print Vellmer's and Roth's rebuttals in full. To the extent that German Protestant church leadership stated their verdict, it was clearly negative against Linnemann.

One can measure scholarly response to her life change by observing that shortly after her conversion, Linnemann sent personal letters explaining her shift in outlook to all her fellow German university theologians. Few even replied, and fewer still, Linnemann reports, were in any way supportive. As for her first post-conversion book,[19] since it was not written for an academic audience *per se* or published by an academic press, it is no wonder that German scholars ignored it in academic journals.

North America and Britain: Reaction to *Historical Criticism of the Bible*

An awareness of Linnemann in English-speaking circles began at the 1988 national meeting of the Evangelical Theological Society in Wheaton, Illinois.[20] Several American publishers expressed interest in the word about Linnemann's conversion and new book.[21] This resulted in the 1990 release of *Historical Criticism of the Bible*, of which some fifteen published reviews appeared by the spring of 1991.[22] At one end of the spectrum of response is David Watson, who has no word of negative criticism, calling

Linnemann's book simply "a magnificent testimony!"[23] David P. Kuske's remarks are equally free of disagreement.[24]

Slightly more reserved is David E. Lanier, who raises rhetorical questions about the extreme tone and substance of some of Linnemann's statements, yet declines to censure her. In his words, "the present writer will refuse to chide her for writing out of the deepest passion of her repentance any more than he would have chided Paul for writing off the teachings of Gamaliel as so much *skubala* ('garbage')."[25] Joe Blair, echoing Lanier's benign assessment, raises a couple of questions but points to no fundamental flaws.[26] William F. Warren, Jr., likewise raises no criticisms, noting only that Linnemann "at times overstates her position."[27] Hardly any more critical is the three-sentence assessment of E. Earle Ellis, who wrote the following:

> While [Linnemann] sometimes paints with too broad a brush and tends to underrate the positive contributions of historical biblical study, she offers important insights and a challenge to all who, within the academic enterprise, seek to be faithful interpreters of the Scriptures as the Word of God.[28]

More strongly worded is the caveat in David Crump's otherwise generally positive review, "Prof. Linnemann draws too many black or white dichotomies for her proposals . . . to be anything more than the enthusiastic trailblazer's rallying cry."[29]

Markedly more reserved is Robert M. Johnston, who points out that Linnemann may sound as intellectually arrogant to some as the critics she denounces. She seems to be unaware of "positive uses of historical-critical *methods* (as distinguished from *ideology*)" by scholars like F. F. Bruce, George Ladd, and Robert Stein.[30] Johnston appears to beg the question that Linnemann raises: Does not the historical-critical *method* in fact necessarily imply an *ideology* hostile to a Christian historiography? Still, his negative remarks are measured and brief, hardly more than ten percent of his total review.

A positive yet discerning analysis is offered by Robert Shirock, who notes that in some ways Linnemann's horizon is too limited to the German scene. He points out, for example, that

> a growing number of young evangelicals have worked their way through the problems which Linnemann raises and have found ways in which they can maintain their conservative beliefs while at the same time pursuing advanced research in Scripture within certain existing university systems,[31]

referring no doubt to the British universities. Yet Shirock urges that everyone engaged in biblical research and exposition read the book, noting the following:

Young evangelicals tend to allow the past forty years of German higher criticism to establish the agenda for their research. We believe that there is much truth in Linnemann's contention that we ought to be on the offensive rather than maintaining a defensive posture.

Equally positive are the remarks of Daniel Clendenin, who notes points of disagreement, including "the annoying form of the book with all its zeal and preachiness and its sometimes simplistic, grim content." Yet he concludes that the book "musters so much prophetic insight, intellectual candor, self-examination and gospel passion that guild Christians everywhere might benefit from it."[32]

Less unabashedly affirming is the essay by Andreas Köstenberger, who raises numerous perceptive questions. Linnemann demonizes Historical Criticism, he notes, but "the alternative remains unclear." (This is precisely the misgiving voiced by another reviewer, Howard Rhys, who in other respects says of Linnemann's book, "Her challenge is well expressed."[33]) More sharply, Köstenberger suggests that Linnemann seems to be headed in the direction of a "devotional" study of Scripture rather than an academically serious one. "Thus Linnemann unfortunately remains largely captive to the very dichotomy between believing and critical inquiry that much of the historical-critical theology itself has helped create."[34] In light of the work Linnemann has published in recent years, one doubts that Köstenberger would accuse Linnemann of a "devotional" method today. Yet even allowing for such criticisms, Köstenberger accords Linnemann grudging praise.

A final positive review comes from Lutheran Church Missouri Synod (LCMS) quarters. Horace D. Hummel writes, "One could easily close his eyes and, with only a few modifications, imagine this book as a product of the intense LCMS conflict about historical-critical exegesis a good two decades ago."[35] "Linnemann deserves better" than Earle Ellis' lukewarm commendation, Hummel thinks, and her "main thrust is surely beyond cavil." He concludes by hinting that the warning that Linnemann's book constitutes for North American evangelicals, whose acceptance of historical-critical thought is at times considerable, also comprises a warning to the LCMS. Is infighting among the LCMS's right wing hampering its attention to the real and far more dangerous challenges from the left? Did the LCMS "win" a pitched theological controversy in the 1960s and 1970s only to be lulled into ultimate loss at the hands of historical-critical impulses now?

Purely negative reactions to Linnemann come from two sources. Casimir Bernas, writing in *Religious Studies Review*, finds Linnemann's conversion touching but her thinking absolutely wrong.[36] "Things are not really as grim as depicted by Linnemann." Following the same Kantian and Bultmannian definition of faith as Vellmer and Roth, who opposed Linnemann in Germany (see the discussion above), Bernas writes, "For those . . . who consider theology to be faith seeking understanding, it is simply erroneous to maintain that critical scholarship is an impediment or danger to either faith, understanding, or gospel proclamation." Behind this assertion appear to lie the convictions (1) that "faith" and "knowledge" are utterly disparate spheres, and (2) that historical study has destroyed whatever factual basis Linnemann might have for her claims.[37]

The second purely negative reaction comes from Gregory A. Boyd.[38] It is interesting to contrast the cautiously appreciative reviews of figures like Ellis and Köstenberger (see the discussion above), who are trained experts in exegesis and methodology, with the spirited review of Boyd, who is not. As an apologetics professor, he writes about his bitter disappointment with Linnemann's book. It is not the kind of book he thinks she ought to have written. He faults her for demonizing philosophy and science, which Boyd wants to view as having Christian roots; for ignoring the church's errors and shortcomings in biblical interpretation; for wanting to transport society back into antiquity, doing away with all scientific and medical advances of modern times; for unqualified fideism in her understanding of the Gospel; and for failing to see the positive conclusions of Literary and Historical Criticism because of her fixation with alleged errors in criticism's assumptions. And so Boyd concludes:

> This is . . . just the kind of over-simplified, non-objective, and certainly unappreciative approach to biblical criticism which contemporary evangelicals do not need. What is needed is a critical dialogue with the biblical critical enterprise which is as appreciative as it is critical, as respectful as it is faithful, and objective as it is committed to scriptural authority. . . . Sadly, despite its sometimes profound insights into the subjective nature of supposedly objective scientific endeavors, Linnemann's book does not contribute to this needed critical dialogue. Unless you are looking for a passionate sermon on the evils of biblical criticism, therefore, I cannot recommend this book to you.[39]

North America and Britain: Reaction to *Is There a Synoptic Problem?*[40]

Linnemann's second post-conversion book, an examination of the so-called Synoptic Problem,[41] has received about eleven reviews of varying length and rigor by the spring of 1995. Among the most positive is that of John Wenham.[42] Wenham points out that "where Mark and Luke are undoubtedly parallel, Luke (if he is redacting) has made about 5,000 changes in Mark and Matthew about 8,000 changes."[43] He agrees that Linnemann's statistics show "in detail the unlikelihood of literary dependence" on the scale accepted by many.[44] Wenham calls Linnemann's third section, dealing with how the synoptics arose apart from literary interdependence, "lightweight." Yet he places himself alongside Linnemann as one who believes "in the verbal independence of the Synoptics" and concludes, "It is heartwarming to welcome this courageous and scholarly addition to the present synoptic problem ferment."

Purely laudatory is Erich H. Kiehl's review.[45] He says her book's "charts and tables reflect the extensive and meticulous study Linnemann has done to demonstrate the accuracy and truthfulness of her study." Unfortunately, little in this review indicates that the reviewer was interested in pointing out flaws, had he sensed any. Only slightly more critical are remarks by Edwin E. Reynolds.[46] He questions mainly formal aspects of the book, although he also wonders "how the statistics would vary if she were to test words for similarity in content rather than for identity." Overall, he writes, "Regardless of what one thinks of her conclusion, her statistical research is impressive, and certainly makes a very significant contribution to synoptic studies. Scholars should be grateful for the wealth of data she has contributed to the field." Robert L. Thomas, though he "does not concur with every minor point along the way," considers her book "probably the most significant volume on the Synoptic Problem to appear thus far in the twentieth century."[47]

William R. Farmer praises Linnemann's debunking of the presumed bases for the classic Two-Source Hypothesis as held by Strecker, Marxsen, and Koester based on Wilke, Weisse, and Holtzmann.[48] But Farmer thinks Linnemann's main argument, that "the Gospels are independent literary works based on eye-witness testimony," is "unconvincing." He does concede that Linnemann correctly exploits a gap in current criticism, which has "failed thus far in explaining Luke's use of Matthew."

David W. Jurgens, like Farmer, is skeptical of Linnemann's main thesis.[49] And he is less appreciative of her rejection of the Two-Source Hypothesis and with it Marcan priority. Jurgens suggests that Hans-Herbert Stoldt's list of fifty-seven agreements of Matthew and Luke against Mark may in fact be a sign that Matthew and Luke *did* use Mark. Jurgens contends, "If Matthew omits 6,593 words of Mark, and Luke omits 11,025 words of Mark, they would naturally have omitted many of the same words without ever having consulted each other." It can be asked whether this statement adequately answers Stoldt's objections to the Two-Source Hypothesis.[50]

Jurgens' other criticism of Linnemann runs like this: Robert Stein in *The Synoptic Problem: An Introduction* states that he believes in Scripture's inspiration, and that when gospel compilers edited traditions as determined through Source, Form, Redaction, and Literary Criticism, those interpretations are still "divinely inspired, canonical, and authoritative." In other words, Jurgens, like Stein, is willing to extend divine inspiration to whatever means gospel transmitters, compilers, or redactors used over the decades of gospel formation. Linnemann's arguments for eyewitness testimony are, then, unnecessary, for Stein's extended doctrine of inspiration abolishes the need for assured and direct eyewitness accounts. This point will receive further attention in the next section of this chapter.

Five reviews remain, each more critical than the preceding. Peter Head finds "the major weakness" in Linnemann's statement that "given the assumption of literary dependence, one would expect similarities of nearly 100 percent."[51] He calls this "a false premise," though he discusses none of Linnemann's observations supporting her statement and alleges that no evidence is available to prove it in light of certain literary parallels like "the Targums and the Masoretic Text; the Gospel of Peter and the canonical Gospels; or Josephus' use of the OT and Aristeas." In a much fuller treatment, Matt Williams makes nearly the same observation, though he seeks to ground it at greater length.[52] This chapter will review his arguments below. He adds the criticism that Linnemann fails to interact with non-German scholars—like Streeter, Sanday, and Farmer—who have argued for literary dependence. In fairness to Linnemann, however, she explicitly takes on the two-source hypothesis as it originated and exists in Germany and is taught in the university there, not all literary dependence theories elsewhere that have sprung up subsequently. It might surprise Williams to learn that German New Testament scholars feel no need to take Streeter, Sanday, and Farmer into account, so they clearly do not. This is, therefore, not a very telling criticism.

Rainer Riesner has some kind words to say of Linnemann.[53] But he says her book "contains too many onesided and imprecise statements." Riesner shows that her handling of the history of the Synoptic Problem is flawed and that her use of patristic sources lacks cogency. His summary of her extensive use of statistics deserves quotation:

> In general L.[innemann], like many of her historical-critical opponents, places too much faith in the view that statistics are decisive for the synoptic question. Although this reviewer has long maintained that the oral gospel tradition must be taken very seriously, he does not believe that it suffices to explain the synoptic phenomena in their entirety. On cultural-historical grounds alone it seems virtually unthinkable that prior to the synoptic gospels, which L. places in the mid-60s, nothing had been written down. I share with L. the concern that broad segments of New Testament science underrate the reliability of the synoptic gospels. But in conservative evangelical exegesis the early written recording was actually seen as a factor supporting this reliability.

In a somewhat more critical vein Dan G. McCartney concedes that Linnemann "certainly deserves commendation" for "her criticism of the naturalistic assumptions lying behind literary dependence theories."[54] But he charges her with a "misunderstanding of the nature of the problem" she is dealing with. Even if it can be shown that only 46 percent of Mark shows verbal identity with Matthew, McCartney says that is significant. He compares the situation with two student examinations he might grade, noting that 46 percent agreement between the two would cause him to suspect literary dependence immediately.

But this analogy is surely defective. What if McCartney were to test two students from an oral culture on what they had learned from a religious teacher in that culture, and what if they had lived with that teacher for three years and had received systematic instruction from him, often repeated verbatim? Would 46 percent agreement in their reminiscences, especially when remembering the words of their master, mean they had copied from each other? McCartney's comparison is hardly to the point. McCartney goes on to allege two other examples of Linnemann's basic misunderstanding of her topic. He charges her with making sweeping conclusions at times and with condemning all criticism of the Gospels because "most German criticism operates on unbelieving presuppositions." McCartney does not allow for Linnemann's self-restriction to the German scene, dominated as it is by the Two-Source Theory. Nor does he recognize that in academic gospels-study in Germany there is no other game in town except for the one controlled by such presuppositions, apart from a relatively tiny enclave of scholars making up the New Testament segment of the *Arbeitskreis für evangelikale Theologie* (a Tyndale Fellowship-like group) numbering no more than a dozen professional New Testament scholars. McCartney concludes that "in spite of her overstatements, she has some good points to make," but that "it is sad she has couched her arguments . . . in such a way that her valid observations will be easy for people to ignore."

One critical review remains, that by John S. Kloppenborg.[55] Generally speaking, it is a withering blast, repaying in kind the absence of "critical, courteous, and fair-minded interchange" he finds in Linnemann's book. Kloppenborg's charges are these: (1) Linnemann fails to set the views of figures like Lessing and Holtzmann "within a historical context"; (2) Linnemann limits her view to the German scene; (3) "her procedure involves both fragmentation of the data and curious statistical operations," an assertion for which Kloppenborg advances some arguments; and (4) Linnemann is wrong in assuming that literary dependence ought to result in nearly 100 percent reduplication of the original source, in this case Mark. Kloppenborg concludes, "If there is a case to be made for the independence of the Synoptics, let it be made. But let it be done with care, attention to the richly nuanced conversation that continues within the academy, and without baseless assertions of prejudice and bad faith." Clearly, in his view Linnemann is guilty of all these, as well as ignorance of bibliography and issues that would justify writing her off as at least emotionally imbalanced and perhaps just plain incompetent.[56]

CONTRIBUTION TO SCHOLARSHIP?

In two books and a number of articles that are impossible to explore in detail here, Linnemann has challenged the monopolistic gospel studies enterprise of German university scholarship as epitomized in the standard textbooks used there. In this she is hardly alone, as Bray has pointed out: "Historical criticism came under attack [in the 1970s and since] from many different sources, including from within the discipline itself."[57] Is Linnemann's voice yet another important word of caution, or even dissent, against Historical Criticism in the strict sense? Should one even move in the direction of looking askance at synoptic study operating within literary dependence parameters on the basis of her findings? With thousands of copies of her books in print and sales still lively, those questions cry out for informed answers from everyone involved in formal gospels studies, whether for preaching or for scholarly purposes. To answer these questions, an additional weighing of criticisms catalogued in the previous section—besides the minor ones already dealt with—is in order. This should also give a basis for additional insights into the question of the viability of Linnemann's proposals, a question involving a few perspectives and considerations that reviewers so far have either not noticed or decided not to mention.

Weaknesses and Merits of *Historical Criticism*

(1) The contentions of Vellmer, Roth, and other mainline German Protestant leaders that true faith is untouched by Historical Criticism because faith does not deal with empirical truth anyway, just religious experience, will carry weight only with those whose notion of Christian faith excludes any admixture of cognitively apprehended facts. This has admittedly been the shape of Christian faith for many since Lessing and Kant. It is a popular conception of faith today among various groups. Examples would include those who identify with an existentialist gospel à la Bultmann, those who utterly reject the role of reason in saving faith à la Barth, and those whose postmodern world view denies the knowable existence of truth generally and in religion particularly. ("If there is a mountain out there, there are any number of ways to get to the top.") Persons identifying with those views might be New Age types desiring a Christian flavor in their religious mix, old-line liberals of mainline denominations, evangelicals zealous for Barth, or pietists of any persuasion who so stress the Spirit and direct experience that Scripture and knowledge assume secondary importance.

But it is difficult to regard criticisms of Linnemann based on this outlook as fatal to her case, for so much in the Bible, in the history of the church, and even in recent hermeneutical discussion argues against it as a compelling position.[58] And in fact those criticisms came against Linnemann only from her German colleagues and from Casimir Bernas in North America. It seems fair to set them aside as insufficient grounds for calling in question the academic merit of Linnemann's arguments as a whole.

(2) Complaints that Linnemann tends to generalize and overstate, on the other hand, recur in reviews and must be taken seriously. To the extent that these tendencies detract from the substance of the arguments, or even replace argument with rhetoric, Linnemann's modus operandi has weakened her own case. It is likewise lamentable that she fails to concede positive contributions by critical scholarship. For example, do not New Testament exegetes everywhere make heavy use of the Greek lexicon that Walter Bauer, no theological conservative, compiled over a lifetime of diligent labor? Common courtesy calls for more fairness here.

On the other hand, the other side could argue that university scholarship in Germany during the last century would have produced a Hellenistic Greek lexicon anyway. After all, Bauer's predecessor, Cremer, a rock-ribbed confessionalist, proved that one need not share Bauer's critical views to produce quality lexical work. The post-Enlightenment, anti-orthodox conceptions of New Testament scholars *per se*, which "Historical Criticism" as Germans understand it enshrines, deserves little or no credit for Bauer's production. Possibly better lexical work, and more of it, could have come into being if there had been more appreciation for the truth and beauty of the Christian Scriptures and fewer million man-hours and monographs devoted to showing how true Christian faith, or early Christian history, is nothing like what the surface claims of the New Testament and the traditional teachings of the church imply.

Moreover, if one praises German criticism and demands reverence for its scholarly achievements, is it right to overlook its complicity in two World Wars, Germany's tragic anti-Semitism, and the West's widespread religious skepticism at the end of the twentieth century? Though it would be quite wrong to blame Historical Criticism for those disasters, it is equally dubious to call for respect for Historical Criticism's accomplishments while saying nothing about its liabilities. More than one German responding to Vellmer and Roth spoke about their country's empty churches and desolate soul as the result of the ravages of critical theology in the universities, and ultimately in the churches, over many generations. As the manifold failures of the twentieth century's Marxist experiments continue to come to light, it should never be forgotten that Karl Marx learned much about the New Testament at the feet of Bruno Bauer, a notable historical critic of the nineteenth century. Those are all sentiments that may sound churlish to voice but probably deserve a hearing.

(3) The investigation of reviews in the previous section indicated that the major set of arguments against Linnemann came from Boyd.[59] Some of his evident pique seems to be a classic case of a book not containing what the reviewer thinks it should. This irritation leads him to accuse Linnemann of fideism, a curious charge when one remembers that Germans like Vellmer thought she sounded rationalistic. His displeasure with Linnemann's statement that a Christian philosophy is a contradiction in terms makes sense in North America, where a Christian like Alvin Plantinga can be a leading philosopher, but fails to appreciate the German setting, which regards "philosophy" as a body of knowledge that rules out the viability of classic Christian belief and renders dialogue with it passé. North American academia has analogies at this point, as Alan Bloom and more recently Phillip Johnson have pointed out. It is naive to think that even Alvin Plantinga is causing historical critics in Germany (or, so far, in North America[60]) to rethink their hermeneutic.

Boyd's claim that Linnemann wishes to return humankind to classical antiquity is likewise hardly to be taken seriously. It constitutes an unfortunate overreaction to Linnemann's rhetorical critique of modernity's pretensions that it is leading the world into utopian splendor in all areas of life, whether medical or educational or technological. Here Linnemann is merely echoing similar critiques by many secular thinkers who call attention to the Trojan horse of "modern" approaches to medicine, technology, the environment, and even private life, and who point out that post-industrial "progress" is often more than offset by harmful side effects. For example, despite the mechanization of the American home by all kinds of time saving devices, why do we have so much less discretionary time than a generation ago? Further, what has a generation of post-60s educational philosophy and values clarification done for the SAT scores, morals, and character of American school children?[61] "New" or "modern" is often not better at all. This is Linnemann's point, as most reviewers were able to recognize.

Boyd's charge that Linnemann fails to point out modern science's Christian roots are historically well founded. But they are irrelevant for science as it exists in the sphere in which Linnemann is dealing. In that realm a stark naturalism has mostly hijacked the scientific enterprise inaugurated centuries ago by thinkers who were, as Boyd correctly implies, Christian in their worldview. Boyd, unlike other reviewers, seems to lack adequate grasp of the shape of "historical critical" thought as it actually exists in the German university system. He seems to see it as a benign set of ground rules amenable to at least two underlying metaphysical (or anti-metaphysical) rationales: a Christian rationale and a post-Enlightenment, non-Christian one. But this is not how "historical critical" thought exists in the halls of learning of the European continent, especially in Germany. In the end Boyd's criticisms point more to failure to understand the German system, a system not without analogies in North America, than to a systemic failure on Linnemann's part.

Boyd's decision not to recommend the book to those not looking for a passionate sermon on "the evils of biblical criticism" is understandable. There are plenty of non-Christians or historical critics to whom this writer would not want to give a copy of *Historical Criticism* for fear the tone would do more harm than good. Yet Boyd's words appear to trivialize those "evils," when in fact Linnemann is on firm ground in seeing them for the dangers they are. Boyd also seems to assume that people do not *need* to hear sermons they do not *want* to hear. The opposite is not seldom the case.

The value of Boyd's remarks is that they alert readers to the limitations of Linnemann's style of response. This writer has finally concluded, in the course of preparing this essay and cataloguing reviewers' responses, that a defense is possible for what she has written from the standpoint of who the writer was, when she wrote (shortly after conversion), and just which set of ills she sought to address (those prevailing in the German system, of which she had long been an insider). But Boyd is correct to warn that Linnemann's approach is not to be universalized, at least not *in toto*, even by others who share many of her basic convictions. Her words could fan the flames of an anti-intellectual, militia mentality already too common in conservative American religion. They might cause college or seminary students to be haughty and dismissive of ideas they have not yet taken the time to understand. They might encourage young preachers to adopt a Rush Limbaugh tone that would be disastrous for any gracious presentation of gospel claims. The need exists for an evenhanded, restrained, and highly trained interaction with historical-critical ideas long typified by scholars in, say, the Tyndale Fellowship tradition, a tradition of learned and dispassionate inquiry, yet still palpably Christian in orientation, with precedents as varied as the work of J. B. Lightfoot, Adolf Schlatter, and J. Gresham Machen.

Yet there is room from time to time for a prophetic voice calling attention to imminent dangers and warning against complacency, unwitting complicity, and misplaced hopes. With many reviewers, this writer concurs that limitations of Linnemann's popular-level diatribe against Historical Criticism should not obscure its important, valid insights. Despite its flaws and intentional popular appeal, Linnemann's *Historical Criticism* furthers scholarship by sharpening one's vision of what it is and ought to be.

Weaknesses and Merits of *Is There a Synoptic Problem?*

(1) Reviewers of *Is There a Synoptic Problem?* have repeatedly pointed out the weakness of Linnemann's positive proposals regarding how the Gospels found their way into writing in the mid-A.D. 60s. Though her appeal to external, patristic evidence is refreshing when compared to common critical fixation with internal evidence alone,[62] it is not as sophisticated as it might be. Wenham, Riesner, and others appear to have valid criticisms here.

Linnemann is also more dependent on Zahn's history of synoptic studies than is desirable. Here, too, Riesner has shown the weakness of Linnemann's reliance on secondary literature, expertly citing relevant original sources to show the derivative nature of her knowledge of certain points. But this does not mean that Kloppenborg is justified in claiming that Linnemann fails to set figures "within a historical context." Linnemann is broadly correct that an anti-Christian animus worked in figures like Lessing, and that biblical scholars taking their cues not from data but from the *Zeitgeist* transformed New Testament scholarship into a discipline serving philosophical idealism rather than the empirical ideals normally associated with historical science. F. C. Baur and the Tübingen school illustrate that point. Still, if Linnemann wishes to place weight on her reading of the history of the discipline, she needs to do more careful primary-source investigation.

Of course, Linnemann could respond that her reading of history is no more sketchy and tendential than Bultmann's reading of the history of New Testament theology, which is at least as skewed as Linnemann's in the direction he wanted it to go.[63] This is not to advocate letting Linnemann off the hook because Bultmann does the same thing. It is only to point out that a weak ancillary section does not necessarily detract from a book's central arguments. Clearly Linnemann's account of the remote history of gospel studies is not the main point of her book, any more than is her reconstruction of gospel composition on the basis of patristic sources—especially Irenaeus.

(2) Jurgens' appeal to Robert Stein[64] in an effort to minimize the importance of eyewitnesses calls for careful reflection. Linnemann is obviously

concerned to uphold apostolic authorship of the synoptics, whether direct (Matthew) or indirect (Mark, Luke), along the lines envisioned by ancient tradition, the titles of the earliest manuscripts themselves, and Luke's prologue. Jürgens seems to think that the process of gospel composition is of less importance than the final form, which is at the end of the day what God inspired. But the issue is not so simple. At the inaugural level of "historical-critical" study of the Gospels as it exists today is D. F. Strauss (1808–1874). And foundational to his demolition of the aura of reliability that had surrounded the Gospels for centuries was his conviction that the Gospels are not, and must not have been, produced by direct eyewitnesses:

> It would most unquestionably be an argument of decisive weight in favour of the credibility of the biblical history, could it indeed be shown that it was written by eyewitnesses, or even by persons nearly contemporaneous with the events narrated. For though errors and false representations may glide into the narrations even of an eye-witness, there is far less probability of unintentional mistake (intentional deception may easily be detected) than where the narrator is separated by a long interval from the facts he records, and is obliged to derive his materials through the medium of transmitted communications.[65]

Linnemann's sensitivity to the eyewitness question is probably an intuitive response to the German setting where the ongoing task of upholding Strauss' denial of eyewitness status to the Gospels is an underlying, if tacit, function of Source, Form, and Redaction Criticism. It is worth noting that Bultmann wished to dedicate the first edition of his *History of the Synoptic Tradition* to Strauss but was advised against it by his teacher Wilhelm Heitmüller for political reasons.[66] His desire confirms his commitment to the ideal Strauss established.

It is ironic, then, to see defense of the authentic (namely, true-to-historical-fact) *result* of gospel formation—such as Stein argues for—when most historical critics understand that material to contain either no direct eyewitness material, or only such as has been handed along, processed perhaps several times, and eventually set in final form generations after the events described. To illustrate, contemporary study of Abraham Lincoln gives the authenticity of sayings attributed to him an A rating in the case of a direct quote recorded soon after its utterance, B if an indirect quote recorded soon after its utterance, and C for quotes reported only after the passage of weeks, months, or years.[67] That seems to be a reasonable ranking system, with its analogies in criteria established to rank the authenticity of what Jesus may have said. But if applied to Jesus' words with the understanding that all the synoptic material is the result of a complex tradition process that first crystallized two generations or more after Jesus' death, few of the synoptic words of Jesus are likely to be regarded as necessarily genuine. Divine inspiration becomes a *deus ex machina* to preserve what historical probability and common sense argue against.

Though Linnemann may try to prove too much with her theory of radical non-interdependence among synoptic writers, she is not being naive in her aversion to facile theories of synoptic composition that would retain a high degree of reliability for synoptic sayings while going with the flow of literary criticisms sprouting out of the ashes of the once-reliable gospel edifice that Strauss torched to the ground. If eyewitnesses are primarily responsible for gospel documents, the complicated tradition process *as posited by large segments of synoptic criticism*[68] is both unlikely and unnecessary. On the other hand, if traditional two-source synoptic criticism is largely correct and the whole gospel tradition is mostly hearsay, then claims of eyewitness reliability for the results of the tradition process sound like special pleading, especially when those claims call in the Holy Spirit to guarantee the historical veracity that empirical observation is assumed to have demolished.

(3) Another point touched on repeatedly by reviewers (Head, McCartney, Williams, Kloppenborg) was Linnemann's claim that literary dependence should result in something approaching 100 percent agreement between, say, Matthew and Mark, if Matthew copied Mark. Reviewers claimed that literary dependence could be at work with a much lower percentage of agreement. Discussion above has already suggested that McCartney's comparison of 46 percent agreement between two student test papers, on the one hand, and the Gospels, on the other, is an apples-and-oranges correspondence carrying minimal weight. The same is true of Williams' observation based on local newspaper reports of a supersectional high school basketball game. It is not easy to see what is proved by observing that two reporters gave two quite different accounts.

This yields no basis for the conclusion that to have the degree of verbal similarity they do,[69] the Gospels must reflect some amount of direct literary borrowing. Other explanations are possible. Different on-the-spot reports of a post-season basketball melee bears little resemblance, formal or material, to the apostolic recollection of the deeds and words of the Son of God as He instilled His truths into His followers over the span of several years and in a culture where faithful preservation of holy prophetic utterances had a venerable past.[70]

More weighty here is Head's reference to the Targums and the Masoretic Text, the gospel of Peter and the canonical gospels, and Josephus' use of the Old Testament and Aristeas. In the same vein Kloppenborg refers to Josephus' replication of the Decalogue. Their point is to underscore what Kloppenborg calls "the extremely free way in which classical authors treated their source material."[71] But this is not always the case. Counterexamples like Suetonius and Eusebius spring to mind immediately. From the New Testament writers to Clement of Rome and onward, it is apparent that direct borrowing from scriptural sources commonly results in nearly 100 percent reproduction of the text being cited, at least in the form known to the writer. When the likeness is much less than 100 percent, then one suspects a loose allusion, not direct copying. So the evidence here is not as clearly one-sided as suggested.

Furthermore, for each example cited by reviewers, one could point out factors that show the relatively free citation as observed in some sources to be doubtful analogies for synoptic composition. The express design of the Targums was to expand and interpret the Masoretic Text; the gospel of Peter is clearly bent on augmenting some strands of canonical material with lore of quite different origin; Josephus is well within the bounds of literary license in how he shapes and adapts the material he uses from the Hebrew Scriptures and elsewhere. It is only if one assumes synoptic literary interdependence that these analogies seem immediately to explain synoptic phenomena. But closer scrutiny limits the analogy.

The Targums, for example, are hundreds if not more than a thousand years later than the traditions they gloss. The gospel of Peter is a mid-second century document[72] making obvious free use of canonical sources for docetic purposes. Josephus' various apologetic motivations are well documented. In each of these cases, purely literary dependence, helped along by extra-literary considerations (for example, Josephus could not possibly have been a witness at Mount Sinai), is the only historical explanation possible. Things are different with the synoptics. The time span between document and putative source is drastically reduced.

Admittedly, a literary dependence explanation on the analogy of Targums, New Testament apocrypha, and Josephus is imaginable. But so is the scenario proposed by Linnemann: hand-picked and specially trained followers of Jesus heard His words and recorded them in juxtaposition with His equally striking and memorable deeds, all framed with varying degrees of chronological concern and exact verbal precision within a continuum stretching from birth and boyhood to Galilean days, forays to Judea and elsewhere, and eventually death in Jerusalem. Verbatim similarities among the synoptics, typically exceeding 80 percent in Jesus' words but more often running at around 50 percent or below even in parallel passages, are due to similarity of reminiscence and the lasting impressions His words left. The accounts resemble each other because the things they report happened and were remembered by those later responsible for recording them, not because various non-witnesses relied chiefly on one or two seminal documents (Mark, Q) having equally indirect ties with the original phenomena.

The synoptics differ for many reasons. To name some obvious ones: imprecision of memory, point of view of recollection, varied and repeated forms in which Jesus delivered His wisdom, translation from Semitic forms into Greek, and the inherent fact that identical truths or observations are communicable in quite different verbal combinations, linguistically speaking.

None of this discounts the challenge that reviewers pose at this point. It simply suggests that the reasons they give for discounting Linnemann are thin in substance. Most telling in Linnemann's favor, however, is the obvious conclusion that reviewers seem to use a heads-I-win, tails-you-lose argument. Synoptic agreement is seen as proof of inter-synoptic direct dependence. Yet synoptic divergence is still proof of inter-synoptic direct dependence, reasoning from parallels like those cited above.[73] In this scheme of things no dissent from current consensus is possible—literary dependence theories are, as M. Goulder says of the Q theory, a juggernaut.[74] While one may finally beg to differ with Linnemann's dissatisfaction with the critical tradition that makes use of that logic, it is only fair to grant that she has a point in calling it into question.

(4) A recurring criticism in reviews questioned Linnemann's use of statistics. Richard S. Cervin sent a lengthy and detailed personal letter to Linnemann outlining problems with her method. To summarize his criticism (page references are to Linnemann's *Is There a Synoptic Problem?*):

> I have found a number of problems with some of your statistics. On page 110, you say "We can only assess the data objectively through quantitative means" and on page 59 you acknowledge the need for tests. I agree with you in principle; however, your analysis makes no use of statistical tests—you have simply counted words and figured percentages. How is anyone to know whether your word counts are statistically significant or are the result of mere chance? How is anyone to know whether your samples are large enough to be statistically significant? Merely counting words and providing percentages as you have done is not very meaningful without some statistical tests to demonstrate probability levels, correlations, margins of error, and various other relationships among the data.[75]

Kloppenborg refers to the same problem in complaining that Linnemann "draws conclusions from raw numbers."[76] This is probably the major weakness of Linnemann's book. Yet Cervin goes on to note that he has "yet to see any biblical scholar provide any formula for any probability statement made." He adds that in the course of researching his response to Linnemann, he "found that nearly all of the statistical studies done by biblical scholars that I examined were based on misunderstandings and/or ignorance of statistical procedures and reasoning." In other words, Linnemann is using a method of reasoning similar if not identical to scholars who argue contrasting conclusions. Though it is fair to point out her faulty method, if faulty it is, one must also go on to call in question the statistic-based arguments of the mainline textbooks that Linnemann seeks to refute. Among reviewers, only Riesner recognizes that Linnemann's problem here is one shared by everyone who places too much weight on statistics alone to prove or disprove synoptic theories. If statistical findings *supporting* literary dependence theories receive positive recognition despite their faulty nature (and no one familiar with synoptic literature will suggest they are not receiving that recognition), then it would be consistent to agree that Linnemann using similar methods has formulated an important counterbalance in response to those theories.

Norman E. Reed has pointed out the problem of statistical studies of the Gospels along with the reasonable nature of Linnemann's results seen within that milieu.[77] He notes that B. H. Streeter finds a 51 percent agreement between Matthew and Mark in actual wording. Morganthaler finds 77 percent agreement in overall substance, 38 percent if agreement be defined as identical wording. Carson, Moo, and Morris say that 97 percent of Mark is paralleled in Matthew,[78] citing Robert Stein's *The Synoptic Problem*, which says that "97.2% of the words in Mark have a parallel in Matthew."[79] For support Stein cites Joseph Tyson's and Thomas Longstaff's *Synoptic Abstracts*.[80] Clearly the divergence of figures here—51 percent, 77 percent, 38 percent, 97 percent—suggests that something is awry. Taking the highest of these, Reed shows that Stein's figure is far too high and is based on a dubious interpretation of Tyson and Longstaff.

Tyson and Longstaff analyze the synoptics with computers for verbal agreement using three different criteria.[81] The first is *continuity*. This means "strict verbal agreement of at least two consecutive words between parallel pericopes." Using this criterion, 3,512 of Mark's 11,025 words agree with Matthew.[82] Thus 32 percent of Mark agrees with Matthew. A second, more generous criterion is what Tyson and Longstaff call *identity*. This is defined as "strict agreement of words, but without the requirement that any of the words have to be consecutive." Using this method, 40 percent of Mark's words agree with Matthew. A third criterion is *equivalency*. This "calls for only the root or the meaning of two words to be in agreement within parallel pericopes."

Applied to all of Mark, adding the similarities found by computer search based on all three criteria, 5,357 of Mark's 11,025 words have verbal agreement with Matthew. This is a 49 percent parallel between Mark and Matthew.

Reed shows that when Stein cites Tyson and Longstaff, he appears to base his 97.2 percent figure on the observation that "[o]f the 11,025 words found in Mark, only 304 have no parallel in Matthew."[83] This means that 10,721 are parallel; Stein appears to be reasoning that 10,721 divided by 11,025 is 97.2 percent. The math here is correct, but he has gone beyond what Tyson and Longstaff themselves arrive at, which is 49 percent.[84] Reed comments, "The problem is further compounded when others . . . quote his interpretation of the data in their writings." And in a surprisingly positive assessment of Linnemann, given criticisms recounted elsewhere in this paper, Reed makes the following conclusion:

> Linnemann claims that the parallelism found between Mark and Matthew is 55.25 percent. She also writes that 40.32 percent of the words of Mark have exact verbal agreement [with parallel passages in Matthew]. But she goes on to give a reasonably detailed explanation of the method she has used to arrive at these statistics. Her willingness to include a description of her method adds to the credibility of her claims. It is interesting to note how closely her results, produced by observation and tedious hand calculations, agree with the computer generated results of [Tyson and Longstaff's] *Synoptic Abstract*.

It seems fair to agree with reviewers that Linnemann's work is hampered by the same restrictions inherent in all purely statistical approaches. But it seems equally important to bear in mind that the suggestion that her statistics are wildly improbable or misleading appears to be one-sided.

(5) Two final criticisms of Linnemann need to be assessed. Previous discussion has already touched on one of them: her specific positive proposal, based on Irenaus's statements about Peter in the A.D. 60s, is unconvincing. It is important to note this. But it is equally important to point out that no single positive proposal explaining the data of gospel origins has yet found universal acceptance. Even Reimarus (who proposed greed for financial gain as the historical explanation for apostolic claims) and Strauss (who proposed naive mythological forms of perception and expression), rightly hailed as leaders in the historical-critical tradition, find few to no followers of their specific positive proposals today. What they contributed was the destruction of prior certainties, not the establishment of more lasting ones. With this in mind, one can say that Linnemann's central argument—that the synoptics can be explained on historical and not merely literary grounds—might still merit serious consideration in spite of the weaknesses of her last few chapters. Parts of her other sections may bring about a constructive destabilization of prior but dubious certainties. It is up to others to make constructive use of them, if this is possible.

(6) And finally, Kloppenborg makes much of Linnemann's failure to factor in "the virtual avalanche of literature on the synoptic problem."[85] This is undoubtedly a weakness. Yet the German university textbooks that Linnemann worked with likewise fail to show familiarity with this avalanche. Helmut Koester, for example, in his section on literary criticism of the Gospels, notes only studies by Holtzmann, Wellhausen, Streeter, Lehmann, Farmer, and Stoldt.[86] The work of Streeter, Farmer, and Stoldt he ignores, unless he includes them in his remark that strong objections continue to be raised against "the Two Source Hypothesis," which he presents as "the most widely accepted solution of the Synoptic Problem." In other words, Linnemann is far from alone in doing her work in isolation from other important strands of research.

Like Kloppenborg, this writer is uncomfortable with Linnemann's bibliographical myopia, and it is true that she invites suspicion by not presenting her views in close enough interaction with a broader spectrum of thinkers. But given the studies she has chosen to respond to, her work is hardly more restricted in focus than theirs.

One thinks here of Otto Betz's critique of the Jesus Seminar: "In view of [their] unfounded presuppositions and the homogeneity that these forced presuppositions impose on the Fellows, the number of scholars [voting] doesn't amount to much in the end: even with 400 participants the Seminar's findings would hardly look any different."[87] Linnemann ignores a sizable bloc of synoptic discussion because in the end, it amounts to a single shout of acclaim for literary dependence, which is the very premise that she wants to isolate and call into question. If one should not ridicule Koester (or Bultmann, whose work typically showed the same tendency) for failing to do bibliographical justice to those segments of the community of scholarship that do not agree with his line of thinking, neither should she/he write off Linnemann for mirroring the limited scope of the textbook examples she analyzes.[88]

CONCLUSION

This chapter began by noting Bray's argument that Historical Criticism no longer enjoys its former monopoly status and is being supplanted by at least two other broad and rival forms of intellectually viable analysis. Linnemann's work is symptomatic of the current ferment. Of the criticisms lodged against her, some of them stick. Others lack cogency. She is not a foe of scholarship, it appears, unless that scholarship is unprepared to question its basic premises where this is warranted. But then in what sense is it scholarship?

Linnemann's work as exemplified in her first two post-conversion books is not a model of scholarly disquisition due to its (in places) sermonic form, abrasive tone, and failure to take account of other literature. On the other hand, sermons are sometimes needed where they are not desired. What she seeks to prove—that the synoptics are not literarily interdependent—may turn out to be unprovable using statistics alone, or indeed by any means whatsoever. Yet it is notoriously difficult, in many instances, to furnish positive proof for or against anything that is not and never was true. She may be regarded as a friend of scholarship in terms of the industry, tenacity, and intensity with which she has expended impressive labor in hope of shedding light on a crucial area of inquiry; in her zeal for truth; in her creativity, originality, fearlessness, and sharpness in analysis; and in her willingness to change her mind (humility) after finding herself fundamentally mistaken at the very core of her outlook.

Article output subsequent to her two post-conversion books shows that her work continues to exhibit the strengths just mentioned—and fewer of the weaknesses. It is ironic, and perhaps symptomatic of the troubled state of criticisms of all stripes at the moment, that precisely in an age of tolerance and recognition of the legitimacy of women's voice in biblical scholarship, some have been so quick to stigmatize a female intelligence praised so highly[89] when it served the furtherance of historical-critical assumptions and results.[90]

ENDNOTES

1. Gerald Bray, *Biblical Interpretation, Past and Present* (Downers Grove, Ill./ Leicester, England: InterVarsity, 1996), 467.
2. Ibid., 539.
3. Ibid., 481.
4. For example, "One can no more be a little historical-critical than a little pregnant" (Eta Linnemann, *Historical Criticism of the Bible: Methodology or Ideology*, trans. Robert W. Yarbrough [Grand Rapids: Baker, 1990], 123).
5. Rudolf Bultmann, *Jesus and the Word* (Edinburgh: T & T Clark, 1980 [1935]); idem, *The History of the Synoptic Tradition*, 2d ed. (Oxford: Blackwell, 1968 [1931]. [titles and dates of English translations with dates of the original German works in brackets]).

6. Walter Bauer, *Orthodoxy and Heresy in Earliest Christianity* (Philadelphia: Fortress, 1971 [1934]).
7. In Linnemann's own words, she was "Dozentin am Seminar für kirchlichen Dienst in Berlin."
8. See note 4.
9. For an assessment (now slightly outdated) of the work there, see Klaus Wetzel, "Die Studenten des Bibelinstituts Batu—ihre kirkliche u. geographische Herkunft," *Evangelische Missiologie* 1 (1988): 7–10.
10. Linnemann, *Historical Criticism of the Bible*.
11. Eta Linnemann, *Is There a Synoptic Problem?* trans. Robert W. Yarbrough (Grand Rapids: Baker, 1992).
12. Udo Schnelle, *Einleitung in das Neue Testament* (Göttingen, 1994).
13. Journal publication under negotiation.
14. *Journal of the Adventist Theological Society* 5, no. 2 (1994): 19–36.
15. *Trinity Journal* 17NS (1996): 3–18.
16. *Bible Review* (August 1995): 18–23, 42–43.
17. *Jahrbuch für evangelikale Theologie* 10 (1996).
18. The article and responses to it referred to above are from *Dokumentation: Kasseler Sonntagsblatt. Moderne Theologie und Gemeinde. Der Streit um Eta Linnemann* (Kassel, 1986). I owe Hans Bayer thanks for making this available to me.
19. *Wissenschaft oder Meinung? Anfragen und Alternativen* (Neuhausen: Hänssler, 1986), later translated as *Historical Criticism of the Bible* (n. 4 above).
20. Robert Yarbrough presented a paper entitled "From Bultmannian to Biblicist: Eta Linnemann's Indictment of Contemporary New Testament Scholarship."
21. Namely, *Historical Criticism of the Bible*.
22. One review by David C. C. Watson appeared twice: *Churchman* 105, no. 4 (1991): 373f.; *English Churchman* (July 12 & 19, 1991): 7.
23. Ibid.
24. David P. Kuske, *Wisconsin Lutheran Quarterly* 88, no. 3 (1991): 239.
25. David E. Lanier, *Faith and Mission* 11, no. 2 (1994).
26. Joe Blair, *Grace Theological Journal* 11 (fall 1990): 246–48.
27. William F. Warren, Jr., *Theological Educator* 45 (1992): 149–52.
28. E. Earle Ellis, *Southwestern Journal of Theology* 34 (fall 1991): 82.
29. David Crump, *Criswell Theological Review* 6 (fall 1992): 153–55.
30. Robert M. Johnston, *Andrews University Seminary Studies* 30 (summer 1992): 171–74.
31. Robert Shirock, *Evangelical Quarterly* 64 (July 1992): 275–77.
32. Daniel Clendenin, *Journal of the Evangelical Theological Society* 35, no. 1 (1992): 101f.
33. Howard Rhys, *Sewanee Theological Review* 35 (1992): 212. Rhys is also critical of Linnemann for holding to a view of verbal inspiration of the Bible and for accepting "such historic ascriptions of authorship as that of Paul for the Pastoral Epistles."
34. Andreas Köstenberger, *Trinity Journal* 13NS (1992): 95–98.
35. Horace D. Hummel, *Concordia Journal* 19 (July 1993): 284–87.
36. Casimir Bernas, *Religious Studies Review* 18, no. 2 (April 1992): 140.
37. Bernas says that the issue is "the reconciliation of historical research with religious faith" and advises Linnemann, *"Non arguitur contra factum."*
38. Gregory A. Boyd, *Christian Scholar's Review* 22, no. 1 (fall 1992): 106–9.
39. Ibid., 109.

40. See note 11 above.
41. Usually defined as the set of knotty questions posed by both the similarities among and the differences between Matthew, Mark, and Luke, assuming some kind of literary dependence among the three.
42. John Wenham, *Evangelical Quarterly* 66, no. 3 (1994): 266–67.
43. Cf. John Wenham's own weighty contribution to the synoptic debate: *Redating Matthew, Mark and Luke: A Fresh Assault on the Synoptic Problem* (Downers Grove: InterVarsity, 1992).
44. Wenham argues for a limited literary interdependence and for Luke's use of Mark (ibid.).
45. Erich H. Kiehl, *Concordia Journal* 19 (July 1993): 280–81.
46. Edwin E. Reynolds, *Andrews University Seminary Studies* 33 (Autumn 1995): 309–10.
47. Robert L. Thomas, *The Master's Seminary Journal* 4 (1993): 111–13.
48. William R. Farmer, *Religious Studies Review* 20, no. 4 (October 1994): 337.
49. David W. Jurgens, *Reformed Review* 47 (1993): 63.
50. Summarized in Hans-Herbert Stoldt, *History and Criticism of the Marcan Hypothesis,* trans. and ed. Donald L. Niewyk (Macon, Ga./Edinburgh: Mercer University/T & T Clark, 1980), 18–23.
51. Peter Head, *Anvil* 10, no. 3 (1993): 260–61. Linnemann makes a statement to this effect in *Is There a Synoptic Problem?* 109, and again (with more nuance) on 132.
52. Matt Williams, *Trinity Journal* 14, no. 1NS (spring 1993): 97–101.
53. Rainer Riesner, *Jahrbuch für evangelikale Theologie* 9 (1995): 225–27.
54. Dan G. McCartney, *Westminster Theological Journal* 55 (1993): 348–50.
55. John S. Kloppenborg, *Critical Review of Books in Religion* 6 (1993): 262–64.
56. The dismissive, even contemptuous tone of the review is striking. Kloppenborg might reply that Linnemann pushed first.
57. Bray, *Biblical Interpretation Past and Present,* 461.
58. On Kantian fact-faith dichotimization in currently ascendent pluralist theologies (Hick, Knitter et al.), see Joseph Cardinal Ratzinger, "Zur Lage von Glaube und Theologie heute," *Internationalen Katholischen Zeitschrift Communio* 25 (July/August 1996): 359–72. I am indebted to Werner Neuer for this reference.
59. See above under the heading "North America and Britain: Reaction to *Historical Criticism of the Bible.*"
60. For a tantalizing harbinger, possibly, of better things to come, see Stephen Louthan, "On Religion—A Discussion with Richard Rorty, Alvin Plantinga and Nicholas Wolterstorff," *Christian Scholar's Review* 26, no. 2 (winter 1996): 177–83.
61. This is not to blame schools for children's declining performance; home life is an even greater problem. But schools are an obvious relevant factor in the decline.
62. The fixation goes back to D. F. Strauss (*The Life of Jesus Critically Examined,* ed. Peter C. Hodgson, trans. George Eliot [Philadelphia: Fortress, 1972 (1835)]): "To investigate the internal grounds of credibility in relation to each detail given in the Gospels (for it is with them alone that we are here concerned) and to test the probability or improbability of their being the production of eyewitnesses, or of competently informed writers, is the sole object of the present work" (70). Strauss justified the limitation to internal matters by discrediting patristic testimony, namely, early church tradition. His procedure is somewhat similar to that of Reimarus.

63. Rudolf Bultmann, *Theologie des Neuen Testaments* (Tübingen: Mohr/ Siebeck, 19808), 585–89.
64. Robert H. Stein, *The Synoptic Problem: An Introduction* (Grand Rapids: Baker, 1987).
65. Strauss, *Life of Jesus Critically Examined,* 69. See also n. 62 above.
66. Gerd Lüdemann, *The Resurrection of Jesus,* trans. John Bowden (Minneapolis: Fortress, 1994), 193 n. 76. Thus, though "Rudolf Bultmann hardly ever referred to Strauss," (Colin Brown, *Jesus in European Protestant Thought* [Grand Rapids: Baker, 1988], 204), he may have worked more consciously in Strauss' train than his explicit autobiographical remarks indicate.
67. Don and Virginia Fehrenbacher, *Recollected Words of Abraham Lincoln* (Stanford: Stanford University, 1996), cited in Lewis Lord, "Looking for Lincoln," *U.S. News & World Report* (February 17, 1997): 62–63.
68. The italics are important. I think there was a tradition process, and it was complicated. But I do not find the methods and informing hermeneutic of some segments of guild synoptic studies to be convincing either in their methods or results. Rainer Riesner's *Jesus als Lehrer,* 3d ed. (Tübingen: Mohr/Siebeck, 1988) is an example of an alternate approach that does not oversimplify, yet works in conscious contrast to many received ground rules of synoptic criticism. See also the viewpoints represented in William R. Farmer, ed., *Crisis in Christology* (Livonia, Mich.: Dove Booksellers, 1995). Biblical scholars represented in this volume include C. F. D. Moule, R. T. France, E. Earle Ellis, N. T. Wright, James Dunn, Martin Hengel, Peter Stuhlmacher, Ben F. Meyer, and Farmer himself. While all of these would take exception to much in Linnemann, their work shares with hers a theme of disagreement with the methods, aims, and results of synoptic criticism in many of its current forms.
69. For a summary of many of the statistical findings, see Linnemann, *Is There a Synoptic Problem?* 149.
70. Note, for example, Kenneth E. Bailey, "Middle Eastern Oral Tradition and the Synoptic Gospels," *The Expository Times* (September 1995): 363–67.
71. Kloppenborg, *Critical Review,* 263.
72. Wilhelm Schneemelcher, ed., *New Testament Apocrypha,* rev. ed., trans. R. McL. Wilson, vol. 1 (Cambridge, England/Louisville, Ky.: James Clarke & Co./John Knox, 1991), 221; M. S. Enslin, "Peter, Gospel of," in *The Interpreter's Dictionary of the Bible,* K-Q (Nashville: Abingdon, 1962), 766. The claims that it "circulated in the mid-1st century" and "probably served as one of the major sources for the canonical gospels" (Paul Allan Mirecki, "Peter, Gospel of," in *The Anchor Bible Dictionary,* ed. David Noel Freedman, vol. 5 [New York et al.: Doubleday, 1992], 278), are based on the mutually supporting theories of J. D. Crossan and H. Koester and lack documentary backing.
73. See Linnemann's observations on this phenomenon in *Is There a Synoptic Problem?* 109f. and elsewhere.
74. M. Goulder, "Is Q a Juggernaut?" *Journal of Biblical Literature* 115, no. 4 (1996): 667–81.
75. This and other quotations from Cervin are from a copy of his letter to Linnemann kindly supplied by Cervin.
76. Kloppenborg, *Critical Review,* 263.
77. "How Much of Mark's Gospel Can Be Found in Matthew?" Unpublished paper. Unfootnoted quotations in the next few paragraphs are from Reed. My thanks to Rev. Reed for sharing the results of his research with me.

78. Carson, Moo, and Morris, *An Introduction to the New Testament* (Grand Rapids: Zondervan, 1992), 33.
79. Stein, *Synoptic Problem*, 48.
80. Joseph Tyson and Thomas Longstaff, *Synoptic Abstracts, The Computer Bible* 15 (Wooster, Ohio: College of Wooster, 1978).
81. Ibid., 11.
82. Ibid., 170.
83. Stein, *Synoptic Problem*, 48.
84. Tyson and Longstaff, *Synoptic Abstracts*, 75, 170.
85. Kloppenborg, *Critical Review*, 264.
86. Helmut Koester, *Introduction to the New Testament*, volume 2: *History and Literature of Early Christianity* (Philadelphia, Berlin, and New York: Fortress/Walter de Gruyter, 1980), 43–45.
87. Review of R. W. Funk and Roy Hoover, *The Five Gospels, Theologische Literaturzeitung* 119, no. 11 (1994): 989.
88. In private conversation, Linnemann defends her practice here by noting that it amounts to an *ad fontes* focus. The problem she wrestles with is that the Synoptics are read through the lenses of secondary literature based on dubious assumptions. She attempts to analyze the primary literature, first of all, not to wade into the turbulent, and turbid, waters of secondary discussion.
89. Linnemann's two published doctoral dissertations were accorded critical acclaim. The first of these, *Jesus of the Parables* (New York/Evanston: Harper & Row, 1966), continues in widespread use.
90. My thanks to Steve Kline and to the New Testament Colloquium of Trinity Evangelical Divinity School for constructive comments on this paper.

CHAPTER FIVE

Form Criticism and Tradition Criticism

F. David Farnell

THE HISTORICAL-CRITICAL DISCIPLINES of Tradition and Form Criticism are the outgrowths of historical skepticism stemming immediately from Source Criticism and ultimately from the philosophical roots of the Enlightenment. Thus, they are *philosophically driven* disciplines. They developed from an underlying foundation that was innately hostile to the historicity of the biblical text. For the most part, philosophical movements that comprise the presuppositional foundations of Tradition and Form Criticism are responsible for the ascendance of these methodologies to widespread predominance in biblical interpretation.

Since philosophy forms the basis for all historical-critical methodologies (Source, Form, Redaction, and Tradition Criticism), "ideologies" is a better name for them than "methodologies." Linnemann remarks as follows:

> A more intensive investigation would show that underlying the historical-critical approach is a series of prejudgments which are not themselves the result of scientific investigation. They are rather dogmatic premises, statements of faith, whose foundation is the absolutizing of human reason as a controlling apparatus.[1]

As inherently philosophical ideologies, Tradition and Form Criticism have prescribed agendas that reach foregone conclusions, rendering objectivity impossible. They are incapable of neutrality in analyzing the text of the Bible.

Philosophical presuppositions also affect how Tradition and Form Criticism interpret the text, causing their proponents to read into the text interpretive conclusions foreign to the text (namely, eisegesis) instead of letting the text speak for itself (namely, exegesis). Just as a child's Lego® set is capable of building only certain structures in a certain way, so it is with historical-critical methods. They are acutely subjective and often magnify the capricious biases of the interpreter. In contrast to the grammatico-historical method that seeks objectivity in interpretation, Tradition and Form Criticism inherently promote subjectivity.[2]

Theological liberalism developed Tradition and Form Criticism, for philosophical trends profoundly influence people of that persuasion. Liberals laud the utilization of these disciplines, for the ideology's *a priori* agenda suits their interpretation of the biblical text. The post-Bultmannian Norman Perrin is typical when he calls Form Criticism [hereafter FC] "the single most important development" in the history of gospel criticism, "for it provides what must be regarded as the only satisfactory understanding of the nature of the synoptic gospel material."[3]

Though some evangelicals, especially conservative ones, at first adopted an apologetic stance against such hermeneutical ideologies, many now evidence a greater willingness to accept them. Evangelical Robert Guelich, following the lead of George Ladd, his mentor, promoted an exegesis "that . . . makes use of the literary critical tools including text, source, form, tradition, redaction, and structural criticism" and asserted, "For many to whom the Scriptures are vital the use of these critical tools has historically been more 'destructive' than 'constructive.' But one need not discard the tool because of its abuse."[4] Evangelical Darrell Bock argues, "In the hands of a skilled exegete who uses the tools of interpretation in a way that fits what they are capable of, Form Criticism can be a fruitful aid to understanding and to exposition."[5] As will be demonstrated, however, evangelical attempts to practice modified forms of these ideologies in isolation from their negative underpinnings have failed.

Alister McGrath recently labelled evangelicalism as the "future of Protestantism," "a modern standard bearer of historic, orthodox Christianity," the "mainstream of American Protestant Christianity," and "the Christian vision of the future."[6] This future for orthodox Christianity may be bleak, however, if evangelicals continue pursuing historical-critical ideologies. The bankruptcy of liberalism in the historical-critical handling of gospel material is a reinforcement of this lesson.[7] To ignore lessons from history leads to repeating past errors.

The following discussion will analyze Tradition and Form Criticism, trace their historical developments, and highlight their practice by evangelicals. This will demonstrate the dangers posed by the adoption of these ideologies.

DEFINITION AND DESCRIPTION OF FORM CRITICISM

German theologian Rudolf Bultmann (1893–1976), who popularized and systematized FC, described it as follows:

> I am entirely in agreement with M. Dibelius when he maintains that form-criticism . . . does not consist of identifying the individual units of the tradition . . . placing them in their various categories. It is much rather "to discover the origin and the history of the particular units and thereby to throw some light on the history of the tradition before it took literary form."[8]

British scholar F. F. Bruce preferred a simpler definition:

Form criticism (German *Formgeschichte*, "form history") represents an endeavor to determine the oral prehistory of written documents or sources, and to classify the material according to the various "forms" or categories of narrative, discourse, and so forth.[9]

One must not understand these definitions in isolation from their historical development, for, taken out of context, they might portray Form Criticism as a benign process. Form Criticism involves far more than determining literary categories or alleged "life situations" from which the gospel tradition arose. Chapter 2 of this volume has traced philosophical presuppositions inherent in Historical Criticism. But one must couple these with how FC developed to determine its legitimacy as a hermeneutical discipline for conservative evangelicals.

The expression "Form Criticism" comes from the German word *Formgeschichte* (English, "form history"). The German name reveals its negative philosophical underpinnings through usage of the term *Geschichte* instead of the *Historie*. *Historie* refers to objective facts of history (external and verifiable), while *Geschichte* dichotomizes the concept of history into interpretations of history, namely, history as significance, internal and non-verifiable. According to this distinction, that Jesus was a man who lived in the first century is an objective statement of historical fact, or *Historie*, that may be verified by canons of "historical reason." But the assertion that Jesus was the Son of God is an interpretive statement and belongs to the realm of *Geschichte* in that an assumption of faith is its only verification. Such a distinction allows for something to be interpretively "true" (history as significance) but not "true" in the sense of being objectively verifiable (history as fact). For form critics as Bultmann, no continuity exists between the Jesus of history *(Historie)* and the Christ of faith, namely, *Geschichte*—the Christ of the kerygma.[10]

For Bultmann, the Jesus of history was a Jewish apocalyptist who died a tragic death and remains dead, while the "Risen Christ" is a mythological concept of the early church that creatively thought of the dead Jesus as the risen "Son of Man." In Bultmann's demythologizing of the stories about Jesus' rising from the dead, the resurrection signified Jesus' ascension to become the kerygmatic Christ. The bases of Bultmann's reasoning centered in a virulent anti-supernaturalism.[11]

The Prime Impetuses: Evolutionary Conceptions and Unbelief

Like Source Criticism, FC stemmed from assuming evolutionary progressions from the simple to the complex. Kelber correctly describes Bultmann's form-critical analysis:

> It [Bultmann's concept of the development of the synoptic tradition] was a process as natural as that of biological evolution: simplicity grew into complexity . . . , an effortlessly evolutionary transition from the pre-gospel stream of tradition to the written gospel.[12]

The fundamental assumption "which makes form criticism both necessary and possible" subtly reveals an evolutionary-based philosophy: "The
tradition consists basically of individual sayings and narratives joined together in the Gospels by the work of the authors."[13] These sayings and
narratives circulated independently as brief, rounded, isolated units before being fixed in written form.[14] The assumed oral period extended for
about thirty years, from A.D. 30/33 to A.D. 60/70.[15]

Guthrie notes the peril of such dogmatic speculations regarding an oral
period: "The very fact that our historical data for the first thirty years of
Christian history are so limited means that form critics inevitably had to
draw a good deal on imagination, although none of them were conscious
of doing so."[16] Thus, at its heart, FC is acutely subjective. Since form critics admit that the passion narrative circulated as a continuous narrative,
why could not other narratives also (for example, Mark 1:21–39; 2:1–3:6)?[17]
Birger Gerhardsson and Harald Riesenfeld have shown the Jews to be capable of tremendous feats of memorization that would contribute to the
stability of the tradition.[18] It is quite credible that short narratives written
by the eyewitness apostles may have existed even during Jesus' ministry.[19]
New Testament scholars as a whole have dismissed the relevance of memory
and note-taking by early Christians as contradictory to currently held views
of Source and Form Criticism.

Evolutionary thinking also dominated the second generation of form
critics. For example, although Caird rejected "radical" conclusions of earlier form critics like Bultmann, especially in terms of the historicity, he
supported the validity of many form-critical principles. He boldly asserts,
"Nobody is likely to dispute that some process of *natural selection* has
been at work in the formulation of the gospel tradition."[20]

Due to philosophically motivated prejudices, form critics allege that they
reflect the post-Easter faith of the early church and are not the writings of
eyewitnesses (Matthew, John) or near-eyewitnesses (Mark, Luke) of Jesus'
earthly life. The Gospels do not reflect the teaching of Jesus or any direct
attestation of His words, but were compositions made long after the eyewitness period. Similar to biological evolutionists, form critics posit a
gradual development of the gospel tradition. For example, Bultmann argued that although the "date of the gospels cannot be accurately determined," Mark "was not the work of a disciple of Jesus or a member of the
primitive community; and the same is true of Matthew and Luke." Bultmann
felt that Mark was the oldest gospel, being composed around A.D. 70, and
stated, "The composition of the Gospels of Matthew and Luke may be
placed in the period from 70–100 A.D., probably nearer 100 than 70."[21]
R. H. Lightfoot, whose work served as the bridge between Form and Redaction Criticism, wrote the following:

> It seems, then, that the form of the earthly no less than of the heav-
> enly Christ is for the most part hidden from us. For all the inesti-
> mable value of the gospels, they yield us little more than a whisper
> of his voice; we trace in them but the outskirts of his ways.[22]

Fundamental Contradictions to Form Criticism

In Bultmann's *History of the Synoptic Tradition*, the term "eyewitness" does not occur. The lack of eyewitness involvement in the gospel tradition is a necessary supposition of early FC. Nineham notes why: "According to form-critics, eyewitnesses played little direct part in the *development* of the Gospel tradition, however much they may have had to do with its original formulation. . . . This opinion is no accidental or peripheral feature of the form-critical position," especially since "characteristics" and "key features" [of form-critical analysis] "are incompatible with any theory of much direct eye-witness influence after the initial stage."[23] Form critic Dibelius honestly admits the strategic significance of eyewitnesses for the tradition: "At the period when eyewitnesses of Jesus were still alive, it was not possible to mar the picture of Jesus in the tradition."[24] Eyewitnesses would contradict form critical speculation and affirm the stability of the tradition.

FC postulates that through time, stories about Jesus gradually acquired accretions (in other words, fabrications and embellishments) that were not historical, especially miraculous elements. Varied circumstances of Christian communities determined what accretions to add and how such accretions took shape. The early church was not interested in tradition for historical and literary purposes but for preaching purposes.[25] According to the developers of FC, the words of Jesus have been lost due to conversion motivations of the early church. No biographical interest existed in the Christian community to preserve the words of Jesus. A basic assumption is that through time, changes (namely, evolutionary developments) in the tradition occurred.

Yet, the New Testament indicates a fundamental biographical interest of the Christian community in the words and deeds of Jesus Christ—for example, 1 Corinthians 7:10, 12, 25 where Paul distinguishes his words from those of Jesus; Luke 1:1–4 where Luke indicates that many had drawn up accounts based on reports handed down to them from those who were "eyewitnesses and servants" from the very beginning of Jesus' ministry and that Luke's research was based on careful investigation of those eyewitness accounts; Acts and other New Testament books contain constant appeal by first-century Christians that they were eyewitnesses of the events about which they spoke (for example, Acts 2:32; 3:15; 10:41; 1 Cor. 15:1–8).

Eyewitnesses prove the concept of an unstable tradition to be untenable, for eyewitnesses would prevent any substantial changes. If the apostles and their eyewitness contemporaries wrote the twenty-seven books of the New Testament, then the New Testament offers *no* support for the form-critical evolutionary hypothesis of the tradition as brief, rounded units circulating for long periods of time, that eventually became part of a gospel record created by the "Christian community." The tradition in the Gospels is what came from the minds of the apostles and their eyewitness contemporaries as they composed their works, reflecting on either their own personal reminiscences or those of eyewitnesses. The true repository of tradition is the New Testament rather than some later, hypothetical, nebulous entity known as the "Christian community."

The Goals of Form Criticism

To account for a substantive change in the tradition through time, FC applies to the Gospels certain literary criteria or laws of tradition (for example, length of episode, addition of details, and presence of Semitisms) to determine relative age, original form, and historical veracity. The inferred criteria stem from (1) an evolutionary assumption of gradually increasing complexity, (2) an antisupernatural bias against miraculous happenings, and (3) an assumption that proposed laws of folk tradition apply to the gospel tradition in determining what aspects are late accretions to and modifications (in other words, inauthentic) of the tradition. Bultmann wrote, "Narratives pass from mouth to mouth, or when one writer takes them over from another, their fundamental character remains the same, but the details are subject to the control of fancy and are usually made more explicit or definite."[26] Bultmann tried to establish laws of literary transmission by viewing the way Matthew and Luke altered Mark and Q (namely, the *Logia*), how the apocryphal gospels altered the canonical gospels, and how the populace in general transmitted folk-takes, anecdotes, and folk-songs.[27]

During this oral period, the early church shaped individual units of tradition as preachers, teachers, and story-tellers continually recounted them. Davies summarized the form-critical posture well: "It is the first assumption of Form Critics that the Gospels are from the Church, by the Church, for the Church."[28]

Form critics suppose that over time the church added these fabricated accretions and gospel literature took on fixed forms through constant repetition. These forms varied according to the function that they served in the Christian community. The technical term to refer to the sociological setting giving rise to different rhetorical forms (for example, legends, sayings, and miracle stories) is *Sitz im Leben* (literally, "setting in life" or "life situation").[29] Hermann Gunkel first employed this term in his form-critical analysis of the Old Testament. Under Gunkel's influence, Dibelius and Bultmann applied the concept to the New Testament, especially the Gospels.[30]

Eventually, anonymous gospel writers collected and arranged the individual stories into written narratives that reflected the needs and interests of their particular communities. Form Criticism assumes the Two- or Four-Source hypothesis, which contends that an unknown evangelist (identified as Mark by tradition) wrote his gospel first.[31] Utilizing both Mark and a hypothetical (namely, postulated, non-extant) document known as "Q" (German, *Quelle*, "source"),[32] the unknown evangelists identified as "Matthew" and "Luke" composed their respective gospels. The gospel writers were mere collectors of tradition, not unique contributors. Dibelius argued, "The authors of the Gospels, at least of the synoptics are not 'authors' in the literary sense, but mere collectors."[33]

With these presuppositions in mind, Dibelius delineated the purpose of Form Criticism:

The method of Formgeschichte has a twofold objective. In the first place, by reconstruction and analysis, it seeks to explain the origin of the tradition about Jesus, and thus to penetrate into a period previous to that in which our Gospels and their written sources were recorded. But it has a further purpose. . . . We must examine the sayings of Jesus and ask with what intention these churches collected them, learnt them by heart and wrote them down.[34]

Dibelius immediately admitted a further purpose of FC: "The method of Formgeschichte seeks to help in answering the historical questions as to the nature and trustworthiness of our knowledge of Jesus, and also in solving a theological problem properly so-called."[35]

Similarly, Bultmann wrote that FC's is "discovering what the original units of the Synoptics were, both sayings and stories, to try to establish what their historical setting was, whether they belong to a primary or secondary tradition or whether they were the product of editorial activity."[36]

In summary, the methodological practice centers on three overall objectives: (1) classification of the individual pericopes (self-contained units of teaching or narrative) of the gospel materials according to form; (2) assigning each form to a *Sitz im Leben* in the early church from which the material arose; and (3) recovery of the original form of the material during the oral period through laws of tradition (see "Tradition Criticism" below).[37]

Historical Background of Form Criticism

A review of the historical developments that gave rise to FC is vital in evaluating its legitimacy for an evangelical as a hermeneutical discipline. A methodology can be only as legitimate as its presuppositional foundation, since that foundation provides its reason for existence (see chapter 2). Evangelical attempts to modify form-critical principles or practice the method in isolation from its antecedents, thereby eliminating the effects of its presuppositions, are futile for such attempts cannot change the justification for FC's existence. The vestiges of the method's foundation will remain.

The roots of FC center in the Enlightenment. Deist and rationalist Hermann Samuel Reimarus (1694–1768), a professor of Oriental Languages in Hamburg, wrote the "prologue" to its development. Though a deist writer, a four-thousand page manuscript entitled *An Apologetic for the Rational Worshipers of God* is perhaps his most famous work, one that remained unpublished during his lifetime.[38]

Between 1774 and 1778 Gotthold Ephraim Lessing (1729–1781), motivated by a profound belief in rationalism and historical skepticism, published parts of Reimarus' work in *Fragments of an Unnamed Author*.[39] The sixth and seventh of these published fragments purposed to discredit Christianity. The sixth fragment, *Concerning the Resurrection Story* (1777), listed alleged inconsistencies in the gospel accounts of the Resurrection and asserted that the writers were mistaken about the

Resurrection. The seventh fragment, *On the Purpose of Jesus and His Disciples* (1778), contended that Jesus was an unsuccessful political messianic pretender and that the disciples allegedly were disappointed phonies who stole the body of Jesus and invented the Christian faith after the crucifixion rather than work for a living.[40]

Reimarus represented the age of deism, rationalism, and skepticism when thinkers were interpreting the Gospels not as historical documents but as dogmatic, theological documents designed to promote belief rather than convey facts. Perrin calls Reimarus the father of "Life of Jesus research."[41] Schweitzer credited him with discovering "a creative element in the tradition."[42]

David Friedrich Strauss (1808–1874), who became part of FC's origin by popularizing the "mythical" view of Scripture, praised Reimarus and held views close to his (see chapter 2). In 1862, Strauss published a tribute to Reimarus, who maintained a rationalistic interpretation of Jesus' life,[43] and in 1835–36, *Das Leben Jesu, kritisch bearbeitet* (English, "The Life of Jesus Critically Examined"), which set forth the concept of "myth" in the gospel accounts. Strauss advocated a closed-continuum of cause and effect that allowed no divine intervention. Whenever the biblical data presents the supernatural or abnormal, the mythopoeic faculty (see chapter 2) has been at work. Strauss considered the vast majority of the Gospels to be myth.[44] Bultmann followed Strauss' mythological approach in his form-critical analysis.[45]

Chapter 2 has described the effect of evolutionary thought on Historical Criticism in general. In particular, that mold of thinking had its special impact on FC. It permeates Source Criticism, especially the Two- and Four-Document Hypotheses that see Mark as the simplest and earliest gospel and Matthew and Luke as the more complex and therefore later gospels (see chapters 4 and 5). These hypotheses form the working bases for form-critical analysis.[46]

The perceived weakness of Source Criticism was that it could not push behind Mark and the hypothetical sources Q, M, and L, into a hypothesized oral period before the Gospels took written form. This left a gap of some twenty to thirty years between the time of Jesus and the first written documents. The desire to explore this period gave rise to form-critical speculation and conjecture.[47]

Form Criticism arose first in analyzing the Old Testament, when Johannes Heinrich Hermann Gunkel (1862–1932) interpreted Genesis with form-critical methods in his work *Sagen der Genesis* (English, "The Stories of Genesis").[48] In this work, Gunkel embraced Old Testament Source Criticism, which negated the Mosaic authorship of the Pentateuch. Under evolutionary influences, he viewed Genesis (and the rest of the Pentateuch) as developing gradually over a long period of time from documents known as JEDP. These are sources suggested by the Graf-Wellhausen hypothesis.[49] Individual stories existed in oral form, being modified as time went on, before the writing of the documents.[50] Gunkel held that the stories were largely mythological in character, especially the accounts of creation and the flood.[51] Kümmel observes, "Gunkel's method . . . prepared the way in decisive fashion for the investigation of the gospel traditions by K. L. Schmidt and the other form critics."[52]

The Old Testament scholar and source critic, Julius Wellhausen (1844–1918), helped bring form-critical thinking into New Testament studies. He formed a bridge between Old and New Testament studies.[53] He established three theories about Mark that eventually developed into major form-critical axioms: (1) the original source for material in the gospel is oral tradition circulating in small independent units; (2) the material came together and underwent revisions in various ways at different stages, the writer's redaction being only one of these stages; and (3) the material furnishes information about the beliefs and circumstances of the early church as well as about Jesus' ministry.[54] In his *Das Evangelium Marci* (English, "The Gospel of Mark," 1903), Wellhausen contended that the writer superimposed editorial additions on the primitive tradition in Mark under the influence of early church theology rather than the historical situation of Jesus. Wellhausen's hypothesis gave impetus to speculation that the original shaping of material did not come from apostolic eyewitnesses but from the Christian community.[55]

For a time, source criticism had postulated that Mark was the earliest gospel, and although it reflected mythological elements like the other gospels, it contained more primitive history than they, being closer to eyewitnesses and therefore a better historical source. But in *The Messianic Secret* (1901, German, *Das Messiasgeheimnis in den Evangelien*), Wilhelm Wrede (1859–1906), following Reimarus' lead, rejected Mark's historicity. Wrede asserted that Mark's gospel contains creative, dogmatic ideas that the writer imposed on the tradition. For example, Jesus never claimed to be Messiah during his lifetime. Rather, the church superimposed this post-Resurrection idea on Jesus' lips.[56] Perrin remarks, "Wilhelm Wrede (1859–1906) . . . sounded the death knell" for the historicity of Mark "by demonstrating that a major aspect of the Marcan narratives was precisely the 'mythic.'"[57]

Although Wrede's view received strong criticism at first,[58] it exerted a powerful influence on early form critics, who presupposed that the contextual framework of the gospel narratives and stories was suspect and of little importance.[59] Bultmann, for example, concurred with Wrede's conclusions, arguing that Mark is not history, for it "is really dominated by the theology of the Church and by a dogmatic conception of Christ."[60] Benoit relates, "This [Wrede's view] is exactly the same attitude adopted by the Form Critics. All they add to Wrede's position is a more methodological research into the way in which Christian dogma was created and elaborated by the primitive Community."[61] Wrede's work is therefore the forerunner of Form and Redaction Criticism.

With a large portion of New Testament scholars viewing Mark as "mythical" and theological rather than historical, the way opened for Karl Ludwig Schmidt (1891–1956) to do his work. In *Der Rahmen der Geschichte Jesu* (1919, English, "The Framework [or Story] of Jesus"),

Schmidt concentrated on the chronological and geographical framework of the early Christian community created for Mark. He asserted that the episodes in the gospel were isolated units of tradition linked together by the author. References to time, place, and geography were not factual and had little value. The writer merely pieced the scenes together unhistorically and artificially. Schmidt concluded, "On the whole there is [in the Gospels] no life of Jesus in the sense of a developing story, as a chronological outline of the history of Jesus, but only isolated stories, pericopes, which have been provided with a framework."[62]

Eliminating the chronological and geographical framework of the Synoptics left units of material in isolation. Schmidt speculated that these "independent" pericopes arose in the Christian community to meet the needs of worship. He, however, did not utilize the tools of FC to pry into an oral period before the Gospels.[63]

Martin Dibelius (1883–1947) and Rudolf Bultmann (1884–1976) fully developed and refined FC in the New Testament. Dibelius was the first to apply the method to the synoptic tradition in *From Tradition to Gospel* (German edition, 1921; English edition, 1934). The term *Formgeschichte* (English, "form criticism [or history]") originated from Dibelius' use of it in his title. Dibelius worked out a system for identifying isolated gospel episodes and classifying their literary form.

Rudolf Bultmann developed FC more fully than Dibelius or Schmidt and is most responsible for the method's thoroughness and maturation. Bultmann's epoch-making work was *The History of the Synoptic Tradition* (German, 1921; English, 1963).[64] Evolutionary dogma influenced him heavily in the formulation of his system. Many of his professors came from the history-of-religions school that advocated an evolutionary development of religions.[65] Kant's philosophy also swayed Bultmann. Morgan writes, "His theology was shaped above all by the pious neo-Kantianism of his teacher Herrmann (1846–1922), a devout follower of Ritschl (1822–89)."[66] The existentialist thinking of Kierkegaard and especially Heidegger also deeply influenced Bultmann.[67] Becoming disillusioned with the historical Jesus of the liberal school, he sought to emancipate the need for any historical demonstration of the Christian faith. For Bultmann, the most important element in the Christian faith was an existential encounter (namely, "a leap of faith") that entailed a decision apart from historical proof (see chapter 2).

An important motivation of Bultmann was a desire to "modernize" the Gospels.[68] He sought to demythologize them, with Strauss' concept of "myth" being a strong influence.[69] To Bultmann, the canonical gospels contained pre-scientific conceptions that are outdated by modern scientific knowledge.[70] He defined myth as follows: "Myth is used here in the sense popularized by the 'History of Religions' school. Mythology is the use of imagery to express the other worldly in terms of this world and the divine in terms of human life, the other side in terms of this side."[71] Any miraculous conceptions of a Divine Being or Son of God, demon possession, angels, resurrection, voices from heaven, so on, are first-century man's primitive understanding of the world that needs to be demythologized and put in twentieth century terms.[72] Bultmann sought to "demythologize" the Gospels: *"Man's knowledge and mastery of the world* have advanced to such an extent through science and technology that it is no longer possible for anyone seriously to hold the New Testament view of the world—in fact, there is no one who does."[73] This presupposition focused attention on literary forms in the gospel and the desire to discover the "essence of the gospel apart from these 'forms' (for example, miracle stories)."[74]

To Bultmann, the form critic must discover the historical- or life-situation that produced the literary materials in the Gospels. He asserted that the gospel material, rather than reflecting the historical situation of Jesus, owed its present shape to the practical needs of the community, reflecting the post-Easter beliefs of the Christian community rather than the pre-Easter period.[75] His method removed supernatural elements in the Gospels because of his presuppositional conclusion of a closed-continuum of cause and effect, as advocated by Troeltsch's historical-critical approach.[76] The result of this thinking was crucial: "I do indeed think that we now can know almost nothing concerning the life and personality of Jesus, since the early Christian sources show no interest in either, are moreover fragmentary and often legendary; and other sources about Jesus do not exist."[77]

Bultmann theorized a greater element of creativity by the early church than did Dibelius.[78] Dibelius saw the evangelists as collectors of material, thereby allowing a greater possibility of determining the original form and function, but Bultmann saw a more radical working of the material, implying that the tradition did not reflect a historical core.[79] Both men rejected the historicity of miraculous events in the Gospels. Yet, "this difference is one of emphasis rather than essence."[80] Because Bultmann analyzed the entire synoptic tradition, his "name and method of analysis have been more closely associated with form criticism than has the name of Dibelius."[81]

FC was the product of the philosophical milieu of the nineteenth and twentieth centuries (see chapter 2), which provided the fertile background for its emergence. Benoit has observed that FC's purpose is to deny the supernatural and that its fundamental thesis is a philosophical one, dependent on such Enlightenment philosophers as Hegel and David Strauss.[82]

Since a credible case exists for the historical, chronological, and geographical integrity of the gospel units, the dismantling of the Gospels into isolated pericopes via FC is tenuous.[83] History offers a conspicuous testimony against current evangelical attempts to associate with that methodology.

Classification of Literary Forms

No agreed-upon list of literary forms exists among form critics, though similar categories appear frequently.[84] It is therefore difficult to summarize them. Any effort to do so must be selective.[85] Acute subjectivity reflecting an antisupernatural bias has characterized the development of various categories.

Legends or Myths

Often classification depends not on form but content, especially if a passage involves the miraculous. For example, Bultmann's category of "Historical Stories and Legends" demonstrates a pronounced antihistorical and antisupernatural bias. These are stories about extraordinary, sometimes miraculous, events; for example, Jesus' baptism, temptation, transfiguration, and resurrection narratives. These, Bultmann says, "instead of being historical in character are religious and edifying."[86] Though he calls the category "Historical Stories," he does not believe they are historically true:

> If at the same time I naturally do not deny that historical happenings may underlie legends, I mean that "unhistorical" applies to the idea of legend negatively in the sense that legends not only have no special interest in history (Dibelius) but that they are not, in the modern scientific sense, historical accounts at all.[87]

Dibelius' category of "myth" designates *"stories which in some fashion tell of many-sided doings of the gods."*[88] These are narratives where the supernatural invades the human scene to authenticate Jesus. Dibelius' "myth" category overlaps with Bultmann's "legend," for Bultmann has no "myth" category. This confusion complicates efforts at analysis.

Like Bultmann, Dibelius held the baptism, temptation, transfiguration, resurrection, and ascension of Jesus to be unhistorical, calling them "myths."[89] He asserted,

> The letters of Paul are an unambiguous proof that there once was a *Christ mythology*. At the same time they are proof that this mythology could not be supported directly from the tradition of the life of Jesus. . . . The Christ-myth . . . had no need of the data handed down.[90]

Over time, early Christians, because of Hellenistic influences, reputedly added miraculous elements to the historical Jesus (for example, Jesus' descent from His heavenly realm to the earth, His resurrection, and ascension back to heaven).[91]

The category of "legend" or "myth," however, is quite suspect. Travis notes, "To describe 'legends' or 'myths' as forms, when no common shape is discernible . . . is not form criticism."[92] Such categories indicate a presuppositional agenda rather than an effort at categorization.

Miracle Stories or Tales

The category of "miracle stories" (Bultmann) or "tales" (Dibelius) is another example where antisupernatural biases emerge. The category's basis is the nature of the miracle not the form. Bultmann, affected by the "history-of-religions school" outlook, asserted as follows:

Yet it would not be right to consider the gospel miracle stories in the bounds of the NT only. The less the miracle stories as such are truly historical reports the more we need to *ask how they have found their way into the Gospel tradition*. . . . The process of transferring some available miracle story to a hero (or healer or even a god) is frequently to be found in the history of literature and religion.[93]

Bultmann, evidencing his evolutionary bias, argued that elapsed time brings "an *increase of the miraculous element*" in regard to details.[94] He asserted, "This story [Mark 10:46–52] shows its secondary character in giving the name of the blind man . . . and it is the only name in any miracle story in the synoptics, apart from Mark 5:22."[95] Guthrie remarks, "Both Dibelius and Bultmann reject the miraculous and therefore the historicity of the gospel accounts of miracles. This is not so much on the basis of 'form' as on philosophical and theological grounds."[96]

Form critics took pagan folklore tales of the miraculous to be parallel with the gospel tradition, and thereby explained the rise of miraculous stories in the tradition.[97] However, the alleged parallels are qualitatively different. Bultmann admitted this: "In general, however, the New Testament miracle stories are extremely reserved in this respect [in describing cures], since they hesitate to attribute to the person of Jesus the magical traits which were often characteristic of the Hellenistic miracle worker."[98] Gospel miracle-stories have no magical incantations and fanciful activities that appear in Hellenistic stories.

Since folklore took hundreds of years to develop, the analogy is false. A period of only about thirty years existed between Jesus and the earliest gospel. Kenyon noted, "There is simply not time for elaborate processes of literary workmanship and development."[99] Eyewitnesses would have prevented substantive changes in the tradition.

Redlich argued that much of the synoptic material defies form category classification:

> We conclude therefore that the assumption that the material can be classified according to their form is only true in part and in a very restricted manner. The only classification that can be made is that (a) as regards the sayings, there is a group with form, if we omit poetical form, namely the Parables, and (b) the narrative portions contain two groups which possess form, namely Apothegm-Stories and Miracle-Stories. The greater part of the material is "form"-less.[100]

Lightfoot echoed that sentiment in reference to Mark 1–13: "It seems at least possible that the new study has here achieved a valuable and lasting result, and that it has succeeded in distinguishing and classifying two types of stories, both of which are prominent in Mark."[101] But how much can a method contribute that can identify clearly only two literary forms?

Mixed Forms

The categories are not as distinct as form critics might imply. They often categorize with extreme subjectivity, curiously mixed forms reflecting their preconceived agendas rather than objective analysis. For example, Dibelius identifies Mark 3:1–6 (the man with a withered hand) as pure but contends that Mark 10:46–52 (blind Bartimaeus) is a "less pure" paradigm, and Mark 5:25–34 (the woman with the hemorrhage) is a tale.[102] All such distinctions originate in the form critic's mind and not the text. Dibelius claims that didactic motives are central, and the healing is incidental in Mark 3:1–6, so it is a paradigm. Yet, the pericope concludes with a miracle and its effect on the Pharisees rather than with a saying about the Sabbath.[103] To overcome this inconsistency, Dibelius asserted that in this paradigm "the original ending in Mark iii, 6, is concealed." Mark 10:52 ends with a saying, yet Dibelius says it is not a pure paradigm (most likely due to the miraculous healing). And Mark 5:34 ends in a saying, but because of its miraculous nature Dibelius deprecates it as a "tale." Dibelius' conclusions illustrate the subjective nature of FC.[104]

Classification comes entirely from the subjective whims of the form critic. For instance, in Bultmann's classification of the sayings of Jesus, he divides them into several groups—Wisdom Sayings, Prophetic and Apocalyptic Sayings, Legal Sayings and church rules, and "I" Sayings.[105] Bultmann divides the Wisdom Sayings into three subclasses based on his conception of genuineness: Jesus' use of existing sayings, Jesus' own creation of sayings, and the church's attribution of sayings to Jesus that He did not speak.[106] Bultmann assigns much to the third subclass,[107] commenting, "It will only be in very few cases that one of the logia can be ascribed to Jesus with any measure of confidence."[108]

Bultmann treated similarly the "I" Sayings of Jesus, in which He made specific demands or special claims. Bultmann interpreted them as words the community placed on Jesus' lips to meet the community's needs in a particular situation. For example, His statements about persecution in Matthew 10:34–36 and Luke 12:51–53 were utterances of Christian prophets long after His ascension, when early communities faced serious threats because of their faith.[109]

Bultmann accepted only about forty sayings as genuinely attributable to Jesus. He considered only the bare facts of Jesus' life and death to be authentic. The rest is attributable to the fabrication or adaptation of the community, which had no biographical interest in the life of Jesus or desire for historical accuracy. In later life, Bultmann moderated his position but only very slightly.[110]

Since Luther and the Reformation (1517), the grammatico-historical method has demonstrated its sufficiency to distinguish "forms" in the gospel material (parables, allegories, proverbs, types, poetry, and so on) rendering the need for any "form-critical" analysis suspect and unnecessary.[111] Current attempts at reforming form-critical postures, labeled as "New" Form Criticism, underscore the *inappropriateness* of FC as a viable option for exegesis, because they partake of many of the same weaknesses.[112] They

also supply an aberrant understanding of FC (presuppositionally, historically, and practically), for the words of the father and systematizer of FC,
Bultmann, make clear the purpose of the discipline, which is "to discover
the origin and the history of the particular units and thereby to throw some
light on the history of the tradition before it took literary form."[113] Bultmann
continued, "Form criticism . . . not only presupposes judgements of facts
alongside judgements of literary criticism, but must also lead to judgements
about facts (the genuineness of a saying, the historicity of a report and
the like)."[114] In contrast to evangelicals who gloss over FC's true nature,
Bultmann's candor is refreshing.

TRADITION CRITICISM

Tradition Criticism[115] (German, *Traditionsgeschichte*) relates closely
to FC in that its principles developed in conjunction with FC. Now, however, it receives attention as a separate discipline.[116] For many critics, especially those who advocate a hermeneutical role for Form and Redaction
Criticism, an important task is to assess the authenticity of each gospel
unit. They seek the earliest form of the tradition-unit through peeling away
layers of narrative, resulting from the *Sitz im Leben* of the early community. They apply "tradition criteria" to the text to determine the relative
antiquity and historical veracity of the these units and to distinguish the
authentic teaching of Jesus from what is non-authentic. So Tradition Criticism is the study of the origin, history, and development of a given saying,
especially in the Gospels but also throughout the New Testament.

Criticism of traditions contained in the Gospels adopts two tactics: (1)
recovering the earliest and most authentic forms of the tradition by application of certain laws of tradition; and (2) making critical judgments on
the historicity of each saying by applying "criteria of authenticity" to discover the origin of these traditions, either Jesus Himself ("authentic") or
the Christian communities (Palestinian, Hellenistic, or Gentile).[117] In identifying embellishments by the communities, Tradition Criticism finds its
most prominent expression.

Operational Bases of Tradition Criticism

Tradition Criticism arose from the same antisupernatural sources as
FC. Negative historical presuppositions of the Enlightenment lie at the heart
of the method. Doty remarks, "The basic presuppositions for the modern
historical-critical approach to the NT writings were set in the last part of
the eighteenth century under the influence of deism and rationalism."[118]
When evangelicals isolate Tradition Criticism from its presuppositions, they
consciously or unconsciously employ its dubious hermeneutical methodology (see chapter 2).

The criteria of authenticity—the principle of discontinuity (dissimilarity), multiple attestation, and consistency of content (coherence)—stem
from a negative view of historicity propagated by Bultmann and his theological descendants (for example, Käsemann, Conzelmann, and Perrin).[119]
In the absence of good reasons for accepting gospel traditions, they are

inherently suspect. In other words, Tradition Criticism places the "burden of proof" on viewing the Gospels as authentic, as Perrin stated it: *"The nature of the synoptic tradition is such that the burden of proof will be upon the claim to authenticity."*[120] The instigator of the "New Quest" for the historical Jesus, Ernst Käsemann, echoes a similar thought: "Historical criticism has shattered this good faith [in the historical reliability of the Gospels] as far as we ourselves are concerned. We can no longer assume the general reliability of the Synoptic tradition about Jesus."[121]

A primary task of Tradition Criticism is to apply laws of tradition to the material in order to discover an "original" or earlier form. Bultmann argued as follows:

> We may accurately observe how the Marcan material is altered and revised by Matthew and Luke, and how Matthew and Luke have presumably edited the text of Q (the Sayings-document). If we are able to deduce a certain regularity in this procedure, then we may certainly assume that the same laws held good even earlier, and we may draw conclusions as to the state of the tradition prior to Mark and Q.[122]

Bultmann, Dibelius, and other form critics also argued that the gospel traditions fell into the category of "folk tradition," and observations about how folklore traditions functioned reveal the same rules that the gospel traditions followed in their development.[123] Assumed parallel developments with German folklore, Greek literature, rabbinic and patristic literature, and the apocryphal gospels served as guides in developing these laws.[124]

Another questionable assumption in the development of laws of tradition was the idea that Matthew and Luke used Mark and the Q source in developing their gospels. By assuming Matthew and Luke used Mark and Q, form critics extrapolated that Mark used oral traditions in a similar fashion.[125] Such a conjecture, however, is highly speculative in light of increasing suspicions and outright rejections of the Two- and Four-Source approaches (see chapters 3 and 4). This factor magnifies the subjectivity of Tradition Criticism.[126]

Tradition Criticism also inherently includes an evolutionary viewpoint of the development of tradition. Discussion earlier in this chapter has shown how evolutionary concepts had a profound influence on Bultmann, Dibelius, and others in the development of form-critical principles. Both Bultmann's methodological analysis of the "accretions" to the tradition and the rules utilized to remove these accretions are replete with evolutionary-philosophical precepts.

Bultmann argued, "The original tradition was made up almost entirely of brief single units (sayings and short narratives), and . . . almost all references to time and place which serve to connect up the single sections into a larger context are the editorial work of the evangelists."[127] Gradually the stories increased from simplicity to complexity with the addition of details. For example, Mark used unnamed persons in his pericopes, but the other synoptics tended to identify these (compare Mark 14:13 with Luke 22:8; and Mark 7:17 with Matt. 15:15). Not only did "later" tradition identify figures, but Matthew and Luke almost invariably identified Jesus' opponents as scribes and Pharisees though Mark or Q left them unidentified. Bultmann also concluded that though some polemical words of Jesus addressed to scribes and Pharisees may be historical (for example, Mark 12:38–40; most of Matt. 23:1–31), "the schematic representation according to which the Pharisees and scribes are from the outset the sworn enemies of Jesus is certainly unhistorical."[128]

Dibelius held that several features reflected a narrative's primitivity: its shortness, because elapsed time allowed the community to expand; a lack of the miraculous elements, because the community added these; and paradigms told in a simple and artless manner. With passage of time, the Christian community expanded the primitive elements as they imitated the world's technique of story-telling, thereby giving birth to a lengthier form called the "tale." Tales reflect Greek and Oriental influences in representing Jesus as a miracle worker and therefore are suspect as historical sources. A later stage was the development of "legends," which were even less trustworthy. Legends accommodated themselves to the world by speaking of Jesus as secular folklore spoke of its holy men.[129]

Another indicator of lateness appears in Matthew's and/or Luke's direct discourse compared to Mark's indirect discourse. Tradition critics assume that transmission by the community transformed the gist of a statement into the very words of gospel characters. For example, Mark 8:32 has Peter rebuking Jesus in general terms, while Matthew 16:22 reports the very words of Peter. Also, the inarticulate cry from the cross in Mark 15:37 becomes specific in Luke 23:46 (also compare Mark 14:23 with Matt. 26:27).[130]

According to Bultmann, Dibelus, and Taylor, the presence of Semitisms in contrast to Hellenistic elements is often an indication of a tradition that is very early or even authentic.[131] Bultmann reasoned, "Since our gospels arose out of Greek Christianity, the distinction provides us with a criterion which frequently enables us to determine whether this or that feature belongs to the older tradition or was composed later."[132] Two contemporary advocates of Semitisms as a test for antiquity are Joachim Jeremias and Matthew Black.[133]

Such logic is tenuous, however. One reason is that by the period of the New Testament, Judaism and Hellenism had experienced considerable interpenetration, as evidenced even by New Testament terminology. For instance, the Jewish institution called "the Sanhedrin" derived its name from the Greek word *synedrion*, reflecting the deep influence of Greek thought on the very heart of Palestinian Judaism.[134] The Talmud also indicates this penetration.[135] Lieberman has demonstrated that Rabbis quoted not only from Jewish sources but also from Greek sources (for example, Greek proverbs).[136]

Another argument against using Semitisms to test for antiquity lies in indications that Jesus and His contemporaries may have spoken Greek as much as they did Aramaic.[137] Gundry makes the following elaboration:

> We can be sure that the tradition about Jesus was expressed from
> the very first in Hebrew, Aramaic, *and Greek.* . . . We cannot na-
> ively work on the assumption that everything was originally in
> Aramaic, that we should seek Aramaic equivalents wherever pos-
> sible, and that wherever Aramaic equivalents cannot be traced we
> must reject authenticity.[138]

Jesus, living in the city of Nazareth in the region of Galilee dominated
by Gentiles who spoke Greek (for example, "Galilee of the Gentiles," Matt.
4:15), most likely knew Greek His whole life. Peter, Andrew, James, and
John also probably knew Greek, if they sold their fish in Gentile markets
of Galilee. This factor, coupled with the missionary emphasis of the gospel (cf. Matt. 28:19; Acts 1:8; 6:1), ensured that the message occurred
both orally and in writing from the very beginning in the *lingua franca*
(namely, Greek) of the civilized world as well as in Aramaic. Argyle notes,
"If Jesus and his disciples were as familiar with Greek as with Aramaic,
the transition from the oral Aramaic stage to the Greek literary stage would
have been natural and easy."[139]

A third reason for rejecting Semiticisms as time indicators is that indications exist to date Mark later rather than earlier. For example, Mark's
Latinisms (for example, *kentyriōn, xestēs, spekoulatōr, hikanon poiein*[140])
and his translation of Aramaic expressions (for example, Mark 5:41; 15:22,
34) for the sake of those who did not know Aramaic may indicate that
Mark was later rather than earlier (as suggested by tradition critics).

Tradition critics also consider writing style an indication of earliness
and trustworthiness of the tradition. Bultmann related the following:

> While with Mark the art of the evangelist appears to be quite unde-
> veloped, Luke displays a fine editorial artistry. Even the casual reader
> may note the difference if he will observe the quite distinct man-
> ners in which Matthew and Luke [in composing their own gospels]
> introduce material from the Sayings-document into Mark.[141]

Redlich counters, "The stylistic methods of writers are no evidence of
laws of tradition; they are indications of the standard of scholarship of the
writers."[142] Then too, if Matthew and Luke did not use Mark, Bultmann's
argument proves nothing.

If the Gospels were written by the apostles or the writers whose names
they bear, some of whom witnessed the events about which they wrote,
the laws of tradition have *no* substantial credibility. The more credible case,
supported by the consistent testimony of church history, is that the Gospels reflect either direct apostolic testimony (Matthew, John) or eyewitness accounts (Mark based on Peter's preaching, Luke based on thorough
research [1:1–4]). Instead of indicating an evolutionary "development"
of tradition or secondary elements, individual gospel pericopes in Matthew,
Mark, and Luke reveal selectivity in what the eyewitnesses chose to convey and stylistic characteristics of the writers.

Tradition critics, in developing their "laws of tradition," exhibit selectivity in argumentation by choosing only examples that appear to support their position, while ignoring other tendencies and factors that convolute their hypotheses. Sanders, after examining form-critical laws of tradition, concludes that the tradition does not progress from simple to complex:

> There are no hard and fast laws of the development of the Synoptic tradition. On all accounts the tradition developed in opposite directions. It became both longer and shorter, both more and less detailed, and both more and less Semitic. Even the tendency to use direct discourse for indirect . . . was not uniform in the Synoptics themselves. For this reason, *dogmatic statements that a certain characteristic proves a certain passage to be earlier than another are never justified.*[143]

Caird concurs, citing the example of the triple-tradition feeding of the five thousand. The "green grass" in Mark 6:39 disappears in Luke 9:14, the exact opposite of what one would expect if these laws of tradition were true. Caird concludes, "A law which tells us that tradition may either amplify or abbreviate, may either add details or omit them, is very little help in determining which of two accounts is the more original."[144]

Strategically, if one rejects central presuppositions of Form and Tradition Criticism (for example, antisupernaturalism, evolution, and the Two-Document [or, Four-Document] Hypothesis), these laws of tradition have *no* substantial basis, for they operate on the tacit assumption of these presuppositions.

Criteria of Authenticity for the Words of Jesus

Because form critics postulated that the Gospels incorporate the creations of the Christian community rather than preserving the actual words of Jesus, they attempted to distinguish "genuine" sayings of Jesus from the embellishments of the Christian community. To do so, they developed "criteria of authenticity." These criteria inherently impugn the gospel record through an initial assumption of inauthenticity. Subsequent analysis will demonstrate these principles are often mutually contradictory and eliminate the authenticity of the majority of Jesus' sayings.

The recent work of Funk, Hoover, and others associated with the "Jesus Seminar" uses Tradition Criticism to negate the authenticity of the Gospels.[145] Like Bultmann,[146] the Jesus Seminar rejects most (82 percent) sayings of Jesus, the remainder (18 percent) being doubtfully authentic.[147]

The presuppositional foundation of the "Jesus Seminar" is the "Seven Pillars of Scholarly Wisdom": (1) a distinction between the Jesus of history and the Christ of faith; (2) a distinction in historical value between the Synoptic Gospels (containing some reflection of the historical Jesus) and the gospel of John (containing only a "spiritual" Jesus and having little historical value); (3) the priority of Mark; (4) recognition of a hypothetical "Q" as the source of material common to Matthew and Luke but not found in Mark; (5) a distinction between Schweitzer's eschatological Jesus (the kingdom is entirely future and cataclysmic) and the Seminar's assertion of a non-eschatological view of Jesus' teaching (the kingdom is already here, namely, "God's imperial rule"); (6) a fundamental contrast between Jesus' predominately oral culture and today's written culture; and, (7) the investigator's operating axiom—for which no further demonstration is necessary—that the burden of proof rests on establishing authenticity, not inauthenticity. As a result, the investigator has "no final guarantees" as to what Jesus claimed and taught. The Seminar calls these axioms "safeguards offered by the historical methodologies practiced by all responsible scholars."[148]

Carson notes, "The criteria by which so much gospel material ascribed to Jesus is dismissed as inauthentic are not much more than restatements of old fashioned Form and Redaction Criticism."[149] The Seminar's final presuppositional "test" is "beware of finding a Jesus entirely congenial to you." The "test" applies especially to the Jesus Seminar, who *a priori* have determined the nature of the "historical Jesus" by adopting biased presuppositions,[150] thereby producing a "Jesus" wholly "congenial" to themselves.

Claiming to be more "scientific" because of "the new lens of historical reason and research" instead of "the perspective of theology and traditional creedal formulations," the Jesus Seminar is far from objective.[151] They cannot be objective, for the anchor of their research is the negative presuppositional foundation of Historical Criticism. They hold the Gospels to be memories of Jesus "embellished by mythic elements . . . and by plausible fictions."[152]

Barbour divides tradition-critical axioms into two categories: formal and material criteria. Formal criteria deal with the form in which the material was allegedly handed down or from the place which it occupies in the gospel tradition (for example, multiple attestation, Aramaisms, poetic form, and parallelism). Material criteria deal with the actual content of the material itself (dissimilarity, coherence).[153] Analysis of some of these criteria will show their methodological bankruptcy—namely, they are not valid or capable of producing what they allege and cannot be "objective" or "scientific."

The criterion of *multiple attestation* is one of the earliest formulated, being advocated by Burkitt.[154] Assuming the Two-Document solution to the Synoptic Problem, it stipulates that when a saying or activity of Jesus appears in more than one of these sources, it is more likely to be authentic. British-trained tradition critics generally rely more heavily on this principle than do those under Bultmannian influence, for it builds on the solution to the Synoptic Problem that the British prefer (namely, the Four-Source Hypothesis—Mark, Q, M, L).[155] McArthur terms multiple attestation "the most objective of the proposed criteria."[156] But if that is the most objective principle, the whole system has acute problems.

Serious flaws render the principle tenuous: (1) The basis of the criterion is a highly questionable synoptic hypothesis, which automatically gives it a built-in bias. If the Two- or Four-Source Hypothesis is invalid (see chapters 3–4), this criterion proves *nothing*, the "layers of tradition" being figments of scholarly imagination. (2) No valid reason exists to deny the authenticity of a saying merely because it is found in only one alleged "source." The criterion is inherently negative, for it implies that one biblical witness is not sufficient because it is errant.

Related to multiple attestation is the criterion of *multiple forms*. C. H. Dodd was the first to suggest this principle. Heavily influenced by FC, this principle suggests that a gospel motif may be authentic if it appears in multiple forms, namely, in different form-critical categories (for example, pronouncement and miracle stories).[157]

Counter-arguments similar to those for multiple attestation apply to this category. One witness is quite sufficient to confirm what Jesus said or did. The acute subjectivity of form-critical categories (see above under "Classification of Literary Forms") also indicates the highly speculative nature of this criterion.

The criterion of *Aramaic linguistic phenomena* asserts that the presence of Aramaisms in gospel material suggests "primitiveness" of a particular tradition, and hence indicates an increased likelihood of authenticity. Dalman, Burney, and Torrey were the earliest advocates of this hypothesis, but Black and Jeremias used it most extensively.[158] Fuller goes so far as to say that "any saying of Jesus, if it is authentic, should exhibit Aramaic features, and if it has the structure of Aramaic poetry this increases the presumption that the saying is authentic."[159]

Decisive considerations militate against using Aramaic phenomena to determine authenticity: (1) This chapter has already demonstrated that Aramaisms are not indications of earliness (see above under "Operational Bases of Tradition Criticism"). (2) The principle is hermeneutically misguided. Inerrancy and the grammatico-historical hermeneutic require the inspiration of the autographs, not of hypothesized sources that lay behind them.

The criterion of *Palestinian environmental phenomena* sees the presence of Palestinian social, domestic, agricultural, religious, or other customs as a sign of earliness, because they indicate a tradition was not a creation of a Greek or non-Palestinian church. A tradition representing the time and environment of Jesus has a higher likelihood of authenticity. Jeremias argued that if the "pictorial element" of the tradition betrays Palestinian conditions, then a greater likelihood exists for the genuineness of the tradition.[160]

Yet not all of Jesus' teachings or incidents are exclusively Palestinian, especially since Jesus said things that indicate a Greek environmental influence also. For example, physicians served as models for sententious sayings in many cultures, and some have striking parallels to Jesus' words (compare Mark 2:17 with Meander, *Fragment 591 K*).[161] Traditions, therefore, are not necessarily inauthentic because they lack an exclusively Palestinian background.

In addition to the above "formal criteria," two important "material criteria" exist: the criteria of dissimilarity and coherence. Although its origin is uncertain, the criterion of *dissimilarity* (or, distinctiveness) is among the most decisive tradition-critical and useful factors in Tradition Criticism. France comments, "This is the essential criterion, around which all others revolve" and "All others [i.e. criteria] are extensions of it, or are used only to check and confirm its findings."[162] It is deeply rooted in the methodology of FC's founders.[163]

This criterion has found its most fervent expression in the works of Perrin and Fuller. Fuller argues, "As regards the sayings of Jesus, traditio-historical criticism eliminates from the authentic sayings of Jesus those which are paralleled in the Jewish tradition on one hand (apocalyptic and Rabbinic) and those which reflect the faith, practice and situations of the post-Easter church as we know them from outside the gospels."[164] Perrin highlights dissimilarity: "The criterion of dissimilarity . . . must be regarded as the basis for all contemporary attempts to reconstruct the teaching of Jesus."[165] The essence of this criterion is that one can establish authenticity *only* when a tradition does not fit within either the Christian community that transmitted it or the Jewish world in which Jesus lived and taught.

Several serious flaws render this criterion unconvincing. First, it blatantly assumes the inauthenticity of traditions. Automatically tradition is suspect and unreliable. Second, it inherently eliminates the great majority of the gospel material, since most does not conflict with Judaism or the early church. Third, its basis is an argument from silence. Knowledge of first-century Judaism and the early church is limited. To eliminate material based on a limited knowledge of these periods is precarious. Fourth, *acute* subjectivity reigns in applying this principle. Scholars constantly differ as to whether a particular item is more "natural" against the background of primitive Christianity or against the background of Jesus' ministry.[166]

Fifth, this principle erroneously presupposes no connection between Jesus and contemporary Judaism to which He belonged and between Jesus and the Old Testament. A continuity would have naturally existed between Jesus and His contemporaries. To exclude such agreement would lead only to a distortion of what Jesus taught and result in a minimalistic Jesus, namely, "a critically assured *minimum*."[167] Sixth, this method directly conflicts with the criteria of Palestinian environmental and Aramaic linguistic phenomena, which hold that an "authentic" saying of Jesus should reflect first-century Palestine. The tradition critic eliminates material if it has parallels in first-century Palestinian Judaism and also if it has a background that cannot be consistent with it. According to his own inclinations, he can eliminate most, if not all, material.

The criterion of *coherence* functions as a buttressing corollary to that of dissimilarity. Its validity depends upon the validity of the other principles discussed. If those principles are wrong, then data accepted through coherence is also invalid. Without explicitly formulating this principle, Bultmann used this type of criterion in such places as Matthew 12:28, where he argued that the verse "can, in my view, claim the highest degree of authenticity which we can make for any saying of Jesus: it is full of that feeling of eschatological power which must have characterized the activity of Jesus."[168]

Regarding coherence Perrin remarked, "Material from the earliest strata of the tradition may be accepted as authentic if it can be shown to cohere with material established as authentic by means of the criterion of dissimilarity."[169] Important considerations render this criterion unsubstantial. First, since this principle depends so heavily upon the criterion of dissimilarity, it automatically inherits the same problems as dissimilarity. Second, acute subjectivity reigns in its formulation. What standards determine coherence? What may seem coherent to modern scholars may not have seemed so to a Jew or Christian in the first century. This is brazenly whimsical.

In sum, tradition critics have carefully chosen their criteria to ensure intended results. Minds already closed to the legitimacy of tradition have devised principles to reinforce their preconceptions. They did not design these principles to confirm, but to underscore their negativity about the reliability of tradition. At best, they allow only a bare minimum of credibility to the tradition, and they predetermined these results by designing criteria to yield them. It is circular reasoning in its most malignant form, betraying a philosophically preconceived agenda without any hope of objectivity. Perhaps more significantly, these so-called tradition criteria rule out any concept of an inspired biblical text.

GROWING EVANGELICAL PRACTICE
OF FORM AND TRADITION CRITICISM

A recent article in evangelically oriented *Christianity Today*, entitled "Who Do Scholars Say That I am?" decried with indignation the Jesus Seminar's wholesale questioning of the words and works of Jesus.[170] In the past, other articles have castigated the members of the Jesus Seminar for their "liberal theological persuasion" in deciding "what Jesus did and did not say."[171] Recent works written by evangelicals have also spotlighted the Seminar's negative pronouncements.[172]

The finger-pointing by evangelicals is, however, to a large extent misleading, for many evangelicals are using the very historical-critical methodologies that they so strongly oppose. They operate from a similar presuppositional grid, resulting in the same type of dehistoricizing of Jesus' words and works as the anathematized Jesus Seminar. Increasingly, the pertinent question for evangelicals no longer can be "who do the *Jesus Seminar* scholars say that Jesus is?" but "who do *evangelicals* say that Jesus is?" The growing evangelical practice is evident especially in the practice of Form and Tradition Criticism. The following will sample evangelical usage of these methods.

For many years, conservative evangelicals tended to reject FC. Gundry observed the following:

It is obvious that a consistent, thorough-going form criticism will have no appeal to those who desire to recognize the inspiration of the Scriptures and the historical continuity between the Lord Jesus and the early church. And let all "conservatives" who are inclined to adopt some form critical terminology and viewpoints be apprised of the basic nature of that to which they are accommodating themselves.[173]

Apparently, many conservative evangelicals have not realized the pernicious basis of form-critical speculation. Gundry wrote that the fundamental assumption of FC—namely, "Gospel tradition first existed as brief, rounded units, circulating orally in the Christian community"—could be "quite innocuous," perhaps without realizing the tacit evolutionary presuppositions behind that fundamental assumption.[174] One cannot overstress that this fundamental assumption is extremely suspect in light of FC's historical development (see "Historical Background of Form Criticism" above). One must not divorce form speculation from the history and presuppositions that led to its development.

Discussion earlier in this chapter has also demonstrated that the basis of this hypothesis of brief, rounded units was the radical skepticism of K. L. Schmidt, who labeled contextual connections of the units as unhistorical and embellished. If those connections are historically and chronologically trustworthy, evangelicals should reject this "fundamental" assumption of FC. No form-critical dismantling of individual pericopes is justifiable, for no one can with accuracy or certainty identify pericopes as isolated units circulating independently. The pericopes are integral to the Gospels and primarily reflect the personal reminiscences of the apostles and other first-century eyewitnesses. The pericopes give no real proof of circulation in isolation (as form critics theorize).

Evangelicals must take care to elucidate presuppositions and historical developments that gave rise to form critical speculation, for as Linnemann has correctly noted, historical-critical practices are in essence ideologies rather than methodologies.[175] Similarly, Donald Guthrie's words are telling: "When all the limitations are taken into account the scope of a true form-critical approach will be seen to be severely restricted. Yet with such restrictions it may well be asked whether such a movement can really make any effective contribution to gospel criticism."[176]

Yet a growing inclination among evangelicals appears to be toward engaging in various "modified" versions of Historical Criticism (for example, Form and Tradition Criticism) with a goal of "dialogue" with liberal theological scholarship. Kingsbury observes this inclination in a comment regarding a recent work by several German- and British-trained evangelical theologians: "New Testament Criticism and Interpretation constitutes a bold and imaginative undertaking: to bring American scholarship into dialogue with the contemporary guild of biblical scholarship."[177] Unfortunately, in this dialogue evangelicals have changed substantially, not contemporary liberal scholarship. Prominent evangelicals have adopted not only the terminology but also the methodology of Historical Criticism.

Perhaps it is their hope that practicing a "modified" version of FC will refute the charge of liberals and other evangelicals that conservative evangelicals are "closed-minded" to current methodological practices.[178] Perhaps it is their desire to exhibit scholarship that has driven the growing evangelical trend toward Historical Criticism. It is clear, however, that liberal definitions of "scholarship" have molded evangelical perceptions of what scholarship is, but liberal methodologies are actually philosophical agendas, not genuine "scholarship."

The current state of affairs has produced another unrealistic situation. Conservative evangelicals, those who do not subscribe to form-critical suppositions, are sometimes the objects of subtle *ad hominem* arguments and downright ostracism within the theological community for failing to conform to these practices.[179] Methods must be "theologically correct," or else the system drowns out dissenting voices that expose the true nature of Form and Tradition criticism.

Some impose a tactic like Davies, who has written, "All serious students of the New Testament today are to some extent Form Critics."[180] He implies that those who question FC are not serious students of the New Testament.

Several individuals will illustrate the tendency of evangelical New Testament scholars to embrace Form and Tradition Criticism.

George Ladd

McKnight cites George Ladd as "an evangelical scholar who is the product of the American fundamentalism of the 1920s" who accepts form-critical analysis.[181] McKnight calls attention to Ladd's acknowledgment that FC contains "valid elements" and "has thrown considerable light on the nature of the gospels and the traditions they employ. Evangelical scholars should be willing to accept this light."[182] McKnight recommends the discipline on the basis of one evangelical's example without evaluating FC's negative bent. Is this wise?

Ladd's approach advocated a modified version of FC,[183] based on his acceptance of the Two-Source Theory as "a literary fact."[184] Yet he admitted that people with a low view of the Bible formulated the Two-Source Theory "because they had been set free from any dogmatic view of biblical inspiration" and could deal with the Gospels as historical documents.[185] Discussion earlier in this chapter and in chapters 3 and 4 has demonstrated the questionable nature of the presuppositional and historical motives behind the Two- and Four-Source Hypotheses, raising strong questions about Ladd's assertion that the theory is "literary fact."

Ladd's position was that FC's "skepticism is not a result of the method by itself but of form criticism coupled with a rationalistic view of the nature of history."[186] Earlier discussion in this chapter and in chapter 2 has demonstrated that FC's fundamental assumptions are inseparable from the method itself.

Ladd's modified FC included belief in an exclusively oral period and categorically rejected any concept of early written documents.[187] The theory of an exclusively oral period is an assumption that has become a dogma.

Credible arguments exist that during Jesus' ministry, His disciples may have written notes on the main aspects of His teaching.[188]

Ladd argued, "A second valid contention of form criticism is that the Gospels are not 'neutral, objective, impartial' records but are witnesses to the faith of Christian believers."[189] Although he qualified this statement, he concluded the following:

> The redemptive events recorded in the Gospels are "objective" in the sense that they really happened in space and time, but their nature is such that they stand apart from merely human "histori- cal events" . . . for they cannot be understood by ordinary human observation but only by the response of faith.[190]

But can an evangelical separate faith-history from other objective his- tory? Can he say that all objective history is not the same, some of it be- ing "merely human"? Asked another way, can he separate the scientific from the spiritual without doing violence to the spiritual? Geisler illustrates:

> Evangelicals cannot look at historical and scientific affirmations in Scripture as purely symbolic or mythical. In short, we cannot separate science from the Scripture. When the Bible declares that Jesus was born of a virgin, then it affirms a biological truth as well as a spiritual one. . . . The scientific cannot be separated from the spiritual without doing violence to the spiritual.[191]

If Jesus was not born of a virgin, the significance of Christ's death and all other redemptive acts become suspect in the New Testament as well.

Robert Stein

Robert Stein is another evangelical who reflects significant agreement with historical-critical assumptions. Like other form critics, he accepts the Four-Source Hypothesis,[192] basing interpretive conclusions on this. Yet, scholarly opinion opposing this theory is growing.[193]

Stein is also positive about the primary assumption of FC:

> One of the positive contributions of form criticism is the recogni- tion that in general the Gospel traditions circulated as indepen- dent oral units before being incorporated into the Gospels. Some material, however, was collected into larger complexes such as Mark 1:21–39 (45); 2:1 to 3:6; and 4:1–34 before being incorpo- rated into our Gospels.[194]

As argued above, the Gospels offer no proof for such an assertion. Because the period before the Gospels were written is largely unknown, dogmatic pro- nouncements concerning the nature of the tradition are speculative at best.

Stein furthermore embraces K. L. Schmidt's thesis, which denigrates the historical, geographical, and chronological connections in the Gospels:

It would appear that there is a great deal to be said for Schmidt's thesis. When one looks at much of the material in the Gospel of Mark, it appears that the accounts were, for the most part, joined together on a non-chronological basis and that they indeed existed as independent units of tradition.[195]

Identification of specific independent units, however, is quite subjective, depending on the whim of the interpreter. Instead of independent units evolving in the church over a period of time, Mark may reflect the personal recollections of the eyewitness and apostle Peter. For example, these could be recollections that Peter emphasized in his preaching.[196]

Regarding the "criterion of multiple attestation," Stein argues, "It is . . . true that this tool cannot provide historical certainty but only probability, but in historical matters this is all we can ever hope to achieve. Faith and belief may have unique access to historical certainty; but historical research can only deal with probabilities."[197] Does this mean that what Jesus said and did can never be known for certain? Is certainty possible only through the eyes of faith? Is an existential leap required? Interestingly, Stein bases probability of the historicity of the tradition upon multiple attestation among four documents, three of which are hypothetical (namely, Mark, Q, M, L). Such a criterion based on a weak hypothesis assumes the falsity of tradition rather than fostering an objective approach to the historical accuracy of tradition.

Regarding the "Criterion of Divergent Patterns from Redaction," Stein argues, "Materials in the Gospels that reflect a writer's unique theological emphasis are probably less authentic or historical, especially if they appear only in his unique material (M in Matthew and L in Luke) or in his redactional work (summaries, explanatory clauses, seams, etc.)."[198] Along with more radical form and tradition critics, Stein allows that elements that appear to be "historical" can actually be unhistorical.

Stein also allows for the possibility of "inauthentic" but "authoritative" sayings attributed to Jesus:

> If a saying attributed to Jesus in the Gospels were inauthentic, its authoritative quality would remain, for the Evangelists not only recalled what the historical Jesus said and did but were taught by the Spirit and empowered by Him to interpret what the historical Jesus said and did (John 14:26; 16:14). Thus in the Gospels the risen Christ also speaks through his Spirit by means of his prophets and apostles. These words are also authoritative even if not authentic. As a result, if the inauthenticity of a saying should be demonstrated this should not be taken to mean that this saying lacks authority.[199]

For example, in Matthew 5:31–32, Stein argues that the exception clause "is an interpretive comment added by Matthew" and that the version without the exception clause in Mark, Luke, and Q "is more authentic." According to Stein's logic, although the words are Matthew's, not from Jesus, making them inauthentic, they are still authoritative.[200] Stein's position, however, results in a quasi-concept of inspired deception within the gospel record. How could Matthew's readers recognize this "interpretation" in context as distinct from historical tradition? They could not. The text contains no indications that the exception clause is an interpretation instead of a historical statement.

For Stein, even if the Gospels were written by eyewitnesses of the events,

> it does not follow that eyewitness accounts of historical events are *a priori* accurate historical accounts. . . . We cannot . . . assume that we have proven the historicity of the gospel accounts even if we can demonstrate that behind them stands the testimony of an eyewitness. . . . If eyewitness testimony of the gospel material should be established, then the burden of proof should rest upon those who would deny the historicity of the events reported.[201]

In other words, Stein can never be sure of historicity, even if eyewitnesses are present. Eyewitnesses shift the burden of proof, but doubt always remains.

Stein supports the criterion of multiple forms: "It would appear reasonable to suppose that the appearance of a tradition or motif in multiple forms is supportive, even if not conclusive, evidence for . . . authenticity."[202] This criterion includes the tendencies of the developing tradition whereby a gospel writer changed the audience of a pericope. For example, Luke 15:4–7 preserves the original audience to whom Jesus spoke the parable of the lost sheep, but Matthew 18:12–14 changed the original audience from Jesus' opponents to the church in order to fulfil Matthew's theological purposes in his own situation.

Thus, one can never be sure what the original audience of a pericope was, for the evangelist was free to change material to fit some hypothesized life situation. By recognizing "certain of the 'laws' which the tradition experienced during the oral period, such as the changing of audience in the first and second/third *Sitz im Leben*" one can "be better able to ascertain what is authentic."[203] This criterion ignores the possibility that as an itinerant preacher, Jesus may have repeated His parables to different audiences and adapted His message to different situations in His own time. Stein allows a subjective postulation of hypothetical life situations to control the determination of what is authentic and what is not.

Stein calls multiple attestation "a helpful tool for ascertaining the authenticity of the Gospel tradition." Indeed, he argues that "the multiple attestation of a tradition places the burden of proof upon those who would argue against the authenticity of a such a tradition."[204] Since the historical foundation of this criterion places the burden of proof on the tradition, one wonders how the burden of proof can be reversible. The intent of the criterion is to cast suspicion on the tradition, not to confirm the tradition. No amount of modification can overcome this built-in intent, for it is impossible for something predicated on acute skepticism to produce positive results.

Stein considers "the Sermon on the Mount (Matt. 5:1–7:29) and the Sermon on the Plain (Luke 6:20–49)" to be "literary creations of Matthew and Luke in the sense that they are collections of Jesus' sayings that were uttered at various times and places and have been brought together due to topical considerations, i.e. in order to have an orderly account ([Luke] 1:3)." Although "there is no need . . . to deny that a historical event lies behind the scene," no "Sermon on the Mount" or "on the plain" ever took place as presented in the Gospels but was a creative, fabricative embellishment of the evangelist.[205]

Stein supports the classification of forms, preferring Taylor's method. Stein admits, however, that of three major classification systems (for example, Bultmann, Dibelius, Taylor), "Only two of the categories possess a distinct form—the pronouncement stories and miracle stories. The remaining types of material are essentially formless" and classification often "does not depend upon form as much as upon content."[206] Stein concludes that such "classification systems are helpful in that they provide convenient handles to refer to the various gospel traditions."[207] Yet, such admittedly meager abilities of FC demonstrate the vastly superior nature of the grammatico-historical hermeneutic and tenuous nature and subjectivity of form analysis. Stein, like other evangelical form critics, makes so many qualifications to an evangelical approach to FC that the validity and usefulness of the practice is suspect.

Robert Guelich

Robert Guelich, in introducing his commentary on the Sermon on the Mount, followed the lead of George Ladd, his mentor:

> This commentary offers a *critical* exegesis in that it makes use of the literary and historical critical tools including text, source, form, tradition, redaction, and structural criticism . . . For many to whom the Scriptures are vital the use of these critical tools has historically been more "destructive" than "constructive." But one need not discard the tool because of its abuse.[208]

Guelich chose to ignore this history of abuse, for he asserts, "Like any other 'tool,' these of literary and historical criticism are basically neutral and often reflect the tendencies of the person using them. . . . . But they have been refined to the extent that they offer the best instruments to date in exegeting the text."[209] On the contrary, Literary and Historical Criticism are anything but "neutral" tools (see chapter 2).

As with other form critics, Guelich assumes the Four-Source Hypothesis.[210] This presupposition controls many of his hermeneutical decisions, producing his many extrapolations regarding the Sermon.[211] Though he allows that the tradition "most likely" stems from Jesus' ministry, he does not see the gospel account of the Sermon as being preached by Jesus, but as the literary product of the gospel writer.[212] Guelich agrees with Dibelius that "even this underlying tradition resulted from the early community's compilation of various traditional units to meet their own catechal needs."[213] In light of this, "the actual 'Sermon' as such came into being when the tradition was combined into its present form in the post-Easter community, a process that makes moot the question of when and where Jesus 'preached' the Sermon."[214] In other words, although both Matthew and Luke portray Jesus as preaching the "Sermon on the Mount [or Plain]," He did not, for the sermon was the product of the Christian community and the gospel writers. Guelich contended that "Matthew has considerably changed the extent and profile of the Sermon tradition."[215]

Guelich asserts that originally the Beatitudes were three (see Luke 6:20–21; Matt. 5:3–4, 6). A fourth Beatitude (Luke 6:22–23; Matt. 5:11–12) was "a separate traditional saying" that also goes back to Jesus.[216] Guelich elaborated further:

> These four Beatitudes underwent further modification in the tradition with the change of person, with the expansion in number to eight in Matt. 5:5, 7–9, the first relating to the Beatitude of 5:3 and the other three corresponding in context to the three admonitions that followed in the tradition, and with the formulation of the antithetically parallel Woes in Luke 6:24–26, either in the tradition or by Luke. Therefore, Matthew found eight beatitudes in his Sermon tradition which he then adapted redactionally for his own purposes.[217]

The evangelist created one beatitude (Matt. 5:10), while four more (Matt. 5:5, 7–9) are the later products of the Christian community.[218] Guelich encapsulated his thesis as follows:

> The Beatitudes of Matt. 5:3–12 indicate several stages of development. First, the core (5:3, 4, 6 par. Luke 6:20–21) had roots extending to Jesus' ministry to the desperate ones of his day. . . . The fourth Beatitude (5:11–12, par. Luke 6:22–23) depicts the continuing struggle in this age for God's people. . . . Second, these four Beatitudes, brought together to make a clear declarative statement as the opening of the Sermon tradition, were later expanded by the use of the Psalms and Jesus' sayings to form four additional Beatitudes (5:5, 7–9) commensurate with Jesus' teachings and preaching as found in the tradition. Third, Matthew expressly adapted these Beatitudes (5:3, 4, 5, 6, 10) to Isaiah 61 in order to underline Jesus' person and work. . . . Throughout the entire process of development, these nine Beatitudes remain consistent with the Jesus of the tradition.[219]

For Guelich, the Sermon on the Mount is essentially non-historical. Many have decried the Jesus Seminar's decision to vote out the fourth beatitude, but evangelicals like Guelich do the very same thing.[220]

Guelich contended, "Matthew's Gospel and the Sermon in particular reflect the portrait artist's freedom to modulate, modify, relocate, rearrange, restructure, and restate as exercised by the community in the traditional process and by the evangelist's redaction."[221] Dealing with three life situations (namely, Jesus', the Christian community's, and the writer's), an interpreter must detect the layers of change by the community and the writer in order to isolate what Jesus actually said—a hopeless task.

Guelich contended the following regarding Matthew 5:17–20:

> In no other section of the Sermon does the meaning of the passage depend so much on the use of tradition and redaction. . . . Consequently, the primary focus of the exegesis of 5:17–20 centers on the literary questions of form, source, and redaction.[222]

Guelich saw the unit as having "differing, at times conflicting, meanings."[223] Guelich has an extended discussion of Matthew 5:17–20 in which he attributes ineptitude, awkwardness, and misuse of tradition to the writer.[224] After reading Guelich's analysis of the section, one wonders whether Jesus actually spoke 5:17–20, whether or to what extent the tradition actually existed in the community, or to what extent the imagination of the evangelist was working and how poorly it was operating. Would Matthew's initial readers have detected the esoteric signals that indicate the alleged modifications of tradition? The writer presents 5:17–20 as coming directly from Jesus' lips, and this is the most natural reading of the passage. The probability is quite high that this is how they understood it.

Guelich leaned toward Schmidt's view of the artificial nature of geographical and chronological connections. Guelich doubted that one could ever be sure that the Gospels do not reflect "a theological tendency to localize events such as with calling of the Twelve, the Sermon, the Transfiguration, and the Olivet Discourse on a mountain" and to what extent they provide "a historically accurate description of the location of the events." Guelich continued with the following observation:

> The ultimate answer to this question lies beyond our historical control. . . . The combination of the Sermon tradition with the traditional mountain setting for the calling for the Twelve may have resulted merely from the Church's catechetical interest in the Q Sermon material for new "disciples" in the early church.[225]

In other words, geographical and chronological items in the text may result from creativity in the Christian community and redaction by the writer.[226] Guelich seems to be suggesting that the early church was so devoid of historical interest that they misrepresented historical features in order to instruct disciples. He does not know whether the Sermon on the Mount took place on a mountain because of the early church's alleged lack of interest in such details.[227] Guelich's analyses throughout are thoroughly preconditioned by the negative presuppositions of Historical Criticism.

Darrell Bock

Darrell Bock, another evangelical form critic, maintains, "In the hands of a skilled exegete who uses tools of interpretation in a way that fits what they are capable of, Form Criticism can be a fruitful aid to understanding and to exposition."[228] He favors Klaus Berger's form-critical approach,[229] but admits that it is a "slimmed down version" that strictly speaking may not be FC.[230] He correctly notes this discrepancy in that the approach does not entail a negative conclusion regarding historicity (as FC presuppositionally and historically does).

Yet, if FC's purpose is only to describe and not to evaluate historicity, as Berger holds, it fulfills no useful purpose and is unnecessary. Hooker observes, "I do not think it is particularly illuminating to be told that a miracle story is a miracle story, or that a paradigm is a paradigm . . .; one can learn that by watching TV commercials."[231] A repetition of Bultmann's definition of FC is relevant:

> It [Form Criticism] does not consist of identifying the individual units of the tradition according to their aesthetics or other characteristics and placing them in their various categories. It is much rather "to discover the origin and the history of the particular units and thereby to throw some light on the history of the tradition before it took literary form."[232]

From the outset FC's purpose has been to go beyond mere description. Thus Bock's definition of the discipline is aberrant, for it ignores its history. Its founders declared its goal to be making judgments on historicity. It views the Gospels as products of the Christian community rather than of eyewitness reports of the apostles and others. Evangelicals should not enervate terminology as a pretext for exhibiting "scholarly" involvement in Historical Criticism. Bock's attempt to distance himself from normal FC by redefining the name attests to the bankruptcy of FC and its inherent dangers. Form Criticism has a predilection toward allowing for errors in the Gospels; grammatico-historical exegesis presupposes inerrancy and has for centuries supplied genre descriptions without negative conclusions regarding historicity and the miraculous therein.

Grant confirmed FC's inseparability from reaching historical judgments:

> It was maintained . . . that form criticism had nothing to do with the historicity of events whose purported records had been handed down orally, but only with the outward form of the tradition; but this was an impossible view. All literary criticism of the New Testament is ultimately Historical Criticism.[233]

The high incidence of evangelicals negating gospel historicity through use of historical-critical methods confirms that assessment of FC.

Bock not only redefines FC, but he also confuses the life situation of the early church with that of Jesus: "As long as one does not deny that the origins of the tradition go back to the participants, this search for the *Sitz im Leben* in the church need not be a problem and in fact can help show the way to methods one might use to teach the account today."[234] Grammatico-historical interpretation concerns itself with the gospel author's intended meaning for his original readers, not with how the Christian community applied tradition to their own life situation, and is unconcerned with any historical situation different from that of Jesus. The form critic's speculation regarding life situations in the early church is so subjective and baseless that it is impossible to confirm. The gospel writers never intended this for the early church was interested in the historical Jesus and wanted to know what He taught and did. Any alleged "signals" in the text to the contrary are the fruit of the unchecked imaginations of form critics.

Hooker, though somewhat favorable to form analysis, notes the discipline's subjectivity:

> We have no independent knowledge of the groups which formed the pericopes which we are discussing, and we can only deduce the needs and interests of the community which shaped the material from the material itself. The *Sitz im Leben* to which a pericope is assigned—often with great confidence—is only a hypothesis, and sometimes one feels that the hypotheses demonstrate an excessive endowment of imaginative ability on the part of those who put them forward . . . whether or not the early Church was adept at thinking up stories about Jesus to fit Church situations, the form-critics are certainly adept at thinking up Church situations to fit the stories of Jesus.[235]

Proposed life situations for isolated units of tradition in the early church are purely speculative. But the goal of sound hermeneutics is to avoid subjectivity as much as possible and not to read into a text a foreign meaning. Form Criticism has done the exact opposite, and so cannot be "a fruitful aid to understanding and to exposition." Even "modified" FC (as proposed by Bock) regards gospel material as owing its present shape to the practical needs of the early Christian community. It assumes a dichotomy between the pre-Easter and post-Easter periods of Christianity by hypothesizing different life situations for them. This is an unhealthy assumption for evangelicals to make as they exegete the biblical text.

Another hermeneutical hitch in the theory of Bock and other evangelical form critics lies in applying biblical inspiration and inerrancy to the period behind the Gospels and not to the text itself. One can learn what Jesus taught and understand the Gospels without FC, for the Gospels are not reinterpretations of the life of Christ to fit later historical circumstances in the Christian community. They present one life situation, that of Jesus Himself. To go beyond that and hypothesize an additional one impugns the text and courts hermeneutical disaster.

Bock illustrates this undesirable tendency in his proposal that the parallels to Luke 8:4–15 in Matthew 13 and Mark 4 are most likely "topical groupings" or "anthologies."[236] Bock's suggestion deprecates the historical validity of Matthew 13:1–3 and 13:53 (cf. Mark 4:1–2, 33–35). He states, "Mark 4 is seen as a collection of distinct sayings, since that grouping is also anthological. But it need not be assumed that, because an anthology of parables is present in Mark 4 (a point that is likely), every parable or saying in it was originally uttered in a distinct setting."[237] Bock's acceptance of the Four-Source Theory of gospel origins lies behind his dehistoricizing conclusions regarding Matthew 13, Mark 4, and Luke 8.[238]

Bock elaborates on form critical categories in a way that minimizes the antihistorical basis of the terminology. He downplays the significance of the term "legend": "The name 'legend' is unfortunate because in English it suggests that the accounts are false. To comment on historicity is not the intent of the title."[239] He says that both "legend" and "Historical Stories" are "simply intended to describe an account that is interested in the life and adventures of Jesus for its own sake, without being concerned to recount his saying or other such things."[240]

Redefining categories is misleading, however. Bultmann and other originators of FC clearly negated historicity of "legends" or "stories of Jesus," especially when they entailed anything miraculous:

> I naturally do not deny that historical happenings may underlie legends, I mean that "unhistorical" applies to the idea of legend negatively in the sense that legends not only "have no special interest in history" (Dibelius) but that they are not, in the modern scientific sense, historical accounts at all. . . . Instead of being historical in character . . . [legends] are religious and edifying.[241]

Bultmann's category for Luke 4:16–30 is "apophthegm," which he regards as unhistorical in various aspects.[242] Bock calls the same section a "pronouncement account."[243] Berger has an entirely different system of categories in classifying the section.[244] Fitzmyer is undecided on which category the section belongs in.[245] Variety in categorization is visible elsewhere.[246] The lack of agreement from one critic to the next highlights the subjectivity of the whole system (see above under *"Mixed Forms"*).

Bock follows the lead of Bultmann, Fitzmyer, Berger, and Theissen in calling Luke 5:12–16 "a miracle story, specifically, a healing."[247] He consistently assigns miracles and sayings of Jesus to form categories whose names in the writings of the original form critics imply unhistoricity.[248] No exegetical benefit comes from such classifications. Why then associate the biblical text with form categories that are clearly hostile to historical accuracy? The negative connections of the terms are distinctly anti-evangelical, no matter how much one modifies them. Besides, evangelicals who use form-critical terminology such as "legend," if they are inerrantists, are guilty of the same deception as neo-orthodox theologians who use such terms as "resurrection" and mean something entirely different from an orthodox understanding.

Another illustration of such misuse of terminology is Bock's employment of "multiple attestation" to argue for the historicity of the healing of the leper in Luke 5:12–16, in opposition to the Jesus Seminar's dehistoricizing of the passage.[249] Yet that very criterion came into existence to engender an inherent suspicion of historicity. Can the reverse use of their own principle ever convince liberals that the Gospels are historically accurate?

David Catchpole

Catchpole advocates the use of tradition critical principles: "The gospel tradition itself compels us to engage in tradition-historical inquiry. . . . We can hardly avoid attributing to the later post-Easter stage both the redaction of material, and, on occasion, its creation."[250] Using tradition-historical principles, Catchpole indicates that Matthew 18:17 could not have been spoken by Jesus for it is "most unlike the historical Jesus" who freely commended and accepted Gentiles and tax collectors (Matt. 13:11ff.; Mark 2:14–17; 11:15–17; Luke 7:9, 34; 10:12–14; 11:31f.; 15:1ff.).[251] Catchpole bases his conclusion on a subjective perception of an inconsistency in Jesus' teaching, not on solid objective evidence. This is a dangerous hermeneutical procedure to follow when interpreting Scripture.

Catchpole ignores Matthew's emphasis on Jesus' mission to the Jews: the offer of the kingdom to the Jews (Matt. 4:17, 23) that was promised in the Old Testament (Isa. 42:1–3), Jesus' warning His disciples to not go to the Gentiles or Samaritans in proclaiming that message of the kingdom (Matt. 10:5–6), and Jesus' exclusive mission to "the lost sheep of the house of Israel." This focus is consistent with Old Testament promises that the Messiah would offer salvation to Israel first and also be a light to the Gentiles (Isa. 42:5–9; 61:1–3; cf. John 4:22).

Furthermore, the focus of Matthew 18:17 is not so much upon deprecating Gentiles and tax-gatherers as on the prevailing Jewish attitudes in excluding such groups. Jesus' point is that in the same way that Jews exclude Gentiles and tax-collectors, so should the church treat a sinning member who does not repent. The focus is on manner of exclusion, not deprecation.

Also, the likelihood of the post-Easter church creating something like Matthew 18:17 is minimal, for the church came to realize Jesus' ministry to Gentiles long before the writing of the gospel. In fact, this realization came as early as Paul's first missionary journey in the early forties. The preservation of this saying and others like it is a clear testimony to the authenticity of such statements coming from the very lips of Jesus. Conservative evangelicals must recognize this.

Catchpole also doubts the authenticity of Matthew 23:2–3, finding it more approving of Pharisaic traditional teaching and more acceptable to Moses as the final court of appeal than Jesus would have been. Catchpole attributes the statement to "Pharisaic membership and theological influence within the church."[252] He takes this as an example of something the Christian community attributed to Jesus which He never spoke. Like radical form and tradition critics, Catchpole distinguishes between the words and deeds of the historical Jesus and those embellishments by the early church that became a part of the gospel accounts.

Finally, Catchpole affirms the basic distinction between the form-critical concepts of *Historie* and *Geschichte*:

> The gospels do belong to Jesus and also to the churches. For Jesus this means that he is seen as not merely *historisch*, a figure of the past, but also one whom we can see within the developing tradition as truly *geschichtlich*, that is, a person whose relevance is explored and exploited ever and again in places far removed from Galilee and Jerusalem and in times long after A.D. 30.[253]

Grant Osborne

Osborne also supports "a positive reappraisal of criteria for studying development tradition." He argues that "criteria should build on a positive foundation and seek to authenticate rather than disprove genuineness."[254] Once again, Osborne tries to revise principles that *inherently* make the tradition suspect. Ultimately the question centers in this: to whom does he want to demonstrate authenticity? If to a group (historical critics) that will not accept his *a priori* assumption of the genuineness of the tradition, no matter how much he tries to refine tradition critical principles, they will not change. No amount of attempted "positive" spin on these inherently negative principles will sway them. If he wants to demonstrate authenticity to evangelicals already inclined to accept it, at best all his tradition-critical principles can offer is a unsubstantial possibility of authenticity. Even Osborne admits that his criteria "can do no more than show probability" and are therefore "tentative."[255]

> There is no reason to ignore or repudiate *Traditionsgeschichte* as a positive tool for investigating the life and unfolding theology of the early Church. When we control the negative dangers and wield the tool with honesty and sensitivity, the results will magnify the Word of God and continue the exciting discovery of ultimate truth for our time.

Osborne speaks about controlling "the negative dangers" of *Traditionsgeschichte*,[256] yet he himself has not done so. Earlier in his career, he advocated that Matthew had expanded the wording of the Great Commission to make it a triadic rather than "an original monadic formula" and concluded that Jesus did not speak the Great Commission as it appears in Matthew's gospel.[257] Matthew allegedly expanded Jesus' original monadic stipulation into the triadic baptismal formula to "interpret the true meaning of Jesus' message for his own day."[258] Due to "widespread dissatisfaction" with his approach, Osborne later revised his explanation.[259]

CONCLUSION

Several conclusions emerge: first, historical and presuppositional developments must enter into an evaluation of Historical Criticism. Form and Tradition Criticism cannot exceed their presuppositional and historical foundation in value. If the foundations are tenuous, so is the practice of that methodology. Radical and virulent antisupernaturalism along with evolutionary dogma are part and parcel of the presuppositions and history of Form and Tradition Criticism.

Second, evangelicals who advocate "modified" versions of these disciplines either ignore the presuppositional and historical impetuses behind fundamental assumptions or operate with aberrant definitions of them. In either case, the high failure rate of evangelicals in avoiding negative presuppositions demonstrates that negative presuppositions are inseparable from the practice.

Third, since the Gospels are eyewitness accounts of Jesus' life, they reflect only one life situation, that of the earthly life, death, and resurrection of the Messiah. Moreover, the Holy Spirit supernaturally guided and aided the writing of the gospel records (John 14:26; 16:13). The practice of Form and Tradition Criticism by evangelicals questions the role of the Holy Spirit by positing errors in the Gospels. Although the Gospels convey theology and are selective not exhaustive (John 21:30), they are also accurate historical and biographical records of Jesus' life.

Fourth, since the Reformation, the grammatico-historical method of interpretation has been the safeguard in hermeneutics, for it downplays subjectivity and emphasizes the need for objectivity in exegeting Scripture. Evangelicals who practice Form and Tradition Criticism depart from this foundational hermeneutic and court interpretive disaster. Inspiration and inerrancy pertain to the autographs of Scripture, not to a hypothesized oral period or to sources behind the Gospels. The time-honored hermeneutic is capable of identifying all literary genres without negative presuppositions about authenticity.

Form and Tradition Criticism are tenuous and philosophically-motivated agendas rather than objective purveyors of truth. An irony is that evangelicals implement principles inherently hostile to the Word to "confirm" the authenticity of the Scripture. These principles cannot lead to certainty regarding the Gospels, for objectivity is not the inherent purpose of Form and Tradition Criticism. How then can they be effective weapons against the liberal findings of non-historicity, especially since they were intended to do the opposite?

For some reason, evangelicals have tried to fit the radical mold by their use of Historical Criticism. Perhaps their goal is to influence the liberal camp. Their efforts, however, have been fruitless in changing liberals to a more conservative stance. On the other hand, a significant number of evangelicals have willingly fallen under the influence of Historical Criticism to the point that they now impugn the authenticity of historical elements in the Gospels. Their efforts at dialogue have backfired.

Robert Yarbrough, in an article entitled "Evangelical Theology in Germany," catalogued an interesting development: a significant trend in current German scholarship from "a dissenting voice, small but hardly still" is toward abandoning historical critical methods as bankrupt methodologies.[260] It calls "for spiritual renewal and biblical fidelity in a land which has done much to undermine, or at least radically redefine, both of these in recent generations."[261] According to Maier, Historical Criticism "has arrived at the end of a blind alley."[262] Evangelical New Testament scholars need to join the trend noted by Yarbrough and Maier. Rather than continuing to dance on the edge of hermeneutical and theological disaster, they should categorically reject historical-critical methods and fulfill their desire to be truly on the cutting edge of scholarship by using exclusively the grammatico-historical approach to interpreting Scripture.

ENDNOTES

1. Eta Linnemann, *Historical Criticism of the Bible, Methodology or Ideology?* trans. Robert W. Yarbrough (Grand Rapids: Baker, 1990), 111.
2. The grammatico-historical method's "fundamental principle is to gather from the Scriptures themselves the precise meaning which the writers intended to convey. . . . The grammatico-historical-exegete . . . will accept the claims of the Bible without prejudice or adverse prepossession and, with no ambition to prove them true or false, will investigate the language and import of each book with fearless independence" (Milton S. Terry, *Biblical Hermeneutics* [reprint, Grand Rapids: Zondervan, n.d.], 173; cf. Walter C. Kaiser, Jr. *Toward an Exegetical Theology* [Grand Rapids: Baker, 1981], 87–88).
3. Norman Perrin, *Rediscovering the Teaching of Jesus* (New York: Harper and Row, 1976), 218.
4. Robert A. Guelich, *The Sermon on the Mount, A Foundation for Understanding* (Waco, Tex.: Word, 1982), 11–12, 23; cf. George E. Ladd, *The New Testament and Criticism* (Eerdmans: Grand Rapids, 1967).
5. Darrell L. Bock, "Form Criticism," in *New Testament Criticism and Interpretation,* ed. David A. Black and David S. Dockery (Grand Rapids: Zondervan, 1991), 192.
6. Alister McGrath, "Why Evangelicalism is the Future of Protestantism," *Christianity Today* (June 19, 1995): 18–23.
7. Gerhard Maier, *The End of the Historical Critical Method,* trans. Edwin W. Leverenz and Rudolf F. Norden (St. Louis: Concordia, 1977), 11–49.
8. Rudolf Bultmann, *The History of the Synoptic Tradition,* trans. John Marsh, rev. ed. (reprint of Basil Blackwell ed., 1963, Peabody, Mass.: Hendrickson, n.d.), 3–4.
9. F. F. Bruce, "Criticism," in *ISBE,* 1:822.
10. Rudolf Bultmann, *"Historie; Geschichte/geschichtlich; historisch,"* in *Handbook of Biblical Criticism,* ed. Richard N. Soulen (Atlanta: John Knox, 1981), 88–89.
11. Bultmann, *Jesus Christ and Mythology,* 11–21; cf. M. J. A. Horsnell, "Myth," in *ISBE,* 3:461–63.
12. Werner H. Kelber, *The Oral and the Written Gospel* (Philadelphia: Fortress, 1983), 5–6.
13. McKnight, *What Is Form Criticism?* (Philadelphia: Fortress, 1969), 18.

14. An exception to this principle is the passion narrative (Vincent Taylor, *The Formation of the Gospel Tradition* [London: Macmillan, 1935], 169–70).
15. This period varies among form critics (cf. Martin Dibelius, *From Tradition to Gospel* [New York: Charles Scribner's Sons, n.d.], 9–10; Taylor, *Formation of the Gospel Tradition*, 168).
16. Donald Guthrie, *New Testament Introduction*, rev. ed. (Downers Grove, Ill.: InterVarsity, 1990), 210.
17. Guthrie, *New Testament Introduction*, 231.
18. Birger Gerhardsson, *Memory and Manuscript* (Lund: C. W. K. Gleerup, 1961); idem, *The Origins of the Gospel Traditions* (Philadelphia: Fortress, 1977); Harald Riesenfeld, *The Gospel Tradition* (Philadelphia: Fortress, 1970).
19. Robert H. Gundry, *The Use of the Old Testament in St. Matthew's School: With Special Reference to the Messianic Hope* (Leiden: E. J. Brill, 1967), 182–83; Edgar J. Goodspeed, *Matthew, Apostle and Evangelist* (Philadelphia: John C. Winston, 1959), 115, 159–60.
20. George B. Caird, "The Study of the Gospels: II. Form Criticism," *Expository Times* LXXXVII (February 1976): 139 [italics added].
21. Rudolf Bultmann, "The Study of the Synoptic Gospels," in *Form Criticism, Two Essays on New Testament Research*, trans. Frederick C. Grant (New York: Harper & Brothers, 1934), 15, 21.
22. Richard H. Lightfoot, *History and Interpretation in the Gospels* (New York and London: Harper and Brothers, 1934), 225.
23. D. E. Nineham, "Eyewitness Testimony and the Gospel Tradition—I," *Journal of Theological Studies* 9 (April 1958): 13.
24. Dibelius, *From Tradition to Gospel*, 293.
25. Ibid., 295.
26. See Bultmann, "The Study of the Synoptic Gospels," in *Form Criticism, Two Essays on New Testament Research*, trans. Frederick C. Grant (New York: Harper & Brothers, 1934), 32.
27. Rudolf Bultmann, "The New Approach to the Synoptic Problem," *Journal of Religion* (July 1926): 345.
28. William D. Davies, *Invitation to the New Testament, A Guide to Its Main Witnesses* (Garden City, N.Y.: Doubleday, 1966), 98.
29. Martin J. Buss, "The Idea of Sitz-im Leben—History and Critique," *Zeitschrift für die Alttestamentliche Wissenschaft* 90 (1978): 157–170; cf. Richard N. Soulen, *"Sitz-im-Leben," Handbook of Biblical Criticism* (Atlanta: John Knox, 1981), 178–79.
30. Dibelius, *From Tradition to Gospel*, 9; Bultmann, *History of the Synoptic Tradition*, 1–7; E. Basil Redlich, *Form Criticism, Its Value and Limitations* (London: Duckworth, 1939), 17–19; Robert H. Lightfoot, *History and Interpretation in the Gospels* (New York and London: Harper and Brothers, 1934), 7–15; Taylor, *The Formation of the Gospel Tradition*, 5–9.
31. William R. Farmer, *The Gospel of Jesus* (Louisville: Westminster/John Knox, 1994), 36–38; G. R. Beasley-Murray, "The Synoptic Problem," in the *Dictionary of Jesus and the Gospels*, ed. Joel B. Green, Scott McKnight, and I. Howard Marshall (Downers Grove, Ill.: InterVarsity, 1992), 786–87.
32. Friedrich Daniel Ernst Schleiermacher, "Ueber die Zeugnisse des Papias von unsern beiden ersten Evangelien," *Theologische Studien und Kritiken* (1832), 735–68; cf. William R. Farmer, *The Synoptic Problem* (Macon, Ga.: Mercer, 1976), 15.

33. Dibelius, *From Tradition to Gospel*, 59; Bultmann, *History of the Synoptic Tradition*, 350.
34. Dibelius, "Author's Preface," *From Tradition to Gospel*, n.p.
35. Ibid.
36. Bultmann, *History of the Synoptic Tradition*, 2–3; cf. 6.
37. C. Blomberg, "Form Criticism," in *Dictionary of the Gospels and Jesus*, ed. Joel B. Green, Scot McKnight, and I. Howard Marshall (Downers Grove, Ill.: InterVarsity, 1992), 243.
38. German title, *Apologie oder Schutzschrift für die vernünftigen Verehrer Gottes*. Reimarus was a "prologue" rather than a beginning, for his ideas did not directly sway others working on the historical study of Jesus. But the forces that affected his thought also influenced others who did cause later developments leading to FC (Edgar V. McKnight, *What Is Form Criticism?* [Philadelphia: Fortress, 1969], 3–4).
39. German title, *Fragmente eines Ungenannten;* cf. Ralph S. Fraser, *Reimarus: Fragments*, ed. Charles H. Talbert (Philadelphia: Fortress, 1970).
40. German titles of the sixth and seventh fragments are *Ueber die Auferstehungsgeschichte* and *Von dem Zwecke Jesu und seiner Jünger;* cf. Fraser, *Reimarus: Fragments*, 61–269.
41. Norman Perrin, *What Is Redaction Criticism?* (Philadelphia: Fortress, 1969), 4.
42. Albert Schweitzer, *The Quest of the Historical Jesus*, trans. W. Montgomery, Introduction by James M. Robinson (New York: Macmillan, 1968), 24.
43. See Strauss, "Hermann Samuel Reimarus and His Apology," in *Reimarus: Fragments*, 44–57.
44. David Friedrich Strauss, *The Life of Jesus Critically Examined*, ed. Peter C. Hodgson, trans. George Eliot (Philadelphia: Fortress, 1972), 52–91; cf. Stephen Neill and Tom Wright, *The Interpretation of the New Testament, 1861–1986*, 2d ed. (Oxford: Oxford University, 1988), 14.
45. For example, Rudolf Bultmann, "New Testament and Mythology," in *Kerygma and Myth*, ed. Hans Werner Bartsch, trans. Reginald H. Fuller (New York: Harper & Row, 1961), 1–44; idem, "The Case for Demythologizing," in *Kerygma and Myth II*, ed. Hans-Werner Bartsch, trans. Reginald H. Fuller (London: SPCK, 1962), 181–194; idem, *Jesus Christ and Mythology* (New York: Charles Scribner's Sons, 1958).
46. Pierre Benoit, "Reflections on 'Formgeschichtliche Methode,'" in *Jesus and the Gospel*, trans. Benet Weatherhead (New York: Herder and Herder), 1:11–45.
47. Guthrie, *New Testament Introduction*, 210.
48. See Hermann Gunkel, *The Stories of Genesis*, trans. John J. Scullion, ed. William R. Scott (Berkeley, Calif.: BIBAL, 1994); cf. idem, *The Legends of Genesis: The Biblical Saga and History*, trans. W. H. Carruth (New York: Schocken, 1964).
49. Gunkel, *Legends of Genesis*, 93–119.
50. Ibid., 29–31.
51. Ibid., 11–12, 71–72, 78.
52. Werner Georg Kümmel, *The New Testament: The History of the Investigation of Its Problems* (Nashville: Abingdon, 1972), 330.
53. Kümmel, *The New Testament*, 281–284; Perrin, *What Is Redaction Criticism?* 13–14.
54. Julius Wellhausen, *Einleitung in die drei ersten Evangelien* (Berlin: Georg

Reimer, 1905), 43–57; cf. also Lightfoot, *History and Interpretation of the Gospels*, 23; Perrin, *What Is Redaction Criticism?* 14.

55. Guthrie, *New Testament Introduction*, 211.
56. James D. G. Dunn ("The Messianic Secret in Mark," in *The Messianic Secret*, ed. Christopher Tuckett [Philadelphia: Fortress, 1983], 116–31) has refuted Wrede's assertions.
57. Perrin, *What Is Redaction Criticism?* 7.
58. For example, A. E. J. Rawlinson, *St. Mark* (London: Methuen, 1947), 258–62; cf. C. M. Tuckett, ed., *The Messianic Secret*.
59. Guthrie, *New Testament Introduction*, 211.
60. Bultmann, *Form Criticism, Two Essays*, 23; cf. idem, "New Approach to the Synoptic Problem," in *Existence and Faith* (Cleveland and New York: World, 1960), 37.
61. Benoit, "Reflections on 'Formgeschichtliche Methode,'" 1:41.
62. Karl L. Schmidt, *Der Rahmen der Geschichte Jesu* (reprint of 1919 ed., Darmstadt: Wissenschaftliche Buchgesellschaft, 1969), 317. The work has never been translated into English.
63. McKnight, *What Is Form Criticism?* 15.
64. Bultmann, *History of the Synoptic Tradition*.
65. Roger A. Johnson, Editor, *Rudolf Bultmann, Interpreting Faith for the Modern Era* (Minneapolis: Fortress, 1991), 9–10; cf. Bultmann, "Autobiographical Reflections," in *Existence and Faith*, 284.
66. Robert Morgan, "Rudolf Bultmann," in *The Modern Theologians*, vol. 1 of *An Introduction to Christian Theology in the Twentieth Century*, ed. David F. Ford (New York: Basil Blackwell, 1989), 109.
67. Martin Heidegger taught at Marburg University with Bultmann from 1922–1928. For further information on Heidegger's influence, see Bultmann's personally written history, "Autobiographical Reflections," in *Existence and Faith*, 283–88.
68. Guthrie, *New Testament Introduction*, 212.
69. M. J. A. Horsnell, "Myth," *ISBE*, 3:455–63 (esp. 461–63).
70. Bultmann, "New Testament and Mythology" and "Demythologizing in Outline," in *Kerygma and Myth I*, 1–44; idem, "The Message of Jesus and the Problem of Mythology" and "The Christian Message and the Modern World-View," in *Jesus Christ and Mythology*, 11–21, 35–59.
71. Bultmann, *Kerygma and Myth I*, 10 n. 2.
72. Ibid., 1–2.
73. Ibid., 4.
74. Guthrie, *New Testament Introduction*, 212.
75. Rudolf Bultmann, "The Study of the Synoptic Gospels," in *Form Criticism*, 11–76.
76. Bultmann, "Is Exegesis Possible Without Presuppositions? in *Existence and Faith*, 291–92.
77. Rudolf Bultmann, *Jesus and the Word*, trans. Louise Pettibone Smith and Erminie Huntress Lantero (New York: Charles Scribner's Sons, 1958), 8–9.
78. Perrin, *What Is Redaction Criticism?* 18–19.
79. Cf. Taylor, *Formation of the Gospel Tradition*, 14.
80. Perrin, *What Is Redaction Criticism?* 18–19.
81. McKnight, *What Is Form Criticism?* 16.
82. Benoit, *Jesus and the Gospel*, 1:39.
83. Guthrie, *New Testament Introduction*, 231.

84. Blomberg, "Form Criticism," in *Dictionary of Jesus and the Gospels,* 243.
85. The following provide further details about classification: McKnight, *What Is Form Criticism?* 20–33; Taylor, *Formation of the Gospel Tradition,* 44–167; E. Basil Redlich, *Form Criticism, Its Value and Limitation* (London: Duckworth, 1939), 50–55; Stephen H. Travis, "Form Criticism," in *New Testament Interpretation,* ed. I. Howard Marshall (Grand Rapids: Eerdmans, 1977), 155–57; Bock, "Form Criticism," in *New Testament Criticism and Interpretation,* 181–188; Guthrie, *New Testament Introduction,* 213–23.
86. Bultmann, *History of the Synoptic Tradition,* 244.
87. Ibid., 244–45 n. 1.
88. Dibelius, *From Tradition to Gospel,* 266.
89. Ibid., 269, 271.
90. Ibid., 267–68.
91. Ibid., 267–73.
92. Travis, "Form Criticism," in *New Testament Interpretation,* 158.
93. Bultmann, *History of the Synoptic Tradition,* 228.
94. Ibid.
95. Ibid., 213.
96. Guthrie, *New Testament Introduction,* 217.
97. For example, Bultmann, *History of the Synoptic Tradition,* 209–44.
98. Bultmann, "The Study of the Synoptic Gospels," in *Form Criticism,* 38.
99. Frederic G. Kenyon, *The Bible and Modern Scholarship* (London: John Murray, 1948), 52.
100. Redlich, *Form Criticism, Its Value and Limitation,* 55.
101. Lightfoot, *History and Interpretation in the Gospels,* 43.
102. Dibelius, *From Tradition to Gospel,* 51–52, 55, 71.
103. Travis, "Form Criticism," in *New Testament Interpretation,* 158.
104. Cf. Bruce's classification(s) of Mark 2:1–12 as a further illustration (Bruce, "Criticism," *ISBE,* 1:823).
105. Bultmann, *History of the Synoptic Tradition,* 69–179.
106. Ibid., 101.
107. Ibid.
108. Ibid., 105.
109. Ibid., 110, 112–125, 127–128, 154–55.
110. Rudolf Bultmann, "Allgemeine Wahrheit und christliche Verkündigung," *Zeitschrift für Theologie und Kirche* 54 (1957): 244–54; cf. J. M. Robinson, *A New Quest of the Historical Jesus* (London: SCM, 1959), 20 n. 1.
111. For example, Terry, *Biblical Hermeneutics,* 161–600.
112. For example, Berger subjectively finds four new and different form-critical categories (*Sammelgattungen* or "Collected Forms," *Symbuleutische Gattungen* or "Behavior Forms," *Epideiktische Gattungen* or "Demonstration Texts," and *Dikanische Gattungen* or "Decision Texts"), and also assumes the Two-Document Hypothesis (Klaus Berger, *Formgeschichte des Neuen Testaments* [Heidelberg: Quelle & Meyer, 1984], 25–366).
113. Bultmann, *History of the Synoptic Tradition,* 3–4.
114. Ibid., 5.
115. Catchpole has said, "The term 'tradition criticism' would be better abandoned and replaced by the term 'tradition history', interpreted in the sense of an on-going process of development in the form and/or meaning of concepts or words or sayings or blocks of material" (Catchpole, "Tradition History," in *New Testament Interpretation,* 165).

116. Guthrie, Catchpole, and Osborne associate Tradition Criticism more closely with Redaction Criticism, but Blomberg discusses Tradition Criticism under Form Criticism. Stein closely associates Form and Tradition Criticism, but notes that the terms "technically . . . are not synonymous but in practice they essentially are" (Robert H. Stein, "The 'Criteria' for Authenticity," in *Gospel Perspectives*, ed. R. T. France and David Wenham [Sheffield: JSOT, 1980], 226, 254; cf. Guthrie, *New Testament Introduction*, 243–47; Catchpole, "Tradition History," in *New Testament Interpretation*, 165–80; Grant R. Osborne, "The Method of Redaction Criticism," in *New Testament Criticism and Interpretation*, 204–7; Blomberg, "Form Criticism," in *Dictionary of Jesus and the Gospels*, 248–49).

117. R. S. Barbour, *Traditio-Historical Criticism of the Gospels* (London: SPCK, 1972).

118. William G. Doty, "The Discipline and Literature of New Testament Form Criticism," *Anglican Theological Review* (October 1969): 286.

119. For example, Bultmann, *History of the Synoptic Tradition*, 205; Ernst Käsemann, *Essays on New Testament Themes* (Philadelphia: Fortress, 1964), 34–37; Norman Perrin, *Rediscovering the Teaching of Jesus* (New York: Harper and Row, 1976), 39–43.

120. Perrin, *Rediscovering the Teaching of Jesus*, 39.

121. Käsemann, *Essays on New Testament Themes*, 34; cf. James M. Robinson, *The New Quest of the Historical Jesus* (London: SCM, 1959), 9–25.

122. Bultmann, *Form Criticism, Two Essays*, 29.

123. For example, Bultmann, *History of the Synoptic Tradition*, 67; idem, *Form Criticism, Two Essays*, 36–63; Dibelius, *From Tradition to Gospel*, 287–95.

124. For example, Bultmann, *History of the Synoptic Tradition*, 236; Dibelius, *From Tradition to Gospel*, 133–77.

125. Bultmann, *History of the Synoptic Tradition*, 6.

126. Hans-Herbert Stoldt, *History and Criticism of the Marcan Hypothesis* (Macon, Ga.: Mercer, 1980).

127. Bultmann, *Form Criticism, Two Essays*, 25.

128. Ibid., 32–35.

129. Dibelius, *From Tradition to Gospel*, 287–93.

130. Bultmann, *Form Criticism, Two Essays*, 34.

131. Bultmann, *History of the Synoptic Tradition*, 48, 55; Dibelius, *From Tradition to Gospel*, 34–35; Vincent Taylor, *Gospel According to St. Mark*, 2d ed. (Grand Rapids: Baker, 1966), 65.

132. Bultmann, *Form Criticism, Two Essays*, 18.

133. Joachim Jeremias, *The Parables of Jesus*, 2d rev. ed. (New York: Charles Scribner's Sons, 1972), 15; Matthew Black, *An Aramaic Approach to the Gospels and Acts*, 3d ed. (Oxford: Clarendon, 1967), 271; idem, "The Problem of the Aramaic Element in the Gospels, *Expository Times* LIX (1947–48): 171–76.

134. Franz E. Meyer, "Einige Bemerkungen zur Bedeutung des Terminus 'Sanhedrion' in den Schriften des Neuen Testaments, *New Testament Studies* 14 (1967–68): 545–51.

135. *The Talmud of Babylonia, An American Translation*, vol. XVII, Tractate Sotah, Brown Judaic Studies 72, trans. Jacob Neusner (Chico, Calif.: Scholars, 1984), 287.

136. Saul Lieberman, *Greek In Jewish Palestine*, 2d ed. (New York: Philipp Feldheim, 1965), 38–40.

137. Philip Edgcumbe Hughes, "The Languages Spoken by Jesus," in *New Dimensions in New Testament Study,* ed. Richard N. Longenecker and Merrill C. Tenney (Grand Rapids: Zondervan, 1974), 127–43.

138. Robert H. Gundry, "The Language Milieu of First-Century Palestine," *Journal of Biblical Literature* 83 (1964): 408. [Emphasis in original]

139. A. W. Argyle, "Greek among the Jews of Palestine in New Testament Times," *New Testament Studies* 20 (1973): 88–89; cf. Stanley E. Porter, "Did Jesus Ever Teach in Greek?" *Tyndale Bulletin* 44, no. 2 (November 1993): 199–235; J. N. Sevenster, *Do You Know Greek? How Much Greek Could the First Jewish Christians Have Known?* (Leiden: E. J. Brill, 1968), 176–91. Porter supports Argyle's view, contending that Jesus both spoke and taught Greek.

140. Though additional Latin words appear in the other gospels *(denarion, kensos, kodrantes, krabattos, legion),* the words listed here are in Mark only (Taylor, *Gospel According to St. Mark,* 45).

141. Bultmann, *Form Criticism, Two Essays,* 26.

142. Redlich, *Form Criticism,* 75.

143. E. P. Sanders, *The Tendencies of the Synoptic Tradition* (Cambridge: At the University, 1969), 272. [Emphasis in original]

144. Caird, "The Study of the Gospels: II. Form Criticism," 140.

145. Robert W. Funk, Roy W. Hoover, and the Jesus Seminar, *The Five Gospels, What Did Jesus Really Say?* (New York: Macmillan, 1993). The "Jesus Seminar" includes the gospel of Thomas as a quasi-canonical gospel, as the number in the title reflects.

146. Funk attempts to distance himself from Bultmann, preferring to look to the post-Bultmannian "New Quest for the Historical Jesus" (inaugurated by Käsemann in 1953) that is not quite so radical. However, Funk's results are essentially the same as those of Bultmann: the Gospels have little, if anything, about the "historical Jesus" (Charlotte Allen, "Away with the Manger," *Lingua Franca* 5 (January–February 1995): 26.

147. Funk et al., *Five Gospels,* 5, 35; cf. D. A. Carson, "Five Gospels, No Christ," *Christianity Today* (April 25, 1994), 30–33.

148. Funk et al., *Five Gospels,* 3–5.

149. Carson, "Five Gospels, No Christ," 32.

150. Funk et al., *Five Gospels,* 5.

151. Ibid., 2.

152. Ibid., 4–5.

153. R. S. Barbour, *Traditio-Historical Criticism of the Gospels* (London: SPCK, 1972), 3.

154. F. C. Burkitt, *The Gospel History and Its Transmission* (Edinburgh: T & T Clark, 1911), 147–148.

155. Harvey K. McArthur, "Basic Issues, A Survey of Recent Gospel Research," *Interpretation* 18 (1964): 48; cf. B. H. Streeter, *The Four Gospels* (London: Macmillan, 1953), 151–200.

156. McArthur, "Basic Issues," 48.

157. C. H. Dodd, *History and the Gospel* (London: Nisbet, 1938), 91–103.

158. Gustav Dalman, *Jesus-Jeshua, Studies in the Gospels* (New York: KTAV, 1971[first published in 1929]), 1–30; C. F. Burney, *The Poetry of Our Lord* (Oxford: Clarendon, 1925), 5–11; C. C. Torrey, *Our Translated Gospels* (New York and London: Harper, 1936), ix–lx; Black, *Aramaic Approach to the Gospels and Acts,* 1–49; Joachim Jeremias, *The Parables of Jesus,* 2d rev. ed. (New York: Charles Scribner's Sons, 1972), 25–27.

159. Reginald H. Fuller, *The New Testament in Current Study* (New York: Charles Scribner's Sons, 1962), 33; cf. Joachim Jeremias, *New Testament Theology* (New York: Charles Scribner's Sons, 1971), 8; Henry E. W. Turner, *Historicity and the Gospel* (London: A. R. Mowbray, 1963), 77–78.

160. Jeremias, *Parables of Jesus*, 11–12.

161. Also, compare Matt. 7:2, Luke 6:37–38, and Mark 4:24 with Hesiod, *Works and Days*, 349–50; Publilius Syrus, *Sentences* [A] 2; for these and other such texts, see Charles E. Carlston, "Proverbs, Maxims, and the Historical Jesus," *JBL* 99 (1980): 87–105.

162. R. T. France, "The Authenticity of the Sayings of Jesus," in *History, Criticism and Faith*, ed. Colin Brown (Downers Grove, Ill.: InterVarsity, 1976), 108–9.

163. For example, Bultmann, *History of the Synoptic Tradition*, 205 (cf. 101, 104–5); cf. Paul W. Schmiedel, "Gospels," in *Encyclopaedia Biblica*, ed. T. K. Cheyne and J. Sutherland Black (New York: Macmillan, 1903), col. 1881–83; cf. Käsemann, *Essays on New Testament Themes*, 37.

164. Reginald H. Fuller, *The Foundations of New Testament Christology* (New York: Charles Scribner's Sons, 1965), 18.

165. Norman Perrin, *Rediscovering the Teaching of Jesus* (New York: Harper & Row, 1976), 43.

166. The word *Abba* illustrates this point. The word is Aramaic in form but no exact parallel exists in Judaism. It was, however, used by the early church (Rom. 8:15; Gal. 4:6). By strict application of Dissimilarity, it should be eliminated, but tradition critics accept it almost universally (for instance, Perrin, *Rediscovering the Teaching of Jesus*, 41; cf. Morna Hooker, "On Using the Wrong Tool," *Theology* 72 [1972]: 577).

167. Nils A. Dahl, "The Problem of the Historical Jesus," in *Kerygma and History*, ed. Carl E. Braaten and Roy A. Harrisville (New York and Nashville: Abingdon, 1962), 156; cf. Barbour, *Tratitio-Historical Criticism of the Gospels*, 50 n. 11.

168. Bultmann established sayings with the "feeling of eschatological power" as authentic through the Criterion of Dissimilarity. He accepted them because they "contain something characteristic, new, reaching out beyond popular wisdom and piety and yet are in no sense scribal or rabbinic nor yet Jewish apocalyptic" (Bultmann, *History of the Synoptic Tradition*, 162, 105; cf. 205).

169. Perrin, *Rediscovering the Teaching of Jesus*, 43.

170. James R. Edwards, "Who Do Scholars Say That I Am?" *Christianity Today* (March 4, 1996): 15–20.

171. Walter W. Wessell, "Voting Out the Fourth Beatitude, The Jesus Seminar decides what Jesus did and did not say," *Christianity Today* (November 12, 1986): 34; cf. Mark A. Kellner "Away with the Manger, The new Jesus Seminar discounts the Virgin Birth," *Christianity Today* (November 14, 1994): 92–93; Robert J. Hutchinson, "The Jesus Seminar Unmasked," *Christianity Today* (April 29, 1996): 28–30.

172. E.g., Michael J. Wilkins and J. P. Moreland, gen. eds., *Jesus Under Fire* (Grand Rapids: Zondervan, 1995); Ben Witherington III, *The Jesus Quest, The Third Search for the Jew of Nazareth* (Downers Grove, Ill.: InterVarsity, 1995); Gregory A. Boyd, *Cynic Sage or Son of God* (Wheaton, Ill.: Victor, 1995).

173. Stanley N. Gundry, "A Critique of the Fundamental Assumption of Form Criticism (Part Two)," *Bibliotheca Sacra* 123 (April 1966): 149.

174. Stanley N. Gundry, "A Critique of the Fundamental Assumptions of Form Criticism (Part One)," *Bibliotheca Sacra* 123 (January 1966): 32.

175. See Linnemann, *Historical Criticism of the Bible: Methodology or Ideology?* 83–123.
176. Guthrie, *New Testament Introduction,* 233.
177. Rear-cover endorsement of David A. Black & David S. Dockery, eds., *New Testament Criticism and Interpretation* (Grand Rapids: Zondervan, 1991).
178. Two recent criticisms have been Mark A. Noll, *Between Faith and Criticism* (Grand Rapids: Baker, 1986), and George Marsden, *Reforming Fundamentalism* (Grand Rapids: Eerdmans, 1987).
179. Linnemann illustrates this ostracization in connection with limited opportunities to publish (Eta Linnemann, *Historical Criticism of the Bible, Methodology or Ideology?* 89).
180. W. D. Davies, *Invitation to the New Testament* (Garden City, N.Y.: Doubleday, 1966), 97.
181. McKnight, *What Is Form Criticism?* 2.
182. Ibid.; cf. Ladd, *New Testament and Criticism,* 148, 168–69.
183. Ladd, *New Testament and Criticism,* 149.
184. Ibid., 141.
185. Ladd, *The New Testament and Criticism,* 141–42.
186. Ibid., 147–48.
187. Ibid., 148–49.
188. In addition to sources cited in this chapter's earlier section *"The Prime Impetuses: Evolutionary Conceptions and Unbelief,"* see Heinz Schürmann, "Die vorösterlichen Anfänge der Logientradition," in *Der historische Jesus und die kerygmatische Christus: Beiträge zum Christusverständnis in Forschung und Verkündigung,* Herausgegeben von Helmut Ristow und Karl Matthiae (Berlin: Evangelische Verlagsanstalt, 1962), 342–70.
189. Ibid., 153.
190. Ibid., 154.
191. Norman L. Geisler, *Biblical Errancy, An Analysis of Its Philosophical Roots* (Grand Rapids: Zondervan, 1981), 21.
192. Robert H. Stein, *The Synoptic Problem* (Grand Rapids: Baker, 1987), 129–38, 142–43. Stein qualifies his acceptance in acknowledging that "Q" may be a layer of tradition rather than a single document.
193. For example, Bo Reicke, *The Roots of the Synoptic Gospels* (Philadelphia: Fortress, 1986); Eta Linnemann, *Is There a Synoptic Problem?* trans. Robert W. Yarbrough (Grand Rapids: Baker, 1992); John Wenham, *Redating Matthew, Mark, and Luke* (Downers Grove, Ill.: InterVarsity, 1992).
194. Robert H. Stein, *The Method and Message of Jesus' Teaching* (Philadelphia: Westminster, 1978), 156 n. 62.
195. Stein, *The Synoptic Problem,* 166–67. He qualifies this by saying not all pericopes may have circulated as independent units (for instance, the passion narrative, Mark 1:21–39; 2:1–3:6; 4:1–34; 4:35–5:43; 7:1–23; 8:1–26; 12:13–37).
196. Eusebius records the words of Papias, who was a personal acquaintance of the apostle John, in *Ecclesiastical History* 3.39: "And John the Presbyter also said this, Mark being the interpreter of Peter whatsoever he recorded he wrote with great accuracy but not however in the order in which it was spoken or done by our Lord." As Guthrie notes, evidence from Papias "cannot so easily be ignored" (Guthrie, *New Testament Introduction,* 83).
197. Stein, *Synoptic Problem,* 142.
198. Ibid., 143.

199. Robert H. Stein, "The 'Criteria' for Authenticity," in *Gospel Perspectives,* vol. 1, ed. R. T. France and David Wenham (Sheffield: JSOT, 1980), 229.
200. Robert H. Stein, *The Synoptic Problem,* 151–52; cf. also idem, *Luke,* vol. 24 of the *New American Commentary,* David S. Dockery, gen. ed. (Nashville, Tenn.: Broadman, 1992), 420.
201. Stein, "'Criteria' for Authenticity," 226.
202. Ibid., 233.
203. Ibid., 238–39.
204. Ibid., 232.
205. Stein, *Luke,* 198; Stein, *Synoptic Problem,* 219–20.
206. Stein, *Synoptic Problem,* 171–72.
207. Ibid.
208. Robert A. Guelich, *The Sermon on the Mount, A Foundation for Understanding* (Waco, Tex.: Word, 1982), 23.
209. Ibid.
210. Ibid., 33–34.
211. Ibid., 33–36.
212. Ibid., 33.
213. Ibid., 35.
214. Ibid.
215. Ibid., 36.
216. Ibid., 35.
217. Ibid., 35–36.
218. Ibid., 35–36, 116–18.
219. Ibid., 117–18.
220. Walter Wessell, "Voting Out the Fourth Beatitude, The Jesus Seminar decides what Jesus did and did not say" *Christianity Today* (November 12, 1986): 34–35.
221. Guelich, *Sermon on the Mount,* 25.
222. Ibid., 135.
223. Ibid.
224. Ibid., 138–43.
225. Ibid., 58–59.
226. Ibid., 58–59.
227. Ibid.
228. Bock, "Form Criticism," in *New Testament Criticism and Interpretation,* 192.
229. Bock, "Form Criticism, 191; cf. Berger, *Formgeschichte des Neuen Testaments,* 366.
230. Bock, "Form Criticism," 187.
231. Hooker, "On Using the Wrong Tool," 571.
232. Bultmann, *History of the Synoptic Tradition,* 3–4.
233. Frederick C. Grant, *The Earliest Gospel* (New York: Abingdon, 1943), 41.
234. Bock, "Form Criticism," 187.
235. Hooker, "On Using the Wrong Tool," 572.
236. Darrell L. Bock, *Luke Volume 1: 1:1–9:50,* ed. Moisés Silva (Grand Rapids: Baker, 1994), 718, 742–43.
237. Ibid., 742.
238. Ibid., 8–12, 742–43.
239. Bock, "Form Criticism," 184.
240. Ibid.; cf. idem, *Luke Volume 1,* 398 n. 12 (cf. 334 n. 3).

241. Bultmann, *History of the Synoptic Tradition*, 244–45 n. 1; cf. Dibelius, *From Tradition to Gospel*, 108–9; idem, *A Fresh Approach to the New Testament and Early Christian Literature* (reprint of 1936 ed., Westport, Conn.: Greenwood, 1979), 43; Taylor, *Formation of the Gospel Tradition*, 32.
242. Bultmann, *History of the Synoptic Tradition*, 31–32.
243. Bock, *Luke Volume 1*, 398.
244. Berger, *Formgeschichte des Neuen Testaments*, 30, 113, 119, 263–64, 347.
245. Joseph A. Fitzmyer, *The Gospel according to Luke (I–IX)*, vol. 28 in the Anchor Bible (New York: Doubleday, 1979, 527–30.
246. Bock, *Luke Volume 1*, 451–52 n. 9; 633; 692 n. 3 also.
247. Ibid., 470 nn. 12 and 13; cf. Bultmann, *History of the Synoptic Tradition*, 66.
248. Bock, *Luke Volume 1*, 758, 769, 826, 879, 893.
249. Ibid., 468.
250. Catchpole, "Tradition History," in *New Testament Interpretation*, 168.
251. Ibid., 167–68.
252. Ibid., 168.
253. Ibid., 178.
254. Grant R. Osborne, "The Evangelical and *Traditionsgeschichte*," *Journal of the Evangelical Theological Society* 21 (June 1978): 122.
255. Ibid., 126.
256. Ibid., 130.
257. Grant R. Osborne, "Redaction Criticism and the Great Commission: A Case Study Toward A Biblical Understanding of Inerrancy," *Journal of the Evangelical Theological Society* 19 (spring 1976): 80.
258. Ibid., 80, 85.
259. Grant R. Osborne, "The Evangelical and Redaction Criticism: Critique and Methodology," *Journal of the Evangelical Theological Society* 22 (December 1979): 311.
260. Robert W. Yarbrough, "Evangelical Theology in Germany," in *Evangelical Quarterly* LXV (October 1993): 329; cf. Maier, *End of the Historical-Critical Method*, 8–10, 11–92.
261. Yarbrough, "Evangelical Theology in Germany," 353.
262. Gerhard Maier, *End of the Historical-Critical Method*, trans. Edwin W. Leverenz and Rudolph F. Norden (St. Louis: Concordia, 1977), 49.

CHAPTER SIX

Redaction Criticism

Robert L. Thomas

IN EXAMINING THE ROOTS of Historical Criticism, earlier discussion has reviewed several areas: how the ancient church viewed gospel relationships (chapter 1); the philosophical and theological basis for Historical Criticism (chapter 2); the foundational building block of Historical Criticism, namely, Source Criticism—the Two-Source Theory in particular—(chapter 3); the role of a contemporary opponent of Historical Criticism (chapter 4); and the function of Tradition Criticism and Form Criticism as parts of Historical Criticism (chapter 5). The present chapter will summarize and elaborate on earlier remarks and culminate with a review of the aspect of Historical Criticism called Redaction Criticism (hereafter RC).

THE FOUNDATION OF REDACTION CRITICISM: SOURCE CRITICISM

Both historically and conceptually the starting point of RC is Source Criticism. What is Source Criticism? Before answering this question, it is important to note that Matthew, Mark, and Luke are referred to as the "Synoptic Gospels." This is because the three take a more or less common view of the Lord Jesus' life. Supposing that extensive agreement among the three indicates some sort of direct literary collaboration among their writers, much New Testament scholarship of the past century or two has tried to explain the nature of that literary relationship. A complicating factor in such efforts, however, is a substantial number of cases where one gospel describes matters differently from one or both of the others. The name given to the difficulty encountered in devising a scheme of literary dependence to account for combinations of similarities and dissimilarities within the Synoptic Gospels is the "Synoptic Problem," and the field of studies devoted to solving the problem is "Source Criticism."

The Synoptic Problem was not an issue that early Christians tried to resolve, for they assumed that the gospel writers drew upon personal memory and firsthand reports rather than upon one another's writings or a common written source (see chapter 1 of this work for further details about early views on sources of the Synoptic Gospels). The early church historian Eusebius indicated that Matthew, one of the twelve apostles, was first to write a gospel account.[1] Before Matthew left the Palestinian area, he supplied a written substitute for his oral teaching, which he apparently obtained largely from his apostolic experience. According to Eusebius and other early writers, Matthew's first writing was in the Hebrew or Aramaic language. However, church fathers before Eusebius connect Matthew's Greek gospel closely in time with whatever he wrote in his own tongue. For example, Clement is specific that the two gospels with genealogies, one of which was Matthew, were the first written (see chapter 7 for further discussion about Luke's prologue).[2] Definitive information about the relationship between Matthew's Hebrew composition and the gospel he wrote in Greek is unavailable to us. But the times of writing for the two accounts were close enough together for early Christians to consider them as having been penned prior to the other gospels.[3]

Luke, according to his own word (Luke 1:1–4), drew from a number of both oral and written source. His written sources did not include Matthew or Mark. Clement of Alexandria wrote that Mark based his gospel on apostolic tradition through Peter.[4] According to Clement, only John was aware of the contents of other canonical gospels before he wrote his gospel. Writing at a much later time, he chose to pen an account significantly different from the others. Rather than copying from Matthew, Mark, or Luke, John verified their truthfulness and supplemented their contents with material that is largely missing from the synoptics.[5]

The Two-Source Theory

As noted above, the early church maintained that no synoptic writer saw the work of another before writing his own gospel. A near-unanimous consensus existed in the church until the mid-eighteenth century,[6] when scholars began exploring various hypotheses as to how one writer may have depended on others or on a single source also available to the others. Theories of one source used by all three and of various orders of writing, with the second writer depending on the first and the third on the other two, were typical hypotheses prior to the appearance of the Two-Source (or Two-Document) Theory. This approach eventually gained wide acceptance among New Testament scholars. That theory proposes the writing of Mark first and the later writing of Matthew and Luke. Mark and another source called "Q"—a written but now nonextant source—were the two sources used by Matthew and Luke.[7] Another theory, closely allied with the Two-Source Theory, is the Four-Source Theory. It says that the two sources in addition to Mark and Q were a document M used by Matthew and a document L used by Luke.[8]

For most of the twentieth century, the majority of New Testament scholars cited Streeter's five arguments as definitive in support of the prior writing of Mark.[9] Those arguments together with responses to them are as follows:

(1) Most of the material in Mark appears in Matthew and Luke (90 percent in Matthew and 55 percent in Luke). Because it seemed

inconceivable to Streeter that Mark would have abbreviated the other two, he concluded that Matthew and Luke must have expanded Mark.[10]

Assuming literary dependence for the sake of argument, one could conclude just the opposite of what Streeter asserted. Mark may have had a special reason for condensing one or both of the other gospels. In fact, literary practice in English writings shows the tendency of a writer to shorten the work of another when editing it.[11] If one applies the same tendency to Greek writers, the likelihood of Mark's being last rather than first is just as strong, perhaps stronger.

But the phenomenon of so much of Mark being present in Matthew and Luke is explainable best without any literary dependence. Material common to the three Synoptic Gospels could very well have come from a common tradition of oral and brief written accounts of Jesus' life. In this case, Mark probably never saw Matthew's and Luke's gospels before writing his own, nor did they see his or each other's gospel before writing their own. The common tradition best explains the origin of all three Synoptic Gospels.

(2) Though agreeing often with Mark in the actual words used, Matthew and Luke do not agree with each other when they diverge from Mark.[12] Allowing for exceptions to this generalization, Streeter accounted for the deviations as being either irrelevant, deceptive, agreements because of an overlap of Mark and Q (Matthew's and Luke's other major source), or agreements because of textual corruption.[13] Streeter used Matthean-Lucan diversity to prove their dependence on Mark.

This argument of Streeter touches upon what is probably the most glaring weakness of a theory of Markan priority: the exceptions to the generalization or the agreements of Matthew and Luke against Mark in sections of triple tradition. With the presence of those agreements, it is possible to argue the priority of Matthew or Luke as well as of Mark, if one assumes literary dependence. Though not as numerous as agreements between Matthew and Mark against Luke or Mark and Luke against Matthew, they are substantial enough to indicate the independence of Matthew and Luke in all sections of triple tradition where the Two-Source Theory says they were dependent on Mark.

Since the agreements of Matthew and Luke against Mark are the most glaring weakness of the Two-Source Theory,[14] a more detailed discussion of those agreements will follow.[15] Agreements of Matthew and Luke against Mark coupled with the agreements with Matthew and Mark against Luke and the agreements of Mark and Luke against Matthew will strengthen the case for literary independence of each of the three Synoptic Gospels.

(3) The order of events in Mark is original, for wherever Matthew departs from Mark, Luke supports Mark's order, and wherever Luke departs from Mark, Matthew agrees with Mark's order.[16] According to Streeter, that demonstrates Markan priority in proving that the other two gospels are secondary—in other words, the two never agree with each other when they do not follow Mark's order.

In chapter 3 of *The Jesus Crisis*, Edgar demonstrated the invalidity of this argument.[17] He showed the plausibility that all three writers worked from an order dictated by a tradition agreed upon by eyewitnesses and transmitted in varieties of ways among early Christians. Occasionally, all three deviated from the traditional sequence for one reason or another.

Ladd has carried Streeter's argument from order further in comparing the selection and arrangement of material in Matthew, Mark, and Luke.[18] Ladd argues for a relatively close interdependence on the basis of the three writers' choice of the same events from the very many episodes in Jesus' life that they could have selected. Ladd then tests passages parallel to Matthew 4–12 in Mark and Luke to observe the relative order of the sections. On the basis of these comparisons, Ladd concludes that Mark must have been first, for Matthew and Luke never agree with one another in order against Mark.

Two criticisms of Ladd's reasoning are pertinent. First, he has chosen a bad section for making comparisons. Mark has no parallel to Matthew 5–7, and no one recognizes Matthew 8–9 as being chronological. Ladd also parallels sections that represent separate occurrences in the life of Christ (for example, Matt. 12:22–45 = Luke 11:14–23). Factors like those make Ladd's comparisons meaningless.

Second, Ladd vastly underestimates the memories of first-century Near-Eastern people in detecting interdependence. The core events that the synoptics have in common are easily explainable through repetitious preaching about the life of Jesus in Jerusalem shortly after the day of Pentecost. Many people, not just the three writers, heard the apostles teach repeatedly about certain episodes that became the core curriculum of early Christian education. That the three Synoptic Gospels should choose many of those core events in common with one another is no great surprise. Albright and Mann comment on the sharpness of memory in ancient times: "[I]t seems generally true that the memory of words and stories is better in the ancient East than in the modern West."[19] Gerhardsson writes along the same lines:

> Memorization is thus an original and elementary method of study, the origins of which are lost in prehistory. It played an essential role in ancient educational theory within the cultural areas in which we are interested. The general attitude was that words and items of knowledge must be memorized.[20]

The degree of similarity that modern Westerners would attribute to literary interdependence was for the ancients a matter of information they had committed to memory. The memorized material would extend even to the sequence of details within each pericope. Hearing an event described dozens of times by the same eyewitness would easily fix the same sequence of happenings in the minds of numbers of listeners. The retelling of that same story in an identical sequence by two or even three gospel writers is no proof that they copied one another. Instead it attests to the sharpness of first-century memories among those who listened. If Mark wrote his gospel so that readers could memorize the very words of Peter's preaching (as Clement of Alexandria reportedly said),[21] it is probable that the Lord's disciples memorized His words and early Christians did the same with the words of the apostles and other eyewitnesses.

So Ladd's argument from selection and arrangement of material to prove interdependence and hence Markan priority is without force.

(4) The primitive nature of Mark, as compared with Matthew and Luke, demonstrates Mark's priority.[22] To illustrate, Matthew uses *kurie* ("lord") nineteen times and Luke sixteen times, compared with the word's single appearance in Mark. Streeter takes this to indicate a more developed reverential attitude toward Jesus than displayed in Mark, and hence a later date for the two longer gospels.[23]

The facts of the case neutralize that evidence, however. Matthew uses *kurie* as a form of address seven times when referring to mere man (Matt. 13:27; 21:29; 25:11 [twice], 20, 24; 27:63). Obviously, Matthew did not reserve that title for deity. That renders the argument useless in a chronological placement of Mark.

Other alleged signs of primitivity are likewise useless. Mark's alleged Aramaisms are an overstatement of the situation. Most would classify Matthew as being more Semitic than Mark.[24] Couple with this the indications of Mark's lateness reflected in his use of Latinisms and translation of Aramaic expressions for those who knew no Aramaic,[25] and one has good reason to postulate the chronological priority of Matthew over Mark, a priority that has nothing to do with literary dependence between the two.

(5) The distribution of Markan and non-Markan material in Matthew and Luke shows their dependence on Mark.[26] Supposedly Matthew uses Mark as a framework and arranges his material into that structure, and Luke gives Markan and non-Markan material in alternate blocks.

Yet, granting for the sake of argument, that literary borrowing could have occurred, one could just as easily find it feasible that Mark borrowed from Matthew and Luke. Rather than Matthew's picking words or phrases here and there and weaving them into a smooth, polished narrative, Mark just as probably could have taken Matthew's gospel and added details for vividness. Dropping the assumption of Mark's priority, one could theorize that Luke could have extracted sections from Matthew and, in turn, Mark could have done the same from Luke. Still another possibility is that all three writers drew from a common core of tradition among early Christians, removing the necessity for any type of literary collaboration.

In summary of Streeter's five proofs, it is apparent that his evidence in some cases presupposes the point to be proven and in others rests on overgeneralizations that fail to account for substantial exceptions. Though enjoying wide acceptance for most of the twentieth century, Streeter's arguments have met with increasing opposition and rarely receive the recognition they once did.[27] Even those favoring Markan priority and the Two-Source Theory admit this.[28]

To fill the void left by the demise of Streeter's arguments, other proponents of Markan priority have looked elsewhere to try and bolster that century-old theory. Some have pointed to the success of RC, which is based on the assumption that Mark wrote first and the other two depended on his gospel.[29] Yet fruit from redaction-critical study cannot be an argument for the correctness of an assumed hypothesis, for no one has done extensive redaction-critical investigation based on another hypothesis.[30] In other words, a comparison of fruitfulness is impossible, for nothing is available with which to compare results. So this attempt to support Markan priority has not received wide attention.

Carson has proposed Old Testament quotations and allusions in Matthew and Mark as evidence for Markan priority, noting that those which Matthew and Mark have in common are consistently from the LXX in contrast with those in Matthew alone, which are from a variety of versions and textual traditions.[31] Carson himself admits some weaknesses in the argument,[32] to which D. Wenham adds others.[33]

Styler has still another proposal in defending Markan priority, finding in Matthew inherent flaws that are best explained by his hasty use of Mark and in Luke an artificiality that presupposes his use of a structured narrative such as Mark.[34] Yet Styler is just as guilty as Streeter in presupposing the point to be proven. His "proof" of Markan priority has received no consensus support.

The fact remains: the Two-Source Theory with its insistence on Markan priority continues to be the dominant theory at the dawn of a new century, but it has no commonly accepted foundation on which to rest.

Weaknesses of the Two-Source Theory

Two weaknesses of the Two-Source Theory should have special appeal to those of an evangelical orientation:

(1) Christian Tradition

The priority of Mark raises a serious question about the heretofore unchallenged testimony of early Christian leaders that Matthew the apostle wrote the first gospel. The Two-Source Theory necessitates understanding that Matthew, an eyewitness of Jesus' ministry, depended on Mark, a noneyewitness, for his information. That dependence extends even to Matthew's reliance on Mark for a description of his own conversion (cf. Matt. 9:9; Mark 2:14)! Even excluding that last-mentioned episode, such dependence is improbable, even though Mark, according to tradition, did have the highly respected Peter as his source.[35] Attempts to reduce the improbability of that transmission of information[36] ignore the fact that Markan priority has an authoritative apostle drawing information from a writer whose authority was subject to that of the apostles. Mark's dependence on Peter did not grant Mark apostolic authority. Mark wrote under his own authority as a prophet,[37] whose ministry was under the direction of apostles (cf. 1 Cor. 14:29–32).

A decision regarding authorship of the first gospel boils down to accepting either what the early church fathers said about Matthean authorship or accepting the "discoveries" of nineteenth-century rationalism. The latter, unconcerned about retaining Matthean authorship of that gospel, placed its composition much later than the traditional date of writing, even locating it some time in the second century, and some evangelicals have followed along to the point of doubting Matthean authorship.[38] However, in a choice between the two options, probable accuracy lies on the side of the ancient church, for that generation was much nearer and had access to better information about authorship of the Gospels. It is highly improbable that the church fathers could be so consistently wrong on such a fundamental point regarding the authorship of the first gospel. No substantially significant reasons for doubting the accuracy of the ancient sources have been forthcoming. Thus, the Two-Source Theory falls short of winning the day in that connection.

(2) Personal Contacts between the Writers

The Two-Source Theory grants insufficient attention to the possibility of *personal* contacts between the synoptic writers. Unless one rejects the traditional authorship by Matthew, Mark, and Luke, he/she must allow for opportunities that presented themselves for the three writers to exchange information about the life of Christ orally, without having to resort to a form of documentary dependence.[39] Matthew and Mark must have been close associates during the period following Pentecost, while Christians in Jerusalem used Mark's home as a meeting place (cf. Acts 12:12). Mark and Luke were together during Paul's first Roman imprisonment (Col. 4:10, 14; Philem. 24), if not sooner. Possibly Luke encountered Matthew during his two-year stay with Paul in Israel in the late A.D. 50s (cf. Acts 24:27). If not, in the process of researching for his gospel, Luke must have interviewed with people close to Matthew after Matthew's departure from the area. Personal contacts like these render unnecessary a theory based on literary interdependence, as advocated by the Two-Source Theory.

It appears that composition of the three synoptics came during a relatively short period when distances between their destinations were widely spread geographically. That resulted in no one of the three seeing the results of another's work before writing his own. This is not to say that Luke, for example, could not have told Mark about his written gospel during their time together with Paul in prison in Rome during the early sixties (Col. 4:10, 14; Philem. 24). But having delivered the book to Theophilus earlier, Luke did not have a copy to show Mark. That did not matter, for Mark's purpose was to reproduce the preaching of Peter in his gospel. By the time of Paul's imprisonment, Mark and Luke may or may not have known about Matthew's gospel, which came earlier. In either case, they did not have an opportunity to view its contents before writing their respective gospels.

Three other weaknesses of the Two-Source Theory should have a wider appeal to anyone interested in gospel origins, regardless of their theological preference:

(3) "The Great Omission"

The Two-Source Theory cannot account for the "Great Omission," namely, a large portion of Mark for which Luke has no parallel.[40] If Luke

used Mark as a source, as the theory proposes, why did he omit any reference to Mark 6:45–8:26? An adequate answer to this question has as yet
not come from a two-source proponent. That important section includes
accounts of Jesus' walking on the water, the healing at Gennesaret, a major conflict over the tradition of the elders, the Syrophoenician woman's
faith, the healing of a deaf and dumb man, the feeding of the four thousand, the Pharisees' demand for a sign, the instruction regarding the leaven
of the Pharisees and that of Herod, and the healing of a blind man at
Bethsaida. That is about 9 percent of consecutive material in Mark's gospel—some of which surely would have contributed to Luke's purpose—that
the third gospel writer skips completely.

Explanations that Luke worked from an earlier form of Mark's gospel
lack documentary support.[41] The suggestion that Luke intentionally omitted the material also comes up short. One advocate of Markan priority
acknowledges the Great Omission to be "the most problematic detail against
Marcan priority."[42] He quickly adds, "No view of Synoptic relationships is
problem free."[43] Why does he not suppose that Luke had no access to Mark's
gospel when he wrote? That supposition is problem free.

(4) Impossibility of a Q Document

Twentieth-century archaeological findings have brought an increased
knowledge about first-century Palestinian conditions, and this has made it
increasingly difficult to sustain the argument for Q as a single written body
of tradition. Ancient historical records show that Palestinian traditions did
not tend to unify, but rather proliferated in a random manner.[44] They definitely did not coalesce into one homogeneous body.

Furthermore, if Q had been a single written source (as required by the
Two-Source Theory), changes made by Matthew and Luke are anomalous.[45]
The two writers followed no consistent rational procedure in copying from
Q, as reflected in their divergence from each other in passages where both
allegedly used that hypothetical document as their source. Most will admit this, with some Two- (or Four-) Source proponents going so far as to
acknowledge that Q was not a written homogeneous document, but was
rather "a fluid pool of traditions from which both Luke and Matthew drew."[46]
That kind of admission essentially destroys the substance of the Two- (or
Four-) Source Theory. To acknowledge Q was not a homogeneous written
source marks the end of that theory's claim to validity.

The only justification for retaining Q as a symbol—and it is a doubtful one,
for it misrepresents what the earliest advocates of the theory intended—is to
identify it as gospel material belonging to many different strands of tradition,
both written and oral. Far from being homogeneous and having definable limits,
it has no boundaries and is quite heterogeneous. That redefinition of Q removes any need for literary interdependence and devastates the Two-Source
Theory and any other theory that presupposes literary collaboration among
the three writers. Recognition of a large layer of tradition from which each
gospel writer could have drawn removes all necessity for any sort of dependence on one another by way of copying or editing.

(5) Agreements of Matthew and Luke against Mark

In sections of triple tradition (namely, those covered by Matthew, Mark, and Luke), a considerable number (about 230) of agreements between Matthew and Luke are different from a parallel portion of Mark. "Different from" does not mean that Mark contradicts the other two, but that his wording varies when Matthew's and Luke's agree. This is the major problem for the Two-Source Theory for which the theory's advocates have no *adequate* reply. Hawkins and Streeter offered explanations in the past,[47] and more recently Stein has attempted the same,[48] but they can only conclude with Fitzmyer that these agreements "represent only a small fraction of the data to be considered in the Synoptic Problem. They constitute a problem which cannot be denied; they are one of the loopholes in the Two-Source Theory."[49] Fitzmyer calls this "the biggest chink in the armor of the modified Two-Source Theory."[50]

The agreements of Matthew and Luke against Mark number about 230,[51] and of the fifty-eight sections of triple tradition in the Burton and Goodspeed *Harmony*,[52] only five very short sections—varying from zero to three verses—are void of agreements. In the fifty-three sections where agreements occur, they number from one to twelve. In thirty-six of the fifty-three sections, they spread throughout the section, and in seven, multiple agreements appear in a small part of the section. Ten sections have only one agreement apiece. Put in percentage figures, Matthew-Luke agreements against Mark touch 91 percent of the triple-tradition accounts. Of those sections, the agreements cover 68 percent rather thoroughly and another 19 percent in a more limited way with only a single agreement. These agreements are not as extensive as those between Matthew and Mark against Luke or between Mark and Luke against Matthew, but they are substantial enough to require an explanation in a satisfactory handling of the Synoptic Problem.

A closer look at allegedly accidental agreements—especially analyses of conjunctions and uses of the Greek historical present tense—will illumine the importance of Matthean-Lukan agreements against Mark.

Conjunctions. An explanation for a number of the agreements that is frequently cited by two-source people is Matthew's and Luke's desire for "a more smooth and usual Hellenistic style,"[53] which prompted them to revise 31 of Mark's numerous uses of the conjunction *kai* to *de*.[54] That is the approximate number of accidental agreements to be expected according to the following computations. In triple-tradition sections, Mark has 156 uses of a connective-type *kai* that Matthew or Luke could have revised to *de*. They did it in the same places as each other thirty-one times, or about 20 percent of the total possible. In observing Matthew and Luke separately, one discovers that Matthew uses *de* for *kai* in fifty-seven out of 156 possible places, or 37 percent of the times, while Luke does so eighty-two out of 156 cases for a figure of 53 percent. The predicted coincidental agreements between Matthew and Luke would be 37 percent of 53 percent, or about 20 percent of the 156 possible cases of such, the same figure reached through tabulation of the actual agreements.[55]

The case for accidental agreements based on probability statistics looks good so far, but other factors nullify the theory of Matthew's and Luke's preference for *de*. For example, in two cases where Mark has *de* (2:6; 14:47), Matthew and Luke agree against Mark in their use of *kai*. In four other cases (Mark 9:25; 13:5; 14:1, 70) Matthew has *kai* instead of Mark's *de*. In four additional cases (Mark 13:28; 14:11; 15:15, 37) Luke has *kai* for Mark's *de*. These instances create a serious doubt about Matthew's and Luke's supposed preference for *de*.

Historical presents. Another kind of claimed accidental agreement relates to Mark's use of the historical present tense of Greek verbs. Markan prioritists have Matthew and Luke—because of their supposed distaste for the historical present—agreeing with each other in changing eighteen of Mark's historical presents to other forms that bring them into exact agreement with each other against Mark.[56] Yet statistics work against the Two-Source Theory in this instance. Does Matthew show a distaste for the historical present when he uses it ninety-three times in his own gospel? Is it legitimate to find in Matthew, as compared with Mark, a trend away from the historical present when the former uses it in thirteen places where Mark's corresponding verb is either aorist or imperfect? These considerations, combined with the fact that Matthew does retain the historical present nineteen of ninety times (21 percent) in places corresponding to Mark's historical present, raise strong questions about Matthew's alleged aversion for the historical present.

The verb form *legei* is an oft-cited historical present that Mark uses frequently.[57] That word alone accounts of fifteen agreements of Matthew and Luke, if they used Mark as a source and coincidentally agreed with one another in eliminating it. The initial impression of support for the theory of "accidental" agreements is misleading, however, for Matthew handles Mark's uses of *legei* in six different ways and Luke in nine different ways. Thus, the possibility of "coincidence" is quite remote. Twelve of the fifteen agreements are *eipen*, but following normal frequency rates of Matthew's and Luke's changes to *eipen* elsewhere in the triple-tradition sections, only six such agreements would have been statistically probable. Two of the fifteen agreements are *legōn*. Yet following normal rates of change, no more than one could have come by accident. One of the fifteen agreements is *ephē*, which is completely contrary to expectation, for Matthew makes such a change only three times out of forty-eight and Luke only once out of fifty-three. The probability of accidental agreements of this nature is extremely low.

Another difficulty in proposing a trend such as a Matthean inclination away from the historical present comes in noticing Mark's version of Matthean historical presents. In eight of seventeen cases where Matthew has the historical present, Mark uses an imperfect or aorist. That is about the same ratio as Matthew's alleged revision of Mark.

Agreements in proximity. A factor militating strongly against the Matthean-Lukan agreements against Mark being accidental is the location of those agreements. For example, of the thirty-one cases of agreement where Matthew and Luke have *de* instead of Mark's *kai*, at least seventeen come in conjunction with another agreement of a different type. Twelve of these seventeen have at least one other agreement in the same sentence. Two others have agreements in both the sentence before and the sentence after, while three others have agreements in either the sentence before or the sentence after. These combination agreements obviously reduce radically the statistical probability of anything accidental.

The phenomenon of combination agreements is even more remarkable in places involving Mark's historical presents. All eighteen Matthew-Luke agreements join with other agreements against Mark, so that no single coinciding form is alone. In thirteen of the eighteen places where Matthew and Luke concur against Mark's historical present, another agreement lies in the same sentence. In four of eighteen cases, agreements come in both the sentence before and the sentence after. In the other case, an agreement occurs in the sentence just before. This pattern of coinciding forms could not have happened by accident.

Various other "accidental" agreements appear less accidental when other coincidences are in focus. For instance, Hawkins lists seven agreements of Matthew and Luke caused by cases of asyndeton in Mark (Mark 5:39; 10:14; 12:9, 23, 37; 13:6, 7).[58] Yet in six of the seven, other agreements are immediately adjacent—two cases in the same sentence, in two in sentences both before and after, and two cases in sentences before only. When taking into account that Matthew has sixteen cases of asyndeton where Mark has *kai*, one questions strongly whether Matthew had any tendency at all to eliminate asyndeton.

Hawkins also gives a category of agreements composed of words so ordinary and colorless and so nearly synonymous with Mark's that Matthew's and Luke's agreement may be merely accidental.[59] Hawkins' two illustrations of this category are *eschaton* in Mark 12:22 and *legei* in Mark 12:37. In the former case Matthew and Luke both have *hysteron* and in the latter *kalei*. Yet how can it be merely accidental when in the former case another agreement comes in the following sentence and in the latter two other agreements appear in the same sentence?

Another set of coincidences Hawkins calls obvious amplifications or explanations.[60] He notes five of these that he calls natural for any writer to introduce. That analysis appears quite improbable, however, in light of other agreements in the immediate context with the five. In two cases the added correspondences are in the same sentence, in two the sentence immediately following, and in one the sentence immediately before.

Abbott, after an exhaustive study of the 230 agreements, concluded that they were not trivial, as he had previously viewed them, and that they demanded some explanation.[61] Streeter paid no attention to combined agreements. He "atomized" them into separate categories so as to avoid calling attention to their occurrence in conjunction with one another.[62]

When viewing the agreements in combination with one another, however, the possibility of their being coincidences is infinitesimally small.

Agreements impossible to attribute to accident. That so many agreements arranged as they are could have happened accidentally defies human imagination. It is an intolerably high "accident rate." Furthermore, the array of inexplicable agreements could be expanded rather easily. For instance, just one section (Matt. 19:16–30 = Mark 10:17–31 = Luke 18:18–30) has eighteen Matthean-Lukan agreements against Mark. Six agreements are of the type already discussed above, namely, exact verbal agreements; six are agreements in different forms of the same words; and six are agreements of a common word where Mark is blank.[63] Besides those eighteen, the same section has ten agreements of omission, namely, Matthew and Luke agree in omitting certain material that Mark includes.[64] In just one pericope, that makes a total of twenty-eight agreements!

Space constraints forbid pursuing a statistical survey any further. It only remains to note twenty agreements that everyone concedes are not accidental.[65] All sides acknowledge them as indicating the influence of a common source for Matthew and Luke and as not based on independent revisions of Mark's gospel. These isolated agreements could not have happened coincidentally.

Proposals as to how these could have occurred have ranged from Matthew's and Luke's use of a text differing from that of the present-day Mark to textual corruptions by later scribes. To account for the agreements by theorizing an overlap of Mark and Q in the sections of triple tradition would swell the size of Q to include not only material in sections of Matthean-Lukan double tradition, but also practically everything included in sections of triple tradition. If Q were that big, Markan priority would no longer be a necessity; all three writers could have drawn from Q. Such efforts are instances of special pleading and are not explanations at all. The lack of a satisfactory answer to the twenty passages as well as the other 210 plus agreements renders the Two-Source Theory unacceptable.

To these five weaknesses of the Two-Source Theory, with its assumption of literary interdependence among the synoptic writers, one could add others. But any one of these—not to mention their collective impact— is sufficient to nullify that theory as a viable option in solving the Synoptic Problem.

The Significance of Agreements as to Source:
Literary Independence

What do two-to-one agreements among the synoptists (as stated above under the heading "(5) Agreements of Matthew and Luke against Mark") prove? The situation as it stands allows for grouping the Synoptic Gospels two against one in all possible combinations: Matthew and Mark against Luke (widely acknowledged), Mark and Luke against Matthew (also widely acknowledged), and Matthew and Luke against Mark. If all three worked from a layer of tradition composed of a homogeneous written source with definable limits (such as Q is alleged to have been), one can account for the agreements, but not for the differences in content and order and the various combinations of omissions.

In arguing against literary dependence between Mark and Q, Kümmel alludes to "the erroneous presupposition that parallels between the materials of tradition can be explained only by literary dependence."[66] He adds, "We shall have to visualize the relationship of the gospel writings to one another and to oral tradition as essentially freer."[67] If a two-source advocate such as Kümmel can follow that line of reasoning for Mark and a document he has never seen, he and every other person with his perspective should be willing to apply the same principle to the three Synoptic Gospels. The same linguistic differences he cites between Mark and Q appear in comparisons of Matthew, Mark, and Luke. If Kümmel attributes these to differing strands of oral tradition,[68] the agreements must be traceable to occasions where the strands coincide with one another.

In other words, the combination of agreements and disagreements among the Synoptic Gospels is explainable through understanding the writers to have drawn from a nonhomogeneous layer of tradition composed of a mixture of oral and written material and containing much by way of duplication and varying accounts of the same events and discourses.[69] They need not to have copied—indeed, probably did not copy—from one another. The evidence of agreements of Matthew-Mark against Luke, Mark-Luke against Matthew, and Matthew-Luke against Mark demonstrates a random combination of agreements and disagreements that are explainable only through an independent use by each writer of tradition based on personal memories of eyewitnesses.

The Two-Gospel Theory

Another theory assuming literary dependence has experienced a mild revival. This theory supposes that Matthew wrote first, Luke wrote second and depended on Matthew, and Mark wrote last and depended on Matthew and Luke. William R. Farmer has led an impressive, but relatively small group of scholars in reviving interest in this theory.[70]

Though this theory dispenses with the need for document Q, it is fraught with insoluble problems that two-source proponents are quick to point out. They challenge advocates of the Two-Gospel Theory to provide a credible explanation for why Mark was ever written, and lay heavy emphasis on why Mark would omit the birth accounts and so much other material.[71] They also point to the difficulties encountered by that theory in explaining why Mark omitted the concurrent testimony of Matthew and Luke in places of Matthew-Lukan agreements against Mark.[72]

The truth of the matter is that both the Two-Source and the Two-Gospel theories have insoluble problems,[73] a consideration that makes it quite surprising not to find more New Testament scholars entertaining the possibility that both theories are wrong and that literary independence is a viable option. As seen in the discussion above about the weaknesses of the Two-Source Theory, the existence of all possible two-gospels-against-one combinations militates against any type of literary dependence. The combination that makes the Two-Gospel Theory an impossible solution to the Synoptic Problem is the agreements of Luke and Mark against Matthew.

If Luke used Matthew as a source and then Mark used Matthew and Luke as sources, no reasonable explanation of how Mark and Luke could agree against Matthew is possible, and yet many such agreements occur, as is quite obvious to anyone comparing the Gospels with one another in sections of triple tradition. That phenomenon was a significant cause of the Two-Gospel Theory's downfall in the nineteenth century, and it has never received an adequate answer since then.

Responses to the Alleged Synoptic Problem

In light of the foregoing evaluation of the Two-Source Theory—and any other theories of literary dependence (or interdependence) among the synoptists—a superior response to the Synoptic Problem says that the problem does not exist, for no copying or editing among the writers of the first three gospels occurred. Under the inspiration of the Holy Spirit, each writer worked independently using his best means of obtaining the necessary information about the life of Christ. For Matthew, the best source was his memory of personal experiences with Christ as one of the Twelve. For Mark, early tradition speaks loudly and with unanimity that his main source was the preaching of his mentor, the apostle Peter. For Luke, the path of diligent research was the appointed means, as he records in the prologue of his gospel (Luke 1:1–4).[74] Nothing forbids allowing that Matthew may have prodded his memory through consulting many traditions retained in and around Jerusalem in the days after Pentecost or through utilizing research techniques similar to Luke's. The same is true of Mark. Besides these channels, the three writers had contacts with each other that would have allowed for exchange of information on a personal basis.[75]

But when they penned their gospels, the three writers did so under the dominating control of the Holy Spirit. He utilized their personal characteristics to cause them to write accounts that were free from error. It need not be ruled out that the Spirit even supplied Matthew, Mark, and Luke with information about Jesus that was inaccessible through any other channel, in other words, through direct revelation. After all, the Lord Jesus had promised that (John 14:26; cf. John 16:13).

A STEPPING STONE TO REDACTION CRITICISM: FORM CRITICISM

An Overview of Form Criticism

Chapter 5 above has provided a detailed description of the origin and characteristics of Form Criticism (hereafter FC). A few brief remarks at this point will summarize that methodology—or, more correctly, ideology—from a slightly different perspective.

According to FC, prior to the first written gospel, each early Christian community took fragments of information about Jesus that were available to them and embellished them in such a way as to meet particular needs of their own community. Take as an example the persecution endured by early Jewish Christians when isolated from their families, jobs, and local synagogues because of their public profession of Jesus as the promised Messiah. Their lives became hard and lonely, so the responsibility of finding ways to encourage them fell upon Christian leaders.

Supposedly, on a certain occasion, while delivering a sermon, the speaker was elaborating on Mark 3:31–32, one of the available fragments of information about Jesus: "And His mother and His brothers came and, standing outside [the house where Jesus was], they sent to Him, calling Him. And a crowd was sitting around Him, and they said to Him, 'Behold, Your mother and your brothers are seeking you outside.'" As the preacher spoke, the need to encourage his persecuted listeners occurred to him, so he added to that fragment of historical tradition the thought, "What if Jesus had continued on that occasion with other words?" Then from his own fertile imagination, he added the words of Mark 3:33–35: "And answering He said to them, 'Who is My mother and my brothers?' And looking around at those seated all around Him, he said, 'Behold, My mother and my brothers. For whoever does the will of God, he is My brother and sister and mother.'"

According to form critical theory, those words of embellishment met a pressing need in the lives of the hearers. Their own families had cut them off, but they were now part of the spiritual family of Jesus, which was a far greater relationship. That did much to ease their pain. Furthermore, not only did that bit of embellishment take hold as a permanent part of tradition in that community, but in a very short time it spread to all the other early Christian churches who embraced the addition enthusiastically and without dissent. The same type of process was occurring with other fragments of information about Jesus and in other communities simultaneously so that the large-scale process resulted in a layer of tradition composed of historical facts combined with embellishments. That layer of tradition became the basis for the gospel of Mark and Q, and indirectly for Matthew and Luke as well.

Form critics have proposed that through observation of literary forms in the Gospels, they can separate what is history from the embellishments or, in other words, demythologize the Synoptic Gospels. They call the person portrayed in the Synoptic Gospels "the Christ of Christianity," a person distinctly different from "the Jesus of History" who was the starting point for the tradition.

Weaknesses of Form Criticism

In view of widespread endorsements of FC, even among evangelicals, a brief listing of its weaknesses is important:

(1) A Chronological Weakness

Form critics argue for the types of embellishments they propose by looking to secular sources where similar things occurred. In ancient Greek mythology, stories about mighty figures described in the legendary writings of the ancient Greek writer Homer arose and gained widespread circulation and acceptance. Those mythological events and exploits form a backdrop for the accomplishments attributed to Jesus in the Gospels.

The Gospels are not parallel to the secular mythological writings, however, because of the vast difference in time required for stories to gain acceptance. Hundreds of years elapsed between Homer's writing and the widespread endorsement of his tales about Greek heroes. But some scholars would assume that the embellishments embedded in the Gospels circulated and gained wide acceptance in only three-to-four decades. Such speedy endorsement of embellished tradition by anyone is unprecedented, especially in a period when communications were immeasurably slower than they have become at the dawn of a new century.

(2) An Evidential Weakness

The alleged extensive exchange of embellished stories among early Christians transpired during a period when eyewitnesses of Jesus' life on earth were still alive. Form critics would propose that the embellishments of events and sayings came to the attention of people who were personally present to see and hear those events and sayings without anyone ever raising a voice of dissent. The eyewitness period lasted until the end of the first century A.D., but the earliest gospel, according to Historical Criticism, came during the seventh decade of that century.

It defies imagination that people who knew historic factuality would stand idly by and watch significantly different details added to the facts as they knew them without raising an objection. Were early Christians that far out of touch with reality? Surely not! The integrity of their faith depended on people knowing about the historical Jesus as He was, not as imaginations of later followers distorted the picture of Him. The evidence from the perspective of living eyewitnesses argues strongly against form critical theory.

(3) Logical Weaknesses

Another good reason for questioning FC's proposals about embellishments of historical events lies in well-known characteristics of literary productions. It is illogical that Jesus, who was supposedly incapable of sustained systematic teaching, attracted followers who were capable of producing works that represent the utmost in literary discrimination. The theory is that Jesus' followers took relatively brief historical excerpts of Jesus' words and spontaneously expanded them into masterful pronouncements and discourses that have stood the test of over twenty centuries because of their excellence. The general rule is that leaders attract only those at their own level of capability or a little lower. However, the suggested phenomena of this theory require the general rhetorical level of Jesus' followers to be much higher than His.

Another logical fallacy lies in the supposition that a group of people, most of them without literary discrimination, could collaborate in producing the literary masterpieces of human history. Excellence in authorship does not stem from group efforts; it comes from individuals working independently. Yet form critics would have readers believe that an embellished oral tradition arising in various sectors of the church during the thirty to forty years after Jesus' death resulted in the greatest story every told or written. Clearly, the logic behind FC is a serious weakness of the ideology.

(4) A Historical Weakness

Form critics would have students of the Synoptic Gospels believe that the earliest Christians quickly lost interest in what Jesus actually said and did. Allegedly very soon after His death, they were more interested in what their fertile minds could formulate by way of edifying suggestions than in retaining a historically accurate picture of their Lord. The actions and sayings of Jesus were simply their launching pad for expounding their own ideas about what He might have said or what they wish He had said.

A recognition of human responses to similar situations throughout history reflects the erroneous nature of that analysis. People respond just the opposite from what the critics allege Jesus' followers did. In the last half of the twentieth century, for example, followers of John F. Kennedy and Martin Luther King, after their deaths, hung on every word the two men ever uttered. They have kept careful documentation of the lives of these men so that accurate accounts of those lives would circulate to as many people as possible. They have not embellished the speeches and activities of Kennedy and King, for they appreciate their contributions and know they would open themselves to criticism from eyewitnesses who know the way things actually occurred.

Why would followers of Jesus have reacted any differently? They did not need to embellish and did not want to. Jesus had attracted them to Himself just as He was. That is the way they remembered Him, and that is the way they reported to others about Him. Paul was careful not to put his own words into Jesus' mouth (1 Cor. 7:10, 12, 25). Luke carefully checked with eyewitnesses before penning his gospel (Luke 1:1–4). Early Christians appealed frequently to events in Jesus' life when they had been personally present (for example, Acts 2:32; 3:15; 10:41). Judas' replacement had to be one who had been with Jesus from John's baptism on (Acts 1:21–22). Peter's sermon at Pentecost verifies an early interest in factual events of Jesus' life (Acts 2:22–24). Peter's instructions to the household of Cornelius prove the same (Acts 10:36–42). In Paul's sermon at Antioch in Pisidia, he drew upon his biographical interest in Jesus (Acts 13:23–33).

In light of the above, it is a totally unrealistic approach to the Gospels to hold that early Christians had no historical interest in Jesus after His death.

(5) An Ethical Weakness

Another breakdown in the theory of FC comes in its view of the integrity of early Christian communities. The theory supposes that those responsible for writings upholding the highest standards of ethics the world has ever known did not practice those ethics. In other words, they were not truthful in their reporting about Jesus. Whether termed "white lies" or "exaggerations," their embellishments misled others by not representing accurately the facts of Jesus' life.

That too is contrary to what one knows about everyday happenings. A person whose descriptions are even slightly off-target does not become an authority on truthfulness. Only those who consistently represent facts exactly as they occurred are qualified to speak with authenticity about telling the truth. If early Christians lacked that integrity, they could not have produced tradition that resulted in the writing of the Synoptic Gospels. At some point, their sham would have surfaced and the integrity of the Gospels would have come into question. That integrity has not, however, been subject to question in this way until the emergence of Historical Criticism in general and FC in particular around the middle of the twentieth century.

The old suggestion that ethics among people of the first-century did not measure up to modern-day ethics meets its refutation in the documents that earliest Christians produced. Those documents present and defend truth in its highest form, higher than standards maintained in any other circles, even standards commonly recognized almost two thousand years later. Practically everyone recognizes that the standards set in New Testament writings are still supreme. It is thus contradictory to argue that people who could not or did not distinguish truth from embellishment produced traditions contained in those documents.

THE EMERGENCE OF REDACTION CRITICISM

Historical Criticism reached its inevitable goal with the emergence of RC. FC focused on the Christian community and its input of embellishments, but it could not explain differences between the three Synoptic Gospels. That attention should eventually shift to the writers of those gospels was inescapable. Redaction Criticism began as a subdiscipline of FC, but soon earned the status of a separate discipline.

Form Criticism specialized in studying the literary forms to distinguish embellishments from historical facts, but RC (*Redaktionsgeschichte,* sometimes called "redaction history," but a good translation could be "redaction story"[76]) examines the editorial changes made by an author to distinguish actual happenings and community embellishments from elements of the text that are traceable to the theological emphases the writer wanted to bring. An element of overlapping between FC and RC is inevitable, for gospel writers were parts of their communities and naturally reflected their respective communities' theological outlooks. They could not separate from the people they served.

For the most part, redaction critics do not embrace traditional viewpoints of authorship of the Synoptic Gospels. They view the originators of the synoptics as later theological editors to whose works the names of Matthew, Mark, and Luke were attached for the sake of prestige. The anonymous writers, then, are the ones whose theological views are under consideration in this type of research. Those theological emphases differ significantly from any specific, systematic teaching Jesus may have given.

RC arose as a separate discipline around the middle of the twentieth century. Most prominent among its early advocates were Günther Bornkamm, Hans Conzelmann, and Willi Marxsen.[77] Each man concentrated his efforts on one gospel—Bornkamm on Matthew, Conzelmann on Luke, and Marxsen on Mark. In discussing this mode of criticism, the following will center attention on these three along with Norman Perrin as representatives of RC.[78]

Theological Analysis of the Writers

Theology of Mark

Redaction Criticism (as most commonly practiced) endorses the priority of Mark, as do the Two- (Four-) Source Theory and FC, for the latter two ideologies are the foundation on which RC builds. That makes Mark a suitable starting point for theological analysis. Redactional analysis of Mark is more difficult due to the unavailability of sources used by its writer.

Nevertheless, Marxsen detected editorial tendencies that enabled him to conclude that Mark joined, edited, and expanded isolated units of tradition in accordance with four guidelines: (1) the passion story is linked to the rest of the gospel by Mark's addition of predictions about its occurrence; (2) Mark invents the messianic-secret theory to explain the late (post-Easter) emergence of messianic teaching; (3) Mark introduces the new literary concept of a "gospel" (euangelion); it is the "proclamation of a message of salvation," and owes its origin to Paul; and (4) Mark weaves into the narrative a geographical orientation toward Galilee. The resultant force of the gospel is, therefore, not a historical account of Jesus' life but a proclamation of the salvation to be expected by Christians subsequent to the Easter (namely, resurrection) "experience." The gospel writer anticipates an imminent return of Christ and directs his readers to make their way to Galilee, where he expects the parousia ("coming") to happen.[79]

Theology of Matthew

Redaction critics have an easier time discovering the theological leanings of Matthew and Luke, for those gospels contained editorial changes of a known source (Mark) and a reconstructed source (Q). Bornkamm held that Matthew's writer composed his gospel in the A.D. 80s or 90s in a location somewhere between Palestine and Syria. Bornkamm understood the book to reflect a deep cleavage between Judaism and Christianity, and more specifically, a turmoil within the church between Jewish and Gentile Christians.

In siding with the Gentile position, the writer arranged his sources (Mark and Q plus some special Matthean material, namely, M) and added material so as to create a teacher who has captured the true essence of the law of Moses that Pharisaic Judaism had missed. Unlike His predecessors, this "rabbi" taught with authority supported by miracles, and His disciples never cease to learn from Him. The new system had much in common with Judaism, but is distinct from it, earning its own title of "church" (ekklēsia). According to form-critical analysis, this is a term put into Jesus' mouth by the Christian community. Unlike the Jewish synagogue, which is local, the church has become universal. The Lord's presence with His church (in place of the law and the temple) is a unifying factor. But the church has not yet attained ultimate perfection. Its constituency needs to obey Jesus' teachings, especially in light of future judgment that will result in promised salvation.[80]

Bornkamm's view of Matthew's scheme, then, has Matthew replacing Mark's exclusive attention to Christ's imminent return with a joint emphasis on the church and the imminent return. Late first-century Christian thought experienced the growing realization that the Messiah's return was not to be immediate. Consequently, Christians reputedly invented the concept of a new institution, the church, to fill the period before the return.

Theology of Luke

In Conzelmann's view, Luke, which was written at about the same time as Matthew or later (perhaps around A.D. 90 or afterwards), delineates three distinct periods: the period of Israel, the period of Jesus' ministry, and the period since the ascension. The writer keeps the second and third periods distinct from each other. The era of Jesus' life and ministry on earth was the time of salvation, when Satan was far away and temptation was nonexistent. Since Jesus' passion, however, Satan has returned and temptations are prevalent and very real. The work of the Spirit in the church essentially fulfills prophecies of the "last days." Hence Luke reflects a more general, somewhat weakened, eschatological expectation in the church of his time. His motif is, then, the delay of Christ's return.[81]

The shift in emphasis from Mark means that Luke changes from his predecessors' focus on a short time of waiting to dealing with a Christian life of longer duration. That shift entails a development of ethical standards, among which perseverance is prominent. It also leads to a development of a complete redemptive plan and the replacement of an imminent end with one that is "endlessly" remote.

It is worth repeating that redaction critics attribute none of these theological emphases to Jesus Himself. That applies to Marxsen's analysis of Mark and Bornkamm's treatment of Matthew as well as to Conzelmann's view of Luke.

Examples of Incorporation of Theological Emphases

Examples from each of the Synoptic Gospels illustrate how redaction critics think the writers edited available material to direct attention to various theological points.

Mark's treatment of the narrative about Caesarea Philippi. In Mark 8:27–9:1, the writer reports questions and answers as coming from the lips of Jesus and Peter. In reality, RC alleges that the titles are from the Christological vocabulary of early Christians, not from the historical occasion when Jesus taught His disciples. Furthermore, though characters in the story bear the names of individuals and groups connected with Jesus' ministry, the principal reference is to circumstances in the church of the late A.D. 60s. "Jesus" and His sayings represent the Lord from heaven and His message to this church. "Peter" pictures misled believers, who confess correctly but interpret their own confession erroneously. "The multitude" stands for the total church membership, to whom the Lord from heaven directs the teaching. In other words, redaction critics see this story as bearing the form of a history about Jesus, but it actually purposed to convey the risen Lord's message, as conceived by Mark, to the church. The impression of a historical incident is merely a vehicle, and the story is not that of an actual happening during Jesus' life on earth.[82]

Matthew's reworking of the narrative about Caesarea Philippi. Matthew took Mark's account of the same incident and reworked it to bring out different theological themes needed by the church of his day. He reshaped Mark's narrative to emphasize ecclesiastical interests by inserting a formal blessing of Peter. That, of course, never occurred before Jesus' death, but it laid a foundation for Peter to assume full authority as founder and leader of the early church (Matt. 16:17–19). For Matthew the church was the sole medium of salvation. In fact, to the person within this church, salvation is assured. In effect, Matthew moved the "Son of Man" reference from 16:21 (cf. Mark 8:31) to 16:13, because unlike Mark, Matthew did not want to generate a Christological discussion. Matthew's interest was in a formal proclamation by Jesus regarding the Christian church.[83]

Luke's reworking of the narrative about Caesarea Philippi. In Luke's handling of the event (Luke 9:18–27), the writer removed the Markan urgency based on an imminent return so that he could highlight a consistent life of testimony over a considerable period of time. Such touches as the addition of "daily" to Luke 9:23 and the omission of "in this adulterous and sinful generation" and "come with power" from 9:26–27 changed the account's complexion drastically. This resulted from Luke's rethinking of Mark's outlook regarding eschatology and introduction of his own emphasis on delay. By attention to details like these, the redaction critic purposes to detect this or that theological point being made by a gospel writer.[84]

Characteristics of the Method

Three characteristics of RC stand out:

(1) The redaction critic views the role of the gospel writers as that of theologians, not historians. He sees Mark as wholly dependent on isolated units of tradition identified by FC and Matthew and Luke as having access to Mark and Q, along with some special sources of their own. The task of the three writers consisted of adopting and connecting the units in ways dictated by their theological purposes, and attributing to Jesus viewpoints and emphases they deemed most crucial for nurturing the faith of the churches of their times. That made them theological editors, but not recorders of historical happenings. It was inconsequential to them that they falsely attributed to Jesus and His associates many things they never said or did. Their prime concern was constructing a theology to meet the needs of the church, even if doing so successfully meant fabricating a lie about Jesus to enforce the credibility of their systems.

(2) The philosophical basis used by redactionists to give respectability

to their systems of falsification is similar to that behind the neoorthodoxy of Karl Barth and the demytholigizing of Rudolf Bultmann. That philosophy contends for two realms of reality, the obvious one where space, time, and the physical senses prevail and a less obvious realm that they term the realm of faith. Anything someone within his own mind believes to be true comprises the realm of faith and is viewed as real regardless of whether it coincides with the other realm of space and time. For example, the postresurrection faith of early Christians was so strong that the resurrection of Christ they believed in became confused with space-time happenings. In fact, many convinced themselves that the physical body of Jesus rose from death, leaving an empty tomb. To the redaction critic, as to the form critic, that mental persuasion is not wrong, even though they cannot support Jesus' resurrection as a fact of history. To early Christians who believed in Jesus' physical resurrection, that "fact of faith" has proven to be health-giving, and that was enough to make it a "real" event. A coinciding with history is unnecessary and even irrelevant. Similarly, as a whole, the Synoptic Gospels need not portray the historical Jesus in toto. It is enough for them to prove beneficial in the spiritual formation of the early Christian church.

(3) The philosophical system behind RC assigns so much of the Gospels to that nonhistorical realm of reality that it eliminates the Gospels as a possible basis for reconstructing a life of Jesus or determining a theology of Jesus. Just as FC says the events recorded in the Gospels are fabrications of the early church, RC says that the theological teachings in the Gospels are those of the individual writers, not of Jesus. The concept of those two methodologies is that early Christians did not follow the modern concept of "historical" (in other words, "factual"). Motivated by a strong religious experience, they had no qualms about imputing to the historical Jesus words He never spoke. The Gospels and the traditions behind them, therefore, are to the redaction critic primarily reflections of the early church's experience and theology. Only by stringent application of carefully contrived criteria for authenticity can one hope to derive accurate data about Jesus' life and teachings. According to the redactionist, whatever one derives in this respect will at most be minimal.

Evaluation of Redaction Criticism

Byproduct Benefits

Benefits of RC for one of conservative-evangelical persuasions are minimal. In fact, they are nonexistent except for a few instances where corrective responses have caused evangelicals to investigate phases of New Testament study more deeply. To put it differently, benefits of RC are merely byproducts, not direct results of redaction critical study.

As a corrective to FC, RC has emphasized that the gospel writers were not just compilers of tradition, but men who wrote, each with a different purpose. That understanding is necessary if one is to find an explanation for the differences in emphasis between the Gospels.

The rise of RC has also revived interest in a comparative study of the Synoptic Gospels, an interest that had lagged because of earlier efforts to merge the three into one strand of tradition. Study of the gospels' relationships with each other is probably more detailed now than ever before. In addition, in its efforts to discover the Christian community's contributions and theological motivation, RC had brought a closer attention to first-century Christianity. That kind of scrutiny of early-church historical backgrounds helps in gaining a better understanding of various parts of the New Testament.

Direct Liabilities

In contrast with the indirect benefits, the redaction critical method of study suffers severely from debilitating weaknesses:

(1) Foundational weaknesses. With the Two- (Four-) Source Theory and FC as its basis, RC inherits all the irresolvable problems associated with those two disciplines, as described earlier in this chapter (see "Weaknesses of the Two-Source Theory" and "Weaknesses of Form Criticism" above). RC is vulnerable at all the same points for it rests on them as its foundation.

(2) Chronological, evidential, and ethical weaknesses. RC compounds the chronological weakness of FC by proposing another step of added embellishments to an already unbelievably short period. First-century Christendom allegedly embraced not only the embellishments of early communities but also those of the synoptic writers. Thirty to forty years during a time of slow communications is simply not long enough for that to happen.

It is likewise impossible for the writers' embellishments to go unchallenged as long as eyewitnesses were alive. If writers of Matthew, Mark, and Luke had attributed to Jesus actions or words that He never did or spoke, someone, remembering what he/she had seen or heard, would surely have brought contrary evidence to the attention of gospel readers.

Redaction critical theories also call into question the integrity of the gospel writers. High standards of truthfulness originated with Christianity in general and the Gospels in particular. Could the writing representatives of such a system be practitioners of extensive falsification regarding the life and teachings of Jesus? Or did the Savior's words and actions (as described in the Gospels) truly come from Himself and were they accurately transmitted by Matthew, Mark, and Luke? The latter alternative is clearly the case.

(3) Abnormal historical study. Redaction critics approach the Gospels differently from the way historians handle other ancient writings. Their initial assumption points toward the nonhistorical character of the bulk of gospel literature, as though some barrier separated the writers from any interest in real happenings during the earlier portion of their century. Redaction critics suppose events and sayings to have been invented or reshaped for theological purposes. That, however, is uncharacteristic of the way historians have treated other teachers in the ancient world, both Jewish and Greek. The initial presumption about them has favored their historical accuracy

until evidence proves otherwise. Like other ancient writers, early Christians had considerable historical interest in Jesus of Nazareth and deserve the same positive assumptions about their historical orientation. Theological purposes of the gospel writers, therefore, were not separate from, but rather anchored in, history. RC's bias against the historicity of the documents it investigates is another serious impediment for the system.

(4) Biased philosophical basis. The philosophical basis of RC is also questionable. A serious analysis must reject acknowledging the existence of a set of "faith realities" when those "faith realities" stand in opposition to physically observable historical data. Only a mind thoroughly conditioned by theories of secular rationalism can envisage two realms of reality in conflict with each other, and yet regard each realm as equally valid. An endorsement of such a state of affairs calls one's intuitive appreciation of reality into serious question. That dualistic concept is quite artificial and strains human logical capacities beyond their limits.

(5) Unregulated subjectivism. RC is weak because of its unregulated subjectivism. That, of course, results from the system's underlying philosophy. Redactionists become their own norms so that they often distort their interpretations of the text. For example, Perrin's explanation of "Peter" as Mark's representation of misled believers is traceable to Perrin, not to Mark (cf. Mark 8:27–9:1).[85] Someone else besides Perrin could just as easily take "Peter" in his confession as representing discerning and obedient believers.[86] Only factual data about who Peter was can rescue one from the dilemma of endlessly conflicting opinions about what this section says about the apostle. Objective criteria must control conclusions about the text. In other words, multiple possible "faith realities" must become one "faith reality" by affirming the only reality to be the one that is historical. "Peter" was either a historical person or the figment of someone's imagination. He cannot be both.

Differences of opinion among redaction critics reflect their personal bias in their assumptions. That they have taken unjustified liberties in arguing for various emphases in each author could not be clearer than their disagreements with one another reflect. For instance, theories about Mark's purpose variously hold his guideline to be an attack on false Christology,[87] the new Moses,[88] the liturgical calendar,[89] an apology for the Cross,[90] the sovereign authority of Jesus,[91] a geographical-theological outline,[92] Pauline theology,[93] and others. If redaction proponents cannot agree what theological theme Mark sought to inaugurate, it is probable he was not trying to inaugurate any such theme; the alleged theological theme originates in the mind of the modern redactionist, not the gospel writer. Various foundational assumptions by different modern scholars create a hodgepodge of opinions, which they then read back into the gospel. That does great injustice to the ancient record.

(6) Method for identifying "authentic Jesus material." RC's method for recognizing "authentic Jesus material" is also quite subjective and even slanted against historical accuracy in the Synoptic Gospels. The three criteria—distinctiveness, multiple attestation, and consistency[94]—stem from

the presupposition that tradition about Jesus contains much that is unhistorical.[95] With that as the foregone conclusion, examining historical sources without bias becomes an impossibility. The verdict is already in before the trial begins. It is not a question of whether the jury will find a person guilty, but of how and when they will find that defendant guilty. RC has determined in advance what it will discover, so the results of the method can be nothing short of devastating to the Synoptic Gospels as historical records.

Evangelicals and Redaction Criticism

Methodology

Some evangelical scholars have argued that redaction critical methodology is a neutral tool and does not require negative conclusions about the Gospels' historicity.[96] They point out that "redact" is just another way of saying "edit" and all evangelicals acknowledge that the writers edited their material to some extent. That response necessitates a closer look at what RC really means by the term "redact."

The methodology has divided editorial activity into four categories: selectivity, arrangement, modification, and creativity.[97] (1) *Selectivity* means that writers of the Gospels did not use all the material available to them, but chose only the parts best suited to the demonstration of their theological emphases. How could Matthew, for example, have included all his recollections from years of personal contact with Jesus? It is true that evangelicals, in line with tradition, have viewed the writers as selecting only material relevant to their purposes, but an evangelical redaction critic may hold the purpose to be purely theological and exclusive of historical objectives. That is contrary to a traditional orthodox perspective that does not view theological and historical purposes as mutually exclusive of each other. Clearly the Gospels devote themselves to both goals, the writers selecting materials from the life of Jesus that would fulfil both theological and historical purposes.

(2) *Arrangement* means that synoptists did not always arrange their material in chronological order. Sometimes they put it in thematic sequence to put emphasis on some particular aspect of the life of Jesus, such as Matthew's grouping of a number of Jesus' miracles in Matthew 8–9 to highlight the authority of Jesus. In that passage, note that Matthew gives no indication that he is describing the miracles in chronological order. That view of arrangement is not a new discovery of RC; it has been a longstanding view of orthodox Christianity.

The situation is different in such passages as Matthew 5–7, however, for the writer begins and closes his account of the Sermon on the Mount with formulas indicating that Jesus spoke the words on a single occasion. When evangelical redactionists interpret the Sermon as a collection of sayings spoken on different occasions,[98] they run roughshod over the historicity of the Sermon's introductory and concluding formulas. That is not a legitimate understanding of editorial principles used by gospel authors.

(3) *Modification* means that Matthew, Mark, and Luke modified the available materials in line with their personal habits and purposes in writing. Sometimes their modifications were of a minor nature, changes so as to conform material to stylistic preferences of each individual author. Long before the advent of RC, evangelical statements of biblical inspiration incorporated that kind of alteration as a valid analysis.

However, other modifications identified by evangelical redactionists are far more extensive. They allow for molding accounts in accord with the theological interests of the evangelists and their communities rather than portraying the situation in Jesus' day. These major modifications step outside the boundaries of conservative evangelical views of inspiration and delve into the realm of radically liberal RC. They include such proposals as Matthew's invention of the "exception clauses" in Matthew 5:32 and 19:9 and a distorted view of the Pharisees of Jesus' day.[99]

(4) *Creativity* means that the editorial activity of the writers allowed them freedom to shape their gospels creatively by radically altering historical narratives and putting on Jesus' lips words that He never spoke. The postulating of that type of editorializing clearly violates a conservative view of biblical inspiration. Evangelical redaction critics have exemplified their favoring of creativity in their handling of passages such as the genealogies of Matthew and Luke and the beatitudes of Matthew 5:3–12.[100]

In summary of evangelical RC, the general effect of its methodology is the dehistoricizing of gospel accounts of Jesus' life in deference to the editorial activities of the writers. Evangelical RC obviously does not do so to the same degree as radical RC, but the same basic problem besets evangelical RC. In other words, evangelical redaction critics are guilty of questioning the historical accuracy of the Gospels. Even though some might claim this is not the case,[101] the written comments of evangelical redactionists belie that claim.

Issues Raised by Redaction Criticism

In raising questions about the historicity of certain facets of the Synoptic Gospels, evangelical RC also touches on other issues of biblical and theological thought. Each time it does so, it comes into apparent conflict with traditional Christianity.

(1) *Theological purpose versus consistent historical accuracy.* Recent RC writings by evangelicals assume that the theological purposes of the authors automatically excludes the possibility that they wrote with consistent historical accuracy.[102] The longstanding position of evangelicalism, however, is that theological purpose and historical accuracy can coexist, and that accepting the gospel accounts at face value (as the ordinary first-century reader would have understood them) is valid. Of course, this viewpoint allows for the presence of figurative language, such as parables, but excludes subtle literary "signals" such as modern RC proposes.[103]

(2) *Impossibility of thorough harmonization.* Evangelical RC minimizes and in some cases absolutely denies the possibility of harmonizing parallel accounts of the same events and discourses of Jesus and, consequently, rejects the possibility of reconstructing a continuous chronological sequence

in the life of Christ.[104] Gundry has written, "The old method of harmonizing what we can and holding the rest in suspension has seen its day."[105] Osborne has expressed the same opinion: "I agree that we can never completely 'harmonize' the synoptics and John—for instance, to attain a so-called chronological 'footsteps of Jesus'—but we should seek a basic picture."[106] The rejection of harmonies is conspicuously out of step with what has been the approach of historic Christianity to the relationships among the Gospels.[107] From the beginning, Christians recognized the legitimacy and advantages of studying the life of Jesus by intermingling the accounts of His life.

(3) Hidden theology of Jesus. Evangelical redaction critics contend that the theology of the gospel writers has hidden at least partially the theology of Jesus Himself. Doctrinal features contrived by the writers cause their gospels to reflect the theologies of the separate redactors. For example, in his apologetic that defends ancient Pharisaism as a positive movement, Hagner has written, "It is this matter [namely, the intramural debate between Jesus and the Pharisees] that underlies the growing hostility between the synagogue and church that has undoubtedly left its impact upon the material present here."[108] In other words, Matthew has colored his account of the historical realities of Jesus' life in a way to put the Pharisees in a much worse light than Jesus actually depicted them (cf. Matthew 23). Their theology was actually less different from His than Matthew portrayed it to be.

It is true that each of the gospel writers was an author in his own right who emphasized theological truths different from the other writers,[109] but it is wrong to question the historical accuracy of what they wrote. Theological purpose and historical accuracy are perfectly compatible when one recognizes that each writer retained parts of Jesus' theological emphasis. By combining those emphases, a reader can arrive at the theology of Jesus Himself, one that is undiluted and undistorted by theological emphases originating with the writers alone.

(4) Loss of Jesus' words. Redaction critical analyses seldom, if ever, allow that the Gospels record the exact words of Jesus.[110] Instead, the Gospels contain either theological modifications of the teachings of Jesus or religious statements that the writers themselves invented. On the other hand, evangelicals have traditionally maintained that, according to the doctrine of biblical inspiration, the text conveys the true meaning of the words of Jesus when it records them. Biblical inspiration also insists that Matthew, Mark, Luke, and John, in their citations, have not changed the intention of Jesus' teachings. In fact, in many cases the Gospels retained His exact words as He spoke them.[111] The issue of *ipsissima vox* ("the very same voice") versus *ipsissima verba* ("the very same words") has tantalized students of the Gospels for many generations, but the latter alternative has more in its favor than what evangelical redaction critics acknowledge.

(5) Overriding of grammatical-historical interpretation. Evangelical RC in particular and Historical Criticism in general have significantly

modified the hermeneutics of traditional Protestantism. That set of guidelines has governed conservative exegetes in their handling of Scripture at least since the Reformation. Redactionists, however, allow critical considerations to add to and usually distort considerations of grammar and history, a practice that evangelicals have rejected traditionally.[112]

(6) *Loss of evidence through dependence theories.* For centuries, Christians held that the four gospels are four independent witnesses to the words and deeds of Jesus, proving by their agreement with each other the historical accuracy of their separate accounts. Around A.D. 400, John Chrysostom, the leading exegete during the Nicene period of church history, wrote the following:

"What then? Was not one evangelist sufficient to tell all?" One was indeed sufficient; but if there be four that write, not at the same times, nor in the same places, neither after having met together, and conversed one with another, and then they speak all things as it were out of one mouth, this becomes a very great demonstration of the truth.[113]

With the relegating of the gospel of John to a secondary role through assigning it a late date,[114] theories of literary interdependence among the other three gospels have reduced the evidence for historicity to a single voice, a single voice that is subject to question because of alleged embellishments by early Christians and gospel writers. Against the majority of opinion of modern New Testament scholars, the ancient church held that Matthew wrote first, basing his gospel largely on his personal recollections,[115] that Mark wrote largely in dependence on the preaching of Peter,[116] and that Luke used information derived from Paul and diligent research in a large number of written sources and oral reports.[117]

In the following words, Meeks evaluates a sample of the evidence that represents ancient tradition: "Both Papias and Clement write as if there were no literary connection between any of the gospels. . . . Neither [Clement nor Origen] has a word to say about dependence."[118] Zahn says that Augustine (late fourth and early fifth centuries) was the first and, until the mid-eighteenth century, only one to advance a theory of literary dependence in connection with the Synoptic Gospels,[119] but it is questionable whether even Augustine advocated literary dependence (see chapter 1 of this volume for further discussion).

Beyond this unanimous tradition favoring the priority of Matthew and near-unanimous, perhaps unanimous, testimony as to literary independence, data on the issue of literary dependence comes from the gospels themselves. Based on that internal evidence, a decision favoring interdependence is at best tenuous, and can only prevail because of a critic's predisposition toward it. The stronger conclusion must be that three different individuals did not produce the Synoptic Gospels by creatively modifying the historical details and didactic essence of a common source or common sources available to them. Rather, the Holy Spirit—the Spirit of *truth*

(John 14:17; 15:26; 16:13)—inspired the writers independently to guarantee that all information in each gospel is an accurate report of the life and teachings of Jesus.

From each issue raised by evangelical use of RC—theological purpose versus consistent historical accuracy, impossibility of thorough harmonization, hidden theology of Jesus, loss of Jesus' words, overriding of grammatical-historical interpretation, and loss of evidence through dependence theories—comes an additional reason for evangelicals to reject RC in particular and Historical Criticism in general. From its beginning, it has demonstrably shown itself to be an ideology, not a methodology—one whose bent is to reach conclusions that undermine the integrity of the Synoptic Gospels.

A far superior course is to concur with the earliest Christian leaders in concluding that the three synoptists wrote without depending on each other in a literary way. To conclude otherwise raises questions about their integrity and ultimately about the inspiration of the three Synoptic Gospels. However faulty may have been his views on other matters, Schaff has spoken truth on this issue:

> The whole theory [dependence of one gospel on another] degrades the one or two Synoptists to the position of slavish and yet arbitrary compilers, not to say plagiarists; it assumes a strange mixture of dependence and affected originality; it weakens the independent value of their history, and it does not account for the omissions of most important matter, and for many differences in common matter. For the Synoptists often differ just where we would expect them to agree. . . . What should we think of a historian of our day who would plunder another historian of one-third or one-half of the contents of his book without a word of acknowledgment direct or indirect? Let us give the Evangelists at least the credit of common honesty, which is the basis of all morality.[120]

ENDNOTES

1. Eusebius, *Ecclesiastical History* 3.24.6.
2. Ibid., 6.14.5.
3. For further discussion of the reliability of ancient Christian tradition, see A. C. Perumalil, "Are not Papias and Irenaeus Competent to Report on the Gospels?" *The Expository Times* 91 (August 1980): 333; F. F. Bruce, *Peter, Stephen, James & John: Studies in Non-Pauline Christianity* (Grand Rapids: Eerdmans, 1979), 128–38; Anthony Meredith, "The Evidence of Papias for the Priority of Matthew," in *Synoptic Studies*, ed. C. M. Tucket (Sheffield, England: Department of Biblical Studies, University of Sheffield, 1984); R. T. France, *Matthew, Evangelist and Teacher* (Grand Rapids: Zondervan, 1989), 52–66; Donald Guthrie, *New Testament Introduction*, 4th rev. ed. (Downers Grove, Ill.: InterVarsity, 1990), 44–53. Massaux has examined the influence of the gospel of Matthew on Christian literature before Irenaeus and shown that this gospel enjoyed preferential treatment by the earliest Christian writers (Édouard Massaux, *The Influence of the Gospel of Saint Matthew on*

Christian Literature before Saint Irenaeus, New Gospel Studies 5, no. 2, trans. Norman J. Belval and Suzanne Hecht, 3 vols. [Macon, Ga.: Mercer University, 1990], 3:183–89). Massaux's immense work compares the texts of various early works with the *Greek* text of Matthew, showing the many correspondences. That evidences the dominance of Matthew's Greek gospel from the earliest period of Christian writing.

4. Cited by Eusebius, *Ecclesiastical History* 6.14.5–6.
5. Ibid., 3.24.7; 6.14.7; cf. Friedrich Bleek, *An Introduction to the New Testament,* William Urwick, ed. (Edinburgh: T & T Clark, 1873), 1:192. Writing 200 years after Clement, Augustine indicates no gospel writer was ignorant of gospels written before his (*The Harmony of the Gospels* 1.2.4), but obviously at least the first one to write could not have known the content of gospels written after his. Clement's information seems to be more accurate in this case.
6. For example, John Chrysostom, *The Gospel according to Matthew* Homily I.5.
7. R. H. Stein, "Synoptic Problem," in *Dictionary of Jesus and the Gospels,* Joel B. Green, Scott McKnight, and I. Howard Marshall, eds. (Downers Grove, Ill.: InterVarsity, 1992), 787–91.
8. Ibid.; the remainder of this discussion of Mark and Q will treat the Two-Source and Four-Source Theories as essentially interchangeable.
9. For a background of the Markan priority hypothesis before Streeter, see William R. Farmer, *The Gospel of Jesus* (Louisville, Ky.: Westminster/John Knox, 1994), 146–60; Hajo Uden Meijboom, *A History and Critique of the Origin of the Marcan Hypothesis 1835–1866,* New Gospel Studies 8, John J. Kiwiet, trans. and ed. (Macon, Ga.: Mercer University, 1993). Also see chapter 2 of this volume, specifically the section entitled "9. Darwin: Evolution."
10. Burnett Hillman Streeter, *The Four Gospels: A Study of Origins* (New York: Macmillan, 1925), 151, 159–60.
11. Roland Muchat Frye, "The Synoptic Problems and Analogies in Other Literatures," in *The Relationships Among the Gospels: An Interdisciplinary Dialogue,* William O. Walker, Jr., ed. (San Antonio, Tex.: Trinity University, 1978), 271–74. Frye also notes the proclivity of writers to condense the total length of someone else's work while expanding certain details and episodes of a source document (ibid., 277–78); contra D. A. Carson, "Matthew," in vol. 8 of *The Expositor's Bible Commentary,* Frank E. Gaebelein, gen. ed. [Grand Rapids: Zondervan, 1984], 14). That would explain Mark's shortness overall combined with his longer accounts of individual pericopes, if Mark had drawn from Matthew and Luke.
12. Streeter, *Four Gospels,* 151, 160–61.
13. Ibid., 179–81.
14. Robert H. Stein, *The Synoptic Problem, An Introduction* (Grand Rapids: Baker, 1987), 132.
15. See (5) under "Weaknesses of the Two-Source Theory" below.
16. Streeter, *Four Gospels,* 151, 161–62.
17. Cf. also Malcolm Lowe, "The Demise of Arguments from Order for Markan Priority," *Novum Testamentum* 24 (1982): 27–36.
18. George Eldon Ladd, "More Light on the Synoptics," *Christianity Today* (March 2, 1959): 12–16.
19. W. F. Albright and C. S. Mann, *Matthew,* vol. 26 of *The Anchor Bible* (Garden City, N.Y.: Doubleday, 1971), xxxviii.

20. Birger Gerhardsson, *Memory and Manuscript: Oral Tradition and Written Transmission in Rabbinic Judaism and Early Christianity* (Lund: Gleerup, 1961), 123–24.

21. Clement of Alexandria, "Fragments from the Latin Translation of [M. Aurelius] Cassiodorus," 1.1, in *The Ante-Nicene Fathers,* Alexander Roberts and James Donaldson, eds. (Grand Rapids: Eerdmans, n.d.), 573.

22. Streeter, *Four Gospels,* 151–52, 162–64. For further discussion of the evolutionary arguments based on Aramaisms that lie behind the Markan priority hypothesis, see chapter 5 and the section dealing with "The Prime Impetuses: Evolutionary Conceptions and Unbelief."

23. Ibid., 162.

24. For example, R. T. France, *Matthew: Evangelist and Teacher* (Grand Rapids: Zondervan, 1989), 64, 96–97, 128.

25. For example, William L. Lane, *The Gospel according to Mark,* NIC (Grand Rapids: Eerdmans, 1974), 24–25.

26. Streeter, *Four Gospels,* 152, 164–68.

27. France, *Matthew,* 37.

28. For example, G. M. Styler, "The Priority of Mark," in *The Birth of the New Testament,* ed. C. F. D. Moule, 3d ed. (San Francisco: Harper & Row, 1982), 289–93, and France, *Matthew,* 32–37.

29. J. M. Robinson, "On the *Gattung* of Mark (and John)," in *Jesus and Man's Hope,* David G. Buttrick, ed., 2 vols. (Pittsburgh, Pa.: Pittsburgh Theological Seminary, 1970), 1:101–2; Stein, *Synoptic Problem,* 76–81; France, *Matthew,* 39–41.

30. France, *Matthew,* 39.

31. D. A. Carson, "Matthew," vol. 8 in *EBC,* Frank E. Gaebelein, gen. ed. (Grand Rapids: Zondervan, 1984), 15–16.

32. Ibid., 16 n. 39.

33. David Wenham, "The Synoptic Problem Revisited: Some New Suggestions about the Composition of Mark 4:1–34," *Tyndale Bulletin* 23 (1972): 12.

34. Styler, "Priority of Mark," 293–98, 304–9.

35. Bruce, *Canon of Scripture* 257–58; Harris, *Inspiration and Canonicity* 255, 281–82.

36. Robert H. Gundry, *Matthew: A Commentary on His Handbook for a Mixed Church under Persecution,* 2d ed. (Grand Rapids: Eerdmans, 1994), 621.

37. Cf. Thomas, "Correlation of Revelatory Spiritual Gifts with NT Canonicity," *The Master's Seminary Journal* 8, no. 1 (spring 1997): 19–24.

38. For example, Donald A. Hagner, *Matthew 1–13,* vol. 33A of *Word Biblical Commentary,* David A. Hubbard and Glenn W. Barker, gen. eds. (Dallas: Word, 1993), lxxv–lxxvii.

39. Merrill C. Tenney, *New Testament Survey, Revised,* revised by Walter M. Dunnett (Grand Rapids: Eerdmans, 1985), 142–43.

40. Albright and Mann, *Matthew,* xl–xli.

41. Darrell L. Bock, *Luke 1:1–9:50,* Moisés Silva, gen. ed. (Grand Rapids: Baker, 1994), 821, 950–51.

42. Ibid., 951.

43. Ibid.

44. Albright and Mann, *Matthew,* xlii, xlvii, xlix, lxii–lxiii.

45. Ibid., xlix.

46. Bock, *Luke 1:1–9:50,* 9; cf. ibid., 915: "Thus, Q is a convenient way to say that Matthew and Luke share a similar tradition at this point, though not necessarily the same document." Cf. Stein, *Synoptic Problem,* 111.

47. J. C. Hawkins, *Horae Synopticae* (reprint, Grand Rapids: Baker, 1968), 208–11; Streeter, *Four Gospels,* 295–331.
48. Stein, *Synoptic Problem,* 113–28.
49. Joseph A. Fitzmyer, *To Advance the Gospel* (New York: Crossroad, 1981), 15.
50. Joseph A. Fitzmyer, *The Gospel According to Luke I–IX,* vol. 28 of *The Anchor Bible* (Garden City, N.Y.: Doubleday, 1981), 72.
51. For a more detailed discussion of these agreements, see Robert L. Thomas, "An Investigation of the Agreements between Matthew and Luke against Mark," *JETS* 19 (spring 1976): 103–12.
52. E. D. Burton and E. J. Goodspeed, *A Harmony of the Synoptic Gospels in Greek* (Chicago: University of Chicago, 1947), see sec. nos. 17–19, 20, 24, 27–32, 51–54, 66–68, 70f., 76–78, 86–90, 92, 99, 136f., 139, 141, 144, 146, 148, 150, 152–56, 160–64, 170, 172–79, 181.
53. For example, Hawkins, *Horae Synopticae,* 209.
54. Ibid., 150–52.
55. Lumis differs with this calculation. As cited by W. R. Farmer (*The Synoptic Problem* [New York: Macmillan, 1964], 111), he says that on the basis of chance Matthew and Luke could have been expected to agree only half as many times.
56. Cf. Hawkins, *Horae Synopticae,* 143–49.
57. Ibid., 143.
58. Ibid., 137–38.
59. Ibid., 209.
60. Ibid.
61. Farmer, *Synoptic Problem,* 94–95, citing Edwin A. Abbott's 1879 *Encyclopaedia Britannica* in contrast with Abbott's 1901 position expressed in *Diatessarica Part II, The Corrections of Mark Adopted by Matthew and Luke* (London, 1901), 300ff.
62. Streeter, *Four Gospels,* 296–305; cf. Farmer, *Synoptic Problem,* 118–19; 131–32.
63. See Robert L. Thomas, "The Rich Young Man in Matthew," *Grace Theological Journal* 3, no. 2 (fall 1982): 235–46.
64. Ibid., 236–39, 240.
65. Hawkins, *Horae Synopticae,* 210–11.
66. W. G. Kümmel, *Introduction to the New Testament* (Nashville: Abingdon, 1966), 55.
67. Ibid.
68. Ibid., 60.
69. Thomas, "Agreements of Matthew and Luke against Mark," 108–11.
70. William R. Farmer, *The Synoptic Problem, A Critical Analysis* (Dillsboro, N.C.: Western North Carolina, 1976); cf. France, *Matthew,* 30–31.
71. Stein, *Synoptic Problem,* 133.
72. Ibid., 136.
73. Ibid.; Carson, "Matthew," 13–16.
74. Henry Clarence Thiessen, *Introduction to the New Testament* (Grand Rapids: Eerdmans, 1943), 121–27.
75. Tenney, *New Testament Survey,* 142–43.
76. The closest English counterpart to the German *Geschichte* is the word "story." A story can be historically factual, but it can also be fiction. The same is true with the German term. *Redaktionsgeschichte* seeks to distinguish what is purely fiction from what is factual by analyzing the alleged redactional activity of the writer.

77. Silva has mounted an effort to demonstrate that Ned Stonehouse's research in redactional studies antedated those of his liberal counterparts (Moisés Silva, "Ned B. Stonehouse and Redaction Criticism," *Westminster Theological Journal* 40 [1977–1978]: 77–88, 281–303). Silva's efforts in this regard have not gained significant backing, however.

78. This discussion recognizes that many changes in redactional critical views have occurred since the times of the theory's earliest advocates (and are still occurring). Rather than try to capture a single moment in the ever-changing perspectives, the present treatment will derive general characteristics of the movement by examining those responsible for its beginning.

79. Willi Marxsen, *Introduction to the New Testament*, trans. G. Buswell (Philadelphia: Fortress, 1968), 136–42; idem, *Mark the Evangelist*, trans. James Boyce, Donald Juel, and William Poehlmann with Roy A. Harrisville (Nashville: Abingdon, 1969), 30–95; cf. Norman Perrin, *What Is Redaction Criticism?* (Philadelphia: Fortress, 1969), 33–39.

80. Günther Bornkamm, *The New Testament: A Guide to Its Writings*, trans. Reginald H. Fuller and Ilse Fuller (Philadelphia: Fortress, 1973), 57–62; idem, Gerhard Barth, and Heinz Joachim Held, *Tradition and Interpretation in Matthew*, trans. Percy Scott (Philadelphia: Fortress, 1963), 15–57; cf. Perrin, *What Is Redaction Criticism?* 25–28.

81. Hans Conzelmann, *The Theology of St. Luke*, trans. Geoffrey Buswell (New York: Harper, 1960), 9–17, 137–234; cf. Perrin, *What Is Redaction Criticism?* 28–33.

82. Perrin, *What Is Form Criticism?* 41–43.

83. Ibid., 57–62.

84. Ibid., 62–63.

85. Cf. Perrin, *What Is Redaction Criticism?* 42.

86. Cf. Gundry, *Matthew*, 334.

87. Theodore J. Weeden, "The Heresy That Necessitated Mark's Gospel," in *The Interpretation of Mark*, William R. Telford, ed., 2d ed. (Edinburgh, T & T Clark, 1995), 89–104.

88. J. A. Ziesler, "The Transfiguration Story and the Markan Soteriology," *ExpTim* 81 (1969–70): 263–68.

89. P. Carrington, *The Primitive Christian Calendar: A Study in the Making of the Markan Gospel* (Cambridge: University Press, 1952), 31–44, 117–230; M. D. Goulder, *The Evangelist's Calendar* (London: SPCK, 1978), 241–306.

90. Robert H. Gundry, *Mark: A Commentary on His Apology for the Cross* (Grand Rapids: Eerdmans, 1993), 1022–26.

91. Lane, *Mark*, 12–17.

92. Marxsen, *Mark the Evangelist*, 54–216.

93. R. Martin, *Mark, Evangelist and Theologian* (Grand Rapids: Zondervan, 1972), 156–62.

94. M. D. Hooker, "Christology and Methodology," *NTS* 17 (1970–71): 480–87.

95. See chapter 5 above under the heading "Operational Bases of Tradition Criticism."

96. For example, William W. Klein, Craig L. Blomberg, and Robert L. Hubbard, Jr., *Introduction to Biblical Interpretation* (Dallas: Word, 1993), 95; Robert H. Stein, *The Synoptic Problem, An Introduction* (Grand Rapids: Baker, 1987), 217–18; Craig L. Blomberg, *The Historical Reliability of the Gospels* (Downers Grove, Ill.: InterVarsity, 1987), 20; James R. Edwards, "Who Do Scholars Say That I Am?" *Christianity Today* 40, no. 3 (March 4, 1996): 20.

97. Donald A. Hagner, "Interpreting the Gospels: The Landscape and the Quest," *Journal of the Evangelical Theological Society* 24 (1981): 29–32.
98. See under the heading "Arrangement of Material" in the introduction to this volume.
99. See discussion under the heading "Modifying of Material" in the introduction to this volume. Another example of major modification is Stein's theory about changes that Luke made to Mark's account of the Olivet Discourse, which reflect—according to Stein's dating—that Luke wrote his gospel after the A.D. 70 destruction of Jerusalem (Robert H. Stein, *Luke*, in vol. 24 of *The New American Commentary*, David S. Dockery, ed. [Nashville, Tenn.: Broadman, 1992], 25, 512).
100. See the "Introduction" to the volume under the heading "Creation of Material."
101. For example, William L. Lane, *Commentary on the Gospel of Mark*, NIC (Grand Rapids: Eerdmans, 1974), 7. Craig L. Blomberg (*The Historical Reliability of the Gospels* [Downers Grove, Ill.: InterVarsity, 1987], 151–52) calls the Gospels historically reliable, but he means that they are *generally* reliable. He allows for historical errors created by editorial activities, but calls the gospel writers more reliable than ancient secular historians.
102. For illustrations, see below in chapter 9, "Impact of Historical Criticism on Hermeneutics."
103. For illustrations of these "literary signals," see chapter 9, "Impact of Historical Criticism on Hermeneutics."
104. For various arguments for why a harmony is impossible, see "Is a Harmony of the Gospels Legitimate?" in *The NIV Harmony of the Gospels*, ed. Robert L. Thomas (San Francisco: Harper & Row, 1988), 249–51.
105. Gundry, *Matthew*, 639.
106. G. R. Osborne, "Round Four: The Redaction Debate Continues," *Journal of the Evangelical Theological Society* 28, no. 4 (1985): 409.
107. See Thomas and Gundry, "A History of Harmonies," *NIV Harmony of the Gospels*, 254–59; Robert H. Stein, *The Synoptic Problem, An Introduction* (Grand Rapids: Baker, 1987), 15–25.
108. Donald A. Hagner, *Matthew 14–28*, vol. 33B of *Word Biblical Commentary*, gen. eds. David A. Hubbard and Glenn W. Barker (Dallas: Word, 1995), 655.
109. For an example of how to detect what emphasis of Jesus a writer retains, without assuming literary interdependence among the synoptics, see Robert L. Thomas, "The Rich Young Man in Matthew," *Grace Theological Journal* 3, no. 2 (fall 1982): 251–60.
110. For example, Darrell L. Bock, "The Words of Jesus in the Gospels: Live, Jive, or Memorex?" in *Jesus under Fire*, eds. Michael J. Wilkins and J. P. Moreland (Grand Rapids: Zondervan, 1995), 73–99.
111. See below in chapter 11, "Impact of Historical Criticism on the Theological Understanding and Apologetic Value of the Gospels."
112. See below in chapter 9, "Impact of Historical Criticism on Hermeneutics."
113. John Chrysostom, *The Gospel according to Matthew*, Homily I.5. Chrysostom obviously does not mean that the writers never met one another or discussed the life of Christ among themselves, but he specifically says they did not discuss their writing projects with each other.
114. M. M. Thompson, "John, Gospel of," in *Dictionary of Jesus and the Gospels*, ed. Joel B. Green, Scot McKnight, and I. Howard Marshall (Downers Grove, Ill.: InterVarsity, 1992), 370–71.
115. Papias, cited by Eusebius, *H.E.*, 3.39.16; Irenaeus, *Adv. Haer.*, 3.1; Clement

of Alexandria, cited by Eusebius, *H.E.*, 6.14.5; Origen, cited by Eusebius, *H.E.*, 6.25.5; Eusebius, *H.E.*, 3.24.6.

116. Papias, cited by Eusebius, *H.E.*, 3.39.15; Justyn Martyr, *Dial. with Trypho*, cvi; Irenaeus, *Adv. Haer.*, 3.1; Clement of Alexandria, cited by Eusebius, *H.E.*, 2.15.1, 6.14.6; Tertullian, *Adv. Marc.*, 4.5; Origen, cited by Eusebius, *H.E.*, 6.25.5.

117. Justin Martyr, *Dial. with Trypho*, 100.22; *Muratorian Fragment; Anti-Marcionite Prologue to the Third Gospel*; Irenaeus, *Adv. Haer.*, 3.1.2; Tertullian, *Contra Marc.*, 4.2; Clement of Alexandria, *Strom.*, 1.21; idem, cited by Eusebius, *H.E.*, 6.14.5; Origen, cited by Eusebius, *H.E.*, 6.25.6; Eusebius, *H.E.*, 3.24.7.

118. Wayne A. Meeks, "Hypomnemata from an Untamed Sceptic: A Response to George Kennedy," in *The Relationships Among the Gospels*, ed. William O. Walker (San Antonio, Tex.: Trinity University, 1978), 170–71.

119. Theodor Zahn, *Introduction to the New Testament*, trans. John Moore Trout et al. (Grand Rapids: Kregel, 1953), 2:402–3, 421–22.

120. Philip Schaff, *History of the Christian Church* (Grand Rapids: Eerdmans, 1910), 1:598–99, 602. The common redaction critical rejoinder that plagiarism was the rule among ancient historians errs in two respects: (1) early Christian writers commonly credited their sources when quoting or copying from another writer, and (2) gospel writers differ from other ancient historiographers in the high standards of ethics and truthfulness they represent. It was those high morals that have permeated literary standards of modern times. The gospel writers did not cite written sources; they were recording speeches and deeds firsthand.

The Fruits of
Historical Criticism

CHAPTER SEVEN

Literary Dependence
and Luke's Prologue

Paul W. Felix

INTRODUCTION

EACH GOSPEL WRITER BEGINS his gospel differently from the others. Matthew commences his with "the book of the genealogy of Jesus Christ" (Matt. 1:1) and proceeds to trace the Lord's genealogy from Abraham to Joseph. Mark abruptly begins with the words "the beginning of the gospel of Jesus Christ, the Son of God" (Mark 1:1 NASB). The apostle John introduces his gospel with a prologue that unfolds some of the major themes developed through the rest of the book. John's prologue begins with the declaration that Jesus is God: "In the beginning was the Word, and the Word was with God, and the Word was God" (John 1:1). Luke introduces his gospel with a prologue too,[1] but his introduction differs from John's as it does from the other two gospels.[2] Luke 1:1–4 constitutes his prologue.

Luke's prologue is unique for several reasons.[3] First, its literary style stands out among the writings of the New Testament because of its close similarity to contemporary secular writings of the period. The author of the third gospel began his work the same way that other ancient writers did, that is, with a preface that fell into a prescribed format. Luke followed that convention very closely.[4]

A second reason for the uniqueness of Luke's preface lies in the attention that Historical Criticism has focused upon it in its attempt to force the passage to contribute a certain kind of information regarding the origin of the Synoptic Gospels. Among the gospel writers, Luke alone partially divulges his method of research and the nature of his research materials.[5] Historical critics have taken alleged information in the prologue and have fashioned it into a standard for judging theories about the origin of the Gospels.[6]

A third and final reason for the uniqueness of Luke's prologue relates to the second. That is its role in discussions of the Synoptic Problem.[7] Virtually all dialogues on this issue refer to the preface of Luke in one way or the other. The many individuals who hold that Matthew, Mark, and Luke depended on each other in some literary way use Luke's prologue as a basis of proving he used either the gospel of Mark or the gospel of Matthew as one of his sources for research.[8] On the other hand, the few who hold that the first three gospels did not depend on each other in a literary way confirm literary independence by referring to the opening verses of the gospel of Luke.[9]

These last two areas of uniqueness deserve attention when considering the relationship of the first four verses of Luke's gospel to literary dependence and the Synoptic Problem. Since Luke alone tells how his gospel came into existence, the possibility of that impacting discussions of gospel relationships renders it necessary to investigate this passage thoroughly to determine what it contributes to the issue of literary dependence versus independence among the synoptic writers.

The following discussion will undertake this task, first through an exegetical study of Luke 1:1–4 and then through an analysis of the prologue with the specific aim of applying the results of the exegetical process to the particular issue of the Synoptic Problem. A limitation will be made on the discussion of those results to what is relevant in the prologue.

THE INTERPRETATION OF LUKE'S PROLOGUE

An English text[10] of Luke 1:1–4 and a transliterated Greek text within brackets following each word or phrase is as follows:

1Inasmuch as *[epeidēper]* many *[polloi]* have undertaken *[epecheirēsan]* to compile *[anataxasthai]* an account *[diegēsin]* of *[peri]* the things accomplished *[tōn peplērophorēmenōn]* among *[en]* us *[hēmin]*, 2just as *[kathōs]* those who *[hoi]* from *[ap']* the beginning *[archēs]* were *[genomenoi]* eyewitnesses *[autoptai]* and *[kai]* servants *[hypēretai]* of the Word *[tou logou]* have handed them down *[paredosan]* to us *[hēmin]*, 3it seemed fitting *[edoxe]* for me as well *[kamoi]*, having investigated *[parēkolouthēkoti]* everything *[pasin]* carefully *[akribōs]* from the beginning *[anōthen]*, to write *[grapsai]* it out for you *[soi]* in consecutive order *[kathexēs]*, most excellent *[kratiste]* Theophilus *[Theophile]*; 4so that *[hina]* you might know *[epigōs]* the exact truth *[tōn asphaleian]* about *[peri]* the things *[hōn logōn]* you have been taught *[katēchēthēs]*.

The Greek text of the four verses consists of one long sentence. The extended sentence is called "the period" and reflects the elegant style of the preface.[11] The structure includes a protasis (1:1–2) and an apodosis (1:3–4). Both the protasis and the apodosis contain three parallel phrases.[12] "Many" in verse 1 parallels with "for me" in verse 3, "compile an account" in verse 1 compares with "to write it out for you in consecutive order" in verse 3, and "exact truth" in verse 4 answers to "eyewitnesses" in verse 2.[13] The following table reflects the correspondences more graphically:

Luke 1:1–2	Luke 1:3–4
Inasmuch as *many*	it seemed fitting *for me* as well
have undertaken to *compile an account* of the things accomplished among us,	having investigated everything carefully from the beginning, *to write it out for you in consecutive order,* most excellent Theophilus;
just as those who from the beginning were *eyewitnesses* and servants of the Word have handed them down to us,	so that you might know the *exact truth* about the things you have been taught.

As noted earlier, the structure of Luke's introduction closely resembles the prefaces used by ancient Greek writers in their works. Yet, one must avoid the mistake of not taking each word and phrase in the prologue seriously.[14] Luke is not just another secular or ancient writer. He wrote under the superintendence of the Holy Spirit in composing his prologue. Therefore, in keeping with a proper view of inspiration, an adequate exegetical study must regard each word and phrase as important.

An interpretation of Luke's prologue is no simple task. In fact, those who seek to understand this passage face a number of obstacles and challenges as they encounter almost every word and phrase.[15] There are many interpretive issues. But this study's purpose dictates concentration on matters that have a direct bearing upon the issue of literary dependence/independence among the Synoptic Gospels.

An outline of Luke's preface is as follows:

I. The context of Luke's writing project (1:1–2).
   A. The activity of Luke's contemporaries (1:1).
   B. The activity of the eyewitnesses (1:2).
II. The commentary on Luke's writing project (1:3–4).
   A. The credentials of the writer (1:3).
   B. The purpose of the work (1:4).

The Context of Luke's Writing Project (1:1–2)

The activity of Luke's contemporaries (1:1). Before Luke comments on the specifics of his writing project (1:3–4), he takes time to discuss the historical context in which he produced his gospel (1:1–2). Two leading factors led to his creation of the third gospel: first, the literary activity of his contemporaries (1:1); and, second, the communication of eyewitnesses regarding the events about which Luke writes (1:2).

A stately compound conjunction that was frequent in classical Greek and was suitable for issuing a solemn warning begins Luke's preface: *epeidēper* ("inasmuch as"). As frequent as were its occurrences in classical Greek, the conjunction does not occur elsewhere in biblical Greek, neither in the LXX nor in the New Testament.[16] Further, its position at the beginning of the sentence is unusual. It normally introduces a causal clause following a main clause. Luke's use of the conjunction expresses a reason for some fact or condition already known.[17] The cause for the writing of the gospel of Luke is the literary activity of people living during Luke's time and a generation before him. Their writings were foundational for Luke's task of producing a gospel. Somehow earlier efforts to record the words and works of Jesus had either created a need or left a void that placed on Luke the obligation of writing his gospel.

The preface does not identify the earlier writers by name, but simply describes them as being "many" (polloi). That designation raises two critical questions: "how many individuals is Luke referring to?" and "to whom does the expression refer?" In answering these questions, it is important that the interpreter not allow an assumption of literary dependence and his personal opinion about a solution to the Synoptic Problem influence his answer.[18]

Is it even legitimate to ask how many individuals Luke is referring to when he uses the term "many"? Some would say that it is not. They would dismiss the question because ancient speeches and documents employed the term frequently in a formal manner at beginnings of speeches and documents. In such cases, a literal understanding of the word was unnecessary. The emphasis was not on the number of a writer's predecessors, but on the legitimacy of his claims to be associated with them.[19] Even though this may be true in secular writings, the New Testament uses the "many" elsewhere in similar book introductions with a clear-cut emphasis on specific numbers (cf. Acts 1:3; Heb. 1:1).[20] Therefore, it is valid to think of a definite number of individuals.

However, those who agree that the question is legitimate are not unanimous as to the number indicated by "many." Proposals range from three[21] to a larger number that no one knows for sure.[22] Surely Arndt is correct when he says, "How many persons Luke has in mind one cannot say."[23] Yet, this does not rule out the conclusion that the term implies plentiful activity in the production of elementary "gospels."[24] This conclusion harmonizes with the context, which gives the impression that Luke is emphasizing "many" as opposed to a "few."

With regards to the second question ("to whom does the expression refer?"), a complete answer must await an examination of more of the preface. In anticipation of that answer, it is possible to eliminate writers of extant apocryphal gospels since they wrote their works much later.[25]

Epecheirēsan ("Have undertaken") characterizes the literary activity of the "many," that is, Luke's predecessors in writing about Jesus. The word literally means "to put the hand to," "to take in hand," or "to attempt."[26] Two elements comprise this compound word: the preposition epi ("upon") and the noun cheir ("hand"). Epecheirēsan occurs frequently in classical Greek literature, but appears only rarely in the New Testament. Use of the word has produced a lively discussion concerning whether the term is neutral or pejorative. The issue confronting the interpreter is to determine whether Luke views his predecessors in a positive light or as having failed in some way in the task they have put their hands to.

A majority of interpreters favors assigning the term a neutral force.[27] They offer impressive support for their position.[28] First, Luke identifies himself with the literary activities of his contemporaries by saying "for me as well" *(kamoi)* in verse 3.[29] He undertakes the same task as his predecessors. Second, the term is a natural one to use for composing an account.[30] Third, this word is common in the papyri for undertaking a project, in which usages no hint of failure appears.[31] In addition, if the writer wanted to deprecate those who wrote before him, he would not have used the causal conjunction "inasmuch as" *(epeidēper)*, but the concessive "although."[32] The final piece of evidence for this view has to do with the dependence of the accounts written by the "many" upon the witnesses and ministers of the word in verse 2. In Acts, Luke regards the witnesses and ministers of the word quite positively (for example, Acts 1:8, 22; 2:32; 3:15; 26:16).[33]

Despite the impressive case that takes "have undertaken" in a neutral sense, some argue that the verb is pejorative. Several evidences support the negative sense. One is that the term occurs only two other times in the New Testament, each time in Luke's writings (Acts 9:29; 19:13). In both uses it describes unsuccessful attempts.[34] In itself, the word speaks only about an attempt, not about a successful attempt. The context must tell whether the attempt was successful. The early church historian Eusebius viewed attempts of the "many" as unsuccessful when he wrote, "Luke has himself at the beginning of his treatise prefixed the cause which had led him to its composition: showing that many others had somewhat rashly taken it upon them to compose *a narrative* of those *things* of which he had *been fully persuaded*."[35] In other words, "What others have somewhat rashly attempted I [Luke] will remedy. I will correct what those others have written."[36] Though *epecheirēsan* may not be so strongly negative in its reflection on earlier attempts as Eusebius indicates, Luke's preface contains at least a slight allusion to the insufficiency of earlier attempts.[37] Otherwise, Luke would not have undertaken the task of writing his gospel. The existence of it is evident testimonial to that.

In addition, Luke's stress on accuracy and research shows that the previous works needed some improvement.[38] Though the church fathers are not always correct in their interpretations, it is significant to note that prominent individuals like Origen and Jerome also took the term in a negative sense.[39] Besides this, if Luke had been entirely satisfied with what his forerunners had written, he would not have found it necessary to write his gospel.[40] Fitzmyer says the following about Luke in this connection:

> The contrast of himself with them and his pretensions to accuracy, acquaintance, completeness, and order as well as his claim to offer "assurance" *(asphaleia)* suggest that he envisages his task as one needed in the church of his day. Their works seemed perhaps mere attempts to record the tradition about the momentous events that had taken place. They were faced with the problem of handing on a tradition; Luke is conscious of this task too and proposes to do it again, in his own better way.[41]

Deciding between the two views of the meaning of *epecheirēsan* is not easy. But in light of the fact that Luke is going to put great emphasis on his credentials for writing this gospel, it is inescapable that he saw a need to improve upon earlier reports about Jesus. This does not mean that Luke's contemporaries utterly failed at their task. Yet, it is clear that, in the mind of Luke, there was room for improvements. The nature of the improvements surfaces in verse 3.

The "many" put their hands "to compile an account" *(anataxasthai diēgēsin)*. The verb that Luke uses for "to compile" *(anataxasthai)* is a rare one. It has the sense of "to draw up" or "to compile," perhaps to draw up an orderly account in writing in contrast to oral tradition.[42] Yet, the verb implies more than oral tradition or a mere written fixation of oral tradition. It emphasizes the idea of the account being orderly.[43] That would not be applicable to oral recitals of isolated facts. Luke stresses that others had attempted the very thing he was seeking to achieve in writing his gospel.

The term that Luke uses for "an account" *(diēgēsin)* is just as infrequent as is *anataxasthai*. This is the only time *diēgēsin* appears in the New Testament. Arndt states, "It is derived from *hēgeomai*, 'to lead,' and refers to something that takes a person through *(dia)* a series of events."[44] Among ancient historians, *diēgēsin* was a technical expression for different kinds of recounting. The term is broad enough to refer to oral or written accounts.[45] The context would tip the scales in favor of Luke's having written accounts in mind.

A natural question to ask relates to the identity of the earlier accounts. Do they include canonical Matthew and/or Mark? Luke could not have referred to Matthew, for he distinguishes the "many" of verse 1 from the apostolic eyewitnesses of verse 2. Since Matthew was one of those eyewitnesses, Luke could not have had his gospel in mind.[46] On the other hand, Mark was not an apostle. Yet according to tradition, he was an eyewitness (Mark 14:51–52) and wrote under the auspices of the apostle Peter.[47] It is also highly improbable that Luke would have chosen to use the somewhat derogatory "have undertaken" to refer to a work received by the church as one of the essential documents about the life of Jesus.[48] If Matthew or Mark had been one of Luke's sources, he would more likely have given it the recognition of "Scripture," as Paul did for Luke's gospel just a few years later (cf. 1 Tim. 5:18).

According to tradition, Matthew wrote earlier than Luke, but Luke's careful wording makes it clear that he had not seen Matthew's gospel before he wrote his own. Luke may have seen Aramaic material written by Matthew, material referred to as "the oracles" *(ta logia)* by an early church father named Papias, but that writing differed from Matthew's gospel in the Greek language.[49] In all probability, the three Synoptic Gospels writers wrote without having seen the works of each other. That means that the works to which Luke refers are writings whose incompleteness condemned them to extinction as the three canonical gospels spread throughout the early church.

Luke is not explicit about whether he used those now-nonextant written accounts in penning his own gospel, but he probably used every speck of information he could locate to compare with other sources to be sure he had his information correct. However, his primary dependence would have been on the "eyewitnesses and servants of the word." They were principal sources on whom the "many" also depended for their attempts at compiling accounts.

Luke describes the literary activities of his predecessors as centering on "the things accomplished among us" (tōn peplērophorēmenōn en hēmin). When used in reference to persons, "accomplished" (peplērophorēmenōn) means "to persuade fully" or "to convince." In reference to things, as here, it means "fulfilled" or "accomplished."[50] The idea of "fulfilled" fits nicely, for Luke puts emphasis on the fulfillment of God's plan in both Luke and Acts (for example, Luke 1:20, 57; 2:6, 21–22; 4:21; Acts 9:23; 13:25; 24:27). These fulfilled events and time periods refer to the carrying out of God's plan in the world in connection with the person and work of the Lord Jesus Christ.

Luke declares these events to have been fully accomplished "among us" (en hēmin). Whom does Luke have in mind when he uses the pronoun "us"? The answers have ranged from first generation witnesses of God's fulfilled plan all the way to Christendom as a whole. The pronoun undoubtedly includes those who witnessed firsthand the events of the Jesus' life. But it also must include Luke and his contemporaries in the sense that they experienced the continual results of these events.[51]

The activity of the eyewitnesses (1:2). In verse 2, Luke shifts attention from the activity of fellow compilers to that of the earlier generation of eyewitnesses. Individuals who provided the foundation for Luke and his literary predecessors to build on comprise that first generation. Compilation of the earlier accounts was in harmony with the communicative activity of the eyewitnesses ("just as," kathōs). Was this correlation one of strict exactness[52] or general exactness?[53] Strict exactness is improbable because of the unlikelihood that the "many" intended to transmit a word-for-word reproduction of what had been handed down to them. As Evans has noted, "This would deprive 'compiled' of its force."[54] The agreement of the later written accounts with eyewitness reports lies in the area of "the things accomplished" (1:1). That is what the apostles and others handed down and what became the basis for the writings of the "many." Luke thereby affirms the general reliability and soundness of the previous narratives, even while he strongly implies (through his use of epecheirēsan in verse 1 and in his undertaking of a similar project) shortcomings in those accounts.

Luke calls the individuals responsible for initiating the communication "eyewitnesses" (autoptai) and "servants" (hypēretai). These are not two separate groups but one group that has a twofold role. The latter view is preferred not so much because the terms are governed by a single article (hoi). With plural nouns, a single article governing two nouns connected by kai may or may not constitute a single entity.[55] But the position of the participle (*genomenoi*, "were") after the second noun justifies this interpretation. The participle does not separate the two nouns "eyewitnesses" and "servants." Instead, it separates the noun "servants" from the genitive "of the word" (*tou logou*).[56] A further factor favoring a reference to one group instead of two is the position of the prepositional phrase "from the beginning" before the first term "eyewitnesses." That has the syntactical effect of viewing the two nouns as a single entity. In light of these considerations, it is best to see the group as those who began as "eyewitnesses" and then became "servants" of the word.[57]

The word "eyewitnesses" (*autoptai*) occurs only here in the New Testament. As the source of the English medical term "autopsy," *autoptai* literal meaning is "to see with one's own eyes." Luke uses the word to inform his readers that what he and others have written comes straight from people who were directly in contact with events being reported.[58] These "eyewitnesses" are not recent additions to the Christian movement. Rather, they were "from the beginning" (*ap' archēs*) observant participants in the life and ministry of Jesus. That beginning was in particular the baptism of Jesus by John the Baptist (Luke 3:23; cf. Acts 1:21–22; 10:37).[59]

The second term highlights the ministry of these individuals. They were simply servants, helpers, and assistants. Marshall points out, "The term emphasizes that they were not propagandists for their own views of what happened with Jesus but had unreservedly put their persons and work in the service of Jesus' cause."[60] They were ministers "of the word" (*tou logou*); that is, they proclaimed a gospel whose substance was the words and works of Jesus Christ.

Who were these "eyewitnesses and servants"? The group included some of the apostles at least. Luke later notes one of the qualifications for apostleship was to have been an eyewitness from the beginning (Acts 1:21–22). It is clear that these were Luke's predecessors. That Luke was not one of their number is evident from his own description of his task in 1:3–4. That the group included others besides apostles is probable, but their identity is unknown. Because of the content of Luke's first two chapters, one of them may have been the mother of Jesus.

The nature of the activity of the eyewitnesses is described as "have handed them down" (*paredosan*). The verb that Luke uses is a technical term for passing on official tradition, whether orally or in writing, as authoritative teaching.[61] Paul used the verb's cognate noun *paradosis* to refer to Christian tradition that eventually acquired a fixed verbal form.[62] He instructed the Thessalonian church to hold fast to the "traditions" (*paradoseis*) they had been taught (2 Thess. 2:15). The eyewitnesses about whom Luke speaks made it their business to pass on what they saw and knew, thereby laying the foundation for a much larger body of tradition. And they passed it on to those whom Luke identifies as "us." This term does not allude to the same "us" as in verse 1. The personal pronoun in verse 2 refers to Luke, his literary predecessors, and other unidentifiable Christians.[63] In other words, its scope is narrower in verse 2.

The Commentary on Luke's Writing Project (1:3-4)

The credentials of the writer (1:3). The first two verses of the prologue focus on the writing activities of others (1:1-2). Next Luke describes to the reader his own literary undertaking (1:3-4). In verse 3 he presents his credentials for launching such a major task as his gospel turned out to be. As pointed out earlier, this verse comprises the main clause and apodosis of the sentence of which "inasmuch as many have undertaken" (vv. 1-2) is the protasis. Verse 4 gives the purpose of Luke's undertaking, which is also the reason why his monumental project is worth the effort.

In light of the literary activity of his predecessors (1:1) and the transmittal activity of the eyewitnesses (1:2), Luke put his hand to a task similar to what others had done, or as he says, "It seemed fitting for me as well" (1:3). He made a personal decision to involve himself in a venture similar to those of the "many." Did this resolve of Luke imply a certain superiority in comparison to the efforts of the "many"? Despite the fact that Luke does not contrast himself with his predecessors, and even honors them,[64] he does claim a certain advantage they did not have. This is evident first of all in that there was no need to add another collection to the narratives concerning Jesus, if Luke felt he had nothing new to contribute.[65] He ranks himself with the others as possessing the same advantages as they, but implies he is really better positioned than they in some way.[66] Furthermore, his scrupulous description of his credentials argues that he is really better situated than those who wrote before.[67] He did not confine himself simply to collecting bare apostolic traditions, but took the necessary steps to select, supplement, arrange, and check the materials furnished through oral reports. Discussion above has excluded canonical gospels from the earlier materials available to him, removing any possible derogatory implications regarding them.

"Having investigated" *(parēkolouthēkoti)* sums up Luke's qualifications for undertaking such a work. The Greek verb means literally "to follow along a thing in mind," "to trace carefully," or "to accompany." These meanings frequent the pages of ancient Greek literature.[68] The author's use of the perfect participle of this verb has drawn much attention.[69] The present discussion will center on the two major views. The first one holds that the word refers to following closely the progress of certain events, so that it means to keep up with a movement. In this sense, Luke depicts himself as somehow keeping in touch with the events as they occurred. This interpretation emphasizes the literal meaning of the word. Also implied in this view is that Luke did not investigate anything; he simply followed along as events unfolded.[70] In other words, Luke was one of the eyewitnesses and servants of the word. The other view interprets the word as referring to an investigation of past events. The approach takes the word in a figurative sense of mentally following along beside the events.[71]

An inherent weakness of the former view lies in the meaning it must assign "from the beginning" *(anōthen)* in 1:3, for it is clear that Luke was not an eyewitness of Jesus' baptism and other early events of His life. Advocates of the view assign the meaning "a long time" to the phrase, but this is impossible.[72] It is better to give a meaning similar to "from the beginning" *(ap' archēs)* in verse 2, although the starting point for "the beginning" is different in the two cases. Also, the idea of an individual being *intimately* associated "carefully" *(akribōs)* does not register a good sense.[73] Furthermore, the author distinguishes himself from the eyewitnesses in the immediate context. Luke clarifies that he is not an eyewitness, but is dependent on them for his information.[74]

The strengths of the latter interpretation further confirm that *parēkolouthēkoti* is referring to a following of past events through research. This was the meaning in such ancient writers as Josephus and Nicomachus.[75] The concept also fits Luke's remarks about his investigation in the remainder of verse 3.

Luke expands upon his qualifications for this task by making four comments about the procedures he utilized. First, he investigated "everything" *(pasin)*. He was comprehensive and thorough in studying the subject matter. He carefully sought out anything available on the subject and weighed it carefully in preparation for writing. Second, he did his work "carefully" *(akribōs)*. This refers not only to his method of writing, but also to the quality of his research. He claims accuracy for his findings. Third, the starting point for his research was "from the beginning" *(anōthen)*. As stated above, some understand this as a reference to how long Luke worked at his project.[76] But it is better to take the adverb as synonymous with the prepositional phrase "from the beginning" in verse 2.[77] The presence of the birth narratives following the prologue would also argue for this interpretation. Luke's investigation went back to the birth stories as its starting point.

The fourth comment about Luke's research relates to its intended result: "to write it out in consecutive order" *(grapsai kathexēs)*. He wanted his work to be in "consecutive order." What does Luke mean by "consecutive order"? The term *kathexēs* means "in order, one thing after another" (cf. Acts 11:4; 18:23) or "as follows, the following" (Luke 8:1; Acts 3:24).[78] The natural meaning would be chronological order. But Stein, for example, argues a case that Luke's order is literary-logical by pointing out sequences of narrative in the gospel that are not chronological.[79] Yet, allowing for details that may not be strictly in temporal order, the gospel does follow a broadly chronological arrangement in treating the life of Christ.[80] The debate on the type of order indicated by *kathexēs* is widespread,[81] but it is hard to deny compelling evidence provided by a lexical study of this word. Such a study leads to only one conclusion: Luke is referring to some type of chronological and historical order. The use of the word and its cognates by Luke himself is the best evidence of that (Luke 8:1; Acts 11:4; 18:23).

The recipient of this monumental work is "most excellent Theophilus" *(kratiste Theophile)*. The epithet that is translated "most excellent" often applies to individuals of rank in the sequel to this gospel. In Acts, it refers to Felix (23:26; 24:3) and Festus (26:25). Yet, Theophilus is not necessarily a person of rank (cf. Acts 1:1, where his name lacks the adjective). One cannot be dogmatic in concluding that Theophilus held a high position.

But Luke clearly held him in high esteem. This was probably due to the recipient's social standing. Attempts at identifying Theophilus as a symbolic name for "pious Christians" are tenuous. Frequent occurrence of this name for both Jews and Greeks from the third century B.C. onward make such an association highly improbable.[82] Also, the vocative rendered "most excellent" argues that a particular person is in mind.[83] Even though the spiritual status of Theophilus has no bearing on the Synoptic Problem, it is best to view him as either a believer or a person with a serious interest in Christianity.

The purpose of the work (1:4). Assuming the traditional authorship of the third gospel,[84] Luke's credentials for writing his gospel (1:3) are impressive, but his purpose for doing so (1:4) was also worthy. He undertook to compile an account of Jesus' life so that the recipient of the account "might know the exact truth" *(epigōs tōn asphaleian)* concerning the things he had been taught. Thus, this gospel in the hands of Theophilus demonstrated the truthful quality of the instruction he had received. To accomplish this, Luke must have done a thorough job of research and writing.

THE IMPLICATIONS OF LUKE'S PROLOGUE

What relation do the opening verses of Luke's gospel have to the issue of literary dependence/independence among the gospel writers? Does Luke acknowledge his dependence in a literary way upon Matthew or Mark? Neither his prologue nor any other single passage can completely resolve the issue. Yet a careful interpretation of Luke's prologue results in important information that must be part of that discussion. Frequent references to that preface to prove that he used the gospel of Mark or Matthew as one of his sources of research necessitate some attention to it. Does an exegesis of Luke 1:1–4 substantiate such a claim?

The meaning of the prologue of Luke has several ramifications with regards to the issue of the interrelationship of Matthew, Mark, and Luke. First, the opening verses of Luke's gospel do not indicate, as many purport they do, that its author used any canonical gospel (namely, Matthew or Mark) as a source. Of course, it is not possible to deny that Luke used sources, but to claim that these sources included the gospel of either Matthew or Mark is merely an assumption read into the text of the prologue by an interpreter. Nothing in the four verses identifies one of the other Synoptic Gospels as a source. Those who use Luke's prologue to justify a written gospel as a source read that into the passage without adequate exegetical evidence.[85] In fact, some who believe in literary dependence between the first three gospels readily admit that fact.[86]

Second, the preface of the third gospel does not state that its author is directly dependent on two or three sources such as Mark, Q, and L. Luke 1:1 establishes the existence of "many" literary predecessors.[87] The relationship of these writings to Luke's research is ambiguous in the eyes of some.[88] Since Luke acknowledges thorough research in his preparation, it is a reasonable conclusion that he examined the writings that preceded his. But it is unwarranted to conclude that he relied on these heavily, in other words, with the type of reliance mandated by those who advocate literary dependence on another canonical gospel. Luke had many sources, both oral and written. For him to depend primarily on one or two of them does not harmonize with his methodology of a thorough examination of Christ's life in composing his gospel. The extensive research that Luke claims (cf. 1:3) is not necessary for a person who is simply copying or editing an earlier writing. His self-described meticulous methodology argues against that simple a procedure.[89]

Third, Luke's prologue argues against his using either Matthew or Mark as a source. Several lines of reasoning substantiate this. It is unlikely that Matthew or Mark was one of the "many" who were his literary predecessors. The "many" (1:1) did not include the apostle Matthew, for he was among "those who from the beginning were eyewitnesses and servants of the word" (1:2). And even though Mark was not an apostle, Luke probably would have considered him to be an eyewitness. The two were acquaintances (cf. Col. 4:10, 14; Philem. 24), so Luke knew at least what modern New Testament scholars know about Mark, namely, that he was an eyewitness to some events in Jesus' life and that he was closely familiar with the preaching and teaching of Peter.[90] Conceivably, Mark could have been among Luke's "eyewitnesses and servants of the word" on whose oral reports he depended.

There is additional evidence that supports Luke 1:1–4 in its argument against Luke using the gospel of either Matthew or Mark as a source. Luke states that conducting a thorough investigation was part of his method of operation in preparing for the writing of his gospel. Remember too that Luke saw some inadequacy[91] in accounts done before his with which he was familiar. Would Luke question the writing of one he knew to be an apostle (cf. Luke 6:13–15)? Would he sense the need to investigate the writing of Mark, whose close acquaintance with Peter he well knew. It is implausible that Luke would do a thorough investigation on a document that was written by an apostle or one so close to an apostle.

Furthermore, it is highly unlikely that Luke would consider either Matthew's or Mark's gospel as unsuitable to give to Theophilus to furnish him with the exact truth concerning the things he had been taught.[92] The authors of both of these gospels considered them sufficient to be given to the church independently, rather than packaged as a trilogy. Likewise, the use of these two gospels in the history of the church has demonstrated their ability individually to stand on their own in declaring the good news about the words and works of Jesus Christ.

A fourth implication of Luke's introduction relates to its author's special attention to writing out "in consecutive order" (1:3) the details of Christ's life and ministry. Though dogmatism is impossible, it is highly probable that this phrase refers to some type of chronological order. One of the arguments used by proponents of literary dependency among the first three gospels is that Matthew and Luke followed the order of events in Mark.[93] If, for the sake of argument, this is the case, then Luke did not need to highlight this feature of his gospel, since it was also true (even more so) of the gospel of Mark. The implication of the phrase "in consecutive order" is that this was not a distinguishing trait of the writings of the "many." But it has to have been if Luke was dependent on Mark for the order of events in the life of Christ.

A final ramification of the prologue is that it provides the reader with insight into some possible sources that Luke used. His use of written sources is probable. As part of his "investigation," he checked these resources for accuracy. Luke also relied upon the testimonies of eyewitnesses. The form of these testimonies was more than likely oral as opposed to written. As a companion of the apostle Paul, Luke had several opportunities to contact those who were eyewitnesses from the beginning and servants of the word. His relationship with Paul also afforded him occasions to discuss matters with Paul.[94]

CONCLUSION

Luke 1:1–4 is significant in a study of the origins of the canonical gospels, as well as having important input regarding the Synoptic Problem. In order for the verses to have their full say in the discussion, their interpretation must be accurate. Too often, an individual view about literary dependence has dictated or been a part of the meaning assigned to Luke's prologue. The proper approach, and the one that this study has attempted to follow, is to understand first the meaning of the verses grammatically and historically. Then, the interpreter must allow the meaning of the passage to have its impact on the issue of interrelationships of Matthew, Mark, and Luke.

The impact of a proper interpretation of Luke's preface has major implications for those who hold to literary dependence among the first three gospels. This is not to suggest that the opening verses of Luke's gospel alone solve the Synoptic Problem. But they do clarify some issues involved. They rule out certain proposed solutions or suggest that no such problem exists because no literary dependence exists. One eliminated theory is that Luke used the gospel of Mark as a source. Another discarded theory is that he used the gospel of Matthew as a source. Exegetically, the use of Luke 1:1–4 to support the idea that a relationship of literary dependence exists among the gospels written by Matthew, Mark, and Luke is quite improbable.

ENDNOTES

1. "Prologue," "preface," and "introduction" are used interchangeably in the following discussion.
2. Craig A. Evans, *Luke* (Peabody, Mass.: Hendrickson, 1990), 17; Joseph A. Fitzmyer, *The Gospel According to Luke I–IX*, vol. 28 of *Anchor Bible Dictionary* (Garden City, N.Y.: Doubleday, 1981), 287; Walter Liefield, "Luke," in vol. 8 of *The Expositor's Bible Commentary*, gen. ed. Frank E. Gaebelein (Grand Rapids: Zondervan, 1984), 821.
3. Several years ago Cadbury noted the importance of the prologue of Luke to biblical studies. He wrote, "In the study of the earliest Christian history no passage has had more emphasis laid upon it than the brief preface of Luke.

It is the only place in the synoptic gospels where the consciousness of authorship is expressed, containing as it does the only reference outside the gospel of John to the origin or purpose of the evangelists record. It has naturally been repeatedly treated in special monographs, as well as in introductions and commentaries, and has been cited in connection with every problem of early Christian literature" (Henry J. Cadbury, "Commentary on the Preface of Luke," *The Beginning of Christianity*, ed. F. J. Foakes Jackson and Kirsopp Lake [Grand Rapids: Baker, 1979], 2:489).

4. I. Howard Marshall, *Commentary on Luke* (Grand Rapids: Eerdmans, 1978), 39. For a more detailed discussion on the use of prologues by secular writers of the time, see C. F. Evans, *Saint Luke* (Philadelphia: Trinity, 1990), 116–20; Fitzmyer, *Luke I–IX*, 288.

5. Cf. Ray Summers, *Commentary on Luke* (Waco, Tex.: Word, 1972), 19.

6. For example, Plummer has written, "This prologue contains all that we really know respecting the composition of early narratives of the life of Christ, and it is the test by which theories as to the origin of our Gospels must be judged. No hypothesis is likely to be right which does not harmonize with what is told us here" (Alfred Plummer, *A Critical and Exegetical Commentary on the Gospel According to S. Luke*, ICC [Edinburgh: T & T Clark, 1896], 2).

7. A simple definition of the Synoptic Problem is as follows: "The difficulty encountered in devising a scheme of literary dependence to account for the combinations of similarities and dissimilarities has been labelled the *Synoptic Problem*" (Robert L. Thomas and Stanley N. Gundry, *A Harmony of the Gospels* [Chicago: Moody, 1978], 274).

8. Numerous books and commentaries are the basis for this observation. Examples of those works include Marshall, *Luke*, 41; Robert H. Stein, *Luke* (Nashville: Broadman, 1992), 63; John M. Creed, *The Gospel According to St. Luke* (London: Macmillan, 1957), 3; William F. Arndt, *The Gospel According to St. Luke* (St. Louis: Concordia, 1956), 39; William R. Farmer, *The Gospel of Jesus* (Louisville: Westminster/John Knox Press, 1994), 25–38.

9. For example, Eta Linnemann, *Is There a Synoptic Problem?* (Grand Rapids: Baker, 1992), 190; Thomas and Gundry, *Harmony*, 19.

10. All Scripture quotations are from the New American Standard Bible.

11. "The period" is "the organization of a considerable number of clauses and phrases into a well-rounded unity." Its use in the New Testament is rare, but the construction occurs frequently in Hebrews (F. Blass and A. Debrunner, *A Greek Grammar of the New Testament and Other Early Christian Literature*, trans. Robert W. Funk [Chicago: University of Chicago Press, 1961], §464).

12. Fitzmyer, *Luke I–IX*, 288.

13. Stein, *Luke*, 63.

14. Dillon commits this mistake when he writes, "The exegete is inevitably tempted to extract from the concise, somewhat ornamental phraseology of the passage more of a self-portrait than the author meant to give. Just as with ecclesiastical pronouncements which hew strictly to conventional formulas, here too, virtually any viewpoint can be justified by working the language beyond its wonted limits" (Richard J. Dillon, "Previewing Luke's Project from His Prologue [Luke 1:1–4]," *Catholic Biblical Quarterly* 43 [1981]: 205–6).

15. A number of writers have expressed this sentiment. An example is John Nolland, who has written, "Despite Luke's careful composition, the sense of

almost every element of the prologue has been disputed" (*Luke 1:1–9:20*, vol. 35A of *Word Biblical Commentary* [Dallas: Word, 1989], 5).

16. Plummer, *Luke*, 2.
17. Fitzmyer, *Luke I–IX*, 290–91.
18. Too many commentators are guilty of discussing the meaning of "many" in light of their solution to the Synoptic Problem. Inevitably—if they think that the gospel writers depended on each other, thereby creating the Synoptic Problem—results of their exegesis matches their conclusion about the nature of literary dependence and colors the identity and number of the "many" they assign. Pate, among others, exemplifies this when he writes, "Who the 'many' were is not specified, but probably included at the very least Mark's gospel, a collection of the sayings of Jesus (Q), and Luke's own special material" (C. Marvin Pate, *Moody Gospel Commentary: Luke* [Chicago: Moody, 1995], 43).
19. Marshall, *Luke*, 41. Stein adopts the same position. He views "many" functioning as a "topos" (in other words, a commonplace notion or stereotyped expression), thereby eliminating any special emphasis on the word (Robert H. Stein, "Luke 1:1–4 and *Traditionsgeschichte*," *Journal of the Evangelical Theological Society* 26, no. 4 (December 1983): 422.
20. In Acts 1:3, *pollois* indicates the large number of "sure signs" by which Jesus showed Himself alive repeatedly over a period of forty days following His resurrection (cf. Richard N. Longenecker, "The Acts of the Apostles," in *Expositor's Bible Commentary*, gen. ed. Frank E. Gaebelein [Grand Rapids: Zondervan, 1981], 254). In Heb. 1:1, the prefixing of the adverbs *polymerōs* and *polytropōs* with *poly-* (from the adjective *polys*) indicates the many parts and the many ways God used to communicate His revelation in the Old Testament (cf. Marcus Dods, "The Epistle to the Hebrews," in *Expositor's Greek Testament*, ed. W. Robertson Nicoll [Grand Rapids: Eerdmans, 1956], 247–48).
21. Fitzmyer is certain that the term must mean at least three persons, but not necessarily limited to three. Yet his solution to the Synoptic Problem has obviously influenced his conclusion. He states, "Luke is dependent on the Markan source, the source 'Q,' and a source, not necessarily written, which is called 'L'" (*Luke I–IX*, 66).
22. Archibald Thomas Robertson, *Word Pictures in the New Testament*, 6 vols. (Grand Rapids: Baker, 1930), 2:3.
23. Arndt, *St. Luke*, 39.
24. Bruce states, "The term is not an exaggeration, but to be taken strictly as implying extensive activity in the production of rudimentary 'Gospels'" (Alexander B. Bruce, "The Synoptic Gospels," *The Expositor's Greek Testament*, ed. W. Robertson Nicoll [Grand Rapids: Eerdmans, 1974], 1:459). Lenski agrees with this when he writes, "How many are included in *polloi* we have no means of knowing, but quite a number must be referred to" (R. C. H. Lenski, *The Interpretation of St. Luke* [Minneapolis: Augsburg, 1946], 24).
25. Plummer, *Luke*, 2.
26. Ibid., 2.
27. For example, Darrell L. Bock, *Luke 1:1–9:50*, ed. Moisés Silva (Grand Rapids: Baker, 1994), 56; Marshall, *Luke*, 40–41; Fitzmyer, *Luke I–IX*, 291; Stein, *Luke*, 63.
28. Ned B. Stonehouse (*The Witness of Luke to Christ* [Grand Rapids: Eerdmans, 1951], 31–32) gives a good representation of the evidence for the neutrality of the term.

29. Stein, "Luke 1:1–4," 423.
30. Darrell L. Bock, "Understanding Luke's Task: Carefully Building on Precedent (Luke 1:1–4)," *Criswell Theological Review* 5, no. 2 (1991): 188.
31. Robertson, *Word Pictures*, 2:3. The passages cited by Moulton and Milligan (cf. J. H. Moulton and G. Milligan, *The Vocabulary of the Greek Testament* [Grand Rapids: Eerdmans, 1974]) confirm the neutrality of the term according to Bock (*Luke 1:1–9:50*, 55).
32. Pate, *Luke*, 43.
33. Stein, *Luke*, 63.
34. C. F. Evans, *St. Luke*, 123.
35. Eusebius *Ecclesiastical History* 3.24.15.
36. A paraphrase of Eusebius' words by William Hendriksen, *Exposition of the Gospel According to Luke*, in New Testament Commentary (Grand Rapids: Baker, 1978), 54–55.
37. F. Godet, *A Commentary on the Gospel of St. Luke*, trans. from 2d French ed. by E. W. Shalders, 2 vols. (Edinburgh: T & T Clark, n.d.), 1:55.
38. Fitzmyer, *Luke I–IX*, 292.
39. C. F. Evans, *St. Luke*, 123.
40. Creed, *St. Luke*, 3; cf. James Orr, *The Resurrection of Jesus* (Cincinnati: Jennings & Graham, n.d.), 70–72.
41. Fitzmyer, *Luke I–IX*, 291–92.
42. Marshall, *Luke*, 41. The noun for "an account" (*diēgēsin*) does not necessarily exclude a reference to oral tradition (Fitzmyer, *Luke I–IX*, 292). See below.
43. I. I. Du Plessis, "Once More: The Purpose of Luke's Prologue (LK I 1–4)," *Novum Testamentum* 16, no. 4 (1974): 262–63.
44. Arndt, *St. Luke*, 39.
45. Bock, "Understanding Luke's Task," 189.
46. Godet, *St. Luke*, 1:56.
47. Ibid., 1:57.
48. Ibid.
49. Ibid., 56. Matthew probably wrote his Greek gospel after leaving the Aramaic-speaking territory of the Jews, and did so not too long before Luke researched for his gospel. Because of distance and timing and because of slow communications of the time, Matthew's work in Greek was unavailable to Luke, who sought out sources in the area where Jesus lived and ministered, but not throughout the Mideast. Luke did not have access to information, for example, from Antioch, the city where Matthew perhaps composed his Greek gospel. See chapter 1 of *The Jesus Crisis* for further discussion of ancient tradition regarding the origin of the Gospels.
50. Plummer, *Luke*, 3.
51. For a detailed discussion on this matter, consult Richard J. Dillon, *From Eye-Witness to Ministers of the Word* (Rome: Biblical Institute Press, 1978), 271–72. In particular, see his discussion about the perfect tense of *peplērophorēmenōn* with its inclusion of abiding results of completed action.
52. Plummer, *Luke*, 3.
53. C. F. Evans, *St. Luke*, 125.
54. Ibid., 125.
55. Daniel B. Wallace, *Greek Grammar beyond the Basics* (Grand Rapids: Zondervan, 1996), 278. Of the five possibilities when the substantives are plural, the present combination would fall in the category of both groups

being identical (cf. ibid., 281–83) because of placement of the participle *genomenoi* and of the phrase *ap' archēs*. See below.
56. Fitzmyer, *Luke I–IX*, 294.
57. Fitzmyer's discussion of this issue is helpful (*Luke I–IX*, 294).
58. Earle E. Ellis, *The Gospel of Luke* (Grand Rapids: Eerdmans, 1966), 65.
59. For further elaboration, see Plummer, *Luke*, 3 and Nolland, *Luke 1–9:20*, 7. John 15:27; 16:4 verifies that this is the beginning of which Luke speaks.
60. Marshall, *Luke*, 42.
61. The verb also occurs in Mark 7:13; Acts 6:14; 1 Cor. 11:2, 23; 15:3; 2 Peter 2:21; Jude 3 (cf. Marshall, *Luke*, 41–42).
62. Friedrich Büchel, *"didōmi, dōron, k. t. l.," TDNT*, 2:171–73.
63. "The eyewitnesses and ministers of the Word delivered the gospel matters 'to us,' i.e., to the Christians in general, including the many and also Luke" (Lenski, *St. Luke*, p. 28).
64. Bock, *Luke 1:1–9:50*, 59. Plummer states, "He does not blame the 'many'; he desires to imitate and supplement them. It is their attempts that encourage him to write. What they have done he may do, and perhaps he may be able to improve upon their work" (Plummer, *Luke*, 4).
65. Godet, *St. Luke*, 1:60.
66. Fitzmyer, *Luke I–IX*, 296.
67. Godet, *St. Luke*, 60; Fitzmyer, *Luke I–IX*, 296.
68. Robertson, *Word Pictures*, 2:6; Marshall, *Luke*, 42.
69. For a full treatment of this subject see the following: Henry J. Cadbury, "The Knowledge Claimed in Luke's Preface," *The Expository Times* 24 (1922): 401–22; A. T. Robertson, "The Implications in Luke's Preface," *The Expository Times* 35 (1924): 319–21; John Wenham, "The Identification of Luke," *The Evangelical Quarterly* 63:1 (1991): 16–32. Various commentaries also furnish helpful information on this subject (for example, Marshall, Fitzmyer, and Plummer).
70. Cadbury, "Knowledge Claimed," 401–21.
71. This is the popular view (Bock, "Understanding Luke's Task," 193–94; Robertson, "Implications," 319).
72. Stonehouse points out the weakness of Cadbury's argument that the term means a "long time" (*Witness of Luke*, 36).
73. Fitzmyer, *Luke I–IX*, 297.
74. Ibid., 297.
75. Nolland, *Luke 1:1–9:20*, 9.
76. Marshall gives this as a possible meaning (*Luke*, 42–43).
77. Acts 26:4–5 is an example that would argue this point (Bock, "Understanding Luke's Task," 194).
78. Marshall, *Luke*, 43.
79. Robert H. Stein, *Luke*, vol. 24 of *The New American Commentary*, gen. ed. David S. Dockery (Nashville, Tenn.: Broadman, 1992), 65.
80. Marshall, *Luke*, 43; Bock, *Luke 1:1–9:50*, 62.
81. A good summary of the debate appears in an article: Gregory J. Lockwood, "The Reference to Order in Luke's Preface," *Concordia Theological Quarterly* 59, no. 1–2 (January–April 1995): 101–4.
82. Nolland, *Luke 1:1–9:20*, 10.
83. Bock, *Luke 1:1–9:50*, 63.
84. Some question Lukan authorship of the third gospel (cf. Fitzmyer, *Luke I–IX*, 35–59), but the present study accepts it on the basis of strong testimony from the ancient church and the "we" sections in Acts.

THE FRUITS OF HISTORICAL CRITICISM

85. Stein is one who does this in his work on the Synoptic Problem (Robert H. Stein, *The Synoptic Problem* [Grand Rapids: Baker, 1987], 29–44).
86. For example, "Not Luke's statement about his relationship to these preexisting Gospels, but the patterns of similarity and dissimilarity between the Synoptic Gospels as we have them, have convinced the world of scholarship that there is dependence, almost certainly of a literary kind, between the three Gospels" (Nolland, *Luke 1:1–9:20*, xxix).
87. Linnemann's position is that the accounts of the "many" were exclusively oral: "Literally, Luke states that many had undertaken to develop a lengthy narration (description) of Jesus' life. There is no hint that such narration was extant in written form. To translate *anataxasthai* (from *anatassomai*, which the NIV translates 'draw up') in Luke 1:1 as 'write' or 'compose' is misleading" (*Synoptic Problem*, 190). Her point is the same, however: neither Matthew nor Mark were among the "many."
88. Some commentators suggest the possibility that the prologue does not say one way or the other whether Luke used the literary works of his contemporaries. Evans comments, "Thus, even if the mention of the 'many' who had previously written accounts of the Christian events is more than simply conventional, Luke does not indicate whether he had read or used them" (C. F. Evans, *St. Luke*, 15). Arndt concurs with this statement when he says, "While he speaks of compositions about Christ that had come into existence prior to his own writing, and while he states that these productions were intended to set forth the reports made by the original apostles, there is no express declaration that he availed himself of either one of these possible sources" (Arndt, *St. Luke*, 8).
89. Paul Benware, *Luke* (Chicago: Moody, 1985), 19.
90. Geldenhuys has written, "It is, moreover, noteworthy that Luke was very intimately associated with Mark. The latter is the author of the second Gospel and had himself very probably been an eyewitness of at least some events in the life of Jesus. In any case he was an intimate follower of Peter, and it is generally recognised that his Gospel is mainly a rendering of Peter's preaching concerning Jesus" (Norval Geldenhuys, *Commentary on the Gospel of Luke* [Grand Rapids: Eerdmans, 1954], 24).
91. Recall the slight pejorative force of *epecheirēsan* in 1:1 and Luke's improved perspective in 1:3.
92. Thomas and Gundry, *Harmony*, 19.
93. Caird, who is a staunch supporter of some type of documentary connection between the Gospels, has this to say: "Matthew and Luke have abbreviated, polished, corrected; but even so, in the parallel passages, they still reproduce respectively 51 percent and 53 percent of Mark's actual words, and they follow his order so closely that there is only one small incident which is differently placed in all three Gospels" (G. B. Caird, *The Gospel of St. Luke*, [Baltimore: Penguin, 1968], 18). Wenham, coming from a different perspective, agrees with Luke's use of the chronology of the gospel of Mark. He comments, "Perhaps Luke's *kathexēs* (1:3) may suggest that he too was aware of Mark's interest in chronological order. If Luke knew Matthew (as I am inclined to believe), it is nonetheless Mark's order that he follows with great fidelity" (John Wenham, *Redating Matthew, Mark & Luke* [Downers Grove: InterVarsity, 1992], 107).
94. For a good discussion on Luke's oral sources, see William Hendriksen, *Exposition of the Gospel According to Luke* (Grand Rapids: Baker, 1978), 28.

CHAPTER EIGHT

Impact of Historical Criticism on Gospel Interpretation: A Test Case

Kelly Osborne

THIS CHAPTER WILL ANALYZE Luke 18:18–23, which records Jesus' encounter with the rich ruler. The goal is to examine how Historical Criticism of the Synoptic Gospels has affected evangelical interpretation of Jesus' words and deeds. But before considering this matter in detail, an historical overview will be conducted of commentaries on the first three gospels to furnish essential background information.

HISTORICAL BACKGROUND

A sampling of post-Reformation works commenting on the rich ruler mentioned in Luke begins with John Calvin, who treats the Synoptic Gospels as a "continuous line" or "harmony." He provides for his readers a "useful shortcut" by commenting in the same place on all three versions of the story.[1] This kind of "harmony"[2] of the Gospels is not found in all commentaries prior to the rise of Source Criticism and its influence.[3] But authors such as Calvin tended to treat harmonistically passages that have parallels in one or both of the other Synoptic Gospels. This meant that the commentator considered the separate parallel accounts of a given passage and endeavored to fit the various data in each together into a noncontradictory whole, that is, harmoniously or harmonistically. For studying the person, actions, and words of Jesus, that approach yields a more complete and detailed picture, and ultimately, one hopes, leads to "a deeper understanding of [Him], His life, death, and resurrection."[4]

For example, Thomas Scott's commentary in its numerous editions before 1851 has extensive comments under the Matthean version of the rich young man (19:16–30 = Mark 10:17–31 = Luke 18:18–30), but very little under the parallel section in Mark, and even less for the Lukan passage. Scott dealt with most of the relevant material in the notes on Matthew's text.[5] Such English-language commentaries on the Greek text as Dean Alford's New Testament commentary and the *Expositor's Greek Testament* follow much the same pattern,[6] even though, by the time the latter was published in 1897, Source Criticism of the Synoptic Gospels was already taking root in Great Britain.[7]

About this time (1896), Plummer's critical commentary on Luke appeared.[8] He accepted a form of Markan priority. For example, in his notes on 18:18–30, Plummer occasionally refers to Lukan omissions or insertions to explain the writer's alleged use of his Markan source. Nevertheless, traces remain of the more traditional tendency toward harmonization.[9] In just over a decade later, however, W. C. Allen's commentary on Matthew in the same series appeared and was replete with references to the Gospel's revisions of Mark. The more traditional harmonistic approach had essentially disappeared.[10] Clearly, a major shift in scholarly approach to the Gospels was in process, one that eschewed a harmonistic approach to the Synoptic Gospels in favor of one that identified the sources for each writer's work and the manner in which he copied, modified, or otherwise used those sources.[11]

Nowhere is this change in approach illustrated more dramatically than in the publication of two different works on Luke's gospel in the Cambridge Greek Testament for Schools and Colleges. In 1921, Cambridge University Press reprinted the commentary by F. W. Farrar, which had originally appeared in 1881. When commenting on Luke 18:18–30, the author follows a harmonistic approach to the passage in comparing it with Matthew and/or Mark and ignores the results of Source Criticism.[12] But a mere twelve years later, H. K. Luce's comments on the same passage not only emphasize Luke's "use" of Mark, but also endorse a liberal view of the person of Christ.[13] Other English-language commentaries of about this same time likewise place a great deal of emphasis on Source Criticism.[14]

After World War II, a concerted effort by evangelicals worldwide began to cultivate scholarship aimed at being both conservative in theological outlook and critically informed. One of the results was the launching of the New International Commentary series [NIC], initially under the editorship of N. B. Stonehouse, then F. F. Bruce, and currently G. D. Fee.[15] The initial trickle of postwar evangelical commentaries on the Synoptic Gospels grew in the 1970s with the publication of two other NIC works,[16] as well as others[17] It continued unabated in the 1980s and 1990s.[18] Every one among this flood of evangelical commentators assumes the Two-Source Theory as the correct explanation of the origin of the Synoptic Gospels.[19]

With such a strong evangelical consensus of opinion favoring the Two-Source Theory over the last half century, discovering whether the theory has affected evangelical interpretation of the Synoptic Gospels is important. An examination of the rich ruler incident recorded in Luke 18:18–30 will help answer that question. That portion of Scripture is fitting to consider for the following three reasons. First, with its parallels in Matthew 19:16–30 and Mark 10:17–31, Luke 18:18–30 is one of the passages that Streeter used to demonstrate that Matthew and Luke allegedly improved the wording of Mark's gospel in order to remove apparent threats to theological orthodoxy found in the text of the second gospel.[20] Second, it is Luke 18:18–30 that Professor Ned B. Stonehouse, formerly of Westminster Theological Seminary and a leading evangelical New Testament scholar of his day, found to be convincing evidence in support of the Two-Document

Hypothesis.[21] Third, Luke 18:18–30 has a sufficient amount of text to function as a typical example of traditional (harmonistic) interpretation. The passage also has recently been treated in depth by a number of evangelical exegetes.[22] Analysis of the text using the traditional approach will come first.

A TRADITIONAL INTERPRETATION OF LUKE 18:18–23

Luke 18:18

The context of Luke's account of the rich ruler is Jesus' last journey to Jerusalem. It occurs after He passed between Samaria and Galilee (17:11) and arrived in the trans-Jordan part of Judea (Matt. 19:1).[23] After Jesus had entered a house along the way, probably in order to rest from the journey,[24] and after blessing the children (Luke 18:15–17), "a certain ruler questioned Him" (*epērōtēsen tis auton archōn,* Luke 18:18) as He was leaving a house (*ekporeuomenou autou,* Mark 10:17). Only Mark mentions that the man came running and knelt before Jesus (Mark 10:17, *prosdramōn . . . kai gonupetēsas*), and only Mark records the sort of dramatic detail that characterizes his gospel.[25] Only Luke records that Jesus' questioner was some kind of official. But Luke does not specify the area of the ruler's authority, whether synagogue or Sanhedrin[26] or (which is less likely) something more secular in nature.[27] Whatever his precise office, he belonged to the ruling class.[28]

The man addressed Jesus as "Good Teacher" (*didaskale agathe,* 18:18). The man appears to have used this appellation sincerely, though it was an unusual one,[29] and was not employing "thoughtless flattery" or merely a polite formality.[30] The ruler's sincerity is obvious, for Mark later says Jesus looked at him and loved him (Mark 10:21). Perhaps the man had heard the Lord's teaching and, having also seen Him bless the children, was motivated by what he had observed to "address himself with a weighty question to Jesus."[31]

Until recently, most Protestant commentators have taken the question asked by the ruler—"What shall I do to inherit eternal life?" (18:18, NASB; literally, "By doing what shall I inherit eternal life?" *ti poiēsas zōēn aiōnion klēronomēsō)*—as an indication that he wanted to accomplish something that would merit eternal life.[32] Whatever the man's reason, whether dissatisfied with the teaching of Moses or the rabbis, or simply lacking assurance that he would partake of the life in Messiah's kingdom at the resurrection,[33] he apparently sought to do some heroic or benevolent deed, or to expend a large amount of wealth in some benefaction.[34] The ruler himself saw a causal relationship between the "doing" and "obtaining" of eternal life, for both Matthew and Mark have the conjunction *hina* ("in order that"), which introduces a purpose clause *(ti poiēsō hina zōēn aiōnion klēronomēsō),* indicating the connection in the questioner's mind (Matt. 19:16; Mark 10:17).[35] The ruler's later emphasis on having kept the commandments (Luke 18:21) is further evidence that he was seeking to *do* something in addition to what he claimed to have already faithfully observed.

Luke 18:19

Jesus said to the ruler, "Why do you call Me good? No one is good except One—God" (Luke 18:19, *ti me legeis agathon; oudeis agathos ei mē heis ho theos*). The Savior's reply has provoked much comment over the centuries. Some say Jesus was denying His own deity or acknowledging His own sinfulness by rejecting the title of "good."[36] The Lord did not, however, explicitly reject the title so much as question its use by the ruler ("why do you call Me good?" *ti me legeis agathon;*). He knew that the man did not realize the full implication of this form of address, and thus sought to make him consider it more carefully.

It is true that in the context Jesus was pointing to God's goodness (Luke 18:19, "No one is good except One—God," *oudeis agathos ei mē heis ho theos*) and subsequently to God's revealed will, as set forth in the law (18:20, "you know the commandments," *tas entolas oidas*).[37] Nevertheless, as many patristic writers and an abundance of modern commentators have contended, one of the possible understandings of Jesus' reply is that by calling Him good, the ruler must realize that he is addressing Jesus as God.[38] The later command to sell all and follow Him (18:22) adds support that this was one issue that Jesus wanted to raise with the ruler. The commitment to become a disciple is surely on a par with the requirement of the first commandment to love God with the whole heart (Deut. 6:5) and would certainly necessitate faith in "the One who was issuing the order."[39]

Luke 18:20

Having dealt with the superficiality of the ruler's address to Him, Jesus then answered one of his questions. God's unique goodness (Luke 18:19, "No one is good except One—God," *oudeis agathos ei mē heis ho theos*) is also the beginning of the reply to the question "What shall I do to inherit eternal life?" The divine standard of goodness, God's perfection shown in His holiness and righteousness and revealed in the law,[40] is also the standard for human beings. Jesus therefore follows His statement about God with a reference to the commandments (Luke 18:20). Matthew is more detailed here and adds, "If you wish to enter into life, keep the commandments" (Matt. 19:17, *ei de theleis eis tēn zōēn eiselthein, tēreson tas entolas*), to which the young man replied "What sort of [commandments]?" (Matt. 19:19, *poias*).[41] At this point Mark and Luke report that Jesus said, "You know the commandments" (18:20 = Mark 10:19, *tas entolas oidas*).[42] Both word order and the initial asyndeton of the sentence emphasize "the commandments."[43] Though the ruler was seeking something in addition to the law, Jesus emphatically turned his attention back to God's already-revealed will for people.[44]

Having mentioned "the commandments," Jesus chose to cite mainly the second table of the Decalogue, namely, the precepts focusing on human and social relationships (Luke 18:20, "Do not commit adultery, do not kill, do not steal, do not bear false witness, honor your father and mother," *mē moicheusēs, mē phoneusēs, mē klepsēs, mē pseudomarturēsēs, tima ton patera sou kai tēn mētera*). After "do not bear false witness," Luke has omitted the phrase "do not defraud" (Mark 10:19, *mē aposterēsēs*). This may have been a summary of the tenth commandment on covetousness, for Jesus placed it after the ninth, which prohibits false witness.[45] More likely it is that in "do not defraud" Jesus provided a general summary of four negative commandments of the second table.[46]

Next Jesus turned to a positive command, the fifth, about honoring father and mother "in order to emphasize its importance in view of its practical abrogation by the oral law."[47] Last of all, the Lord enlarged the scope of the second table's specific prohibitions and the positive duty to one's parents by adding the obligation to love one's neighbor as oneself (Lev. 19:18, reported by Matthew 19:19 only). This formed a positive conclusion and summary to the whole second table, and included anything not covered by what Jesus had already explicitly stated.[48] Without a mention of the Decalogue's first four commandments, these sufficiently test the ruler's external obedience to the law and faithfulness to God.[49] Jesus' purpose in reciting so many commandments was evidently to show His eager questioner, if he would carefully consider it, the impossibility of keeping the law and thereby obtaining eternal life.[50]

Luke 18:21

"I kept these all from youth" was the ruler's response, according to Luke (*tauta panta ephulaxa ek neotētos*, 18:21). Jesus had quoted both negative and positive commandments. Perhaps this is the reason the ruler gave his answer with two separate forms of the verb, one an aorist active (*ephylaxa [<phylassō]* = "I observed" or "I kept," namely, by doing the positive commandments) recorded by both Luke and Matthew (19:20), the other an aorist middle (*ephylaxamēn* = "I kept (myself)," namely, from the things prohibited in the negative commands) recorded only by Mark (10:20). Although some maintain the two forms reflect only stylistic variation between the evangelists,[51] it is more likely that the difference indicates two separate statements by the ruler.[52] Thus, Luke (and Matthew) records only one of the two verbs the ruler used to describe his own faithfulness to the law, while Mark recorded the other.

"From youth" (*ek neotētos*, Luke 18:21) may only signify "since I was a child," or it may point to an early religious, even Pharisaic, training for the man. For years, at any rate, this man had assiduously applied himself to keeping the law, including the specific commandments just recited. Though his answer was sincere and displayed a certain self-confidence—just as the apostle Paul's response would surely have been before his conversion (cf. Phil. 3:5–6)[53]—nonetheless, the ruler was dissatisfied with his own situation relative to "eternal life."[54] His added question, recorded only by Matthew, "What am I still lacking?" (*ti eti husterō*; Matt. 19:20), shows this.

Luke 18:22

Only Mark notes that Jesus fixed His eyes with a searching gaze upon the young man and loved him (10:21).[55] This confirms the sincerity of both the ruler's initial inquiry and his latest affirmation and question. He had an earnestness, a "natural amiableness," and a moral uprightness that were attractive.[56] He was indeed different from the scribes, Pharisees, and others who tested Jesus, who sought to trap Him in His speech or to destroy Him.[57] Yet the ruler had by his question expressed dissatisfaction with his own situation ("what do I still lack?" Matt. 19:20), so the Lord—without directly affirming or refuting his claim to having obeyed the commandments—responded to the ruler's question, "You are *still* lacking one thing" (*eti hen soi leipei,* Luke 18:22),[58] indicating that the man had not kept the law perfectly.[59] In this way Jesus endeavored to bring the ruler to recognize the true cause of his anxiety about eternal life.

It is unclear whether the beginning of Jesus' reply in Mark, "You lack *one thing*" (*hen se husterei,* 10:21; with *hen* emphasized in the initial position)[60] followed Luke's "You are *still* lacking one thing" (*eti hen soi leipei,* Luke 18:22) as a repetition with a slightly different emphasis, or whether it followed Matthew's "If you wish to be perfect" (*ei theleis teleios einai,* 19:21) as the apodosis to Matthew's protasis.[61] Whichever order is correct, Matthew and Mark continue their narratives with Jesus saying, "Go" (*hupage,* Matt. 19:21 = Mark 10:21). Luke, on the other hand, moves immediately to the next element—found in all three gospels—Jesus' command to sell all and follow Him (*panta hosa echeis pōlēson . . . kai deuro akolouthei moi,* Luke 18:22; cf. Matt. 19:21; Mark 10:21).

Though Matthew has Jesus' initial emphasis as "*sell* your belongings" (*pōlēson sou ta huparchonta,* 19:21), Mark and Luke, using a different word order, give what appears to be the Lord's reiteration of the command, which further clarified the scope of the requirement ("whatever you have, sell," *hosa echeis pōlēson*). Only Luke has emphasized the command's full import with the word *panta* ("*all* that [literally, "*whatever*"] you have, sell," *panta hosa echeis pōlēson*), although the other synoptists seem to imply as much. Even with this Jesus had not finished. The rest of the command included systematically distributing one's possessions to poor people and returning to follow Jesus ("distribute [the proceeds from the sale of your goods] to the poor [people], . . . and come follow me," *kai diados ptōchois, . . . kai deuro akolouthei moi,* Luke 18:22).[62] In giving this charge, Jesus identified the ruler's great weakness, the one great obstacle or stumbling block that stood in the way of his obtaining eternal life, namely, love for his wealth.[63] In addition, the Lord showed the ruler his failure to keep the two "great" commandments, loving God and one's neighbor.[64]

Since the command to sell forms part of a series of imperatives ("go, sell, . . . and come follow," *hupage, pōlēson . . . kai deuro akolouthei,* Matt. 19:21 = Mark 10:21 = Luke 18:22 [which omits "go," *hupage*]), Jesus' definition included both the man's need to rid himself of his possessions and his need to become Jesus' disciple. He could not do one without the other.[65] Following Jesus would entail the ruler's obedience to the command to come and follow. In this way he would show his personal commitment and trust in the Lord, that Jesus was who He claimed to be and that what He said was true. But the first step of this faith-commitment entailed the ruler's going and selling all that he had. Obedience to the charge and faith in both the person of Jesus and the rightness of His command are insepa-rable.[66] In giving the ruler this command, Jesus was not adding a statute to the law. If he had kept the law perfectly, Jesus would not have needed to add something more. Therefore, the ruler must have failed to keep the law, with Jesus' command constituting a replacement for that broken law.[67] Obeying Jesus' command to sell will not go unrequited. The giving up of earthly possessions to follow Jesus will be more than recompensed with an everlasting reward of treasure in heaven ("and you will have treasure in [the] heavens," *kai hexeis thēsauron en tois ouranois,* Luke 18:22). This statement is not simply equivalent to offering the ruler salvation,[68] for the latter is equated with obtaining eternal life and entering the kingdom (Luke 18:24–26).[69]

In contrast to that future treasure is a present aspect to eternal life and life in the kingdom found in the rewards experienced "in this present age" (*en tǭ kairǭ toutǭ,* Luke 18:30) by followers of Jesus.[70] Rather than being related to the present age, the "treasure in heaven" recalls the Lord's teach-ing in the Sermon on the Mount about storing up treasures, not on earth, but in heaven, where they will be untouched by temporal deterioration or loss (Matt. 6:19–21). In that passage Jesus spoke about heavenly treasures immediately after His remarks about being rewarded by "your heavenly Father" (Matt. 6:16–18). That connection resembles the conversation with the ruler with the close connection—found in all three synoptics—Jesus made between the ruler's giving up all earthly wealth and acquiring heav-enly treasure (Luke 18:22 = Matt. 19:21 = Mark 10:21). Thus Jesus did not mean that by selling his goods he could obtain eternal life in exchange. After all, people cannot earn or buy salvation/eternal life. It is a free gift from God.[71] But if the ruler had put his faith in Jesus and demonstrated that faith by obeying the command to sell all and become His disciple, he would have received eternal life. He also would have received some addi-tional, though unspecified, heavenly reward to more than replace what-ever earthly rewards he had sacrificed.

Luke 18:23

Though Matthew and Mark both note that the ruler left after hearing Jesus' command, Luke gives only his reaction, shown in his change of attitude ("when he heard these things, he became sorrowful," *ho de akousas tauta perilupos egenēthē,* Luke 18:23). His disappointment may have signalled an inner struggle taking place as a result of Jesus' command. When he first came to the Lord, the ruler had wanted to add something to his prior record of law-keeping in order to guarantee obtaining eternal life. But Jesus had not told him something additional. Instead He had given him an altogether different requirement. Mark uses an aorist participle to describe the ruler's facial expression in response (*stugnasas,* "upon becoming gloomy/sullen," Mark 10:22) to Jesus' shocking command to him. Reflected in his countenance was the sudden disappointment of being "asked to part with what he valued most."[72] He now had to choose between love for his wealth and obedience to Jesus' command.

All three gospels give a similar reason for the man's disappointment and grief: he was very wealthy (*ēn gar plousios sphodra*, Luke 18:23; "for he had many possessions," *ēn gar echōn ktēmata polla*, Matt. 19:22 = Mark 10:22). His desire to hold on to the wealth he possessed outweighed his desire to inherit eternal life.[73] He was drawn to Jesus, but the cost of following Him was too great. The man could not bear to give up his material riches, even though he was guaranteed to receive treasure in heaven. Since he could not serve both God and Mammon (Matt. 6:24 = Luke 6:13), he chose to reject Jesus' call and keep his temporal wealth. This has been eloquently called "the great refusal."[74] No one today knows whether this ruler ever repented. Scripture provides no basis for believing that he did.[75]

RECENT EVANGELICAL INTERPRETATION OF LUKE 18:18–23

This section will examine those points of evangelical commentary on this passage in which the effects of Historical Criticism appear. Earlier documentation has reflected that recent evangelical interpreters echo some comments made by traditional commentators, but in addition to these, they add elements that those interested in harmonizing the Gospels would never have made.

Journey Setting

According to Marshall, who assumes Luke's dependence on Mark, in 18:18 Luke has omitted Mark's "journey setting" (namely, of Jesus going out into a road, *ekporeuomenou autou eis hodon*, Mark 10:17), as well as the personal details of the man's approach to Jesus, since they are unnecessary and he wants rather to emphasize the connection between this incident and the one immediately preceding.[76] Here and elsewhere, however, Mark has recorded details that surely reflect "derivation from the reminiscence of an eyewitness."[77]

On the other hand, the lack of a journey setting here may mean only that in doing his research for writing the gospel, Luke spoke to someone who had witnessed this particular incident, but who did not mention that Jesus was coming out of a house as a certain wealthy ruler approached Him. It is clear from a study of the third gospel that Luke has his own journey setting. It is one that emphasizes the moral and spiritual aspects of Jesus' approach to Jerusalem more than, but—it must be reiterated—not in contradiction to, the physical steps toward the city. Beginning with 9:51, "when the days of His being received up were being fulfilled" (a clear reference to Christ's eventual ascension), Luke tells that Jesus "firmly set His face to journey to Jerusalem." Then from time to time Luke reminds his reader that this journey continues (9:57; 10:1, 38; 13:22, 33; 17:11; 18:35; 19:1, 11, 28–29, 37, 41, 45; 24:50–51).[78]

With this the case, one would have expected Luke to use Mark's "journey setting" if it had been available to him in the text of Mark's gospel.[79] That he did not do so is explained as well or better by the fact that he did not know about Jesus' departure from a house, for he had not seen Mark's gospel.

Furthermore, not only does Luke omit the journey setting, but Matthew does as well. Marshall calls this agreement in omission "probably coincidental, since there is no other evidence of significant agreement between Lk. and Mt. here."[80] The facts are very much the contrary, however, for in his own discussion about the passage (Luke 18:18–23), Marshall mentions not one or even two, but six "minor agreements" between Luke and Matthew![81] Moreover, an examination of the remainder of the passage, namely, Luke 18:24–30, reveals up to eighteen such "minor agreements," with its Matthean parallel (19:16–30) against Mark.[82] According to the logic of the Two-Source Theory, the probability of so many and varied agreements occurring coincidentally in a passage of such length would be "infinitesimally small."[83] In other words, it would be impossible. Yet none of the five evangelical commentators selected for this study (see n. 22) seriously addresses the full consequences of the accumulation in number and variety of these "minor agreements."[84]

A Ruler or Not?

Still on verse 18, Marshall only mildly defends the historicity of the detail in Luke's account that the man who came to Jesus was a ruler *(archōn)*. Marshall suggests that Bultmann was mistaken to consider the description as *novellistisch* (a folk-tale, namely, a fictional element added by the early Christian community),[85] and that the detail could have been passed on through oral tradition. But then Marshall concedes, "It is possibly a deduction from the fact of the man's riches."[86] Rather than a deduction, however, Luke probably had done his homework and it was known fact that Jesus' questioner was indeed a ruler. Such a conclusion derives in part from the testimony of Luke himself and his claim to have researched thoroughly the material contained in his gospel (Luke 1:1–4). This suggests certainty rather than guesswork or deductive logic in Luke's identification of the man's status.

Wording of the Ruler's Question

Marshall, in explaining the divergence between Luke and Matthew/Mark, states that Luke "has altered M[ar]k's formulation" of the ruler's question. But a more probable explanation is that when the ruler rushed up to Jesus and knelt (Mark 10:17), he stated his question more than once, a possibility that Mark hints at by his use of the imperfect tense for the Greek verb introducing the question ("began asking," NASB; *epērōta*).[87] Coming with haste, the ruler may have started the conversation as follows: "Teacher, good teacher, by doing what will I inherit eternal life? I mean, what should I do in order to inherit eternal life?" As previously noted, this would be a typical way for an ordinary conversation to proceed.[88] Historical-critical theory is unnecessary to explain the difference between Mark and Luke here.

Wording of Jesus' Answer

Verse 19 and its parallels in Matthew (19:17) and Mark (10:18) provide what one might call the *locus classicus* for discussing evangelical use of historical-critical hypotheses. The divergence here between Mark and Luke on the one hand and Matthew on the other led Prof. Ned B. Stonehouse of Westminster Theological Seminary over thirty-five years ago to accept the Two-Document Theory as an explanation of the origin of the Synoptic Gospels. In the account of the rich young ruler, he argued that Matthew had changed Mark's version of the Lord's reply from "Why do you call me good? There is none good except one, God" (*ti me legeis agathon; oudeis agathos ei mē heis ho theos*, Mark 10:18 = Luke 18:19) to "Why do you ask me about the good? There is only one who is good" (*ti me erōtais peri tou agathou; heis estin ho agathos*).[89]

Although Stonehouse denied that Matthew made the change to protect against a denial of Jesus' deity allegedly posed by Mark's "why do you call me good?" at the same time Stonehouse demonstrated hostility to the long-honored principle of harmonizing divergent accounts. He called this method "conservative and simple," and proceeded to describe what was in his judgment "a sounder attitude to most problems of harmonization." That "sounder attitude," he contended, "is marked by the exercise of greater care in determining what the Gospels as a whole and in detail actually say as well as greater restraint in arriving at conclusions where the available evidence does not justify ready answers." He contended that orthodox Christians or those who defend the "infallibility of Scripture" should *not* maintain that the evangelists, "in reporting the words of Jesus . . . must have been characterized by a kind of notarial exactitude."[90] Thus, "infallibility is not properly understood if it is supposed that it carries with it the implication that the words of Jesus as reported in the Gospels are necessarily the *ipsissima verba*." What we have in the Gospels then are not Jesus' precise words, but "an accurate and trustworthy *impression* of the Lord's teachings" recorded by human authors under the guidance of the Holy Spirit.[91]

If this is true, Christians have for almost two millennia been wrong to maintain "Jesus said this or that," when they really should have been saying "Jesus may have said something like this or that." The harmonistic approach, by contrast, maintains that the text of the Gospels gives the actual words of Jesus, not merely a vague representation of them.

Technically, of course, Stonehouse's discussion centered only on the divergences between Matthew and Mark. Nevertheless, the topic is appropriate here because, of the recent evangelical commentators examined in this chapter (see n. 22), only Bock mentions the variation in wording between Matthew and Mark/Luke. No one of the five attempts to explain it. Though the silence about divergences may be attributable to editorial decisions by publishers not to introduce unnecessary Matthean material into commentaries on Luke, it may be that the acceptance of the Two-Document Theory by evangelical scholars has rendered harmonization unnecessary. The reasoning would be that the important differences are those between Matthew (or Luke) and Mark, whose text the other two supposedly copied and modified to suit their own theological purposes. When considering how older commentators dealt with this difficulty, one must keep in mind that the Received Text had the same wording for Jesus' reply in Matthew as in Mark ("why do you call me good?" *ti me legeis agathon*, 19:17 = Mark 10:18), so that the divergence in this passage did not become an issue for commentators until the last quarter of the nineteenth century, especially after the appearance of the Westcott and Hort text in 1881.[92] Since that time, some have sought to explain the difference between Matthew and Mark/Luke to mean that each evangelist had recorded only part, not all, of the conversation.[93] Thus, the rich young ruler addressed Jesus as both "teacher" and "good teacher." Matthew recorded only the first of these, while Mark and Luke recorded only the second. On the other hand, of the two questions with which Jesus responded to him, "why do you ask me about the good?" and "why do you call me good?" Matthew records only the first while Mark and Luke give only the second.

This is the kind of divergence to be expected among three *independent* accounts of the same conversation, in which the man asked two rather different questions and two writers have preserved one of them while the third writer recorded the other question. As can be seen from the earlier exposition, the traditional approach holds that *Luke, Matthew, and Mark have independently, yet accurately, recorded various portions of both the actions and words of Jesus from a particular incident* during His public ministry. At points the three independent accounts overlap, so all three have retained virtually the same actions and words of Jesus.[94] At other points, however, but still during the same incident, two of the accounts have preserved or omitted the same material.[95] At still other points in the text, each evangelist has recorded unique data that simultaneously diverge from each of the other two synoptists and, when combined with an omission by one of the remaining two, gives each gospel account a distinctive wording.[96] At any rate, the combined phenomena of similarities and differences between the three synoptic records in the present passage are explainable by three independent versions of the same incident more readily than by recourse to the Two- (or Four-) Source Hypothesis or any other theory based on literary interdependence, such as the Two-Gospel Hypothesis proposed by Griesbach.[97]

About Jesus' reciting of the commandments (Luke 18:20), Stein confidently asserts, "Matthew and Luke excluded Mark's 'do not defraud' (10:19) because it is not found in Exodus 20:1–17."[98] This explanation of why the command "do not defraud" does not appear in the text of either Matthew or Luke is *pure speculation*. Only assuming the Two-Document Hypothesis compels someone to explain why neither Matthew nor Luke incorporated the material in Mark's text into their own, for the two writers supposedly decided to do so independently. On the other hand, no such difficulty faces those who espouse the independence of the synoptics, for this line of thinking considers it impossible to know what sources a particular writer employed. Rather than speculate about sources, the important task for the independence approach is to ascertain how the various accounts fit into a harmonious (in other words, noncontradictory) whole. Although one can never be sure of having all the words of a given conversation, nevertheless, as demonstrated earlier in this chapter, he/she can obtain a proper understanding of the passage without resorting to speculation about hypothetical sources.

Commenting on why Jesus postponed the commandment to honor father and mother until after the sixth through the ninth, Marshall writes, "The post-placing of the fifth commandment suggests that it is an addition to an originally briefer text."[99] He apparently means that although in the original conversation with the ruler Jesus only referred to commandments six through nine (or possibly ten), Mark (or his source), copied by Matthew and Luke, decided to improve the record of this incident by having the Lord speak the commandment to honor father and mother *when in reality He had not mentioned it at all.* This, however, like Stonehouse's treatment of Matthew 19:17, forces upon the reader a dual crisis of confidence. First, there is a crisis of confidence in the integrity of the evangelist, who is guilty of putting words in the mouth of Jesus that He never spoke. Second—as a direct result of the first—comes a crisis of confidence in the accuracy of the report of what Jesus actually said and did. The logic of this kind of statement pushes further, however. If this respected evangelical scholar's statement is true, no one can have full confidence in the credibility of the gospel writer or—which is even more disastrous—any secure knowledge of what Jesus actually said (or did).

Who is to say, for example, that a gospel writer who felt the freedom to add something inauthentic here would not have added something equally untrue elsewhere, perhaps in the birth, death, or resurrection narratives? That approach casts serious doubt on the truth of the Virgin Birth and, consequently, Jesus' full deity and/or humanity, His substitutionary atonement, and His victory over death and sin in His resurrection from the dead. And even if writers did not make such egregious alterations elsewhere, how can anyone today be certain that they did not?[100] It is also worth pointing out that an alternative explanation for the order of the commandments has already been offered in the traditional exposition. Furthermore, the first-century Christians' high view of Jesus' person, His words, and work is evidence that they would have been far more interested in preserving accurately the record of those words and deeds than in changing or adding to them for the sake of their own needs or theological purposes.[101]

The Ruler's Response

In verse 21, three of the five selected evangelical commentators, using a historical critical approach, note that both Matthew and Luke independently improved Mark's use of the aorist middle form of the verb *phulassō* ("to guard" or "keep") by changing it to the aorist active.[102] But, as shown in the traditional exposition of the verse, the ruler could have used both forms of the verb to affirm his careful adherence to the commandments since his youth. That explanation is more probable than an alleged redactional improvement, especially in view of the fact that later, in the larger context, one of these five scholars says Mark has retained a more appropriate tense of the verb (the perfect) than Matthew and Luke, who have apparently "dis-improved" the Markan original by using the aorist (*ēkolouthēkamen*, "we have followed," Mark 10:28 vs. *ēkolouthēsamen*, "we followed," Matt. 19:27 = Luke 18:28)![103]

Jesus' Correction

The next verse yields difficulties for evangelical historical critics, and these difficulties cluster around three issues: (1) the absence of a reference to Jesus looking at the ruler and loving him (absent from Matt. 19:21; present in Mark 10:21); (2) Jesus' use of *eti* ("still") in response to the ruler's claim to have kept the law (absent from Mark 10:21); and, (3) the presence of *panta* in Jesus' command to sell all and follow Him (absent from Matt. 19:21; Mark 10:21).

On the first point one remarks that "Luke (as Matthew) is less comfortable with attributing emotion to Jesus . . . and has eliminated this Markan clause (as has Matthew)."[104] Once again, this betrays the influence of the Two-Document Hypothesis and the guess work resorted to in explaining why Matthew and Luke agreed in omitting something in Mark. Alternatively, if one accepts the independence of the three Synoptic Gospels, the absence of a reference to Jesus' gaze at and love for the ruler needs no explanation. It may (or may not) have been lacking in Luke's research source(s). Since Luke's sources are unknown, further speculation is useless.

In addition, many—even the Twelve—may not have noticed the Lord's response to the ruler's apparently sincere claim to have kept all the law, if one pictures the ruler facing Jesus about two or three feet away and the disciples crowding around to listen. In such an interview, perhaps only two or three might have noticed the Lord's actions and facial expression(s). That could even explain why one disciple, Peter—the principal source of Mark's gospel—noticed the reaction while another disciple and eyewitness (Matthew) did not, thus accounting for its absence in his gospel. Moreover, while it may be accurate to say that Luke does not refer to Jesus' emotions as much as Mark, it is misleading to say that Luke is "less comfortable with attributing emotion to Jesus." After all, Luke is the only writer to mention that Jesus wept over Jerusalem (Luke 19:41), to record two lamentations of Jesus for Jerusalem (13:34–35; 19:41–44), to indicate the depth of Jesus' agony in the garden of Gethsemane resulted in His sweating great drops of blood (22:44), and to give the forcefulness of Jesus' desire to eat the Passover with the Twelve before His arrest (22:15). These examples suffice to show that Luke is certainly not uncomfortable "in attributing emotion to Jesus."

The treatment of Jesus' statement "you still lack one thing" varies only a little between the five commentators. Using Mark's text as the standard for comparison, Marshall annotates merely "*eti* is also [namely, in the same way as Luke] added by Matt[hew], but in the previous verse."[105] Thus, Matthew adds to the ruler's words something that he never said, as Luke does to Jesus' words. Discussion above about Stonehouse's treatment of

Matthew 19:17 (parallel to Luke 18:19) has dwelled on the problems of such an approach to Luke's text. Although their statements are not as direct, both Liefeld and Bock in their respective commentaries appear to agree with Marshall on this issue.[106] Those of the five who comment on the presence of *panta* ("all") in the Lord's command to the ruler to sell all agree that Luke has added the adjective "all."[107] This is a small but significant addition to Jesus' words, an addition of something that He did not actually say. It thus casts grave doubt on whether Luke has reliably recorded Jesus' words elsewhere in his gospel. The limiting of the addition to only a single word ought not to blind anyone to the seriousness of the issue. Did the Lord actually use the word "all" or not? If He did not, then how much of Luke's account gives the reader Jesus' actual words, and how much gives us what is merely close to His words?

The Ruler's Dejection

Marshall's comment on verse 23 is rather puzzling: "Luke omits mention of the young man's emotion (*stugnasas epi tọ logọ* ["shocked/saddened at the word," Mark 10:22]), but retains the fact of his grief (*perilupos*, . . . diff. Mk *lupoumenos*)."[108] If by emotion Marshall means *kind* of emotion, that is, gloom as opposed to anger or joy, that makes a little better sense. But to contrast *stugnasas* with either the adjective *perilupos* ("sad," NASB) or the participle *lupoumenos* ("grieved," NASB) is odd, for both describe an emotion of some kind.

Somewhat more problematic is Nolland's remark that "Luke's omission of Mark's departure statement probably leaves the ruler present to hear the development in vv. 24–30."[109] If the record of Matthew and Mark is chronological, it should be clear that once the ruler was disappointed by Jesus' command to follow Him, he went away grieved. After his departure, Jesus spoke to the disciples about the difficulties of entering the kingdom of heaven (Matt. 19:23) or of God (Matt. 19:24; Mark 10:23, 24, 25). This would be the simplest and most natural understanding of the passages' meaning. If Nolland is right about Luke's omission of Mark's departure statement, Luke fundamentally contradicts Matthew and Mark. If, however, as might have seemed obvious to Luke, the ruler's disappointment led to his immediate departure—and what reason would he have to stay?—no conflict between the writers exists. Alternatively, if Mark's (and Matthew's) phrase "he went away grieved" (*apēlthen lupoumenos,* Mark 10:22 = Matt. 19:22) is a summary statement about the eventual (though not chronologically precise) departure of the ruler, who briefly lingered to listen further to the Lord's teaching to His disciples, the three synoptics would have no contradiction, for Luke's account makes no mention, chronological or otherwise, of the ruler's departure.

CONCLUSION

This chapter has presented a brief historical review, an exposition of Luke 18:18–23 (using a traditional harmonistic approach), and an examination of a number of points in the same passage where the historical critical thinking of recent evangelical scholars has deviated from the traditional understanding. The parallel passages make good exegetical sense without resorting to any theory of literary dependence among the synoptic writers. In light of this, recent evangelical interpretation of this passage is open to serious objections.

The first objection is the failure of two-source advocates to explain satisfactorily the "minor agreements" between Matthew and Luke against Mark. In the discussion of Luke's "omission" of Mark's journey setting, at least eight "minor agreements" occur, but explanations of only a few of these have been forthcoming. Two-source proponents simply dismiss them as coincidental or ignore them without comment.[110] Since evangelical synoptic scholarship that is built upon the foundation of the Two-Document Hypothesis and Markan priority has been unable to give a reasonable explanation for the numerous minor agreements, it must either come up with the goods or be abandoned as being wrong-headed or—what is worse— inaccurate to the extent that it bases its conclusions about the text on the foundation of a hypothesis that demonstrably lacks credibility. Indeed, in the more than seventy years since the classic formulation of the case for Markan priority by B. H. Streeter, no adequate explanation for the "minor agreements" has appeared, and it is unlikely that any ever will. On the other hand, any theory of composition or origin of the Gospels that has no difficulty explaining the minor agreements ought to commend itself as a superior alternative. The independence of the three Synoptic Gospels is such a theory!

A second objection to recent evangelical synoptic interpretation is that it, for the most part, rejects the use of harmonization in order to explain the divergences between the gospel accounts. Marshall, for example, hints at this rejection when he allows for the possibility that Luke's observation about Jesus' questioner may be a deduction from the fact of his wealth, or Nolland suggests that by not mentioning his departure in verse 23, Luke leaves the ruler present to hear Jesus' subsequent remarks in verses 24–30. Discussion has noted more serious examples of non-harmonization in verse 19 with the question "why do you call me good?" as compared to Matthew's "why do you ask me about the good?" (19:17), and in verse 22 with the placement of "still" (compared with Matt. 19:20) and the use of "all" (compared with Matt. 19:21; Mark 10:21). In these last three cases, evangelical scholars see Luke and Matthew responsible for adding words to the Lord's and yet portraying these additions as having been spoken by Him.

No matter what the alleged motives of the writers in so doing, that kind of action is fundamentally problematic at best and dishonest at worst. It is problematic, for it obscures the reader's knowledge of what Jesus actually said. And it is dishonest, for the Lord appears to be saying something He did not say. Even if done out of the best of motives, that kind of redactional activity amounts to doing evil that good may come of it, an ethic clearly condemned elsewhere in Scripture (Rom. 3:8). Now if those who reported those words and deeds of Jesus took such liberties with what He said in that case, how trustworthy can they be elsewhere? Perhaps Jesus was not born of a virgin. Perhaps He only said that He was the Way and the Life, not the Truth, and so on. There is no sure means of distinguishing between what He actually did or said and what this or that writer has added. This in turn leaves the reader in a morass of subjective judgment about the historical Jesus. This means, in effect, that members of the Jesus Seminar are right after all! If evangelicals defend that methodology as accomplished under the guidance of the Holy Spirit, the only effect is to shift the culpability from human agents to a divine person. To do so, however, flies in the face of what the Bible teaches about the character of God, namely, His truthfulness (Num. 23:19) and His holiness (1 John 1:5). Indeed, to say that the Holy Spirit prompted such additions is to make a mockery of the testimony of Scripture about the Person of the Trinity known as the Spirit of truth, for Jesus promised His disciples that this same Spirit of truth would guide them into all truth (John 16:13).

To any reader of this chapter who believes that the New Testament is God's infallible Word, inspired by God the Holy Spirit, the consequences of adopting the Two-Document Hypothesis as a methodology for studying the Synoptic Gospels should cause great alarm, for they compel one to ascribe to God what orthodox believers in Christ throughout the centuries would normally have considered blasphemy. I cannot bring myself to believe that the scholars whose work has been examined in this chapter have intended to bring shame on God's character in this way. Nevertheless, I believe that this is precisely what they have done.

By contrast, however, if one accepts the independence of the three Synoptic Gospels, the kinds of difficulties just discussed disappear. If the accounts are indeed independent, harmonization becomes not only a viable option but the one that is most important and utilized before considering any other possibilities. The exposition earlier in this chapter illustrated this approach. For example, when the words spoken by Jesus are similar but not identical between Luke and Matthew, the assumption should not be that one is more authentic than the other, but that the Lord reiterated the same idea in a similar but not identical manner. When two of the gospel writers agree in omitting a phrase, it is probably the result of coincidence in sources and sometimes of coincidence in composition. Conversely, when two gospel accounts include the same material, the included material traces its origin to words or actions in the original situation. This does not provide facile solutions to all difficulties in the text, but it avoids the need to say that one or another evangelist inserted into the text of his gospel words or phrases never actually spoken by Jesus.

One final observation needs to be made about the independence of the synoptics and the use of harmonization. It is imperative to retain the traditional orthodox Christian emphasis on the Gospels as accurate records of what Jesus said and did. If Matthew, Mark, and Luke knew Jesus as the Son of God, the Messiah, the Savior of the world, and the King of Israel, they were surely far more interested in accurately preserving His words and deeds than in changing or making editorial embellishments of what

He had said and done. Therefore, exegetes should not obscure the picture of Jesus (as we have it from the hands of the gospel writers) by conjecturing how each writer has interpreted His words and actions. Rather, the approach that harmonizes the Synoptic Gospels based on the assumption of their independence gives due weight to a full understanding of the Savior, which can come only from combining the witness of each gospel into one well-rounded picture.

ENDNOTES

1. J. Calvin, *A Harmony of the Gospels Matthew, Mark and Luke,* vol. I, Calvin's Commentaries, A. W. Morrison, trans.; D.W. Torrance and T. F. Torrance, eds. (Grand Rapids: Eerdmans, 1972), xiii–xiv; 2:253–64. He comments mainly on the accounts of Matthew and Mark.

2. This kind of commentary differs from what most call a harmony today, namely, one in which only the text of three or four of the Gospels appears in parallel columns. J. J. Griesbach introduced this latter type in 1776, in connection with which he coined the term "synoptic" ("viewed together") for the first three gospels. W. G. Kümmel, *Introduction to the New Testament,* H. C. Kee, trans., rev. ed. (Nashville: Abingdon, 1975), 36.

3. H. Olshausen, *Biblical Commentary on the New Testament,* trans. and ed. A. C. Kendrick and D. Fosdick, Jr. (New York: Sheldon, Blakeman & Co., 1858), vols. I–II, does use this type of harmony, however.

4. R. L. Thomas and S. N. Gundry, eds., *A Harmony of the Gospels* (Chicago: Moody, 1978), 5; cf. also A. T. Robertson, *A Harmony of the Gospels for Students of the Life of Christ* (New York: Harper & Brothers, 1922), viii. These words apply to both kinds of harmonies.

5. Thomas Scott, *The Holy Bible, Containing the Old and New Testaments, according to the Authorized Version; with Explanatory Notes, Practical Observations and Copious Marginal References,* vol. V, stereotype ed. from 5th English ed. (Boston: Crocker and Brewster, 1851); for Matthew, see 146–50; for Mark, 263; Luke, 412. So also, Albert Barnes, *Notes on the New Testament: Matthew and Mark,* R. Frew, ed. (reprint of 1884–85 ed.; Grand Rapids: Baker, n.d.), 197–201, 203–4 for comments on Matthew; for Mark, 368–70; Barnes has no comments for the Lukan version, referring the reader to the notes on Matthew and Mark, see A. Barnes, *Notes on the New Testament: Luke and John,* R. Frew, ed. (reprint of 1884–85 ed.; Grand Rapids: Baker, n.d.), 130.

6. H. Alford, *The Greek Testament,* vol. I, *The Four Gospels,* 7th ed. (London: Rivingtons/Cambridge, 1874); for Matthew, 195–99; for Mark, 383–86; for Luke, 616–17. A. B. Bruce, "The Synoptic Gospels," in *The Expositor's Greek Testament,* vol. 1, W. Robertson Nicoll, ed. (reprint of 1897 ed.; Grand Rapids: Eerdmans, 1990); for Matthew, 248–53; for Mark, 409–12; for Luke, 600–1. Cf. also the earlier German work by J. A. Bengel, *Gnomon of the New Testament,* A. R. Fausset, trans., rev. and ed. (Edinburgh: T & T Clark, 1860); for Matthew, vol. I, 361–68; for Mark, I, 545–49; for Luke, vol. II, 173.

7. See, for example, A.B. Bruce, *EGT,* 4–13. On Source Criticism and Markan priority, see chapters 3 and 6 of this volume.

8. A. Plummer, *A Critical and Exegetical Commentary on the Gospel according to S. Luke,* International Critical Commentary (Edinburgh: T & T Clark, 1896).

9. Plummer, *Luke*, 421–27; regarding traces of harmonization, see his mention of Markan details in v. 22.
10. W. C. Allen, *A Critical and Exegetical Commentary on the Gospel according to S. Matthew*, International Critical Commentary (Edinburgh: T & T Clark, 1907), 207–14.
11. This shift in scholarly approach to the Gospels was at the commentary level. Among trailblazing historical critics, however, the shift in scholarly opinion had occurred much earlier (see chapters 2, 3, 5, and 6 of this volume). It took a while for the impact of historical critical theories to spread their influence to those writing commentaries on the Synoptic Gospels, however.
12. F. W. Farrar, *The Gospel according to St. Luke in Greek*, Cambridge Greek Testament (Cambridge: University Press, 1921), 333–37; see esp. his dismissive comments about the theory of Markan priority in the "Introduction," xxii.
13. H. K. Luce, *The Gospel according to St. Luke*, Cambridge Greek Testament, ed. A. Nairne (Cambridge: University Press, 1933), 283–89; see esp. 285 for Luce's comments on Christ's sinlessness.
14. For example, J. M. Creed, *The Gospel according to St. Luke* (London: Macmillan, 1930), 225–27, and B. S. Easton, *The Gospel according to St. Luke: A Critical and Exegetical Commentary* (New York: Scribner's Sons, 1926), 272–74.
15. Published in Grand Rapids by Eerdmans, beginning in 1951 when N. Geldenhuys's *Commentary on the Gospel of Luke* first appeared.
16. L. Morris, *The Gospel according to John* (Grand Rapids: Eerdmans, 1971), and W. L. Lane, *The Gospel according to Mark* (Grand Rapids: Eerdmans, 1974).
17. William Hendriksen, *New Testament Commentary: Exposition of the Gospel According to Matthew* (Grand Rapids: Baker, 1973); commentaries on both Mark (1975) and Luke (1978) soon followed. Also, I. Howard Marshall, *The Gospel of Luke: A Commentary on the Greek Text*, New International Greek Testament Commentary (Grand Rapids: Eerdmans, 1978), and L. Morris, *Luke*, Tyndale New Testament Commentary, L. Morris, ed. (Grand Rapids: Eerdmans, 1974).
18. R. H. Gundry, *Matthew: A Commentary on His Handbook for a Mixed Church under Persecution* (Grand Rapids: Eerdmans, 1982), now in a 2d ed. (1994); idem, *Mark: A Commentary on His Apology for the Cross* (Grand Rapids: Eerdmans, 1996); D. A. Carson, "Matthew," W. W. Wessel, "Mark," W. L. Liefeld, "Luke," in *The Expositor's Bible Commentary*, vol. 8, ed. F. E. Gaebelein (Grand Rapids: Zondervan, 1984); in the Word Biblical Commentary series, J. Nolland, *Luke*, vols. 35A, B, C, ed. D. A. Hubbard, Glenn W. Barker et al. (Dallas: Word, 1989–93); R. A. Guelich, *Mark*, vol. 34A (Dallas: Word, 1993), D. A. Hagner, *Matthew*, vols. 33A, B (Dallas: Word, 1993, 1995); R. H. Stein, *Luke*, The New American Commentary, vol. 24, D. S. Dockery et al., eds. (Nashville: Broadman, 1992); D. L. Bock, *Luke*, 2 vols., Baker Exegetical Commentary on the New Testament (Grand Rapids: Baker, 1994, 1996). Nor is this an exhaustive list!
19. In spite of "salutary warnings against a simple overall scheme" of literary dependence on Mark by the other two synoptists, R. T. France still opts for Markan priority as his working hypothesis in *The Gospel according to Matthew*, Tyndale New Testament Commentary, ed. L. Morris (Grand Rapids: Eerdmans, 1985), 38; although Morris writing on *Luke* seems a bit more cautious about the Two-Document Theory (56, 59).

20. B. H. Streeter, *The Four Gospels: A Study of Origins* (reprint of 5th imp., 1936; London: Macmillan, 1964), 151–52, 162–64.

21. Ned B. Stonehouse, *The Origins of the Synoptic Gospels* (Grand Rapids: Eerdmans, 1963), 93–112. See chapter 11 of this volume for further discussion of Stonehouse's handling of this passage.

22. Of recent (in other words, since 1975) commentators on this passage, I have chosen the following as most representative of evangelical interpretation: Bock, *Luke*, vol. 2; Liefeld, "Luke," *EBC*, vol. 8; Marshall, *Luke*; Nolland, *Luke, 9:51–18:34*, WBC, vol. 35B, and Stein, *Luke*, NAC, vol. 24; for full bibliographic details, see notes 17, 18 above.

23. J. Foote, *Lectures on the Gospel According to Luke*, 2d ed. (Edinburgh: Johnstone, 1849), 3:71.

24. Geldenhuys, *Luke*, 457.

25. Hendriksen, *Mark*, 19–23.

26. Cf. Luke 8:41, 14:1; so W. Grundmann, *Das Evangelium nach Lukas* (Berlin: Evangelische Verlagsanstalt, 1974), 354.

27. G. Delling, *TDNT*, 1:489. E. H. Plumptre, "The Gospel according to St. Matthew, St. Mark and St. Luke," in *A Bible Commentary for Bible Students*, vol. VI, *The Four Gospels*, C. J. Ellicott, ed. (reprint; London/Edinburgh: Marshall Brothers, n.d.), 118, identifies the ruler as Lazarus, whom Jesus raised from the dead (John 11), though he admits that this is no more than "conjectural inference."

28. Morris, *Luke*, 292.

29. Marshall, *Luke*, 684.

30. So Calvin, *Harmony*, 253–54; cf. J. N. Darby, *Notes of Addresses on the Gospel of Luke* (London: F. E. Race, 1922), 205, who writes thus about the ruler: "Morally attracted [to Jesus], he came to learn to do good, without a doubt of his own competence. In Jesus he . . . saw a perfectly good man, and one therefore eminently able to advise and direct him in the same path." For flattery or politeness, Morris, *Luke*, 292; D. Gooding, *According to Luke: A New Exposition of the Third Gospel* (Grand Rapids: Eerdmans, 1987), 295.

31. J. J. Van Oosterzee, "The Gospel according to Luke," *A Commentary on the Holy Scripture: Critical, Doctrinal, and Homiletical*, J. P. Lange, ed.; P. Schaff and C. C. Starbuck, trans., 6th ed. (New York: Charles Scribner, 1870), 278.

32. For example, Calvin, *Harmony*, 2:254; Bengel, *Gnomon*, 1:361, 545; Van Oosterzee, "Gospel according to Luke," 278; F. Godet, *A Commentary on the Gospel of St. Luke*, M. D. Cusin, trans. (Edinburgh: T & T Clark, 1879), 2:206; J. C. Ryle, *Expository Thoughts on the Gospels*, vol. 2, *Luke* (reprint; Grand Rapids: Zondervan, 1951), 271; Plummer, *Luke*, 422; Hendriksen, *Luke*, 831; A. T. Robertson, *Word Pictures in the New Testament*, vol. II, *The Gospel according to Luke* (New York: Harper, 1930), 235; Morris, *Luke*, 292; Liefeld, "Luke," 1003.

33. Plummer, *Luke*, 422; for a possible Pharisaic view concerning the connection between eternal life and resurrection, cf. 2 Macc. 7:9; 4 Macc. 15:3, Bock, *Luke*, 2:1476. For supplementing rabbinical teaching, see W. Grundmann, *Das Evangelium nach Markus* (Berlin: Evangelische Verlagsanstalt, 1973), 210; for supplementing Moses, F. W. Danker, *Jesus and the New Age*, rev. ed. (Philadelphia: Fortress, 1988), 299; Liefeld, "Luke," 1003.

34. Contra Stein, *Luke*, 315–16, who in commenting on Luke 10:25–26, where

a lawyer asked the very same question about Jesus, states that "this is a good question, not to be confused with an attempt to earn salvation." He then cites the present reference, Acts 2:37, and 16:30 to show that "eternal life" is "a synonym for being 'saved' or entering God's kingdom. . . . The four responses should be understood as variant ways of giving the same answer." But, at least in 10:25ff., when Jesus replies to the lawyer, "do this [referring to the first commandment to love God and the 'next' one to love one's neighbor (10:27)] and you shall live," He is attempting to make His listeners realize that no one can keep the law perfectly, whatever His contemporaries might believe, thus indicating that something was wrong with the original inquiry (R. C. H. Lenski, *The Interpretation of St. Luke's Gospel* [Minneapolis: Augsburg, 1946], 601; cf. the apostle Paul's complaint about his countrymen in Rom. 9:30–10:3; Gal. 3:21). Thus, Jesus' reply here could also indicate that there was something amiss with the original question.

35. F. Blass, A. Debrunner, *A Greek Grammar of the New Testament and Other Early Christian Literature*, R. W. Funk, trans. and ed. (Chicago: University of Chicago, 1961), 186, §369; hereafter BDF.

36. B. B. Warfield refuted this view in "Jesus' Alleged Confession of Sin," *Princeton Theological Review* 12 (1914): 177–228, reprinted in *Christology and Criticism*, E. D. Warfield et al., eds. (New York: Oxford University Press, 1929), 97–145, although the issue has resurfaced since (see references in Bock, *Luke*, 2:1477). As V. Taylor pointed out, acknowledgment of Jesus' own sinfulness by Himself would be "at variance with the entire Synoptic portraiture of Jesus" (*The Gospel according to St. Mark*, 2d ed. [London: Macmillan, 1966], 426) as well as the rest of the New Testament (cf. 2 Cor. 5:21; Heb. 4:15).

37. So Calvin, *Harmony*, 2:254; Warfield, *Christology and Criticism*, 139; Bock, *Luke*, 2:1477, following J. A. Fitzmyer, *The Gospel according to Luke (x–xxiv)*, vol. 28A of *The Anchor Bible* (New York: Doubleday, 1985), 1199.

38. So, for example, Ambrose, *De Fide* 2.1; Cyril, *Commentary on St. Luke*, Homily 122; cf. John Chrysostom, *Homilies on St. Matthew* 63, *ad loc.* Among moderns, so (more or less chronologically) Scott, V, *Holy Bible*, 146, col. a; Bengel, *Gnomon*, 1:545–46; Alford, *Greek Testament*, 383; Farrar, *Luke*, 333; Geldenhuys, *Luke*, 458; Morris, *Luke*, 292. Lenski (*Luke*, 913–14) goes so far as to say that when Jesus responded "No one is good except one—God," He was asserting His deity, and not merely trying to get the ruler to consider the possibility, by causing him "to look upon Jesus in the true light, as the One who bestows salvation, i.e., as himself being God." While it is true that the enclitic *me* ("me") shows that Jesus was not emphasizing His own person (and deity) with the counter question (Warfield, *Christology and Criticism*, 104), the logic of the situation is impossible to escape. The ruler had just addressed Him as "good." Jesus immediately responded with not only the question—parentheses here denote the enclitic *me*—"why do you call (Me) good?" but also with the additional statement, "no one is good except One—God." How could the thought not have crossed the ruler's mind, "If that is so, then I have addressed this man as God"?

39. Hendriksen, *Luke*, 834; Geldenhuys, *Luke*, 458; Lenski, *Luke*, 914; cf. Alford, *Greek Testament*, 1:197, citing Stier; also, "by following Jesus, he would have indicated his allegiance to God" (Liefeld, "Luke," 1003).

40. Bock, *Luke*, 2:1478; Hendriksen, *Luke*, 832.

41. For the ruler's reply, see A. B. Bruce, *EGT*, 1:249. Those who object to harmonizing the various accounts in this way and who maintain that two

evangelists have copied (intact) or adapted material from a third must argue that Jesus cannot or would not have conducted a conversation in such a manner and that nothing or little more transpired in the interview than all three synoptists record. But this is to go beyond what is known and engage in speculation about compositional techniques and editorial activities, none of which can be substantiated. In fact, in the course of a conversation like this, one would expect a certain amount of give and take, question and response, or question and counter-question, perhaps even of questions or statements repeated or rephrased with slightly different shades of meaning (See R. L. Thomas, "The Rich Young Man in Matthew," *Grace Theological Journal* 3 [1982]: 256). Such a conversation characterizes normal communication under sometimes even ideal circumstances. Given, however, the hasty approach of the ruler, the public nature of the exchange, with the disciples and others probably standing or milling around, and the location of the encounter on a well-travelled road outside a house, it is highly improbable that any other pattern of conversation would be credible. Hence this conversation recorded by the evangelists most probably constitutes only a summary of everything spoken on the occasion (cf. the apostle John's similar testimony about Jesus' deeds, John 21:25), with each gospel writer reporting a different part or emphasis of a particular conversation, sometimes with an overlap of what another has written and sometimes giving almost entirely different subject matter (cf. Matt. 24:3, Mark 13:4, and Luke 21:7, where the disciples apparently asked three different but related questions, about the destruction of the temple, the return of Christ, and the end of the age [Thomas and Gundry, *Harmony,* 195, with note], with the possibly even a different interlocutor or listener/audience). This principle also assists in the understanding of other parts of the passage.

42. So Foote, *Lectures,* 76; R. Jamieson, A. R. Fausset and D. Brown [JFB], *A Commentary: Critical, Practical and Explanatory, on the Old and New Testaments, vol. I, New Testament: Matthew–Corinthians* (Toledo: Hood Brothers, 1888), 330; Farrar, *Luke,* 334; a different order is presented in Tatian's *Diatessaron,* where "you know the commandments" comes just after "no one is good except One—God," rather than last, just before the listing of the commandments (28.44–45).

43. So R. H. Gundry, *Mark: A Commentary on His Apology for the Cross* (Grand Rapids: Eerdmans, 1993), 553.

44. Plumptre, "The Gospel," 119; cf. also F. W. Grant, *The Numerical Bible: The Gospels* (New York: Loizeaux, n.d.), 195–96.

45. Hendriksen, *Mark,* 393, notes that *mē aposterēsēs* ("do not defraud"), apparently derived from Exod. 21:10 and/or Deut. 24:14, would be a better summary for the eighth commandment, "do not steal."

46. H. B. Swete, *The Gospel according to St. Mark* (reprint of 3d ed.; Grand Rapids: Eerdmans, 1951), 224.

47. Cf. Mark 7:10–13; Swete, *Mark,* 225.

48. The textual evidence regarding the order of commandments in Mark is mixed, sometimes supporting the order of the seventh commandment before the sixth (for example, Luke) and sometimes the sixth before the seventh (for example, Matthew). Luke's order is that of the Septuagint (LXX) translation in Deut. 5:16–21, not that of the Hebrew Masoretic Text (MT), so that Jesus placed the seventh ("do not commit adultery," *mē moicheusēs*) before the sixth ("do not murder," *mē phoneusēs*)—an order also found in Rom. 13:9 and James 2:11. Matthew, though retaining the exact form of the LXX, cites

them in the order of the MT (R. H. Gundry, *The Use of the Old Testament in St. Matthew's Gospel*, Supplement Novum Testamentum 18 [Leiden: Brill, 1967], 17–19), possibly thus deferring to the sensibilities of his original and primarily Jewish readers (D. Guthrie, *New Testament Introduction*, 4th ed. [Downers Grove, Ill.: InterVarsity, 1990], 28–29, 32–33). On the occasion, Jesus probably cited the commandments at least twice in varying orders.

49. Calvin, *Harmony*, 2:255; cf. Marshall, *Luke*, 685. Gundry, *Mark*, 561, objects that "obedience to the second table [cannot] demonstrate obedience to the first table, for non-murderers may practice idolatry, non-adulterers may break the Sabbath, and so on." But in a first century Palestinian Jewish context, where someone is concerned about "eternal life," a person's meticulous attention to keeping the (relatively) external commands in the second table would almost certainly guarantee that he (or she) was likewise attentive to the requirements of the first table. Apparent solicitousness for the first table would not necessarily guarantee similar concern for the second table, as Jesus' frequent criticism of the Pharisees demonstrates (cf. Matt. 5:17–48; 6:1–7; 15:1–20; 23:1–36).

50. Lenski, *Luke*, 915; Olshausen, *Biblical Commentary*, 2:109; cf. Van Oosterzee, "Gospel according to Luke," 279.

51. For example, Marshall, *Luke*, 687.

52. R. H. Gundry, *Matthew*, 386–87, points out the difference in meaning between "I have guarded myself [from the conduct prohibited in the commandments quoted]" (cf. Acts 21:25; 2 Tim. 4:15), and "I have kept [the commandments]." Gundry adds, however, that it is "better to see no difference between the two. . .," since the verb is "often deponent" in the LXX and "since the negative meaning of the reflexive understanding does not fit the last quoted command to honor father and mother" (387; although, commenting on Mark 10:20, Gundry thinks the middle force of the verb is significant [*Mark*, 562]).

If, however, one examines some of the Pentateuchal passages where the verb *phulassō* is used in the middle (for example, Lev. 18:4; 20:8, 22; 22:9), he finds either its use in parallel with an active form of *poieō* to speak of keeping the Lord's commands and judgments (*prostagmata, krimata*), or its use in connection with a set of commands that are mostly negative (Lev. 22:9; contra A. Plummer, *The Gospel according to St. Mark*, Cambridge Greek Testament for Schools and Colleges, rev. ed. [Cambridge: Cambridge University, 1926], 259).

Furthermore, "the negative meaning of the reflexive," while obviously inappropriate for the positive command to honor parents, is quite proper for the five negative commands that Jesus quoted. If, as I have suggested, the ruler responded separately to both the positive and negative commands, the inappropriateness disappears. It would have made perfect sense for the ruler to say "I kept myself from the behaviors [of (namely, forbidden in) the negative commandments] and I kept the [positive] command to honor father and mother, as well as, to love neighbor as self."

Moreover, (1) since the ruler seems to have been a thorough man, to judge by his initial question to the Lord about inheriting eternal life, and (one may surmise) given even the man's prior accumulation or retention of wealth and advancement to a position of authority in society or synagogue, it is not surprising if, to Jesus' admonition to keep the commandments, he had given a twofold answer with *both* the active and the middle forms; (2) the appropriateness of both forms of the verb to the conversation may explain the later confusion among early copyists over whether to have the active or the middle forms; (3) the ability of scholars—twenty centuries removed from the original situation—to detect some significant difference between the active and middle forms in their evaluation of the language of those who could undoubtedly speak and comprehend the koiné Greek tongue better than anyone today (or anyone who has lived in the last several centuries!), opens the possibility of some difference of usage (between active and middle voice) in the original situation. Only when this approach fails should we concede that the two forms have "no difference of meaning" (Gundry, *Matthew*, 387).

53. Bock, *Luke*, 2:1480; Stein, *Luke*, 457; cf. H. L. Strack and P. Billerbeck, *Kommentar zum neuen Testament aus Talmud und Midrasch* (München: Becksche, 1922), 1:814.

54. W. Kelly, *An Exposition of the Gospel of Luke*, ed. E. E. Whitfield (London: Alfred Holness, 1914), 302; Van Oosterzee, "Gospel according to Luke," 278.

55. W. Kelly, *An Exposition of the Gospel of Mark*, ed. E. E. Whitfield (New York: Loizeaux, n.d.), 151; Swete, *Mark*, 225, who cites Grotius: "Christ loves not only virtues, but also the seeds of virtues"; cf. Calvin, *Harmony*, 2:258, "there is no absurdity in God loving the good seed which He has sown in some natures, while rejecting their persons and their works on account of their corruption." Although Hendriksen (*Mark*, 395–96) tries to explain *ēgapēsen* ("loved") as Jesus' admiration and pity for the young man, since He would not have begun to love him "immediately after this man revealed his very superficial attitude towards God's holy law," JFB (*Commentary*, 330) call Mark's observation "a lesson to those who see nothing lovable save in the regenerate." Cf. also W. Kelly's very useful discussion in *Lectures on the Gospel of Matthew*, rev. ed. (New York: Loizeaux, n.d.), 377–78.

56. Scott, *Holy Bible*, 268; Foote, *Lectures*, 78.

57. For testing Jesus, see Luke 10:25–37; for catching Jesus in His words, see Luke 20:1–38; Matt. 21:23–46; 22:15–40; Mark 12:13–34; for seeking to destroy Jesus, see Luke 6:6–11; Mark 3:1–6; Matt. 12:10–14.

58. H. A. W. Meyer, *Critical and Exegetical Handbook to the Gospels of Mark and Luke*, R. E. Wallis, trans.; W. P. Dickson and M. B. Riddle, eds. (New York: Funk & Wagnalls, 1884), comments on *eti hen soi leipei* that it "does not presuppose the *truth*, but the *case* of what is affirmed by the *archōn*" (505). In His reply, Jesus not only echoes the *eti* ("still") of the ruler's question (cf. Plumptre, "The Gospel," 333), but He also emphasizes it in His own statement by placing it first (BDF 248, §472).

59. A number of ways to explain Jesus' statement that one thing was still lacking are possible: (1) the ruler had been relying on his own self-righteousness in general with a mere external adherence to the law and therefore utterly failed to keep it in its true, spiritual sense (so Godet, *Luke*, 2:208; Lenski, *Luke*, 917); (2) he had loved his wealth more than God, having thus become an idolater (so Geldenhuys, *Luke*, 459; Olshausen, *Biblical Commentary*, 110); (3) he "had broken the first commandment [idolatry] by breaking the last [covetousness]," namely, he had coveted riches to such a degree that they had become his god (so Liefeld, 1003; cf. "Jesus . . . put His finger on the covetousness that ruled him," J. N. Darby, *Synopsis of the Books of the Bible*, vol. III, *Matthew-John*, rev. ed. [New York: Loizeaux, 1942], 383). It is difficult to say which understanding is best, but surely the second became true when he refused to obey Jesus' call. Cf. Stein, *Luke*, 457, who states that "since

the ruler lacked eternal life/entrance into the kingdom ([Luke] 18:24–25), he must not really have 'kept' the commandments."

60. On emphasis and word order, see n. 58.

61. On this order of the phrases, see Tatian's *Diatessaron* 28.49. On the term "perfect" *(teleios)*, Bock (*Luke*, 2:1480) and Thomas ("Rich Young Man," 257) agree that it means "keeping all the commandments." Gundry (*Matthew*, 388) denies that it connotes "complete [sic] sinlessness and full virtue as matters of fact." In light of the ruler's claim to have kept all the commandments, however, Jesus' use of the term must go beyond his claim, namely, the proper observation of all the commandments plus the one He is about to enjoin. To hold that "perfect" means less than this makes nonsense of this part of the conversation.

62. Each of the three forms of *diadidōmi* in the New Testament occurs in contexts where a systematic rather than haphazard or random giving is in view (cf. Luke 11:22; John 6:11; Acts 4:35); cf. J. H. Moulton G. Milligan, *The Vocabulary of the Greek New Testament* (London: Hodder & Stoughton, 1930), s.v., 148.

Matt. 19:21 (= Mark 10:21) has *dos* ("give!"). Some see here an insignificant variation between "distribute" and "give" (Bock, *Luke*, 2:1481). In exactly the same manner, however, as the Lord further clarified the extent of "sell your belongings" with "all that you have, sell," so here, He appears to encourage a more orderly or systematic disposition of the ruler's wealth. Only Van Oosterzee (*Luke*, 278) seems to approximate the thought of systematic giving in his comment on *diados*. That kind of giving would put the wealth in the hands of those who had the greatest need. Could Jesus thus also have been showing a special concern for those over whom this ruler exercised authority? Cf. the effect of Jesus upon Zacchaeus (Luke 19:8–10).

63. So Geldenhuys, *Luke*, 458. Lenski (*Luke*, 917) calls it "the chief sin," while Hendriksen (*Luke*, 834) calls it "his Achilles' heel, his most vulnerable spot" and describes the Lord's command as a test of whether the ruler would trust in Him. Cf. also Calvin, *Harmony*, 2:258, "that Christ bids him sell everything is . . . a testing of his latent vice."

64. In a lengthy discussion, Bock (*Luke*, 2:1482) objects that the text never explicitly says that this is what Jesus is doing with the ruler. But the subsequent refusal to sell all and follow Jesus is surely evidence that he was guilty of breaking the first commandment. Moreover, if at that time poor people were in need (cf. Matt. 26:11, Luke 19:8, John 12:5–6), then the ruler's refusal to sell all and distribute is evidence that he did not love his neighbor as himself.

65. Lenski, *Luke*, 917; Stein, *Luke*, 458. Strangely, Plummer (*Luke*, 424) sees two charges—one to go and sell and one to come and follow—but says they may not be separated. If so, then surely they constitute a single command to become Jesus' disciple.

66. Hendriksen, *Luke*, 834; Morris, *Luke*, 293; Bock, *Luke*, 2:1483.

67. Contra Bock, *Luke*, 2:1480; Marshall, *Luke*, 685; Nolland, *Luke*, 888. Later, Jesus, during His follow-up conversation with the disciples, commented about how difficult it is for the wealthy to enter the kingdom of God, an indication that the ruler had not entered the kingdom, for he had not kept the commandments perfectly (Stein, *Luke*, 457); cf. also Calvin, *Harmony*, II, 258; Lenski, *Luke*, 917.

68. So Stein, *Luke*, 458; Taylor, *Mark*, 429; Plummer, *Luke*, 424.

69. Stein, *Luke*, 315–16, 456; cf. Bock, *Luke*, 2:1475.
70. Cf., for example, John 3:14–16, 36; 5:24–25; 6:54; 10:10, 28; 11:25–26; 20:31; Gal. 2:20; Eph. 2:1–5; 1 John 5:11, 13.
71. Lenski, *Luke*, 917–18.
72. Plummer, *Mark*, 240–41; cf. Hendriksen, *Mark*, 397.
73. Gooding perceptively comments: "That is the difficulty with those who are in any way rich. . . . Their present possessions make the kingdom of God appear very much less than the one supremely valuable thing. It becomes at best a thing which they would gladly have in addition to their riches if they could conveniently do so, but not something to be chosen if need be to the exclusion of all else. And as long as they think of the kingdom like that, it is doubtful if they will ever enter it" (*Luke*, 296).
74. "*Il gran rifuto*," Dante Alighieri, *Inferno* 10.27.
75. Hendriksen, *Luke*, 835; Foote, *Lectures*, 80.
76. Marshall, *Luke*, 684.
77. Probably the apostle Peter, cf. C. E. B. Cranfield, *The Gospel according to Saint Mark*, Cambridge Greek Testament Commentary, C. F. D. Moule, ed.; rev. ed. (Cambridge: University Press, 1977), 11; Hendriksen, *Mark*, 12–13, 19–23; Gundry, *Mark*, 1026–45.
78. Gooding, *Luke*, 179.
79. In fact, Bock (*Luke*, 2:1477) finds it curious that Luke "lacks the journey note." It is curious only if one assumes Marcan priority.
80. Marshall, *Luke*, 684, a sentiment clearly shared by Bock, *Luke*, 2:1477, who refers to "a few, mostly stylistic differences among the Synoptic parallels." Nolland does point out other agreements between Matthew and Luke against Mark but concludes that "none of these warrants appeal to a second source"— in other words, dispensing with the Two-Document Hypothesis (*Luke*, 2:884).
81. Marshall, *Luke*, one each on 684, 686, four on 685; on 684, the agreement in the absence of the "journey setting" (Luke 18:18 = Matt. 19:16); on 685, the absence of "do not defraud" (18:20 = Matt. 19:18), the absence of "teacher," the use of the aorist active form of *phulassō*, not the aorist middle form as in Mark (18:21 = Matt. 19:20), and the absence of how Jesus looked at the young man and loved him (18:22 = Matt. 19:21); on 686, the use of *akousas* ("having heard," 18:23 = Matt. 19:22). Marshall mentions four more minor agreements in the verses immediately following Luke 18:18–23 (one each on 687 and 689, and two on 688).
82. For a full discussion about these, see Thomas, "Rich Young Man," 236–46. See also chapters 3 and 6 of this volume for more detail on the Two-Source Theory.
83. Thomas, "Rich Young Man," 246.
84. See chapter 6 of this volume for further discussion of the "minor agreements." Though some use these agreements to argue for Matthean priority—namely, the dependence of Luke on Matthew, and the dependence of Mark on Matthew and Luke—that line of reasoning is not cogent, for agreements of two of the Gospels against the other occur in all three combinations: Matthew and Luke against Mark, Matthew and Mark against Luke, and Mark and Luke against Matthew.
85. R. Bultmann, *History of the Synoptic Tradition*, J. Marsh, trans. (rev. ed.; Oxford: Blackwell, 1963), 67–69.
86. Marshall, *Luke*, 684.
87. Thomas, "Rich Young Man," 256, following Warfield, 109. C. L. Blomberg, "The Legitimacy and Limits of Harmonization," in *Hermeneutics. Authority*

and Canon, D. A. Carson and J. D. Woodbridge, eds.; rev. ed. (Grand Rapids: Baker, 1995), 159, dismisses this explanation of the imperfect to describe a series of questions by saying, "The grammatical thread on which this hangs . . . is extremely slender," and by adding in a footnote, "Mark . . . uses the imperfect of *erōtaō* and its compound form much more often than the aorist, and few of these references suggest an iterative emphasis" (394 n. 119). The facts contradict Blomberg. The "iterative emphasis" is certainly appropriate where Mark uses the imperfect form of these verbs in the plural (cf. for *erōtaō,* 4:10; for *eperōtaō,* 7:17; 9:28; 10:2; 10:10; 12:18), for it is probable that each case involves multiple questions by a number of individuals. Also, when Jesus asked His disciples a question, He probably had to repeat it more than once in order to communicate it clearly to all of the Twelve and perhaps others who may have been present. Interestingly, Mark 13:3 uses the imperfect (3d person singular) to describe a series of questions posed by some of the disciples. I suspect that Mark employed most of his imperfects similarly when he reported only one question in the text itself to summarize the whole series.

88. See n. 41 above.

89. Stonehouse, *Origins,* 93–112. See chapter 11 of this volume for further discussion of Stonehouse's view on this passage.

90. All citations from ibid., 109.

91. Ibid., 109–10 [emphasis added].

92. B. M. Metzger, *The Text of the New Testament: Its Transmission, Corruption and Restoration,* 3d ed. (New York/Oxford: Oxford University, 1992), 129–35.

93. Lange, *Matthew,* 344; Hendriksen, *Matthew,* 723–25, with n. 692; E. J. Young, *Thy Word Is Truth* (Grand Rapids: Eerdmans, 1957), 131.

94. For example, "teacher," "what," "eternal life" (*didaskale, ti, zōēn aiōnion,* Matt. 19:16 = Mark 10:17 = Luke 18:18), "said to him" (*eipen autǭ,* Matt. 19:17 = Mark 10:18 = Luke 18:19), *mē moicheusęs, mē phoneusęs, mē klepsęs, mē pseudomarturēsęs, . . . tima ton patera . . . kai tēn mētera,* Matt. 19:18–19 = Mark 10:19 = Luke 18:20 (on the slightly different form and order of Matthew's account, see n. 48); "to [the] poor, and you will have treasure in heaven [or, the heavens], and come follow me" (*ptochois, kai hexeis thēsauron en ouranǭ* [or, *tois ouranois*], *kai deuro akolouthei moi,* Matt. 19:21 = Mark 10:21 = Luke 18:22).

95. For example, for omission of material by two writers (= retaining by one), Jesus' leaving the house, the man running to and kneeling before Him (Luke 18:18 = Matt. 19:16), "a ruler" (*tis archōn,* Matt. 19:16 = Mark 10:17), "why do you ask me about the good?" (*ti me erōtąs peri tou agathou;* Mark 10:18 = Luke 18:19), "if you wish to enter into life" (*ei de theleis eis tēn zōēn,* Mark 10:18 = Luke 18:19), the commandment "do not defraud" (*mē aposterēsęs,* Matt. 19:18 = Luke 18:20), "the young man" (*ho neaniskos,* Mark 10:20 = Luke 18:21), "what do I still lack?" (*ti eti husterō,* Mark 10:20 = Luke 18:21), "and Jesus, having looked intently at him, loved him" (*ho de Iēsous emblepsas autǭ ēgapēsen,* Matt. 19:21 = Luke 18:22), "if you wish to be perfect" (*ei de theleis teleios einai,* Mark 10:21 = Luke 18:22), "sell your belongings" (*pōlēson sou ta huparchonta,* Mark 10:21 = Luke 18:22), "all" (*panta,* Matt. 19:21 = Mark 10:21), "the young man" (*ho neaniskos,* Mark 10:22 = Luke 18:23).

For retaining by two writers (= omission by one), "good [teacher]" (*agathe,* Mark 10:17 = Luke 18:18), "in order that" (*hina,* Matt. 19:16 = Mark

10:17), "why do you call me good? No one is good except one, God" (Mark 10:18 = Luke 18:19), "I kept" (aorist active, *ephulaxa*, Matt. 19:20 = Luke 18:21), "go" (*hupage*, Matt. 19:21 = Mark 10:21), "whatever you have" (*hosa echeis*, Mark 10:21 = Luke 18:22), "upon hearing" (*akousas*, Matt. 19:22 = Luke 18:23), "he went away sorrowful, . . . having many possessions" (*apēlthen lupoumenos*, . . . *ēn gar echōn ktēmata polla*, Matt. 19:22 = Mark 10:22).

96. For example, on the ruler's approach to Jesus, Luke has nothing except "a certain ruler asked him, saying" (18:18), Mark has the most detailed account, "and as [Jesus] was going into the road, someone ran to Him and, upon kneeling before Him, began asking Him" (Mark 10:17), while Matthew has "And behold, someone approached and said to Him" (Matt. 19:16), namely, having more than Luke about the approach, but without a narrative reference to "asking." Similarly, in Jesus' response to the ruler's claim about keeping the Law, Matthew has only "Jesus said to him" (19:21), Mark again has the fullest account, "and Jesus, upon looking intently at him, loved him and said to him" (10:21), while Luke has "now when Jesus heard [this], He said to him" (18:22), in other words, having more than Matthew about Jesus' reaction to the ruler's statement, but minus Mark's detail about the Lord's gaze and love.

97. See chapters 3 and 6 for further information on Griesbach's Four-Source Theory.

98. Stein (*Luke*, 457), although Nolland (*Luke*, 2:886) writes in a slightly more cautious manner, "Since 'you shall not defraud' is not among the Ten Commandments, its omission by both Matthew and Luke is understandable."

99. Marshall, *Luke*, 685.

100. Nor is Marshall's equivocation, evidenced in the word "suggests," of any help here, for though his use of that word does not promote inauthenticity as much as a stronger term would have, it still shows his openness to the likelihood that Jesus never spoke the fifth commandment to the rich ruler.

101. Cf. John 1:1–18; 6:66–69; 2 Pet. 1:16–18; 1 John 1:1–4.

102. Marshall, *Luke*, 685; Nolland, *Luke*, 2:886; Stein, *Luke*, 457.

103. Marshall, *Luke*, 688.

104. Nolland, *Luke*, 2:886; cf. Stein, *Luke*, 453, 457; Marshall (*Luke*, 685) thinks that by Luke's omission of Jesus' emotion "in this way the story is generalised."

105. Marshall, *Luke*, 685.

106. Liefeld ("Luke," 1003–4) comments, "Luke's report of this part of the conversation—'You still lack one thing'—corresponds to Matthew's—'If you want to be perfect' (19:21)—in the same way that Luke 6:36—'Be merciful'—corresponds to Matthew 5:48—'Be perfect.' In each case, the record in Matthew speaks generally of righteousness, whereas that in Luke (and also Mark) concentrates on that which is yet needed in order to produce righteous perfection." By themselves, these remarks seem innocent enough, but Liefeld's discussion of the phrase "be merciful" in Luke 6:36 (894) is as follows: "Since Luke omits a discussion of the Law and Pharisees that would not be appropriate for his readership, he omits the imperative about being perfect and replaces it with one about being merciful."

Everything hinges on whether Jesus actually spoke the replacement phrase "be merciful" on this occasion either before or after the command recorded in Matthew 5:48, "be perfect." If so, the problem disappears. If not, however, the problem remains, for it is difficult to take commands to be perfect and to be merciful as equivalent. If they are equivalent, Luke is guilty of obfuscating the Lord's words. If they are not equivalent, Luke is responsible for putting in the Lord's mouth words that He never spoke. Either of these problems is extremely serious and weighs heavily on the question of reliability of the gospel record about Jesus.

Similarly, Bock (1480) writes, "Matthew's account is fuller, for he alone notes that the ruler asked an additional question about what was still lacking. This suggests that the ruler is disappointed with Jesus' reply and wants to know if that is all there is to his answer. In contrast, Mark 10:21 = Luke 18:22 note how Jesus initiates the idea that the ruler still lacks something. This difference may well be the result of their telescoping the conversation." Again, in his remarks about "telescoping the conversation," Bock apparently means that Luke has taken the *eti* ("still" or "yet") from Matthew's text (or rather from a source used by Matthew), where the ruler spoke it and made it part of Jesus' reply. Along the same lines, Bock refers to Luke's portrayal of Jesus, rather than the ruler, as initiating the suggestion that the ruler still lacked one thing. If this were true, one would have to decide between the reliability of Matthew's or Luke's (and Mark's) account of the conversation, for there is a good deal of difference between the ruler initiating an idea and Jesus initiating it. In the context of the whole interview, however, it should be obvious to any reader of the full incident (Luke 18:18–30) that the ruler first broached the thought that he still lacked something. Else, why would he have come to Jesus at all?

107. Marshall (*Luke,* 685) writes, "He [Luke] . . . adds the antecedent *panta,* of which he is fond"; cf. Nolland, *Luke,* 2:886; Stein, *Luke,* 457.

108. Marshall, *Luke,* 686.

109. Nolland, *Luke,* 2:887.

110. For ignoring without comment, see Marshall, *Luke,* esp. 685–86; cf. Nolland (*Luke,* 2:884), who, after mentioning most of the minor agreements identified in n. 81 above, writes "none of these warrants an appeal to a second source."

CHAPTER NINE

Impact of Historical Criticism on Hermeneutics

Robert L. Thomas

As INDICATED IN CHAPTER 6, Redaction Criticism is in some senses one of the final stages of Historical Criticism.[1] Some have questioned the legitimacy of the expression "*evangelical* redaction criticism," for the practice of Redaction Criticism by evangelicals has never made a clean break with the roots of the ideology.[2] Others adamantly defend the propriety of the expression.[3]

One reason for the great disparity between these two viewpoints is the lack of a consensus definition of "Redaction Criticism." Some see connotations arising from the disciplines' historical origination and development.[4] With that framework as part of the signification, excluding the radical presuppositions of redaction critics like Bornkamm, Marxsen, and Conzelmann is impossible. Those positions are clearly inimical to an evangelical stance. Yet others plead that Redaction Criticism can exist apart from the associations of its historical roots.[5] They argue that the discipline itself is atheological and need not carry the implications attached to it by its originators. The present chapter will focus on this latter group.

The other reason for the great divergence in viewpoints about the legitimacy of "*evangelical* redaction criticism" stems from differences of opinion about the meaning of "evangelical." Some people associated with the International Council on Biblical Inerrancy define an evangelical as one who can subscribe to the "Chicago Statement" of 1978.[6] To others, however, an evangelical is anyone who is more conservative than someone else, whoever that someone else may be. Such a person prefers to talk about biblical authority rather than biblical inerrancy.[7]

The present chapter does not purpose to resolve the debate about either of the above two issues connected with "evangelical redaction criticism," but rather it will examine certain hermeneutical principles currently being implemented under the heading of "evangelical redaction criticism." By comparing these principles with standards set by the traditional grammatical-historical method of exegesis, the following discussion will seek to measure how current practices match up with that system of interpretation.

317

Evangelical redaction critics have written a good number of articles and books about the Synoptic Gospels, but since it is not possible to deal with every nuance of every evangelical redaction critic, primary attention will go to three of the earliest commentaries of this type that blazed a trail for others to follow: Robert H. Gundry's work on Matthew,[8] William L. Lane's on Mark,[9] and I. Howard Marshall's on Luke.[10]

Evangelical practitioners of Historical Criticism have given indirect signs that they are aware of some of their methodology's impact on hermeneutics. Lane has written, "That redaction criticism is a valid hermeneutical approach to understanding the text of Mark and the intention of the evangelist has been assumed in this commentary."[11] That statement appears to reflect a consciousness of something new and different by way of interpretive methodology. Marshall is more direct when he says that his work on Luke "will . . . attempt to provide a theological understanding of the text, based on *historical-critical-linguistic* exegesis."[12] Though implying in his discussion a difference between his methodology and that practiced in earlier times (presumably the grammatical-historical), Marshall does not state explicitly what that difference is.[13] He only says that the added element is "the recognition of the primarily theological character of the books of the New Testament."[14]

The goal of the present chapter is to isolate some of the differences in interpretive methodology and evaluate the magnitude of departures from earlier evangelical understandings of the Gospels. That will reflect the kinds of changes made through the addition of the "critical" component to grammatical-historical interpretation.

ALTERATIONS TO WHAT HAS
BEEN CONSIDERED HISTORICAL

Probably the most conspicuous effect on hermeneutics from historical-critical presuppositions is in the area of historicity. Regarding the abuses of Historical Criticism, hermeneutical expert Milton S. Terry wrote these words back in the nineteenth century:

> The various rationalistic theories of interpretation, which ignore or deny the supernatural, and proceed on the assumption that any of the sacred writers feign a historical standpoint which they did not really occupy, are continually changing, and lead only to confusion.[15]

Terry expressed no sympathy for the position that biblical writers "feigned" a historical viewpoint. He insisted on taking at face value what the Bible says about historical perspectives.

A respected twentieth-century hermeneuticist, Bernard Ramm, addresses the issue of gospel historicity thus:

> It has been hard to assess the literary genre of the Gospels. To some the Gospels are pure historical reporting and to radical critics of the nineteenth and twentieth centuries they are mythological

(pious and well-meaning elaborations and additions of the early Church but nonetheless non-historical fabrications). Most modern New Testament scholarship does not think the Gospels are biographies in the usual sense of the term. By this they mean no "life of Christ" can be decoded or deciphered from them. The films, novels, and plays that so construct a life of Christ are at variance with the nature of the Gospels themselves. Also most modern scholars (*and by this expression we are including evangelicals* [emphasis added]) believe that the Gospels are *witnessing* or *kerygmatic* or *preaching* or *teaching* [emphasis in the original] materials. How authentic the materials are depends on the convictions about inspiration and revelation of the scholar. *The evangelical accepts them as authentic materials* [emphasis added].[16]

Ramm notes two kinds of evangelicals: those who agree with radical critics in dehistoricizing the Gospels and those who accept everything in the Gospels as historically authentic. His last sentence evidences his placement of the latter group in the line of historical orthodoxy.

Among evangelical advocates of Historical Criticism, however, that assumption of historical authenticity does not hold. They display a pronounced tendency to use various formulas to explain away apparent actuality of narrative events and quotations. No longer is their initial assumption on the side of historicity. Rather, the theological bias of a gospel writer takes precedence over this and at times negates a historical reference. In contrast with grammatical-historical interpretation, which initially presupposes historicity in narrative-type literature, every text is initially in a "suspect" category before an analysis declares it to be either historical or unhistorical. With that approach, it does not take substantial evidence to overthrow historicity.

Lane exemplifies the tendency toward suspicion. After writing in his introduction, "There is no necessary reason why redaction criticism should lead to dehistoricizing the NT Gospel,"[17] he proceeds to use Redaction Criticism to do so in numbers of instances. He speaks about "the 'commentary character' of verse 10" when discussing Mark 2:10.[18] By this he identifies a speaker of words that in the flow of Mark's narrative come from Jesus. This commentary character is, according to Lane, a Markan invention. Jesus on the occasion of His healing miracle never said anything about the forgiveness of sins such as the statement of v. 10. The words are simply an editorial comment reflecting the writer's understanding of the significance of the healing for his readers several decades later.

In contrast to Lane, Marshall finds no problem in accepting the historicity of Luke's account of Jesus' utterance at the time of this healing.[19] Neither does Gundry in the Matthean account.[20] The difference of opinion among the three reflects the subjectivity of redaction critical methodology, according to which every person does what is right in their own eyes. Grammatical-historical interpretation, of course, accepts that Jesus did utter the words.

Yet the favorable conclusion of Gundry and Marshall regarding Mark 2:10 and its parallels does not rule out their inclination to identify nonhistorical elements in narrative portions. Regarding Luke 3:21–22, Marshall writes as follows:

> The question then is whether the narrative reflects an account of Jesus' actual experience (which must have been handed down by him in esoteric teaching to his disciples) or represents the attempt of the early church to explain for Christians the significance of Jesus in terms of the calling with which his ministry must have begun. . . . The case that Jesus' ministry was preceded by some kind of "call"-experience is strong . . . and the account may well express in concrete form the consciousness of divine calling with which he began his ministry; historical study can scarcely go beyond this possibility.[21]

In this case, Marshall disallows that evangelical historical research can go so far as to assert that the events described in conjunction with Jesus' baptism were actual historical happenings.

Regarding the genealogy of Jesus in Luke 3:23–38, Marshall opines, "At the very outset, however, the possibility of a historical record seems unlikely."[22] At one point in his discussion of this genealogy, Marshall seems to revert to a more traditional grammatical-historical approach. This is when he says, "It is only right, therefore, to admit that the problem caused by the existence of the two genealogies [namely, one in Matthew and one in Luke] is insoluble with the evidence presently at our disposal."[23] Yet his broader discussion does not withhold judgment on these difficulties until further information comes to light, as the statement might imply.[24] It rather pronounces the genealogy in Luke to be unhistorical.

Marshall criticizes Lane for accepting the historicity of two visits to Nazareth by Jesus instead of one: "Whatever the historical basis to the incident, Mark and Luke have brought out its significance in different ways. (The view of Lane, 201 n. 2, that *two* different visits are recorded in the Gospels is most unlikely.)"[25] In evaluating this narrative, Marshall not only sees the two writers as having edited their accounts so heavily that they made one visit look like two, but also questions whether either has retained more than a small fraction of what transpired during the visit. The rest of their descriptions are editorial accretions.

In comparison with Gundry, however, the nonhistorical findings of Lane and Marshall are mild. Writing about Matthew 2:7–8, Gundry describes the author as follows: "Matthew is not so historically concerned as to imply that Herod needed secrecy in order to forestall a spiriting away of his dangerous rival by parents and revolutionaries."[26] After reading Gundry's explanation of the narrative about the coming of the Magi, one wonders whether Matthew is historically concerned at all. Matthew has transformed the Jewish shepherds that appear in Luke 2 into Gentile Magi.[27] He has changed the traditional manger into a house.[28] For Gundry, then, the nonexistent house was where the nonpersons called Magi found Jesus on the occasion of their nonvisit to Bethlehem.

Such is the tenor of Gundry's entire treatment of the first gospel, all the way to Matthew 28:19, about which he made the following comments:

> Matthew edited the story of Jesus' baptism so as to emphasize the Trinity (see comments on 3:16–17; cf. 12:28); yet only Jesus' name is associated with baptism in Acts 2:38; 8:16; 10:48; 19:5; 1 Cor. 1:13, 15 (cf. Rom. 6:3; 1 Cor. 6:11; 10:1–4). Therefore Matthew seems to be responsible for the present formula.[29]

In other words, the trinitarian baptismal formula originated with Matthew, not with Jesus. One could have hoped that Gundry would have taken Osborne's revised explanation of the Matthew 28 great commission under advisement before settling upon such a conclusion about this formula.[30]

Gundry speaks plainly in describing his theory about Matthew's treatment of historic events:

> Matthew' subtractions, additions, and revisions of order and phraseology often show changes in substance; i.e., they represent developments of dominical tradition that result in different meanings and departures from the actuality of events. . . . The data of the text understood against the backdrop of ancient literary genres, not a presumption that narrative style in the Bible always implies the writing of history, should govern our understanding of authorial intent.[31]

Gundry shows his estimate of the traditional grammatical-historical approach in these words:

> Radical historical reductionism has caused a recoil into conservative historical positivism, i.e., a system of orthodox belief based solely on the positive data of historical experience. Such an empiricism, blended as it is with a fixation on history, tends to exclude literary possibilities that would diminish even slightly the amount of history contained in the Bible. But nobody has the right to insist that Scripture conform to standards of writing he happens to feel comfortable with and rule out those he does not.[32]

In other words, to Gundry the grammatical-historical method is a reactionary and extreme position derived from subjective prejudice about the nature of narrative literary style. He understands his own position as a compromise between that extreme and the extreme of radical criticism, which sees little or no history in the Matthean account. Clearly from Gundry's perspective, "historical" should not be the first presumption. Instead literary genres discovered through redaction-critical techniques should come first, and "historical" is the conclusion only when these techniques are fruitless in coming up with some other sense. "Grammatical-critical-historical"[33] is a more appropriate name for that approach, for criticism takes precedence over historical probability.

Marshall's concept of his method is very similar to Gundry's. In discussing the narrative about the birth of John the Baptist (Luke 1:5–25), Marshall concludes in part that "the history of the present narrative cannot be positively established."[34] In the larger discussion from which these words come, Marshall, like Gundry, seeks for a middle ground between granting historicity to narrative sections and outright rejection of that historicity. As a result, he settles upon a mixture of the historical and the unhistorical.

It is quite clear from this brief survey that the grammatical-historical method has become the grammatical-critical-historical method, with history taking a back seat to Historical Criticism. History is no longer the first assumption with evangelical redaction critics. To quote Gundry: "We must remind ourselves that taking Matthew's intent to be solely historical is as much of a critical judgment (conscious or unconscious) as taking it to be a mixture of the historical and unhistorical."[35] Nonhistory is just as strong a presumption as history when Redaction Criticism becomes a hermeneutical maxim, whether it be because of Mark's alleged "wilderness theology,"[36] Luke's "considerably" substantial editorial policies,[37] or Matthew's midrashic or haggadic interpretations.[38]

Many evangelicals justifiably respond negatively to giving Historical Criticism that kind of role in gospel interpretation. Of the grammatical-historical method, Terry wrote, "It is an old and oft-repeated hermeneutical principle that words should be understood in their literal sense unless such literal interpretation involves a manifest contradiction or absurdity."[39] Only evidence of the strongest type can change that positive approach to the Gospels. To this point, no such evidence has appeared. The functionings of the idealogy of Historical Criticism fall far short of the kind of evidence needed to overthrow an initial assumption of authenticity.

REJECTION OF THE PRINCIPLE OF HARMONIZATION

The evangelical redaction critic does not accept the principle of harmonization of the Gospels as a consistent guide in gospel research. If an apparent discrepancy between two parallel accounts surfaces, his usual reaction is to explain it as a redactional change of one or both accounts. He gives only passing notice to the possibility that a reasonable explanation may bring the two passages into agreement with each other.

Gundry summarizes this principle most succinctly when pointing out that "whatever synoptic theory we adopt—and even though we remain agnostic on the synoptic problem—somebody was making drastic changes."[40] When writing about Matthew's tendentious (in other words, biased) patterns of diction, style, and theology, Gundry states, "These patterns attain greatest visibility in, but are by no means limited to, a number of outright discrepancies with the other synoptic gospels."[41] He considers harmonization as traditionally conceived to be outmoded: "The old method of harmonizing what we can and holding the rest in suspension has seen its day, like worn-out scientific theories that no longer explain newly discovered phenomena well enough. In Matthew we have a document that does not match even a selective report of Jesus' words and deeds."[42] These opinions are a far cry from the position of grammatical-historical hermeneutics. In his full description of that method, Terry approved of J. A. Alexander's appraisal:

> The true use of harmonies . . . is threefold, Exegetical, Historical, and Apologetical. . . . And, lastly [regarding the apologetical use], by the endless demonstration of the possible solutions of apparent or alleged discrepancies, even where we may not be prepared to choose among them, they reduce the general charge of falsehood or of contradiction, not only *ad absurdum,* but to a palpable impossibility. How *can* four independent narratives be false or contradictory which it is possible to reconcile on so many distinct hypotheses? The art of the most subtle infidelity consists in hiding this convincing argument behind the alleged necessity of either giving a conclusive and exclusive answer to all captious cavils and apparent disagreements, or abandoning our faith in the history as a whole. This most important end of gospel harmonies has been accomplished.[43]

Alexander adds the following to the above words: "It has been established, beyond all reasonable doubt, that however the evangelists may differ, and however hard it may be often to explain the difference, they never, in a single instance, contradict each other."[44]
Later Terry adds the following:

> In view of the marvellous harmonies and the all-embracing scope and purposes of the written gospels of our Lord, how unworthy the skepticism that fastens upon their little differences of statement (which may be explained by divers reasonable suppositions), and magnifies these differences into contradictions with design to disparage the credibility of the evangelists.[45]

Traditional harmonization lies within the framework of grammatical-historical hermeneutics. That, of course, does not include fanciful or extreme proposals of harmonization that ignore historical, contextual, grammatical, and other hermeneutical features. The abuses of harmonization do not constitute a legitimate reason for ruling against a hermeneutically sound approach to harmonizing parallel accounts.
Gundry is not alone in departing from the principle of consistent harmonization. After an extensive discussion of differences between Luke 5:36 and its Markan parallel, Marshall writes, "Whereas in Mk., the deficiencies of Judaism cannot be mended simply by a Christian 'patch', in Lk. the emphasis is on the impossibility of trying to graft something Christian

onto Judaism."[46] Marshall leaves his readers ignorant as to which of the two emphases Jesus brought on the historical occasion and unable to judge whether Mark or Luke is responsible for changing the meaning of Jesus' words. Marshall also leaves open the possibility that both made editorial changes, leaving unanswered the question about what Jesus Himself said in this historical situation.

Blomberg, who has written extensively about harmonization, summarizes his conclusions thus:

> Two fundamental conclusions . . . do merit more widespread acceptance than they have received. First, "additive" [namely, traditional] harmonization is entirely legitimate as one among many tools for alleviating tension between Gospel parallels, but a survey of the classic "contradictions" suggest that in most cases it is not the best tool. Second, the newer branches of Gospel study (source, form, and redaction criticism), far from necessarily proving Scripture's errancy, regularly enable the exegete to reconcile apparent contradictions in a much less contrived and artificial manner than traditional harmonization. Of course, complex problems regularly require a combination of methods, and the innovative conjunction of redaction criticism with harmonization emerges as a powerful but little-used tool for breaking down some of the most resistant barriers to belief in the accuracy of the Evangelists' narratives.[47]

Blomberg allows for traditional harmonization in some cases, but does not feel that it is adequate to handle all the "discrepancies" in the parallel gospel accounts. He even suggests that Redaction Criticism helps prove the accuracy of the gospel accounts, which is another way of saying that editorial activities of the writers introduced historical inaccuracies in order to emphasize a theological point.

Blomberg suggests, for instance, that Matthew modified Mark's record of the rich young ruler's dialogue with Jesus (Matt. 19:17 = Mark 10:18) to change the focus from Christology to the law of Moses.[48] Blomberg proposes that Jesus replied to the young man in a manner deliberately designed to allow for two meanings. Matthew attached the meaning that suited his purpose in emphasizing the law, while Mark interpreted the words to accord with his focus on Christology.[49] Blomberg's proposal not only violates what the grammatical-historical method says about harmonizations, but it also runs roughshod over the method's principle of assigning each text one meaning and one meaning only.

So far are they from showing any inclination to harmonize the Synoptic Gospels that at times evangelical historical critics appear to find delight in magnifying differences that allow them to implement the tools of their trade—Source, Form, and Redaction Criticism. They thereby gain opportunities to detect different nuances in meaning that they can attribute to editorializing, thereby furnishing more grist for their mill. A typical example of this is the way that Marshall uses the divergence of Luke's genealogy from Matthew's to conclude that Luke's genealogy is unhistorical. And Gundry uses the divergence of Matthew's genealogy from Luke's to show that Matthew's genealogy is unhistorical.[50] Neither favors a possible reconciliation between the two.

The antiharmonistic stance of evangelical RC is an outgrowth of the dehistoricizing tendency of that discipline, and further alienates the idealogy from the grammatical-historical method.

ALLEGORIZATION AS A MEANS OF EXPLAINING DIFFICULTIES

Another hermeneutical mark of evangelical RC is its tendency to avoid harmonistic and other types of difficulties by interpreting ostensibly literal passages in an allegorical manner. A few examples will illustrate the tendency.

According to Lane's theory, in Mark's "wilderness-theology" lies the reason for Mark's inappropriate calling of the land around Capernaum a "wilderness" or "desert" (Mark 1:35).[51] Lane reasons that it was historically wrong to call the area around Capernaum a wilderness, for the area was cultivated during the period Jesus was there. Lane explains that geographical inaccuracy as Mark's way of saying that Jesus found a place of solitude where He experienced a temptation reminiscent of the ones He endured in the wilderness at the hands of Satan.

Gundry is more radical in the use of allegorizing techniques: "Moreover, in their numbers and in their following Jesus during his earthly ministry, the Jewish crowds symbolize the international church, including the many Gentiles who were later to become disciples (4:25–5:1 with 7:28–8:1; 21:8–9, 11)."[52] Gundry apparently means that there were no Jewish crowds, that they were a literary symbol of Matthew's pen. However, one cannot help wondering by what rationale Jewish crowds can be a suitable symbol for Gentile Christians.

Marshall does not differ from Lane and Gundry in following the principle of allegorization:

> Jesus' message is brought first of all to the people of his home town. But when Jesus goes on to speak by implication of the preaching of the gospel and the performance of mighty works among the gentiles, Nazareth begins to take on the symbolic meaning of the Jewish nation. So the narrative takes on more than literal significance; it becomes a paradigm not merely of the ministry of Jesus but also of the mission of the church.[53]

Apparently in Marshall's eyes, the latter portions of this episode could not have occurred on the occasion of Jesus' visit to Nazareth, and he averts the historical difficulty by attributing to Luke highly allegorical language. The statements did not come from Jesus.

Often the allegorical explanation of a difficulty stems from an alleged authorial theme that the critic has conceived in his own mind. These preconceived themes, such as the intermingling of the priestly line with the kingly line and emphasis on brotherhood in the church in Matthew's genealogy,[54] are sometimes utterly fanciful and even incredible to all but the critic himself. The attractiveness of allegory to redaction critics certainly does not commend RC as a viable alternative to the grammatical-historical approach. Terry's words are wise:

[I]ts [namely, the allegorical method of interpretation] habit is to disregard the common signification of words, and give wing to all manner of fanciful speculation. It does not draw out the legitimate meaning of an author's language, but foists into it whatever the whim or fancy of an interpreter may desire. As a system, therefore, it puts itself beyond all well-defined principles and laws.[55]

Later Terry adds, "It is an old and oft-repeated hermeneutical principle that words should be understood in their literal sense unless such literal interpretation involves a manifest contradiction or absurdity."[56] In the above-cited allegorisms, absurdity is definitely descriptive of historical critical conclusions.

AUTHORIAL INEPTITUDE IN EDITORIAL PROCEDURES

Another marked tendency of evangelical RC is its identification of inferior editorial procedures on the parts of the gospel writers. The focus is on the humanness of the authors and their proneness to make mistakes rather than on their inspiration by the Holy Spirit. The Spirit allegedly did not prevent them from committing various forms of literary blunders as they put their gospels together. Those ineptitudes necessitate corrective measures prescribed by redaction-critical analysis.

In this vein, Marshall, though taking issue with those who reject the historicity of Luke 1:34 by calling it a literary device, agrees with them in disallowing the verse's historicity. He denies historical validity on grounds of history and psychology rather than on literary grounds. Regarding the Lukan editorial addition, he writes, "Mary's question is puzzling, since, if the promised child is to be a descendant of David, she is already betrothed to a member of the house of David and can expect to marry him in the near future and bear his child."[57] In essence, Marshall accuses Luke of spoiling the smooth flow of the context by his insertion of an unhistorical question that is a literary misfit. Marshall says Luke committed the blunder in the process of retelling the event "in the light of the Christian understanding of the verse"—namely, in the light of the Christian belief in Jesus' virginal conception and birth.[58]

Terry's elaboration on the nature and degree of inspiration rules out any conclusion such as Marshall has reached:

On this point we affirm the proposition, that a particular divine providence secured the composition of the Scriptures in the language and form in which we possess them. . . . Many revelations may have been given which are not recorded, as well as many facts and experiences which would have been profitable for religious instruction. But the Divine Wisdom guided the human agents in selecting such facts and reporting such truths as would best accomplish the purpose of God in providing a written revelation for the world. We see no good reason for denying that the divine guidance extended to all parts and forms of the record.[59]

Terry contends that because of the ministry of the Holy Spirit in inspiring the writers, grammatical-historical hermeneutics allow for no human gaffes in recording their descriptions.

Yet others join Marshall in identifying human fallibility on the part of the authors. Lane holds the same opinion about Mark's editorial ability. In writing about Mark 2:10–11, Lane had this to say:

The thought that the Lord affirmed his dignity and function before the scribes during his Galilean ministry is in conflict both with general probability and more particularly with Mark's testimony concerning Jesus' consistent refusal to reveal himself to the scribes, priests and elders who challenged his authority (cf. Ch. 11:33). To hold that he did so in Galilee contradicts the posture he assumed before unbelief throughout his earthly ministry.[60]

To rephrase Lane's appraisal, Mark was incapable of presenting a consistent picture of Jesus. At times like this, he lapsed into attributing to Jesus something that did not happen during His lifetime, thereby marring the picture that Mark himself was drawing.

In connection with the same passage, Lane attributes to Mark an "awkward syntactical structure" that he calls "deliberate and functional."[61] It is hardly appropriate to label a writing inspired by the Spirit as "awkward," whether Mark did it intentionally or not. Yet the humanness of the author is so dominant that the evangelical redaction critic scarcely notices the involvement of the Holy Spirit in the penning of Scripture.[62]

In Gundry's opinion, human fatigue is a factor that explains some editorial phenomena: "At first Matthew freely rearranged his Markan materials in addition to inserting other materials (often shared with Luke). But editorial fatigue set in, so that in the latter half of his gospel he stuck close to Mark's order even when continuing to insert other materials."[63]

But fatigue is not all Gundry finds. Regarding Matthew 3:11, he writes the following:

Since Matthew has avoided saying that the Pharisees and Sadducees came to be baptized, *hymas* has to be understood in his text as a general "you" despite the uninterrupted addressing of the Pharisees and Sadducees from v. 7 onward. This inconcinnity favors that the crowds in Luke were the original addressees.[64]

In other words, Matthew misrepresents who Jesus was addressing. Matthew was so unskillful in his arrangement of the parts of his narrative that he commits a classic blunder. Of course, his original readers would have completely missed that literary error, for they did not have Luke's gospel to compare—a consideration that Gundry fails to notice.

It is astounding how unwilling evangelical RC is to give the gospel writers the benefit of the doubt when a decision such as this could go either of two ways. After all, Matthew could have had a different statement in mind than the one in Luke. Redaction-critical proponents are much more willing to accept an ineptitude on the writers' parts in deference to a redaction-critical principle than to seek a grammatical-historical explanation.

DENIAL OF PERSPICUITY OR ASSUMPTION
OF AN ESOTERIC COMMUNICATION

Of strategic importance to evangelical RC is the presence in the text of a variety of literary signals that alert the critic to narrative portions that are not historical. Critics are not always clear as to whether these signals were evident to the original readers. In any case, the assumptions of their presence is another deviation from the grammatical-historical approach.

For Marshall, Luke's three mentions of time in Luke 1:26, 36, 56 constitute a clue to show the nonliterality of the delay in the announcement of Elizabeth's pregnancy that he mentions in Luke 1:24–25.[65] Another example of a literary signal is Mark's "intercalation of one account within another" that sometimes, according to Lane, enhances the sources of opposition faced by Jesus, sometimes shows a lapse of time, and sometimes sharpens a contrast.[66] By this Lane means Mark has constructed an artificial chronological sequence for a literary purpose, but his doing so gives the impression that events happened together when actually they did not.

Gundry's work is also full of such alleged signals. His comment about "the king of the Jews" in Matthew 2:2 is an example: "Since Jesus has already been introduced as David's son, Matthew expects his readers to catch such allusions; or he takes private delight in them."[67] Since Gundry holds the coming of the Magi to be a nonhappening, he attributes this statement of the Magi to Matthew's editorial creativity. "The king of the Jews" is to him a literary signal of nonhistoricity that Matthew hoped his readers would catch or else a signal that Matthew inserted for his own enjoyment.

Gundry's indecision about why Matthew used that signal raises the issue of how evangelical RC views the perspicuity of Scripture. Were those signals incorporated with no intention of their being detected by the general readership? Or were they posed as a sort of secret code that only the intellectually elite could break? In either case, critics ignore the convincing principle that God intended the average reader to be able to understand the Bible. If He designed it to be a book of mysteries solvable only by a select few, a gnostic type of situation prevails with its extreme subjectivity and endless stream of conflicting meanings. Evangelical RC falters badly in its efforts to justify that feature of its conclusions.

Gundry advocates that Matthew's Jewish readers were of a mentality that the "scrabble-like" games he attributes to Matthew would impress them. In describing how Matthew fictitiously substituted reigning kings first and then well-known priests into Jesus' genealogy,[68] Gundry stimulates curiosity about how thoroughly Jewish minds of the first century had been conditioned to that sort of thing. Would a fictional genealogy drawing on the fancies of a writer who is given to stating nonexistent relationships persuade them that Jesus was the promised Messiah? Jesus never taught the Jews in that manner. It is incredible that Matthew, a follower of Jesus, would have done so either. The probability is much higher that such arguments would have been ludicrous to Jewish readers of the time. That "Matthew may intend to play with . . . history for the sake of an unhistorical point"[69] would have carried no weight with those readers. Were it otherwise, evidence of that kind of practice elsewhere in New Testament teachings to Jewish audiences would certainly be apparent.

So it is still unproven that the original readers of Matthew, Mark, and Luke deciphered any of the alleged codes attributed to them by evangelical redaction critics. Gundry contends that the burden of proof rests on those who say the readers did not decipher them.[70] But where is his evidence? Certainly it is not in the teachings of Jesus directed to some of these same Jews. The burden of proof rests on one who claims that the disciple used a technique so radically different from his Master. Jesus clearly regarded narrative style as appropriate only for pure history, as in His words about the ministry of Elijah to the widow of Zarephath and that of Elisha to Naaman the Syrian in Luke 4:26–27.

In the theological postscript to his volume, Gundry argues at length that biblical clarity does not require a biblical writer to distinguish the historical from the unhistorical.[71] He seems to agree that widespread misunderstanding of Matthew's alleged intention has prevailed from the early church fathers down to the present and that this misunderstanding has been universal. Gundry states, "The Spirit of Christ directed the editing, so that its results, along with the historical data, constitute God's Word."[72] But could the result of the Spirit's direction be that Christians throughout the era of the church until the present are totally ignorant of the truth about what Matthew wrote? This clearly is not the way of an omniscient and omnipotent God, who is seeking to reveal Himself through the inspired writings of the Synoptic Gospels.

Gundry adds, "It takes only a comparison of Matthew with other gospels to discover that even where Matthew spins out the tradition he is developing dominical motifs."[73] But how could the earliest readers of Matthew have detected this? They had no other gospels for comparison. Furthermore, how can one detect such "spin-outs"? A comparison with other gospels could be misleading, for the other gospels may have been "spinning out" too. If the church had followed this theory through to its logical end, Christians would be ignorant about the facts of Jesus' life. Certainty about anything would be impossible.

The denial of perspicuity by evangelical redaction critics is diametrically opposed to grammatical-historical interpretation, which teaches the following:

> It is commonly assumed by universal sense of mankind that unless one designedly put forth a riddle, he will so speak as to convey his meaning as clearly as possible to others. Hence that meaning of a sentence which most readily suggests itself to a reader or hearer, is, in general, to be received as the true meaning, and that alone.[74]

That method advocates that an author never "intends to contradict himself or puzzle his readers."[75] Grammatical-historical hermeneutics do not assume an esoteric message requiring special keys to unlock the meaning. Rather, they follow the usual laws of language, which advocate that the Gospels mean what they say, without any special coding—such as midrashic or haggadic style or any other type of literary signals—necessary to unlock the meaning.

OTHER PRINCIPLES OF HERMENEUTICS

A goodly number of other historical-critical principles differ from grammatical-historical hermeneutics. At least a few of them are worthy of mention.

One principle is the marked tendency to see a synoptic writer as the ultimate source of what he has written about Jesus or those in contact with Him, rather than tracing the sayings to the lips of the historical persons who uttered them. For example, Lane attributes parenthetical statements and rhetorical questions to Mark, even though Mark presents them as coming from Jesus or His disciples (cf. Mark 2:10a; 4:41).[76] Also, Gundry traces the words of Matthew 2:5–6 to Matthew, not to the chief priests and scribes, the ones to whom the text attributes them.[77] At times, by doing this, the critics place gospel writers at odds with the meaning of Jesus' original statement. Gundry, Guelich, Stein, and Hagner understand Matthew to have added to what Jesus said about divorce in a manner that contradicted Jesus' original teaching (cf. Matt. 5:32).[78] That interpretation violates the grammatical-historical principle of letting the text have its plain sense.[79]

Another differing practice of evangelical RC lies in its proneness to ignore the original historical setting of a statement. Both Hagner and Guelich conceive of the Sermon on the Mount as a collection of statements of Jesus made on different occasions,[80] but Matthew presents the sermon as having been preached on a single occasion (Matt. 5:1–2; 7:28–29). Marshall takes the sayings of Luke 6:43–45 to have come from a different setting than where Luke places them, with the result that the original purpose of the sayings is uncertain.[81] Gundry says that Jesus' people are Jews and Gentiles, not just Jews, as Jesus' historical setting would have required.[82] Again, these interpretations violate the plain sense of Matthew's and Luke's writings by ignoring the historical context in which the writers place the happenings.[83]

Another mark of the redactional school is its de-emphasis on the role of eyewitnesses. An instance of this is Gundry's view that Matthew conflated a number of scattered Markan phrases in Matthew 4:23; 9:27–31; 10:40 and in quite a few other places.[84] That raises questions about Matthew's integrity as an eyewitness of what he records. In his discussion of eyewitnesses, Stein has a curious remark: "For Luke, there is no distinction between *Historie* (the historical events of Jesus' life surrounding his ministry) and *Geschichte* (his resurrection and ascension)."[85] Does Stein distinguish between events that are objectively verifiable *(Historie)* and those that are not *(Geschichte)?* Is he saying that the assumption of faith is the only verification of Christ's resurrection and ascension? If Stein is, he contradicts the testimonies of eyewitnesses of that Resurrection and Ascension. Grammatical-historical interpretation, on the other hand, views the Gospels as impeccable products of apostolic, eyewitness testimony.[86]

An additional device of evangelical RC is to allow for more than one interpretation of a given passage. An instance to illustrate this is Gundry's theory that Matthew added *ph* to Asa's name in his genealogy at 1:8 to give a secondary allusion to the psalmist Asaph.[87] A reference to two persons at the same point in a genealogy, however, violates a basic grammatical-historical principle: a word can have one meaning and one meaning only. Terry has written, "A fundamental principle in grammatical-historical exposition is that words and sentences can have but one signification in one and the same connection. The moment we neglect this principle we drift out upon a sea of uncertainty and conjecture."[88]

Another feature of evangelical RC is a reticence to allow that Jesus may have repeated the same or similar words on different occasions. Rather than understanding Him to have done so, redactionists usually explain similar accounts in different settings in the Gospels as a relocating of His single utterances into various contexts by the writers to serve their own differing theological purposes. Gundry contends that Matthew relocates an eschatological parable into Matthew 6:22–23 (cf. Luke 11:34–36), thereby giving it a different meaning.[89] Gundry is unwilling to see Jesus as using the same illustration in two different settings. Silva seems to lean in that same direction, namely, that the burden of proof is on those who advocate that Jesus repeated Himself rather than on those who say He did not.[90] Warfield was of a different opinion, however. He favored assigning instances of similar wording to Jesus' use of the same illustration or parable on different historical occasions, rather than explaining the phenomenon as editorial liberties taken by the writers.[91] With that viewpoint, Warfield stood in the lineage of grammatical-historical interpretation.

Finally, grammatical-historical interpretation has better controls over the subjective whims of the interpreter than does evangelical RC, a subjectivism that is evident not only in the fanciful extremes to which some interpreters go, but also in their radical disagreement with one another. An example of fanciful extremes is Gundry's theory that Matthew transformed the offering of two turtledoves or two young pigeons (Luke 2:24) into Herod's slaughter of the babies in Bethlehem (Matt. 2:16).[92] Earlier discussion in this chapter has noted examples of radical disagreement among critics, such as Lane's understanding of two visits to Nazareth versus Marshall's view that only one occurred (see "Alternatives to What Has Been Considered Historical" earlier in this chapter) and Marshall's and Gundry's difference regarding which genealogy is unreliable (see "Rejection of the Principle of Harmonization" above). In contrast, grammatical-historical interpretation reduces subjectivism substantially by insisting that interpretation be in light of the laws of grammar and the facts of history as they existed during the period of writing the books.[93] Those guidelines go a long way in eliminating the elements of subjectivism that are so rampant among evangelical redaction critics.

CONCLUSION REGARDING COMPATIBILITY

The above survey comparing the hermeneutics of evangelical RC with grammatical-historical hermeneutics has evidenced conclusively the incompatibility of the two systems. They view historicity differently, which in turn causes varying approaches to harmonization and allegorization. Differing views of historicity also necessitate differences of perspective regarding authorial capability and the readership's ability to comprehend. Added to these divergences are others: the ultimate source of what gospel writers penned, an ignoring of historical settings, de-emphasis on the roles of eyewitnesses, single versus multiple interpretations, repetitions of Jesus' sayings, and degrees of subjectivism in interpretation.

The preceding analysis contradicts opinions of some evangelicals to the effect that evangelical RC is quite compatible with grammatical-historical exegesis.[94] The obvious facts of the case belie the conclusion that the two are compatible. The two systems of interpretation are mutually exclusive of each other. An exegete must choose either evangelical RC principles or the grammatical-historical method. He cannot follow a "both/and" approach to the two.

ENDNOTES

1. Composition Criticism may eventually win recognition as a separate discipline from Redaction Criticism. Composition Criticism examines the arrangement of material by a writer that is motivated by his theological understanding and intention (cf. Stephen S. Smalley, "Redaction Criticism," in *New Testament Interpretation,* I. Howard Marshall, ed. [Grand Rapids: Eerdmans, 1977], 181).

2. H. Lindsell, *The Battle for the Bible* (Grand Rapids: Zondervan, 1976), 73, 81–82, 86–87, 204–5; J. W. Montgomery, "The Fuzzification of Biblical Inerrancy," in *Faith Founded on Fact: Essays in Evidential Apologetics* (Nashville: Nelson, 1978), 220–21; H. Lindsell, *The Bible in The Balance* (Grand Rapids: Zondervan, 1979,), 308–11.

3. For example, W. L. Lane, *Commentary on the Gospel of Mark,* NICNT (Grand Rapids: Eerdmans, 1974), 7; R. A. Guelich, "The Gospels: Portraits of Jesus and His Ministry," *Journal of the Evangelical Theological Society* [namely, *JETS*] 24, no. 2 (1981): 125; D. A. Hagner, "Interpreting the Gospels: The Landscape and the Quest," *JETS* 24, no. 1 (1981): 35–37.

4. Cf. for example, Eta Linnemann, *Historical Criticism of the Bible: Methodology or Ideology?* Robert W. Yarbrough, trans. (Grand Rapids: Baker, 1990).
5. Hagner, "Interpreting," 23–24; M. Silva, "Ned B. Stonehouse and Redaction Criticism. Part I: The Witness of the Synoptic Evangelists to Christ," *WTJ* 40 (1977): 78; William W. Klein, Craig L. Blomberg, and Robert L. Hubbard, Jr., *Introduction to Biblical Interpretation* (Dallas: Word, 1993), 95; Robert H. Stein, *The Synoptic Problem, An Introduction* (Grand Rapids: Baker, 1987), 217–18; Craig L. Blomberg, *The Historical Reliability of the Gospels* (Downers Grove, Ill.: InterVarsity, 1987), 20; James R. Edwards, "Who Do Scholars Say That I Am?" *Christianity Today* 40, no. 3 (March 4, 1996): 20.
6. Article XVIII, "Articles of Affirmation and Denials, The Chicago Statement on Biblical Inerrancy," International Council on Biblical Inerrancy (Chicago, 1978); cf. also Article XV, "Articles of Affirmation and Denials, The Chicago Statement on Biblical Hermeneutics," International Council on Biblical Inerrancy (Chicago, 1982).
7. For example, J. Rogers, "The Church Doctrine of Biblical Authority," in *Biblical Authority* (Waco, Tex.: Word, 1977), 15–46.
8. R. H. Gundry, *Matthew, a Commentary on His Literary and Theological Art* (Grand Rapids: Eerdmans, 1982).
9. Lane, *Mark.*
10. I. H. Marshall, *Commentary on Luke* (Grand Rapids: Eerdmans, 1978).
11. Lane, *Mark,* 7.
12. Marshall, *Luke,* 13 [emphasis added]. G. R. Osborne calls Redaction Criticism a tool of the grammatico-historical method ("Round Four: The Redaction Debate Continues," *JETS* 28, no. 4 [1985]: 404, 407–8), but in practice he struggles with the "historical" aspect of the method in the employment of "redactional" tools. See n. 42 below.
13. Marshall, *Luke,* 13, 15.
14. Ibid., 13.
15. Milton S. Terry, *Biblical Hermeneutics,* 2d ed. (reprint; Grand Rapids: Zondervan, n.d.), 242.
16. Bernard Ramm, *Protestant Biblical Interpretation: A Textbook of Hermeneutics,* 3d rev. ed. (Grand Rapids: Baker, 1970), 145.
17. Lane, *Mark,* 7.
18. Ibid., 97. Hurtado agrees with Lane in suggesting that the title "Son of Man" may have been inserted in some sayings attributed to Jesus by the gospel writers in imitation of Jesus' general usage (Larry W. Hurtado, *Mark,* New International Biblical Commentary, W. Ward Gasque, ed. [Peabody, Mass.: Hendrickson, 1989], 41–42). Cranfield also prefers that explanation (C. E. B. Cranfield, *The Gospel according to St. Mark,* Cambridge Greek Testament, C. F. D. Moule, ed. [Cambridge: Cambridge University, 1977], 100). For another example of dehistoricizing, see R. A. Guelich, *The Sermon on the Mount, A Foundation for Understanding* (Waco, Tex.: Word, 1982), 112–18. Guelich traces only three beatitudes to Jesus, theorizes that the Christian community added four (or five) more, and that Matthew himself added one. Gundry, on the other hand, attributes four of the eight beatitudes to Matthew's creativity (*Matthew,* 69).
19. Marshall, *Luke,* 214–16.
20. Gundry, *Matthew,* 164–65.
21. Marshall, *Luke,* 151. Regarding the same event Nolland agrees with Marshall: "An estimation of the historicity of the voice from heaven is finally beyond

the scope of critical inquiry. . . . The perspective is that of Christian affirmation. . . . [T]he differences already in the words from heaven in the canonical gospel tradition show that we are dealing with formulations of Christian
faith, the value of which for reconstruction of the historical Jesus can only
be maintained in close conjunction with other historical Jesus materials"
(John Nolland, *Luke 1–9:20*, vol. 35A of *Word Biblical Commentary*, David
A. Hubbard and Glenn W. Barker, gen. eds. [Dallas: Word, 1989], 159).
Nolland considers the voice from heaven to be an addition made by the early
church in its preaching, the only thing that really happened being a psycho-
logical phenomenon within the consciousness of Jesus. Bock concurs with
Nolland's understanding of the voice (Darrell L. Bock, *Luke 1:1–9:50*, Baker
Exegetical Commentary of the New Testament, Moisés Silva, ed. [Grand
Rapids: Baker, 1994], 333–34).

22. Marshall, *Luke*, 157–58.
23. Ibid., 159.
24. See E. J. Young, *Thy Word Is Truth* (Grand Rapids: Eerdmans, 1957), 124–25.
    Young represents a more traditional grammatical-historical posture of waiting
    for further light.
25. Marshall, *Luke*, 179.
26. Gundry, *Matthew*, 30.
27. Ibid., 31. Nolland, on the other hand, expresses certainty that neither Mat-
    thew 2 nor Luke 2 could have been written with an awareness of the other
    (Nolland, *Luke 1–9:20*, 22).
28. Gundry, *Matthew*, 31.
29. Ibid., 596. Gundry also attributes a special focus on the Trinity to Matthew's
    editing at Jesus' baptism in Matthew 3:16 (52). Blomberg joins Gundry in
    accepting that the trinitarian baptismal formula may have originated with
    Matthew (Craig L. Blomberg, *Matthew*, vol. 22 of *The New American Com-
    mentary*, David S. Dockery, gen. ed. [Nashville, Tenn.: Broadman, 1992],
    432–33).
30. G. R. Osborne, "The Evangelical and Redaction Criticism: Critique and
    Methodology," *JETS* 22, no. 4 (1979): 311, where Osborne reverses an ear-
    lier position similar to Gundry's regarding the trinitarian formula and al-
    lows that Jesus referred to the Trinity as a part of a larger discussion on the
    occasion. See also Grant R. Osborne, "Redaction Criticism," in *New Testa-
    ment Criticism & Interpretation*, David Alan Black & David S. Dockery, eds.
    (Grand Rapids: Zondervan, 1991), 217.
31. Gundry, *Matthew*, 623, 628.
32. Ibid., 629.
33. Compare this terminology with Marshall's "historical-critical-linguistic"
    method (Marshall, *Luke*, 13) in which "linguistic" equals "grammatical."
34. Ibid., 51. See also Guelich, *Sermon on the Mount*, 24–25, where the author
    sees the Gospels as portraits contrasted with snapshots—namely, an uncriti-
    cal approach—and abstract paintings—namely, a critical approach. He takes
    the Gospels as close approximations but not precise representations of the
    historical Jesus. See also Hagner, "Interpreting," 24. This is also the opin-
    ion of Blomberg (*Historical Reliability of the Gospels*, 8–12).
35. Gundry, *Matthew*, 633. Contrast Hagner, "Interpreting," 32: "There is, of
    course, something fundamentally wrong with an *a priori* negativity which
    must then produce criteria of authenticity such as these. In fact, the character
    of the gospel tradition by its conservative nature is such that the burden of
    proof should never have shifted from inauthenticity to authenticity. As in

any *bona fide* historical study the presumption must lie in favor of (or at least not against) the sources until and unless it is reasonably demonstrated that they are basically untrustworthy (as in the courts the fairest rule is 'innocent until proven guilty,' not vice versa)." Yet Hagner falls into the same camp as Gundry with his negative assumptions.

36. Lane, *Mark*, 81.
37. Marshall, *Luke*, 197.
38. Gundry, *Matthew*, 633.
39. Terry, *Biblical Hermeneutics*, 247.
40. Gundry, *Matthew*, 625.
41. Ibid., 624.
42. Ibid., 639. Grant Osborne admits to reversing his position on this issue so as to allow for harmonization, but in an apparently contradictory vein, two pages later he states, "I agree that we can never completely 'harmonize' the synoptics and John—for instance, to attain a so-called chronological 'footsteps of Jesus'—but we should seek a basic picture" ("Round Four," 407, 409).
43. J. A. Alexander, "Harmonies of the Gospels," *The Biblical Repertory and Princeton Review* 28 (July 1856): 395–96; cf. Terry, *Biblical Hermeneutics*, 555.
44. Alexander, "Harmonies of the Gospels," 396.
45. Terry, *Biblical Hermeneutics*, 564–65.
46. Marshall, *Luke*, 227.
47. Craig L. Blomberg, "The Legitimacy and Limits of Harmonization," in *Hermeneutics, Authority, and Canon*, D. A. Carson and John D. Woodbridge, eds. (Grand Rapids: Baker, 1995), 161.
48. Ibid., 159.
49. Ibid.
50. Marshall, *Luke*, 159–160; Gundry, *Matthew*, 15.
51. Lane, *Mark*, 81. Brooks agrees with Lane that there was no desert near Capernaum and concludes that the word suggests the same kind of spiritual testing as in Jesus' temptation in Mark 1:12, 13 (Brooks, *Mark*, 53). For another example of allegorization, see Guelich, *Sermon on the Mount*, 42, 50–52. Guelich says the audience on location during the Sermon on the Mount are redactional creations, not historical realities. He adds, "The Sermon on the Mount, as we know it, is ultimately the literary product of the first evangelist," by which he means Jesus did not preach it to a crowd as Matthew says he did (33). Wilkins also says the addition of the crowd was a Matthean redaction: "[T]his writer suggests that Matthew . . . has added that the crowds were also there, but as a secondary object of teaching because of their interest in his mission (4:23–25)" (Michael J. Wilkins, *The Concept of Disciple in Matthew's Gospel, As Reflected in the Use of the Term Mathētēs* [Leiden: E. J. Brill, 1988], 149–50). These men mean that readers should not understand Matthew to be talking about literal crowds that heard the sermon.
52. Gundry *Matthew*, 8–9.
53. Marshall, *Luke*, 178; cf. also p. 70.
54. For example, Gundry, *Matthew*, 14–18.
55. Terry, *Biblical Hermeneutics*, 164.
56. Ibid., 247.
57. Marshall, *Luke*, 69. Nolland finds the same difficulty in Luke 1:34, but rather than accusing Luke of clumsiness at that point, he attributes Luke 1:27 to

Luke's editorial activity. He implies that Mary was not at that point betrothed to Joseph as Luke says she was (Nolland, *Luke 1–9:20*, 49, 53–54). Neither commentator considers the possibility that Mary understood Gabriel's announcement to mean she would give birth to a son *before* consummating her union with Joseph. They find it more convincing to attribute to Luke questionable editorial procedures.

58. Ibid., 70.
59. Terry, *Biblical Hermeneutics*, 143.
60. Lane, *Mark*, 97. Stein agrees with Lane about Mark's literary lapses in characterizing his literary skills as "lesser" than those of Matthew and Luke and in calling attention to his use of "an incorrect form of the verb" in Mark 10:20 (Stein, *Synoptic Problem*, 52–53). He also finds an example of ineptitude in Matthew (ibid., 75–76).
61. Lane, *Mark*, 97.
62. Cf. Hagner, "Interpreting," 26. Redaction critic Hagner insists on a focus on "the humanity of Scripture," and says that does not necessitate the presence of "errors" in the Bible (26 n. 11). But the practical results of excessive attention to the human writer are evident. Such excess concludes that inspiration by the Spirit did not exclude human error from the written record.
63. Gundry, *Matthew*, 10.
64. Ibid., 49. Contra B. B. Warfield, *Christology and Criticism* (New York: Oxford, 1929), 112–15. Warfield rejects the suggestion that Matthew "bunglingly" composed his gospel.
65. Marshall, *Luke*, 62.
66. Lane, *Mark*, 28. Stein detects "seams" in the verses that connect various episodes together, and on that basis concludes that Mark joined them together in a non-chronological sequence (Stein, *Synoptic Problem*, 165–66).
67. Gundry, *Matthew*, 27.
68. Ibid., 15.
69. Ibid., 636.
70. Ibid., 635.
71. Ibid., 632.
72. Ibid., 640. Regarding the parable of the sower (Luke 8:4–15), Stein has written, "If the interpretation is not authentic, then what we possess is an inspired interpretation of the parable by Jesus' authoritative spokesmen—the apostles and Evangelists. It need not be denied that the interpretation of the parable reflects the situation and vocabulary of the early church. After all, the Evangelists were interpreters of Jesus' words, not mere stenographers. Luke in particular interpreted this parable in light of his own theological interests" (Robert H. Stein, *Luke*, vol. 24 of *The New American Commentary*, David S. Dockery, gen. ed. [Nashville, Tenn.: Broadman, 1992], 243). Like Gundry, Stein would have his readers believe that Luke supplied the interpretation of that parable, even though for centuries the gospel of Luke has presented both the parable and the interpretation as coming from Jesus on a single historical occasion.
73. Gundry, *Matthew*, 640.
74. Terry, *Biblical Hermeneutics*, 205.
75. Ibid.
76. Lane, *Mark*, 27.
77. Gundry, *Matthew*, 29.
78. Gundry, *Matthew*, 91; Guelich, *Sermon on the Mount*, 206–9; Stein, *Synoptic Problem*, 152–53; Donald A. Hagner, *Matthew 1–13*, vol. 33A of *Word*

Biblical Commentary, ed. David A. Hubbard, Glenn W. Barker et al. (Dallas: Word, 1993), 123.

79. Terry, *Biblical Hermeneutics,* 205.

80. Hagner, *Matthew 1–13,* 83; Guelich, *Sermon on the Mount,* 33.

81. Marshall, *Luke,* 271. Stein contends that Matthew relocated the parable of the lost sheep into another context where it was addressed to His disciples, whereas Jesus had originally spoken the parable to the Pharisees and scribes (Matt. 18:12–14; cf. Luke 15:3–7; Stein, *Synoptic Problem,* 249). That different historical setting radically changes Jesus' meaning of the parable in Matthew.

82. Gundry, *Matthew,* 23–24.

83. Terry, *Biblical Hermeneutics,* 205, 231.

84. Gundry, *Matthew,* 63, 177, 201.

85. Stein, *Luke,* 194.

86. Terry, *Biblical Hermeneutics,* 557–58.

87. Gundry, *Matthew,* 15.

88. Terry, *Biblical Hermeneutics,* 205.

89. Gundry, *Matthew,* 113.

90. M. Silva, "Ned B. Stonehouse and Redaction Criticism. Part Two: The Historicity of the Synoptic Tradition," *Westminster Theological Journal* 40 (1978): 290–91 n. 12.

91. Warfield, *Christology and Criticism,* 108–10.

92. Gundry, *Matthew,* 34–35.

93. Terry, *Biblical Hermeneutics,* 203.

94. For example, K. S. Kantzer, "Redaction Criticism: Handle with Care," *Christianity Today* 29, no. 15 (1985): 12.

Impact of Historical Criticism on Preaching

Dennis A. Hutchison

RECENTLY, THE NEWS MEDIA broke a story about a well-known talk-show host who paid another comedian $2,000 for an anecdote. It seems that after hearing the other comedian tell the story, the host decided it would be a great addition to his own autobiography. In other words, he paid another person a sum of money for a story so that he could tell it as though it had happened to him. It did not matter that it had nothing to do with the truth. All that counted was that it was funny and he knew he wanted it in his book. Unfortunately, many today would have us believe that the gospel writers acted similarly as they wrote about Jesus. In their quest for the "historical Jesus" or the theological intent of a gospel writer, such individuals pick and choose between what actually occurred during Jesus' life on earth and what an individual writer added because of his own ecclesiastical or theological situation, or, as some moderns call it, his own "horizon." In the meantime, very few are examining the eventual impact of this methodology on the task of Bible exposition.

Bible exposition has always been a solemn task and an awesome responsibility. The clear and accurate proclamation of the Scriptures is a God-given mandate (Matt. 28:19–20; 1 Tim. 4:13; 2 Tim. 2:2; 4:2; Titus 2:1; cf. Neh. 8:8). Ultimately, God will judge every preacher for the manner in which he fulfills this obligation (2 Tim. 2:15). Many pastors and teachers will face God's negative adjudication for not living up to the charge of this commission (2 Tim. 4:1–2). Reasons for failure in preaching are numerous, and certainly include more than lack of training and laziness. John MacArthur points to a noteworthy reason when he emphasizes that "our commitment to inerrancy is somewhat lacking in the way it fleshes out in practical ministry."[1] He blames this shortcoming for the drift of many preachers toward "an experience-centered, pragmatic, topical approach in the pulpit."[2]

A further reason for failure lies in an inadequate foundation or preparation for Bible exposition. Recent scholarship has attempted with some success to redefine hermeneutics, namely, the rules for interpretation.

338

Scholars have accomplished this through a shift from the grammatical-historical method of exegesis to less sound approaches.[3] They now advocate including practical application of a text to contemporary Christian living as a part of determining the meaning of that text.[4]

In the same vein, many evangelicals have advocated the historical-critical approach in studying the New Testament, especially the Gospels.[5] The result has been an overemphasis on the "horizon" of the individual writers as a basis for contemporary preaching. In terms of the Gospels, they have relegated the horizon of Jesus to a secondary position or, in some cases, excluded it almost entirely. Therefore, in spite of calls for a return to biblical preaching both in the past[6] and in more recent years,[7] the task is impossible without a return to a more sound set of hermeneutical rules. This need becomes quite evident when examining the potential impact of adopting a historical-critical method of exegesis as preparation for preaching the Synoptic Gospels.

THE GRAMMATICAL-HISTORICAL APPROACH TO EXEGESIS

In the past, pastors and teachers who were committed to expository preaching had an equal commitment to a definite set of hermeneutical principles that governed a procedure called the "grammatical-historical" approach to exegesis. According to Milton Terry, that approach is "the method which most fully commends itself to the judgment and conscience of Christian scholars."[8] It is a study designed to discover the meaning of a text that is dictated by the principles of grammar and the facts of history. It seeks to find the meaning that the authors of Scripture intended to convey.[9]

Traditionally, those committed to the grammatical-historical method have advocated following a definite sequence of certain disciplines leading to the final outcome of Bible exposition. The order or process includes four levels made up of one or more fields of study. Understanding the place of each area of concentration in sequence within that process is prerequisite to assuring precise and accurate conclusions.[10]

The foundation of all other disciplines lies at level one. Included here are three basic disciplines: biblical introduction, biblical languages, and hermeneutics. Biblical introduction deals with particular issues related to each book of the Bible: location (namely, where it was written), process of writing (namely, as a unit or in parts), time of writing, background of the writer, immediate recipients, culture, and so on. Also included in biblical introduction is Textual Criticism, namely, the process that establishes the exact words that came from the hand of the author.

A proficiency in the biblical languages also finds its place at level one. Because languages differ from one another, any translation to a different language loses at the very least some nuances. Therefore, to be a competent exegete, one must be able to read the text in the language used by an author and understood by his original readers.

The final discipline located at this level is hermeneutics, that is, the rules for interpretation. Concerning the place of hermeneutics as relates to exegesis, Bernard Ramm has written the following:

As a theological discipline hermeneutics is the science of the correct interpretation of the Bible. It is a special application of the general science of linguistics and meaning. It seeks to formulate those particular rules which pertain to the special factors connected with the Bible. . . . Hermeneutics is a science in that it can determine certain principles for discovering the meaning of a document, and in that these principles are not a mere list of rules but bear organic connection to each other. . . . [Hermeneutics] stands in the same relationship to exegesis that a rule-book stands to a game. The rule-book is written in terms of reflection, analysis, and experience. The game is played by concrete actualization of the rules. The rules are not the game, and the game is meaningless without the rules. Hermeneutics proper is not exegesis, but exegesis is applied hermeneutics.[11]

Therefore, sound exegesis is the application of sound hermeneutical principles.

Only after a reasonable mastery of biblical introduction, biblical languages, and hermeneutics is one ready to proceed to level two, which includes biblical exegesis and nothing else. Exegesis is the step that investigates the meaning of a biblical text. It is the step used to determine the one meaning an author under the inspiration of the Holy Spirit intended to convey to his original readers. That is the meaning determined by employing "the valid principles of Hermeneutics in connection with the data supplied by Biblical Introduction and the Biblical Languages."[12] The order of these steps is crucial. No one can do justice to exegesis without pursuing fields of study at level one, and, at the same time, it is impossible to move to level three without exegesis.

Level three includes a number of disciplines: systematic theology, biblical theology, philosophy of religion and apologetics, Christian counseling, Christian education, Christian administration, missions, evangelism, and homiletics (namely, the organization of the products of exegesis for public presentation). Even Church history, especially as it relates to historical theology, fits into level three.

Lastly, level four constitutes the final product or the fruit of levels one through three: biblical exposition. It is important to note that even though the heart of Bible exposition is exegesis, the two are not the same. Indeed, biblical exposition, or expository preaching, is not equal to any of the other disciplines. It consists of setting forth the fruit of exegesis or the teaching of the passage in a more popular form, accompanied by other helpful material from the rest of the fields.

EXPOSITORY PREACHING

Until recently, the definition of expository preaching has linked it inseparably to the "grammatical-historical method of exegesis." Thomas believes, "The distinguishing mark of expository preaching . . . is the biblical interpretation communicated through the sermon."[13] Haddon

Robinson, in his excellent book on homiletics, says that expository preaching is

> the communication of a biblical concept, derived from and transmitted through a historical, grammatical, and literary study of a passage in its context, which the Holy Spirit first applies to the personality and experience of the preacher, then through him to his hearers.[14]

For Robinson, expository preaching is more a philosophy than a method. He posits that every expositor must first honestly answer the question: "Do you, as a preacher, endeavor to bend your thought to the Scriptures, or do you use the Scriptures to support your thought?"[15] On this basis, he gives five elements to follow in the order prescribed: (1) the passage governs the sermon; (2) the expositor communicates a concept; (3) the concept comes from the text; (4) the concept is applied to the expositor; (5) the concept is applied to the hearers.[16] Thus, according to Robinson, a Bible expositor is one who follows a definite order or pattern of thought as he progresses toward a finished product.

It is important to note that although an application of the text is an important part of the final product, it is not part of the step of interpretation. Application comes at level three in the correct sequence, not at levels one or two. An exegete following the grammatical-historical approach recognizes the oft-stated principle: there is only one valid interpretation, but many possible applications.[17]

Traditionally, a philosophy that views the Bible as God's inspired and inerrant Word has gone hand-in-hand with grammatical-historical exegesis. That philosophy enhances the responsibility of the expositor and, therefore, his commitment to its accurate interpretation and communication. In the recent past, evangelical scholars reaffirmed that philosophy by coming to a consensus that the grammatical-historical method of exegesis is the only interpretive approach compatible with biblical inerrancy.[18] Thus it is strange that so many evangelicals now herald Historical Criticism—namely, the historical-critical method—as their interpretive approach of choice.[19]

RESPONSIBILITY OF THE EXPOSITORY PREACHER

The apostle Paul wrote the following:

> I solemnly charge you in the presence of God and of Christ Jesus, who is to judge the living and the dead, and by His appearing and His kingdom: preach the word; be ready in season and out of season; reprove, rebuke, exhort, with great patience and instruction. For the time will come when they will not endure sound doctrine; but wanting to have their ears tickled, they will accumulate for themselves teachers in accordance to their own desires; and will turn away their ears from the truth, and will turn aside to myths. (2 Tim. 4:1–4 NASB)

Elsewhere, Paul pointed out to Timothy that his task included exposing false teaching (1 Tim. 4:1–6), retaining the standard of the Word (2 Tim. 1:13), and guarding the Word (2 Tim. 1:14). Thus, the basic task of the expository preacher is essentially twofold: he is to teach the Word of God and he is to warn against error and false doctrine.

Understood in all those instructions is that the expository preacher must study thoroughly in order that he may handle the Word of God accurately (2 Tim. 2:15). Therefore, in terms of the Synoptic Gospels, the obvious question is this: "Which method of exegesis best equips the expositor as he stands behind the pulpit to handle the text accurately and/or explain God's intended meaning in the text?"

In determining the best approach for personal study, certain steps are indispensable. The exegete should become thoroughly familiar with the historical background of the passage.[20] He should also become as familiar with the text as possible by reading and rereading it in both the original language and in several English translations. Finally, he will come to interpretation proper, that is, a detailed lexical and syntactical study, in which he seeks to determine the correct interpretation (where differences of opinion exist) and ultimately arrive at the precise meaning of the passage.[21]

THE HISTORICAL-CRITICAL APPROACH
TO THE SYNOPTIC GOSPELS

Historical Criticism is a broad heading that includes a number of sub-disciplines: Source Criticism, Tradition Criticism, Form Criticism, and Redaction Criticism. All but Source Criticism, which is a product of the nineteenth century, arose at various points in the twentieth century. Concerning these disciplines, Thomas writes, "The stated purpose of all the subdisciplines is to *test* the historical accuracy of NT historical narrative, but in one way or another, they *reduce* the historical accuracy of the Synoptic Gospels."[22]

Historical Criticism in its most radical form is the methodology that characterizes the philosophy behind the highly publicized Jesus Seminar.[23] Although evangelicals have been loud in their denunciation of the Jesus Seminar, they have not denounced the method of exegesis that it uses. Indeed, in what may seem like a strange turn of events, many evangelical scholars have felt compelled to adopt a "watered-down" version of this liberal-based philosophy as a foundation for their own exegetical work. Although these evangelicals maintain that Historical Criticism as widely practiced in evangelical circles does not contradict the presumption that the Gospels are historically accurate, the interpretations resulting from their exegesis leaves their claim open to question.[24]

From the standpoint of historical accuracy, the expositor must be alert to the fact that the historical-critical method differs fundamentally from the grammatical-historical method in a number of its presuppositions. First, whereas the latter always assumes the gospel accounts to be historically accurate, the initial assumption of the historical-critical approach is to view their historicity with suspicion.[25] In terms of the Gospels, the "horizon" of the early church and the "horizon," or theological bias, of a gospel writer are as important, if not more important, than that of Christ. Consequently, that approach views a significant amount of gospel material as without any historical basis, for the early church and the gospel writers allegedly created it.[26] One subdiscipline, Redaction Criticism, furnishes an excellent example of how Historical Criticism presumes the Gospels to be less than historically accurate.[27] Grant Osborne's definition, if it does not state it explicitly, certainly implies that presumption. He defines Redaction Criticism as "a historical and literary discipline which studies both the ways the redactors/editors/authors *changed* their sources and the seams or transitions they utilized to link those traditions into a unified whole."[28]

Second, Historical Criticism rearranges levels of the various disciplines leading to Bible exposition. Hermeneutics is no longer just the rules for interpretation, but is now part of exegesis proper.[29] Likewise, application has become part of exegesis,[30] and theology has become the basis of exegesis, rather than vice versa.[31]

Again, Redaction Criticism furnishes an excellent example of how the gospel writer's theological bias influences the interpretation of whether material came from him or from an earlier source. Osborne asserts, "The purpose of this approach is to recover the author's theology and setting."[32] Those words, in conjunction with Osborne's earlier definition of Redaction Criticism, according to which one or more of the gospel writers researched and edited material already in existence, mean that later gospel writers purposely changed the earliest gospel to suit their own editorial or theological objectives. That conclusion is inevitable, for all theories of literary dependence assume that the first synoptic gospel written was a source for the other two.[33]

Although all exegetes and homileticians must concern themselves with each gospel writer's intent and purpose, they must recognize that the historical-critical approach goes beyond what is acceptable. When the approach assumes that the author has changed what was originally written, either the accuracy of the prior document is brought into question, or the theological bias of a later gospel writer receives precedence over the assumption of historicity.[34]

THE HISTORICAL-CRITICAL METHOD AND THE DILEMMA OF THE EXPOSITORY PREACHER

The historical-critical method creates several dilemmas for the expositor. How does the preacher reach exegetical conclusions about the life and ministry of Jesus with such a subjective approach?[35] If parts are historically accurate and others are not, who decides between the two? What is the preacher to tell his audience? Are all the Gospels equally credible? Is historical accuracy not included in an evangelical definition of inspiration and inerrancy? Does the theology of the writer take precedence over a historically accurate portrayal of both the Lord's activities and teachings? Finally, how does one teach the ethics of Scripture when the gospel writers seem to have violated so many ethical principles?

The Preacher and the Historical Relevance of the Gospels

In 1 Corinthians 2:1–5, the apostle Paul wrote the following:

> And when I came to you, brethren, I did not come with superiority of speech or of wisdom, proclaiming to you the testimony of God. For I determined to know nothing among you except Jesus Christ, and Him crucified. . . . And my message and my preaching were not in persuasive words of wisdom, but in demonstration of the Spirit and of power, that your faith should not rest on the wisdom of men, but on the power of God.

For Paul, the content of his message centered in Jesus Christ. Paul says nothing that would indicate a lack of concern for history or that he was part of a creative Christian community that formulated its own accounts of what Jesus said and did. The historicity of Christ's crucifixion was of particular importance to Paul. Indeed, everything he wrote gives evidence that his readers shared the same concern for the historical reliability of existing traditions and also records. For instance, later in 1 Corinthians, Paul evidences his emphasis on the historical reliability of reports about Jesus' life when he summarizes the Savior's actions and teaching in connection with His institution of the Lord's supper: "For I received from the Lord that which I also delivered to you" (11:23–25).

With the possible exception of Matthew's readers, the vast majority of those who received original New Testament manuscripts had not seen Jesus during His lifetime or after His resurrection. For them as well as for succeeding generations, the object of faith was Jesus Christ as revealed in the Gospels. Little, if any, evidence indicates that those first-century readers were less interested in history than believers around the close of the twentieth century. With this in mind, biblical expositors and preachers have traditionally approached Scripture with the understanding that the gospel accounts accurately portray events and teachings as they actually happened. The first assumption of the exegete following the grammatical-historical method is that harmonizations are possible for apparent contradictions in the Gospels.

On the other hand, the exegete following the historical-critical method takes the opposite view with regard to history. Robert Gundry has written the following:

> Radical historical reductionism has caused a recoil into conservative historical positivism, i.e., a system of orthodox belief based solely on the positive data of historical experience. Such an empiricism, blended as it is with a fixation on history, tends to exclude literary possibilities that would diminish even slightly the amount of history contained in the Bible. But nobody has the right to insist that Scripture conform to standards of writing he happens to feel comfortable with and rule out those he does not.[36]

In this statement, Gundry has attempted to turn the tables on those who are orthodox in doctrine and interpret Scripture following the grammatical-historical method. He portrays the grammatical-historical method of exegesis as reactionary, at the opposite extreme from "radical historical reductionism." Between the two, he places an evangelical approach to Historical Criticism, which devalues the historical accuracy of the Gospels. Concerning this he has written, "The data of the text understood against the backdrop of ancient literary genres, not a presumption that narrative style in the Bible always implies the writing of history, should govern our understanding of authorial intent."[37] In other words, although Gundry has admitted that evangelical Historical Criticism would "diminish even slightly the amount of history contained in the Bible," he posits that its loss does not affect an understanding of what the gospel writers were trying to convey. Yet, despite Gundry's claim, the loss, however small, creates a serious dilemma for the preacher. How does he know what is historical and what is not? How much history is really lost, and does it matter? What does he do with apparent contradictions? How much does he really know about Jesus, the one whom he claims to trust? What about the preacher's audience, and what does he convey to them?

How does the preacher know what is historical and what is not? The evangelical redaction critic claims that a variety of clues or signals should alert readers to the fact that a part of the narrative is not historical.[38] For Marshall, the three mentions of time in Luke 1:26, 36, and 56 is such a clue. Seeing these, he says the interpreter should know that the delay in the announcement of Elizabeth's pregnancy should not be taken literally (Luke 1:24–25).[39] For Gundry, Matthew's comment about "the king of the Jews" in Matthew 2:2 is the signal to alert his readers that the account of the Magi is really a non-literal event. Gundry posits, "Since Jesus has already been introduced as David's son, Matthew expects his readers to catch such allusions; or he takes private delight in them."[40] Concerning this, Thomas correctly notes the following:

> Gundry's indecision on this point raises the issue of how evangelical redaction criticism stands regarding the perspicuity of Scripture. Were these signals incorporated with no intention of their being detected by the general readership? Or were they posed as a sort of secret code that could be broken only by the intellectually elite? In either case the convincing principle that the Bible was written to be understood by average readers, at least in general terms, is ignored. . . . Evangelical redaction criticism falters badly in efforts to justify this feature of its conclusions.[41]

Certainly, the subjective nature of these alleged clues renders them useless to the exegete who is preparing a sermon.

How much history is lost and does it matter? Although, as mentioned above, Gundry posits only a small amount of history is lost through the use of Historical Criticism, the evidence indicates that this is a gross understatement. An examination of various works of those using an "evangelical" approach to Historical Criticism provides a list of items that they claim to be neither historical nor accurate. A partial list includes Jesus' genealogies in both Matthew[42] and Luke,[43] the account of the Magi,[44] the historicity of events surrounding the birth of John the Baptist,[45] a denial that Jesus spoke the words of Mark 2:10,[46] the events surrounding Jesus' baptism as described in Luke 3,[47] the assertion that the Sermon on the Mount, the parables of Matthew 13 and Mark 4, and the Olivet discourse are composites from various ministries of Jesus and not historical events,[48] a denial that some of the beatitudes came from the lips of Jesus,[49] a denial of Matthew's account that Jesus commissioned the Twelve on a single occasion,[50] and a denial that the words of Matthew 28:19 are those of Jesus.[51]

Obviously, that list incorporates more than a small amount of history, especially in light of the list's being only *representative* of many more episodes. In the meantime, it appears that no one has asked the obvious question, "How does an evangelical approach to Historical Criticism facilitate the task of the expository preacher who feels the responsibility to preach God's Word accurately with confidence and conviction?" The obvious answer is that it provides no help at all. Indeed, what is the benefit of an embellished portrayal of the Lord Jesus Christ? Equally perplexing is the subjectivity of all this. No unanimity prevails among those following the historical-critical method about any of the "redactions" listed above.

Again, Thomas correctly observes the following:

> Finally, evangelical redaction criticism has as yet devised no means for controlling the subjective whims of the critic. The subjectivism is seen not only in the fanciful extremes to which some interpreters go but also in their radical disagreement with one another.[52]

Instead of teaching with conviction and answering questions, the preacher has the unenviable task of asking questions and leaving his audience in doubt as to what Jesus actually said or did, or for that matter, who Jesus really is.

The Preacher and Harmonization of Apparent Conflicts in the Gospels

Closely related to the discussion of historical accuracy is the topic of harmonizing Scripture. Until the nineteenth century, harmonizing the Gospels was a common and accepted practice.[53] However, with the rise of areas of Historical Criticism, many New Testament scholars no longer consider harmonization to be a valid tool for studying the Gospels. Thomas summarizes Redaction Criticism's position on this when he writes the following:

> The evangelical redaction critic does not accept the principle of harmonization of the gospels as an accurate guide in gospel

research. If an apparent discrepancy between two parallel accounts is found, his usual reaction is to explain it as a redactional change of one or both accounts. Little or no attention is given to the possibility that there may exist an explanation that will bring the two passages into agreement with each other.[54]

Issues affected by harmonization include the differences in genealogies in Matthew 1 and Luke 3, the exception clause related to divorce and re-marriage found in Matthew 5:32 and 19:9, but omitted in Mark 10:11, differences in wording in the accounts of Jesus' dialogue with the rich man in Matthew 19:16–17 and Mark 10:17–18, the length of Jesus' ministry, and many others.

So what is the expository preacher to do with the apparent disagreements he encounters in the gospel accounts? The traditional approach (grammatical-historical) would look for an explanation that would bring the two accounts into agreement with each other. On the other hand, the historical critic would be more apt to explain it as "a redactional change of one or both accounts."[55] In his opinion, the writers took the traditions handed down to them and molded them to reflect the theology they were attempting to develop. This leaves unharmonized apparent discrepancies that the critic considers inaccurate in many instances. Treatments of the genealogies of Jesus in Matthew and Luke offer an excellent example of those alleged inaccuracies. Marshall finds Luke's account inaccurate as he compares it to Matthew.[56] Gundry, on the other hand, concludes that the genealogy in Matthew is incorrect when he compares it with the one in Luke.[57]

For the expository preacher, the removal of traditional harmonization[58] as a viable tool is an unacceptable option. It is granted that each of the gospel writers was setting forth his picture of Jesus from his own distinct perspective. And each one had a definite purpose for writing. Nevertheless, *it is unnecessary, unjustifiable, and unsatisfactory to conclude that they altered the facts of history to achieve their objectives.*

The apostle Paul wrote in 2 Timothy 3:16–17, "All Scripture is inspired by God and profitable for teaching, for reproof, for correction, for training in righteousness; that the man of God may be adequate, equipped for every good work." The foundation for preaching is the inspired Word of God. The preacher's message can be no more credible than the accuracy of the text from which he preaches. If harmonization of the gospels is impossible because of historical inaccuracies introduced by each evangelist, then at least three adjustments arise for the expository preacher. First, he has to redefine the doctrine of inspiration to include the possibility of errors in the text. Second, the subjectivity of the historical-critical approach makes it nearly impossible for the expository preacher to determine what can be harmonized and what cannot, so he must be content to preach uncertainties about Jesus.[59] And third, the preacher must rethink the value of a historically inaccurate text in accomplishing the purpose Paul espoused in 2 Timothy 3:16–17.

Those adjustments undercut the preacher's primary purpose in preaching, for it is ultimately important for him that his audience know what Jesus said and did. The only Jesus that people know is the one described in the four gospels. Without that historical foundation provided consistently in all four gospels, the task of the expository preacher is not only illogical, but also impossible. Why be so concerned with a text that does not reflect an accurate account of what really transpired in the life of the Person who is the subject of the preaching?

The Preacher and the "Horizons" of the Evangelists

By definition, the purpose of the redaction critic is to "recover the author's theology and setting,"[60] or in recent parlance, the author's "horizon."[61] Concerning the process Osborne writes, "Redaction critics work also with the results of form and tradition criticism, assuming the process of tradition development but studying primarily the final stage, the *changes* wrought by the Evangelists themselves."[62] What this means is that the redaction critic focuses less on the biographical interests of the gospel writers, and lays stress on their purpose or theology. Osborne states further:

> In short, redaction criticism has enabled us to rediscover the Evangelists as inspired authors and to understand their books for the first time as truly Gospels; not just biographical accounts but history with a message. They did not merely chronicle events but *interpreted them and produced historical sermons.*[63]

Thomas and Gundry give a more conservative look at how Redaction Criticism views the Gospels when they write, "The writers purportedly took the traditions handed down to them and molded them so as to reflect the church's and their own understanding of the *kerygma* (i.e., proclamation; the preached Word; gospel)."[64]

Although Blomberg warns against creating a false dichotomy between history and theology, he provides few, if any, guidelines to help the exegete avoid the dilemma.[65] In reality, the dichotomy is absent only for the redaction critic. For those pursuing a grammatical-historical approach, the dichotomy continues. Blomberg concludes his discussion on the intentions of the evangelists by saying, "[L]ittle if any material was recorded solely out of historical interest; interpreters must recognize theological motives as central to each text."[66]

How then does all this flesh out for the expository preacher who views the text from the historical-critical approach? Numerous examples exist which indicate that even redaction critics of evangelical persuasions hold that the gospel writers changed the words of Jesus in order to set forth their own theology. Consequently, knowledge of a writer's theology must precede the task of exegesis so as to distinguish what part is his and what part of an account describes the historical Jesus. This is a reversal of the traditional pattern of the grammatical-historical approach, which dictates that exegetical study (level 2 in the discussion earlier in this chapter) must precede theological conclusions (level 3). A few examples will demonstrate the point.

As mentioned above, Gundry rejects Matthew's genealogy as being an accurate account of the lineage of Joseph. Instead, Gundry believes Matthew merely listed "royal prototypes of Jesus King of the Jews."[67] In Gundry's opinion, Matthew included it for entirely theological reasons. His intent was to provide "a large figure of speech for Jesus' messianic kingship."[68] Additionally, Matthew embeds within the framework of this "figure of speech" other sub-theologies, such as the inclusion of Gentiles in the church pictured by Tamar, Rahab, and Ruth.[69] In Gundry's view, Matthew *created* all this in setting forth his theology of Jesus.

Aside from reading Gundry's commentary and the use of a creative imagination, how is the exegete to reach these conclusions? In some mysterious way, apart from traditional grammatical-historical exegesis, he must determine the theology of the evangelist before "true" exegesis is possible. Once more, the realm of total subjectivity governs the expositor's preaching. The meaning is in the mind of the interpreter, not in the text.

Also previously mentioned was Gundry's postulation that the account of the Magi was an invention of Matthew. Gundry concludes that Matthew transformed a visit by local shepherds into a visit by Gentile royalty from a foreign country. In addition to changing the people, he also changed the setting by making the stable into a house.[70] Again, Gundry asserts that Matthew's theological bias necessitated the changes. He altered history to show that at a later time—namely, Matthew's time and "horizon"—God would bring Gentiles into the church.[71]

Another favorite theory of alteration deals with the exception clauses connected with Jesus' forbidding of divorce and remarriage in Matthew 5:32 and 19:9. Among the three reasons Hagner gives for concluding that the exception clauses do not go back to Jesus is the opinion that "the clause is an accommodation to the common understanding of Deut. 24:1, which probably reflects the practice of Matthew's community."[72] It came not from the lips of Jesus, but from the pen of Matthew and originated because of Matthew's "horizon." Gundry calls this "an editorial insertion to conform Jesus' words to God's Word in the OT."[73] Gundry goes on to explain that Matthew purposed to put words into Jesus' mouth to stress the responsibility of the husband so that he would demonstrate compassion on his wife.[74] Ultimately, Gundry not only has Matthew putting words into the mouth of Jesus, but by his own admission, he sees Matthew creating a "new version" of Jesus. Gundry declares, "But it is not for nothing that *Matthew's Jesus* demands a surpassing sort of righteousness."[75]

Concerning Jesus' dialogue with the rich man in Matthew 19:16–17 and Mark 10:17–18, many believe that Matthew intentionally changed the words of Jesus and the rich man because he found them to be theologically unacceptable as set forth in Mark. In highlighting the problem of harmonization between the two passages, D. A. Carson states, "A majority of modern scholars hold that Matthew has transformed the exchange because, at a later time of writing, the church can no longer live with the suggestion that Jesus himself is not sinless."[76] Regarding Matthew 19:16–22, Hagner concludes, "Matthew has extensively reworked the passage, more so than is usually the case with a number of his own special interests in mind."[77] In verse 17 Hagner concludes that Matthew—because of his "horizon" of Christological interests—modified Jesus' question and His answer in Mark 10:18 to avoid the implication in Mark that Jesus is not good and therefore not God.[78]

Undoubtedly, this approach to differing "horizons" teaches a careful Bible student unacceptable practices and bad conclusions. Closer examination shows that the methodology creates particular theologies or theological perspectives so as to explain away apparent discrepancies (for example, Jesus' genealogy or His discussion with the rich man). Sometimes the so-called theology of the evangelist leads to allegorization in order to explain a difficulty in the text. For instance, Matthew's intense interest in the evangelization of the Gentiles and their inclusion into the church is seen as an explanation of why Matthew mistakenly included Rahab in his genealogy. Furthermore, the theory of this same theological concern by Matthew for the evangelization of the Gentiles caused an alleged rewriting of history (for example, Matthew's changing the shepherds into Magi).

Clearly, that kind of analysis oversteps the bounds of common sense and creates problems for the exegete whose concern is preparing an expository sermon. Thomas and Gundry take a much better approach when they set forth the proper mind-set for one following the grammatical-historical approach:

> It may be agreed that each gospel writer had a distinctive purpose in mind, but it is unwarranted to conclude that he altered the facts at hand in order to attain this purpose. Matthew, Mark, Luke, and John were truthful men writing about a system of truth built around Him who is the Truth. To arbitrarily attribute to them an almost endless stream of lies, even "white lies," as does the redaction critic, is to impugn the truth itself.[79]

The Preacher and Historical Criticism's Ethical Dilemma

The above discussion has set forth numerous examples to show that the evangelical historical critic believes that the gospel writers changed or added to the words of Jesus, created historical events, and developed their own theologies to make them appear to come from Jesus. This is done while somehow trying to support the inspiration and inerrancy of Scripture. Even though Gundry argues that biblical clarity does not require Matthew to identify the unhistorical elements of his gospel,[80] Christian integrity dictates that someone ought to question Matthew's ethics (so also those of Mark, Luke, and John) in all of this. How can the author of a book purportedly teaching the highest possible ethics be so unethical as to misrepresent the source of his material? In addition, what does that system imply about the God who inspired the Gospels? Finally, what does it say about the preacher who teaches it as though it were fact? Once more, the historical-critical method leaves the expository preacher with a hopeless dilemma.

CONCLUSION

An examination of the evangelical historical-critical approach to exegesis has revealed a number of things. First, it leaves the expository preacher with no concrete historical basis for preaching the Gospels. Historical accuracy is no longer an assumed by-product of inspiration and inerrancy. Second, the rules of hermeneutics have changed. Application is now part of interpretation. In addition, Historical Criticism has changed the sequence of interpretive steps, forcing the preacher to derive an evangelist's theology before finding the meaning of the text. Third, the subjective nature of the historical-critical approach leaves the expository preacher with more questions than answers for his audience. It is impossible for those following this method to reach 100 percent agreement as to whether a text contains the words of Jesus or is simply a statement created by the gospel writer. Fourth, harmonization is no longer a valid tool for exegesis or sermon preparation under this system. Fifth and finally, the approach leaves the expository preacher with an unresolvable ethical dilemma. How does one preach about ethics from texts purporting to contain the words of Jesus, when in fact He may not have spoken them at all?

John MacArthur writes the following:

> Exegesis can now be defined as the skillful application of *sound hermeneutical principles* to the biblical text in the original language with a view to understanding and declaring the author's intended meaning both to the immediate and subsequent audiences.[81]

Although, evangelical Historical Criticism may lay claim to sound hermeneutical principles, clearly that method of exegesis falls short of the stated goal. In reality, it creates serious problems for an exegete preparing an expository sermon. In fact, so many problems are created that a warning of its dangers needs to be sounded to all those whom God has called to pulpit ministry.

ENDNOTES

1. John MacArthur, Jr., "The Mandate of Biblical Inerrancy: Expository Preaching," in *Rediscovering Expository Preaching*, Richard L. Mayhue, ed. (Dallas: Word, 1992), 23.
2. Ibid. For additional examples see Richard L. Mayhue, "Rediscovering Expository Preaching," in *Rediscovering Expository Preaching*, ed. Richard L. Mayhue (Dallas: Word, 1992), 5–6.
3. Thomas cites several examples, Robert L. Thomas, "Exegesis and Expository Preaching," *Rediscovering Expository Preaching*, Richard L. Mayhue, ed. (Dallas: Word, 1992), 140–41.
4. Osborne writes, "We cannot finally separate exegesis from application, meaning from significance, because they are two aspects of the same hermeneutical act. To derive the 'meaning' of a text is already to arrive at its significance, because the horizon of your preunderstanding has united with the horizon of the text, and exposition has become the beginning of significance" (G. R. Osborne, *The Hermeneutical Spiral* [Downers Grove, Ill.: InterVarsity, 1991], 318).

5. For example, G. R. Osborne, "The Evangelical and Redaction Criticism: Critique and Methodology," *JETS* 22, no. 4 (1979): 315; D. A. Hagner, "Interpreting the Gospels: The Landscape and Quest," *JETS* 24, no. 1 (1981): 35–37; William L. Lane, *Commentary on the Gospel of Mark* NICNT (Grand Rapids: Eerdmans, 1974), 7.

6. C. H. Spurgeon, "Sermons—Their Matter," Lecture 5, Book 1, *Lectures to My Students* (reprint, Grand Rapids: Baker, 1977), 72; John A. Broadus, *A Treatise on the Preparation and Delivery of Sermons* (New York: Hodder & Stoughton, 1898), xi–xii, 1–2; G. Campbell Morgan, *Preaching* (Westwood, N.J.: Fleming H. Revell, 1964), 11; Merrill F. Unger, *Principles of Expository Preaching* (Grand Rapids: Zondervan, 1955), 11–15.

7. Brian Bird, "Biblical Exposition: Becoming a Lost Art?" *Christianity Today* 30, no. 7 (April 18, 1986): 34; Richard L. Mayhue, "Rediscovering Expository Preaching," in *Rediscovering Expository Preaching*, Richard L. Mayhue, ed. (Dallas: Word, 1992), 3–21.

8. Milton Terry, *Biblical Hermeneutics* (New York: Eaton & Mains, 1890), 70.

9. Terry, *Biblical Hermeneutics*, 101.

10. For a fuller discussion of this process, see Thomas, "Exegesis and Expository Preaching," 143–47.

11. Bernard Ramm, *Protestant Biblical Interpretation*, 3d rev. ed. (Grand Rapids: Baker, 1970), 11.

12. Robert L. Thomas, "Introduction to Exegesis" (unpublished class syllabus, The Master's Seminary, 1987), 13; cf. idem, "Exegesis and Expository Preaching," 139–42.

13. Thomas, "Exegesis and Expository Preaching," 137.

14. Haddon W. Robinson, *Biblical Preaching* (Grand Rapids: Baker, 1980), 20.

15. Ibid.

16. Ibid., 20–29.

17. Cf. Ramm, *Protestant Biblical Interpretation*, 113.

18. Article XVIII, "Articles of Affirmation and Denial, The Chicago Statement of Biblical Inerrancy," International Council on Biblical Inerrancy (Chicago, 1978); Article XV, "Articles of Affirmation and Denial, The Chicago Statement on Biblical Hermeneutics," International Council on Biblical Inerrancy (Chicago, 1982).

19. For example, Robert H. Stein, *The Synoptic Problem* (Grand Rapids: Baker, 1987), 139–43.

20. In terms of the Synoptic Gospels, this information is available in New Testament introductions, Bible dictionaries and handbooks, introductory material in commentaries, and so on.

21. For a detailed approach to exegesis, see Thomas, "Introduction to Exegesis," 29–138.

22. Robert L. Thomas, "Evangelical Responses to the Jesus Seminar," *The Master's Seminary Journal* 7, no. 1 (spring 1996): 80.

23. A group of liberal scholars under the leadership of Robert Funk began meeting in 1985 under the name Jesus Seminar. They examined the four gospels and the pseudepigraphal gospel of Thomas. Ultimately, they denied the authenticity of 82 percent of what the four canonical gospels indicate that Jesus said (Robert W. Funk, Roy W. Hoover, and the Jesus Seminar, *The Five Gospels: The Search for the Authentic Words of Jesus* [New York: Macmillan, 1993]). See chapter 2 of this volume for detailed information about the philosophical foundation of Historical Criticism.

24. See Thomas, "Evangelical Responses to the Jesus' Seminar," 83–102, for

ten examples of conclusions arising from an evangelical use of the historical-critical method of exegesis.

25. From a large assortment of examples of this suspicion among evangelicals,
the following are two: (1) Wilkins holds that the presence of the crowds to
hear Jesus preach the Sermon on the Mount is a Matthean addition and is
not historical (Michael J. Wilkins, *The Concept of Disciple in Matthew's
Gospel, As Reflected in the Use of the Term* Mathētēs [Leiden: E. J. Brill,
1988], 149–50; cf. Matt. 5:1–2; 7:28); (2) Bock discounts the historical worth
of the introduction and conclusion to the parabolic teaching of Matthew
13:4–52 by advocating that Jesus taught the parables on separate occasions
and that Matthew grouped them in Matthew 13 for topical reasons (Darrell
L. Bock, *Luke 1:1–9:50*, in Baker Exegetical Commentary, ed. Moisés Silva
[Grand Rapids: Baker, 1994], 718, 742–43).

26. For example, a majority of modern scholars believe that Matthew reworded
the exchange between Jesus and the rich man for theological reasons (D. A.
Carson, "Matthew," *The Expositor's Bible Commentary,* Frank E. Gaebelein,
gen. ed. [Grand Rapids: Zondervan, 1984], 422).

27. For examples of the dehistoricizing effect of Source and Form Criticism,
see chapters 3 and 5 of this volume.

28. G. R. Osborne, "Redaction Criticism," *Dictionary of Jesus and the Gospels,* Joel B. Green, Scot McKnight, I. Howard Marshall, eds. (Downer Grove,
Ill.: InterVarsity, 1992), 662 [emphasis added].

29. Osborne, *The Hermeneutical Spiral,* 318.

30. Ibid.

31. Carson, "Matthew," 422 n. 23.

32. Ibid.

33. Most redaction critics hold to either a Two-Source or a Four-Source Theory.
The Two-Source Theory is usually based on the assumption of Markan priority and another document named "Q," the existence of which is at best
questionable, for there is no extant copy of Q. In recent years some scholars have returned to the traditional view that Matthew wrote first.

34. For example, concerning the account of the Magi in Matthew 2, Gundry
writes, "Matthew now turns the visit of the local Jewish shepherds (Luke
2:8–20) into the adoration by the Gentile magi from foreign parts" (Robert
Gundry, *Matthew, A Commentary on His Literary and Theological Art,* 2d
ed. (Grand Rapids: Eerdmans, 1994), 26.

35. The increase of imprecise definitions relating to hermeneutics and exegesis
illustrates this point. For a discussion of a growing confusion about definitions of common interpretive terms and a related growth of subjectivism,
see Robert L. Thomas, "Current Hermeneutical Trends: Toward Explanation or Obfuscation?" *JETS* 39 [1996]:241–56.

36. Gundry, *Matthew,* 629.

37. Ibid., 627–28.

38. For a more complete discussion of these literary "signals," see Robert L.
Thomas, "The Hermeneutics of Redaction Criticism," *JETS* 29, no. 4
(1986):456–58. He examines some of the "signals" that Gundry in his com-
mentary on *Matthew,* that William L. Lane (*The Gospel according to Mark,*
NIC [Grand Rapids: Eerdmans, 1974]), and that I. Howard Marshall (*The
Gospel of Luke,* New International Greek Testament Commentary [Grand
Rapids: Eerdmans, 1978)] have identified.

39. Marshall, *Luke,* 62.

40. Gundry, *Matthew,* 27.

41. Robert L. Thomas, "Hermeneutics of Evangelical Redaction Criticism," 456.
42. Gundry, *Matthew*, 15.
43. Marshall, *Luke*, 157–65.
44. Gundry, *Matthew*, 27.
45. Marshall, *Luke*, 51.
46. Lane, *Mark*, 97–98.
47. Marshall, *Luke*, 150–51.
48. Robert A. Guelich, *The Sermon on the Mount, A Foundation for Understanding* (Dallas: Word Publishing, 1982), 33; C. L. Blomberg, "Gospels (Historical Reliability)," *Dictionary of Jesus and the Gospels*, Joel B. Green, Scot McKnight, and I. Howard Marshall, eds. (Downers Grove, Ill.: InterVarsity, 1992), 295; Darrell L. Bock, *Luke 1:1–9:50*, Baker Exegetical Commentary of the New Testament, Moises Silva, Gen. ed. (Grand Rapids: Baker, 1994), 742–43.
49. Donald A. Hagner, *Matthew 1–13, vol. 33A*, Word Biblical Commentary, David A. Hubbard, Glenn W. Barker, gen. eds. (Dallas: Word, 1993), 90.
50. D. A. Carson, "Matthew," 241–42.
51. Gundry, *Matthew*, 596.
52. Thomas, "Hermeneutics of Evangelical Redaction Criticism," 459. See his footnotes for examples.
53. For a history of gospel harmonies, see "A History of Harmonies," *A Harmony of the Gospels*, Robert L. Thomas and Stanley N. Gundry, eds. (San Francisco: Harper & Row, 1978), 269–73.
54. Thomas, "Hermeneutics," p. 452. From the historical-critical perspective, Gundry writes, "The old method of harmonizing what we can and holding the rest in suspension has seen its day, like worn out scientific theories that no longer explain newly discovered phenomena well enough. In Matthew we have a document that does not match even a selective report of Jesus' words and deeds" (*Matthew*, 639).
55. Thomas, "Hermeneutics," 452. Blomberg has written, "[T]he newer branches of Gospel study (source, form, and redaction criticism) . . . regularly enable the exegete to reconcile apparent contradictions in a much less contrived and artificial manner than traditional harmonization" (Craig L. Blomberg, "The Legitimacy and Limits of Harmonization," in *Hermeneutics, Authority, and Canon*, D. A. Carson and John D. Woodbridge, eds. [Grand Rapids: Zondervan, 1986], 161). Those "newer branches of Gospel study" furnish the interpreter with license to deviate from attributing historical accuracy to the gospel accounts.
56. Marshall, *Luke*, 157–60.
57. Gundry, *Matthew*, 14–18.
58. Blomberg refers to traditional harmonization as "additive" harmonization and accepts its legitimacy in such instances as harmonizing the sequence of events surrounding Jesus' resurrection and the stages of His trials (Blomberg, "Legitimacy and Limits of Harmonization," 160–61). But he rejects traditional harmonization in reference to Jesus' instruction to the Twelve about a staff and sandals (Matt. 10:10; Mark 6:8–9; Luke 9:3), Jesus' rebuke of the disciples before/after the stilling of the storm (Matt. 8:26; Mark 4:39–40), Jesus curing of blind Bartimaeus before/after entering Jericho (Matt. 20:29; Mark 10:46; Luke 18:35), the thrust of the rich man's question to Jesus (Matt. 19:17; Mark 10:18), and the centurion's cry at Jesus' crucifixion (Mark 15:39; Luke 23:47) (ibid., 154–60).
59. Thomas notes, "The controls of the grammatical-historical method—namely,

the principles of grammar and the facts of history—are lost in this newer approach" ("Hermeneutics," 459).

60. Osborne, "Redaction Criticism," 662.

61. S. Greidanus, "Preaching from the Gospels," *Dictionary of Jesus and the Gospels*, Joel B. Green, Scot McKnight, I. Howard Marshall, eds. (Downers Grove, Ill.: InterVarsity, 1992), 473. See also Anthony C. Thiselton, *The Two Horizons* (Grand Rapids: Eerdmans, 1980).

62. Osborne, "Redaction Criticism," 663 (emphasis added).

63. Ibid., 668 [emphasis added].

64. Robert L. Thomas and Stanley N. Gundry, eds., "Is the Harmony of the Gospels Legitimate?" in *A Harmony of the Gospels* (San Francisco: Harper & Row, 1978), 266.

65. Blomberg, "Gospels (Historical Reliability)," 294. His opinion is that the Gospels parallel "the more historically reliable Jewish and Greco-Roman biographies and histories." He feels this feature of secular literature explains why the gospel writers did not give equal treatments to all aspects of the life of Jesus; why they wrote topically, rather than chronologically; why they were selective in the material they included in order to reinforce the morals they wished to inculcate; why they abbreviated, explained, paraphrased, and contemporized in whatever ways they felt benefitted their audiences. Blomberg notes, "All of these features occur in the Gospels, and none of them detracts from the Evangelists' integrity" (ibid.).

66. Ibid.

67. Gundry, *Matthew*, 15.

68. Ibid., 15.

69. Ibid.

70. Ibid. 26–27.

71. Ibid., 27.

72. Donald A. Hagner, *Matthew 1–13*, in vol. 33A of *Word Biblical Commentary*, David A. Hubbard and Glenn W. Barker, gen. eds (Dallas: Word, 1993), 123; cf. Gundry, *Matthew*, 90, and Stein, *Synoptic Problem*, 151–53. Guelich says Matthew modified the tradition he received to include the exception clause because of the mission situation among the Gentiles that he faced: "His motivation . . . for inserting the clause in 19:9 would thus have been in confronting the more practical concerns of the Gentile mission and its consequences for a mixed community of Jewish and Gentile Christians." (Guelich, *Sermon on the Mount*, 209).

73. Gundry, *Matthew*, 90.

74. Ibid.

75. Ibid., 91 (emphasis added).

76. Carson, "Matthew," 422.

77. Donald A. Hagner, *Matthew 14–28*, in vol. 33B of *Word Biblical Commentary*, David A. Hubbard and Glenn W. Barker, gen. eds. (Dallas: Word, 1995), 556.

78. Ibid., 555, 557; cf. Gundry, *Matthew*, 385.

79. Thomas and Gundry, *Harmony*, 266.

80. Gundry, *Matthew*, 632.

81. MacArthur, "Mandate of Biblical Inerrancy," 29 (emphasis added).

CHAPTER ELEVEN

Impact of Historical Criticism on Theology and Apologetics

Robert L. Thomas

THE LAST SECTION OF CHAPTER 6—"Issues Raised by Redaction Criticism"—made brief mention of some of the effects of Historical Criticism (HC) in general and of Redaction Criticism (RC) in particular. Three of those were a loss of apologetic evidence for the defense of Christianity, the hiding of Jesus' theology, and a loss of Jesus' words. The present chapter purposes to examine those effects in greater detail so as to show more fully the range of HC's effects.

LOSS OF EVIDENCE FOR THE DEFENSE OF CHRISTIANITY

Evangelical scholars who have built their whole approach to gospel study on unproven theories of gospel relationships—including theories of literary interdependence and Markan priority—have ruled out the centuries-old view that the synoptic writers worked independently of each other[1] and have thereby created a number of dilemmas for themselves and those under their influence. In allowing for such a degree of the encroachments of editorial liberty, they have focused so much attention on the theologies of the writers that they have obscured the theology of Jesus Himself. They have raised serious questions about whether students of the Gospels have any hope of recovering the precise teachings of Jesus. They have reduced to mere human judgment the question of who is correct about the accuracy of the Gospels: the radical historical critics or the evangelical historical critics.

Editorial Liberties

If the gospel writers did take editorial liberties of the type evangelical redaction critics propose, what was the extent of those liberties? Silva has illustrated the difficulty in answering this question with the following discussion and illustration:

> Indeed someone may object that we are opening the door for a radically negative assessment of the gospel story [i.e., by allowing for editorial liberties by the writers]. We can illustrate the

nature of the problem most effectively by noticing some of the gradations that are possible when dealing with historical accuracy. The items in the left column represent a hypothesis (merely for the sake of the argument) as to what Jesus may have actually said or done.

Actual Event (?)	Event as Reported
(a) "Blessed are you poor"	"Blessed are you poor" (Luke 6:20)
(b) "And when you hear of wars . . . be not alarmed" (cf. Mark 13:7)	"And you will hear of wars . . . ; see that you are not alarmed" (Matt. 24:6)
(c) "Why do you call me good?" (cf. Mark 10:18)	"Why do you ask me concerning the good?" (Matt. 19:17)
(d) The Father "will give good things to those who ask him" (cf. Matt. 7:11)	The Father "will give the Holy Spirit to those who ask him" (Luke 11:13)
(e) "Blessed are you poor" (cf. Luke 6:20)	"Blessed are the poor in spirit" (Matt. 5:3)
(f) "Woe to you who are full now, for you will be hungry" (cf. Luke 6:25)	"Blessed are those who hunger . . . , for they will be filled" (Matt. 5:6)
(g) "baptizing them in my name" (cf. Acts 2:38)	"baptizing them in the name of the Father, and of the Son, and of the Holy Spirit" (Matt. 28:19)
(h) One demoniac healed in Capernaum and another one after Jesus crossed the lake (Mk. 1:21ff.; 5:1ff.)	*Two* demoniacs healed after Jesus crossed the lake (Matt. 8:28ff.)
(i) Jesus descends from a mountain to a level place and speaks (cf. Luke 6:17)	Jesus goes up to a mountain to speak (Matt. 5:1)
(j) The Holy Family returns to Nazareth quite soon after Jesus' birth (cf. Luke 2:39)	The Holy Family travels to Egypt, some time after Jesus' birth, before returning to Nazareth (Matt. 2:13ff.)[2]

THE FRUITS OF HISTORICAL CRITICISM

After elaborating on some of the difficulties created by the gradations in agreement, Silva concludes that a suitable limit to editorial liberties would be to go as far as Stonehouse did in allowing for them and perhaps even a little further.[3]

His solution does not solve the problem, of course, but he illustrates the nature of the difficulty. How far did Stonehouse go in his allowance of editorial liberties? The issue arises in his discussion of point "(c)" in Silva's illustration above. Stonehouse, assuming that Matthew used Mark as a source—note the influence of the Two-Source Theory on him—held that Matthew reworded Mark's "Why do you call me good?" and put on Jesus' lips a significantly different question: "Why do you ask me concerning the good?"[4] Stonehouse proposed that Matthew did not make the change because of questions of Christology raised by Jesus' words as recorded in Mark, but did so to focus more specifically on the lesson of discipleship and obedience to the divine command.[5] Regardless of Matthew's motivation, however, Stonehouse still suggests that Jesus never spoke the words of Matthew 19:17; they rather resulted from the editorial liberties of the writer Matthew. Stonehouse proceeds further to suggest that Matthew used freedom in the writing of Matthew 19:16–17 as a whole, namely, in the recording of the young man's question—"what good thing should I do that I may have eternal life"—and the formulation of the rest of Jesus' answer—"one is good; but if you desire to enter into life, keep the commandments."[6]

Apparently conscious that he had raised an issue inconsistent with or at least difficult for an inerrantist view of Scripture, Stonehouse then embarked on a discussion of the larger issue of the trustworthiness and harmony of the Gospels.[7] In this section, he dealt "with the possible criticism that his conclusion damages the doctrine of inspiration."[8] He distanced himself from "pedantic precision" that seeks to weave the Gospels together into a harmonious whole, even to the point of insisting they contain the *ipsissima verba* of Jesus. Stonehouse recommended allowing for *some* liberty of composition whereby the gospel writers made changes to actual historical happenings and speeches. Yet he did not say how much liberty, but in the case of the rich young man passage in Matthew 19, he allowed that Matthew put words into Jesus' mouth that changed the meaning of what Jesus actually uttered on that historical occasion. Stonehouse cited Warfield in support of his view,[9] but a closer examination of Warfield shows Stonehouse to support a view opposite to that of Warfield, who wrote, "And in general, no form of criticism is more uncertain than that, now so diligently prosecuted, which seeks to explain the several forms of narratives in the Synoptics as modifications of one another."[10]

It is incongruous that Stonehouse cited Warfield in support of his treatment of the rich young man passage in Matthew 19, for Warfield expressed himself emphatically in opposition to the very position that Stonehouse defended, namely, that Matthew changed Mark's wording:

That Matthew should be gratuitously charged with falsifying the text that lay before him in the interests of his doctrinal views is an indefensible procedure. There is no reason to believe Matthew capable of such dishonesty. And why the narrative as it lies in Mark's account should have been less acceptable to Matthew than it was to Mark himself and to Luke remains inexplicable. It is not doubted that the dogmatic standpoint of Matthew was fully shared by Mark and Luke. . . . A critical theory which is inapplicable except on the assumption of stupidity and dishonesty on the part of such writers as the Evangelists show themselves to be, is condemned from the outset.[11]

How then did Warfield explain Matthew's different wording? He reasoned as follows:

The two narratives [namely, Matthew and Mark] are in substance completely consentaneous. It is not to be supposed that either has reported in full detail all that was said. Actual conversations are ordinarily somewhat repetitious: good reports of them . . . in condensation. . . . Each selects the line of remark which seems to him to embody the pith of what was said; and the skill and faithfulness with which they have done this are attested by such a phenomenon as now faces us, where, amid even a striking diversity in the details reported, a complete harmony is preserved in the substance of the discourse. . . . *Each gives us in any case only a portion of what was said.* It may be plausibly argued, indeed, that Mark intimates as much by his employment of the imperfect tense when introducing the words reported from the lips of the questioner: *epērōta.* . . . It lies in the nature of the case that two accounts of a conversation which agree as to the substance of what was said, but differ slightly in the details reported, are *reporting different fragments of the conversation,* selected according to the judgment of each writer as the best vehicles of its substance.[12]

So Stonehouse in his conclusion regarding the rich young man passage—and regarding editorial liberties of the gospel writers in general—broke ranks with his Reformed heritage. He adopted a presupposition that B. B. Warfield found to be quite repulsive. Having come to this position shortly before his death in 1962, Stonehouse probably never envisioned how evangelicals would eventually use his concession to the principle of editorial changes to justify some of the extreme positions advanced by those in their ranks since his death. Robert Gundry is an example of those whom Stonehouse may have influenced. Gundry has cited Stonehouse's example on this point to justify the way he interprets Matthew as going beyond the boundaries of present-day historians.[13] Most evangelicals would probably agree that Gundry has excessively dehistoricized Matthew.[14] Carson compares Gundry with Stonehouse and concludes that the only difference between the two is in the degree of restraint exercised by Stonehouse that Gundry lacks.[15] Their presuppositions regarding interdependence and Markan priority are the same.

Carson himself follows the same presuppositions, but criticizes Gundry for the way he uses the presuppositions.[16] Carson may as well have criticized Stonehouse for the same, because Carson comes to a different conclusion regarding the rich young man passage in Matthew, saying that Matthew did not change the meaning of Jesus' words.[17] Yet Carson grants Matthew an equivalent editorial latitude by questioning the writer's accuracy in introducing and concluding the commissioning of the Twelve in Matthew 10, as though all the commissioning occurred on the same occasion. Carson supposes that Matthew has combined the commissioning of the seventy (Luke 10) with the commissioning of the Twelve in that discourse, necessitating two commissionings on separate occasions that Matthew treats as one commissioning on one occasion.[18]

Perhaps Stonehouse had an inkling of where the presuppositions of interdependence and Markan priority might ultimately lead and disapproved of the destination. That may have been the reason he waited so long in committing himself to that position.[19] Yet he took the step and, in a sense, led the way to the present state of confusion regarding the historical accuracy of the Gospels among evangelicals.

What degree of editorial liberty is allowable? That of Stonehouse? Of Gundry? Of Carson? Or even of the Jesus Seminar? All have the same presuppositions regarding interdependence and Markan priority. Qualitatively their methodology is the same. The only distinction is in the matter of personal restraint, an unreliable subjective safeguard.

The Resurrection of Christ

An important element in the defense of Christianity's truthfulness centers in the gospel accounts of the empty tomb and Christ's postresurrection appearances. Grant R. Osborne has devoted a special volume to this subject, in which he strives to separate what is redactional from what is historical in those accounts.[20]

Osborne calls the time notes regarding the arrival of the women at the tomb redactional. Whether it was "at dawn" (Matthew, Luke), "while it was still dark" (John),[21] or "just after sunrise" (Mark), is not an issue to be harmonized. Each writer was free to stress whatever fitted his account best.[22] The number and names of the women at the tomb is also different in the four accounts: three: Mary Magdalene, Mary the mother of James, and Salome (Mark); two: Mary Magdalene and Mary the mother of James (Matthew); three plus: Joanna, Mary Magdalene, Mary the mother of James, and the other women (Luke); and one: Mary (John). Without trying to harmonize the differences, Osborne concludes that redactional factors eliminate the need to bring the four gospels into agreement, but that the nucleus of the account—the empty tomb—is all that matters.[23]

Osborne proceeds to examine other parts of the empty tomb narratives whose historicity critics have challenged: the motive of the women, the guards at the tomb, the stone before the tomb, the earthquake and tomb events, the race to the tomb, the angels at the tomb and their message, Galilee vs. Jerusalem as sites of Jesus' postresurrection appearances, and the deception by the priests (Matt. 28:11–15).[24] In almost every case, Osborne handles an apparent contradiction by reasoning in favor of a redaction by one or more gospel writers, but at the same time arguing for a general historical validity. In summarizing the empty-tomb descriptions, Osborne finds in the episodes a traditional base, but concedes redactional characteristics added by the writers to meet specific needs of the readers.[25] He cites especially the guard episode and the race to the tomb where he finds unusually conspicuous redactions that correspond to the large number of discrepancies pointed out by radical opponents of the empty tomb's historicity.

Next, Osborne examines the postresurrection appearances of Christ.[26] He identifies the appearance to Peter and the Twelve mentioned in 1 Corinthians 15:5 with Luke 24:43–44, but suggests that the appearance to the five hundred (1 Cor. 15:6) was something Paul added for apologetic purposes.[27] Osborne concludes that the gospel writers omitted the appearance to James (1 Cor. 15:7) for editorial purposes and that the appearance to "all the apostles" (1 Cor. 15:7) took place at the Ascension (Luke 24:50–51; Acts 1:1–2), "all the apostles" referring to both Jews and Gentiles in church leadership.[28] Osborne continues to deal similarly with the appearances to Paul (1 Cor. 15:8–10), to the women (Matt. 28:9–10; John 20:14–18), the Emmaus pericope (Luke 24:13–35), the Great Commission (Matt. 28:16–20), the appearance to the Twelve (Luke 24:36–49; John 20:19–23), the Thomas pericope (John 20:24–29), the fishing appearance (John 21:1–14), the reinstatement of Peter (John 21:15–17), the prophecy regarding Peter (John 21:18–19), the prophecy regarding the beloved disciple (John 21:20–23), and the Ascension (Luke 24:50–53; Acts 1:9–11).[29] Osborne finds in all of these episodes a combination of actual events with redactional additions and changes by the writers. For instance, he argues that the originator of the command to baptize was Jesus Himself, but the trinitarian formula contained in the command was a Matthean redaction of a monadic formula.[30]

To a degree, Osborne is to be commended for his tireless efforts in answering critics whose historical critical views are more extreme than his, but how can he answer the obvious rebuttal of those critics? If gospel writers handled actual events as loosely as he proposes, what proves that they did not handle all the data that loosely? With witnesses who were that free in transmitting evidence, who would ever believe that a resurrection ever occurred? If a witness embellished at any single point in his testimony, he may have invented the whole testimony. Those given to exaggeration tend to stretch the truth to any imaginable limit. The view of evangelical redaction critics is that "the presence of discrepancies in circumstantial detail is no proof that the central fact is unhistorical."[31] But the presence of those discrepancies demonstrates the general unreliability of the witnesses and also raises an aura of doubt around their testimony regarding the central fact.

George Ladd also allowed for discrepancies in the resurrection accounts, though he went into far less detail than Osborne. In contrasting the reactions of the women in Mark 16:8 with those Matthew 28:8 and Luke

24:9, he spoke about the "unimportant discrepancies which mark the Synoptic Gospels."[32] Ladd blames the discrepancy on changes made by Matthew and Luke in the reports they had received. That type of reconstruction of events damages the credibility of the writers and therefore the case that contends that Jesus did rise from the dead.

Redaction critical approaches essentially eliminate the apologetic value of the gospel accounts of the empty tomb and Christ's resurrection appearances. John Wenham's presuppositional construct—besides being a normal way to approach the synoptics—provides a far superior vindication of the truthfulness of Jesus' resurrection in particular and of Christianity in general. Wenham is one of the few whose views of the origin of the Synoptic Gospels frees him from the drastic implications of HC and allows him to treat the resurrection accounts as independent of one another. He holds that the accounts "are independent variants of the form of instruction hammered out in the early Jerusalem church."[33] He writes the following:

> It is important to realise that the critical procedures which have whittled away the authority of different parts of the gospels are neither infallible nor sacrosanct. It is valuable, even if only as an experimental exercise, to break away from these procedures and to work on the supposition that the evangelists may have got their facts right, and see what happens. This is an exercise which can stand on its own feet without paying much attention to the many critical questions which have been raised and which need answering in their own place.[34]

Approaching the scriptural accounts with that frame of reference, Wenham has no significant difficulty in harmonizing the resurrection accounts in a traditional way. For example, he finds no insuperable problem in John's description of the race to the tomb (John 20:1–10). Wenham must suppose no redactional activity on the writer's part to explain alleged discrepancies in that description.[35] Nor does he find it necessary to use editorial liberties to explain away difficulties in the guard episode (Matt. 28:1–15)[36] or in the time of arrival of the women at the tomb (Matt. 28:1; Mark 16:2; Luke 24:1; John 20:1).[37]

Wenham's explanation of the empty tomb and Christ's appearances closely approximates the traditional method of earlier evangelicals in harmonizing the different passages, before the inroads of HC into evangelical ranks. That is why the resurrection of Christ has been such a powerful apologetical tool for defending the Christian faith through the centuries.

Machen saw the historicity of the Resurrection as an indispensable element in the founding of the Christian church:

> The great weapon with which the disciples of Jesus set out to conquer the world was not a mere comprehension of eternal principles; it was an historical message, and account of something that had recently happened, it was the message, "He is risen."[38]

Machen surely would have lamented the way evangelicals of the latter part of his own century are tampering with the accounts of Jesus' resurrection to the point of dismissing certain parts of them as unhistorical.

Substantial Loss of Evidence

The tremendous apologetic price that these relatively new presuppositions have cost evangelicalism is obvious. Instead of pointing to the Gospels as invincible witnesses to the words and works of Jesus, defenders of Christianity must now debate among themselves which parts are historical and which are not. About a century and a half ago, Joseph Addison Alexander wrote about "the grand and comforting impression of the Church's strong faith in the absolute consistency of these divine records [namely, the four gospels]."[39] He spoke about reducing the general charge of contradiction in the Gospels "not only *ad absurdum*, but to a palpable impossibility."[40] He affirmed beyond a reasonable doubt the conclusion that the gospel writers "never, in a single instance, contradict each other."[41] He continued, "This is a grand result, well worthy of the toil bestowed upon it by Fathers and Reformers and Divines for eighteen hundred years."[42]

Evangelical redaction critics near the turn of this century cannot make statements such as those. They rather point to the inconsistencies and contradictions that the writers' editorial liberties have introduced into the text. Gundry speaks about the tendentious (namely, biased) patterns of diction, style, and theology in the gospel of Matthew that are visible in "a number of outright discrepancies with the other synoptics."[43] Gundry also speaks about "a vast network of tendentious changes" that cause these discrepancies.[44] He further notes differences between gospel accounts so great that "suggested harmonizations look pathetic."[45]

Blomberg joins Gundry in spirit—if not in pejorative expression—when he judges, "[A] redaction-critical explanation may account for the differences between the Gospels more often than a traditional harmonization."[46] By that Blomberg means, of course, that editorial liberties of the writers explain the harmonistic discrepancies more often than traditional attempts to do so. Later he expresses the same:

> [A] survey of the classic "contradictions" suggests that in most cases it ["additive" or "traditional" harmonization] is not the best tool. . . . [T]he newer branches of Gospel study (source, form, and redaction criticism) . . . regularly enable the exegete to reconcile apparent contradictions in a much less contrived and artificial manner than traditional harmonization.[47]

Note the vast difference in outlook between Alexander, a respected nineteenth-century orthodox scholar, and Gundry/Blomberg, two end-of-the-twentieth-century evangelical redaction critics. Then answer the question, "Who is in best position to defend Christianity against those who question its historical authenticity?" For Alexander, the Synoptic Gospels were historical records, reliable in every respect. For Gundry and Blomberg, they are full of editorial changes that significantly reduce the historical worth of what they record.

All the more alarming is the fact that some evangelical redaction critics speak about traditional attempts at harmonizing with demeaning terminology such as "pedantic precision,"[48] "like worn-out scientific theories,"[49] and "shallow harmonization."[50] That attitude toward traditional harmonization is quite unfortunate. Alexander, many years ago, lamented the existence of that same attitude among German rationalists and other opponents of orthodoxy toward harmonization:

> We mean the flippant and contemptuous ignoring of all harmonizing methods, where there seems to be a discrepancy on the surface, and treating them not only as inadequate, and even silly, but as unmanly and dishonest. To those who are at all familiar with the history and literature of the subject, there is something quite amusing in the air with which some recent and by no means first-rate writers, try to put out of existence, by a peevish exclamation or a wave of the hand, problems and methods of solution, which have been deemed worthy of profound thought and laborious exertion, not merely now and then, or here and there, but by many of the great minds of the Christian Church, in every country and in every age.[51]

Do the disparaging attitudes of evangelical redaction critics toward traditional harmonization portend a direction of their movement toward more radical forms of RC? In other words, how much of gospel historicity will evangelicals surrender? Where will their movement toward a Jesus-Seminar approach to the Gospels end? Is this the leaven that will leaven the whole lump?

With their view of interdependence among the synoptic writers, *all* evangelical redaction critics lack substantially in apologetic ammunition in comparison with ancient church fathers such as John Chrysostom, who wrote, "[I]f there be four that write, not at the same times, nor in the same places, neither after having met together, and conversed one with another, and then they speak all things as it were out of one mouth, this becomes a very great demonstration of the truth."[52] Chrysostom and the rest of the early church writers knew that the gospel writers worked independently of each other;[53] thus "editorial liberties" were not an issue with them.

HIDING OF JESUS' THEOLOGY

With RC's focus on the editorial liberties taken by the gospel writers has come an emphasis on the theology of the individual writers. That emphasis has obscured or even obliterated attention to the theology of Jesus. A few examples will illustrate how evangelicals have given little or no attention to the doctrinal positions of Jesus Himself.

In connection with Matthew 5:17–20, Hagner observes that Matthew "was hardly a passive transmitter of the tradition available to him. He is responsible at least for the present juxtaposition of these four separate verses, a juxtaposition that lends emphasis to the whole."[54] Hagner adds that Matthew "has probably put his own stamp on the traditional material, shaping it so as to make the strongest possible impact upon his Jewish-Christian readers."[55] Hagner proposes that the emphatic thrust of this section in its downgrading of the scribal and Pharisaic righteousness resulted from a need in the Christian community for whom Matthew composed his gospel. The emphasis did not come from Jesus.

Regarding Matthew 5:19–20, Gundry comments as follows: "Therefore we may fairly judge that in vv. 19–20 he [namely, Matthew] continues to expand the traditional saying lying at the core of v 18. The state of Matthew's church demanded this forceful attack on antinomianism."[56] Matthew 5:20, which is the theme verse of the Sermon on the Mount, originated with Matthew, not with Jesus, according to Gundry. Matthew put those words on Jesus' lips to meet a pressing need in the church of his time; thus they do not explicitly represent the teaching of Jesus.

The opinions of Hagner and Gundry raise questions about the theology of Jesus Himself. If the writer of Matthew "doctored" the tradition on which he based his gospel, who is to say what Jesus Himself taught regarding the status of the scribes and Pharisees. Perhaps He was not nearly so harsh in reprimanding their externalism as Matthew portrays Him to be.

In a similar vein, Hagner insists that the correct understanding of Matthew 23 derives from understanding the growing hostility between the synagogue and the church of Matthew's day.[57] Jesus never spoke the words on a single occasion. Rather, Matthew put the seven woes together so as to obtain the emphasis he desired.[58] Thus the harshness comes from Matthew. But that assertion leaves open the question of what Jesus' specific position was on this issue.

For Gundry, Matthew 23–25 contains a portrait of Jewish officials who were persecuting the church of his (namely, Matthew's) day. These chapters also direct their criticism against antinomian ecclesiastics whose influence the church of the apostle's day was feeling.[59] Like Hagner, Gundry holds that Matthew 23 is a collection of traditional material that Matthew pieced together with additions to form a continuous lecture. As throughout the gospel, in 23:1 Gundry takes the disciples to represent original Jewish Christians in the church of Matthew's day, and the crowds represent the larger body of Gentile converts.[60] In all Gundry's allowance for editorial liberties, he and other similar commentators hide the theology of Jesus.

Stein proposes that Luke intended the sayings of 6:43–49 to apply to believers. Stein also suggests that Jesus' intention was the same, but Stein claims that Matthew changed the sayings to pertain to false prophets (Matt. 7:16–18; 12:33–37).[61] But who is to say what Jesus' intention was? Could it not have been the same as Matthew expresses rather than what Luke presents? So, once again, a commentator such as Stein raises questions about the theology of Jesus.

Stein also holds that Luke changed Mark's illustration of the garment and cloth in three ways (compare Luke 5:36 with Mark 2:21).[62] That changed the main lesson of the illustration from spoiling the old economy to tearing apart the new one.[63] However, Stein is not clear about which lesson Jesus taught regarding the old and new economies. Did He teach it as Mark has it or as Luke gives it?

Stein furthermore suggests that Luke's interpretation of the parable of the soils (Luke 8:4–15) is not authentic; in other words, it did not come from Jesus.[64] The interpretation, Stein says, reflects the situation and vocabulary of the early church. Luke must have interpreted the parable in light of his own theological interests.[65] Again, however, that kind of redactional addition leaves open the question of what meaning Jesus attached to the parable.

In Luke 21:20, Stein holds that the writer changed "abomination of desolation" to "desolation" to keep his readers from confusing Jerusalem's fall in A.D. 70 with events connected with Christ's second coming.[66] That change entailed a change in the other two gospels' reference to a desolation of the holy place into a desolation of the city of Jerusalem. If Jesus never spoke what Luke records, the revised meaning amounts to a high degree of editorial freedom taken by the writer. What was Jesus' position on that detail of eschatology?

Brooks suggests that Jesus may not have taught His substitutionary death in Mark 10:45. (This verse is considered by some to be the key passage of that gospel.) Brooks' idea is based on the assertion that the preposition translated "for" may have come from Mark, not from Jesus.[67] This would imply that Jesus Himself did not teach that He would die as a vicarious sacrifice for the sins of many. Brooks also proposes that Jesus spoke the words of Mark 4:10–12 on an occasion other than where Mark places the words. Brooks claims they apply to the whole of Jesus' ministry, not just to the parables recorded in Mark 4.[68] This suggestion, of course, would give the words of Jesus a different meaning from what they have in the context of Mark 4.

To one degree or another, evangelical redaction critics see the synoptics, not as theological teachings of Jesus, but as theological teachings of individual writers who altered or supplemented the teachings of Jesus to cater to the needs of particular Christian communities at a time much later than Jesus' days on earth. For example, Greidanus recommends preaching the Gospels from the horizon of the early church, not from the horizon of Jesus, and transferring the past relevance from the early church to the church today.[69] Greidanus reasons that the Gospels "are not transparent windowpanes, but colored presentations of the historical Jesus."[70] Greidanus apparently means that the Gospels do not present the real historical Jesus, but only the picture of a Jesus that a later generation had painted.

K. Giles seems to lean toward interpreting the forty-day resurrection appearances of Christ (Acts 1:3) as a Lukan redaction.[71] If that were the case, one wonders whether Jesus ever uttered the important words of Acts

1:4, 7–8. Did the command to be witnesses throughout the earth come from Luke's attempt to create a postresurrection account that would give direction to the church of the late first century? That would not be beyond the guidelines of evangelical HC.

Gundry characterizes Matthew's theology in the following ways: his great concern over the problem of a mixed church, true disciples in the church suffering persecution at the hands of the Jews, false disciples making public disclaimers of Jesus under the leadership of church officials who have adopted an easygoing attitude and policies of accommodation, development of an antinomianism in the church that resembles Jewish legalism in failing to require true righteousness, and the Jewish crowds symbolizing the international church (including many Gentiles).[72] Gundry concludes, "All in all, Matthew writes his gospel to keep persecution of the church from stymieing evangelism."[73] In essence, the gospel of Matthew presents the theology of Matthew, not the theology of Jesus. It deals with doctrinal themes relevant to the church of Matthew's day, not themes taught by Jesus Himself. So for Gundry and other evangelical historical critics the theology of Jesus remains shrouded in mystery.

LOSS OF JESUS' WORDS

Evangelical HC now has the evangelical world wondering what words Jesus spoke. The general impact of that field of scholarship has been on the side of assuming the gospel writers *never* reported His exact words or the *ipsissima verba*—the very words—of the Lord.

Ipsissima Vox

Ironically, an extensive discussion of this subject has appeared as a chapter in a volume directed against the excessive dehistoricizing of the Jesus Seminar.[74] It advocates that the Gospels do not contain the words of Jesus, but only His "voice"—namely, the *ipsissima vox*. In that chapter, Bock argues that the Gospels consistently give the gist of Jesus' teaching, not His very words.[75] Bock maintains that the Gospels retained the "central thrust" of Jesus' words,[76] but that the writers consciously changed His words in accord with the purposes of their reports.[77] Stein concurs with Bock on this point:

> [T]hey [namely, the Evangelists] felt free to paraphrase, modify certain terms, and add comments, in order to help their readers understand the "significance" of what Jesus taught. The Evangelists had no obsession with the *ipsissima verba*, for they believed that they had authority to interpret these words for their audience.[78]

Bock gives three supports for the *ipsissima vox* position: (1) Jesus spoke a Semitic language that someone had to translate into Greek; (2) accounts of Jesus' speeches are shorter than the original speeches, and therefore revision was necessary to produce the condensations; and (3) New Testament citations of the Old Testament are not word for word.[79] Of Bock's three reasons, the second is certainly valid. In summarizing Jesus' Sermon on the Mount (or Plain), for example, both Matthew and Luke have obviously omitted material, as a comparison of the two accounts reflects. That means that transitions from one part of the sermon to another, where omissions occurred, had to be constructed, but through inspiration of the Spirit, the writers surely did an accurate job of representing how Jesus moved from part to part. They just did it with fewer words.

Bock's first point, however, is subject to debate. A growing realization among contemporary scholars recognizes the wide use of Greek among the Jews of Jesus day.[80] The assumption that Jesus never spoke Greek is certainly unfounded. It is amazing how much some try to build on their conclusion that He always used Aramaic. Osborne, for example, sees evidence of heavy redactional activity in John 21:15–17, partly on the basis of the inability of Aramaic to express a distinction between two Greek words for "love," *agapan* and *philein*.[81] Similarly, Blomberg concludes that in Matthew 16:18 Peter must be the rock on which Jesus built His church, for Aramaic could not distinguish between two Greek words for "rock," *petros* and *petra*.[82] Both of those conclusions are poor, for they rest on a wrong assumption that Jesus always spoke Aramaic.

The case that Jesus spoke Greek is quite strong. His half-brother James wrote an epistle using literary koiné Greek,[83] demonstrating the advanced knowledge of Greek in the family. Greek was the *lingua franca* of the Roman Empire, and was determinative of the linguistic and cultural character of lower Galilee during the first century A.D. The New Testament documents have existed in the Greek language from their earliest appearance. Diverse epigraphic evidence, significant literary evidence, and several significant contexts in the Gospels (for example, Matt. 27:11–14; Mark 15:2–5; Luke 23:2–5; John 18:29–38) add to those considerations.[84] All of these factors severely weaken Bock's first argument against *ipsissima verba*. In fact, Porter finds a very high likelihood that the Gospels do in some cases record the actual words of Jesus.[85]

Bock's third argument concerning the New Testament citations of the Old Testament is also weak. That usage is not parallel to gospel quotations of Jesus' words. The conspicuous difference between the two types of citations lies in the availability of the Old Testament for comparisons with the gospel writers' Old Testament quotations. Anyone could tell immediately just by looking at the quotation alongside the Old Testament source whether a writer quoted verbatim or whether he quoted loosely or paraphrased. However, with Jesus' sayings that was not possible. No other authoritative written source of Jesus' words was available, so readers were dependent solely on what the gospel writers reported. If their reports varied even slightly from Jesus' actual words, they had nothing to correct the wrong reporting.

Ipsissima Verba

On the other side of the issue, much evidence favors the *ipsissima verba* perspective. On occasions when Jesus used the Greek language—which conceivably could have been most of the time—it is quite possible that His listeners took down what He said in shorthand or retained what He said in their highly trained memories. A general consensus acknowledges that minds of that day in that culture were much more adept in remembering details than the average Western mind of the twentieth century.[86] Jesus' followers had all the more reason to remember His words, as Linnemann has noted:

> *Memory includes a personal relationship and intensifies to the extent that this relationship has significance for the one who remembers.* Things of little importance are readily forgotten; but we graphically recall something that engages the heart. Both the quantity and the quality of recollection depend on the personal relationship to what is remembered. Eyewitnesses to Jesus' words and deeds would be expected to possess graphic memories. They *remembered* what their Lord and Savior had said and done![87]

If the Gospels do contain the very words of Jesus, what is one to make of their disagreements in wording when recording the same discourse or conversation? The fact that no single gospel records everything spoken on a given occasion furnishes an adequate response to that challenge. It is probable, in fact, that no combination of parallel accounts records the entirety of a speech or dialogue. Christ undoubtedly repeated some of His teachings with slightly differing wording on different occasions. He very probably did so on the same occasion too. So instances where parallel accounts report the same substance in slightly different forms may easily be traceable to different but similar statements on the same occasion, with each writer selecting for his account only a part of what was said.

Warfield elaborates on this characteristic:

> It has been said that Jane Austen records the conversations at her dinner-parties with such, not faithfulness but, circumstantiality that her reports bore the reader almost as much as the actual conversations would have done. There is no reason to suppose that the Evangelists aimed at such meticulous particularity in their reports of our Lord's conversations. Not all that he said any more than all that he did (Jno. xx. 30, xxi. 25), has been recorded. Each selects the line of remark which seems to him to embody the pith of what was said; and the skill and faithfulness with which they have done this are attested by such a phenomenon as now faces us, where, amid even a striking diversity in the details reported, a complete harmony is preserved in the substance of the discourse. . . . Each gives us in any case only a portion of what was said.[88]

On the very occasion about which Warfield writes—Jesus' dialogue with the rich young man—Mark confirms the repetitious nature of the conversation. Immediately after the young man's departure, Mark records Jesus' words to His disciples: "How hard it will be for those who are wealthy to enter the kingdom of God!" (Mark 10:23 NASB). In the very next verse, Mark quotes Jesus again: "Children, how hard it is to enter the kingdom of God!" (v. 24).[89] The two statements say essentially the same thing, but they say it with different words. This erases any doubt that Jesus, like anyone else in His day or in any other time, was repetitious in His conversations and teachings.

Warfield observes that in Mark 10:17, the use of the imperfect verb *epērōta* when introducing the young man's question(s) is another clue indicating repetition. The young man *kept on asking* Jesus about the issue that was troubling him. Warfield, aware of the claim of some that Mark's imperfects are insignificant because he interchanges them with aorists, responds to those who dispute his contention by pointing out that the present, aorist, and imperfect come in close contiguity, bringing attention to the shades of implication of the tenses. He then observes the following:

> It lies in the nature of the case that two accounts of a conversation which agree as to the substance of what was said, but differ slightly in the details reported, are reporting different fragments of the conversation, selected according to the judgment of each writer as the best vehicles of its substance.[90]

The additive-harmonization approach—the name assigned to traditional harmonization by recent critics of the method—to this passage does not hang on an "extremely slender" grammatical thread.[91] It has strong grammatical, contextual, and hermeneutical support.

Other passages illustrate how repetition clarifies differences in parallel-passage wording. Matthew's wording of the first beatitude is, "Blessed are the poor in spirit, for theirs is the kingdom of heaven" (Matt. 5:3). But Luke writes, "Blessed are you who are poor, for yours is the kingdom of God" (Luke 6:20). Most probably Jesus repeated this beatitude in at least two different forms when He preached His Sermon on the Mount/Plain, using the third person once and the second person another time and referring to the kingdom by two different titles. We know that neither gospel records the whole sermon, and that repetition of thoughts with different wording is the most effective way to preach and teach. Each writer selected the wording that best suited his purpose.[92]

The parable of the mustard tree (Matt. 13:32; Mark 4:32) furnishes another illustration of repetition. Matthew has Jesus saying that the birds of the air rest "in its branches," but Mark has them resting "under its shade." Jesus probably told the parable in both ways.

In Jesus' Olivet Discourse did He cite the claim of future imposters as "I am the Christ" (Matt. 24:5) or as "I am (He)" (Mark 13:6; Luke 21:8)? In an extended discourse as this must have been, He probably used both wordings.

In other places the variations are more significant. The difference between "because" (Matt. 13:13) and "in order that" (Mark 4:12) is far-reaching. Did Jesus use parables because His rejectors were already spiritually blind, as Matthew says, or did He do so in order to produce their blindness, as Mark indicates? Is the difference due to editorial liberties by one or both writers, or did Jesus say both? He probably said both. His rejectors had already indicated their blindness through commission of the unpardonable sin (cf. Matthew 12), and the parables served to confirm them in their blindness more fully.

The alleged displacement of Matthew 13:12 in Mark 4:25 and Luke 8:18b most likely has the same explanation: In the context of Matthew's account, the words speak about Jesus' enemies, and in the other two gospels, about His disciples. The difference in meaning is substantial. Do the words mean that the mysteries of the kingdom of heaven will be withheld from the rejectors (Matthew), or that the "good seed" will receive even more than they already have (Mark and Luke)? To contend that the wide variation in meaning came from any other source than Jesus' direct teaching on the occasion would be hard to reconcile with a doctrine of biblical inerrancy. Editorial liberty would attribute at least one of the meanings to a gospel writer, not to Jesus. No, Jesus must have uttered the same principle at least twice on the same occasion, but in different contexts of the same discourse to teach two different lessons.

At this point, the sage reminder of J. I. Packer strengthens the discussion:

> Our point here is simply that the Church must receive all teaching that proves to be biblical, whether on matters of historical or of theological fact, as truly part of God's Word.
>
> This shows the importance of insisting that the inspiration of Scripture is *verbal*. Words signify and safeguard meaning; the wrong word distorts the intended sense. Since God inspired the biblical text in order to communicate His Word, it was necessary for him to ensure that the words written were such as did in fact convey it. We do not stress the verbal character of inspiration from a superstitious regard for the original Hebrew and Greek words . . . ; we do so from a reverent concern for the sense of Scripture. If the words were not wholly God's, then their teaching would not be wholly God's.[93]

Packer echoes the earlier opinion of A. A. Hodge and B. B. Warfield, who wrote as follows:

> It is evident, therefore, that it is not clearness of thought which inclines any of the advocates of a real inspiration of the Holy Scriptures to deny that it extends to the words. Whatever discrepancies or other human limitations may attach to the sacred record, *the line* (of inspired or not inspired, of infallible or fallible) *can never rationally be drawn between the thoughts and the words of Scripture.*[94]

Even the slightest redactional change of Jesus' words by a gospel writer would have altered the meaning of Jesus' utterances on a given historical

occasion. It is important to a sound view of biblical inspiration that readers have the precise intended sense of Jesus' teaching, not an altered sense
that a writer conveyed because of a particular theological theme he wanted
to emphasize.

Another factor often overlooked by evangelicals in the whole issue of
literary independence versus interdependence is the role of the Holy Spirit
in enabling the memories of the eyewitnesses of Christ's life. Jesus promised His apostles that very assistance after His departure: "But the Helper
[parakletos], the Holy Spirit, whom the Father will send in My name, will
teach you all things and will remind you of all things that I have spoken to
you" (John 14:26; cf. also 16:13 and the promise that the Spirit would
"guide . . . into all truth"). Most often Bock, Blomberg, and others will
compare the Gospels with secular historical writings with little or no regard for this supernatural boost to the memories of eyewitnesses and writers.[95] The ministry of the Spirit in quickening the memories and inspiring
the writing of the Gospels deserves more attention than that. It is worthy
of major emphasis in gospel composition. It puts those books into a category by themselves in regard to their precision, which is notably superior to secular historical writings.

The Spirit's work in reminding and inspiring is a supernatural work,
guaranteeing a degree of accuracy and precision that is without parallel in
the annals of human historiography. That accounts for the approximately
eighty percent agreement in the synoptics' reporting of the words of Jesus.[96]
That is an extremely high figure for writers working independently of each
other and attests to the precision of the writers' Spirit-enabled memories.
Of course, a historical critic would attribute that to literary dependence
and copying, but if copying occurred, he then must account for the other
twenty percent where disagreements appear. Why did the writers not copy
there?

An advocate of literary independence would attribute the disagreements
to Jesus' repetitious conversations and teaching/preaching methodology.
The reported wording is true to what He actually said at one point or another. It is historically accurate.

Presuppositional Probability

When faced with some of the same critical pressures that face contemporary evangelicalism, A. A. Hodge and B. B. Warfield expressed themselves
thus:

> In testing this question by a critical investigation of the phenom-
> ena of Scripture, it is evident that the stricter view, which denies
> the existence of errors, discrepancies, or inaccurate statements
> in Scripture, has the presumption in its favor, and that the *onus
> probandi* rests upon the advocates of the other view. The latter
> may fairly be required to furnish positive and conclusive evidence
> in each alleged instance of error, until the presumption has been
> turned over to the other side. The *prima facie* evidence of the

claims of Scripture is assuredly all in favor of an errorless infallibility of all Scriptural affirmations. This has been from the first
the general faith of the historical Church, and of the Bible-loving,
spiritual people of God.[97]

In application of their principle to the words of Jesus, the presumption
must favor that each of the writers has recorded Christ's very words. Only
positive and conclusive evidence to the contrary could prove a discrepancy caused by factors such as a gospel writer's editorial liberty.

Blomberg dismisses this presuppositionalist approach as invalid, claiming
that widely accepted historical criteria can demonstrate "the *general
trustworthiness* of the gospels."[98] But "general trustworthiness" is not
sufficient for those holding a doctrine of *verbal* inspiration of inerrant
gospels. As noted above, one's doctrine of inspiration becomes very
subjective, elastic, and essentially meaningless unless it adheres to the very
words themselves.

So presuppositional probability must be on the side of the Gospels'
containing the *ipsissima verba* of Jesus. Recognizing the necessity of
condensation in some accounts of His conversations and discourses, an
outside possibility exists that some are not His very words. Yet in the absence
of any way to identify what those instances are, a person can only assume
that a gospel account has exactly what Jesus spoke on any given occasion.

Ancient resources are unavailable to prove absolutely one side or the
other in this debate. No one has an airtight case for concluding whether
they are Jesus' very words or they are only the gist of what Jesus said. For
one whose predisposition is toward evangelical HC and its primary focus
on the human element in the inspiration of Scripture, he will incline toward the *ipsissima vox* position. For one whose inclination leads him to
place highest premium on the Spirit's part in inspiring Scripture, he will
certainly lean toward the *ipsissima verba* view. In some mysterious way
known only to God, the natural merged with the supernatural when the
Spirit inspired the Gospels. Whatever way that happened, however, the
supernatural must have prevailed. Otherwise, the Gospels could not be
inerrant.[99] The Bible is more than just a humanly generated book.

Without denying the human part in inspiration, Hodge and Warfield have
written the following:

> During the entire history of Christian theology the word Inspira-
> tion has been used to express either some or all of the activities
> of God, cooperating with its human authors in the genesis of Holy
> Scripture. We prefer to use it in the single sense of God's contin-
> ued work of superintendence, by which, His providential, gracious,
> and supernatural contributions having been presupposed, He pre-
> sided over the sacred writers in their entire work of writing, with
> the design and effect of rendering that writing an errorless record
> of the matters He designed them to communicate, and hence con-
> stituting the entire volume in all its parts the Word of God to us.[100]

An evangelical with a high view of inspiration must give precedence to the part of the Holy Spirit in inspiring the Bible.

ENDNOTES

1. See chapter 1 of this volume for a detailed discussion of the early fathers' views regarding origins of the Gospels.
2. Moisés Silva, "Ned B. Stonehouse and Redaction Criticism, Part Two: The Historicity of the Synoptic Tradition," *Westminster Theological Journal* 40 (1978): 289–90.
3. Ibid., 298, 298 n. 25.
4. Ned B. Stonehouse, *Origins of the Synoptic Gospels, Some Basic Questions* (Grand Rapids: Baker, 1963), 105.
5. Ibid., 105–8.
6. Ibid., 108.
7. Ibid., 109–12. Silva notes that Stonehouse postponed taking a position on Source Criticism and Form Criticism until later in life—a time that turned out to be shortly before his death—and, having taken that position, he viewed editorial liberties by the gospel writers in a way that represented a "considerable evolution in Stonehouse's thought" (Silva, "Ned B. Stonehouse and Redaction Criticism, Part Two," 282–84).
8. Silva, "Ned B. Stonehouse, Part Two," 285.
9. Stonehouse, *Origins*, 110 n. 17.
10. Benjamin Breckenridge Warfield, *Christology and Criticism* (New York: Oxford, 1929), 155 n. In another work Warfield clarifies his view that complete harmony between the four gospels exists without injecting the element of editorial liberties by the writers. Referring to the Sermon on the Mount, the healing of the centurion's son, the denials of Peter, the healing of the blind man at Jericho, and the time of the institution of the Lord's supper, he and A. A. Hodge wrote, "[I]n each of these, most natural means of harmonizing exist" (A. A. Hodge and B. B. Warfield, "Inspiration," *Presbyterian Review* 2, no. 6 [April 1881]: 252, cf. 252–55, the section entitled "Complete Internal Harmony").
11. B. B. Warfield, "Jesus' Alleged Confession of Sin," *Princeton Theological Review* 12 (April 1914): 192, cf. 191–97.
12. Ibid., 188–91 [emphasis added]. See also Edward J. Young, *Thy Word Is Truth: Some Thoughts on the Biblical Doctrine of Inspiration* (Grand Rapids: Eerdmans, 1957), 127–37. Young prefers Warfield's explanation of the "rich young man" passage and of other passages where critics find apparent discrepancies. For an illustration of a traditional handling of the passage such as Warfield and Young would have approved, see chapter 8 of this volume.
13. Robert H. Gundry, *Matthew, A Commentary on His Handbook for a Mixed Church under Persecution*, 2d ed. (Grand Rapids: Eerdmans, 1994), 623. In principle, Blomberg's position regarding the difference between ancient and present-day historians is similar, namely, standards of objectivity in ancient times did not require the kind of compartmentalizaton of reporting and interpretation that modern-day counterparts require (Craig L. Blomberg, *Matthew*, vol. 22 of *The New American Commentary*, David S. Dockery, gen. ed. [Nashville, Tenn.: Broadman, 1992], 46). Gundry pushes the difference to a much greater extreme than Blomberg, however.
14. Cf. Craig L. Blomberg, "The Legitimacy and Limits of Harmonization," in

Hermeneutics, Authority and Canon, D. A. Carson and John D. Woodbridge, eds. (Grand Rapids: Baker, 1995), 144.

15. D. A. Carson, "Gundry on Matthew: A Critical Review," *Trinity Journal* 3NS (1982): 77.
16. Ibid., 80–81.
17. D. A. Carson, "Matthew," vol. 8 of *Expositor's Bible Commentary,* Frank E. Gaebelein, gen. ed. (Grand Rapids: Zondervan, 1984), 423.
18. Ibid., 241–42.
19. Moisés Silva, "Ned B. Stonehouse and Redaction Criticism, Part I: The Witness of the Synoptic Evangelists to Christ," *Westminster Theological Journal* 40 (1977): 80–88; idem, "Ned B. Stonehouse, Part II," 282–86.
20. I. Howard Marshall, "Foreword" to Grant R. Osborne, *The Resurrection Narratives, a Redactional Study* (Grand Rapids: Baker, 1984), 7. In the Foreword, Marshall states the question the volume seeks to answer: "How much is theological interpretation in the Gospels true and how much actually happened?"
21. Though the main focus of *The Jesus Crisis* is on the Synoptic Gospels, in discussing the harmonization of the resurrection accounts, one must also consider the contribution of the gospel of John.
22. Osborne, *Resurrection Narratives,* 198–99.
23. Ibid., 199–200.
24. Ibid., 200–16.
25. Ibid., 218.
26. Ibid., 225–59.
27. Ibid., 227, 229.
28. Ibid., 230–31.
29. Ibid., 231–70.
30. Ibid., 245.
31. Murray J. Harris, *Raised Immortal: Resurrection and Immortality in the New Testament* (Grand Rapids: Eerdmans, 1983), 68.
32. George Eldon Ladd, *I Believe in the Resurrection of Jesus* (Grand Rapids: Eerdmans, 1975), 85.
33. John Wenham, *Easter Enigma: Are the Resurrection Accounts in Conflict?* 2d ed. (Grand Rapids: Baker, 1992), 8. Yet Wenham does not support complete literary independence of the Synoptic Gospels.
34. Ibid., 127.
35. Ibid., 90–94.
36. Ibid., 76–80.
37. Ibid., 81–84.
38. J. Gresham Machen, *Christianity and Liberalism* (New York: Macmillan, 1923), 28–29.
39. J. A. Alexander, "Harmonies of the Gospels," *The Biblical Repertory and Princeton Review* 28 (July 1856): 394.
40. Ibid., 396.
41. Ibid.
42. Ibid.
43. Gundry, *Matthew,* 624.
44. Ibid., 625.
45. Ibid., 626.
46. Blomberg, "Legitimacy and Limits of Harmonization," 145.
47. Ibid., 161.

48. Stonehouse, *Origin of the Synoptic Gospels*, 109.
49. Gundry, *Matthew*, 639.
50. Grant R. Osborne, "Redaction Criticism," in *New Testament Criticism & Interpretation*, David Alan Black & David S. Dockery, eds. (Grand Rapids: Zondervan, 1991), 214.
51. Alexander, "Harmonies of the Gospels," 401.
52. John Chrysostom, *The Gospel according to Matthew*, Homily I.5.
53. Chapter 1 of this volume shows that Augustine probably agreed with this view held by the other early fathers.
54. Donald A. Hagner, *Matthew 1–13*, vol. 33A of *Word Biblical Commentary*, David A. Hubbard and Glenn W. Barker, gen. eds. (Dallas: Word, 1993), 104.
55. Ibid.
56. Gundry, *Matthew*, 82.
57. Donald A. Hagner, *Matthew 14–28*, vol. 33B of *Word Biblical Commentary*, David A. Hubbard and Glenn W. Barker, gen. eds. (Dallas: Word, 1995), 655.
58. Ibid., 665–66.
59. Gundry, *Matthew*, 453.
60. Ibid.
61. Stein, *Luke*, 214.
62. Ibid., 186.
63. Ibid.
64. Ibid., 243.
65. Ibid.
66. Ibid., 520.
67. James A. Brooks, *Mark*, vol. 23 of *The New American Commentary*, David S. Dockery, ed. (Nashville: Broadman, 1991), 171.
68. Ibid., 82.
69. S. Greidanus, "Preaching from the Gospels," in *Dictionary of Jesus and the Gospels*, Joel B. Green and Scot McKnight, eds. (Downers Grove, Ill.: InterVarsity, 1992), 625–30.
70. Ibid., 625.
71. K. Giles, "Ascension," in *Dictionary of Jesus and the Gospels*, Joel B. Green and Scot McKnight, eds. (Downers Grove, Ill.: InterVarsity, 1992), 48–50.
72. Gundry, *Matthew*, 5–10.
73. Ibid., 9.
74. Darrell L. Bock, "The Words of Jesus in the Gospels: Live, Jive, or Memorex?" in *Jesus under Fire*, Michael J. Wilkins and J. P. Moreland, gen. eds. (Grand Rapids: Zondervan, 1995), 73–99.
75. Ibid., 78, 86, 88, 94.
76. Ibid., 78.
77. Ibid., 95 n. 6.
78. Stein, *Synoptic Problem*, 156.
79. Bock, *The Words of Jesus in the Gospels*, 77–78.
80. Cf. Stanley Porter, "Did Jesus Ever Teach in Greek?" *Tyndale Bulletin* 44 (1993): 195–235; Robert H. Gundry, "The Language Milieu of First-Century Palestine," *Journal of Biblical Literature* 83 (1964): 404–8; Philip Edgcumbe Hughes, "The Languages Spoken by Jesus," in *New Dimensions in New Testament Study*, Richard N. Longenecker and Merrill C. Tenney, eds. (Grand Rapids: Zondervan, 1974), 125–43; Bruce M. Metzger, "The Language of the New Testament," *The Interpreter's Bible* (New York: Abingdon, 1951), 7:43–59; Daniel B. Wallace, *Greek Grammar beyond the Basics* (Grand Rapids: Zondervan, 1996), 24.

81. Osborne, *Resurrection Narratives,* 261 n. 45.
82. Craig L. Blomberg, *Matthew,* vol. 22 of *The New American Commentary,* David S. Dockery, gen. ed. (Nashville, Tenn.: Broadman, 1992), 252.
83. Metzger, "Language of the New Testament," 46–52. With the writing of James placed in the late 40s, James would hardly have had time to develop such mastery of literary koiné between Herod Agrippa I's persecution (Acts 12:1; approximately A.D. 44)—the cause of the dispersion to whom James wrote (James 1:1)—and his writing of the epistle. He would have had no occasion to do so before that time.
84. Porter, "Did Jesus Ever Teach in Greek?" 204.
85. Ibid., 223.
86. See comments in chapter 6 of this volume for more discussion about the keenly developed memories of the earliest Christians.
87. Eta Linnemann, *Is There a Synoptic Problem? Rethinking the Literary Dependence of the First Three Gospels,* Robert W. Yarbrough, trans. (Grand Rapids: Baker, 1992), 183, cf. 182–95 [emphasis in the original].
88. Warfield, "Jesus Alleged Confession of Sin," 189.
89. Cf. Robert L. Thomas, "The Rich Young Man in Matthew," *Grace Theological Journal* 3, no. 2 (fall 1982): 255–56.
90. Warfield, "Jesus Alleged Confession of Sin," 190–91.
91. Contra Blomberg, "The Legitimacy and Limits of Harmonization," 158–59, 394 n. 119.
92. Cf. Young, *Thy Word Is Truth,* 134.
93. J. I. Packer, *'Fundamentalism' and the Word of God: Some Evangelical Principles* (Grand Rapids: Eerdmans, 1958), 89–90.
94. A. A. Hodge and B. B. Warfield, "Inspiration," *The Presbyterian Review* 2, no. 6 (April 1881): 235 [emphasis in the original].
95. Bock, "The Words of Jesus in the Gospels," 78–81; Craig L. Blomberg, *The Historical Reliability of the Gospels* (Downers Grove, Ill.: InterVarsity, 1987), 8–12. Bock mentions the ministry of the Spirit as promised in John 12–14, but implies that His guidance included editorial departures from the actual historical words cited (98 n. 25). Blomberg refers to John 14:26 and 16:13, but only to say that the Spirit kept the writers from adding information to the Gospels that was not based on historical tradition (41). Later he interprets the verses to explain John's differences from the Synoptic Gospels because of his interpreting the significance of Jesus' words rather than reporting more precisely His actual words (184). This guidance he also calls "safeguarding . . . [the] accuracy" of the memories of the eyewitnesses (ibid.), which is a very loose use of the word "accuracy."
96. Cf. Linnemann, *Is There a Synoptic Problem?* 106, 149.
97. Hodge and Warfield, "Inspiration," 241.
98. Blomberg, *Historical Reliability,* 9–10 [emphasis added].
99. Hodge and Warfield, "Inspiration," 230–32.
100. Ibid., 232.

Epilogue

Robert L. Thomas

THE CRISIS SUMMARIZED

A CRISIS IN STUDIES OF JESUS is present. The surrounding terrain of gospel studies raises a question about how much of the truth about Jesus will survive. On the one hand, the Jesus Seminar and its aggressive proliferation of literature decimates the Gospels and the factual data about Jesus recorded therein. On the other hand, those expected to stand against a demolition of the inspired text—namely, evangelical New Testament scholarship—practice the same methodology as the Jesus Seminar and are dehistoricizing the Gospels too. They may not do so as extensively as the Jesus Seminar, but they raise serious questions about the accuracy of the Synoptic Gospels. That is the way the fundamentalist-modernist debate began earlier in the twentieth century. Some contemporary evangelicals reflect the same symptoms as liberals did in those earlier days. Current developments portend bad omens for the future of evangelicalism.

On many fronts, Historical Criticism (HC) has made enormous inroads into New Testament scholarship—evangelical New Testament scholars not excluded—raising the question of how much of gospel truth about Jesus will scholars—evangelical ones in particular—surrender. For those who cherish a high view of inspiration, the prospects appear grim, for they recognize that the method of gospel study these scholars are teaching will in only a few years be the one that prevails in churches throughout the land and the whole world. Those scholars are respected instructors in evangelical institutions where pastors and church and missionary leaders of the future are receiving their training in how to disciple the church of Jesus Christ. Apart from a major turnabout in the present situation, the Jesus crisis will spread like gangrene. "A little leaven leavens the whole lump" (Gal. 5:9).

The crisis is very real and poses an extremely dangerous threat to the survival of truth about Jesus. If allowed to progress without challenge, the movement can only deteriorate further as evangelical scholarship imbibes ever more deeply of the principles of HC. Thus far the tendency has been for new generations of historical critics to have less restraint than their mentors in applying historical-critical principles, with the result that their conclusions about Jesus are veering further and further away from historicity. Without a major reversal, the problem can only get worse before it gets any better.

The Jesus Crisis has surveyed HC from two general perspectives: how did it originate (part 1) and what does it cause, or what are its effects on various Christian principles and practices (part 2)?

(1) HC originated, not in the ancient church (cf. chapter 1), but with an antisupernaturalistic bias that the Enlightenment engendered (cf. chapters 2 and 5). Antisupernaturalism brought with it the assumption of literary dependence in the writing of the Synoptic Gospels (cf. chapters 3 and 6), an assumption that has devastated a historical understanding of the Gospels. Furthermore, HC tolerates no deviation from its presuppositions as attested by treatment its advocates extend toward those who dare to question its ideological standards (cf. chapter 4).

(2) The practical effects of HC have been equally drastic. It has radically affected the exegetical handling of Synoptic Gospel texts, forcing on the Lukan prologue an unnatural meaning (cf. chapter 7) and changing the basic interpretive process for gospel parallels (cf. chapter 8). Its ideological outlook has brought about a departure from principles of grammatical-historical exegesis (cf. chapter 9) and erected a major obstacle to expository preaching of the biblical text (cf. chapter 10). HC has also severely reduced the apologetic value of the Gospels for those who would defend Christianity against its adversaries, for it has substantially minimized attention to the theology and words of Jesus (cf. chapter 11).

The Crisis Exacerbated

And yet, a goodly number of evangelical New Testament scholars view HC as a useful tool in studies of the Gospels. This must be one of the greatest mysteries of this century! How can those who profess to believe in the inerrancy of the Bible openly advocate a methodology—actually an *ideology*—that is so blatantly contrary to historical accuracy in Synoptic Gospel texts? This defies rational explanation. The situation is reminiscent of the predicament that arose in the first-century Colossian church to whom Paul wrote, "Beware lest there should be anyone who leads you captive through philosophy and vain deceit according to the tradition of men, according to the rudiments of the world and not according to Christ" (Col. 2:8). A present-day ideological system has a stranglehold on evangelical New Testament scholarship that is choking to death what is supposed be the bastion of truth. Yet few recognize the blindness that is contributing to the deterioration of the gospel records.

What is even more inexplicable is the attitude of some evangelical historical critics toward those who choose the traditional view of independence among the synoptic writers. They take delight in belittling anyone who prefers a literary independence view. An example of this is the stinging review of Linnemann's book on HC by Gregory A. Boyd (see chapter 4). He criticizes her for demonizing philosophy and science, for transporting society back to antiquity, for her fixation on alleged errors in critical assumptions, and the like. Others obscure the real issues involved through demeaning expressions against people with the traditional view, such as "a Rush Limbaugh tone," acting like a "knee-jerk conservative," or being "diehards." That type of interaction does not advance the cause of biblical scholarship. It is rather a way of covering up a scholar's inability to respond effectively to a viewpoint that is opposite his own.

Evangelical historical critics have displayed an intense unwillingness to enter into dialogue with people who maintain that the Synoptic Gospels originated independently from each other. They have failed to respond specifically, directly, and substantively to presentations at theological societies, published journal articles, and private conversations dealing with the subject of gospel origins. In fact, most are unwilling to discuss the basic issues involved, but are content with the status quo—namely, interdependence among the gospel writers, usually combined with preference for the Two-Source Theory. That furnishes another reason for asserting that a crisis exists among evangelicals in regard to defending the historicity of the gospel accounts of Jesus' life, death, and resurrection. Those who have been willing to contribute chapters to the present volume are happy exceptions, but not many of that quality live in the evangelical world today. This adds to the seriousness of the crisis.

Impact of the Crisis on Inspiration

It is anomalous that a person on one hand professes a belief in biblical inerrancy, a position that of necessity places highest value on the Holy Spirit's part in inspiring the Bible, and on the other hand, minimizes the same Spirit's part in generating accuracy in the part of that Bible that deals with Jesus. Chapter 11 of this work has dwelt upon the balance between man's part and God's part in inspiring the Scriptures, and has pointed out that the overshadowing role of the Spirit in ensuring precision regarding the details of Jesus' life. That approach coincides perfectly with viewing the New Testament as being inerrant. An allowance for inaccuracies in the gospel accounts—often excused because the accounts are general in nature rather than precise—magnifies the human part in inspiration to the point of at least straining and probably violating the idea of an errorless Bible.

Some evangelical historical critics mention the Holy Spirit's activity in inspiring the Gospels. Bock mentions the Spirit's ministry as promised in John 12–14, but says the Spirit led the gospel writers to summarize Jesus' words rather than give accounts that were detailed in their precision.[1] At issue here is what degree of precision the Spirit chose to use. At some point, what Bock calls "summarization" becomes factually erroneous, as examples throughout this volume have illustrated. Is the Spirit of God incapable of communicating precise information about the incarnate Son of God? Has He used human authors to pass on information that is anything less that absolutely correct? It is hardly appropriate for finite humans to view an absolutely sovereign God as unable to produce anything less than the ultimate in exactness.

Blomberg sees the Spirit's role in John 14:26 and 16:13 as a safeguard to assure that additions made by the gospel writers rested on historical tradition, contrary to what radical RC advocates.[2] Later in the same book he interprets John 14:26; 15:26; and 16:12–13 to teach the Spirit's function in John's gospel in giving the significance of Jesus' words rather than reporting more precisely His actual words.[3] Yet the verses teach neither of these lessons. John 14:26 explicitly promises, "He [namely, the Spirit] will remind you of all things which I have spoken to you." That promise leaves no room for imprecision, and grants no license for writers to make additions or alterations to suit their own situations. It says nothing about giving the significance of Jesus' words as opposed to reporting exactly what He said. Jesus' promise of the Spirit goes beyond being a pledge of general reliability; it promises detailed accuracy.

Stein understands the promise of guidance "into all the truth" in John 16:13 as saying that the Spirit taught the apostles the meaning and significance of Jesus' words and deeds and that the gospel writers then reported those meanings and significances as coming directly from Jesus' lips.[4] That is not what Jesus promised, however. The pledge of guidance into all truth did not grant license to attribute to Jesus things He never spoke while personally present on earth. That is a misappropriation of what John 16:13 teaches.

Stein goes further in recognizing divine authority in the meanings that the gospel writers' assigned to Jesus' utterances, even though those meanings sometimes introduced unhistorical reports of certain occasions.[5] How can someone believe in an inerrant Bible that at times misrepresents historical incidents it purports to describe? A doctrine of inspiration that condones erroneous reports is indefensible. The Spirit's inspiration cannot be an excuse for historical misrepresentations and for the impartation of divine authority to words that are blatantly wrong. He is the Spirit of truth (John 15:26) and cannot have a part in untruth. For someone to explain how the Spirit inspired the writers to use the tools of HC to communicate falsehood illustrates the folly of saying the method is neutral. Originally, HC came into being as a device for explaining why the Gospels are not true (see chapter 2). To explain the method now as part of inspiration by the Spirit of truth is ludicrous.

The choice is clear. One can accept the ideology of HC and view the Synoptic Gospels as *generally* reliable, with some doubt about particular parts—depending on which New Testament scholar he/she consults—or he/she can reject the validity of HC in approaching those gospels and have confidence in their *full* reliability. The latter position rests on the full independence of the Gospels in relation to each other—namely, three independent witnesses to the words and works of Jesus. The strong evidence for that position has surfaced throughout this volume. That remaining alternative has been the dominant view of the Christian church for the vast majority of her history.

The Remaining Alternative

In view of the consequences of assuming literary dependence among the synoptists, a sane balancing of evidence rules against such an assumption. Yet the most visible scholars in New Testament shun literary independence. Despite their acknowledgment that no solution to the Synoptic Problem is without its problems, they still cling to the theory that the gospel writers depended on the works of each other in some manner. Without such literary collaboration, the Synoptic Problem does not exist,[6] but they practice a wholesale neglect of that possibility. They are content to cite the theory of Matthew's and Luke's dependence on Mark and Q as the majority opinion and to build on that as a foundation. They acknowledge the absence of absolute proof for the theory,[7] and are unable to provide any widely accepted evidence to plug its holes. This is why HC advocate McKnight must admit, "But we can never be totally certain about some of these matters since we can never be totally confident of a solution to the Synoptic Problem."[8] The consequence of that theory's being wrong is a trashing of most of the research done on the Synoptic Gospels over the last hundred years.[9]

Is it not more reasonable to drop the ill-supported and dubious assumption of literary dependence and thus dispense with the insoluble difficulties it creates?[10] Would this not furnish a better basis for responding to the destructive conclusions publicized by the Jesus Seminar? Evangelical responses to this seminar are hopelessly futile, for they are inextricably mired in the same tainted methodology—better, *ideology*—advocated by the seminar. This ideology is contradictory to evangelical standards of inspiration, and therefore self-defeating for the inerrantist perspective.[11] The difference between evangelicals and the Jesus Seminar is only a matter of one person's opinion against another's. For both a gulf is fixed between historical precision and the gospel records. Subjective criticisms of the seminar's findings by evangelicals are at best peripheral. Those of radical persuasion merely turn the tables and show how evangelicals are dehistoricizing just as the radicals do, though perhaps not to the same extremes.[12]

But a verbal, plenary view of the inspired gospels tolerates no degree of dehistoricizing. Such a view of inerrancy guarantees accuracy in every detail. Yes, divine and human elements explain the inspiration of the Scriptures, but the prevalence of the divine over the human guarantees the full accuracy of every part of Bible history.

The Jesus crisis should be a source of serious concern for the Christian church. God will somehow overcome the crisis. His Word will remain intact for He is sovereign and omnipotent. His truth will prevail. He will not allow gospel truth to disappear. But He will carry out His will as the church, Christ's bride, reasserts the integrity of His Word. Believers should exert themselves to alleviate the crisis. Believers do so by maintaining an uncompromising stand on what He has written and not questioning its accuracy at any point. Hopefully, the church will do so immediately by raising her voice against the enemy who already has his foot in the door and is seeking to pry it wide open.

The only way to objectify historical reliability is to accept the historical accuracy of every portion of Scripture. J. Gresham Machen insisted on historical precision, and would have been extremely perturbed if he had known that evangelicals would eventually embrace historical-critical methodology. He voiced the objection of those who in his day advocated a Christianity independent of history when he wrote, "Must we really wait until the historians have finished disputing about the value of sources and the like before we can have peace with God?"[13] To this Machen responded, "If religion be made independent of history there is no such thing as a gospel. . . . A gospel independent of history is a contradiction in terms."[14] In an endorsement of Machen's position, Lippmann wrote the following:

> The veracity of that story was fundamental for the Christian Church. For while all the ideal values may remain if you impugn the historic record set forth in the Gospels, these ideal values are not certified to the common man as inherent in the very nature of things.[15]

Lippmann continues, "The liberals have yet to answer Dr. Machen when he says that 'the Christian movement at its inception was not just a way of life in the modern sense, but a way of life founded upon a message.'"[16]

Harrisville and Sundberg correctly analyze Machen's response to Historical Criticism when they note, "Christianity is wed inextricably to the *particularities* of a history that are open to investigation and have the *specificity* and *integrity* to risk falsification."[17] Christianity in its fundamental nature is "grounded in an historical narrative; it depends upon the claims of external events. To separate the ideas and values of the faith from their history is to cut the nerve of Christianity."[18] Cutting that nerve is exactly what HC does, as Machen seems to have seen years ago. The ideology of HC therefore has no place in evangelical scholarship.

Far better is a resolute stand for the literary independence of the Gospels. Speaking for the early church, John Chrysostom concurred with that approach when he wrote, "[I]f there be four that write, not at the same times, nor in the same places, neither after having met together, and conversed one with another, and then they speak all things as it were out of one mouth, this becomes a very great demonstration of the truth."[19] Historical Criticism contradicts that independence of the Synoptic Gospels and thus has no place in promoting biblical truth. The three writers produced their gospels independently of one another under the guidance of a sovereign God who cannot lie.

ENDNOTES

1. Darrell L. Bock, "The Words of Jesus in the Gospels: Live, Jive, or Memorex?" *Jesus under Fire*, Michael J. Wilkins and J. P. Moreland, gen. eds. (Grand Rapids: Zondervan, 1995), 98 n. 25.
2. Craig L. Blomberg, *The Historical Reliability of the Gospels* (Downers Grove, Ill.: InterVarsity, 1987), 41.
3. Ibid., 184.

4. Robert H. Stein, *The Synoptic Problem* (Grand Rapids: Baker, 1987), 216.
5. Ibid., 270–71.
6. Cf. Eta Linnemann, *Is There a Synoptic Problem?* (Grand Rapids: Baker, 1992), 149–52.
7. For example, Scot McKnight, *Interpreting the Synoptic Gospels* (Grand Rapids: Baker, 1988), 37; R. H. Stein, "Synoptic Problem," *Dictionary of Jesus and the Gospels,* Joel B. Green, Scot McKnight, and I. Howard Marshall, eds. (Downers Grove, Ill.: InterVarsity, 1992), 790; D. A. Carson, "Matthew," in *EBC,* Frank E. Gaebelein, gen. ed. (Grand Rapids: Zondervan, 1984), 8:13–14; Donald A. Hagner, *Matthew 1–13,* vol. 33A of *Word Biblical Commentary,* David A. Hubbard and Glenn W. Barker, gen. eds (Dallas: Word, 1993), xlvii–xlviii; Craig L. Blomberg, *Matthew,* vol. 22 of *The New American Commentary,* David S. Dockery, gen. ed. (Nashville: Broadman, 1992), 40–41.
8. McKnight, *Synoptic Gospels,* 89. Robert H. Stein expresses the uncertainty of the two-document solution by calling it the "least worst!" of the proposed theories ("Is It Lawful for a Man to Divorce His Wife?" *JETS* 22 [June 1979]: 117 n. 8).
9. A. J. Bellinzoni describes the situation thus: "Since Markan priority is an assumption of so much of the research of the last century, many of the conclusions of that research would have to be redrawn and much of the literature rewritten if the consensus of scholarship were suddenly to shift. . . . Were scholars to move to a position that no consensus can be reached about the synoptic problem or that the synoptic problem is fundamentally unsolvable, we would then have to draw more tentatively the conclusions that have sometimes been drawn on the basis of what were earlier regarded as the assured results of synoptic studies" (*The Two-Source Hypothesis, A Critical Appraisal,* ed. Arthur J. Bellinzoni, Jr. [Macon, Ga.: Mercer University, 1985], 9). Such a shift is in progress (cf. R. T. France, *Matthew, Evangelist and Teacher* [Grand Rapids: Zondervan, 1989], 25, 29–49). It remains to be seen how long it will take for the consensus to change.
10. Cf. France, *Matthew,* 41–46.
11. For reminders that evangelical respondents to the Jesus Seminar employ the same flawed methodology, see for example Carson, "Matthew," 15–17; Blomberg, *Matthew,* 37; Michael J. Wilkins, *The Concept of Disciple in Matthew's Gospel, As Reflected in the Use of the Term* Mathētēs (Leiden: E. J. Brill, 1988), 8; Darrell L. Bock, *Luke 1:1–9:50,* in *Baker Exegetical Commentary on the New Testament,* Moisés Silva, ed. (Grand Rapids: Baker, 1994), 9; idem, "The Words of Jesus in the Gospels: Live, Jive, or Memorex?" in *Jesus Under Fire: Modern Scholarship Reinvents the Historical Jesus,* Michael J. Wilkins and J. P. Moreland, eds. (Grand Rapids: Zondervan, 1995) 90, 99; McKnight, *Synoptic Gospels* 37–40; Gregory A. Boyd, *Cynic, Sage, or Son of God?* (Wheaton: Victor, 1995) 136–37, 204, 295–96 n. 13; Ben Witherington III, *The Jesus Quest: The Third Search for the Jew of Nazareth* (Downers Grove, Ill.: InterVarsity, 1995), 46–47, 50–52, 96, 187, 260–61 nn. 29, 30, 32. Compare these with the methodology of the Jesus Seminar (Robert W. Funk, Roy W. Hoover, and the Jesus Seminar, *The Five Gospels: The Search for the Authentic Words of Jesus* [New York: Macmillan, 1993], 9–14). The Jesus Seminar's addition of the gospel of Thomas to the sources Mark, Q, M, and L is the only exception to the parallelism in methodology.
12. John Dart's article about evangelical responses to the Jesus Seminar, "Holy War Brewing over Image of Jesus," illustrates how unconvinced the radical

wing remains in spite of the responses (*Los Angeles Times* [10/28/95]: B12–B13). In assessing the effectiveness of recent evangelical efforts to refute the seminar, Dart concludes, "That traditional [namely, evangelical] viewpoint may also be an increasingly hard sell to a skeptical American public." He adds, "Biola University's Michael Wilkins, co-editor of the first book to take on the Jesus Seminar, said it will be harder to promote orthodox Christianity in the next century, and perhaps easier for the notion of Jesus as a non-divine sage to gain a following."

13. J. Gresham Machen, *Christianity and Liberalism* (Grand Rapids: Eerdmans, 1946), 121.

14. Ibid.

15. Walter Lippmann, *A Preface to Morals* (New York: Macmillan, 1929), 32.

16. Ibid., 33.

17. Roy A. Harrisville and Walter Sundberg, *The Bible in Modern Culture: Theology and Historical-Critical Method from Spinoza to Käsemann* (Grand Rapids: Eerdmans, 1995), 195 [emphasis added].

18. Ibid., 201; cf. Lippmann, *Preface to Morals*, 32f.

19. John Chrysostom, *The Gospel according to Matthew*, Homily I.5.

Index of Ancient Literature

An "n" following a number indicates that the source appears in an endnote.

Select Index of Modern Authors

Index of Scripture

Index of Subjects

LaVergne, TN USA
21 September 2010
197896LV00001B/69/A